UML 2 SEMANTICS AND APPLICATIONS

UML 2 SEMANTICS AND APPLICATIONS

Edited by

KEVIN LANO

WILEY

A JOHN WILEY & SONS, INC., PUBLICATION

Published by John Wiley & Sons, Inc., Hoboken, New Jersey.
Published simultaneously in Canada.

For general information on our other products and services or for technical support, please contact our Customer Care Department within the United States at (800) 762-2974, outside the United States at (317) 572-3993 or fax (317) 572-4002.

Wiley also publishes its books in a variety of electronic formats. Some content that appears in print may not be available in electronic formats. For more information about Wiley products, visit our web site at www.wiley.com.

Library of Congress Cataloging-in-Publication Data:

UML 2 semantics and applications / edited by Kevin Lano.
p. cm.
Includes bibliographical references and index.
ISBN 978–0–470–40908–4
1. Computer software–Development. 2. Application software–Development. 3. UML (Computer science) 4. Formal languages–Semantics. I. Lano, K.
QA76.76.D47U39 2009
005.13'1–dc22 2009008870

10 9 8 7 6 5 4 3 2 1

CONTENTS

CONTRIBUTORS

RICHARD AMPHLETT, Department of Computing and Electronics, School of Technology, Oxford Brookes University, Oxford, UK

LUÍS S. BARBOSA, Department of Informatics, Minho University, Braga, Portugal

IAN BAYLEY, Department of Computing and Electronics, School of Technology, Oxford Brookes University, Oxford, UK

MANFRED BROY, Institut für Informatik, Technische Universität München, München, Germany

MARÍA VICTORIA CENGARLE, Institut für Informatik, Technische Universität München, München, Germany

DAVID CLARK, Department of Computer Science, King's College London, London, UK

HANS GRÖNNIGER, Lehrstuhl Informatik 3 (Softwaretechnik), RWTH Aachen University, Aachen, Germany

ANNEKE KLEPPE, Independent Consultant, The Netherlands

ALEXANDER KNAPP, Institut für Informatik, Universität Augsburg, Augsburg, Germany

KEVIN LANO, Department of Computer Science, King's College London, London, UK

SUN MENG, CWI, Amsterdam, The Netherlands

HERIBERT MÜHLBERGER, Institut für Informatik, Universität Augsburg, Augsburg, Germany

BERNHARD RUMPE, Lehrstuhl Informatik 3 (Softwaretechnik), RWTH Aachen University, Aachen, Germany

EMIL SEKERINSKI, Department of Computing and Software, McMaster University, Hamilton, Ontario, Canada

LIJUN SHAN, Department of Computer Science, National University of Defense Technology, Changsha, China

HONG ZHU, Department of Computing and Electronics, School of Technology, Oxford Brookes University, Oxford, UK

PREFACE

The Unified Modeling Notation (UML) is the most widely adopted software modeling notation in use today, and is an international standard, whose development and maintenance is managed by the Object Management Group (OMG).

UML was introduced to solve the incompatibilities between the hundreds of differing modeling notations that came into use in the 1980s and early 1990s, notations such as OMT, Booch, Syntropy, and object-oriented versions of earlier methods, such as SSADM. This multiplicity of methods meant that tools and developer expertise could not be transferred easily from project to project, and that documentation in one notation might become valueless if the notation was no longer supported.

The advent of UML in the mid-late 1990s partially solved this problem: One standardized notation was now available for software engineers. However, other compatibility issues became apparant:

- Do two different developers use UML constructs in the same way, with the same semantics?
- How can we check that the graphical UML models of a system correctly express the requirements and that the meaning of these models is correctly implemented in an executable implementation of the system?
- If a transformation is applied to a model to improve its quality or refine it to code, how can we verify that the starting model is correctly expressed in the transformed model?

The UML documents concentrated on defining the syntax of models: how the diagram elements could be validly combined (e.g., that no cycles of inheritance are possible). The semantics was only defined informally, and in many cases semantic variation and interpretation were deliberately built into UML (e.g., a composite state might, or might not, be the "abstract" superstate of its contained states).

Semantic correctness became increasingly important with the definition of model-driven architecture and model-driven development. These use model transformations as a central element, principally to transform high-level models toward more implementation-oriented models, but also to improve the quality of models at a particular level of abstraction.

A large number of semantics have been developed or proposed for parts of UML to solve these problems. These semantics include *transformational semantics*, by which a semantics for UML models is provided by translating them into a representation that already has a precise semantics. Translations of UML to B, SMV, finite state machines, Petri nets, and many other formalisms have been defined for this purpose. Another approach is to define, ab initio, a semantic domain and a semantic interpretation of UML in this domain, a *denotational semantics* approach, as followed by the UML semantics project. A related approach is the *axiomatic semantics* technique, which defines an interpretation of UML into a mathematical formalism such as first-order set theory. The *metamodeling* approach uses a subset of UML itself as a semantic domain for UML.

In the first part of the book we introduce UML notations considered as subjects for semantic definition: class diagrams, state machines, interactions, use cases, OCL and activity diagrams. We also provide an overview of different semantic approaches and the role of semantics in contributing to the definition of UML and to supporting the use of UML.

In the main part of the book we present a range of semantic approaches to defining the semantics of UML models. These include well-established approaches (denotational, operational, transformational, and axiomatic) and two more novel approaches (metamodeling and co-algebraic). In Chapter 3 the UML Semantics Project approach to defining a unified semantics for UML is introduced, and in Chapter 4 we give the technical details of the definition of the *system model* upon which this semantics is based. This is a mathematically defined abstract execution environment in which the underlying semantic concepts of UML, such as objects and behavior, can be represented precisely. Chapter 5 focuses on an alternative approach to a unified UML semantics, by directly expressing the structure of models and metamodels in first-order logic. In Chapter 6 we introduce an axiomatic semantics for UML and use this to define a semantics for a large part of the UML class diagram notation and OCL. In Chapter 7 we describe and explain the metamodeling approach to semantics and apply this in particular to the semantics of OCL. In Chapter 8 we introduce an axiomatic semantics for a large part of UML state machine notation, and discuss problems of semantic ambiguity with the notation and describe how these can be resolved. In Chapter 9 we give a detailed denotational semantics for UML interactions and use this to identify problems with the UML standard for interactions and to consider improvements in the standard. In Chapter 10 we introduce the co-algebraic approach to semantics and define a co-algebraic semantics for interaction diagrams, then use this to prove algebraic properties of interaction operators. Chapter 11 defines a transformational semantics for activity diagrams by mapping these into state machines.

The remaining chapters are concerned with applications of UML semantics. Chapter 12 is an overview of verification techniques for UML. In Chapter 13 we define detailed verification techniques for state machines using a translation to B notation, and in Chapter 14 we use a semantics-driven approach to specify and verify a number of widely used model transformations.

KEVIN LANO

CHAPTER 1

INTRODUCTION TO THE UNIFIED MODELING LANGUAGE

KEVIN LANO
Department of Computer Science, King's College London, London, UK

1.1 INTRODUCTION

In this chapter we describe the primary notations of the Unified Modeling Language (UML): class diagrams, state machines, use cases, interaction diagrams, activity diagrams, and deployment diagrams.

The UML consists of a large collection of notations whose purpose is to model software systems in all their aspects: data, state, behavior, communication, services provided, timing properties, and deployment configurations. Each notation itself forms a complex language, and the notations are interrelated and interdependent, making the task of providing a unified semantics for the UML very challenging.

1.2 CLASS DIAGRAMS

Class diagrams are probably the most important of the UML notations. They can be used to describe the entities, data, and static structure of a system at all levels of abstraction from specification to implementation, and together with Object Constraint Language (OCL) constraints can also define the functionality of operations by pre- and postconditions.

As metamodels, class diagrams together with OCL can be used to define the syntax of all the UML notations. The class diagram notation has many elements, based on notations for entities (represented as UML classes), drawn as rectangles, and notations for relationships (represented as UML associations) between entities, drawn as lines between the classes of the related entities. Figure 1.1 shows a class diagram with four classes—*Lift*, *Door*, *LightSet*, and *Light*—and associations between them. This diagram describes lifts with an associated set of light sets (e.g., one light set inside

UML 2 Semantics and Applications. Edited by Kevin Lano

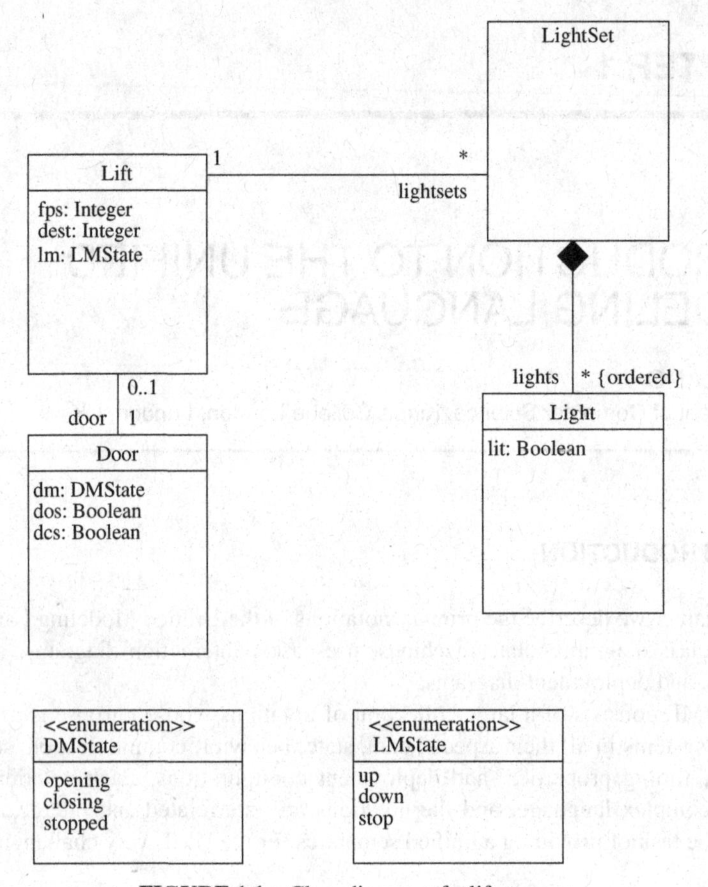

FIGURE 1.1 Class diagram of a lift system.

the lift and others on each floor) to indicate the current position of the lift. Each light set consists of a sequence of individual lights. Figure 1.2 shows part of the UML 2.1 metamodel for class diagrams.

Definitions of the metaclasses *Class* and *Association* [2] follow:

- *Class:* describes a set of objects that share the same specifications of features, constraints, and semantics.
- *Association:* declares that there can be links between objects of the classes it connects. A link is a tuple with one value for each end of the association; each value is an instance of the class at that end.

In other words, a class represents a collection of things that all have a common structure and common properties. The things in the collection are called the *objects* of the class, or *instances* of the class. An association also represents a collection of things: tuples defining connections between objects.

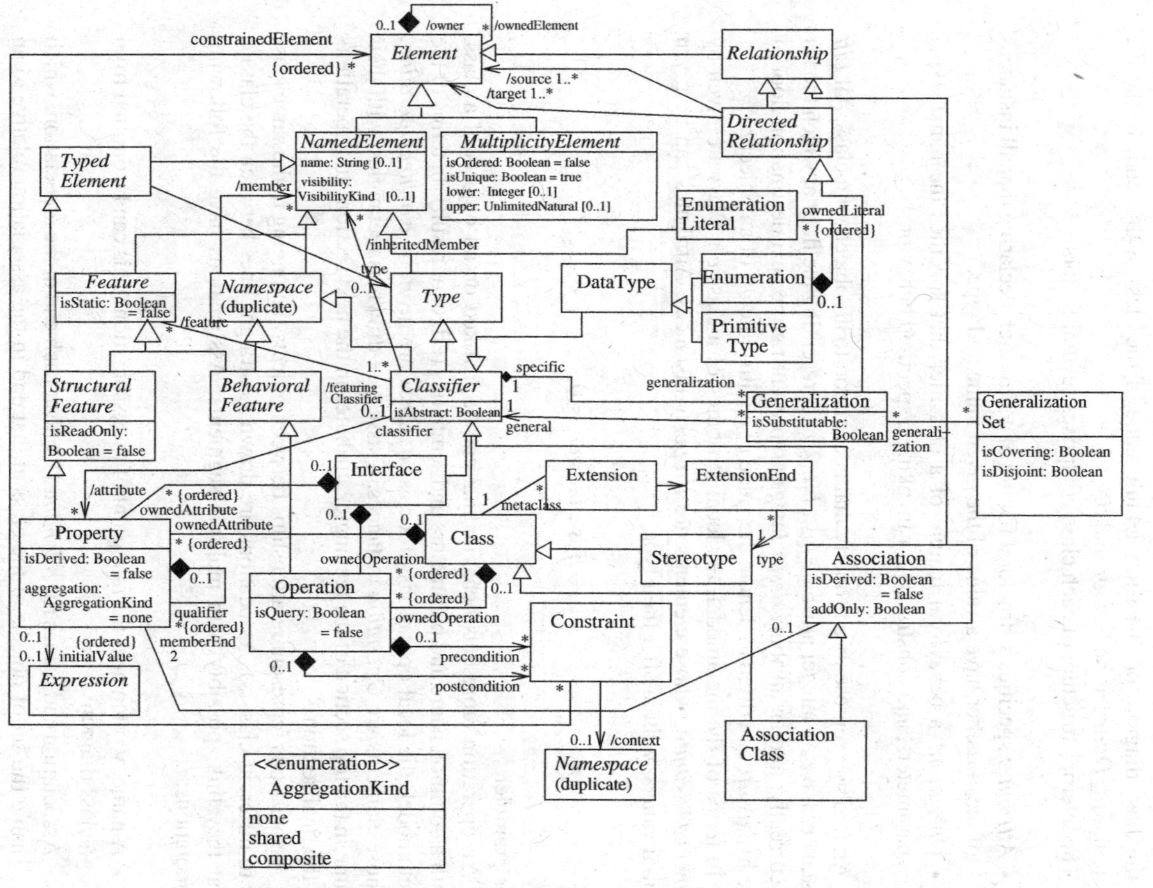

FIGURE 1.2 Part of the UML 2.1 metamodel for class diagrams.

In Figure 1.1 the classes (instances of the metaclass *Class* in Figure 1.2) are *Lift*, *Door*, *LightSet*, and *Light*, the associations (instances of the metaclass *Association*) are *Lift_Door*, *Lift_LightSet*, and *LightSet_Light*. The *memberEnd* sequence for each association identifies its ends (two or more *Property* instances). These can be named in the class diagram or given the default name of the class at that end. In the lift system, *Lift_Door* has ends *door* and *lift*.

The internal structure of each class comprises several factors:

- *Attribute:* specifies a structural feature of a classifier, declaring that all instances of the classifier have a value of the given name and type.
- *Operation:* a behavioral feature of a classifier that specifies the name, type, parameters, and constraints for invoking a specified behavior.

An attribute represents a property that is common to all objects of a class. All *Lift* instances have an integer attribute $fps : Integer$ representing the floor at which the lift is currently; and an attribute $dest : Integer$ representing the next destination floor of the lift. *ax.att* is written to denote the value of an attribute *att* of an object *ax*.

In terms of the metamodel, the local attributes of a class $c : Class$ are given by *c.ownedAttribute*, whose elements are *Property* instances. Attributes can be given initial values, written after their type:

$$fps : Integer = 0$$

for example.

An operation represents behavior that can be invoked on all objects of a class, with a common name and parameters and semantics (effect or result). In terms of the metamodel, the local operations of a class $c : Class$ are given by *c.ownedOperation*, whose elements are *Operation* instances. Classes are drawn as rectangles, with their name in the top section of the rectangle, attributes in the next section, and operations in the final section.

Associations represent relationships between objects (belonging to the same class or to different classes). Assocations are drawn as straight lines between the classes that they link, possibly with multiple segments. Associations have the following annotations:

- A name, written near the mid point of the association. This can be omitted from a class diagram.
- Association end names (or *rolenames*), one at each end of the association, which name the set of objects of the class at that end in the association relative to an object at the other end. A rolename at one end of an association can be considered to be a feature of the class at the *other end* of the association. In other words, the *Property* instances $p1$ and $p2$, which are elements of *r.memberEnd* for an association r, indicate that $p1$ is a feature of the class $p2.type$ of the class located at $p2$'s end of r, and $p2$ is a feature of the class $p1.type$.

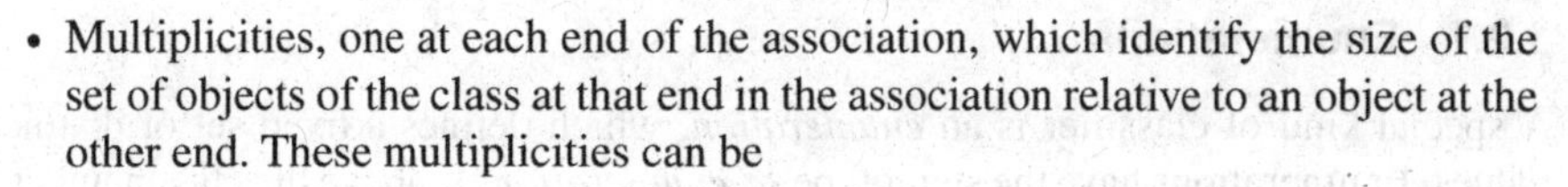

- Multiplicities, one at each end of the association, which identify the size of the set of objects of the class at that end in the association relative to an object at the other end. These multiplicities can be
  — 1
  — n
  — a..b
  — *
  — a..*

  where a, b, and n are particular natural numbers. $*$ represents an unlimited number and is the most general multiplicity. These are parts (meta-attributes *lower* and *upper*) of each *Property*, since this metaclass inherits from *MultiplicityElement*. A feature defined by an association end is termed *many-valued* if its multiplicity is not 1, and *single-valued* if its multiplicity is 1. In versions of UML before UML 2, multiplicities with discontinuous ranges were also possible, such as $m, n..p$ (allows m instances, or any number between n and p inclusive).

A *feature* of a class is therefore any attribute of the class, any operation of the class, or any opposite association end of an association connected to the class. This definition includes inherited features (see Section 1.2.2).

Attributes and association ends can be annotated with the constraint {*readOnly*} (in older versions of UML this was {*frozen*}) to indicate that they cannot be modified after being set initially (e.g., someone's date of birth). Such features are like constants in programming languages. Association ends with multiplicities other than 1 can be marked as {*addOnly*} to indicate that elements cannot be removed from them, only added.

Operations come in two varieties:

- *Query operations*, which only return a value, and do not modify the state of any object.
- *Update operations*, which normally do not return a value, but which modify the object state. Update operations that return a value are also possible.

A query operation is indicated by the constraint {*query*} following the operation in its class box, corresponding to *isQuery* = *true* in the metamodel.

Some standard update operations are *setatt*(*attx* : *T*) to set the value of a nonfrozen attribute *att* : *T* to *attx*, and *addr*(*bx* : *B*) to add *bx* to a nonfrozen association end *r* (of multiplicity not equal to 1).

Attributes and operations may be *static* (in previous versions of UML this was referred to as *class scope*); this means that they are not specific to individual objects of the class, but instead, are independent of such objects. Class scope is indicated by underlining the attribute or operation. A typical example is a *constructor* operation of a class, which produces a new instance of the class.

1.2.1 Enumerations

A special kind of classifier is an *enumeration*, which defines a fixed set of distinct values. Enumerations have the stereotype ≪ *enumeration* ≫ above the class name, to indicate that they are instances of the *Enumeration* metamodel class. Enumerations can be used as the types of attributes elsewhere in the model: for example, *LMState* and *DMState* in the lift example.

1.2.2 Inheritance

Inheritance is denoted by an open-headed arrow pointing from one class (the subclass) to another (the superclass). This is used to express the fact that one class represents a special case of the concept represented by another. All the attributes, roles, and operations of the superclass automatically become attributes, roles, and operations of the subclass. Every instance of the subclass is also an instance of the superclass: If $x : B$ holds, where B is a subclass of A, then $x : A$ holds also.

Inheritance of class c by class d is represented in the metamodel by c : *Class* having $c = g.general$ for some g : *Generalization*, where $d = g.specific$. Inheritance cannot be cyclic: If a class A is a subclass, directly or indirectly, of class B, then B cannot be a subclass of A. However, several classes can be subclasses of the same class (*multiple subclassing*), and one class can be a direct subclass of several other classes (*multiple inheritance*).

A class may be *abstract*, meaning that it has no direct instances of its own, only instances of its subclasses. The notation for an abstract class is to place the class name in italic font, as shown in Figure 1.3. This diagram also shows an example of an abstract operation, *maximumLoad*() : *Integer*. Such operations have no definition in the superclass, but have (potentially different) definitions in the subclasses. Abstract operations are also written in italic. (The meta-attribute *isAbstract* is shown for *BehavioralFeature* in Figure 1.6.)

In general, an operation $op(x : T)$ in a subclass D may redefine an operation with the same name and parameters in its superclasses, so that the definition given in D is used whenever *op* is invoked on an object that actually belongs to D. This is known as operation *overriding*.

A special form of classifier, similar to an abstract class in that it cannot be instantiated directly, is the *interface*, which is a classifier whose purpose is to specify a set of operations that will be defined (implemented) in subclasses of the interface, and which all users (clients) of the interface can rely on being implemented. Interfaces form a bridge between one subsystem of a system (the services of this subsystem are specified as operations in the interface) and other subsystems, which wish to use the services of this subsystem. Interfaces are marked with an ≪ *interface* ≫ stereotype. An interface may be implemented by a number of behaviored classifiers via a relationship of *InterfaceRealization* (analogously to *Generalization*). c : *BehavioredClassifier* implements i : *Interface* if there is r : *InterfaceRealization* such that $i = r.contract$ and $c = r.implementingClassifier$. All features owned by an interface must be public.

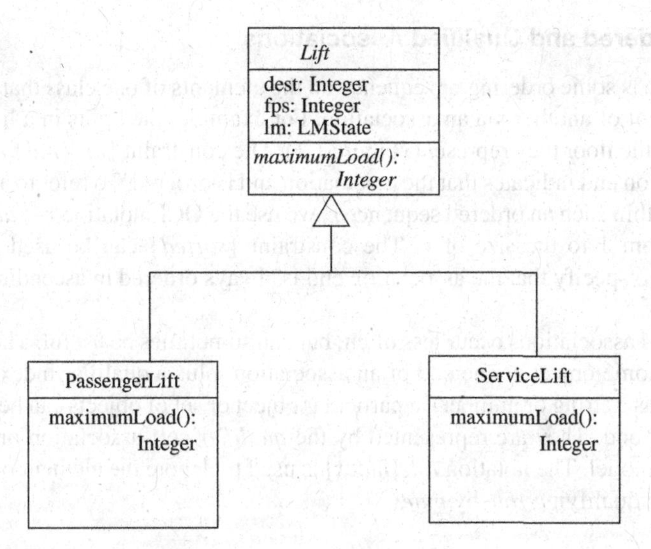

FIGURE 1.3 Abstract class example.

It is normal for the *base class* of a class hierarchy (i.e., the class at the top of the hierarchy, without ancestors) to be abstract. Such classes define the common structure and properties of all their subclasses. A class is termed *concrete* if it is not abstract.

1.2.3 Identity and Derived Attributes

A useful concept that can be defined in UML is that of *identity* attributes. These have the property that their values can be used to identify objects, because no two objects of their class will have the same attribute value. For example, the bank account number of an account within a bank should be unique: No two different accounts can have the same account number. The constraint {*identity*} after an attribute defines it as an identity. These can be expressed as a *Constraint* in terms of the metamodel: Each model element may have any number of constraints attached.

The formal property of an identity attribute *att* of a class *C* is

$$x : C \textit{ and } y : C \textit{ and } x.att = y.att \quad \textit{implies } x = y$$

The concept is the same as that of a *primary key* in a database. Normally, only one attribute within a class is an identity attribute.

Another special form of attribute is the *derived attribute*, attributes whose value can be computed from the values of other elements in a model. Derived attributes are shown annotated by a leading "/." This is expressed by the *isDerived* meta-attribute shown in Figure 1.2. Roles can also be derived, and such roles are shown with a "/" before their name.

1.2.4 Ordered and Qualified Associations

Often, there is some ordering or sequence on the elements of one class that are linked to an element of another via an association. For example, the lights in a light set are ordered by the floor they represent (Figure 1.1). The constraint {*ordered*} attached to an association end indicates that the association end is ordered. To refer to a particular position within such an ordered sequence r, we use the OCL notation $r \rightarrow at(i)$, where i ranges from 1 to the size of r. The constraint {*sorted*} can be used instead of {*ordered*} to specify that the association end is always ordered in ascending order of its elements.

Qualified associations occur less often, but can sometimes be useful. They express that given some object at one end of an association, plus a qualifier index (a simple value such as a string or number), a particular object or set of objects can be identified at the other end. They are represented by the *qualifier* self-association on *Property* in the metamodel. The notation $role[index]$ is used to denote the element or elements obtained by qualifying *role* by *index*.

1.2.5 Aggregation

Another special form of association is an *aggregation* or *composition*. The difference with normal associations is conceptual: A normal association expresses "has a" relationships (e.g., a *Lift* has a set of *LightSet*s that indicate its position). An aggregation expresses "is part of"/"is composed of" relationships, such as a *LightSet* being composed of *Light*s.

The main semantic aspect of such relationships is that the "whole" side, marked with a black lozenge, always has multiplicity at most 1, and that deletion of an object of this class also deletes all part objects aggregated to it (the *deletion propagation* property). If the multiplicity is 1 at the whole end, part objects cannot exist without being attached to a whole object. In the metamodel, the metafeature *aggregation* has the value *composite* for the association end representing the whole side.

UML also has a weaker notion of *simple aggregation*, represented using an unfilled diamond at the container/whole end ($aggregation = shared$). This does not have the strong semantic property of deletion propagation, but is used to indicate that the association has a whole/part aspect. At most one end of an association can be a composition or aggregation.

1.2.6 Association Classes

An association class is an association that is also a class, and it can have attributes and operations in the same way as has any class. Effectively, each link (pair of objects) in the association is able to have its own attributes and operations, just as does a normal object of a class. A class box is attached to the association by a dashed line, and the features of the association class are written in this box.

1.2.7 Stereotypes

A diagram element in UML may be marked with a label in double angle brackets, such as ≪ *enumeration* ≫. These are called *stereotypes* of the element and indicate that the element is a specialized form of the diagram element that uses the same graphical notation: An enumeration is a specialized kind of class, and an implicit association is a specialized kind of association, for example.

Stereotypes enable the basic UML notation to be extended with new notations. This is especially useful in platform-specific models, in order to mark certain model elements as being of a particular kind in this platform (≪ *session bean* ≫ in a Java Enterprise Edition PSM, for example, or ≪ *form* ≫ in a Web application PSM).

1.3 OBJECT DIAGRAMS

Object diagrams are variants of class diagrams in which *object specifications* are denoted instead of classes. Object specifications describe particular objects by means of their attribute values, expressed as equalities,

$$att = val$$

and by their links to other objects, expressed as lines between the connected objects. Object specifications are labeled with an optional name and the name of their class, all underlined. Figure 1.4 shows a lift system with two lifts and five floors as an object

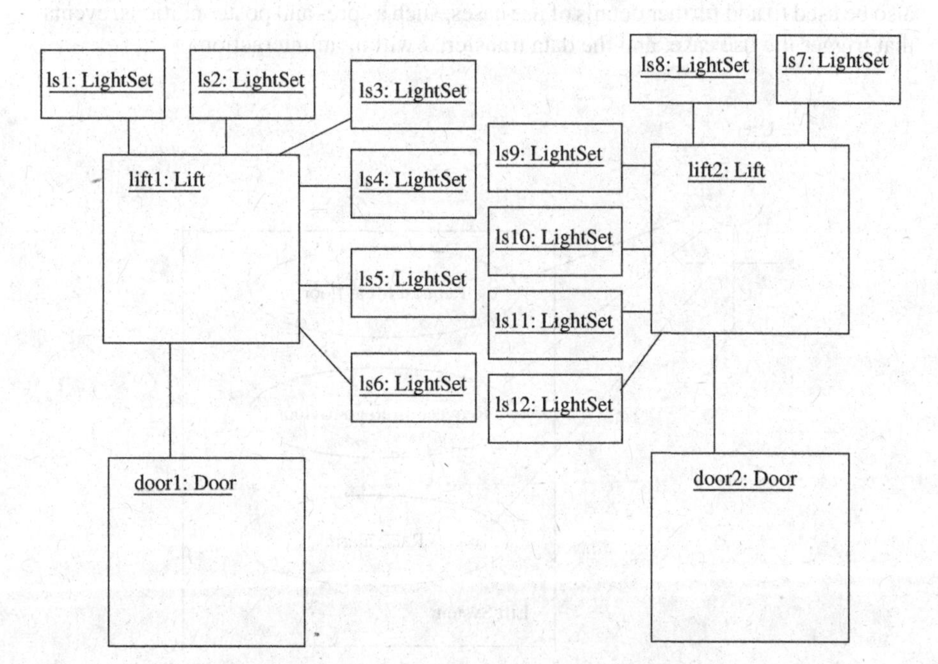

FIGURE 1.4 Object diagram of a specific lift system.

diagram. Notice that a model such as Figure 1.1 can be considered to be an object diagram relative to the UML metamodel as a class diagram.

1.4 USE CASES

Use cases are often the earliest UML modeling notation used within a development. Use cases identify how a system will be used and which categories of external agents (human users or other external agents) can interact with the system. The notation is quite simple, using ovals to represent the use cases and stick figures to represent the agents (known as *actors* in UML).

Figure 1.5 shows the use case diagram of the lift system. This diagram indicates that a user of the system can carry out three functionalities by interacting with it: to request a lift to come to the floor (external request), to request a lift to go to a floor (internal request), and to raise an alarm. Use cases provide a "black box" view of the functionality of the system, omitting the internal details of how the functionality is carried out by the execution of interacting objects.

One use case may inherit from another if it represents a special case of its ancestor. Similarly, one actor may inherit from another actor, to represent that it is a specialized form of its ancestor. In particular, it will inherit all the connections that its ancestor has with use cases.

Part of the metamodel for use cases is shown in the metamodel of Figure 1.6, which includes many of the dynamic modeling elements of UML 2.1. Textual notations can also be used to add further details of use cases, such as pre- and postconditions, events that trigger the use case, and the data transfered within an interaction.

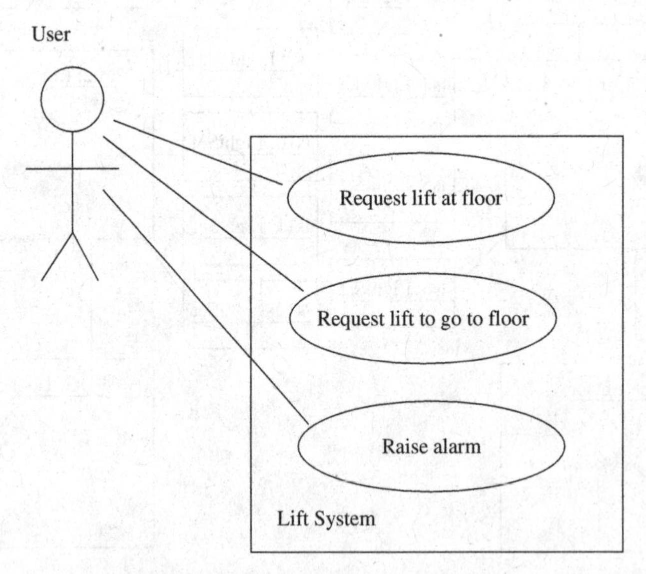

FIGURE 1.5 Use cases of a lift system.

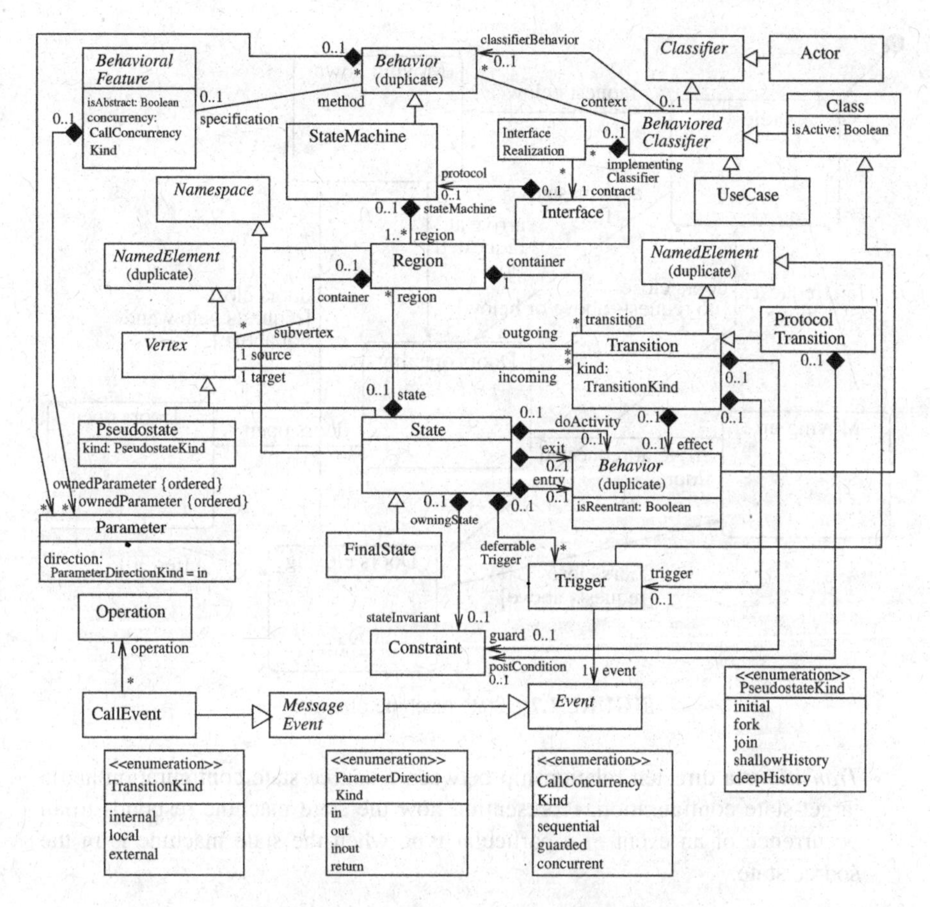

FIGURE 1.6 UML 2.1 behavior metamodel.

1.5 STATE MACHINES

State machines describe how an object or system changes over time and what events (such as operation calls) it may respond to and how it responds to them. Figure 1.6 shows a metamodel for state machines. Note that this metamodel is additive to the class diagram metamodel: Where a metaclass such as *BehavioralFeature* occurs in both metamodels, it is considered to have all the features and generalization relationships specified in both. Figure 1.7 shows the behavior of an individual lift as a state machine.

1.5.1 State Machine Notation

There are two key metaclasses in the state machine notation:

- *State:* models a situation during which some (possibly implicit) invariant condition holds.

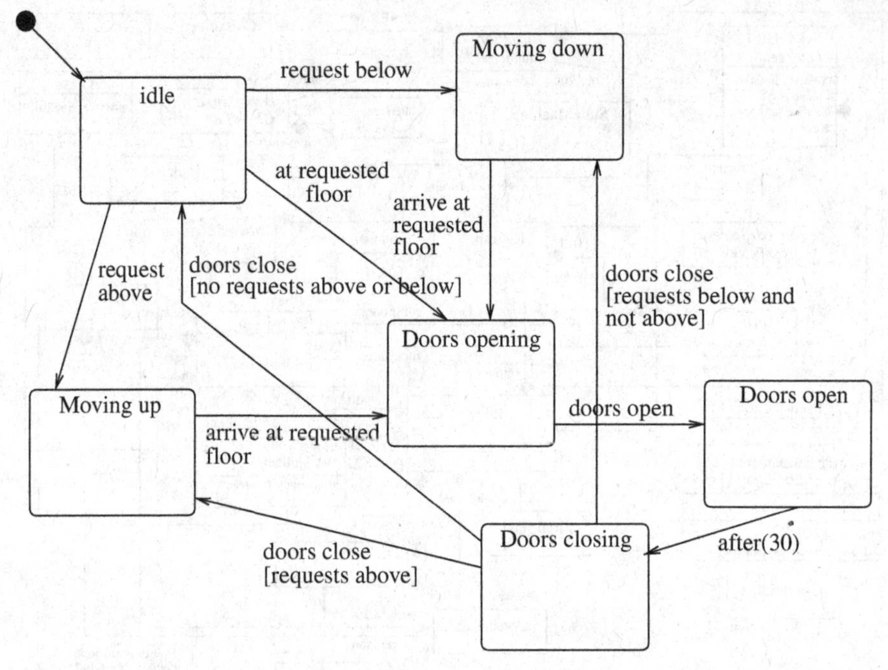

FIGURE 1.7 State machine of a lift.

- *Transition:* a directed relationship between a source-state configuration and a target-state configuration, representing how the state machine responds to an occurrence of an event of a particular type when the state machine is in the source state.

A state represents some phase during the lifetime of an object or system which is significant for its behavior (it may have different behavior in different states). A state is occupied for some interval of time, and is entered and exited by means of transitions. The notation for a state is a rounded rectangle, and transitions are drawn as arrows from their source state to their target state. The initial state, from which the behavior begins, is indicated by a transition whose source is shown by a black circle. An initial state is expressed in the metamodel as a *Pseudostate* with *kind* = *initial*.

State machine diagrams can be used to model both the environment of a system and the system's behavior. The description can be of the behavior of an individual operation (in which case, states in the diagram represent intermediate states during execution of the operation, and transitions represent steps in the algorithm of the operation) or of the behavior of an object over all possible operation executions (states represent states of the object when no operations are executing on it, and transitions show what happens when an operation executes).

States have names, and can also have invariants, written within square brackets inside the state. Invariants of a state are conditions that hold true while the system is in the state.

Transitions are labeled

$$event(parameters)[guard]/actions$$

where *event* represents the event that triggers the transition. If the state machine models the environment, this event can be some real-world event. In models of object/system behavior it is usually an operation call on the object or system described by the state machine. The parameters are then the formal parameters of the operation.

A *guard* is an additional condition that must be true for the transition to take place, and *actions* are actions (such as operation calls on the same or other objects) that take place when the transition is followed (the *effect* of a transition in the metamodel). Alternatively, for protocol transitions, a postcondition [*Post*] can be specified. All of these parts of the transition label can be omitted.

In the situation that an operation has some transition in a state machine, but there is no transition with a true guard for this operation from the current state of this state machine, there are three variations on the semantics:

1. The operation can take place, but has no effect, either on the state or on the values of any feature of any object (*skip semantics*, also known as *ignore semantics*).
2. The operation can take place but has an undefined effect (*error* or *precondition semantics*).
3. The operation cannot take place; any caller of the operation is blocked if they try to execute it in such a case (*blocking semantics*).

Error semantics is the most general; it requires that we explicitly add transitions for all cases (guard conditions) of an operation from a state if the operation has some transition in the model. Blocking semantics is appropriate for shared objects in concurrent systems (e.g., an object that is attempting to place messages in a buffer should be blocked if the buffer is already full).

If an operation has no transition in a model, it is assumed to be state independent and not to change the state (it may, however, change the values of attributes according to the definition of its postcondition in the class diagram).

State machines can describe the detailed steps of an operation; that is, they can define an algorithm (platform independent or specific). In such state machines the transitions have no explicit triggers; instead, they are triggered when their source state is occupied, all internal activity of the state has been completed, and the transition guard is true.

In UML there are two distinct varieties of state machine:

1. *Protocol state machines:* used to specify the intended pattern of calls on an object. In such state machines the transitions have postconditions instead of actions.
2. *Behavior state machines:* used to define object and operation behavior. These have actions instead of postconditions. States in behavior state machines may have *entry actions*, which are executed whenever the state is entered, and *exit actions*, which are executed whenever the state is exited. They may also have

a *do action*, which starts when the state is entered and is terminated when the state is exited (if it has not already finished execution). Skip semantics is usually assumed for behavior state machines.

Transitions may be triggered by time-based events such as timeouts. A transition with trigger $after(t)$ leaving a state s means that the transition is triggered whenever s has been occupied continuously for t time units.

A transition may be *internal* to a state, which means that when it occurs it does not cause exit or entry of the state (or entry or exit of any state contained in the state). Internal transitions of a state are written inside the state, without an arrow.

A *local* transition does not exit its composite source state, but may exit or enter states within the composite state. Local transitions are drawn within the composite state, starting at its boundary and ending at a state within the composite state.

1.5.2 Composite States

States may have an internal structure of states, which represent subphases of the phase (of an object/system life cycle or operation processing) represented by the state. The substates of a state are analogous to the subclasses of a class. In terms of a metamodel (Figure 1.6), a composite state s has $s.region$ nonempty; the elements $r.subvertex$ for $r \in s.region$ are then the substates of s, which can be normal states or pseudostates.

Two special forms of state are *final states*, denoted by a bull's-eye symbol, which denotes termination of the containing state, and the *history state*, denoted by the H symbol. A transition to a history state has as actual target the most recently occupied substate of the composite state containing the history state.

Composite states with single regions (*region* has size 1) are termed *OR states*; composite states with multiple regions are termed *AND states*. When the system is in an OR state, it is in exactly one direct substate of this state; when it is in an AND state, it is in all regions of the state.[1] AND states are divided into concurrent parts (the regions), which describe parts of the life cycle of an object (or operation) that can happen semi-independently.

It is possible to have any number of regions in a concurrent state, and to refer to the state of one region within another. Figure 1.8 shows a lift state machine with three states organized as substates of an OR composite state *At floor*. A transition from a composite state, such as *doors close*, abbreviates a set of transitions, one from each of the immediate substates of the composite state.

Transitions may have multiple sources and multiple targets, but all the sources must be in different regions of some AND state, and similarly for the targets. By default, a region of an AND composite state is entered at its initial state, an action termed *implicit entry*. An example of an AND state is shown in Figure 1.9, where the lift and the lift door are represented as two regions of the same AND composite state. The initial state of this composite state is the tuple $(idle, closed)$ of the initial states of its regions.

[1] UML 2 allows a variant semantics in which membership of an OR state is possible without membership of any contained state (concrete OR state), but this is unusual.

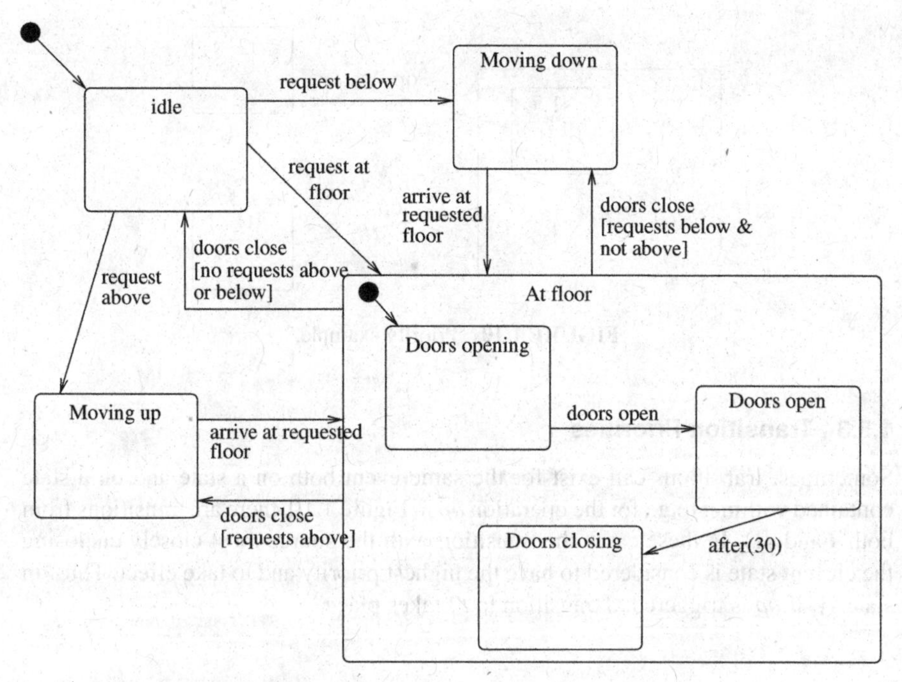

FIGURE 1.8 State machine of a lift with an OR state.

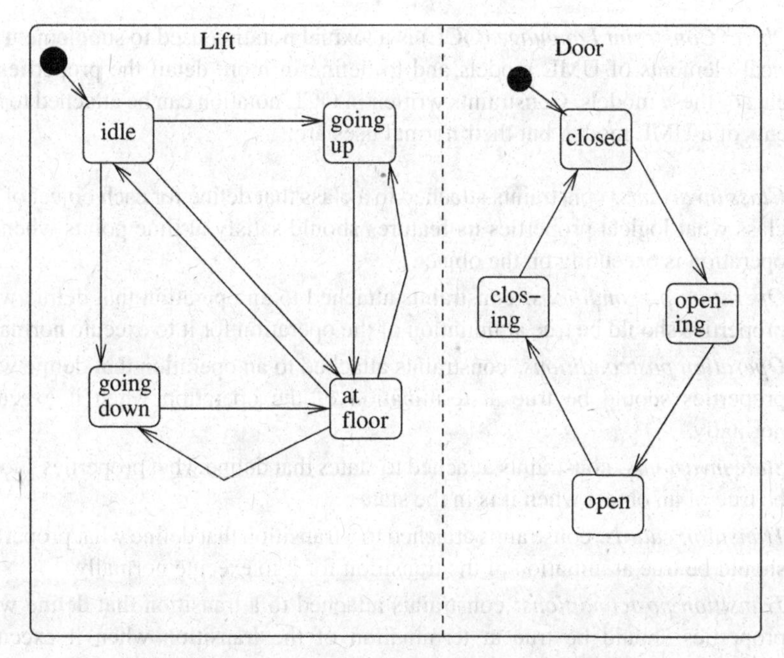

FIGURE 1.9 State machine of a lift with an AND state.

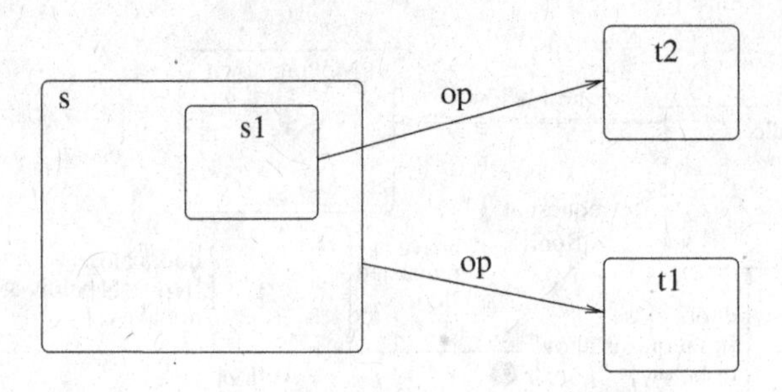

FIGURE 1.10 Priority example.

1.5.3 Transition Priorities

Sometimes, transitions can exist for the same event both on a state and on a state contained within it (e.g., for the operation *op* in Figure 1.10, there are transitions from both *s* and *s*1). In these cases the transition with the source most closely enclosing the current state is considered to have the highest priority and to take effect. Thus, in state *s*1, if *op* is triggered, a transition to *t*2 takes place.

1.6 OBJECT CONSTRAINT LANGUAGE

The *Object Constraint Language* (OCL) is a textual notation used to supplement the graphical elements of UML models and to define in more detail the properties of elements of these models. Constraints written in OCL notation can be attached to any elements of a UML model, but their normal uses are:

- *Class invariants:* constraints attached to a class that define for each object of the class what logical properties its features should satisfy at time points when no operation is executing on the object.
- *Operation preconditions:* constraints attached to an operation that define what properties should be true at initiation of the operation for it to execute normally.
- *Operation postconditions:* constraints attached to an operation that define what properties should be true at termination of the operation when it executes normally.
- *State invariants:* constraints attached to states that define what properties should be true of an object when it is in the state.
- *Transition guards:* constraints attached to a transition that define what properties should be true at initiation of the transition for it to execute normally.
- *Transition postconditions:* constraints attached to a transition that define what properties should be true at termination of the transition when it executes normally.

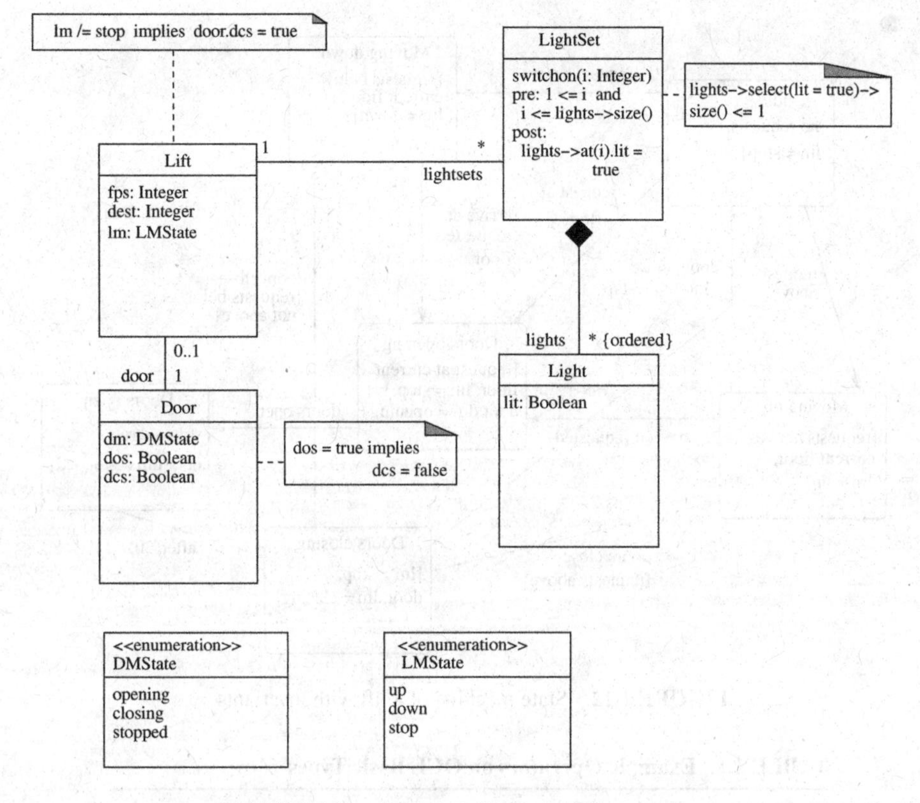

FIGURE 1.11 Lift class diagram with constraints.

A version of the lift class diagram, enhanced with constraints, is shown in Figure 1.11. The class invariant of *Door* expresses that the door open sensor *dos* and door closed sensor *dcs* are never both on:

$$dos = true \quad implies \;\; dcs = false$$

The class invariant of *Lift* specifies that the doors are always closed when the lift is moving:

$$lm \neq stop \quad implies \;\; door.dcs = true$$

The constraint on *LightSet* expresses that at most one light in the set is lit:

$$lights \rightarrow select(lit = true) \rightarrow size() \leq 1$$

The precondition of *switchon*(i : *Integer*) expresses that i is an index of a light in the set:

$$1 \leq i \quad and \quad i \leq lights \rightarrow size()$$

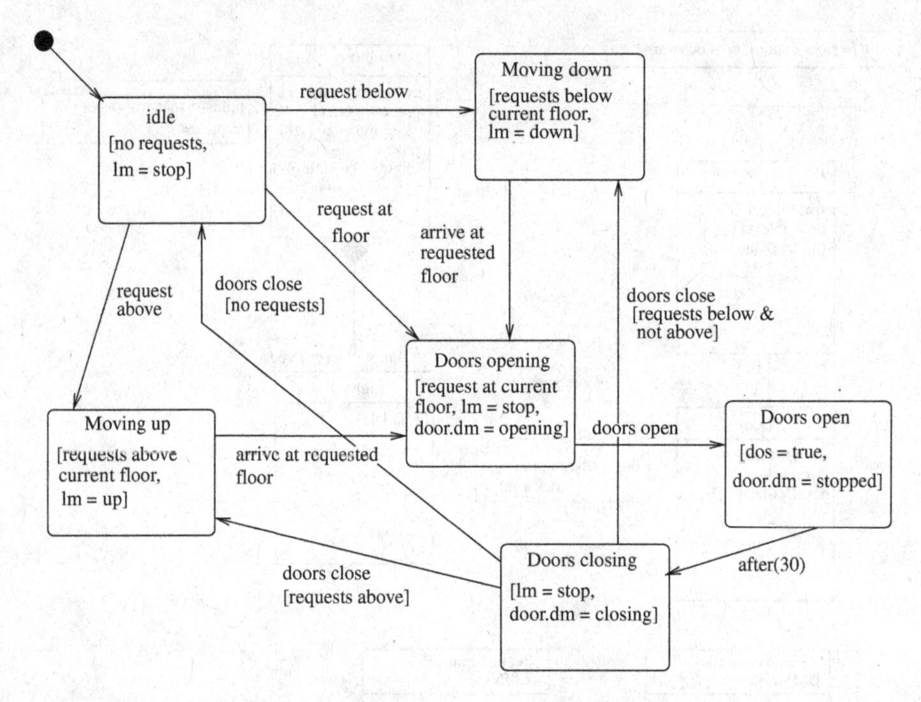

FIGURE 1.12 State machine of a lift with invariants.

TABLE 1.1 Example Operators on OCL Basic Types

Type	Operations
Integer	*, +, −, /, abs()
Real	*, +, −, /, floor()
Boolean	and, or, implies, not
String	size(), concat(s: String), substring(lower: Integer, upper: Integer)

The postcondition sets light i to lit:

$$lights{\rightarrow}at(i).lit = true$$

Figure 1.12 shows the use of state invariants in a lift state machine.

OCL provides the basic types *Boolean*, *Integer*, *Real*, and *String* and the usual operations on these, such as + between numbers and obtaining a substring of a string (Table 1.1).

There are also four types of collection (Table 1.2), corresponding to the four possible combinations of the *isOrdered* and *isUnique* meta-attributes of a *Property* in the metamodel. Sets or bags arise as the values of unordered association ends (e.g., *l.lightsets* for a lift *l*), while ordered sets or sequences arise as the values of ordered association ends (e.g., *s.lights* for a light set *s*).

TABLE 1.2 OCL Collection Types

Type	Properties
Set	unordered collections, without duplicate elements
Bag	unordered collections, possibly with duplicate elements
Sequence	ordered collections, possibly with duplicate elements
OrderedSet	ordered collections, without duplicate elements

TABLE 1.3 OCL General Collection Operations

Operator	Meaning
$s \rightarrow size()$	Number of elements in s, including duplicates
$s \rightarrow includes(x)$	True if $x \in s$, false otherwise
$s \rightarrow excludes(x)$	$not(s \rightarrow includes(x))$
$s \rightarrow count(x)$	Number of times x occurs in s
$s \rightarrow isEmpty()$	True if s has no elements, false otherwise
$s \rightarrow notEmpty()$	True if s has elements, false otherwise
$s \rightarrow sum()$	$+$ combination of all elements of s (numerics)
$s \rightarrow forAll(P)$	True if all elements of s satisfy P
$s \rightarrow exists(P)$	True if some element of s satisfies P
$s \rightarrow select(P)$	Collection of elements of s for which P is true
$s \rightarrow collect(f)$	Collection formed by applying f to each element of s

TABLE 1.4 OCL Specialized Collection Operations

Operator	Meaning
$s \rightarrow union(t)$	For sets: $s \cup t$; for bags: bag union; for ordered sets and sequences: the elements of s followed by those of t
$s \rightarrow at(i)$	The ith element of sequence or ordered set s

Table 1.3 shows some operators that apply to all types of collection. Collection operators are written following an arrow symbol ($\rightarrow$) from the collection in which they operate.

Collect expressions are abbreviated in the common case that one feature is applied after another [e.g.: *l.lightsets.lights* abbreviates *l.lightsets*$\rightarrow$*collect*(*lights*)]. These may result in bags or sequences. In this example the result is effectively a set (a bag without duplicates) because two different lightsets will have disjoint collections of lights. Sets and sequences have additional specialized operators (Table 1.4).

1.7 INTERACTION DIAGRAMS

Interaction diagrams represent the detailed behavior of a system in terms of objects, messages between objects, operation executions, states that hold at particular times, and durations between time points. Two specialized forms of interaction are used in UML: *communication diagrams* (termed *collaboration diagrams* in earlier versions of UML), which focus on the ordering of messages, and *sequence diagrams*, which explicitly represent time.

1.7.1 Sequence Diagrams

The basic elements of a sequence diagram interaction are specifications of operation executions, messages, or points at which conditions hold, on one or more object lifelines (Figure 1.13). In addition, the points at which an object is created or destroyed can be specified. It is also possible to specify the duration between two time points.

Time is shown visually by the y-axis of the diagram, increasing from top to bottom. The vertical lines denote (the lifelines of) objects and are identified by an object name and a class: *object* : *Class*. Messages are shown as arrows between the object lifelines. Returns from synchronous operation calls are shown as dotted-line arrows in the direction opposite to the call, as in Figure 1.13. The execution of an operation

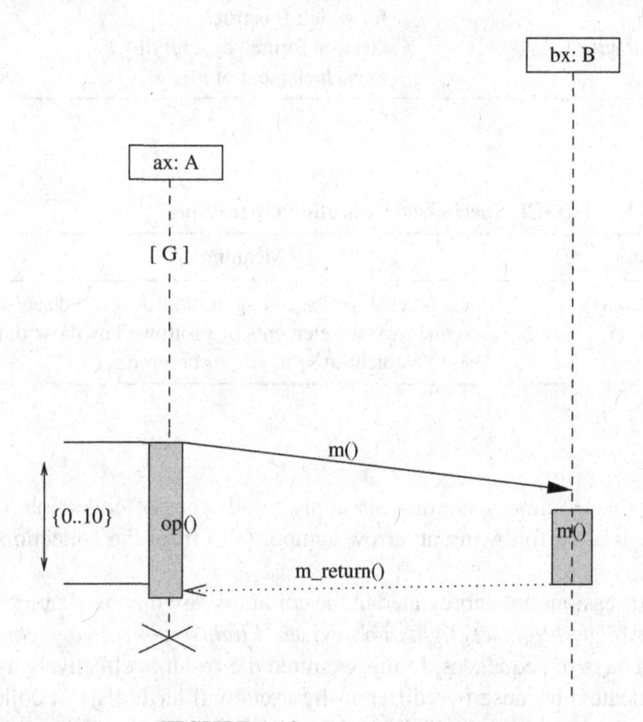

FIGURE 1.13 Sequence diagram.

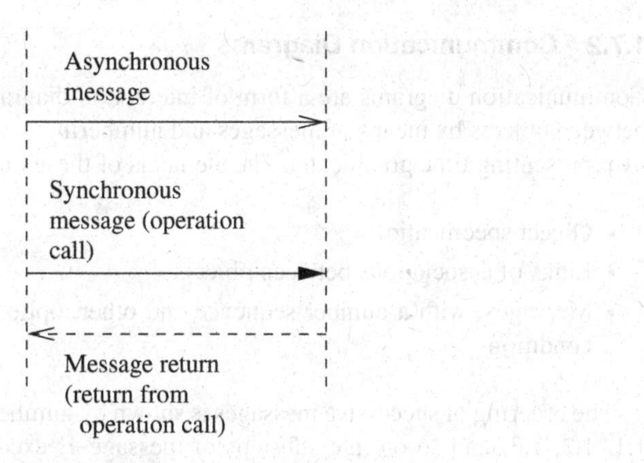

FIGURE 1.14 Message types.

on an object is shown as a shaded rectangle on the lifeline, representing the duration of the execution.

Durations can be specified by identifying two time points; the notation $\{a..b\}$ then refers to the minimum a and maximum b allowed difference between these times. In Figure 1.13 the duration specification asserts that the time between the sending of $m()$ to bx and the reception of the result of this message is no more than 10. Figure 1.14 shows the various types of message that can be drawn between lifelines.

Interactions can be combined by a number of operators:

1. *Ordering along lifelines.* An event time vertically above another on the same lifeline is considered to precede it.
2. *Parallel composition.* $par(I_1, I_2)$ combines two interactions, I_1 and I_2, without any order restrictions on the relative times of their elements. Ordering within I_1 and I_2 is maintained.
3. *Strict sequencing.* The strict sequential composition $strict(I_1, I_2)$ places I_1 entirely above I_2; every event time from I_1 precedes every event time of I_2.
4. *Weak sequencing.* The weak sequential composition $seq(I_1, I_2)$ of two interactions is the union of I_1 and I_2, together with the restriction that for each lifeline, every event time from I_1 on the lifeline precedes every event time of I_2 on the same lifeline.
5. *Alternative.* The meaning of $alt(E, I_1, I_2)$ is the same as I_1 if E holds at the first event occurrence of the interaction; otherwise, it is that of I_2.
6. *Negation.* The traces of I are forbidden traces of $neg(I)$.

Interactions are used to describe intended scenarios of system behavior, such as different cases of execution of a use case.

1.7.2 Communication Diagrams

Communication diagrams are a form of interaction diagram that shows interactions between objects by means of messages and numbering of these messages, instead of by representing time graphically. The elements of these diagrams are:

- Object specifications
- Links of associations between objects
- Messages, with a number sequence and other, optional annotations, such as a condition

The ordering of successive messages is shown by numbering: Messages numbered 1.1, 1.2, 1.3, and so on, are substeps of message 1, executed in order. If, in turn, message 1.1 had subparts, these would be numbered 1.1.1, 1.1.2, and so on.

Conditions placed on a message mean that the message is sent only if the condition is true. Concurrency can be indicated by alphabetical indexes: messages 1.1a and 1.1b execute concurrently within message 1.1.

As on sequence diagrams, asynchronous messages are shown by open arrowheads, and synchronous messages are shown by filled black arrowheads.

Iteration is shown by a condition $*[i = 1..n]$, meaning that a message is to be sent n times.

1.8 ACTIVITY DIAGRAMS

Activity diagrams provide a means to describe behavior composed of collections of tasks (such as the algorithms of operations, or the workflows of business processes), in a graphical manner. UML Superstructure 2.0 [2] defines activities and actions as:

- *Activity:* specification of parameterized behavior as the coordinated sequencing of subordinate units whose individual elements are actions.
- *Action:* represents a single step within an activity: that is, one that is not further decomposed within the activity. An action may be complex in its effect and not atomic.

Activities are a generalization of sequential programming constructs such as sequencing, conditionals, and loops. They can also be regarded as a generalization of state machines in which the states represent actions within the activity. Figure 1.15 shows an activity describing a workflow. The arrowed lines denote sequencing of actions, and there are also choice points (diamonds) and parallel flows (starting and ending at vertical bars).

1.9 DEPLOYMENT DIAGRAMS

Deployment diagrams show how the artifacts (i.e., executable code, data sources, etc.) of a system are allocated to nodes (computational resources). They show a specific

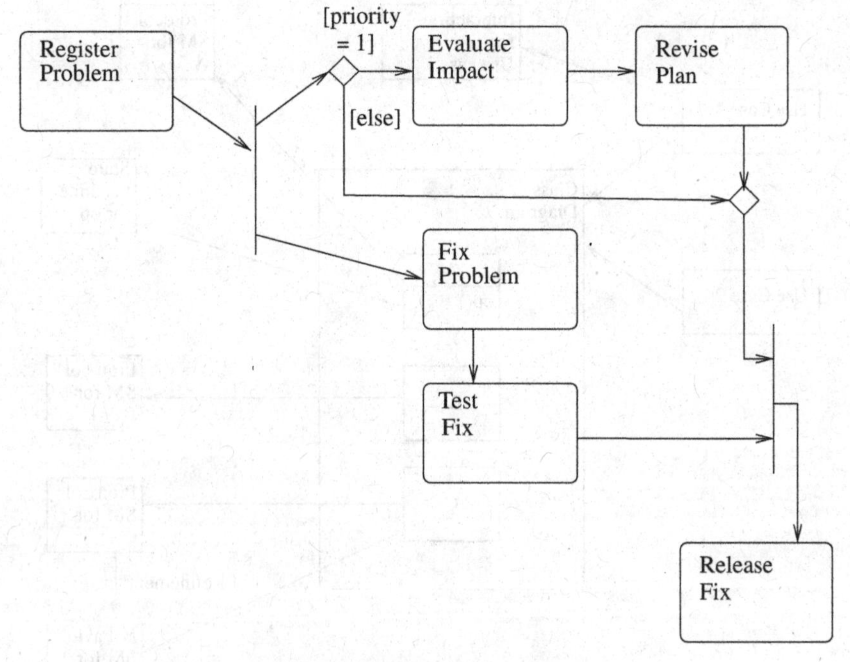

FIGURE 1.15 Problem workflow.

physical architecture of devices upon which the system will operate. Artifacts are drawn as class rectangles with the stereotype ≪*artifact*≫.

Nodes are drawn as three-dimensional cubes. Nodes may represent devices or execution environments; devices are hardware components with computational capabilities, such as a computer or modem. Execution environments are software platforms upon which specific forms of software artifacts can be deployed (e.g., a database server can host particular databases).

Communication paths between nodes are drawn as solid lines, with directionality and multiplicity of the ends indicated. Such paths may represent physical wired connections or wireless data transmission. Deployment of an artifact on a node can be shown by drawing the artifact within the node or by a dashed ≪*deploy*≫ arrow from the artifact to the node.

1.10 RELATIONSHIPS BETWEEN UML MODELS

Typically, a UML specification will consist of a set of interrelated UML models (Figure 1.16):

- A class diagram (CD).
- One or more use cases associated with a CD. Each use case will be related to one of more classes of CD, using instances of these classes and operations on these

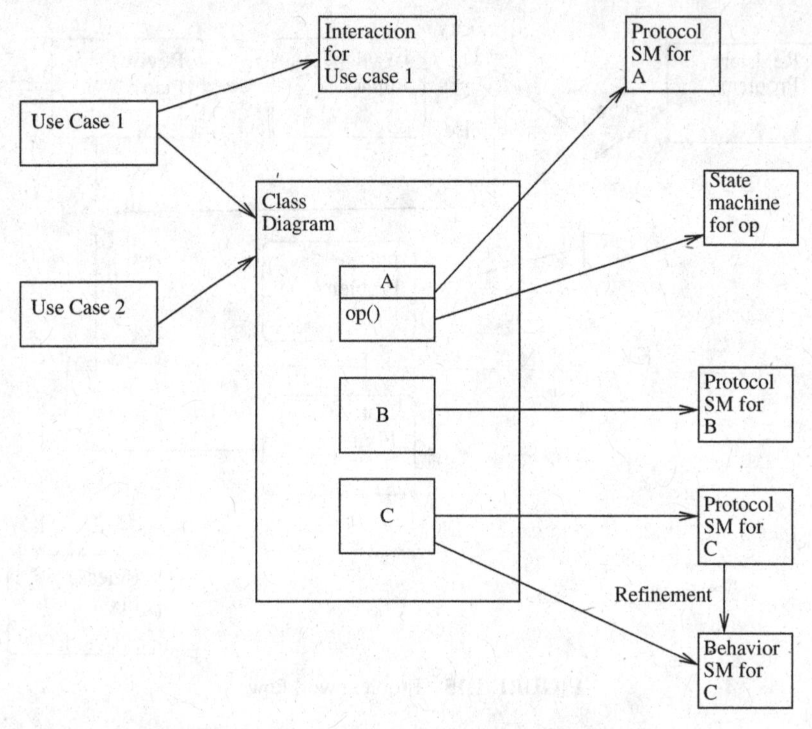

FIGURE 1.16 Relationships between UML models.

instances. The use cases may be given detailed definitions using behavior state machines, or activities, or examples of their behavior can be given by means of sequence diagrams or interactions.

- Each class and interface of CD may have an associated protocol state machine that defines the intended life cycles of its instances. This state machine may be refined to a behavior state machine. Operation behavior can be shown both in the class diagram, using pre- and postconditions, and on the (protocol or behavior) state machine of the class. It is usual to show state-independent and local behavior in the class diagram, and state-dependent behavior and invocation of supplier operations in the state machine.
- Operations of classes in CD may have associated behavior state machines which define detailed algorithms for these operations. These algorithms should satisfy any pre- or postspecification of the operations.

1.11 SUMMARY

In this chapter we have described the main features of the class diagram, state machine diagram, use case, activity diagram, sequence diagram, communication diagram, and deployment diagram notations of UML 2.

REFERENCES

1. OMG. Model-driven architecture. http://www.omg.org/mda/, 2007.
2. OMG. *UML Superstructure, Version 2.0.* OMG Document Formal/05-07-04. Object Management Group, Needham, MA, 2005.
3. OMG. *UML Superstructure, Version 2.1.1.* OMG Document Formal/2007-02-03. Object Management Group, Needham, MA, 2007.
4. OMG. *UML OCL 2.0 Specification.* Final/06-05-01. Object Management Group, Needham, MA, 2006.

CHAPTER 2

THE ROLE OF SEMANTICS

KEVIN LANO
Department of Computer Science, King's College London, London, UK

2.1 INTRODUCTION

In this chapter we explain semantics and the role it plays in the definition and application of a modeling language: specifically, UML.

The term *semantics* has been used in many different, inconsistent ways in computing. For example, *static semantics* is used in UML documents to mean additional syntactic constraints on the notation elements. In this book, *semantics* is defined as follows:

- *Semantics:* a precisely defined mapping of the elements of a language into a precisely defined domain of values.

The mapping is termed the *semantic mapping*. The domain of values is termed the *semantic domain*. To each construction that it is possible to form in the language (e.g., each model that obeys the UML 2.0 metamodel), the semantic mapping gives a precise semantic representation or *denotation* (Figure 2.1).

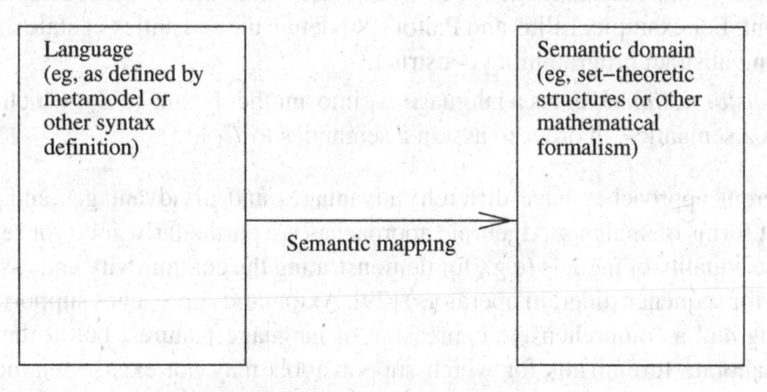

FIGURE 2.1 Semantics of a language.

UML 2 Semantics and Applications. Edited by Kevin Lano

Often, the mapping is neglected in considerations of semantics, but it is an essential part of a semantic definition of a language, and it should be defined so that there are no ambiguities or gaps in the semantic assignment.

The semantic domain may consist of purely mathematical constructs, such as sets, functions, or algebras, or it may itself be a language, such as B, Object-Z, or even a subset of the source language. For example, a UML class C could be interpreted as a set $\overline{C}$, as an Object-Z class, or as a B module.

A semantics is often defined in a *compositional* manner; that is, the elements of a complex language construct are mapped into their own individual representations; then the semantics of the construct as a whole is assembled, according to a rule, from these. The semantics of expressions is usually defined in this way. For example, the OCL expression s->union(t) could be given the semantics $s \cup t$, where s and t are the semantic denotations of the expressions s and t, as mathematical collections, and $\cup$ is the mathematical collection union operator.

2.2 DIFFERENT SEMANTIC APPROACHES

The following are some alternative approaches to assigning semantics to a language that have been used for UML:

- *Algebraic:* maps the language constructs into a mathematical algebra. For example, Meng and Barbosa [29] interpret sequence diagrams as elements of a co-algebra.
- *Axiomatic:* maps language constructs into logical theories, consisting of mathematical structures together with axioms defining their properties. For example, Lano [23] interprets UML models as theories in a real-time logic.
- *Metamodeling:* defines a language $\mathcal{L}_1$ and its semantics as a model in a language $\mathcal{L}_2$ (possibly the same language as $\mathcal{L}_1$) [5].
- *Operational:* maps a language into structures of an abstract execution environment. For example, Lilius and Paltor [26] define the semantics of state machines using abstract programming constructs.
- *Transformational:* maps a language $\mathcal{L}_1$ into another language $\mathcal{L}_2$, which already has a semantics, in order to assign a semantics to $\mathcal{L}_1$ [13].

Different approaches have different advantages and disadvantages and support different forms of analysis. Algebraic approaches are particularly good for reasoning about the equality of models (e.g., for demonstrating the commutivity and associativity laws for sequence diagram operators) [29]. Axiomatic approaches support general reasoning and a comprehensive expression of language features, but at the cost of using elaborate formalisms for which support tools may not exist. Metamodelling and transformation approaches require the existence of a language $\mathcal{L}_2$ with a well-defined semantics. Use can then be made of tools for $\mathcal{L}_2$ to analyze models in $\mathcal{L}_1$. If $\mathcal{L}_1$ and $\mathcal{L}_2$ are quite different (e.g., UML and B), the mapping of languages may be difficult to define and apply. Results of semantic analysis performed in the second language may also be difficult to relate to the original language. If the languages are the same, or $\mathcal{L}_2$ is a subset of $\mathcal{L}_1$, the reduction of $\mathcal{L}_1$ to $\mathcal{L}_2$ introduces a semantic circularity, which must be resolved by giving an independent semantics to $\mathcal{L}_2$.

2.3 APPLICATIONS OF SEMANTICS

The definition of a semantics for any significant language is a substantial task, so we could ask why it is necessary or useful. There are two general categories of application of a language semantics: (1) to the language itself, to ensure its soundness and correctness, and (2) to the use of the language (e.g., to support the definition of tools to create and process models in the language).

In the first category are the following applications:

- *Language validity*. Languages are constructed for a purpose, to enable language users to express concepts using appropriate notations. Defining a semantics for the language can help to check that the notations are complete (they express the full range of concepts they are intended to express) and consistent (the notation is unambiguous).
- *Improving a language*. The semantics may uncover cases where the language has unclear or ambiguous meanings (e.g., the rules for compound transition priorities in UML state machines, or for history states) [6]. Corrections to these problems can be based on the semantics [21].

In the second category are:

- *Model validity*. A semantics provides a way to analyze the meaning of individual models in a language, to check that these models are internally consistent or have other desirable semantic properties. For example, if we translated the class of Figure 2.2 into B, we could apply a theorem-proving tool that would quickly

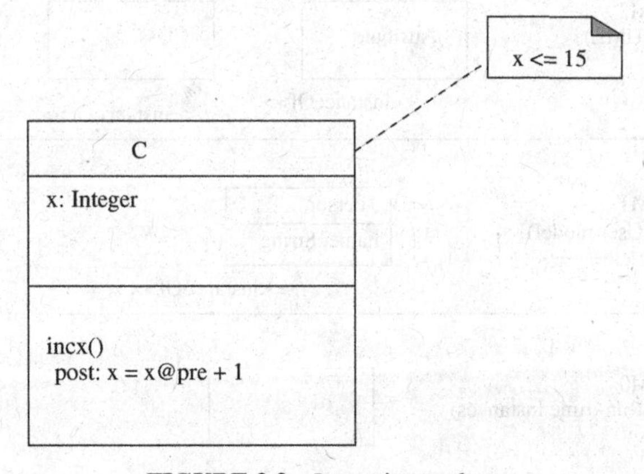

FIGURE 2.2 Inconsistent class.

uncover the inconsistency between the definition of the operation postcondition and the class invariant.

- *Validating transformations.* Transformations of one model into another should normally preserve the semantic properties of the starting model. Proposed transformations can therefore be checked for correctness by comparing the semantics of the start and result models. The situation is similar for code generation from models if a semantics for the resulting implementation language exists.
- *Language tool definition.* Semantics can be used to define tools for the language to ensure that analyses and transformations supported by the tools are semantically correct.

2.4 UML SEMANTICS

The documents of the UML 2 standard use metamodeling to define the syntax of UML and some parts of the semantics. Informal natural language is also used to define the semantics. Specifically, the UML is defined as a model of the metaobject framework (MOF) metamodel, which is itself defined using a subset of UML notation (Figure 2.3). For example, the concept of a class is defined in the UML metamodel by the metaclass *Class*, with associated sequences of *ownedAttributes*, *ownedOperations*, and other features (Figure 2.4).

This metamodel is itself defined in a subset of the class diagram notation of UML. The UML infrastructure document [36] precisely defines this metacircular

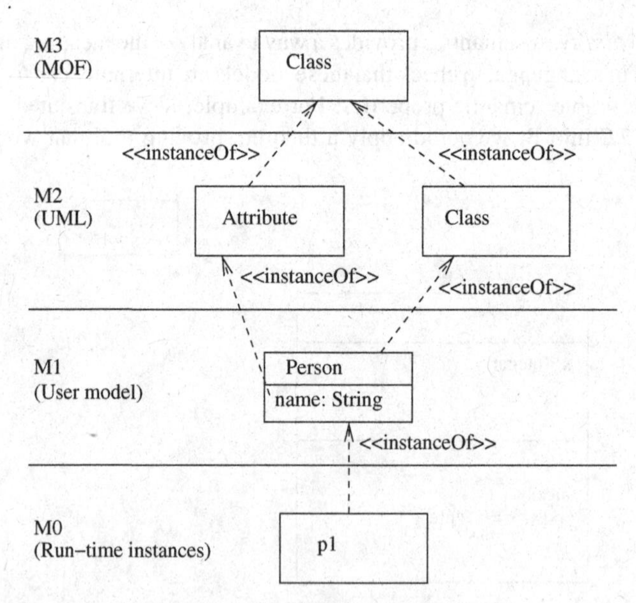

FIGURE 2.3 UML metamodel levels.

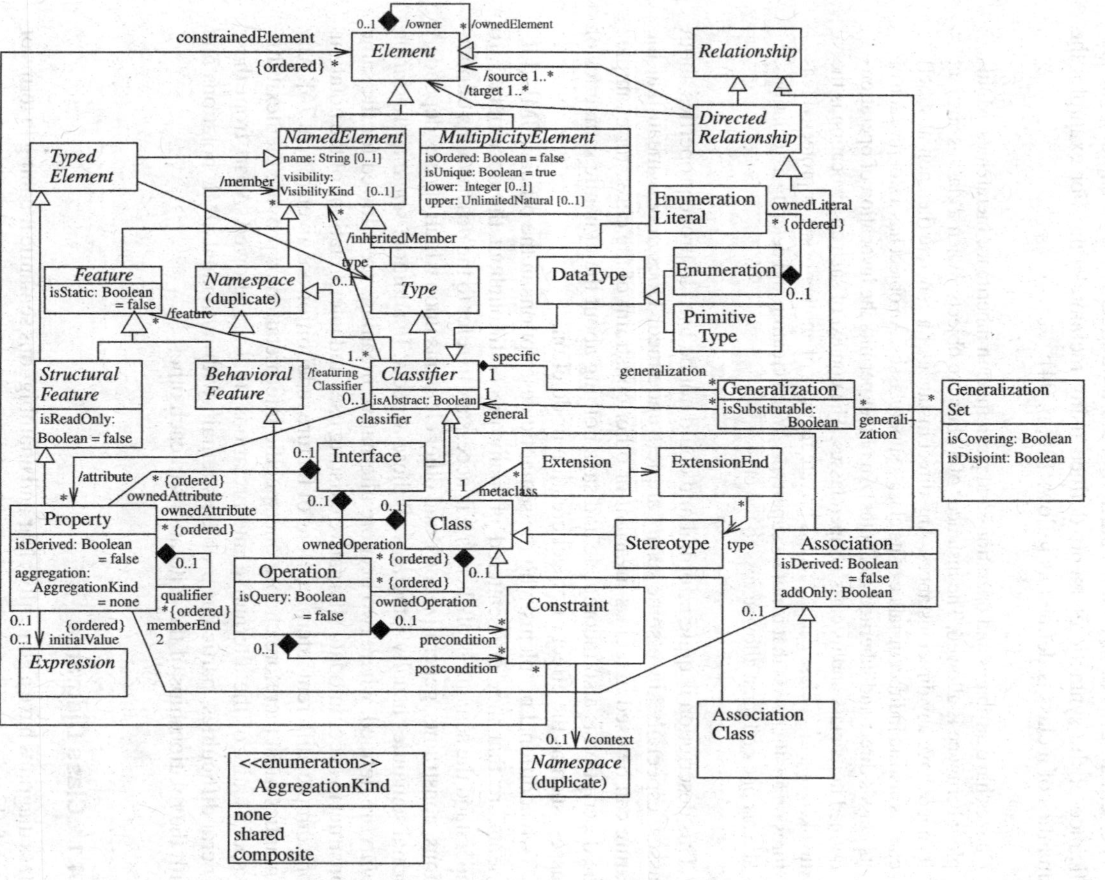

FIGURE 2.4 Part of the UML 2.1 metamodel.

construction, which ultimately relies on an intuitive understanding of the elementary UML constructs of MOF to resolve the circularity. "In order to understand the description of the UML semantics, you must understand some UML semantics" [36, p. 22].

The semantics is described primarily in natural language, which explains the significance of the syntactic elements defined using metamodeling. For example, the semantics of a class is defined as follows [36, p. 94]:

> Classes have attributes and operations and participate in inheritance hierarchies. Multiple inheritance is allowed. The instances of a class are objects. When a class is abstract it cannot have any direct instances. Any direct instance of a concrete (i.e., non-abstract) class is also an indirect instance of its class's superclasses. An object has a slot for each of its class's direct and inherited attributes. An object permits the invocation of operations defined in its class and its class's superclasses. The context of such an invocation is the invoked object. A class cannot access private features of another class, or protected features on another class that is not its supertype. When creating and deleting associations, at least one end must allow access to the class.

This description is quite informal and could not be used to prove properties about classes, especially since some terms are left undefined. Does *access* mean that the feature can be used in a class invariant or other constraint of the class, for example? The description is also incomplete and says nothing about the dynamic semantics of classes, such as the effect of object creation or deletion.

Two additional problems with the semantic descriptions in the official UML documents are that they are scattered in many pieces throughout the documents: To understand the semantics of classes it is necessary to refer to the descriptions of operations, constraints, generalizations, and other elements upon which classes depend. A formal semantics usually integrates all these aspects. In addition, *semantic variation points* are defined, where two or more alternative meanings are allowed for the same construct to accommodate alternative existing uses and interpretations of the notation. For example, different interpretations of feature redefinition are given [36, p. 76]. Any semantics must therefore choose one specific interpretation or provide the flexibility to specify any of the alternative interpretations, that are allowed. Apart from these general difficulties, particular problems remain with individual UML notations and with the relationships of these notations to each other.

2.4.1 Class Diagrams

Class diagrams have a generally clear and unambiguous semantic meaning in terms of sets of objects and relationships between these sets, and most work on the semantics of class diagrams has agreed on the meaning of the main elements of these diagrams. However, particular concepts, such as aggregation and composition, can be given several different semantics, each of which appears consistent with the UML documents [1]. Other concepts, such as the definition of generalization set disjointness, seem to be stated incorrectly in the UML standard.

The notation is necessarily extensive and complex since it serves multiple purposes, being used for system specification, design, and implementation in addition to domain and environment modeling. Some aspects, such as association end ownership and navigability, are relevant primarily to the design uses of class diagrams and so can be omitted from formal semantics of class diagrams used for specification.

2.4.2 State Machines

UML state machines have been given semantics primarily in an operational manner [21, 26]. However, these semantics have uncovered a considerable number of semantic unclarities, ambiguities, and excessive complexities in state machine semantics: for example, in the definitions of transition priorities, history states [6], and the entry and exit actions executed when composite states are entered and exited. In addition, a large number of syntactically similar state machine and state chart notations exist with divergent semantics [4]. These problems may be an indication that state machine concepts, especially those dealing with composite states and history states, need revision and simplification.

Extensions of state machine notation have been proposed as a result of semantic development; in particular, the introduction of state invariants for all forms of UML state machine would be useful to improve the capabilities for state machine verification of operations and objects (Chapters 8 and 13). There may also be scope for rationalization of the state machine metamodel using the similarity of the *State* and *Classifier* metaclasses, for example.

2.4.3 Use Cases

Use case diagrams can be given a semantics by using semantics for class diagrams, state machines, and other behavior notations for UML, since use-case actors are a special kind of *Classifier*, and use cases are special kinds of *BehavioredClassifier*, with an attached *Behavior*, such as a state machine. The relationships *includes* and *extends* between use cases can be given a general meaning in terms of execution occurrences (every execution of the including use case contains an execution of the included use case, and there exists an execution of the extended use case that contains an execution of the extension use case). Fine-grained semantics of use cases is inappropriate, since the notation is intended for use at early stages of development, not for detailed design [39].

2.4.4 Interactions

Interaction diagrams have been given denotational or algebraic semantics which attempt to formalize particular interpretations of the semantics intended for these diagrams described in the UML standard, based on sets of allowed and forbidden traces. The UML documents appear to allow different interpretations, especially for the forbidden traces of interaction operators. The notation itself can be considered misleading, as the use of vertical position in a sequence diagram to indicate relative

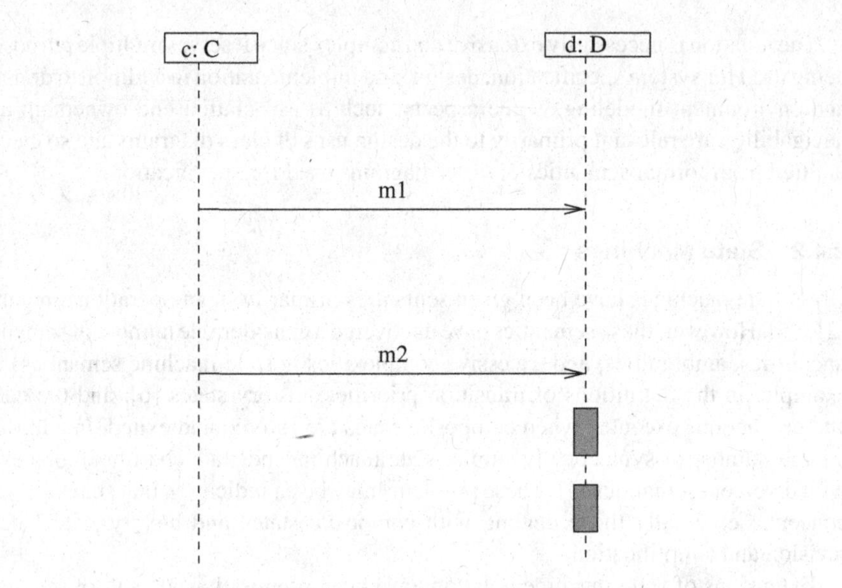

FIGURE 2.5 Misleading sequence diagram.

time of occurrence of events does not always apply if the events are on different lifelines. For example, Figure 2.5 appears to show that the "receive" of *m*1 occurs before the "send" of *m*2, but this is not actually specified by the diagram, which allows the receive of *m*1 to occur after the send of *m*2. In addition, the diagrams do not provide an unambiguous way to connect the reception of a message and the operation execution triggered by it. In Figure 2.5 the temporally first operation execution on *d* may actually arise from *m*2, not from *m*1. Hence, protocols such as "First come, first served" cannot be specified. Further semantic problems with the notation, such as the lack of a notation for event queueing, are identified in Chapter 9.

Unlike state machines and class diagrams, there is also ambiguity over how interactions should be used: Are they simply describing examples of expected or forbidden behavior of a system, or are they specifying in a complete manner the behavior required? For real-time and critical systems the latter would be desirable, but this seems to require revision of the notation [22].

2.4.5 Object Constraint Language

For OCL, different semantics have been defined, and two different semantic definitions, based on metamodeling and set theory, are given in the OCL standard. In general, OCL has a clear and unambiguous semantics, although its semantics depends to a degree on the semantics of the notations with which it is used. The specification notation and semantics of OCLMessage remain incomplete: No timestamps of send or receive times are associated with the message or with the identity of the caller.

2.4.6 Unified Semantics for UML

There have been few attempts at a unified semantics of UML because of the size and complexity of the entire language and the unclear relationships between several models. The overlap between state machines and activities and between the various forms of interaction diagram is one example, as is the lack of a precise relationship between state machines and interactions. Two attempts at a unified semantics are described in this book: the UML Semantics Project system model (Chapters 3 and 4), which defines a mathematical model of the informal global semantics described by the OMG [33, chapter on common behaviors], and the axiomatic semantics for class diagrams and state machines described in Chapters 6 and 8. These do not, however, cover all cases of activity diagrams or interactions.

The current state of UML semantics research enables a "safe" subset of UML to be defined, on which a complete mathematical semantics supporting proof, model checking, and other analyses can be assigned. This subset would include class diagrams using the metamodel of Figure 2.4, state machines without composite states, use cases, and a large subset of OCL.

2.5 APPLICATIONS OF SEMANTICS TO UML

In this section we survey research that has used a precise semantic analysis to identify flaws, such as inconsistencies and incompleteness, in the UML language itself, and to identify possible improvements for future versions of UML.

2.5.1 Core Metamodeling Semantics of UML: The pUML Approach

Evans and Kent [5] propose a precise denotational semantics for a core of UML and use this to identify incompleteness in the informal semantics of the UML documents, particularly with regard to inheritance and instantiation. Two specific omissions from the UML semantics are (1) a constraint enforcing that instances of a classifier should also be indirect instances of the parents of this classifier, and (2) a constraint expressing the fact that instances cannot be instantiated from arbitrary classifiers, only from a direct classifier and its parents. Evans and Kent propose additional OCL constraints to enforce these properties. Incompleteness in the semantics of packages is also addressed.

2.5.2 A UML Semantics FAQ

Gogolla et al. [9] identified several semantic inconsistencies between various UML documents and incompleteness in the informal semantics contained in these documents. One example of incompleteness identified is that it is impossible to determine from the informal semantics if the two alternative ways of entering and exiting an orthogonal state (Figure 2.6) are semantically equivalent. A precise semantics would be able to answer this question.

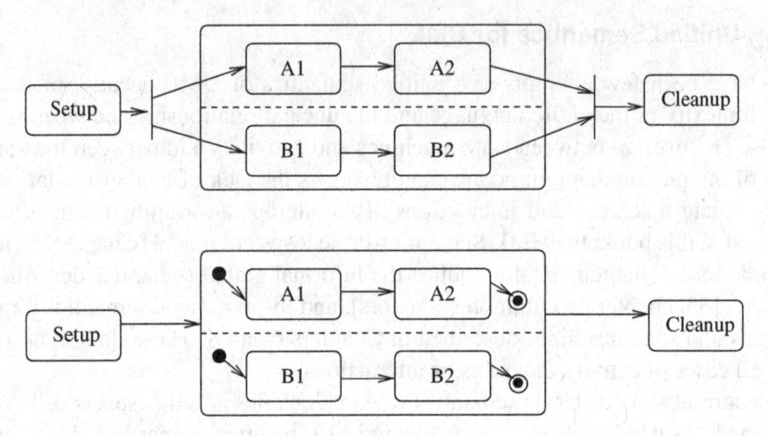

FIGURE 2.6 Alternative orthogonal state models.

2.5.3 Detecting OCL Traps in the UML 2.0 Superstructure

Bauerdick et al. [2] apply the software tool USE (UML-based specification environment) to a semantic analysis of the OCL constraints used in the definition of the UML 2.0 superstructure. Many errors were discovered, ranging from incorrect use of OCL operators to inconsistent use of names for metaclasses and metafeatures between the OCL constraints and the superstructure class diagrams. Syntax and type errors were mainly uncovered; neither theorem proving nor animation was carried out to identify more subtle flaws.

An example of a type error is the OCL defining the operation *visibleMembers*() : *Set(PackageableElement)* of *Package*:

```
visibleMembers(): Set(PackageableElement) =
  member->select( m | self.makesVisible(m))
```

However, *member* of *Package* has type *Set(NamedElement)*, a supertype of the result type required. This problem remains in version 2.1.1 of UML [33, p. 110]. A total of 361 specific errors were found in the 246 OCL constraints in the UML 2.0 superstructure document.

2.5.4 29 New Unclarities in the Semantics of UML 2.0 State Machines

Fecher et al. [6] identify semantic problems with the UML state machine notation, in particular in the definitions of transition priority and the meaning of history states. The authors point out that the informal definitions in the UML documents are incomplete and ambiguous: "The priority of joined transitions is based on the priority of the transition with the most transitively nested source state" [32, p. 547]. UML

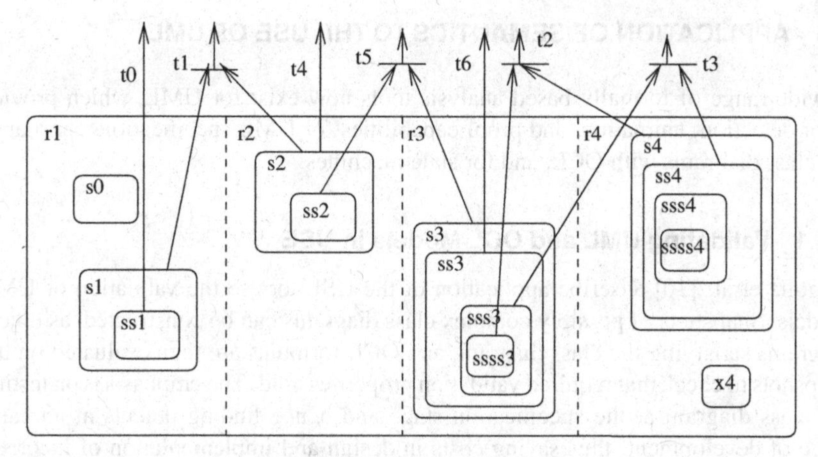

FIGURE 2.7 Priority examples [6].

superstructure 2.0 [32, p. 548] provides an algorithm for calculating the fired set of transitions when an event occurs. This algorithm involves starting from "innermost nested simple states," which does not resolve cases such as Figure 2.7. We assume that all the transitions are triggered by the same event and have *true* guards.

Fecher et al. also identify problems with the semantics of history states:

1. It is not clear if default transitions from history states must go to normal states (not pseudostates or final states).
2. The notion of "last active" state is ambiguous; it is not clear if this can include final states of composite states.
3. Do history states of nested states affect deep history entry to these states?
4. Does the reset of the last active state in a composite state p on entry to p's final state also reset the records of the last active state in its substates?

2.5.5 Semantics of OCL Specified with QVT

Markovic and Baar [28] define a semantic mapping from OCL to a semantic domain by utilizing model transformations to express the evaluation of OCL expressions. The transformations apply to abstract syntax tree representations of OCL expressions and define how value bindings propagate through these trees as composite expressions are evaluated from the values of their components. The transformations are defined using the QVT graphical specification notation for transformations.

To define this semantics, the OCL metamodel needed to be extended to support convenient evaluation of expressions. An interesting point raised is that OCL as defined does not specify if dynamic binding is to be used to evaluate query operations on objects defined in an inheritance hierarchy.

2.6 APPLICATION OF SEMANTICS TO THE USE OF UML

A wide range of formally based analysis tools now exist for UML, which provide error detection, animation, and proof capabilities for UML specifications, primarily for class diagrams with OCL, and for state machines.

2.6.1 Validating UML and OCL Models in USE

Gogolla et al. [10] describe application of the USE tool to the validation of UML models. Snapshots of possibly complex class diagrams can be constructed, as object diagrams satisfying the class diagram, and OCL formulas are then evaluated on the snapshots to check that required validation properties hold. The emphasis is on testing the class diagram at the specification stage and hence finding defects at an early stage of development, thus saving costs in design and implementation of incorrect specifications. The underlying semantics used for OCL is the denotational semantics of Richters and Gogolla [37].

2.6.2 vUML: A Tool for Verifying UML Models

Lilius and Paltor [27] define a technique for verifying UML state machine models automatically, by translating these to the PROMELA language of the SPIN model checker. The model checker can then detect flaws in the state machine, such as deadlocks, livelocks, reaching unintended states, violation of state invariants, event queue overflows, and sending messages to terminated objects. The results of output are presented as sequence diagrams, so users do not need to know the PROMELA notation or use SPIN directly. The operational state machine semantics [26] is used to underpin the translation and verification. A related approach is presented by Jussila et al. [15].

2.6.3 Model Checking UML State Machines and Collaborations

Shafer et al. [38] also use PROMELA and SPIN to verify state machines but encode an operational semantics for state machines as a process (type) in PROMELA instead of statically translating individual state machines into PROMELA. This makes the translation more explicit and visible and easier to modify. The disadvantage is increased computation time. Shafer et al. identified various problems in the state machine language, in particular that the lack of a specified order in many cases of concurrently executed actions (e.g., exit actions of regions of the same AND state) causes inefficiency in verification, since a verifier must consider all possible alternative orders of execution.

2.6.4 Automated Formal Verification of Model Transformations

Varro and Pataricza [45] define a model-checking technique for testing that a transformation preserves selected properties on a model-per-model basis. UML statecharts are translated into Petri nets, with model checking of selected semantic correctness properties p on the source model, and of a corresponding property q on the target model, to verify that p is preserved, in interpreted form, in the target model.

This technique does not provide a means to verify transformations on a global basis (that all properties of the source model are preserved in the target). By considering model transformations as operations on metamodels, specified by pre- and postconditions, we could in principle apply standard verification techniques to prove these operations correct (e.g., by translation into the language of a proof tool such as B) [18].

2.7 SUMMARY

In this chapter we have introduced the concepts of semantics that are used in the remainder of the book and have described some of the issues that need to be addressed when defining semantics for UML. Despite the problems that remain with UML semantics (formal or informal), the UML is the most comprehensive and well developed notation for software modeling. The current state of semantics research for UML already provides a basis for precise specification within a substantial subset of UML and has contributed to the development of powerful analysis tools for UML, and to the evolution of UML itself. Further revision of UML to improve its semantics will extend the scope of research and applications of UML semantics to more comprehensive subsets of the language.

REFERENCES

1. F. Barbier, B. Henderson-Sellers, A. Le Parc-Lacayrelle, and J-M. Bruel. Aggregation and composition in UML: a revised implementation based on whole-part theory. *Transactions on Software Engineering*, 29(5), 2003.
2. H. Bauerdick, M. Gogolla, and F. Gutsche. Detecting OCL traps in the UML 2.0 superstructure. In *UML 2004*. Lecture Notes in Computer Science, vol. 3273. Springer-Verlag, New York, 2004.
3. T. Clark, A. Evans, S. Kent, and P. Sammut. The MMF approach to engineering object-oriented design languages. In *Workshop on Language Descriptions, Tools and Applications (LDTA)*, 2001.
4. M. Crane, and J. Dingel. UML vs Classical vs Rhapsody statecharts: not all models are created equal. *MoDELS 2005*. Lecture Notes in Computer Science, vol. 3713, Springer-Verlag, New York, 2005.
5. A. Evans and S. Kent. Core meta-modelling semantics of UML: the pUML approach. In *UML '99*, pp. 140–155, 1999.
6. H. Fecher, J. Schonborn, M. Kyas, and W.-P. de Roever. 29 new unclarities in the semantics of UML 2.0 state machines. In *Formal Methods and Software Engineering (ICFEM 2005)*. Lecture Notes in Computer Science, vol. 3785, pp. 52–65. Springer-Verlag, New York, 2005.

7. J. Fiadeiro and T. Maibaum. Describing, structuring and implementing objects. In *Foundations of Object Oriented Languages*. Lecture Notes in Computer Science, vol. 489. Springer-Verlag, New York, 1991.
8. M. Glinz. Problems and deficiencies of UML as a requirements specification language. In *Proceedings of the 10th International Workshop on Software Specification and Design IWSSD-10*, pp. 11–22, 2000.
9. M. Gogolla, O. Radfelder, and M. Richters. *A UML Semantics FAQ: The View from Bremen*. University of Bremen, Bremen, Germany, 1999.
10. M. Gogolla, J. Bohling, and M. Richters, Validating UML and OCL models in USE by automatic snapshot generation. *Software and Systems Modelling*, 4(4), 2005.
11. D. Harel and A. Naamad. The STATEMATE semantics of statecharts. *ACM Transactions on Software Engineering and Methodology*, 5(4):293–333, Oct. 1996.
12. C. A. R. Hoare. An axiomatic basis for computer programming. *Communications of the ACM*, 12(10):576–585, 1969.
13. S. Kim and D. Carrington. A formal denotational semantics of UML in Object-Z. *L'Objet*, 7(3):323–362, 2001.
14. A. Knapp and J. Wuttke. Model-checking of UML 2.0 interactions. In *Proceedings of the 5th International Workshop on Critical Systems Development Using Modelling Languages (CSDUML)*. Telenor Report 20/2006, 2006.
15. T. Jussila, J. Dubrovin, T. Junttila, T. Latvala, and I. Porres. Model checking dynamic and hierarchical UML state machines. In *Proceedings Modeva 2*, pp. 94–110, 2006.
16. M. Kyas, H. Fecher, F. de Boer, J. Jacob, J. Hooman, M. van der Kwaag, T. Arons, and H. Kugler. Formalizing UML models and OCL constraints in PVS. In *SFEDL '04*, 2004.
17. K. Lano. Logical specification of reactive and real-time systems. *Journal of Logic and Computation*, 8(5):679–711, 1998.
18. K. Lano. UML to B: formal verification of object-oriented models. In *IFM '04*, 2004.
19. K. Lano. Constraint-driven development. *Information and Software Technology*, 50: 406–423, 2008.
20. K. Lano. Formalising design patterns as model transformations. Chapter VIII in a T. Taibi, (ed.), *Design Pattern Formalisation Techniques*. IGI Publishing, Hershey, PA, 2007.
21. K. Lano and D. Clark. Direct semantics of extended state machines. In *TOOLS '07*, 2007.
22. K. Lano. Formal specification using interaction diagrams. In *SEFM'07 Proceedings*, 2007.
23. K Lano. A compositional semantics of UML-RSDS. *SoSyM*, 8(1): 85–116, 2009.
24. King's College London. UML RSDS toolset, 2007. http://www.dcs.kcl.ac.uk/staff/kcl/umlrsds.
25. K. Lano and A. Evans. Rigorous development in UML. In *FASE'99*. Lecture Notes in Computer Science, vol. 1577, pp. 129–144. Springer-Verlag, New York, 1999.
26. J. Lilius and I. Porres Paltor. *The Semantics of UML State Machines*. Technical Report. Turku Centre for Computer Science, Turku, Finland, 1999.
27. J. Lilius and I. Porres Paltor. *vUML: A Tool for Verifying UML Models*. Technical Report 272. Turku Centre for Computer Science, Turku, Finland, 1999.
28. S. Markovic and T. Baar. Semantics of OCL specified with QVT. *Software and Systems Modelling*, 7(4), Oct. 2008.
29. S. Meng and L. S. Barbosa. A coalgebraic semantic framework for reasoning about UML sequence diagrams. In *QSIC 2008*. IEEE Computer Society, Los Alamitos, CA, 2008.

30. A. Naumenko and A. Wegmann. Triune continuum paradigm and problems of UML semantics. http://icwww.epfl.ch/publications/documents/ IC_TECH_REPORT_200344.pdf, 2003.
31. OMG. Model-driven architecture. http://www.omg.org/mda/, 2007.
32. OMG. *UML Superstructure, Version 2.0.* OMG Document Formal/05-07-04. Object Management group, Needham, MA, 2005.
33. OMG. *UML Superstructure, Version 2.1.1.* OMG Document Formal/2007-02-03. Object Management group, Needham, MA, 2007.
34. OMG. *UML OCL 2.0 Specification.* Final/06-05-01. Object Management group, Needham, MA, 2006.
35. OMG. *Query/View/Transformation Specification.* Technical Report ptc/05-11-01. Object Management group, Needham, MA, 2005.
36. OMG. *UML Infrastructure v2.1.2.* OMG Document Formal/2007-11-04. Object Management group, Needham, MA, 2007.
37. M. Richters and M. Gogolla. On formalising the UML object constraint language OCL. In *Proceedings of the 17th International Conference on Conceptual Modelling.* Lecture Notes in computer Science, Vol. 1502, pp. 449–464. Springer-Verlag, New York, 1998.
38. T. Shafer, A. Knapp, and S. Merz. Model checking UML state machines and collaborations. *Electronic Notes in Theoretical Computer Science*, 47:1–13, 2001.
39. A. Simons and I. Graham. 37 things that don't work in object-oriented modelling with UML. In *2nd ECOOP Workshop on Precise Behavioral Semantics.* TUM-I9813. Technical University Munich, Munich, Germany, 1998.
40. C. Snook and M. Butler, U2B: a tool for translating UML-B models into B, in J. Mermet, ed., *UML-B Specification for Proven Embedded Systems Design.* Springer-Verlag, New York, 2004.
41. M. Richters. OCL semantics. Annex A of [34], 2005.
42. J. Smith, S. DeLoach, M. Kokar, and K. Baclawski. Category theoretic approaches of representing precise UML semantics. In *Proceedings of the ECOOP Workshop on Defining Precise Semantics for UML*, 2000.
43. UML 2 Semantics Project. http://www.cs.queensu.ca/~stl/internal/uml2/bibtex/ref_uml2semantics.html, 2008.
44. L. Tratt. Model transformations and tool integration. *SoSyM*, 4(2): 112–122, 2005.
45. D. Varro and A. Pataricza. Automated formal verification of model transformations. Presented at the CSDUML Workshop, 2003.

CHAPTER 3

CONSIDERATIONS AND RATIONALE FOR A UML SYSTEM MODEL

MANFRED BROY and MARÍA VICTORIA CENGARLE
Institut für Informatik, Technische Universität München, München, Germany

HANS GRÖNNIGER and BERNHARD RUMPE
Lehrstuhl Informatik 3 (Softwaretechnik), RWTH Aachen University, Aachen, Germany

3.1 INTRODUCTION

Semantics definition for the Unified Modeling Language (UML) [8,33] is not an easy task. Although considerable effort has been made, starting in the late 1990s [1,2,19], no commonly agreed formal and integrated UML semantics exists. Broy et al. [3] defined a system model as a semantic domain for the UML. The system model is supposed to form a possible core and foundation of the UML semantics definition. For that purpose, the definitions are targeted toward UML, which means that central concepts of UML have been formalized as theories of the system model.

In this chapter we discuss the general approach and highlight the main decisions. This material is important for an understanding of the system model definition given in Chapter 4. Our work in this chapter is based on the second version of the system model [3], which is the result of a major effort to define the structure, behavior, and interaction of object-oriented, possibly distributed systems abstract enough to be of general value, but also in sufficient detail for a semantic foundation of the UML. The first version of the system model can be found in the work of Broy et al. [4–6].

3.2 GENERAL APPROACH TO SEMANTICS

The semantics of any formal language consists of the following basic parts [44]:

- The syntax of the language in question (here: UML), be it graphical or textual
- The semantic domain, a domain well known and understood based on a well-defined mathematic theory

UML 2 Semantics and Applications. Edited by Kevin Lano

- The semantic mapping: a functional or relational definition that connects both the elements of the syntax and the elements of the semantic domain

This technique of giving meaning to a language is the basic principle of denotational semantics: Every syntactic construct is mapped onto a semantic construct. As discussed in the literature, there are many flavors of these three elements. Syntax can, for example, be specified by grammars or metamodels. To stay formal, our approach intends to use the abstract syntax of UML in a mathematical form that resembles context-free grammars (examples are given by Cengarle et al. [10,11]). The term *system model* was first used by Klein et al. [24] to denominate a semantic domain; it defines a family of systems, describing their structural and behavioral issues. Each concrete syntactic instance (in our case, an individual UML diagram, or even a part of it) is interpreted by the semantic mapping as a predicate over the set of systems defined by the system model. As explained by Harel and Rumpe [21], the semantic mapping has the form

$$Sem : UML \rightarrow \mathbb{P}(Systemmodel)$$

and thus functionally relates any item in the syntactic domain to a set of constructs of the semantic domain. The semantics of a model $m \in UML$ is therefore $Sem(m)$.

Given any two models $m, n \in UML$ combined into a complex $m \oplus n$ (for any composition operator $\oplus$ of the syntactic domain), the semantics of $m \oplus n$ is defined by $Sem(m \oplus n) = Sem(m) \cap Sem(n)$. This definition also works for sets of UML documents, which allows easy treatment of views on a system specified by multiple UML diagrams. The semantics of several views (i.e., several UML documents) is given as $Sem(\{doc_1, \ldots, doc_n\}) = Sem(doc_1) \cap \cdots \cap Sem(doc_n)$. A set of UML models *docs* is consistent if systems exist that are described by the models, so $Sem(docs) \neq \emptyset$. As a consequence, the system model supports both view integration and model consistency verification.

In the same way, $n \in UML$ is a (structural or behavioral) refinement of $m \in UML$, exactly if $Sem(n) \subseteq Sem(m)$. Formally, refinement is nothing other than "*n* is providing at least the information about the system that *m* does." These general mechanisms provide a great advantage, as they simplify any reasoning about composition and refinement operators.

The system model described in this document identifies the set of all possible object-oriented (OO) systems that can be defined using a subset of UML which we call "clean UML" described below. It relies on earlier work on system models [1,2,9,20,24,40].

To capture and integrate all the orthogonal aspects of a system modeled in UML, the semantic domain must have a certain complexity. Related approaches very often contain a relatively small and specialized semantic domain, such as (pairs of) sets of traces for UML interaction [22], template semantics based on hierarchical state machines [42] or Kripke structures [43] for UML state machines, or sets of inequations to give semantics to class diagrams focusing on the satisfiability of association cardinality [8,18,30,38]. However, these approaches fail to give an integrated semantics for different types of UML notations. Approaches with a broader scope are, for example, those of Damm et al. [14], who define a UML subset called krtUML and associate with each model a symbolic transition system. Kuske et al. [27] combine class, object, and state machine diagrams using graph transformations. Engels et al. [15] use dynamic metamodeling (also based on graph transformations) to define the operational semantics of, for example, UML activities. Semantics for class and state machine diagrams have been developed for different purposes. Snook and Butler [39] examine the refinement of associations. Fecher et al. [17] provide a compositional semantics that considers activity groups. Lano [28] additionally supports sequence diagrams and considers timing issues. Consistency between (simplified) state machines and sequence diagrams is checked by Zhao et al. [45] using a model checker. Consistency conditions are also proposed [29,35].

3.3 STRUCTURING THE SEMANTICS OF UML

Our long-term goal is to define the semantics of a comprehensive core of well-defined concepts of UML. The overall strategy of giving semantics to a modeling language is depicted in Figure 3.1. The basic idea expressed by this diagram is as follows:

- Full UML is restricted to a subset (called *clean UML*) that can be treated semantically without overly sophisticated constructs.
- Clean UML is mapped by transformations into *simplified UML*. In doing so, derived constructs of UML are replaced by their definition in terms of constructs of the core so that notational extensions and derived concepts can be eliminated. UML provides a number of derived operators that do not enhance the expressiveness of the language, only the comfort of its use. Derived constructs can be defined in terms of constructs of the core; for example, state hierarchy of UML's state transition diagrams can be neglected without losing expressiveness.
- Finally, simplified UML is mapped to the system model using a predicative approach.

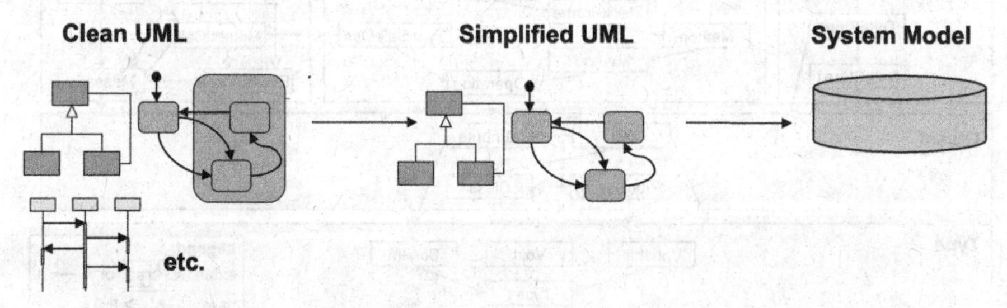

FIGURE 3.1 General strategy for the definition of the semantics of UML 2.0.

The system model describes the "universe (set) of all possible semantic structures (each with its behavior)." The semantic mapping interprets a UML model as a predicate that restricts the universe to a certain set of structures, which represents the meaning of the UML model. To be able to map concepts faithfully from UML to the system model, the system model has to cover a number of basic concepts expressible in UML. Otherwise, the semantic mapping cannot be defined adequately.

The system model itself is defined in a modular fashion. From a global viewpoint, a system in the system model is a state transition system. This semantic universe is introduced in layers of mathematical theories, which are shown in Figure 3.2. Note that this figure shows the full set of theories as defined by Broy et al. [3]; we shorten the definitions slightly, in this chapter. The rectangles in Figure 3.2 contain the names of the theories; the arrows show a relationship among concepts that could be paraphrased as "is defined in terms of." For instance, basic theories for types and objects used to define the data, control, and event state of a system are used in turn to define the state space for the transition systems.

When defining the constituents of the system model, we will state the decisions that have to be made and those that can be left open or do not even occur when staying informal. We clearly identify those decisions either directly or mark them as a *variation point* and leave it to the user of the system model to choose or adopt a variation. The variation points may correspond very nicely to stereotypes on the language side, such that the language designer (and semantics definer) can transfer the freedom of choice to the actual modeler.

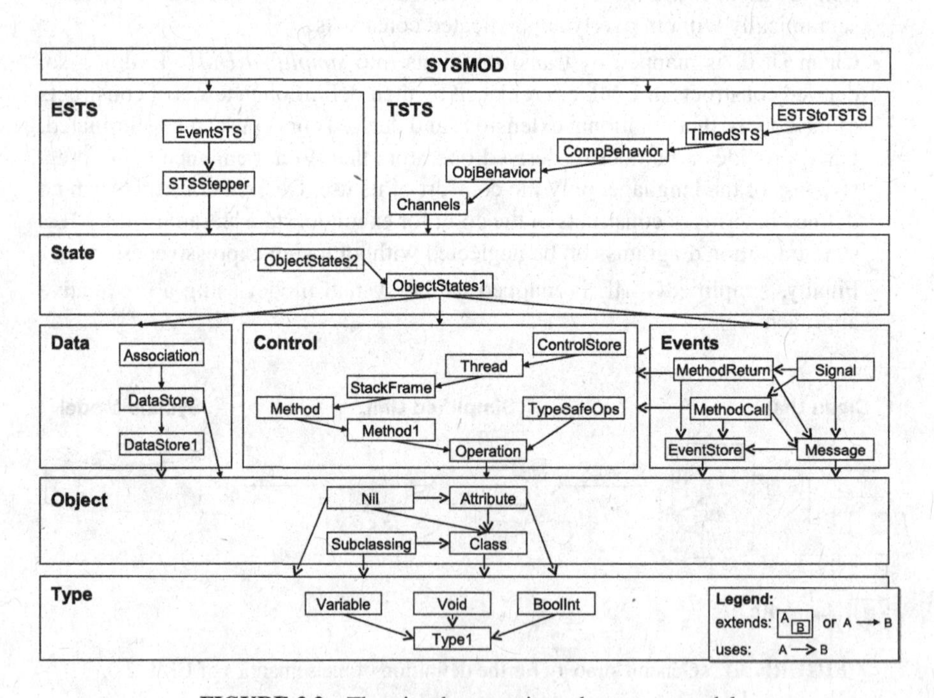

FIGURE 3.2 Theories that constitute the system model.

3.4 THE MATH BEHIND THE SYSTEM MODEL

A precise description of the system model calls for a precise instrument. For our purposes, mathematics is exactly appropriate because of its power and flexibility. Admittedly, reading and understanding mathematics is an effort that requires some training, but it makes it possible to describe things precisely and abstractly that cannot be defined using UML itself. Using UML itself to describe the semantics of UML might seem a pragmatic approach. This approach is somewhat metacircular, however, and necessarily calls for a kind of bootstrap, typically mathematics again. Moreover, understanding the semantics of UML in terms of UML itself demands a very good knowledge of the language whose semantics is about to be given formally. Besides, UML does not conveniently provide the appropriate mechanisms we need (e.g., to handle scheduling and distributed systems, and to deal with underspecification in a precisely controllable way). Of course, whenever appropriate, we use diagrams to illustrate some mathematically defined concepts, but the diagrams do not replace the mathematical formulas.

Instead of relying on basic mathematics, related work often proposes the use of specialized formalisms. Bruel and France [7] and Evans et al. [16] translate UML to the formal language Z, while Sarstedt and Guttmann [37] map to B. Graph transformations are used by Kuske et al. [27]. Activities have been formalized using the π-calculus [26], Petri nets [41], and abstract state machines (ASMs) [37]. Trace-based semantics for interactions have been presented [12,22], and metamodeling techniques have been employed [15]. Template semantics [42] that are based on state machines allow for describing semantic variation points.

We intentionally avoided the use of more specialized notations such as Z, B, and ASMs for two reasons:

1. It is not clear that any of these notations is general and comfortable enough to allow a satisfactory and adequate expression of all concepts in UML.
2. Arguably, all these notations have a certain bias (e.g., for state-based formal specification, analysis with a theorem prover, analysis with a model checker); we kept the system model free of this bias to ensure that we obtain a true reference semantics that, if useful, enables the future use of other notations for, among other uses, analysis purposes.

For these reasons we decided to use only mathematics. The following principles have proven to be useful when defining a system model:

1. Mathematics is used to define the system model. Its subtheories are built on numbers, sets, relations, and functions. Additional theories are built in a layered form. That is, only notation and mathematical definitions, and neither new syntax nor language, are introduced or used in the system model. Diagrams are used occasionally to clarify things but do not contribute formally to the system model.
2. The system model does not constructively define its elements, but introduces the elements and characterizes their properties. That is, abstract terms are used

whenever possible. For example, instead of using a record to define the structure of an object, we introduce an abstract set of objects and a number of selector functions. Properties of the set are then defined through such selectors. Based on our background and knowledge, we claim that we can transform this system model into a constructive version (and actually do this, see the work of Cengarle et al. [9]), but that would probably be more awkward to read and less intuitive, as it requires a lot more mathematical machinery. This will satisfy "constructivists," who aim to make everything constructive or executable.

3. Everything important is given an appropriate name. For example, to deal with classes there is a "universe of class names," UCLASS, and similarly, there is a "universe of type names," UTYPE, which is, however, just a set of names (and not types); see Sections 4.3.4 and 4.3.1.
4. To the best of our knowledge, any underlying assumptions were avoided, according to the slogan: "What is not specified explicitly does not need to hold." If, for example, we do not state explicitly that two sets are disjoint, the two sets might have elements in common. Sometimes these loose (underspecified) ends are helpful to specialize or strengthen the system model and are there on purpose. If you need a property, (a) check whether it is there; (b) if absent, check whether it can be inferred as an emerging property; (c) if not, check if it is absolutely necessary; and (d), if yes, you may add it as an additional restriction.
5. Generally, deep embedding (or explicit representation) is used. This means that the semantics of the embedded language (i.e., UML) is formalized completely within the supporting language: in our case, mathematics. As one consequence, although there are similar concepts in the language describing the system model (which is mathematics) and the language described (UML), these need not be related. For instance, the system model characterizes the type system of UML; however, it does not itself have, and does not need, a type system.
6. Specific points where the system model could be strengthened further have been marked as variation points, which deal with additional elements that can be defined within the system model. We may introduce additional machinery that need not be present in each system modeled. Prominent examples of such variations are the existence of a predefined top-level class called "Object" or an enhanced type of system, including, for example, templates. Furthermore, variations describe changes of definitions that lead to a slightly different system model. Variation points allow us to describe specialized variants of the system model that may not generally be valid, but hold for a large part of possible systems. Examples are single inheritance hierarchies or type-safe overriding of operations in subclasses, which may not be assumed in general.

3.5 WHAT IS THE SYSTEM MODEL?

As indicated in Section 3.3, the system model is a hierarchy of theories that capture a large number of concepts typically found in distributed object-oriented systems.

To obtain an adequate semantic domain, the system model defines concepts such as types and values, classes with attributes and methods, objects, messages and events, or threads.

An object-oriented system can be described basically using one of various existing paradigms. We opted for the paradigm of a global state transition system in order to accommodate a global (and perhaps distributed) state space. The system model thus defines a universe of state transition systems. A state transition system is given by its state space, its initial states, and its state transition function. Note that our notion of state transition system is more basic and does not relate directly to the state machines the UML provides. If detailed enough, the global state transition system is perfectly appropriate to model parallel, independent, and distributed computations. In principle, a system of communicating elementary transition systems could be considered more convenient than a single global machine for describing the semantics of UML models. It is also possible to construct a global transition system by integrating elementary models; however, this is a nontrivial operation. Therefore, it is more appropriate to employ the concept or metaphor of one state transition system at a higher, nonelementary level. In fact, we introduce a composition operator on transition systems representing fragments of larger systems such that these transition systems can be composed, leading to larger systems.

3.5.1 Static and Dynamic Issues

The types and classes are static (i.e., they do not change over the lifetime of a system). Similarly, the sets of defined operations, methods, messages, and events do not change. This information is called the *static information* of a state transition system.

The set of existing objects, the values of the attributes, the computational state of invoked methods, and dispatched and not yet delivered messages passed from one object to another are dynamic (i.e., they may change in transition steps). This is called the *dynamic information* of a state transition system and is encoded in the states of the system. In the database realm, the static part is called *schema* and the dynamic part is the *instance*. The schema instantiation is changeable, whereas the schema itself is not. Schema changes (usually called *schema evolution* in the literature) are not considered, as they usually do not occur within a running system but when evolving and/or reconfiguring it.

Summarizing, the state space of the transition system will be defined in terms of its orthogonal constituents, namely, control and events. Each of these theories contributes static and dynamic information to the system model definitions.

3.5.2 Types, Classes, Objects, and DataStore

The first part of the system model definition (see Section 4.3) is concerned with defining type names, their carrier sets, classes, objects, associations, and the component of a system state that stores information about existing objects and their variable values. Although we do not deal with the peculiarities of various type systems, strong or weak typing, and so on, we outline basic assumptions on the underlying type system, as we need to map the type information of UML to this type system. In that respect, we use a deep embedding of the type system of UML, by representing it through type names and a universe of values only. By "deep embedding" we mean that we do not map types of the UML to a type system of the underlying mathematical structure, but explicitly model types as first-class elements.

Occasionally, we make assumptions that simplify matters but are careful not to lose generality. For example, we assume global variables in the system. In practice, it would be relatively inconvenient if every variable name could be used only once in a program. We then would see a global namespace and thus not have any hiding concepts in the language. In the system model, however, we may accept such a restriction and handle it as follows. As in ordinary programming languages, variables shadow each other when a new variable with the same name is introduced in an inner scope. We assume static binding; thus, each variable name can be statically resolved (as opposed to dynamic binding of variables, by which the resolution of a variable name depends not on the environment of its definition but on the environment of its use, and thus variable resolution can occur only at runtime). Generally, we assume that in the modeling languages we deal with, a consistent and model-wide redefinition of variable names is possible in such a way that each variable is used only once. Then variable shadowing does not occur and any variable is unique. We may handle that systematically through encoding the place of definition or the namespace within each variable. Quite the same thing is done by many compilers anyway.

Class names in the system model are introduced in an abstract fashion. Each class name is associated with a set of object identifiers and with a set of attributes. This is sufficient to define the structure of objects belonging to a class in the form of a tuple, consisting of an object identifier and a mapping of attributes to values.

In the system model, classes are also types. Together with a subclassing relation, the carrier set of a class is the set of object identifiers belonging to the class or to one of its subclasses. This makes it possible to store subclass identifiers polymorphically in places where superclass identifiers are expected. As a consequence, we require object identifiers to be values. However, objects will not be forced to be values. We leave open whether objects are also to be treated as values (variation point). Our relational point of view concerning subclassing also supports multiple inheritance, which is covered by several binary inheritance relationships. As we assume global attribute names, we avoid name conflicts that otherwise could arise.

For the data store, we abstract from a number of details, such as storage layout and physical distribution. We use an abstract global store to denote the data state of an object system. Even if there is no such concept in a real, possibly distributed system, we can conceptually model the system that way by organizing all instances in this single global store. We also allow interleaving, as well as concurrent activities, as can be seen in the control part of the system model in Section 4.4.

Intuitively, the data store models the data state of a system at a certain point in time. Normally, at each point of time the store contains real objects for a finite subset of the universe of all object identifiers. We will, however, see that the data store is not enough to describe the system, but a control store and an event store need to be added. In these stores time progress is modeled by state transitions of the overall state machine.

At each point in time (i.e., in each state of the state machine), when an instance exists, we assume that its attributes are present and their values are defined, but it is not necessarily the case that we know about these values. They may be left underspecified. In particular, it may be that after creation of an instance, its attributes still need to be initialized, that is, come into a known (and thus well-defined) state. Note that this is a usual modeling technique used (e.g., in verification systems to avoid explicit handling of a pseudovalue "undefined" [32]). It also resembles reality; that is, when an uninitialized variable of type *int* is accessed, we do know that it contains an integer, but we do not have a clue which one it is.

One of the core concepts of UML are associations. Associations are relations between classes; and links, which can be regarded as instances of associations, are the corresponding relations between object identifiers at runtime. Although associations are mostly binary, they may be of any arity; in addition, they may be qualified in various ways and may have additional attributes on their own. Furthermore, an association can be "owned" by one or more of the participating objects/classes or can stand on its own, not owned by any of the related objects. In an implementation a basic mechanism for managing those relations is to use direct links or collection classes, but there are other possibilities as well. To capture different variants of realizations of associations semantically, we use a generalized, extensible approach: Retrieval functions extract links from the store. We allow for a variety of realizations of these functions. This approach is very flexible as, on the one hand, it abstracts away from the owner of associations as well as from how associations are stored, and on the other hand, does not restrict possible forms of an association. As a big disadvantage of this approach, we cannot capture all forms of associations in one uniform characterization but need to provide a number of standard patterns that cover the most important cases. If no standard case applies (e.g., for a new stereotype for associations), the stereotype developer has to describe his or her interpretation of the stereotype directly in terms of the system model. We demonstrate this approach by defining variants of binary associations below.

The retrieval function *relOf* depends on the concrete realization of the association. Even after quite a number of years of studying formalizations of object orientation, there is so far no really satisfactory approach that describes all variants of association implementations. Therefore, we provide this abstract function and impose some properties on the function without discussing the internal storage structure. The only decision we made so far is that associations are somehow contained within the store (i.e., they are somehow part of objects, and association relations do not extend the store). This is pretty much in the spirit of the system model, where higher-level concepts are explained using lower-level concepts. To retrieve the links of an association, the state of multiple objects may have to be examined. From the viewpoint of a single object, this is not possible since it has access only to its own state. Hence, we assume that links may be retrieved using an API, a set of special methods that can be called by an object and that return the links.

3.5.3 Operations, Methods, Threads, and ControlStore

The control part defines the constituents of the structure used to model control information such as operations and methods. The control store contains additional information needed to determine the state of a system during computation. In particular, we provide means to express how control flows (as part of method calls) through active and passive objects; what it means for an object to be active or passive; how messages are passed, delayed, and handled; how events are handled; how threads work in a distributed setting; and how synchronization of all these concepts takes place (see Section 4.4).

One result of this section is a flexible mechanism to describe control structures of various kinds, resembling quite a number of implementation languages. This variability is enforced by the UML and leads to a rather complex formalization of control. In fact, UML does not allow us to abstract away from control primitives. In the systems we describe with UML, we do not only have various types of control and interaction, but also very often have their combinations within a single system. Unfortunately, we need rather detailed definitions for stacks, events, and threads that are not very elegant and do not give us much abstraction. However, this lack of elegance covers accurately the lack of elegance in distributed object-oriented systems where method calls, asynchronous signals, and threads of activity are orthogonal concepts that can be mixed in various ways. On the one hand, these concepts provide the system developer with great flexibility. On the other hand, they make it difficult to understand the behavior of the resulting systems. In addition, many orthogonal concepts make it very awkward to describe a system model that uses all of them, because any combination (useful or not) needs to be covered. The resulting complexity becomes apparent in modeling the control part of the system model.

We define operations (signatures) and methods (implementations) as separate entities. Operations are named and have a list of parameter types and one return type. Methods additionally define parameter names and may have an implementation. This approach does not explicitly specify overloading, signature and implementation inheritance, overriding and dynamic binding, but allows specializations in a flexible way to various mechanisms of method binding, that are actually used. This even includes binding mechanisms such as that in Modula-3. These concepts are thus to be decided and defined by the time the mapping from UML to the system model is devised.

In UML, interestingly, subclassing does not impose clear constraints on method implementations, as the implementation may be redefined according to some "compatibility" notion. This notion, however, is a semantic variation point that we therefore also leave open to a semantic specialization (e.g., by adding additional constraints for redefined method behavior). Subclassing in general allows for renaming of parameters in the implementation, as these are not part of the signature. The signatures (in the form of lists of types), however, are either equal or in a generalization or specialization relation. The types of parameters can be generalized, and the type of the return value can be specialized. This is the well-known co/contravariant way (see, e.g., [7]) that ensures type safety in a language. We also impose this constraint in the system model.

UML furthermore provides "out" and "in/out" parameters. However, many authors advise against the use of (in/)out parameters. The recommendation in the present context is to use a variation point where, if several "out"-values are to be assigned, each of these is assigned through method call or message passing. In this way, object encapsulation is kept. However, if needed, the system model allows us to encode these parameters by passing locations of the variables where the "out"-values are to be stored.

In UML there is also the notion of *object behavior*, which, strictly speaking, is not a method. However, for simplification we assume that *object behavior* can be encoded as a special kind of operation associated with the object whose parameters define the signature of the operation.

The computational state of a method is stored in a frame with the obvious information, such as sender, receiver, and values of local variables and parameters. A thread in the system model is associated with a stack of frames. The control store is the part of a system model state that stores information about which threads currently execute methods in which objects.

There are quite a number of approaches to combining object orientation and concurrency. Some approaches argue that each object is a unit of concurrency on its own. Others group passive objects into regions around single active objects, allowing operation calls only within a region and message passing only between regions. The programming languages that are commonly used today, however, have concurrency concepts that are completely orthogonal to objects. This means that various concurrent threads may independently and even simultaneously "enter" the very same object. The system model is abstract enough to allow specializations to any of these approaches. We do, however, have the basic assumption that there is a notion of atomic action. These atomic actions are the basic units for concurrency; their exact definition is deferred to the UML actions definitions. On top of atomic actions, we assume forms of concurrency control that are provided through appropriate concepts in UML (e.g., "synchronized" in Java). However, UML currently does not provide sufficient mechanisms to actually define scheduling and atomicity of actions conveniently. Possible units of concurrency, for example, would be a variable assignment or an operation invocation.

3.5.4 Messages, Events, and EventStore

One crucial question is the choice of the appropriate communication or interaction mechanism. Two basic flavors are asynchronous and synchronous communication. There is no definitive answer as to which one of these two possibilities is better, and both approaches can model each other. The system model is based on the asynchronous approach because of its abstractness. Synchronous method calls within the system model are encoded as asynchronous message passing.[1]

The UML specification distinguishes between event (types) and event occurrences (see [8, Sec. 6.4.2]) and provides a rather general notion of events and event

[1] *Message passing* is the general term; in the system model, events (which include message events) are passed.

occurrences. An event may be a message (which resembles a method call with parameters or return values), a *timeout*, a simple *signal*, or a *spontaneous state change*. Event occurrences, for example, are *sending of a message* or *reception of a message*. In Section 4.5.1 we introduce events and subsets of events that contain messages (which may further contain method calls and returns) as well as signals.

The last constituent of the state of an object is the event store. For each existing object, the event store stores a buffer that contains the events that still need to be processed. Event occurrences correspond to system states in which an event has just been added (sent) or removed (received) from the event store.

3.5.5 States

The state of a system is defined straightforwardly to consist of one data store, one control store, and one event store (see Section 4.6). So in each system state we capture the attribute values, the computational state, and the event buffer of each object. Given a system state, the state of an individual object is consequently the part of each store that holds information for that object. One of the main features of the system model is its compositionality. This means that an object state can be described on an individual basis as well as in any (meaningful) group.

3.5.6 Transition Systems

We provide two different types of transition systems to define object behavior. Event-based state transition systems (see Section 4.7) are suitable to explain object behavior on a fine-grained level. Objects react to incoming events, and their next computational activity is triggered explicitly by a scheduling event. The scheduling may be defined for groups of objects (belonging to the same processor, virtual processor, scheduling domain, etc.). Specific scheduling strategies, however, have not yet been defined.

As with object states, object behavior can be described on an individual basis as well as in groups. Behavior for compositions of groups of objects into larger components can be defined. For this purpose we use the time-aware version of state-transition systems, called *timed STS* (TSTS) (see Section 4.8). Although asynchronous communication is assumed in the system model, the time-based approach allows the use of a simple abstraction on the time scale to look at communication as being synchronous. Communication between objects is dealt with by channels. Channels, on the one hand, help to compose groups of objects into larger units and hide their internal communication. On the other hand, UML provides linguistic constructs such as "pins" in some of its diagrams; the pins resemble communication lines between objects and can be mapped to channels.

3.5.7 Further Extensions

Of course, this system model that can be seen as a hierarchy of algebras may and probably should be extended by adding further functional machinery to ease description of the mapping of UML constructs to the system model. However, we wanted to keep the system model rather simple and therefore did not concentrate much on this additional machinery. "Users" of the system model are really invited to add whatever they feel appropriate. There are also a number of loopholes and particular variation points that can be investigated further by providing additional machinery to clarify a mapping of UML concepts to the system model.

3.6 USAGE SCENARIOS

After discussing the general approach to define the semantics of UML and highlighting the main characteristics of the system model, in this section we present usage scenarios of a system-model-based UML semantics.

3.6.1 Analysis

Assuming that we have defined the semantics for UML using the system model, we are able to express precisely if a model A is well formed [i.e., $Sem(A) \neq \emptyset$]. Similarly, models A and B are consistent if $Sem(A) \cap Sem(B) \neq \emptyset$. It is well known that for models to be well formed, a necessary but not sufficient condition is that they correspond to the language's grammar or metamodel. However, additional syntactic conditions, called *context conditions*, need to be fulfilled. So the challenge is to develop a set of context conditions *coco* that, if fulfilled, guarantees well formedness, [e.g., $coco(A,B) \Rightarrow Sem(A) \cap Sem(B) \neq \emptyset$]. Analyzing the well formedness of models can then be reduced to checking syntactic conditions. Unfortunately, undecidable conditions exist that cannot be checked automatically but, instead, require verification.

3.6.2 Verification

As pointed out above, system-model-based verification of UML models can be necessary to verify context conditions that cannot be checked automatically. In general, we are also interested in proving properties of concrete models using the UML semantics. The semantics characterizes all properties of systems s realizing model(s) A, from which we then try to infer the property of interest ϕ [i.e., $\forall s \in Sem(A) : \phi\ s$]. Verification can also be used to prove transformations or generators correct. Assume, for example, a transformation $\rightsquigarrow$ that refines model A to B: We have to show that $\forall A, B : A \rightsquigarrow B \Rightarrow Sem(B) \subseteq Sem(A)$.

3.6.3 Simulation

The system model is deliberately not defined in an executable way, to support underspecification. It is, however, possible to resolve this underspecification and to encode the declarative specification into an executable simulator that is highly customizable with respect to semantic variation points [9]. Given a mapping from UML to the executable system model, we can validate models and experiment with different choices for semantic variation points via simulation.

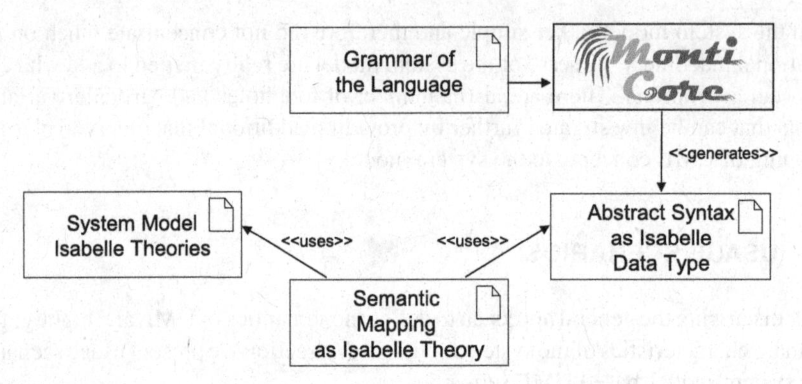

FIGURE 3.3 Approach with tool support.

3.6.4 Tool Support

The general approach to defining the semantics of UML has been outlined in Sections 3.2 and 3.3. To summarize, a precise and adequate semantics is made up of equally precise and adequate definitions for the syntax, the semantic domain, and the semantic mapping. The most flexible way of defining these constituents is by using pencil and paper. To keep most of the flexibility but to benefit from the advantages of a machine-readable semantics that can be (type) checked, used for automated verification, and so on, we use Isabelle/HOL [32] to formalize the system model definitions and also the semantic mapping. As a front end for defining the syntax of the language, MontiCore [25], a framework for the development of modeling languages is used. The overall approach is depicted in Figure 3.3.

1. The syntax is specified as a grammar in the MontiCore grammar definition language, which is basically a context-free grammar.
2. The framework then generates a data type in Isabelle/HOL that represents the abstract syntax.
3. The semantics developer then uses this abstract syntax and the available formalization of the system model theories in Isabelle to encode the semantics of the syntactic constructs as predicates over system models.

3.7 CONCLUDING REMARKS

In this chapter we described our approach to UML semantics and discussed the rationale underlying the system model definition. The system model describes the structure and behavior of object systems on a very detailed and fine-grained basis. It uses the general notion of (timed) state transition systems, which is integrated with the data, control, and event stores. As a general result of system model theory, we have a complete description of how systems are decomposed into objects, what states objects may have, and how objects interact. As motivated in the introduction, the mathematical theory is developed in layers, each building up an algebra that introduces some universe of elements, functions, and laws for these functions. The detailed definitions are provided in Chapter 4.

The key features are support for underspecification and a modular and flexibly extensible definition that is not biased by the choice of a concrete formal language or tool. Even the use of mathematical theories probably will bias the semantics a little, but we hope as little, as possible. Such bias creeps in easily, and we tried very hard to avoid it. In particular, we did not address executability because this includes one of the biggest biases that a modeling language can have: A model should have the ability for underspecification and should be open for a specification of many different implementations. An executable semantics for an underspecified UML model must therefore necessarily contain implicit choices added by the semantic mapping.

To prevent the executability bias, we chose a specific style of description. This form of description allows us to leave open quite a number of definitions. We usually introduce a universe and then characterize the properties of its elements without fully determining how many elements it has or what these elements look like. Sometimes, we describe only a subset of the elements and allow other types of elements to be in the universe as well.

This gives us the chance to specialize variation points according to specific situations. To put it in UML jargon, we could for example define a "system model profile" that specializes the general definitions to sequential, single threaded systems, to static systems without creation of new objects, to systems without subclassing, etc. While the system model is an underlying basis for these kinds of systems, it does not provide such specialization directly; this is matter of further work. Indeed, as one of the results of this work, we have been able to make a number of variation points explicit. Although there are a lot more variation points to explore and their bandwidth to clarify, we regard this approach as a first important step to the formalization and clarification of variation points. On the other hand, the complexity of the system model shows that the integration of objects, threads, state-based behavior and concurrency is complex, has many variations and is therefore somewhat arbitrary. It is particularly complex to model the possible interactions between these, leading us to the assumption that it is particularly difficult to master these not so well integrated concepts. We also described usage scenarios and discussed how a system-model-based UML semantics can be used to analyze, verify, and validate UML models.

The system model defined by Broy et al. [3] and the previous version [4–6] have been used actively to define the semantics of UML sublanguages such as class diagrams [10] and statecharts [11]. A simulator for UML models has been developed by Cengarle et al. [9] based on the system model definitions. This work has been carried out in the context of the DFG rUML project. UML actions have been formalized by Crane and Dingel [13] using the system model as a semantic domain. The system model also forms the basis for characterizing the semantics of model composition [23] as part of the MODELPLEX project.

Acknowledgments

We wish to thank a number of colleagues, especially Bran Selic, Michelle Crane, Jürgen Dingel, Gregor von Bochmann, Gregor Engels, Alain Faivre, Christophe Gaston, Sébastien Gérard, and Martin Schindler for their valuable help.

REFERENCES

1. R. Breu, R. Grosu, F. Huber, B. Rumpe, and W. Schwerin. Systems, views and models of UML. In *Proceedings of the Unified Modeling Language: Technical Aspects and Applications*. Physica Verlag, Heidelberg, Germany, 1998.
2. R. Breu, U. Hinkel, C. Hofmann, C. Klein, B. Paech, B. Rumpe, and V. Thurner. Towards a formalization of the unified modeling language. In *Proceedings of ECOOP'97—Object Oriented Programming, 11th European Conference*. Lecture Notes in Computer Science, vol. 1241. Springer-Verlag, New York, 1997.
3. M. Broy, M. V. Cengarle, H. Grönniger, and B. Rumpe. *Modular Description of a Comprehensive Semantics Model for the UML (Version 2.0)*. Technical Report 2008-06. Carl-Friedrich-Gauß-Fakultät, Technische Universität Braunschweig, Braunschweig, Germany, 2008.
4. M. Broy, M. V. Cengarle, and B. Rumpe. *Semantics of UML—Towards a System Model for UML: The Structural Data Model*. Technical Report TUM-I0612. Institut für Informatik, Technische Universität München, Munich, Germany, June 2006.
5. M. Broy, M. V. Cengarle, and B. Rumpe. *Semantics of UML—Towards a System Model for UML: The Control Model*. Technical Report TUM-I0710. Institut für Informatik, Technische Universität München, Munich, Germany, Feb. 2007.
6. M. Broy, M. V. Cengarle, and B. Rumpe. *Semantics of UML—Towards a System Model for UML: The State Machine Model*. Technical Report TUM-I0711. Institut für Informatik, Technische Universität München, Munich, Germany, Feb. 2007.
7. J.-M. Bruel and R. B. France. Transforming UML models to formal specifications. In P.-A. Muller and J. Bézivin, eds., *International Conference on the Unified Modelling Language: Beyond the Notation (UML'98, Proceedings). Lecture Notes in Computer Science*, vol. 1618. Springer-Verlag, New York, 1998.
8. M. Cadoli, D. Calvanese, G. De Giacomo, and T. Mancini. Finite model reasoning on UML class diagrams via constraint programming. In R. Basili and M. T. Pazienza, eds., *AI*IA*. Lecture Notes in Computer Science, vol. 4733, pp. 36–47. Springer-Verlag, New York, 2007.
9. M. V. Cengarle, J. Dingel, H. Grönniger, and B. Rumpe. System-model-based simulation of UML models. In *Proceedings of the Nordic Workshop on Model Driven Engineering (NW-MODE 2007)*, 2007.
10. M. V. Cengarle, H. Grönniger, and B. Rumpe. *System Model Semantics of Class Diagrams*. Technical Report 2008-04. Carl-Friedrich-Gauß-Fakultät, Technische Universität Braunschweig, Braunschweig, Germany, 2008.
11. M. V. Cengarle, H. Grönniger, and B. Rumpe. *System Model Semantics of Statecharts*. Technical Report 2008-04. Carl-Friedrich-Gauß-Fakultät, Technische Universität Braunschweig, Braunschweig, Gernmay, 2008.
12. M. V. Cengarle and A. Knapp. UML 2.0 interactions: semantics and refinement. In J. Jürjens, E. B. Fernandez, R. France, and B. Rumpe, eds., *Proceedings of the 3rd*

International Workshop on Critical Systems Development with UML (CSDUML'04). Technical Report TUM-I0415. Institut für Informatik, Technische Universität München, Munich, Germany, 2004.

13. M. L. Crane and J. Dingel. Towards a formal account of a foundational subset for executable UML models. In *MoDELS*. Lecture Notes in Computer Science, vol. 5301, pp. 675–689. Springer-Verlag, New York, 2008.
14. W. Damm, B. Josko, A. Pnueli, and A. Votintseva. Understanding UML: a formal semantics of concurrency and communication in real-time UML. In F. de Boer, M. Bonsangue, S. Graf, and W.-P. de Roever, eds., *Proceedings of the 1st Symposium on Formal Methods for Components and Objects (FMCO 2002)*. Lecture Notes in Computer Science Tutorials, vol. 2852, pp. 70–98. Springer-Verlag, New York, 2003.
15. G. Engels, C. Soltenborn, and H. Wehrheim. Analysis of UML activities using dynamic meta modeling. In M. M. Bonsangue and E. B. Johnsen, eds., *FMOODS. Lecture Notes in Computer Science*, vol. 4468, pp. 76–90. Springer-Verlag, New York, 2007.
16. A. Evans, K. Lano, R. France, and B. Rumpe. Meta-modeling semantics of UML. In *Proceedings of Behavioral Specifications of Businesses and Systems*. Kluwer Academic, Norwell, MA, 1999.
17. H. Fecher, M. Kyas, W. P. de Roever, and F. S. de Boer. Compositional operational semantics of a UML-kernel-model language. *Electronic Notes in Theoretical Computer Science*, 156(1):79–96, 2006.
18. I. Feinerer and G. Salzer. Consistency and minimality of UML class specifications with multiplicities and uniqueness constraints. In *TASE*, pp. 411–420. IEEE Computer Society, Los Alamitos, CA, 2007.
19. R. France, A. Evans, K. Lano, and B. Rumpe. Developing the UML as a formal modelling notation. In *Proceedings of the Unified Modeling Language: UML'98 Beyond the Notation. Mulhouse*. Lecture Notes in Computer Science, vol. 1618, pp. 336–348, Springer-Verlag, New York, 1998.
20. R. Grosu, C. Klein, and B. Rumpe. *Enhancing the SysLab System Model with State.* Technical Report TUM-I9631. Technische Univeritát München, Munich, Germany, 1996.
21. D. Harel and B. Rumpe. Meaningful modeling: What's the semantics of "semantics"? *Computer*, 37(10):64–72, 2004.
22. O. Haugen, K. E. Husa, R. K. Runde, and K. Stoelen. STAIRS towards formal design with sequence diagrams. *SoSyM*, 4(4):355–357, 2005.
23. C. Herrmann, H. Krahn, B. Rumpe, M. Schindler, and S. Völkel. An algebraic view on the semantics of model composition. In D. H. Akehurst, R. Vogel, and R. F. Paige, eds., *Model Driven Architecture: Foundations and Applications (ECMDA-FA)*, Haifa, Israel, June 2007. Lecture Notes in Computer Science, vol. 4530, pp. 99–113. Springer-Verlag, New York, 2007.
24. C. Klein, B. Rumpe, and M. Broy. A stream-based mathematical model for distributed information processing systems: the SysLab system model. In E. Naijm and J.-B. Stefani, eds., *Formal Methods for Open Object-Based Distributed Systems (FMOODS'96)*. Chapman & Hall, London, 1996.
25. H. Krahn, B. Rumpe, and S. Völkel. MontiCore: modular development of textual domain specific languages. In *Proceedings of Tools Europe*, 2008.
26. J. Küster, J. Koehler, J. Novatnack, and K. Ryndina. *A Classification of UML2 Activity Diagrams*. IBM ZRL Technical Report 3673, 2006.

27. S. Kuske, M. Gogolla, R. Kollmann, and H.-J. Kreowski. An integrated semantics for UML class, object and state diagrams based on graph transformation. In *Proceedings of the 3rd International Conference on Integrated Formal Methods* (IFM'02), pp. 11–28, London. Springer-Verlag, New York, 2002.
28. K. Lano. A compositional semantics of UML-RSDS. *SoSyM*, 8(1): 85–116, 2009.
29. X. Li. A characterization of UML diagrams and their consistency. In *ICECCS*, pp. 67–76. IEEE Computer Society, Los Alamitos, CA, 2006.
30. A. Maraee and M. Balaban. Efficient reasoning about finite satisfiability of UML class diagrams with constrained generalization sets. In D. H. Akehurst, R. Vogel, and R. F. Paige, eds., *ECMDA-FA*. Lecture Notes in Computer Science, vol. 4530, pp. 17–31. Springer-Verlag, New York, 2007.
31. B. Meyer. *Object-Oriented Software Construction*, 2nd ed. Prentice Hall, Upper Saddle River, NJ, 1997.
32. T. Nipkow, L.C. Paulson, and M. Wenzel. *Isabelle/HOL: A Proof Assistant for Higher-Order Logic*. Springer-Verlag, New York, 2002.
33. OMG. Unified modeling language: infrastructure version 2.1.2. http://www.omg.org/docs/formal/07-11-04.pdf.
34. OMG. Unified modeling language: superstructure version 2.1.2. http://www.omg.org/docs/formal/07-11-02.pdf.
35. G. O'Keefe. Dynamic logic semantics for UML consistency. In A. Rensink and J. Warmer, eds., *ECMDA-FA*. Lecture Notes in Computer Science, vol. 4066, pp. 113–127. Springer-Verlag, New York, 2006.
36. B. Rumpe. Formale Methodik des Entwurfs verteilter objektorientierter Systeme. Herbert Utz Verlag Wissenschaft, 1996. Ph.D. dissertation, Technische Universität München. Munich, Germany.
37. S. Sarstedt and W. Guttmann. An ASM semantics of token flow in UML 2 activity diagrams. In I. Virbitskaite and A. Voronkov, eds., *Ershov Memorial Conference*. Lecture Notes in Computer Science, vol. 4378, pp. 349–362. Springer-Verlag, New York, 2006.
38. K. Satoh, K. Kaneiwa, and T. Uno. Contradiction finding and minimal recovery for UML class diagrams. In *ASE*, pp. 277–280. IEEE Computer Society, Los Alamitos, CA, 2006.
39. C. Snook and M. Butler. UML-B: formal modeling and design aided by UML. *ACM Transactions on Software Engineering Methodology*, 15(1):92–122, 2006.
40. T. Stauner, B. Rumpe, and P. Scholz. *Hybrid System Model*. Technical Report TUM-I9903. Technische Univerität München, Munich, Germany, 1999.
41. H. Störrle and J. H. Hausmann. Towards a formal semantics of UML 2.0 activities. In P. Liggesmeyer, K. Pohl, and M. Goedicke, eds., *Software Engineering*. Lecture Notes in Informatics, vol. 64, pp. 117–128. Gesellschaft für Informatik, Bonn, Germany, 2005.
42. A. Taleghani and J. M. Atlee. Semantic variations among UML state machines. In *MoDELS*, pp. 245–259, 2006.
43. M. von der Beeck. A structured operational semantics for UML-statecharts. *Software and Systems Modeling*, 1(2):130–141, 2002.
44. G. Winskel. *The Formal Semantics of Programming Languages*. Foundations of Computer Science Series. MIT Press, Cambridge, MA, 1993.
45. X. Zhao, Q. Long, and Z. Qiu. Model checking dynamic UML consistency. In Z. Liu and J. He, eds., *ICFEM*. Lecture Notes in Computer Science, vol. 4260, pp. 440–459. Springer-Verlag, New York, 2006.

CHAPTER 4

DEFINITION OF THE SYSTEM MODEL

MANFRED BROY and MARÍA VICTORIA CENGARLE
Institut für Informatik, Technische Universität München, München, Germany

HANS GRÖNNIGER and BERNHARD RUMPE
Lehrstuhl Informatik 3 (Softwaretechnik), RWTH Aachen University, Aachen, Germany

4.1 INTRODUCTION

This chapter is devoted to the definition of a system model tailored toward UML. The hierarchy of theories that compose the system model is introduced setp by step. These theories are combined into a theory of sophisticated state transition systems. The semantics of a word in a UML sublanguage (i.e., a diagram) can then be defined by a set of such transition systems. Given two or more actual diagrams, possibly forming a complete UML model, the semantics of them together is defined by the intersection of their translations into the system model. In other words, consistency of a model is defined by nonempty intersection of the sets containing the transition systems that implement the diagrams individually.

The system model supports underspecification in two manners. On the one hand, the fact that the semantics of a single UML diagram or of a complete UML model is not univocal is a form of underspecification. On the other hand, at the metalevel, the system model can be further constrained in such a way that the ambiguity inherent to the language is reduced or even eliminated. The latter ambiguities are called *variation points*, and the choice of a particular variant reduces the range of possibilities.

Chapter 3 motivates and explains the system model that is introduced below. The system model in this chapter is a simplification of the one presented by Broy et al. [1]. In that work, a number of variation points are also presented. These include, among others, records and Cartesian products within the type system of the system model, subclassing observing structure, objects as values, locations and reference

UML 2 Semantics and Applications. Edited by Kevin Lano

types, qualified and ordered binary associations, active vs. passive objects, and single vs. multithreaded computation.

This chapter is organized as follows. Section 4.3 includes a definition of the structural part of the system model. Sections 4.4 and 4.5 cover the control- and communication-related definitions which form a basis for the description of the state of a system in Section 4.6. Two variants of state transition systems are introduced to define object behavior in Sections 4.7 (event based) and 4.8 (timed).

4.2 NOTATIONAL CONVENTIONS

This section covers the conventions used to structure the mathematical theories that constitute the system model. Definitions, presented as shown in Definition 4.2.1, usually contribute new elements to the system model and/or add constraints to existing elements. Noteworthy derived properties following from a definition are stated as lemmas, presented in a manner similar to that for definitions.

Definition 4.2.1 (This Is a Definition)

DefinitionName
introduction of new elements (sets, functions, ...)
Notation: additional notational abbreviations (optional)
definition of properties that hold
informal, textual explanation (optional)

To simplify the notation, if a formula contains a symbol whose value is irrelevant for the purpose of the fomula, the symbol is replaced by a wildcard $*$. For example, $\forall a : P(a, *, *)$ stands for $\forall a : \exists y, z : P(a, y, z)$, where the variables y and z are unused within the predicate P and are existentially quantified at the innermost level. Also, a number of container structures are used, such as $\mathbb{P}(.)$ for powerset, $\mathbb{P}_f(.)$ for the set of finite subsets of a given set, and *List*(.), *Stack*(.), and *Buffer*(.) for the usual constructs. These structures are defined in mathematical terms with appropriate manipulation and selection functions. For details on these basics, the reader is referred to the work of Broy et al [1].

4.3 STATIC PART OF THE SYSTEM MODEL

The static part of the system model contains the unalterable information regarding the intended systems. The static part is composed of, among other things, some universes of elements that are assumed given and not fully described here. Furthermore, properties of and relationships between those universes may be assumed. Universes are, for example, the universe of type names *UTYPE*, the universe of values *UVAL*, a relation *CAR* that associates a set of values to each type name (see Definition 4.3.1), the universe of class names *UCLASS*, and the universe of object identifiers *UOID* (see Definition 4.3.5). The primitive concept of name is not prescribed further.

Definition 4.3.1 (Tupes and Values)

*Type*1

$UTYPE$
$UVAL$
$CAR : UTYPE \rightarrow \mathbb{P}(UVAL)$

$\forall u \in UTYPE : CAR(u) \neq \emptyset$

UTYPE is the universe of type names.
UVAL is the universe of values.
CAR maps type names to nonempty carrier sets; carrier sets need not be disjoint.

4.3.1 Type Names and Carrier Sets

A type name identifies a carrier set that contains simple or complex data elements called *members* or *values* of (or associated with) the type name. The universe of all type names is denoted by *UTYPE*. Members of all type names are gathered in the universe *UVAL* of values; see Definition 4.3.1.

Any $T \in UTYPE$ is a type *name*, not a type, but may be referred to as type T. In particular, the types of the system model explicitly encode UML types (i.e., deep embedding of types is used).

The definitions above leave open quite a number of possibilities to characterize types. Broy et al. [1] show a few examples which are not formal parts of the system model. For example, we may wish to express that integer and float are type names, that integer and floating-point values are values in the system model, and that integer values are also floats: $Int, Float \in UTYPE$, $CAR(Float) = \mathbb{R}$, and $CAR(Int) = \mathbb{Z} \subseteq \mathbb{R} \subseteq UVAL$.

The value *void* is usually needed when giving semantics to procedures or methods with no return value. This is customary in the semantics of programming languages.

4.3.2 Basic Type Names and Type Name Constructors

Basic type names for basic values such as Boolean and integer values (see Definition 4.3.2) are given by default, together with their typical operations, such as logical connectives and arithmetic operators (not detailed here). The carrier set associated with *Void*, a further basic type name, is a singleton; see Definition 4.3.3.

Definition 4.3.2 (Basic Types)

BoolInt

Bool, Int $\in$ *UTYPE*
true, false $\in$ *UVAL*

$CAR(Bool) = \{true, false\}$

$true \neq false$

$CAR(Int) = \mathbb{Z} \subseteq UVAL$

UTYPE contains at least the type names Bool and Int.
UVAL contains at least Boolean and integer values.

Definition 4.3.3 (Basic Type Void)

Void

Void $\in$ *UTYPE*
void $\in$ *UVAL*

$CAR(Void) = \{void\}$

---

void can be used, for example, to return control without an actual return value.

4.3.3 Variables

The notion of variable (see Definition 4.3.4) permits the encoding of object attributes, method parameters, and method local variables. Each variable name has an associated unique type name.

4.3.4 Class Names and Objects, Subclass Relation

Definition 4.3.5 introduces the universes *UCLASS* of class names, *UOID* of object identifiers, and *INSTANCE* of instances. A class name is associated with a finite set of attributes, which simply are variables. Each class name is, moreover, associated with a set of object identifiers. By use of the association mechanism (see Section 4.3.7), class names can be related to each other. Also, methods can be associated with class names; see Definition 4.4.2.

Definition 4.3.4 (Variables, Attributes, Parameters)

Variable

$UVAR$
$vtype : UVAR \rightarrow UTYPE$
$vsort : UVAR \rightarrow \mathbb{P}(UVAL)$
$VarAssign = (v : UVAR \rightharpoonup vsort(v))$

Notation:
$a : T$ denotes "a is a variable of type T" [i.e., $vtype(a) = T$].

$\forall v \in UVAR : vsort(v) = CAR(vtype(v)) \wedge \forall val \in VarAssign : val(v) \in vsort(v)$

UVAR is the universe of all variable names, each with a unique type associated.
VarAssign is the set of all total and partial assignments of values for variables.

Definition 4.3.5 (Classes and Instances)

Class

$UCLASS$
$UOID$
$INSTANCE$
$attr : UCLASS \rightarrow \mathbb{P}_f(UVAR)$
$oids : UCLASS \rightarrow \mathbb{P}(UOID)$
$objects : UCLASS \rightarrow \mathbb{P}(INSTANCE)$
$objects : UOID \rightarrow \mathbb{P}(INSTANCE)$
$classOf : INSTANCE \rightarrow UCLASS$
$classOf : UOID \rightharpoonup UCLASS$

$\forall oid \in oids(C) : classOf(oid) = C \wedge$
$\quad objects(oid) = \{(oid, r) \mid r \in VarAssign \wedge \mathrm{dom}(r) = attr(C)\}$
$\forall o \in objects(C) : classOf(o) = C$

UCLASS is the universe of class names.
attr assigns a finite set of attributes to each class name.
UOID is the universe of object identifiers.
INSTANCE is the universe of objects of the form $o = (oid, r)$, where *oid* is an object identifier and r is a variable assignment for the attributes of the class name associated with *oid*.
oids assigns a set of object identifiers to a class name.
classOf enforces uniqueness of the class (name) associated with each object and with each identifier.

Except for the object identifier *Nil* (see Definition 4.3.7), there is a bijection between the universes *UOID* and *INSTANCE*. Thus, besides *Nil*, there are no dangling references. As a consequence, each object belongs to exactly one class,[1] and this does not vary over time, whereas the object value can vary, and dereferencing from an object identifier is state dependent. (In particular, structurally equivalent classes are distinguished.)

More precisely, *UOID* contains references to all possible objects, and in a similar way, *INSTANCE* contains all possible objects. These sets are usually infinite because they represent the possible existence of objects. Furthermore, *INSTANCE* contains all object values, thus describing many different object values using the same identifier. At each point in time only a finite subset of objects will actually exist in the data store (see Section 4.3.6) and there will be at most one instance for any identifier.

Definition 4.3.6 introduces the mechanisms for accessing the attributes of an object. A distinguished term is *this*, which can be treated as if it is an attribute although it is not [and thus does not appear in $attr(C)$]. In particular, no type name is associated with *this*; thus, a number of conceptual difficulties, such as recursive type definitions, are avoided. Definition 4.3.7 introduces the special identifier *Nil* and constrains *UOID* to consist exactly of object identifiers and *INSTANCE* of objects only.

Definition 4.3.6 (Attribute Access)

Attribute

$this : INSTANCE \rightarrow UOID$

$getAttr : INSTANCE \times UVAR \rightharpoonup UVAL$

$attr : INSTANCE \rightarrow \mathbb{P}_f(UVAR)$

$attr : UOID \rightarrow \mathbb{P}_f(UVAR)$

Notation:

$o.this$ is shorthand for $this(o)$

$o.a$ is shorthand for $getAttr(o, a)$

$\forall o, (oid, r) \in INSTANCE :$

$this((oid, r)) = oid$

$getAttr((oid, r), a) = r.a$

$attr(oid) = attr(classOf(oid))$

$attr(o) = attr(classOf(o))$

$o.this$ is written in the spirit of attribute selection but is treated differently: *this* is not an actual attribute of the class.

[1] Polymorphism is introduced in Section 4.3.5.

4.3.5 Subclass Relation

The *subclass* (or *inheritance*) relation *sub* is introduced in Definition 4.3.8. There, a type name constructor is also introduced, which associates a type name with each class name; this type name collects in its carrier set all the object identifiers associated with the class name or any of its subclass names. Therefore, object identifiers are values (i.e., $UOID \subseteq UVAL$).

Definition 4.3.7 (Introduction of Nil)

Nil

$Nil \in UOID$

$\forall C \in UCLASS : Nil \notin oids(C)$

$\forall o \in INSTANCE : o.this \neq Nil$

$UOID = \{Nil\} \cup \bigcup_{C \in UCLASS} oids(C)$

$INSTANCE = \bigcup_{C \in UCLASS} objects(C)$

Nil is a distinguished object identifier, the only one not associated to any class or any object. *UOID* and *INSTANCE* consist only of object identifiers and objects, respectively.

Thus, the subclass relation allows a precise definition of the type of a class: The object identifiers associated with the class and any of its subclasses belong to a carrier of the type assigned to the class.

Definition 4.3.8 leaves a number of questions open and thus allows further refinement. For example, the binary relation *sub* is not enforced to be antisymmetric (although this is the case in any implementation language today). Furthermore, subclassing is not based on a structural definition: The sets of attributes of two classes may be in the subset relation; nevertheless, the classes may be unrelated by *sub*.

Definition 4.3.8 (Subclass Relation)

Subclassing

$sub \subseteq UCLASS \times UCLASS$
$.^{\&} : UCLASS \rightarrow UTYPE$

$UOID \subseteq UVAL$

$transitive(sub) \wedge reflexive(sub)$

$\forall C \in UCLASS : CAR(C^{\&}) = \{Nil\} \cup \bigcup_{C_1 \, sub \, C} oids(C_1)$

sub is the transitive and reflexive subclass relation.
The carrier set associated with the type name $C^{\&}$ contains all object identifiers that belong to the carrier set of class name *C* or any of its subclass names.

Definition 4.3.9 (The Data Store)

*DataStore*1

$DataStore \subseteq (UOID \rightharpoonup INSTANCE)$
$oids : DataStore \rightarrow \mathbb{P}(UOID)$

$\forall ds \in DataStore : oids(ds) = \mathrm{dom}(ds)$

$\forall o \in UOID, ds \in DataStore : ds(o).this = o$

DataStore is the set of all data stores or possible snapshot values.
oids(*ds*) is the set of existing objects in a given data store *ds*.

The technique of defining *sub* as a subset relation on object identifiers instead of objects permits a great simplification on the type system within the system model. Furthermore, it allows a redefinition of attribute structures in subclasses without an otherwise necessary loss of the substitution principle.

4.3.6 Data Store Structure

Intuitively, a data store is a snapshot of the data state of a running system. Definition 4.3.9 introduces data stores as functions assigning objects to object identifiers. Any such function assigns an object *o* to an object identifier *oid* only if this is the identifier of that object, which can be retrieved using *o.this*.

A number of convenient retrieval and update functions for data stores are given in Definition 4.3.10. They deal basically with lookup and change of attribute values as well as "creating" a new object in the store.

Various restrictions on the use of retrieval and update functions apply. They involve the use of values of appropriate type, attributes that actually exist in a class, and so on. However, we refrain from defining these restrictions here.

4.3.7 Associations

Definition 4.3.11 introduces the universe *UASSOC* of association names. The function *classes* associates a list of class names with each association name; given an association name *R*, $classes(R) = [C_1, \ldots, C_n]$ is sometimes called the *signature* of *R*. *classes* assigns a list, not a set, of class names to an association name. The order of the classes is relevant as in a self-association such as "parent–child."

Additional values that accompany an association name can be retrieved using the function *extraVals*. Additional values permit qualified associations using one (or more) of them as a qualifier. They also allow nonunique associations: By introducing a value as a distinguishing flag, a tuple can be duplicated.

Given a system snapshot (i.e., a data store), the relation retrieval function *relOf* returns the tuples that constitute the (instantiation of) the association name, each one together with the additional values *extraVals*, in that data store. These tuples contain

Definition 4.3.10 (DataStore Infrastructure)

DataStore

$val : DataStore \times UOID \times UVAR \rightharpoonup UVAL$
$setval : DataStore \times UOID \times UVAR \times UVAL \rightharpoonup DataStore$
$addobj : DataStore \times INSTANCE \rightarrow DataStore$

Notation:
$ds(oid.at)$ is shorthand for $val(ds, oid, at)$

$ds[oid.at = v]$ is shorthand for $setval(oid, at, v)$

$\forall ds \in DataStore, oid \in oids(ds), at \in attr(oid), v \in CAR(vtype(at)))$:

$val(ds, oid, at) = ds(oid).at$

$setval(ds, oid, at, v) = ds \oplus [oid = (oid, \pi_2(ds(oid)) \oplus [at = v])]$

$o.this \notin oids(ds) \Rightarrow addobj(ds, o) = ds \oplus [o.this = o]$

val retrieves the value for a given object and attribute.
setval updates a value for a given object and attribute.
addobj adds a new object.

Definition 4.3.11 (Basic Definitions for Associations)

Association

$UASSOC$
$classes : UASSOC \rightarrow List(UCLASS)$
$extraVals : UASSOC \rightarrow \mathbb{P}(UVAL)$
$relOf : UASSOC \times DataStore \rightarrow \mathbb{P}(UVAL \times UVAL)$

$\forall R \in UASSOC, C_i \in UCLASS(i = 1, \ldots, n), ds \in DataStore$:

$classes(R) = [C_1, \ldots, C_n] \Rightarrow$

$relOf(R, ds) \subseteq (CAR(C_1^{\&}) \times \cdots \times CAR(C_n^{\&})) \times extraVals(R)$

UASSOC is the universe of association names.
classes returns the list of class names related by a given association name.
extraVals of a given association name is the set of further values that accompany the association name.
relOf is the retrieval function to derive the actual links for an *n*-ary association based on the current store.

values of the corresponding types; these types, in turn, are obtained from the class names in the signature of the association name using the type name constructor $\cdot^{\&}$. This means that the tuples of an instantiation of the association name may include object identifiers whose *classOf* is a subclass of the corresponding class in the signature of the association name.

Restrictions on the changeability of an association such as UML class diagrams may impose can be observed or checked only when two consecutive *DataStore*s are compared. This means that the semantics of a class diagram cannot be defined completely using only one snapshot of the *DataStore*.

4.3.7.1 Variation Point: Simple Associations Only Variation Point 4.3.1 is not formally part of the system model but shows how to refine it by adding further constraints. Each constraint may be imposed individually. These constraints restrict the instantiations of association names to finite sets of tuples, disallow additional values for association names, and force association names to be binary or all association names to have multiplicity *1-to-** (which includes *1-to-1*) but not **-to-**. Other variation points may define binary, qualified, and ordered association names as well as realization techniques for them.

Variation Point 4.3.1 (Simplified Associations)

[SimplAssociation]

$\forall R \in UASSOC, ds \in DataStore : \#relOf(R, ds) \in \mathbb{N}$

$\forall R \in UASSOC : \#extraVals(R) = 1$

$\forall R \in UASSOC : \#classes(R) = 2$

$\forall R \in UASSOC, ds \in DataStore, oid \in UOID :$

$\#\{(oid_1, oid_2, x) \in relOf(R, ds) \mid oid = oid_1\} = 1$

4.4 CONTROL PART OF THE SYSTEM MODEL

Having defined the data part, in this and the following section, we focus on the control part of the system model. The control part defines the structure used to store control information. Roughly speaking, this structure is divided into a control store and an event store. The control store contains all the information needed to determine the state of a system during computation.

That is, in addition to its data store as introduced in Definition 4.3.10, a state machine of the system model has a control store. This store contains information about the behavior of the intended system and is used by the state machine to decide which transition to perform next. A control store consists of:

- A stack of method/operation calls, each with its arguments and local variables
- The progress of the running program (e.g., a program counter)
- Possibly information about one or more threads

In any setting, be it distributed or not, any state machine of the system model also has to deal with receiving and sending events that trigger activities in objects. General events such as "message arrived" or "timeout" must be handled by any object. These events are put into an event store, which consists of an event buffer for each object where handling of events is managed. The event store, which is the last constituent of the state of an object, is defined in Section 4.5.

4.4.1 Operations

Objects are accessed through their methods and operations. Here *operation* refers to the signature (or head), whereas *method* also refers to the implementation (or body). Operations can be called, and they may provide a return value as given by the corresponding implementation. Each operation has a name and a signature (which includes arguments and a return value that may be of type *Void*).

Definition 4.4.1 specifies signatures, which consist of a (possibly empty) list of types for parameters and a type for the return value. Note that parameter names are not present in the signature; parameter names are only part of the implementation. For each operation, its signature, its implementation, and the class it belongs to are specified uniquely.

Definition 4.4.1 (Operations)

Operation

$UOPN$
$UOMNAME$
$nameOf : UOPN \to UOMNAME$
$classOf : UOPN \to UCLASS$
$parTypes : UOPN \to List(UTYPE)$
$params : UOPN \to \mathbb{P}(List(UVAL))$
$resType : UOPN \to UTYPE$

$\forall op \in UOPN : parTypes(op) = [T_1, \ldots, T_n] \Rightarrow$

$params(op) = \{[v_1, \ldots, v_n] : v_i \in CAR(T_i)(i = 1, \ldots, n)\}$

UOPN is the universe of operations.
UOMNAME the universe of operation (or method) names.
nameOf returns the name of a given operation.
classOf returns the class to which a given operation belongs.
parTypes returns the list of types of the parameters of a given operation.
params returns all possible arguments of a given operation.
resType returns the result type of a given operation.

The subclassing mechanism lets subclasses inherit operations from their superclasses. This means that subclassing imposes a constraint on signatures and, in many languages, also a constraint on the promised behavior of its related classes. Definition 4.4.2 relates operations in super- and subclasses in a co- and contravariant way (see, e.g., the book of Meyer [7]). An inherited operation in the subclass may accept a superset of parameter values and may return a subset of return values, compared to the possible values of the superclass operation. In this way, the subclass operation can safely substitute the superclass operation.

Definition 4.4.2 (Type Safety on Operations)

TypeSafeOps

$$\begin{aligned}&\forall op_1 \in UOPN, c \in UCLASS : c\ sub\ classOf(op_1) \Rightarrow\\&\quad \exists op_2 \in UOPN : classOf(op_2) = c \wedge\\&\quad nameOf(op_1) = nameOf(op_2) \wedge\\&\quad CAR(resType(op_1)) \supseteq CAR(resType(op_2)) \wedge\\&\quad params(op_1) \subseteq params(op_2)\end{aligned}$$

Any class type-safely inherits operations from any of its superclasses.

Although rather general, Definition 4.4.2 needs not hold in all object-oriented languages. In particular, languages such as Smalltalk, exhibiting "Message not understood" errors to which a program can react, do not enforce this type of safety requirement.

In the system model, operations have exactly one return value. Multiple return values, can be encoded, however: for example, by packing them in a class or record.

4.4.2 Methods

As we noted earlier, *operation* refers only to the signature, whereas *method* also refers to the implementation of an operation. Thus, methods have both a signature and an internal implementation. The signature of a method consists of a list of parameter names with their types. Projected on the list of types, this list coincides with the parameter type list of the associated operation(s).

To provide all information necessary for a detailed understanding of method interactions, a binding mechanism between arguments and corresponding formal parameters is needed, as well as a store for local variables and an abstract notion of a program counter, as given in Definition 4.4.3. Furthermore, a method is equipped with the class name to which it belongs and where it is implemented. Note that *localsOf* and *parOf* result in variable assignments that contain mappings of variables to appropriate values. For convenience, parameters, attributes, and local variables of a method are assumed disjoint (which is allowed by syntactic resolution).

Definition 4.4.3 (Methods)

Method1

$UMETH$
UPC
$nameOf : UMETH \rightarrow UOMNAME$
$definedIn : UMETH \rightarrow UCLASS$
$parNames, localNames : UMETH \rightarrow List(UVAR)$
$parOf : m : UMETH \rightarrow \mathbb{P}(VarAssign|_{set(parNames(m))})$
$localsOf : m : UMETH \rightarrow \mathbb{P}(VarAssign|_{set(localNames(m))})$
$resType : UMETH \rightarrow UTYPE$
$pcOf : UMETH \rightarrow \mathbb{P}_f(UPC)$

$\forall m \in UMETH, v \in UVAR, val \in parOf(m) :$

$\quad v \in \mathrm{dom}(val) \Leftrightarrow v \in set(parNames(m))$

$\forall m \in UMETH, v \in UVAR, val \in localsOf(m) :$

$\quad v \in \mathrm{dom}(val) \Leftrightarrow v \in set(localNames(m))$

$\quad parNames(m) \cap localNames(m) = \emptyset$

$\quad parNames(m) \cap attr(definedIn(m)) = \emptyset$

$\quad localNames(m) \cap attr(definedIn(m)) = \emptyset$

UMETH is the universe of methods.
UPC is the universe of program counter values.

Given a method, *definedIn* returns the class to which the method (implementation) belongs (and where it was defined).
parNames returns the formal parameter variables of a given method.
localNames returns local variables of a given method.
parOf and *localsOf* return sets of variable assignments of formal parameters and of local variables, respectively, of a given method.
resType returns the result type of a given method.
pcOf is the (finite) set of possible program counter values of a method.
Pairwise disjointness of *parNames*, *localNames* and *attr* is assumed for convenience.

The concepts of method (implementation) and operation (signature) are fully decoupled, which allows their mutually independent description. However, there usually is a strong link between methods and operations: A method can only implement operations with compatible signatures. Nevertheless, as implementations can be inherited, multiple operations can refer to the same method as its implementation. In this way, on the one hand, the operation signature can be adapted (e.g., made more specific) without changing the implementations, and on the other, the implementation can be redefined using a new method in a subclass. Definition 4.4.4 describes this relation through a function *impl* that associates a method with a signature; if the class can be instantiated, all operations of that class need to have implementations.

Definition 4.4.4 (Relationship Between Method and Operation)

Method

$impl : UOPN \rightharpoonup UMETH$

$\forall op \in UOPN : m = impl(op) \Rightarrow$

$nameOf(m) = nameOf(op) \wedge$

$classOf(op)\ sub\ definedIn(m) \wedge$

$CAR(resType(m)) \subseteq CAR(resType(op)) \wedge$

$n = length(parNames(m)) \Rightarrow$

$\{[val(parNames(m)_1), \ldots, val(parNames(m)_n)] : val \in parOf(m)\}$

$\supseteq params(op)$

$\forall c \in UCLASS, op \in UOPN : oids(c) \neq \emptyset \wedge classOf(op) = c \Rightarrow$

$op \in \mathrm{dom}(impl)$

impl assigns a method implementation to each operation.

The signature *params*(*op*) of an operation *op* is a set of lists of values, whereas the parameter list *parNames*(*m*) of the corresponding method implementation $m = impl(op)$ is a single list of variables.

4.4.3 Stacked Method Calls

A stack is a well-known mechanism to store the structure necessary to handle chained and (mutually) recursive method calls. A control stack is indispensable for a description of nested operation calls and, in particular, object recursion.[2] Object recursion is a common principle in object orientation and provides much flexibility and expressiveness. Almost all design patterns (e.g., that of Gamma et al. [4]) as well as callback mechanisms of frameworks (e.g., that of Fontoura et al. [3]) rely on this principle.

Thus, the information needed in order for computation to resume after a method has finished is generally stored in a stack. The notion of stack used is abstract; the information stored in the stack is organized in frames which include, among others, program counter values. Although using abstractions, the matter is complicated

[2] That is, a method calls another method of the same object. By contrast, in method recursion, a method that has not yet finished execution is called from a method of another object.

enough to justify an incremental definition of the method call mechanism. First the single-threaded case is considered.

A stack frame, introduced in Definition 4.4.5, contains the relevant information about the method in execution. A frame on top refers to a method executing at the moment or to be started now. A frame below the top of the stack refers to a method executing at the moment that has passed control and is blocked. The relevant information in a frame includes the object identifier to which the method belongs, the name of the method, the current program counter value of the method, the object identifier of the calling object, and the (current) variable assignment for formal parameters and local variables of the method. *StackFrame* defines the minimal information needed for a description of stack frames; additional conditions can be added to further constrain stack frames.

Definition 4.4.5 (Stack Frames)

StackFrame

$FRAME = UOID \times UOMNAME \times VarAssign \times UPC \times UOID$

$framesOf : UMETH \to \mathbb{P}(FRAME)$

$$
\begin{aligned}
framesOf(m) = \{(callee, nameOf(m), val, pc, caller) \mid\ & \\
& \exists op \in UOPN : m = impl(op) \wedge \\
& callee \in oids(classOf(op)) \wedge pc \in pcOf(m) \wedge \\
& val \in parOf(m) \oplus localsOf(m) \quad \}
\end{aligned}
$$

FRAME is the universe of frames;

framesOf is the set of possible frames for a given method.

Derived:

$$
\begin{aligned}
framesOf(m) = \textstyle\bigcup_{op \in UOPN, m = impl(op)} & oids(classOf(op)) \times \{nameOf(m)\} \times \\
& (parOf(m) \oplus localsOf(m)) \times pcOf(m)
\end{aligned}
$$

In the case of a single-threaded system, the only existing thread can be defined as an element of type *Stack*(*FRAME*). A method may fork several control flows. Nevertheless, frames have only one program counter. When a fork takes place, a new thread is started. Each thread is then represented by its own stack of frames, each of which again contains only one program counter. Therefore, the definition of frames also suffices for the multithreaded case; the only difference is that there is more than one stack of such frames.

4.4.4 Multiple-Thread Computation: Centralized View

The concurrency concept of the system model is orthogonal to objects; that is, various concurrent threads may independently and even simultaneously "enter" the same object. In the following, a model of threads is added to the system model definition introduced so far. The increment is general enough to allow specialization to other approaches and is based on an assumed notion of atomic action (whose precise definition is deferred to the definition of UML actions).

In Definition 4.4.6, an (abstract) universe of possibly infinitely many threads is introduced. The control store maps a stack of frames to each thread. These stacks satisfy the following condition: For any two adjacent frames in the stack, the calling object above is the called object below. A central control store with concurrently executing threads is illustrated in Example 4.4.1.

Definition 4.4.6 (Control Store in the Centralized Version)

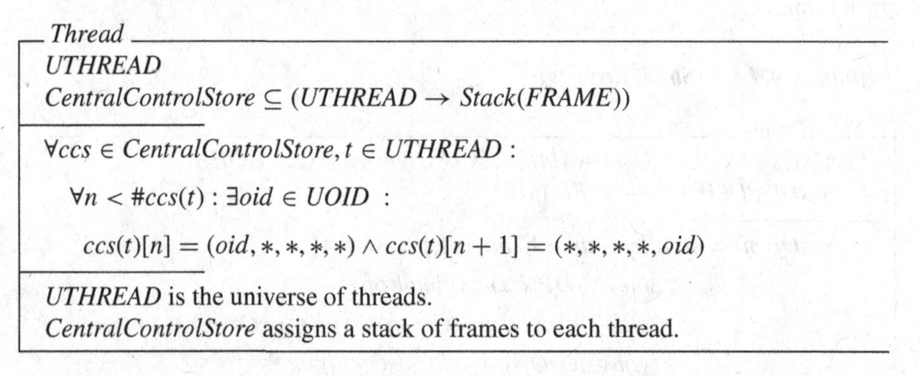

Thread

UTHREAD

$CentralControlStore \subseteq (UTHREAD \rightarrow Stack(FRAME))$

$\forall ccs \in CentralControlStore, t \in UTHREAD :$

$\quad \forall n < \#ccs(t) : \exists oid \in UOID :$

$\qquad ccs(t)[n] = (oid, *, *, *, *) \wedge ccs(t)[n+1] = (*, *, *, *, oid)$

UTHREAD is the universe of threads.

CentralControlStore assigns a stack of frames to each thread.

Example 4.4.1 (Centralized View on Concurrently Executing Threads) The figure below illustrates the situation where two threads are active, and both object recursion as well as concurrency occurs. Here "Frame$x.y$" denotes that the frame is in thread x at position y, where the highest y-numbers denote the active frames.

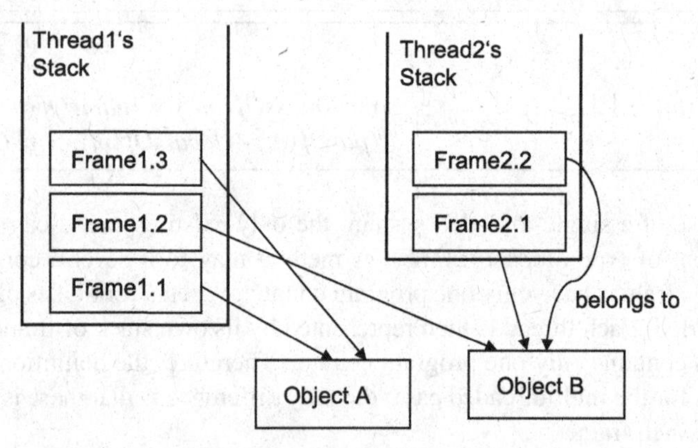

4.4.5 Multiple-Thread Computation, Object-Centric View

The central control store defined above is rather general but so far does not cover how concurrent threads are executed within an object. To enable a general mechanism for scheduling and definition of priorities, the representation of thread-based stacks is rearranged by providing a different view on threads. The key idea is to use an object-centric view of stacks instead of the current thread-centric view as shown in Definition 4.4.7. As an important side effect, objects are then described in a self-contained way. This means that the control information in the system and the object state in full provide a compositional view of object-oriented systems.

Definition 4.4.7 (Control Store in the Object-Centric Version)

ControlStore

$ControlStore \subseteq (UOID \rightharpoonup UTHREAD \rightarrow Stack(FRAME))$
$. \sim . \subseteq CentralControlStore \times ControlStore$

$ccs \sim cs \Leftrightarrow$

$\forall oid \in UOID, t \in UTHREAD:$

$cs(oid)(t) = filter(\{(oid, *, *, *, *)\}, ccs(t))$

ControlStore splits each stack in parts that belong to objects.

$. \sim .$ relates two representations of the control store by essentially filtering the centralized stack with regard to individual objects.

Lemma 4.4.1 (Control Store Representations Are Equivalent)

$\forall ccs \in CentralControlStore : \exists^1 cs \in ControlStore : ccs \sim cs$
$\forall cs \in ControlStore : \exists^1 ccs \in CentralControlStore : ccs \sim cs$

For a *ControlStore* *cs* the stack $cs(oid)(t)$ contains exactly those frames where a method from object *oid* was called in thread t. Note that the relation $. \sim .$ defines an isomorphism as formulated in Lemma 4.4.1. Decentralization into a control store is by definition a function. However, the original stacks can also be reconstructed uniquely because the caller object identifier is part of the frame of the called object. So both representations of the control store provide exactly the same information arranged differently. Example 4.4.2 shows the Example 4.4.1 as represented by an object-centered control store.

According to Definition 4.5.3, an object can easily recognize that it is being called a second time within the same thread. This is important when, for example, scheduling or blocking incoming messages from other threads. The Java synchronization model distinguishes recursive calls from other threads and calls from the same threads, and blocks the former but not the latter.

Example 4.4.2 (Object-Centric View on Concurrently Executing Threads)

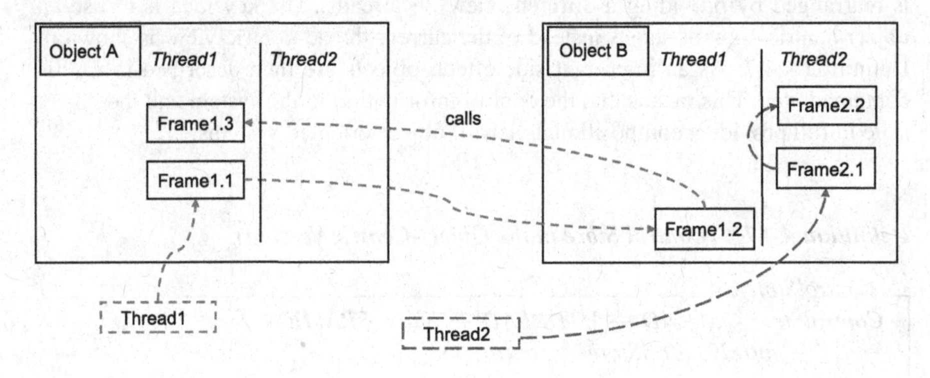

4.5 MESSAGES AND EVENTS IN THE SYSTEM MODEL

In this section, messages and events are specified as well as how they are stored and handled within objects.

4.5.1 Messages, Events, and the Event Store

A uniform handling of events and messages is allowed when messages are considered as events as well, and this gives rise to a general concept also called "events." Events can be handled by an operation being executed, a blocked operation resuming execution (in case of a return event), or ignored. They need not be consumed in the order in which they appear, and a more sophisticated management (scheduling) can be defined individually for each object: Event occurrences may be handled immediately, or their handling may be delayed until it is made possible, or they can even be ignored.

To capture this rather general notion, a universe of events occurring in systems is introduced. Events are not yet structured further; below, certain types of events, such as method call and return, are introduced as special forms of events. Further specializations are left open.

In Definition 4.5.1, the universes *UEVENT* of events and *EventStore* of event stores are introduced. An event store buffers events that have occurred and are waiting to be processed. A buffer is a rather general structure to store and handle messages, deal with priorities, and so on. Event occurrences are instances of events that may store information such as the time the instance occurred and possibly other state information. In the system model, hence, event occurrences correspond to system states in which the event has just been added (sent) to or removed (received) from the event store.

Definition 4.5.2 introduces the universe *UMESSAGE* of messages and the function *MsgEvent*. Messages are a general mechanism to encode any kind of synchronous method call as well as asynchronous message passing. Each message has a unique sender and a unique receiver. That is, a direct description of broadcasting or multicasting is not possible. This means no restriction, though: Multicasting, for example, can be simulated by sending the same message repeatedly to different addressees. Moreover, no further distinction between the various possible forms of messages is enforced.

Definition 4.5.1 (EventStore and Object Event Signature)

EventStore

$UEVENT$
$eventsIn : UOID \to \mathbb{P}(UEVENT)$
$eventsOut : UOID \to \mathbb{P}(UEVENT)$
$EventStore \subseteq (UOID \rightharpoonup Buffer(UEVENT))$

$$events(oid) = eventsIn(oid) \cup eventsOut(oid)$$

$$\forall es \in EventStore : oid \in \mathrm{dom}(es) \Rightarrow es(oid) \in Buffer(events(oid))$$

UEVENT is the universe of events.
eventIn are the events that an object may receive.
eventOut are the events that an object may generate.
EventStore maps an object identifier to a buffer of processable events.

Definition 4.5.2 (Object Message Signature)

Message

$UMESSAGE$
$MsgEvent : UMESSAGE \to UEVENT$
$sender, receiver : UMESSAGE \to UOID$
$msgIn, msgOut : UOID \to \mathbb{P}(UMESSAGE)$

$\forall m \in UMESSAGE, oid \in UOID :$

$$sender(m) = oid \Leftrightarrow MsgEvent(m) \in eventsOut(oid)$$

$$receiver(m) = oid \Leftrightarrow MsgEvent(m) \in eventsIn(oid)$$

$$msgIn(oid) = \{m \mid receiver(m) = oid\}$$

$$msgOut(oid) = \{m \mid sender(m) = oid\}$$

UMESSAGE is the universe of messages.
MsgEvent wraps messages into events that can then be adequately stored. *sender* and *receiver* enforce uniqueness of sender and receiver, respectively, of any message.

4.5.2 Method Call and Return Messages

Common kinds of messages describe method call and return. The well-known technique of encoding method call and return into messages, as practiced in distributed systems, supports, among other things, *remote procedure calls*.

Call messages carry the usual information, such as caller and called objects, method name, parameter values, and thread. All possible invocations for a given caller object, called object, operation, and thread are packed by the function *callsOf* into an appropriate message; see Definition 4.5.3.

Definition 4.5.3 (Method Call Messages)

MethodCall

$callsOf : UOID \times UOPN \times UOID \times UTHREAD \to \mathbb{P}(UMESSAGE)$
$callsOf : UOID \to \mathbb{P}(UMESSAGE)$

$\forall r, s \in UOID, op \in UOPN, th \in UTHREAD$:

$callsOf(r, op, s, th) \subseteq UOID \times UOMNAME \times List(UVAL) \times UOID \times UTHREAD$

$callsOf(r, op, s, th) = \{(r, nameOf(op), pars, s, th) \mid$

$\quad r \in oids(classOf(op)) \wedge$

$\quad pars \in params(op)\}$

$callsOf(r, op, s, th) \subseteq msgIn(r)$

$callsOf(r, op, s, th) \subseteq msgOut(s)$

$callsOf(r) = \bigcup_{op \in UOPN, s \in UOID, th \in UTHREAD} callsOf(r, op, s, th)$

---

callsOf defines the set of all possible method calls from object s to r with operation signature op and run in thread th.

Return messages carry the return value, the thread, and the sender and receiver of the result value. So Definition 4.5.4 differs only slightly from the previous definition of method calls. According to the definition of *returnsOf*, the receiver r of the return message was the sender of the original method call.

The concepts of method calls and returns, on the one hand, and of messages, on the other, can be gathered into a single concept of message passing. Message passing allows handling of the composition of objects and provides a clear interface definition for objects and object groups. Method calls and returns are then just special kinds of messages and can be treated together with other kinds of incoming messages.

4.5.3 Asynchronous Messages

Formally, signals are just asynchronous messages that do not transfer control. Therefore, not every message needs to carry a thread marker. There may, moreover, exist

Definition 4.5.4 (Return Messages)

MethodReturn

$returnsOf : UOID \times UOPN \times UOID \times UTHREAD \to \mathbb{P}(UMESSAGE)$
$returnsOf : UOID \to \mathbb{P}(UMESSAGE)$

$\forall r, s \in UOID, op \in UOPN, th \in UTHREAD:$

$returnsOf(r, op, s, th) \subseteq UOID \times UVAL \times UOID \times UTHREAD$

$returnsOf(r, op, s, th) = \{(r, v, s, th) \mid$

$\quad s \in oids(classOf(op)) \wedge v \in CAR(resType(op))\}$

$returnsOf(r, op, s, th) \subseteq msgIn(r)$

$returnsOf(r, op, s, th) \subseteq msgOut(s)$

$returnsOf(r) = \bigcup_{op \in UOPN, s \in UOID, th \in UTHREAD} returnsOf(r, op, s, th)$

returnsOf defines the set of all possible returns from object *s* to *r* that may occur as a response to a method call in thread *th*.

signals that an object may accept. In this case, the object needs to be "active" in the sense that it already has an internal thread to process the stimulus. It is, furthermore, possible that the object is not itself active, but belongs to a group of objects that has a common scheduling concept for the processing of messages that come from outside the group. This concept resembles the situation in classical language realizations, where one process contains many objects. A concept of regions allows a description of such a common scheduling strategy.

In Definition 4.5.5 the universe *USIGNAL* of signals is introduced, which is a subset of the universe of messages.

Definition 4.5.5 (Signals as Asynchronous Messages)

Signal

$USIGNAL \subseteq UMESSAGE$

$callsOf(*, *, *, *) \cap USIGNAL = \emptyset$
$returnsOf(*, *, *, *) \cap USIGNAL = \emptyset$

4.6 OBJECT STATE

Objects may have an individual state, and groups of objects may have a collective state.

4.6.1 Individual Object States

The signature and the state space of an object comprises data, control, and event stores. The three stores are defined as mappings from *UOID* to the respective state elements. Thus, the state of an object is fully described by a value of *OSTATE* as given in Definition 4.6.1.

Definition 4.6.1 (State Space of An Individual Object)

*ObjectStates*1

$$STATE \subseteq DataStore \times ControlStore \times EventStore$$
$$oids : STATE \rightarrow \mathbb{P}(UOID)$$
$$OSTATE = INSTANCE \times (UTHREAD \rightarrow Stack(FRAME)) \times Buffer(UEVENT)$$
$$state : STATE \times UOID \rightarrow OSTATE$$
$$states : UOID \rightarrow \mathbb{P}(OSTATE)$$

$$STATE = \{(ds, cs, es) \mid \text{dom}(ds) = \text{dom}(cs) = \text{dom}(es)\}$$

$$oids(ds, cs, es) = oids(ds) = \text{dom}(ds)$$

$$\forall oid \in oids(us) : state((ds, cs, es), oid) = (ds(oid), cs(oid), es(oid))$$

$$states(oid) = \{state(us, oid) \mid us \in STATE \wedge oid \in oids(us)\}$$

The state of an object consists of its actual attribute values, events, and the threads belonging to an object. *states* defines the potential states of an object.

Derived:

$$oids(ds, cs, es) = \text{dom}(ds) = \text{dom}(cs) = \text{dom}(es)$$

4.6.2 Grouped Object States

The functions *state* and *states*, introduced in Definition 4.6.2, can be generalized to define the actual and potential set of states for groups of objects. These generalizations use a mapping from object identifiers to their respective contents and are thus structurally equivalent to *STATE*. The structural equivalence of *STATE* and $states(os)$ raises the possibility of using a composition on object states in Lemma 4.6.1 that can also be used to compose state machines in the following section. In particular, $f \oplus g$ is well defined, as $state(us, os_i)$ is equal on the common objects $os_1 \cup os_2$. This also allows us to regard the possible set of object states in *states* as a cross product, where the common object identifiers need to coincide in their state.

Definition 4.6.3 (State Space of Sets of Objects)

ObjectStates2

$state : STATE \times \mathbb{P}(UOID) \rightarrow (UOID \rightharpoonup OSTATE)$
$states : \mathbb{P}(UOID) \rightarrow \mathbb{P}(UOID \rightharpoonup OSTATE)$

$\forall os \subseteq UOID, us \in STATE, oid \in UOID :$

$state(us, os)(oid) = state(us, oid)$

$\forall os \subseteq UOID :$

$states(os) = \{state(us, os) \mid us \in STATE \wedge os \subseteq oids(us)\}$

Function *state* and *states* can be generalized to define the actual and potential set of states for groups of objects.

Derived:

$\forall os \subseteq UOID, us \in STATE : \mathrm{dom}(state(us, os)) = os \cap \mathrm{dom}(us)$
$\forall os \subseteq UOID, f \in states(os) : \mathrm{dom}(f) = os \cap \mathrm{dom}(us)$

Lemma 4.6.1 (State Space Composition)

ObjectStates

$\forall os_1, os_2 \subseteq UOID, us \in STATE :$

$state(us, os_1 \cup os_2) = state(us, os_1) \oplus state(us, os_2)$

$\forall os_1, os_2 \subseteq UOID, os_1 \cap os_2 = \emptyset \Rightarrow$

$states(os_1 \cup os_2) = \{f_1 \oplus f_2 \mid f_i \in states(os_i), i = 1, 2\}$

Function *state* and *states* are compositional with respect to the state of objects.

Derived:

$\forall os, os_1, os_2 \subseteq UOID : os = os_1 \cap os_2 \Rightarrow$

$states(os_1 \cup os_2)$

$= \{f_1 \oplus (f_2 |_{os_2 \setminus os_1}) \mid f_i \in states(os_i)\}$

$= \{(f_1 |_{os_1 \setminus os_2}) \oplus f_2 \mid f_i \in states(os_i)\}$

$= \{(f_1 \oplus f_2) \mid f_i \in states(os_i) \wedge f_1 |_{os} = f_2 |_{os}\}$

Definition 4.6.2 identifies *states*(o) and *states*($\{o\}$) as equivalent, as the latter is a function with a singleton argument only.

4.7 EVENT-BASED OBJECT BEHAVIOR

Based on the notions of state for each object and the corresponding incoming and outgoing events, the behavior of an object is specified in the form of a state transition system. For this purpose the theory of state transition systems (STSs) defined in Appendix A.1 in this chapter is used.

An STS-based representation of basic actions is required. For that purpose an ordinary programming language such as Java is used. The special actions of UML (see [8, Chap. 11]) were disregarded because of the better expressiveness of Java.

4.7.1 Control Flow State Transition Systems

As objects react to incoming events, an STS describing object behavior is basically event based and does not necessarily describe timing aspects. To trigger the next execution step for thread *th* within an object, a pseudoevent $\dagger(th)$ is used as given in Definition 4.7.1. With this trigger as explicit input of an STS, the scheduling can be defined in a separate entity.

Definition 4.7.1 (Stepper for an STS)

STSStepper

$\dagger : UTHREAD \to STEP$

$injective(\dagger)$

$\dagger(th)$ is used as a trigger for the next execution step in thread *th*.

Transitions within the control flow STS (CFSTS) are regarded as atomic actions. A CFSTS is defined such that an object has no direct access to an attribute of any other object but may call methods and send events as desired. The state of a CFSTS is defined by the object's own attributes and the currently active frame. Variation Point 4.7.1 introduces CFSTS and uses STS as introduced in Definition A.1.1.

Note that there are alternative ways to describe the result of method execution: for example, by using actions as defined by the Object Management Group [8, Chap. 11]. An action language may encompass an ordinary programming language but allow additional actions that deal with manipulation of associations, timing and scheduling, and so on.

Indeed, to define such high-level "model-aware" actions is useful, as otherwise such concepts need to be emulated through lower-level concepts if at all possible. This would mean, for example, that associations are encoded as attributes, with scheduling managed through an API of an ordinary object serving as scheduler.[3]

[3] In Java this would be a Thread object.

Variation Point 4.7.1 (Control Flow STS for Methods)

[CFSTS]

$cfsts : UMETH \times UOID \times UTHREAD \rightharpoonup STS(S, I, O)$

$\forall m \in UMETH, oid \in UOID, th \in UTHREAD :$
$classOf(oid)\ sub\ classOf(m) \wedge cfsts(m, oid, th) = (S, I, O, \delta, s0) \Rightarrow$

$S = \{(o, fr) \in objects(oid) \times framesOf(m) \mid$
$fr = (oid, *, *, *, *)\} \wedge$

$s0 = \{(o, fr) \in S \mid \exists start \in StartPC : fr = (*, *, *, start, *)\} \wedge$

$I = \{MsgEvent\ call \mid call \in callsOf(oid, m, *, th)\} \cup STEP \wedge$

$O = eventsOut(oid)$

cfsts assigns a possibly underspecified CFSTS to each method. This describes the implemented behavior of that method in the form of a state machine.

Variation Point 4.7.1 is not constraining CFSTS. Certainly, many states of the CFSTS will never be reached, many outputs that are included in O will not be made. However, it is relatively accurate on the input, as it describes all information about the context that is known.

Note that one CFSTS for each method implementation is attached to each object individually. This gives some freedom, allowing different behaviors for objects of the same class. In practice, however, objects of one class are assigned the same CFSTS. Furthermore, objects of subclasses whose methods are not overridden are assigned the same CFSTS as their superclass objects. This resembles method inheritance on the level of behavior through CFSTS.

4.7.2 Event-Based State Transition Systems

Objects react to incoming events and can therefore be described by an STS. This behavior does not describe timing aspects. An event-based STS (ESTS) handles execution within a single object. Definition 4.7.2 specifies the general structure and

Definition 4.7.2 (Event-Based STS for Objects)

EventSTS

$ests : UOID \to STS(S, I, O)$

$\forall oid \in UOID\ :$

$ests(oid) \in STS(states(oid), eventsIn(oid) \cup STEP, eventsOut(oid))$

ests assigns a possibly underspecified STS to each *oid*, thus making it possible to describe externally visible behavior for an object as a state machine.

signature of ESTS. An ESTS operates on the full object state and is triggered either by real events or by steps indicated by a dagger. Those steps denote only scheduling of steps, not timing.

The nondeterministic transition function δ of an ESTS supports underspecification and thus multiple possible behaviors within the STS. This underspecification may be totally or partially resolved during design time by the developer or during runtime by the system itself, choosing transitions according to some circumstances, sensor input, and so on.

Compared to the CFSTS defined previously, this notion of ESTS is rather general. It embodies all data, control, and event states on a very general level and thus can describe interference of parallel executions as well as handling of incoming events in the buffer. In contrast to an CFSTS, an ESTS embodies the complete object state including the control state and event buffer. A detailed description of the relationship between an CFSTS and an ESTS has been given by Broy et al. [1], who also provided a variation point for ESTS that is composed of several CFSTSs.

4.8 TIMED OBJECT BEHAVIOR

In this section we present a time-aware version of STS, *timed STS* (TSTS), defined in Appendix A.2. TSTS allows a description of individual object behavior and the composition thereof.

A discrete global time is assumed available. Each step of transition of the TSTS corresponds to progress of one time unit. A system executes in steps, each step consuming a fixed amount of time. TSTS are transition systems that deal with this paradigm. Roughly speaking, in each step a finite set of input events is provided to a TSTS, and a finite set of output events is produced by the TSTS.

As a further mechanism, communication channels allow a description of the interaction (communication flow) between parts of the objects and thus of the behavior of objects on a very fine-grained level. As a general result, a complete description of how systems are decomposed into objects is provided, as well as what states objects may have and how objects interact.

4.8.1 Object Behavior in the System Model

In the system model, the object and component instances cooperate by asynchronous message passing. Method invocation is already modeled by the exchange of two events, the method invocation event and the method return event.

Communication between objects is dealt with by channels. A communication channel is a unidirectional communication connection between two objects. The system model defines a universe *UCN* of channels and leaves open how many channels are used between objects.

Each channel has a name (e.g., $c \in UCN$), and the type of events that may flow through c is given by $csort(c)$. Each object has a number of incoming and outgoing channels, and each event is associated with the channel through which it flows (see Definition 4.8.1).

Definition 4.8.1 (Channel Signatures of Objects)

Channels

UCN
$sender, receiver : UCN \rightarrow UOID$
$channel : UEVENT \rightarrow UCN$
$inC, outC : UOID \rightarrow \mathbb{P}(UCN)$
$csort : UCN \rightarrow \mathbb{P}(UEVENT)$

$\forall m \in UEVENT, oid \in UOID :$

$$sender(m) = oid \Rightarrow sender(channel(m)) = oid$$

$$receiver(m) = oid \Rightarrow receiver(channel(m)) = oid$$

$\forall c \in UCN \ :$

$$inC(oid) = \{c \mid receiver(c) = oid\}$$

$$outC(oid) = \{c \mid sender(c) = oid\}$$

$$csort(c) = \{m \in UEVENT \mid channel(m) = c\}$$

UCN denotes the universe of channel names.
sender and *receiver* assign a sending and a receiving object to each channel.
channel assigns a channel to each event.
inC and *outC* denote the channel signature of each object.
The type of each channel *csort*(c) describes the possible events flowing over that channel.

As an important consequence of the definitions above, each channel is in the output signature of only one object, since events are associated with a channel not only but also with its originating object. This ensures the applicability of composition techniques for TSTS, which work only if the output channels of composed objects are disjoint.

Based on channels and their type, the behavior of a single object is defined in Definition 4.8.2. This definition is based on the assumption of a time granularity fine

Definition 4.8.2 (Behavior of Individual Object)

ObjBehavior

$beh : UOID \rightarrow \mathcal{B}^{csort}(I, O)$

$\forall oid \in UOID :$

$$beh(oid) \in \mathcal{B}^{csort}(inC(oid), outC(oid))$$

beh(*oid*) denotes the behavior of a single object.

enough to ensure the independence of the output in one step from the input received in that step. In this way, strong causality is preserved between input and output. Moreover, the composition of state machines is simplified since feedback within one time unit is ruled out, and thus causal inconsistencies are avoided. The actual (real-) time occurrence of events can be abstracted away; thus, only the untimed behavior of objects needs be considered.

Definition 4.8.3 provides a flexible concept of components, including, for example, classical sequential systems (in this case, there is only one input and one output channel). Input and output flow of events can be further restricted, allowing the reception or the dispatch of at most one event in each step. At the other extreme, highly concurrent systems with a large number of input and output events in one state transition step can also be described.

4.8.2 State-Based Object Behavior

The behavior of an object *oid* is defined precisely as *beh*(*oid*). The relationship of this behavior to a state-based view is not yet defined. For this purpose, a timed state transition system to each object is attached as shown in Definition 4.8.4. According to this definition, each object $oid \in UOID$ can be described by a nondeterministic TSTS as introduced in Appendix A.2.

Definition 4.8.3 (Behavior of Object Compositions)

CompBehavior

$beh : \mathbb{P}(UOID) \rightarrow \mathcal{B}^{csort}(I, O)$

$inC, outC : \mathbb{P}(UOID) \rightarrow \mathbb{P}(UCN)$

$\forall os \subset UOID :$

$I = inC(os) = \{c \mid receiver(c) \in os \wedge sender(c) \notin os\}$

$O = outC(os) = \{c \mid sender(c) \in os \wedge receiver(c) \notin os\}$

$beh(os) = \oplus_{oid \in os} beh(oid)$

---

beh(*os*) denotes the behavior of a group of objects where internal communication is not visible anymore.
inC describes the incoming channels for a group of objects; *outC* describes the outgoing channels.

The axiom $\mathbb{S}(tsts(oid)) = beh(oid)$ for any *oid* states that the behavior of each object is defined by an appropriate TSTS. It can be shown that the composition of TSTS and of I/O-behaviors is compatible. This means that it can be switched between a state-based and a purely I/O-based view of object behavior, and moreover,

Definition 4.8.4 (Behavior as TimedSTS)

TimedSTS

$tsts : UOID \rightarrow TSTS^{csort}(S_1, I_1, O_1)$
$tsts : \mathbb{P}(UOID) \rightarrow TSTS^{csort}(S, I, O)$

$\forall oid \in UOID$:

$tsts(oid) \in TSTS^{csort}(states(oid), inC(oid), outC(oid))$

$\mathbb{S}(tsts(oid)) = beh(oid)$

$\forall os \subset UOID$:

$tsts(os) = \bigoplus_{oid \in os} tsts(oid)$

tsts(*oid*) denotes the TSTS-based description of behavior of a single object. The definition is then generalized to a set of objects.

the behavior of objects or groups (components) can be specified individually and afterward composed meaningfully.

Note that each object *oid* has exactly one single TSTS *tsts*(*oid*). However, as *tsts*(*oid*) is a nondeterministic state machine, it allows various forms of underspecification. Therefore, there is no need to add a further concept of underspecification by, for example, assigning a set of possible TSTS to each object. Any UML model, however, may have an impact on the elements of a TSTS. For instance, the sets of reachable states can be constrained, the initial states restricted to be a singleton, or the nondeterminism reduced by enforcing a behavior that is deterministic in reaction and time.

With this last part of the system model, a TSTS for the entire system is available that includes all snapshots and all system states and is thus capable of describing any behavioral and structural restrictions by *tsts*(*UOID*). The overall system *tsts*(*UOID*) does not have any external channels; it incorporates all "objects." This includes objects that have direct connections to interfaces to other systems, mechanical devices, or users and thus can act as surrogates for the context of the system. In other words, the overall system makes a closed-world assumption. Rumpe [9] discusses how to deal with a closed-world assumption to describe open, reactive systems, and what advantages are implied by this assumption. A general mapping from event-based to TSTS is defined by Broy et al. [1].

4.9 THE SYSTEM MODEL DEFINITION

Finally, Definition 4.9.1 introduces the universe of system models.

Definition 4.9.1 (The System Model as a Universe)

SYSMOD

SYSMOD

$sm \in SYSMOD \Rightarrow$

$sm =$

$(UTYPE, UVAL, CAR,$

$UVAR, vtype, vsort,$

$UCLASS, UOID, attr, oids, classof,$

$sub, \&,$

$UASSOC, classes, extraVals, relOf,$

$UOPN, UOMNAME, nameOf, classof, parTypes, params, resType,$

$UMETH, UPC, nameof, definedIn, parNames,$

$localNames, resType, pcOf, impl,$

$UTHREAD,$

$UVENT, eventIn, eventsOut,$

$UMESSAGE, MsgEvent, USIGNAL,$

$ests,$

$UCN,$

$tsts)$

such that all constraints defined above are fulfilled.

APPENDIX A.1: STATE TRANSITION SYSTEMS

As objects react on incoming events, state transition systems are an appropriate way of describing object behavior. Several forms of state transition systems and their compositions are used in theory. Therefore, we introduce the basics of STS as a general technique.

A.1.1. STS Definition

The theory used here is based on the theory of automata but was partly enhanced by Rumpe [9] to describe a form of automata, called I/O^*-automata, where transitions are triggered by one incoming event and the effect of this event: a sequence of possible outputs is the output of the same transition. In contrast to I/O-automata [6], this form allows us to abstract away from many internal states of the automaton, which are necessary if each output is triggered by an individual transition. The application of I/O^*-automata to our description of objects is given in Definition A.1.1.

Definition A.1.1 (I/O*-STS)

STS

$$STS(S,I,O) = \{(S,I,O,\delta,s0) \mid s0 \subseteq S \wedge s0 \neq \emptyset \wedge \delta \in S \times I \rightarrow \mathbb{P}(S \times O^*) \wedge \forall s \in S, i \in I : \delta(s,i) \neq \emptyset\}$$

Notation:

$\delta : s \xrightarrow{i/o} t$ is shorthand for $(o,t) \in \delta(s,i)$

$STS(S,I,O)$ is the set of all, possibly underspecified STSs with given state, input, and output sets. An STS has a complete transition relation as $\delta(s,i) \neq \emptyset$ for all s, i.

As can be seen from the definition, the transition function is nondeterministic. This allows us to model underspecification and thus multiple behaviors in the STS. As discussed by Rumpe [9], this underspecification may be resolved during design time by the developer or during runtime by the system itself taking the choice according to some random circumstances, sensor input, or other factor.

The semantics of such an STS is defined by Rumpe [9] using stream processing functions in the form developed by Broy et al. [2]. These stream processing functions allow composition, behavioral refinement, and other operations of interest. However, STS themselves are not fully compositional regarding the compositionality of the state space. But there are quite a number of techniques to combine smaller STSs into a larger STS.

APPENDIX A.2: TIMED STATE TRANSITION SYSTEMS

Timed state transition systems do not use events directly to make their steps, but time progress. A timed state machine equidistantly performs its steps as time progresses and consumes all events arriving at that time. As a big advantage, we cannot only integrate time into the specification technique, but also have composition operators at hand that are compatible with the composition of streams.

A.2.1. Definition of Timed State Transition Systems

A timed state transition system (TSTS) is an STS in which each transition resembles a time step. Such a time step can handle several input events and produce several outputs.

TSTSs are defined in Definition A.2.1. Here I and O play the roles of channels, which are typed by the channel typing function $c : (I \cup O) \to \mathbb{P}(M)$.

Definition A.2.1 (Timed STS)

*TSTS*1

$$TSTS^c(S, I, O) = \{(S, \mathcal{T}^c(I), \mathcal{T}^c(O), \delta, s0) \in STS(S, \mathcal{T}^c(I), \mathcal{T}^c(O)) \mid$$
$$\forall \delta : s \xrightarrow{i/o} t \Rightarrow \#o = 1 \wedge$$
$$\forall \delta : s \xrightarrow{i/o} t, i' : \exists t' : \delta : s \xrightarrow{i'/o} t'$$
$$\}$$

$TSTS^c(S, I, O)$ is the set of all, possibly underspecified STSs that resemble timed object behavior. A TSTS has a complete transition relation.

The restriction $\#o = 1$ in TSTS is not a real one, as by definition $o \in (\mathcal{T}(O))^*$, which can be regarded as equivalent to $o \in \mathcal{T}(O)$. Instead, we could also use a flattening operator on o. The simplified representation of the timed transition function δ, which will now be used, is thus

$$\delta : (S \times \mathcal{T}^c(I)) \to \mathbb{P}(S \times \mathcal{T}^c(O))$$

where $\mathcal{T}^c(I)$ denotes the set of channel time slices for the channels in I.

The second restriction models the fact that the state transition function describes the behavior of a Moore machine [5]. The output o therefore depends only on the start state s, not on the input x, as for all other inputs x' the same output y is happening, too.

One way to interpret this rule is that the granularity of time is fine enough to trace state changes in such a detailed way that the reaction to an input is always delayed by at least one time unit (one state transition step). As an immediate consequence, feedback cycles include a time step and thus preserve causality. Another consequence is that the output of a transition is independent of the input of this transition and intermediate storage for either the input before being processed or the resulting output in the state space is therefore inevitable.

REFERENCES

1. M. Broy, M. V. Cengarle, H. Grönniger, and B. Rumpe. *Modular Description of a Comprehensive Semantics Model for the UML (Version 2.0)*. Technical Report 2008-06. Carl-Friedrich-Gauß-Fakultät, Technische Universität Braunschweig, Braunschweig, Germany, 2008.
2. M. Broy, F. Dederich, C. Dendorfer, M. Fuchs, T. Gritzner, and R. Weber. *The Design of Distributed Systems: An Introduction to FOCUS*. Technical Report, TUM-I9202, SFB-Bericht 342/2-2/92 A, 1993.

3. M. Fontoura, W. Pree, and B. Rumpe. *The UML/F Profile for Framework Architecture*. Addison-Wesley, Reading, MA, 2001.
4. E. Gamma, R. Helm, R. Johnson, and J. Vlissides. *Design Patterns: Elements of Reusable Object-Oriented Software*. Addison-Wesley, Reading, MA, 1995.
5. R. H. Katz. *Contemporary Logic Design*. Benjamin-Cummings, Redwood City, CA, 1993.
6. N. A. Lynch and M. R. Tuttle. An introduction to input/output automata. *CWI Quarterly*, 2:219–246, 1989.
7. B. Meyer. *Object-Oriented Software Construction*, 2nd ed. Prentice Hall, Upper Saddle River, NJ, 1997.
8. OMG. Unified modeling language: superstructure version 2.1.2. http://www.omg.org/docs/formal/07-11-02.pdf.
9. B. Rumpe. *Formale Methodik des Entwurfs verteilter objektorientierter Systeme*. Herbert Utz Verlag Wissenschaft, 1996. Ph.D. dissertation, Technische Universität München, Munich, Germany.

CHAPTER 5

FORMAL DESCRIPTIVE SEMANTICS OF UML AND ITS APPLICATIONS

HONG ZHU
Department of Computing and Electronics, School of Technology, Oxford Brookes University, Oxford, UK

LIJUN SHAN
Department of Computer Science, National University of Defense Technology, Changsha, China

IAN BAYLEY and RICHARD AMPHLETT
Department of Computing and Electronics, School of Technology, Oxford Brookes University, Oxford, UK

5.1 INTRODUCTION

What is the meaning of a UML diagram? Consider the simple class model of a library system, shown in Figure 5.1. One may interpret its meaning as follows: *The system has two classes, called* Member *and* Book. *There is an association between them, which is called* Borrows. *The multiplicity upper bound of the* Borrows *association at the* Book end *is 10, and the multiplicity upper bound of Borrows at the* Member end *is 1.* An alternative interpretation of the model is: *There are two types of objects in the system, called Member and Book. Members can borrow books. Each member can only borrow up to 10 books at any time, and each book can be borrowed by at most one member at any time.*

In general, "*a model is a set of statements about some system under study,*" to quote Seidewitz [22]. However, the statements themselves differ according to which formalization of UML is being used, and comparing the two interpretations above, we can identify two types.

- *Descriptive statements* describe a system based on a set of basic concepts, such as class, association, and multiplicity upper bound. Such statements can be used

UML 2 Semantics and Applications. Edited by Kevin Lano

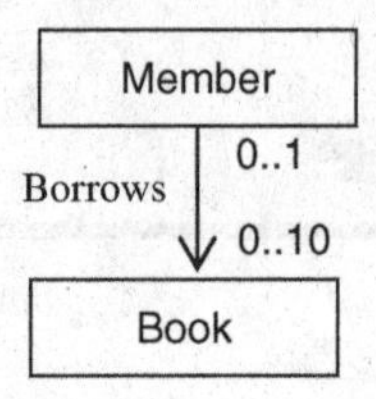

FIGURE 5.1 Library system.

to determine which system in a given subject domain is an instance of a model. For example, consider the statement above that "the system contains two classes, Member and Book." This is a description of the system based on the concept of class without further information about what a class is, but by making an assertion about its construction.

- *Functional statements* define how a system functions at runtime. An example is the statement above that "there are two types of objects in the system, called Member and Book." This makes an assertion about the system's runtime behavior (i.e., the existence of two types of runtime entities).

The differences between these two types of statements become clearer when they are formalized in predicate logic. The statement "the system contains two classes, Member and Book" can be formalized as follows:

$$Class(Member) \wedge Class(Book)$$

where $Class(x)$ is a predicate that asserts that an element x is a class. The formal representation of the statement "there are two types of objects in the system, called Member and Book" in predicate logic would be

$$\exists x \cdot Member(x) \wedge \exists y \cdot Book(y)$$

where the predicates $Member(x)$ and $Book(x)$ mean that element x is of type *Member* and *Book*, respectively. Obviously, the difference between these two statements lies in the domain of the predicates.

These two types of statements reflect two aspects of the semantics of UML: The *functional semantics* defines how an instance of a model behaves, while the *descriptive semantics* describes what an instance of a model "looks like" (i.e., it determines which system in a given subject domain is an instance of a model).

As far as we know, all existing work on the formalization of UML semantics has focused on using functional statements in various formalisms to define the functions of modeled systems. As discussed briefly in Section 5.5, such works are interesting and important for the definition of UML's semantics, especially since they deepen significantly our understanding of object-oriented concepts. However, a number of issues connected with the semantics of UML are neglected, and they are best addressed by descriptive semantics.

```
class Member
{...}
class Staff extends Member
{...}
class Student extends Member
{...}
```

(a) Program P1

```
class Member
{...}
class Staff extends Member
{...}
class Student extends Member
{...}
class MScStudent extends Student
{...}
```

(b) Program P2

```
class Member {
  public enum MemberType {
    Staff, Student }
  public MemberType
    TypeOfMember;
  ...
}
```

(c) Program P3

FIGURE 5.2 Java-like programs.

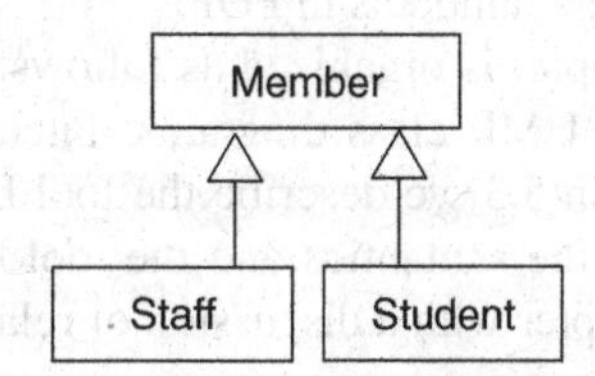

FIGURE 5.3 Classification of members.

For example, consider the Java-like programs depicted in Figure 5.2. Which can be regarded as an instance of the model in Figure 5.3? Unfortunately, the documentation of UML does not answer this question.

To answer questions like this, we proposed [23] an approach to specifying the semantics of UML formally in first-order predicate logic (FOPL) and reported a preliminary version of an automated software tool called LAMBDES for the logic analysis of UML models. The theory and the tool focus on the descriptive semantics of UML and address the following open problems in the formalization of UML semantics.

First, UML models are not limited to modeling computer software systems, and each UML model can be interpreted in many different subject domains. For example, the class diagram of Figure 5.1 can be regarded as a model of libraries in both the physical world and in a computer information system. So the definition of the semantics of UML must be flexible enough to be interpreted in all subject domains.

Second, UML is intended to provide a holistic modeling approach to object-oriented software development. It is designed for use at all stages of software development and to support all software development and maintenance activities. This imposes further flexibility requirements on a formal definition of its semantics. For example, if the model in Figure 5.3 is used as a requirements specification, all three programs in Figure 5.2 should be considered as a correct implementation of the model. If the same model is regarded as a design of a software system, program P3 would be regarded as not following the design faithfully, so it would be an incorrect implementation. But programs P1 and P2 should both be regarded as correct instances of the model. If the diagram is the result of reverse engineering through source code analysis, it is a correct model only for program P1. So a good definition of UML's semantics should be flexible enough to cover all these situations and many more.

Finally, UML is designed to be extensible through the use of profile definitions and new stereotypes in the metamodel. The definition of UML semantics must also cover these extension mechanisms.

In this chapter we present the theory behind and a method for the formal definition of UML's descriptive semantics using FOPL to demonstrate how the difficulties above are overcome in our approach. We report the current state in the development of the tool LAMBDES, which translates graphic models into descriptive semantics in FOPL and enables the formal analysis of models in FOPL by integration with a theorem prover. We also demonstrate how the semantics and the tool together support formal analysis of both models and metamodels in FOPL.

The remainder of this chapter is organized as follows. In Section 5.2 we present the descriptive semantics of UML class diagrams, interaction diagrams, and state machine diagrams. In Section 5.3 we describe the tool LAMBDES, in Section 5.4 demonstrate applications of the semantics and the tool by some examples, and in Section 5.5 conclude the chapter with a discussion of related and future work.

5.2 DEFINITION OF DESCRIPTIVE SEMANTICS IN FOPL

In this section we first outline our approach to a formal definition of UML's semantics and then present mappings from models and metamodels to their descriptive semantics. Then we discuss how to deal with the semantics of models in different development contexts and extension mechanisms.

5.2.1 The Framework

As in all existing approaches to the formalization of UML in FOPL, we define the descriptive semantics of UML through a mapping from UML models to a set of FOPL statements which are constructed from a set of predicate and constant symbols via logic connectives and quantifiers. However, in our approach, these symbols represent the basic concepts of the modeling language rather than the concepts in the system to be modeled. For example, a predicate *Class*(x) is defined to represent the concept *class* in UML. Moreover, our approach differs from existing work in the way that the atomic predicate symbols are derived. Instead of determining the signature of the FOPL system manually, we derive the atomic predicate and constant symbols from the metamodels because the concepts of OO modeling are specified in UML metamodels. The collection of rules that are used to derive signatures from a metamodel is called *signature mapping*.

A metamodel defines not only a collection of concepts but also their interrelationships. The interrelationships between the concepts are properties that all models must satisfy and thus are the axioms of models. We also derive these axioms from a metamodel systematically with a set of rules called *axiom rules*, and we represent them in the FOPL using atomic predicates and constants in the signature derived. These

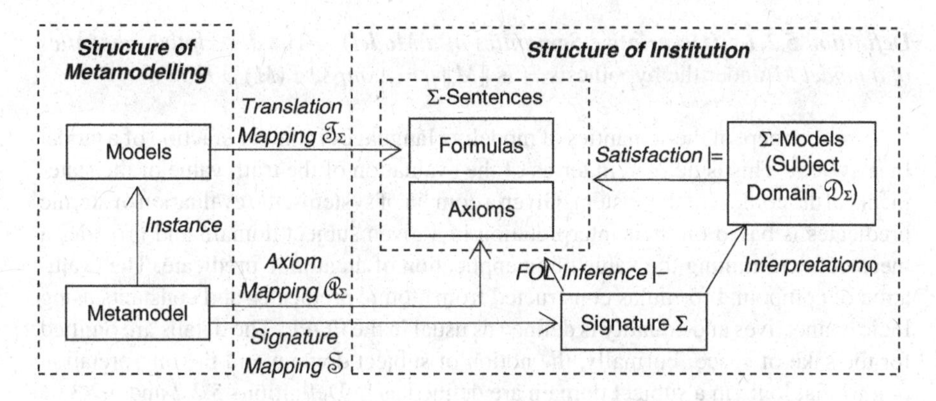

FIGURE 5.4 Overview of the approach to formalizing UML semantics.

axioms are called *axioms of descriptive semantics* to distinguish them from *axioms of functional semantics*, which define the functional semantics using the runtime properties of the basic concepts. A typical axiom of descriptive semantics is

$$\forall x \cdot (Class(x) \rightarrow Classifier(x))$$

which means that if x is a class, it is also a classifier. In contrast, here is an example of an axiom of functional semantics:

$$\forall A, B \cdot (Class(A) \wedge Class(B) \wedge Inherits(A, B) \rightarrow \forall x \cdot (A(x) \rightarrow B(x)))$$

which means that if class A inherits class B, every instance of A is also an instance of B. A full treatment of the functional semantics is beyond the scope of this chapter and will be reported elsewhere.

The descriptive semantics of a UML model is a set of formulas in FOPL that can be derived systematically by applying a set of rules called *translation rules*. In addition, we specify the context in which the model is used by a set of formulas in formal logic using the same signature. These formulas can also be derived from the model by a set of rules, so they are mappings from the model to the formulas and are called *hypothesis mappings*. In different contexts, different rules are applied. Figure 5.4 illustrates the overall structure of our approach to the definition of UML semantics.

5.2.1.1 Notation: In the sequel we use Σ and Axm_D to denote the signature and axioms of the descriptive semantics, derived from a given metamodel that a model M is considered as its instance. We also use $\mathcal{T}(M)$ to denote the translation mapping from models to Σ-sentences and $\mathcal{H}(M)$ to denote a hypothesis mapping from models to Σ-sentences that represent the context in which model M is to be used.

Given a formal definition of UML's semantics in the framework described above, the semantics of a model is defined as in Definition 5.2.1.

Definition 5.2.1 (Descriptive Semantics of a Model) The *descriptive semantics of a model M* under the hypothesis $\mathcal{H}$ is $[\![M]\!]_{\mathcal{H}} = Axm_D \cup \mathcal{T}(M) \cup \mathcal{H}(M)$.

A key concept of the semantics of modeling languages is the satisfaction of a model by a system. This is defined in terms of the evaluation of the truth value of the statements in the context of the system. Given a domain of systems, the evaluation of atomic predicates is based on their interpretation in a given subject domain and provides a means of determining the value of an application of an atomic predicate. The evaluation of compound formulas constructed from atomic predicates and constants using logic connectives and equality is defined as usual in the FOPL. The details are omitted for the sake of space. Formally, the notion of subject domain and the interpretation of a formal logic in a subject domain are defined as in Definitions 5.2.2 and 5.2.3.

Definition 5.2.2 (Subject Domain) A *subject domain Dom* is a triple $\langle D, \Sigma, Eva \rangle$, where D is a collection of systems; Σ is a signature; *Eva* is an evaluation rule (i.e., a mapping from systems s in D and Σ-formulas to the truth value *True* or *False*). Given Σ-formula f and system s in D, $Eva(f, s)$ is called *the interpretation of the formula f in s*. We write $s \models_{Eva} f$ if $Eva(f, s) = true$.

When there is no risk of confusion, we omit the subscript *Eva* in $\models_{Eva}$. For a set F of formulas we write $s \models F$ to denote that for all f in F, $s \models f$.

Definition 5.2.3 (Satisfaction of a Model) Let Σ be a given signature and *Dom* a subject domain of Σ. A system s in D *satisfies a model M* under hypothesis $\mathcal{H}$ according to a semantic definition $[\![M]\!]_{\mathcal{H}}$ if $s \models [\![M]\!]_{\mathcal{H}}$ (i.e., for all formulas f in $[\![M]\!]_{\mathcal{H}}$, $s \models f$). We also say that s is an *instance of model M*, and write $s \models M$.

5.2.2 Semantics Mappings

We now elaborate the approach by defining the semantics mappings. We demonstrate that the descriptive semantics of different types of diagrams can be defined using the same set of semantics mappings.

5.2.2.1 Signature Mapping Given a metamodel, the signature of a formal logic system can be derived by applying the following rules:

S1. For each metaclass C in the metamodel, a unary atomic predicate symbol $C(x)$ is defined to represent the fact that the model element x is an instance of metaclass C.

S2. For each meta-attribute A of metaclass X with Y as its type, and each meta-association from metaclass X to metaclass Y with A as the association end name on Y, a binary predicate $A(x, y)$ is defined to represent the relation between model elements of type X and the elements of type Y.

S3. For each enumeration value V in the metamodel, a constant symbol V is defined.

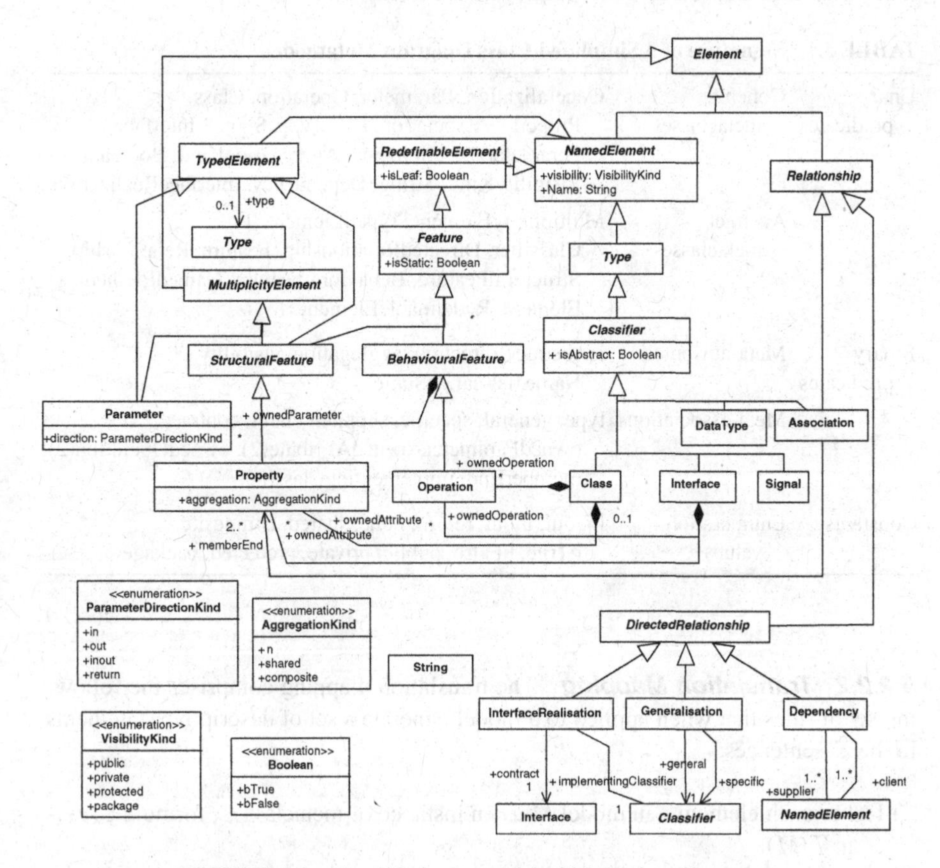

FIGURE 5.5 Simplified metamodel of UML class diagrams.

For example, consider the simplified metamodel of UML class diagrams shown in Figure 5.5. The unary predicate *Class*(x) represents the metaclass *Class*. The binary predicate *specific*(x, y) represents that the association named *specific* connects metaclass x to metaclass y in Figure 5.5. Table 5.1 lists all the unary and binary predicates derived from the metamodel of class diagrams shown in Figure 5.5.

Constant symbols in the signature are also derived from the metamodel. For example, two enumeration values t and f (UML *bTrue* and *bFalse*) are defined in the enumeration metaclass *Boolean* in Figure 5.5, so two constant symbols t and f are derived.

The interpretation of the constant and predicate symbols must be defined in the context of a subject domain. Taking the set of C++ programs as an example, the predicate *Class*(*User*) is true if *User* is a class in the program. The statement *isAbstract*(*User*, t) is true when the class *User* in the program is declared to be abstract. It is worth noting that the formal definition of descriptive semantics is independent of the subject domain and its interpretation. So we leave the definition of the interpretation open so that a model can be interpreted in different subject domains.

TABLE 5.1 Signature of a Simplified Class Diagram Metamodel

Unary predicates	Concrete metaclasses	Generalization, Parameter, Operation, Class, Property, Association, DataType, Signal, Interface, ParameterDirectionKind, AggregationKind, Boolean, VisibilityKind, String, Dependency, InterfaceRealization
	Abstract metaclasses	MultiplicityElement, TypedElement, Type, Classifier, DirectedRelationship, Feature, Relationship, StructuralFeature, BehavioralFeature, NamedElement, Element, RedefinableElement
Binary predicates	Meta-attributes	isAbstract, direction, aggregation, visibility, Name, isLeaf, isStatic
	Meta-associations	type, general, specific, supplier, client, contract, ownedParameter, ownedAttribute(2), ownedOperation(2), memberEnd, implementingClassifier
Constants	Enumeration values	in, out, inout, return, none, shared, composite, bTrue, bFalse, public, private, protected, package

5.2.2.2 Translation Mapping

The translation mapping comprises the following set of rules that when applied to a model generate a set of descriptive statements in the Σ-sentences:

T1. For each element e in model M as an instance of metaclass C, formula $C(e)$ is in $\mathcal{T}(M)$.

T2. For each element e in model M as an instance of metaclass C, if $Attr$ is a meta-attribute of C and v is e's value on the meta-attribute $Attr$, formula $Attr(e, v)$ is in $\mathcal{T}(M)$.

T3. For each pair e_1 and e_2 of elements in model M, formula $R(e_1, e_2)$ is in $\mathcal{T}(M)$, if there is an instance of meta-association R from e_1 to e_2 in M.

For example, consider the class diagram in Figure 5.6. The following formulas are among the statements generated by applying the translation rules:

$$Class(User), Class(Bank), Class(BoxOffice), isAbstract(Clerk, f)$$

5.2.2.3 Axiom Mapping

The axiom mapping for deriving axioms can be defined by the following set of rules:

A1. If $\{C_1, C_2, \ldots, C_n\}$ is the set of concrete metaclasses in a metamodel, the formula $\forall x \cdot (C_1(x) \vee C_2(x) \vee \cdots \vee C_n(x))$ is an axiom.

A2. For each pair of different concrete metaclasses $C \neq C'$, the formula $\forall x \cdot (C(x) \rightarrow \neg C'(x))$ is an axiom.

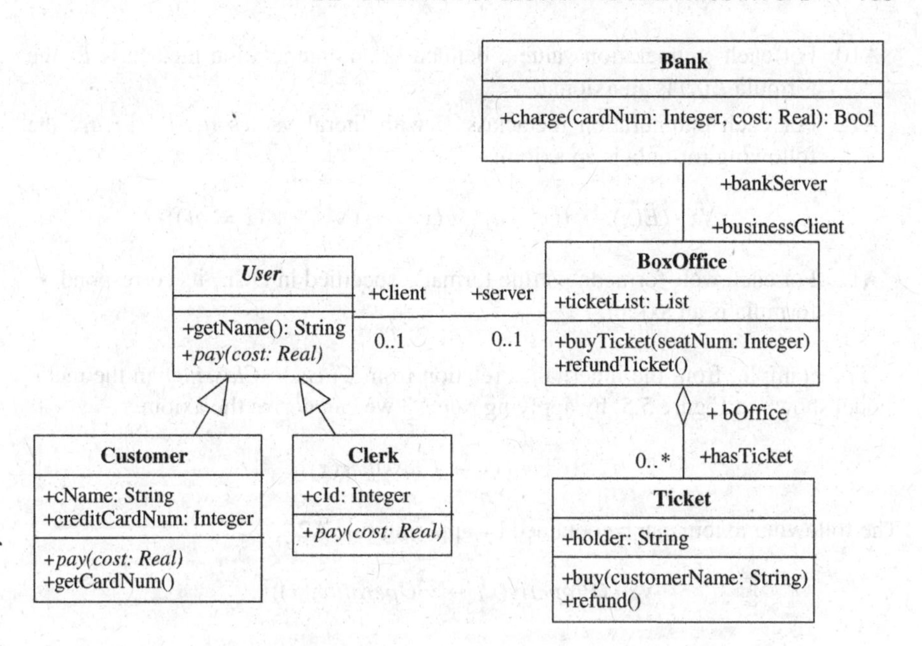

FIGURE 5.6 Ticket office system: class model.

A3. For each generalization relation from metaclass A to B, the formula $\forall x \cdot (A(x) \to B(x))$ is an axiom.

A4. If A is an abstract metaclass and $\{B_1, B_2, \ldots, B_k\}$ is the set of metaclasses specializing A, the following formula is an axiom:

$$\forall x \cdot (A(x) \to (B_1(x) \vee B_2(x) \vee \cdots \vee B_k(x)))$$

A5. For each association A from metaclass C_1 to C_2, the formula $\forall x, y \cdot (A(x,y) \wedge C_1(x) \to C_2(y))$ is an axiom.

A6. For each metaattribute *Attr* of type T in a metaclass C, the formula $\forall x, y \cdot (C(x) \wedge Attr(x,y) \to T(y))$ is an axiom.

A7. For each association A from metaclass C_1 to C_2, if "$e_1 \cdot \cdot e_2$" is its multiplicity value, the following formula is an axiom:

$$\forall x \cdot (C_1(x) \to (e_1 \leq ||\{y|A(x,y)\}|| \leq e_2))$$

A8. For each meta-attribute *Attr* of type *MT* in a metaclass C, if "$e_1 \cdot \cdot e_2$" is its multiplicity value, the following formula is an axiom:

$$\forall x \cdot (C(x) \to (e_1 \leq ||\{y|(Attr(x) = y)\}|| \leq e_2))$$

A9. For each pair of different literal values a and b of an enumeration metaclass, the formula $a \neq b$ is an axiom.

A10. For each enumeration value a defined in an enumeration metaclass E, the formula $E(a)$ is an axiom.

A11. For each enumeration metaclass E with literal values $a_1, a_2, \ldots, a_k$, the following formula is an axiom:

$$\forall x \cdot (E(x) \rightarrow ((x = a_1) \vee (x = a_2) \vee \cdots \vee (x = a_k)))$$

A12. For each well-formedness rule formally specified in OCL, its corresponding formula is an axiom.

For example, from the inheritance relation from *Class* to *Classifier* in the metamodel shown in Figure 5.5, by applying rule A3 we can derive the axiom

$$\forall x \cdot (Class(x) \rightarrow Classifier(x))$$

The following axiom can be obtained by applying rule A2:

$$\forall x \cdot (Property(x) \rightarrow \neg Operation(x))$$

5.2.3 Context of Modeling

As discussed in Section 5.1, a UML model can be understood differently in different contexts of software development. We argue that this variety of meanings can be represented by additional formulas, known as the *hypothesis on the model*. (Meanwhile, the core meaning of a model is still captured in the formulas generated by the translation mapping plus the axioms that all models must satisfy.) Hypothesis mappings can be designed and applied to models on a case-by-case basis to generate the formulas that represent the contexts in which a model is used.

For example, when a model is obtained by reverse engineering all the classes in the source code, we understand that the model is complete as a description of classes in the system. We also assume that each class in the model represents a different class in the source code. Such assumptions can be represented by the following formulas:

$$\forall c \cdot (Class(c) \rightarrow c \in \{c_1, c_2, \ldots, c_k\})$$
$$\forall c, c' \cdot (Class(c) \wedge Class(c') \wedge (Name(c) \neq Name(c')) \rightarrow (c \neq c'))$$

where $\{c_1, c_2, \ldots, c_k\}$ is the set of classes in the model M. Such formulas can be generated by transformation rules called *hypothesis rules*. Some examples of hypothesis rules are as follows:

H1. *Distinguishability*. If $e_1, e_2, \ldots, e_k$ is the set of instances of a concrete metaclass C in the model, to assume that these elements in the model are all different, the following set of formulas are generated as hypotheses:

$$\{e_i \neq e_j | i \neq j \in \{1, 2, \ldots, k\}\}$$

H2. *Completeness of elements.* If $e_1, e_2, \ldots, e_k$ is the set of instances of a concrete metaclass C in the model, to assume that this type of element in the model is complete, the following formula is generated as a hypothesis:

$$\forall x \cdot (C(x) \rightarrow ((x = e_1) \vee (x = e_2) \vee \cdots \vee (x = e_k)))$$

H3. *Completeness of relations.* If $\{(e_1, e_1'), \ldots, (e_n, e_n')\}$ is the set of instances of a relation R contained in the model, to assume the completeness of relation R in the model, the following formula is generated as a hypothesis:

$$\forall x, y \cdot (R(x, y) \rightarrow (((x = e_1) \wedge (y = e_1')) \vee \cdots \vee ((x = e_n) \wedge (y = e_n'))))$$

Next we give examples of each of these rules in turn. First, in Figure 5.6, if we assume that class *Clerk* is different from class *Customer*, the formula *Clerk* $\neq$ *Customer* can be generated by applying rule *H1*. This hypothesis is applicable if the model is considered as a design, as it forces the programmer to implement the two classes *Clerk* and *Customer* separately, but not if it is a requirements specification instead, as then a program would satisfy the model with only one class implementing both.

Second, the assumption that the model in Figure 5.6 contains all classes in the system can be specified as follows and generated by applying rule H2:

$$\forall x \cdot (\mathit{Class}(x) \rightarrow (x = \mathit{Ticket}) \vee (x = \mathit{Clerk}) \vee (x = \mathit{Customer}) \vee (x = \mathit{User}) \vee (x = \mathit{Bank}) \vee (x = \mathit{BoxOffice}))$$

Third, for the model in Figure 5.6, if we believe that all the inheritance relations in the system modeled are depicted in the diagram, we can generate the following hypothesis by applying rule *H3*:

$$\forall x, y \cdot (\mathit{specific}(x, y) \rightarrow (((x = \mathit{CustomerUser}) \wedge (y = \mathit{Customer})) \vee ((x = \mathit{ClerkUser}) \wedge (y = \mathit{Clerk})))$$

It is worth noting that the hypothesis rules above are just examples and are by no means to be considered complete. The point here is that the flexibility of UML for different uses can be revealed explicitly through a set of optional hypothesis mappings. The manner in which the hypothesis rules are related to use of the modeling language will be an interesting problem for further research.

5.2.4 Extendability and Integration of Multiple Views

There are two extension mechanisms in UML: metamodeling and profiles. The former allows the language engineers to use UML class diagrams to define metamodels as far as it can be consistent with the OMG meta object facility (MOF). The latter enables limited extensions of a reference metamodel by introducing new metaclasses in the

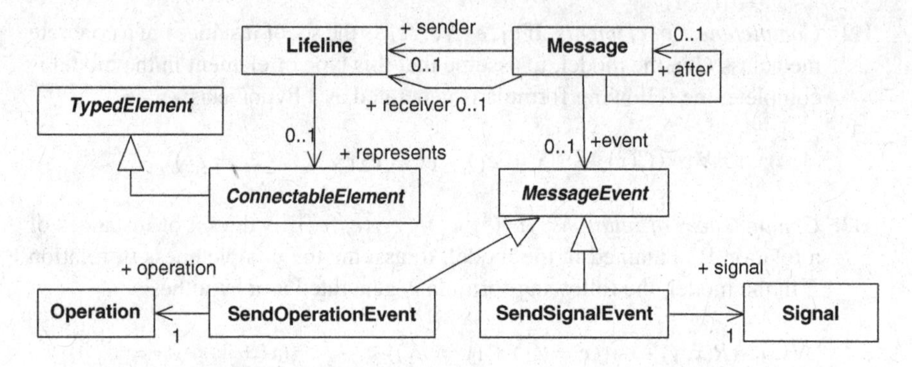

FIGURE 5.7 Simplified metamodel of interaction diagrams.

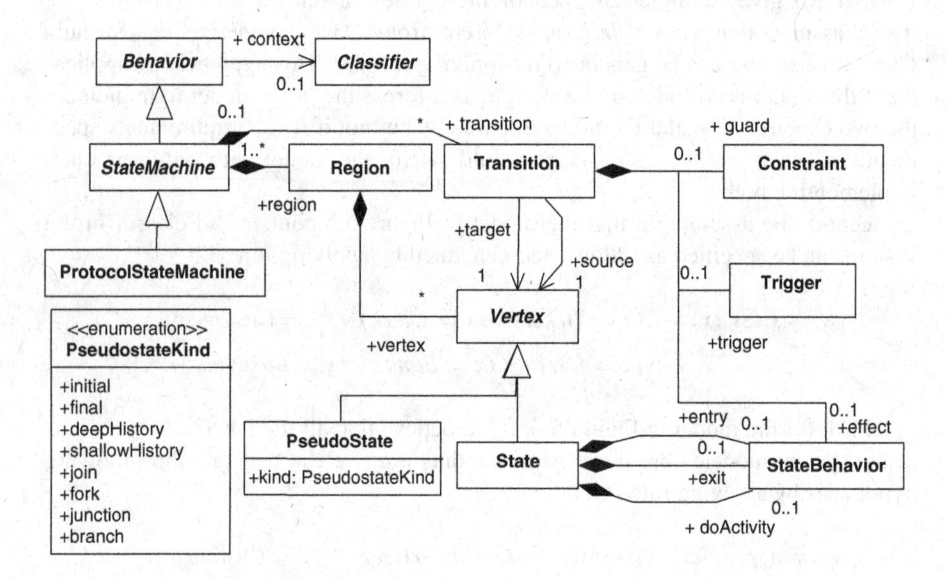

FIGURE 5.8 Simplified metamodel of state machine diagrams.

form of stereotypes, for the purpose of using models in various platforms or domains. To demonstrate that our approach to formal descriptive semantics is applicable to all metamodels, we apply the semantics mappings defined previously to the metamodels of UML interaction and state machine diagrams, shown in Figures 5.7 and 5.8.

It is worth noting that for multiple-view modeling languages such as UML, each view is often defined by using one metamodel that is linked to other metamodel(s) by references to external metaclasses. For example, the metamodel for interaction diagrams refers to the kernel, which is the metamodel of class diagrams. Also, the metamodel of state machine diagrams refers to the metamodel of interaction diagrams.

The references to an existing metaclass in another metamodel may occur in one of two forms: through an association and via inheritance. In the association case, the axioms can be generated by applying exactly the same axiom rules as in the same

TABLE 5.2 Summary of the Logic System for UML Diagrams

	Type of Element	Class Diagram	Interaction Diagram	State Machine
Signature	Unary predicate			
	Abstract metaclass	12	3	4
	Concrete metaclass	16	6	9
	Binary predicate			
	Meta-attribute	7	0	2
	Meta-association	13	7	12
	Constant symbol	13	0	8
Axioms	Implication of specialization	26	3	4
	Completeness of specialization	12	2	3
	Disjointness of classification	120	15	36
	Domain of binary predicate	21	7	14
	Enumeration constants	33	0	37
	Multiplicity of meta-associations	14	9	12
	Completeness of classification	1	1	1

metamodel. However, caution must be paid when implementing the axiom rules because the occurrences of a metaclass in two metamodel class diagrams may be assigned with two different internal identifiers. To ensure that the new occurrences are treated as identical to its original occurrence, the original identifier must be used.

If, on the other hand, a metaclass is referred to via inheritance, new concrete metaclass(es) are introduced. Consequently, the axiom about completeness of the classification of the modeling elements must be modified. In this case, the following axiom rule for cross-metamodel references must be applied instead:

A2′. Let A be a metaclass depicted in two metamodels M_1 and M_2. If $\{B_1, B_2, \ldots, B_k\}$ is the set of metaclasses that specialize A in metamodel M_1, and $\{C_1, C_2, \ldots, C_p\}$ is the set of metaclasses that specialize A in metamodel M_2, we have the following axiom for models defined by M_1 and M_2:

$$\forall x \cdot (A(x) \rightarrow (B_1(x) \vee \cdots \vee B_k(x) \vee C_1(x) \vee \cdots \vee C_p(x)))$$

As defined by the rules given above, the semantics mapping was applied successfully to these metamodels to generate the signatures and axioms. Table 5.2 summarizes the results of applying the rules.

The same translation rules are applicable to interaction diagrams and state machines to generate descriptive semantics of their corresponding models. For example, Figure 5.9 depicts a simple sequence diagram and state machine for the ticket office system. The following formulas are among those generated from the sequence diagram:

$$Message(buyTicket), sender(buyTicket, c)$$

and the following formulas are among those generated from the state machine:

$$State(available), trigger(Transition7, refund), source(Transition7, unavailable)$$

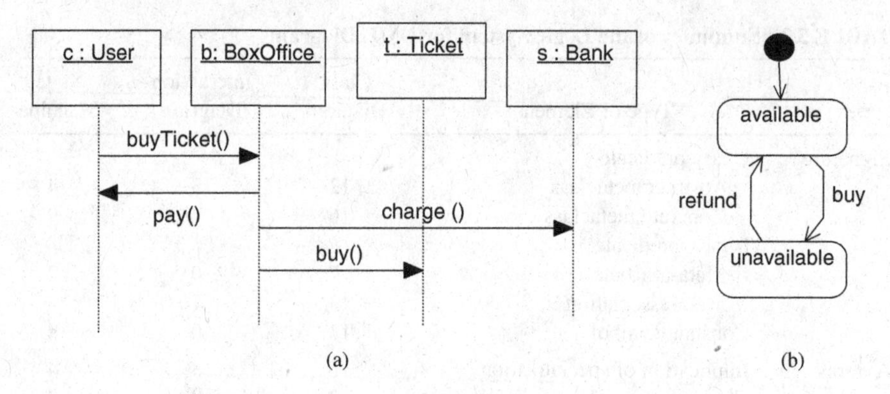

FIGURE 5.9 (a) Sequence diagram; (b) state machine.

5.3 THE LAMBDES TOOL

The descriptive semantics of UML class, interaction, and state machine diagrams have been implemented in an automated software tool called LAMBDES (Logic Analyzer of Models and metamodels Based on DEscriptive Semantics). Figure 5.10 shows its overall structure and main functions. The current version of the LAMBDES toolkit consists of a GUI interface, a number of generators, and a repository of design pattern specifications. It is integrated with the graphic modeling tool StarUML[1] and a theorem prover, SPASS.[2] It takes the model or metamodel's XMI representation produced by StarUML as input to generate a logic system in the format of SPASS's input and invokes SPASS to perform logical analysis of the model and/or metamodel.

SPASS is a general-purpose theorem prover for FOPL with equality. Its input is a text file that represents a logic system with the following parts:

1. *Description:* background information not used in logic inference by SPASS
2. *Signature:* declarations of the predicates and constant symbols of the logic system
3. *Premises:* a list of formulas as the premises of logic inference
4. *Conjectures:* a list of formulas to be proved

Given an input, the execution of SPASS may terminate with a proof of the conjecture from the premises, terminate with a failure to prove, or else run forever without producing any results, because inference in FOPL is NP-hard. SPASS is refutationally complete [28], which means that when it terminates with a failure to prove, the conjecture cannot be proved from the premises in FOPL.

Figure 5.11 shows a snapshot of the tool's interface, where the input XMI file of the model is displayed on the left and the FOPL system generated in SPASS input

[1] Available online at http://staruml.sourceforge.net/en/.

[2] Available online at http://www.spass-prover.org/tutorial.html.

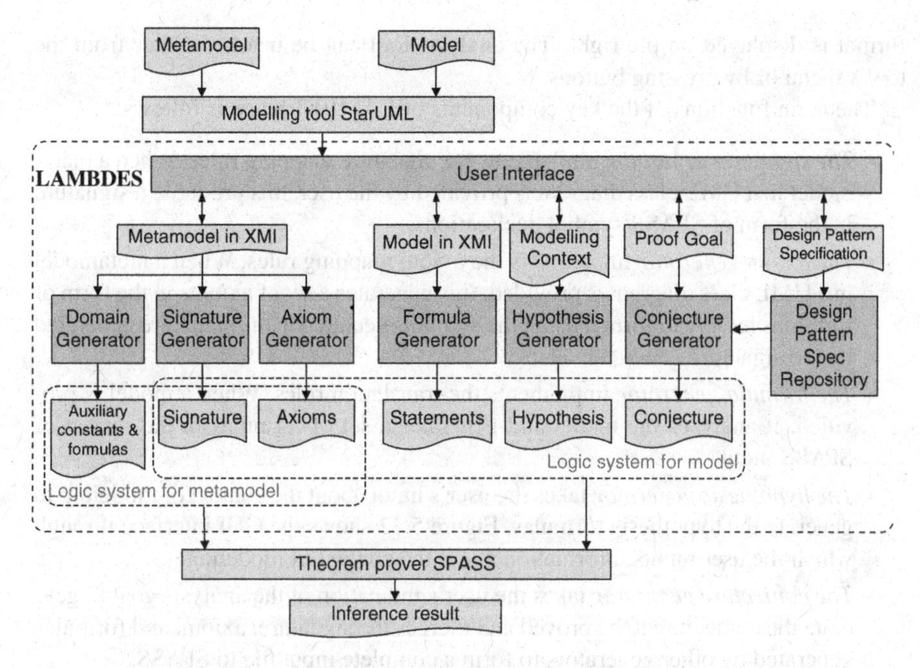

FIGURE 5.10 Overall structure of the LAMBDES toolkit.

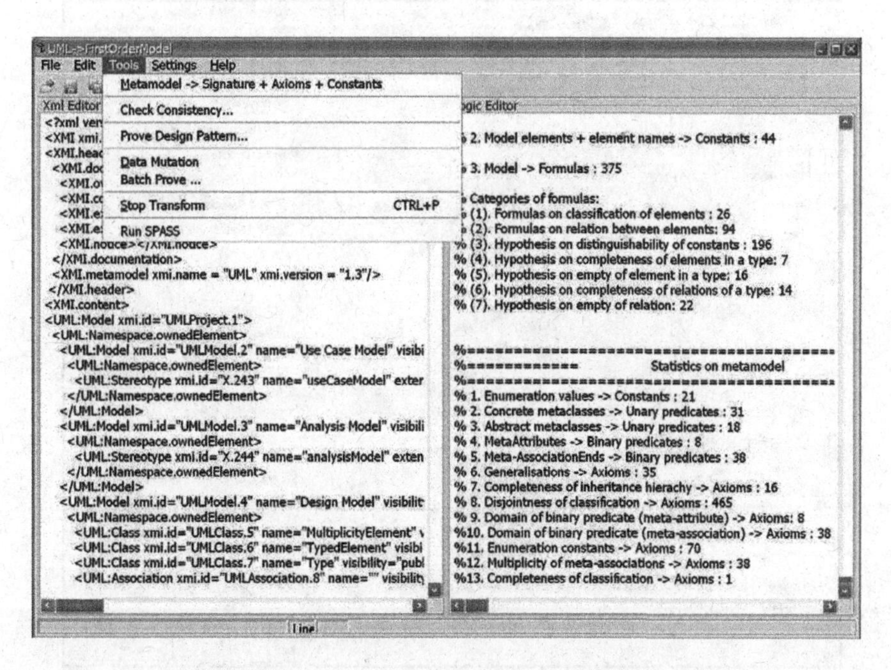

FIGURE 5.11 Screen snapshot of the LAMBDES toolkit.

format is displayed on the right. The analysis tool can be invoked either from the tool's menu or by pressing buttons.

The main functions of the key components of LAMBDES are as follows:

- *The signature generator* implements the signature mapping rules. When a metamodel in a UML class diagram is provided by the user, this produces a signature in the form of SPASS symbol declarations.
- *The axiom generator* implements the axiom mapping rules. When a metamodel in a UML class diagram is provided, this generates a set of axioms in the form of formulas in SPASS format using the symbols declared in the signature generated by the signature generator.
- *The formula generator* implements the translation rules. When a model is provided, it analyzes the model and generates a set of formulas in the format of SPASS input.
- *The hypothesis generator* takes the user's input about the context of modeling to generate the hypothesis formulas. Figure 5.12 shows the GUI interface through which the user inputs information about the context of modeling.
- *The conjecture generator* takes the user's indication of the analysis goal to generate the conjecture to be proved and merges the signature, axiom, and formulas generated by other generators to form a complete input file to SPASS.

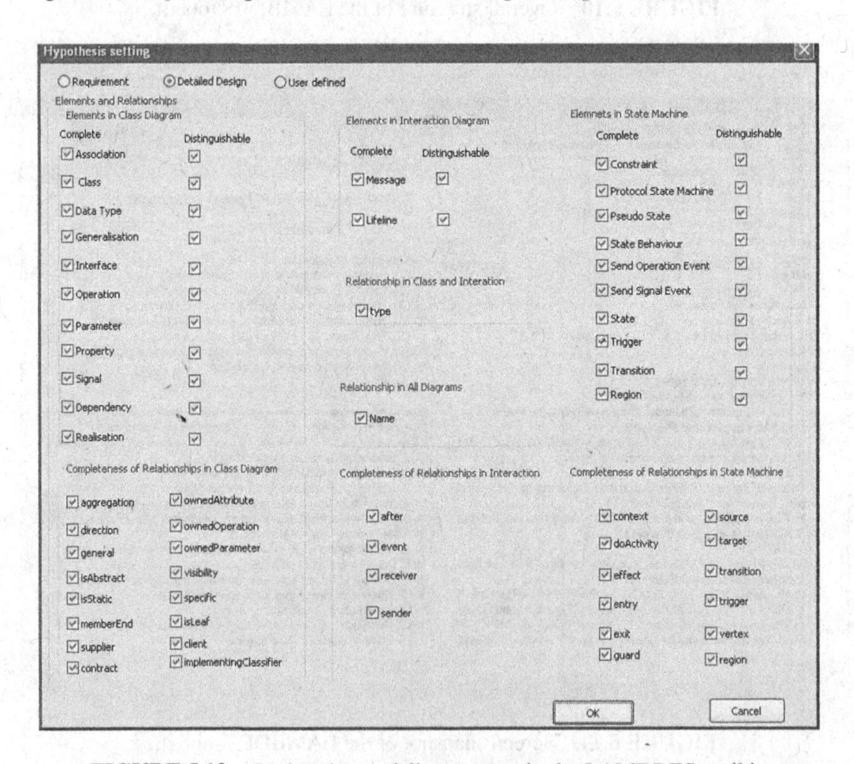

FIGURE 5.12 Setting the modeling context in the LAMBDES toolkit.

- *The design pattern specification repository* stores a set of formal specifications of design patterns in FOPL in the form of SPASS formulas. Currently, it contains the specification of all 23 design patterns of the GoF book [11], based on the work reported by Bayley and Zhu [5]. It supports proofs that a design model conforms to a given design pattern.
- *The domain generator* takes a metamodel as input and generates a set of constant symbols of various types of model elements and instances of various relations to populate the domain when the metamodel is analyzed.

5.4 APPLICATIONS USING MODEL AND METAMODEL ANALYSIS

In this section we demonstrate some applications of descriptive semantics in the logic analysis of models and metamodels.

5.4.1 Consistency Check of Models

Let F be a set of formulas in a signature Σ. As in FOPL, if we can deduce that if $F \vdash false$, then F is inconsistent. Thus, we can check if a model is or is not logically consistent (Definitions 5.4.1 and 5.4.2).

Definition 5.4.1 ***(Logical Consistency)*** Model M is said to be *logically inconsistent in the descriptive semantics* if $[\![M]\!]_H \vdash false$; otherwise, we say that the model is logically consistent in the descriptive semantics.

Definition 5.4.2 ***(Consistent Interpretation of Formulas in a Subject Domain)*** Let $Dom = \langle D, Sig, Eva \rangle$ be a subject domain. The interpretation of Σ-formulas in Dom is consistent with respect to FOPL if and only if for all formulas q and $p_1, p_2, \ldots, p_k$ that $p_1, p_2, \ldots, p_k \vdash q$, and for all systems s in D that $Eva(p_i, s) = true$ for $i = 1, 2, \ldots, k$, we always have $Eva(q, s) = true$.

Shan and Zhu [23] have proved that a logically inconsistent model is not satisfiable in a subject domain, where a consistent interpretation of formulas is applied.

Theorem 5.4.1 *(Unsatisfiability of an Inconsistent Model) A model M that is logically inconsistent in descriptive semantics is not satisfiable on any subject domain whose interpretation of formulas is consistent with respect to FOPL.*

For example, using the LAMBDES tool, we generated the descriptive semantics of the model of the ticket office shown in Figures 5.6 and 5.9 and invoked the SPASS theorem prover to prove that each set of formulas generated from the three diagrams in the model are logically consistent. Their union is also consistent. Therefore, the model is consistent.

We have also made various minor changes to the diagrams in the model ticket office. Some changes led to logically inconsistent sets of formulas, and these were

TABLE 5.3 Summary of Using LAMBDES for Model Quality Checking

Error Description	Represented	Implemented
Severe errors		
Abstract class not inherited	Yes	Yes
Circular association	Yes	Yes
Circular dependency	Yes	Yes
Abstract class inherits from concrete class	Yes	Yes
Class inherits from one or more nonbase classes	Yes	Yes
Interface to class expected but defined improperly	Yes	Yes
Two methods exist in the model with the same signature	Yes	Yes
Two objects exist in the model with the same name	Yes	Yes
Parent accessing attributes/operations of child class	Yes	Yes
Moderate errors		
Number of associations above user-defined threshold	No	No
Number of attributes above user-defined threshold	No	No
Number of methods above user-defined threshold	No	No
Base artifact in an inheritance tree is concrete	Yes	Yes
Number of messages passed to a class above user-defined threshold	No	No
Multiple inheritance	Yes	Yes
Operation has more arguments than user-defined threshold	No	No
Base class in inheritance tree has publicly accessible attributes	Yes	Yes
Low-severity errors		
A dependency has no declared stereotype	Yes	No
Interface not used	Yes	Yes
Missing associations	Yes	Yes
Missing dependencies	Yes	Yes
No classes are dependent on this class	Yes	Yes
Operation missing postconditions	Yes	No
Operation missing preconditions	Yes	No
A class's methods or attributes are unused by other classes	Yes	Yes

detected by theorem prover SPASS. It is therefore possible to check the consistency of models through logic inferences based on descriptive semantics. It is worth noting in general, though, that logical consistency does not guarantee that the model is satisfiable in a subject domain.

In addition to logical consistency, many other quality attributes of models can be expressed in first-order logic and checked through logic inference. For example, Cheng et al. [7] studied 25 quality problems in software models using the tool DesignAdvisor. As shown in Table 5.3, among these quality problems, 20 attributes can be represented in FOPL and 17 attributes are implemented in the LAMBDES tool. Those quality attributes that cannot be checked by the LAMBDES tool include: (1) five quality issues defined on the bases of metrics, which cannot be represented in FOPL without arithmetics; (2) one quality issue related to stereotypes of dependence relations, which the current version of LAMBDES does not deal with; and (3) two quality issues about the missing pre- and postconditions of methods, which are not dealt with in the current implementation of the LAMBDES tool.

5.4.2 Validation of Consistency Constraints

It is often desirable to check models against consistency constraints. The following examples of these consistency constraints show how such constraints can be formally specified as Σ-formulas:

1. A lifeline must represent an instance of a class [8,25]:

$$\forall x, y, z \cdot (\mathit{Lifeline}(x) \wedge \mathit{represent}(x, y) \wedge \mathit{type}(y, z) \rightarrow \mathit{Class}(z))$$

2. A message must represent an operation call of its receiver [8]:

$$\forall x, y, z, u \cdot (\mathit{Message}(x) \wedge \mathit{event}(x, y) \wedge \mathit{SendOperationCall}(y) \\ \wedge \mathit{receiver}(x, z) \wedge \mathit{type}(z, u) \rightarrow \mathit{ownedOperation}(u, y))$$

3. The classifier of a message's sender must be associated to the classifier of its receiver [8]:

$$\forall x, y, z, u, v \cdot (\mathit{Message}(x) \wedge \mathit{sender}(x, y) \wedge \mathit{type}(y, u) \\ \wedge \mathit{receiver}(x, z) \wedge \mathit{type}(z, v) \rightarrow \exists w, m, n \cdot (\mathit{Association}(w) \\ \wedge \mathit{memberEnd}(w, m) \wedge \mathit{AssociateTo}(m, u) \\ \wedge \mathit{memberEnd}(w, n) \wedge \mathit{AssociateTo}(n, v)))$$

4. A protocol state transition must refer to an operation, and that operation must apply to the context classifier of the state machine:

$$\forall x, y, z \cdot (\mathit{ProtocolStateMachine}(x) \wedge \mathit{transition}(x, y) \\ \wedge \mathit{trigger}(y, z) \wedge \mathit{context}(x, u) \\ \rightarrow \mathit{Operation}(z) \wedge \mathit{ownedOperation}(u, z))$$

5. The order of messages in an interaction diagram must be consistent with the order of triggers on transitions in the state machine [8,15]:

$$\forall x, y, z, u \cdot (\mathit{Message}(x) \wedge \mathit{event}(x, z) \\ \wedge \mathit{Message}(y) \wedge \mathit{event}(y, u) \wedge \mathit{after}(x, y) \rightarrow \mathit{Trigs}(z, u))$$

These cannot be derived from the axioms and are not required for logical consistency, so we clearly do need a separate notion of consistency with respect to a set of constraints (Definition 5.4.3).

Definition 5.4.3 ***(Consistency with Respect to Consistency Constraints)*** Given a set of consistency constraints $C=\{c_1,c_2,\ldots,c_n\}$, the consistency of a model M with respect to the constraints C in descriptive semantics is the consistency of the set $U=[\![M]\!]_H \cup C$ of Σ-formulas. In particular, we say that a model M fails on a specific constraint c_k if $[\![M]\!]_H$ is consistent but $[\![M]\!]_H \cup \{c_k\}$ is not.

It is important to know if a consistency constraint is valid and effective. Such formal analysis becomes possible now that the descriptive semantics are defined formally. First, for a consistency constraint to be valid, it must be consistent with the semantics of the modeling language (Definition 5.4.4).

Definition 5.4.4 ***(Validity of Consistency Constraints)*** Let Axm_D be the set of axioms of descriptive semantics. A set $C=\{c_1,c_2,\ldots,c_n\}$ of consistency constraints is *valid* if $Axm_D \cup C$ is logically consistent.

Second, a consistency constraint is not effective if it does not impose additional restrictions on models. This is true if the constraint can be deduced from the axioms in FOPL (Definition 5.4.5).

Definition 5.4.5 ***(Effectiveness of Consistency Constraints)*** Let Axm be a set of axioms. A set $C=\{c_1,c_2,\ldots,c_n\}$ of consistency constraints is *ineffective with respect to the set Axm of axioms* if $Axm \vdash C$.

So a formal analysis of consistency constraints can be performed through logic inference. For example, we have used the LAMBDES tool to prove that the constraints given above are all valid. We have also proven that they are effective by detecting models that are consistent with respect to the axioms but inconsistent with respect to the constraints.

5.4.3 Consistency Check of Metamodels

The LAMBDES tool can also be used to analyze metamodels by proving or disproving the consistency of the axioms generated from the metamodel. If the axioms derived are inconsistent, the metamodel is not well defined.

We have conducted a case study with two metamodels. The first is the UML 2.0 metamodel defined in the *Classes*, *Common Behaviors*, *Interactions*, and *State Machines* packages. The second is the profile of AspectJ proposed by Evermann [10] for aspect-oriented modeling. This case study was intended to demonstrate the applicability of descriptive semantics in the analysis of proper uses of profiles as extension mechanisms. Table 5.4 summarizes the logic system generated from the metamodels.

Two types of errors in the metamodels were detected: incompleteness errors and inconsistency errors. For an example of *incompleteness*, in the UML 2.0 metamodel the data types of meta-attributes are either enumeration types (e.g., *VisibilityKind*)

TABLE 5.4 Summary of the Logic Systems

	Type of Element	UML 2.0 Metamodel	AspectJ Profile
Signature	Unary predicate		
	Abstract metaclass	27	6
	Concrete metaclass	99	25
	Binary predicate		
	Meta-attribute	58	11
	Meta-association	255	12
	Constant symbol	46	7
	Total	*485*	*61*
Axioms	Implication of specialization	133	26
	Completeness of specialization	25	6
	Disjointness of classification	4851	300
	Domain of binary predicate	321	23
	Enumeration constants	196	18
	Multiplicity of meta-associations	222	18
	Completeness of classification	1	1
	Total	*5740*	*392*

or primitive types (e.g., *String*). The enumeration types are defined in the metamodel, while the primitive types are used in the metamodel without definition. This contradicts the statement in the *Classes Package* that "each metaclass is completely described" [18]. Incompleteness errors were detected by the SPASS theorem prover with error reports where symbol declarations were missing.

For an example of *inconsistency*, in the UML 2.0 metamodel, *OccurrenceSpecification* is specified as an abstract metaclass in one diagram and as a concrete metaclass in another. This error has been corrected in UML 2.1 [19]. A more subtle inconsistency detected, this time within the AspectJ metamodel, is that there are two association ends, both named *composee*: one on the association from *PointCut* to *PointCutConjunction* and the other on the association from *PointCut* to *PointCutDisjunction*. Since an association end represents a directed relation that enables navigation between elements, two association ends of the same name from the same metaclass cause ambiguity in the direction of the navigation. This problem is detected by the theorem prover SPASS when checking the consistency of the axioms generated from the AspectJ metamodel, which include the following formulas:

$$\forall x \cdot (PointCutConjunction(x) \rightarrow \neg PointCutDisjunction(x))$$

$$\forall x \cdot (PointCut(x) \wedge composee(x, y) \rightarrow PointCutConjunction(x))$$

$$\forall x \cdot (PointCut(x) \wedge composee(x, y) \rightarrow PointCutDisjunction(x))$$

Another form of inconsistency in metamodels is the violation of the *principle of strict modeling*, which states that *in an n-level modeling architecture* $M_0, M_1, \ldots, M_n$,

TABLE 5.5 Summary of Ambiguity in the UML 2.0 Metamodel

Package	Concrete Supermetaclasses	Concrete Submetaclasses
Classes	InstanceSpecification	EnumerationLiteral
	Class	AssociationClass
	Association	AssociationClass
	DataType	PrimitiveType
	Abstraction	Realization
	Realization	Substitution
	Dependency	Usage
Common behaviors	OpaqueBehavior	FunctionBehavior
	Constraint	IntervalConstraint
	IntervalConstraint	TimeConstraint
	Class	Behavior
Interactions	CombinedFragment	ConsiderIgnoreFragment
	InteractionUse	PartDecomposition
State machines	Transition	ProtocolTransition
	State	FinalState
	StateMachine	ProtocolStateMachine

every element of an M_m*-level model must be an* instance-of *exactly one element of an* M_{m+1}*-level model, for all* $0 \leq m < n-1$*, and any relationship other than the instance-of relationship between two elements X and Y implies that* $level(X) = level(Y)$ [2]. According to this principle, each model element must belong to one and only one concrete metaclass in the metamodel—hence the axiom mapping rules *A1* and *A2*. However, both UML 2.0 and AspectJ metamodels violate this principle. In particular, they contain concrete metaclasses as subclasses of concrete metaclasses. Therefore, a model element can belong to two concrete metaclasses, and the meaning of the model element is ambiguous. Table 5.5 lists such ambiguities in the UML 2.0 metamodel.

5.4.4 Conformance of Design to Design Patterns

Software design patterns are frequently used to share design expertise. They document solutions to commonly occurring design problems. Tool support for patterns has been much reported at the code level [17] but not at the modeling and design stages, and the latter is increasingly important with the advent of model-driven software development methodologies. Here we demonstrate that the descriptive semantics of UML and the LAMBDES tool can be applied to formally prove the conformance of a design represented in a UML model to a pattern formally specified in the FOPL. More details about a case study on this topic will be reported separately.

Bayley and Zhu [3,5], advanced an approach to the formal specification of design patterns using FOPL on UML models. Here a design pattern *P* is specified as a predicate $p = Spec(P)$ such that a design model *M* conforms to a pattern *P* if the evaluation of the predicate p on model M is true. For example, the following is Bayley and Zhu's specification of the *Template Method* pattern [5]:

- Components
  - $AbstractClass \in classes$
  - $templateMethod \in AbstractClass.opers$
  - $others \subseteq AbstractClass.opers$
- Static conditions
  - $templateMethod.isLeaf$
  - $templateMethod \notin others$
  - $\forall o \in others\ .\ \neg o.isLeaf$
- Dynamic conditions
  - The template method calls the nonleaf operations:

$$\forall o \in others\ .\ callsHook(templateMethod, o)$$

The static conditions relate to the class diagram, and the dynamic conditions relate to the sequence diagram. Here, *classes* denotes the set of classes in the class diagram. If C is a class, $C.opers$ denotes the set of operations of class C. If o is an operation, $o.isLeaf$ is true when o is not redefined in a subclass. So the static conditions state that there must be a class *AbstractClass* with a nonredefined operation *templateMethod* that calls a set *others* of separate redefined operations.

Under dynamic conditions, the predicate $callsHook(op, op')$ used above is defined as $\exists C \in subs(C') \cdot calls(op, C.op')$, where $calls(op, op')$ denotes that in the sequence diagram, there exist messages m and m' in *messages*, the set of messages, such that m, labeled with operation op, calls m', labeled with operation op'.

The mix of math and text forming the specification above is meant to be read as a single (commented) predicate in which the variables *AbstractClass*, *templateMethod*, and *others* are existentially quantified, and the four conditions are conjoined together into a single predicate on those three variables. The general form for the predicate is

$$\exists v_1 : T_1 \exists v_2 : T_2 \cdots \exists v_n : T_n \cdot (Pr_s \wedge Pr_d)$$

where Pr_s and Pr_d are the static and dynamic conditions as predicates and the $v_i : T_i$ are free variables in Pr_s and Pr_d.

An assignment α is a mapping from free variables in p to elements in model M. The evaluation of a predicate p on a model M in the context of an assignment α, written $Eva_\alpha(M, p)$, is the truth value of p when the free occurrences of each variable x in p are replaced by $\alpha(x)$. If $Eva_\alpha(M, p) = true$, we say that model M *satisfies* predicate p under the assignment α, and write $M \models_\alpha p$. When there is no free variable in the predicate p, its truth value is independent of the assignment, so the subscript α can be omitted.

From the discussion above it is apparent that although FOPL is used in both the descriptive semantics of UML and the formal specification of design patterns [3–5], the universes of discourses are different. To bridge the semantic gap, the formal specification of design patterns [5] must be translated into Σ-sentences (i.e., in the syntax of the LAMBDES tool). The translation is fairly straightforward because both languages use the same basic concepts of object orientation. For *Template Method* pattern, we get the following:

```
%%%%%%%%%%%%%%%%%%%%%%%%%%%%%%%%%%%%%%%%%%%%%%%%%
% Template Method Pattern Specification         %
%%%%%%%%%%%%%%%%%%%%%%%%%%%%%%%%%%%%%%%%%%%%%%%%%
formula(exists([
%Components:
  xAbstractClass, xTemplateMethod, xOthers],
 and(
%Static conditions:
  Class(xAbstractClass),
  ownedOperation(xAbstractClass,xTemplateMethod),
  ownedOperation(xAbstractClass,xOthers),
  isLeaf(xTemplateMethod,bTrue),
  not(equal(xTemplateMethod,xOthers)),
  isLeaf(xOthers,bFalse)
%Dynamic conditions:
  callsHook(xTemplateMethod,xOthers)
))).
```

The translation mentioned above must meet the general correctness requirement (Definition 5.4.6).

Definition 5.4.6 (Correctness of Translation) Let p be a predicate on models, and p' be a predicate on systems. The predicate p' is a *correct translation* of p if for all models M, we have $M \models p \leftrightarrow \forall s \in \mathcal{D} \cdot (s \models ([\![M]\!] \rightarrow p'))$, where D is a subject domain.

Once a specification $Spec(P)$ of pattern P is translated correctly into $Spec'(P)$, then given a design model M represented in UML diagrams, we can decide whether the design M conforms to pattern P by proving or disproving the logic statement $[\![M]\!] \rightarrow Spec'(P)$ in FOL. For example, the translated specification of the *Template Method* pattern can be deduced from the formulas generated from the class diagram in Figure 5.13.

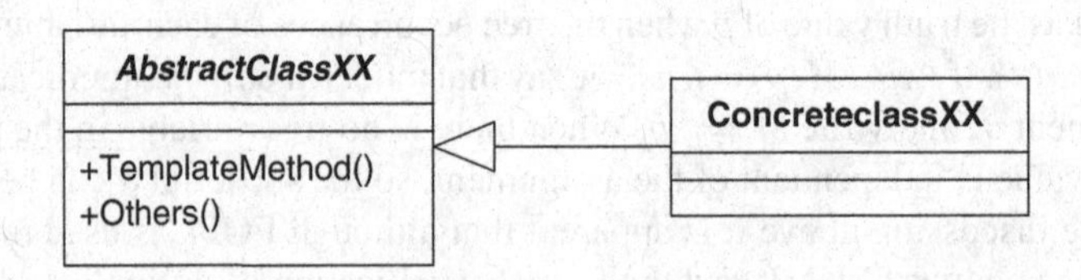

FIGURE 5.13 Example design instance in a template method pattern.

The following theorem states that if we can prove $[\![M]\!] \to Spec'(P)$ in FOPL for model M and pattern P, every system that is an instance of M must conform to pattern P. The proof is omitted for the sake of space.

Theorem 5.4.2 *Suppose that $Spec'(P)$ is a correct translation of the formal specification $Spec(P)$ of pattern P. For all models M, if $[\![M]\!] \Rightarrow Spec'(P)$ is true in FOPL, then for all systems $s \in \mathcal{D}$, $s \models M$ and $M \models Spec(P)$ imply that $s \models Spec'(P)$.*

We have translated into LAMBDES format Bayley and Zhu's specifications [5] for all 23 design patterns in the GoF book. They are stored in a pattern specification repository. The conjecture generator of the LAMBDES tool is implemented to enable the proof (or disproof) of the conformance of a UML design model to a pattern. We have also conducted an experiment with the LAMBDES tool on its ability to recognize patterns in design instances. The experimental results show that the false negative error rate (for rejecting a pattern it should accept) is 0%, while the false positive error rate (for accepting a pattern it should reject) is below 22%. Details of the experiment are omitted here for the sake of space and will be reported separately.

5.4.5 Logic Analysis of Design Patterns

It is worth noting that the specification of a design pattern may contain errors. The conditions to satisfy the pattern may be in conflict with the semantics of the modeling language, or they may be in conflict with each other. Such logic errors can be detected by using the LAMBDES tool and SPASS theorem prover. In particular, let $Spec(P)$ be a specification of a pattern P. If $Axm_D \cup Spec(P) \vdash false$, we can conclude that $Spec(P)$ contains such errors.

In the development of the pattern specification repository, using LAMBDES and SPASS we have proved that for all specifications of design patterns P in the repository, $Axm_D \cup Spec(P) \nvdash false$. So all the specifications in our repository are consistent with the axioms of descriptive semantics.

Another application of LAMBDES and SPASS in the logic analysis of design patterns is to prove relations between patterns: for example, to prove that one pattern is a specialization of another. Bayley and Zhu [4] argued that the relationship that a design pattern P is a specialization of pattern Q can be written as $Spec(P) \to Spec(Q)$. Such a relationship can be proved formally by using LAMBDES and SPASS to infer that $Axm_D \cup Spec(P) \vdash Spec(Q)$. In the context of descriptive semantics, we can now prove the following property of the pattern specialization relation.

Theorem 5.4.3 *Let Dom be a subject domain that is consistent with FOPL. If $Axm_D \cup Spec(P) \vdash Spec(Q)$, then for all systems $x \in Dom$, if x is an instance of P, x is also an instance of pattern Q [i.e., $\forall x \cdot (x \models Spec(P) \to x \models Spec(Q))$].*

5.5 CONCLUSIONS

In this chapter we presented a framework for the formalization of UML semantics and defined a formal descriptive semantics of UML in FOPL. We introduce a tool called

LAMBDES, which translates UML class, interaction, and state machine diagrams to FOPL systems and is integrated with the theorem prover SPASS to enable various logic analysis of models and metamodels. A number of applications of the descriptive semantics and the tool LAMBDES were demonstrated.

5.5.1 Related Work

Remarkable efforts have been made in the past decade to formalize UML semantics so as to address the underspecification and ambiguity in UML's semantics. With regard to the formalization of class diagrams, often considered to be the most important type of UML diagram, a number of proposals have been advanced. Work by Evans et al. defines classifier, association, generalization, and attribute in Z schemas [9]. Relations between objects and classifiers are specified as axioms. Diagrammatical transformation rules are defined as deduction rules to prove properties of UML models. Amalio and Polack [1] survey various approaches to formalizing class diagrams with Z or Object-Z. Berandi et al. used FOPL and description logics (DLs) to formalize class diagrams [6]. By encoding UML class diagrams in DL knowledge bases, DL reasoning systems can be used to reason about class diagrams.

The formalization of other types of diagrams has also been investigated, especially on state machine diagrams. Varro proposed [26] a rule-based operational semantics of state machines based on transition systems. Von der Beeck reported other work on operational semantics of state machines [27]. A coalgebra framework for defining the formal semantics of sequence diagrams was proposed by Mang and Barbosa [14].

Great efforts have also been made to formalize different diagrams in one semantic framework. Considering the semantics of a UML model as a set of acceptable structured processes, Reggio et al. [21] map class diagrams and state machines into algebraic specifications in Casl-ltl [20]. Another work aiming at integrating the semantics of class, object, and state machine diagrams is based on graph transformation [13].

To bridge the gap between UML and formal methods, the extensibility mechanism of UML profiles is used to define specializations of UML. Snook and Butler designed [24] a profile UML-B so that the semantics of specialized UML entities could be defined via a translation into B. Muller et al. [16] used an integrated formal method combining the process algebra CSP with the specification language Object-Z as the intermediate specification language to link UML and Java. A UML profile for CSP-OZ is designed with the aim of generating part of the CSP-OZ specifications from the specialized UML models.

The existing methods described above define the semantics of UML by mapping models into a specific semantic domain, such as labeled transition systems, or OO software systems specified in a formal notation such as Z. The properties of OO systems are specified as axioms and are used to reason about UML models. In other words, they mostly address only the functional semantics of UML. Each method focuses on certain properties of OO systems, so only a certain subset of UML is formalized. However, it is difficult to see how these approaches could work either alone or together for fully fledged UML. Most important, the ambiguity in descriptive semantics is not addressed in these works. Instead, their formalization approaches are based on explicit or implicit assumptions about the descriptive semantics. They do not achieve automatic translation of UML models to formal specifications, and this is necessary to facilitate formal reasoning.

In comparison with the existing works, our approach separates descriptive semantics from functional semantics so that the overall structure of semantics is much clearer and simpler. It also conforms to the theory of institution proposed by Goguen and Burstall [12] for the study of formal specification languages. As we have shown, our approach successfully addressed problems related to the requirement for flexibility in using models in different software development contexts by introducing hypothesis mappings into the semantics framework. It also addressed successfully the problem of extensibility of the semantics definition by defining semantics mappings from the metamodel to the logic system so that when new stereotype metaclasses are introduced, new atomic predicate and function symbols can be derived from profile definitions or even from a completely new metamodel. The universality of semantic mappings are clearly demonstrated by their application to class, interaction, and state machine diagrams as well as in the AspectJ profile case study. Our approach is also independent of the interpretation of the logic in any particular subject domain. Therefore, the semantics can be interpreted in the subject domain of computerized information systems, real-world objects and physical systems, human societies, and so on, as far as the basic concepts of object orientation apply. These are open problems that have not been solved in existing work.

Our approach is scalable, as shown in the case study of the main parts of UML 2.0 containing four large packages and the real example of AspectJ profile, all 23 design patterns in the GoF category, and so on. Our approach is also highly automated in the sense that a graphical model edited by the modeling tool StarUML can be input into LAMBDES to generate formal semantics of the model and to invoke a theorem prover to check its consistency, its conformance to design patterns, and similar factors. Our approach applies not only to models but also to metamodels.

5.5.2 Future Work

We are investigating both how functional semantics can be specified formally and the interplay between descriptive semantics and functional semantics. Static functional semantics has also been developed, and this will be reported separately.

We are also studying the logic properties of the descriptive semantics reported here. It is apparent that the axioms of descriptive semantics are consistent, as proved in the experiment by using SPASS. The particular problems that we are interested in include whether the axioms and various other semantics mappings are complete.

One of the problems that we encounter in the case studies and experiments is the inefficiency of the theorem prover. When the number of formulas in the logic system is more than 1000, the proof that the formulas are consistent does not terminate, and this would appear to be a bottleneck for practical use of the LAMBDES tool.

REFERENCES

1. N. Amalio and F. Polack. Comparison of formalisation approaches of UML class constructs in Z and Object-Z. In D. Bert et al. (eds.), *ZB 2003: Formal Specification and Development in Z and B*, pp. 339–358. Springer-Verlag, New York, 2003.
2. C. Atkinson and T. Kühne. Rearchitecting the UML infrastructure. *ACM Transactions on Modelling and Computer Simulation*, 12(4):290–321, 2002.
3. I. Bayley and H. Zhu. Formalising design patterns in predicate logic. In *Proceedings of SEFM'07*, 2007.
4. I. Bayley and H. Zhu. On the composition of design patterns. In *Proceedings of QSIC'09*, pp. 27–36. IEEE Computer Society, Los Alamitos, CA, 2009.
5. I. Bayley and H. Zhu. Specifying behavioural features of design patterns in first order logic. In *Proceedings of COMPSAC'08*, pp. 203–210. IEEE Computer Society, Los Alamitos, CA, 2008.
6. D. Berardi, A. Cal, and D. Calvanese. Reasoning on UML class diagrams. *Artificial Intelligence*, 168:70–118, 2005.
7. B. H. Cheng, R. Stephenson, and B. Berenbach. Lessons learned from automated analysis of industrial UML class models. In *MoDELS 2005*. Lecture Notes in Computer Science, vol. 3713, pp. 324–338. Springer-Verlag, New York, 2005.
8. A. Egyed. Instant consistency checking for the UML. In *Proceedings of ICSE'06*, pp. 381–390. IEEE Computer Society, Los Alamitos, CA, 2006.
9. A. Evans, R. B. France, K. Lano, and B. Rumpe. The UML as a formal modeling notation. In *UML'98: Selected Papers from the First International Workshop on the Unified Modeling Language*, London, pp. 336–348. Springer-Verlag, New York, 1999.
10. J. Evermann. A meta-level specification and profile for AspectJ in UML. *Journal of Object Technology*, 6(7):27–49, 2007.
11. E. Gamma, R. Helm, R. Johnson, and J. Vlissides. *Design Patterns: Elements of Reusable Object-Oriented Software*. Addison-Wesley, Reading, MA, 1995.
12. J. A. Goguen and R. M. Burstall. Institutions: abstract model theory for specification and programming. *Journal of the ACM*, 39(1):95–146, 1992.
13. S. Kuske, M. Gogolla, R. Kollmann, and H.-J. Kreowski. An integrated semantics for UML class, object and state diagrams based on graph transformation. In *IFM'02: Proceedings of the 3rd International Conference on Integrated Formal Methods*, London, pp. 11–28. Springer-Verlag, New York, 2002.
14. S. Meng and L. S. Barbosa. A coalgebraic semantic framework for reasoning about UML sequence diagrams. In *Proceedings of QSIC'08*, pp. 17–26, IEEE Computer Society, Los Alamitos, CA, 2008.
15. T. Mens, R. Straeten, and J. Simmonds. Maintaining consistency between UML models with description logic tools. In *ECOOP Workshop on Object-Oriented Reengineering*, 2003.
16. M. Muller, E. Olderog, H. Rasch, and H. Wehrheim. Linking CSP-OZ with UML and Java: a case study. In *Integrated Formal Methods*. Lecture Notes in Computer Science vol. 2999, pp. 267–286. Springer-Verlag, New York, 2004.
17. N. Nija Shi and R. Olsson. Reverse engineering of design patterns from java source code. In *Proceedings of ASE'06*, Tokyo, pp. 123–134, Sept. 2006.

18. OMG. *Unified Modeling Language: Superstructure Version 2.0*. Object Management Group, Needham, MA, 2005.

19. OMG. *Unified Modeling Language: Superstructure Version 2.1.1*. Object Management Group, Needham, MA, 2007.

20. G. Reggio, E. Astesiano, and C. Choppy. *Casl-ltl : A Casl Extension for Dynamic Reactive Systems—Summary*. Technical Report DISI-TR-99-34. DISI–Università di Genova, Genova, Italy, 1999.

21. G. Reggio, M. Cerioli, and E. Astesiano. Towards a rigorous semantics of UML supporting its multiview approach. In *FASE'01: Proceedings of the 4th International Conference on Fundamental Approaches to Software Engineering*, pp. 171–186, London. Springer-Verlag, New York, 2001.

22. E. Seidewitz. What models mean. *IEEE Software*, 20(5):26–32, 2003.

23. L. Shan and H. Zhu. A formal descriptive semantics of UML. In *Proceedings of ICFEM'08*, pp. 375–396. Springer-Verlag, New York, Oct. 2008.

24. C. Snook and M. Butler. UML-B: formal modeling and design aided by UML. *ACM Transactions on Software Engineering Methodology*, 15(1):92–122, 2006.

25. R. Van, D. Straeten, J. Simmonds, and T. Mens. Detecting inconsistencies between UML models using description logic. In *Proceedings of DL 2003*, 2003.

26. D. Varro, A formal semantics of UML statecharts by model transition systems. In *Proceedings of ICGT 2002: International Conference on Graph Transformation*. Lecture Notes in Computer Science, Vol. 2505, pp. 378–392. Springer-Verlag, New York, 2002.

27. M. von der Beeck. A structured operational semantics for UML-statecharts. *Software Systems Model*, 1:130–141, 2002.

28. C. Weidenbach. Spass—version 0.49. *Journal of Automated Reasoning*, 18(2):247–252, 1997.

CHAPTER 6

AXIOMATIC SEMANTICS OF UML CLASS DIAGRAMS

KEVIN LANO
Department of Computer Science, King's College London, London, UK

6.1 INTRODUCTION

In this chapter we provide a semantics for the class diagram notation of UML, by translating this notation into a first-order logic known as real-time action logic (RAL).

UML [62] is a large and complex notation in which many aspects of the semantics remain incomplete or imprecise. Specific problems include the following:

1. Lack of semantic consistency properties for individual models and between models of the same system [25]
2. Unclear semantics for transition priority in state machines [20] and for substitutability of a subclass for a superclass
3. Lack of consistent interpretation of concepts [59]

The upgrade of UML to UML 2.0 rationalized the metamodel structure of UML but introduced further semantic complexities by enlarging the UML notation: for example, to include Petri net-style models.

We solve some of these problems by using the following semantics approach:

1. Use a semantic model that is very general and supports treatment of large parts of UML, and extensions of UML, for real-time and hybrid systems.
2. Use structured theories to decompose the semantics of a model into subtheories for individual classes and objects so that instance-level reasoning can be carried out more efficiently.

We show how a complete semantics can be given to a large subset of the UML 2 class diagram notation, including OCL constraints.

UML 2 Semantics and Applications. Edited by Kevin Lano

Although real-time specification is not common in class diagrams (the duration of operations can be specified by comparing *now* and *now*@pre in their postconditions, however), UML contains a number of notations that refer to time, such as time-based triggers in state machines and the notation for interactions [62, Sec. 14]. Specialized UML profiles such as the UML profile for real time [64] also permit specification of concurrent and real-time aspects of a system, such as:

1. Specification of durations of operation executions, and delay in a requested operation being executed
2. Specification of periodic behavior
3. Specification of operation semantics as sequential, guarded, or concurrent
4. Specification of priority policies for request handling, such as "first come, first served"

Therefore, our semantics will support representation of time and properties of execution instances at a detailed level.

A large number of relevant formalisms exist, including real-time logic (RTL) [3,34], temporal logic of actions (TLA) [36], duration calculus [18], and real-time temporal logic [70,71]. We will use a simple but highly expressive formalism, RAL [37], based on RTL.

RAL directly supports the assignment of times to method initiations and terminations, and contains an embedding of linear temporal logic, by interpreting "next time" as "next action invocation time." RAL is an extension of modal logics such as the object calculus of Fiadeiro and Maibaum [22]. RAL has been used to give a semantics to the real-time object-oriented language VDM^{++} [37]. The semantics described here is also used as the basis of the UML2Web tools [45]. In Section 6.2 we define the RAL formalism.

Figure 6.1 shows the metamodel for class diagrams that we will use: it is a subset of the UML 2.1.1 class diagram metamodel. *StructuralFeature* also inherits from *MultiplicityElement*. The metaclasses *Extension*, *ExtensionEnd* and *Stereotype* are defined as in the Profiles package of UML 2.0 [61, Sec. 18].

The following simplifications are made to the UML 2.1.1 class diagram metamodel:

- Qualified associations and aggregation are omitted.
- Associations are binary:

$$memberEnd \rightarrow size() = 2$$

Association ends are never static:

$$memberEnd \rightarrow forAll(isStatic = false)$$

- Association ends are either sets ($isUnique = true$ and $isOrdered = false$) or sequences ($isUnique = false$ and $isOrdered = true$).

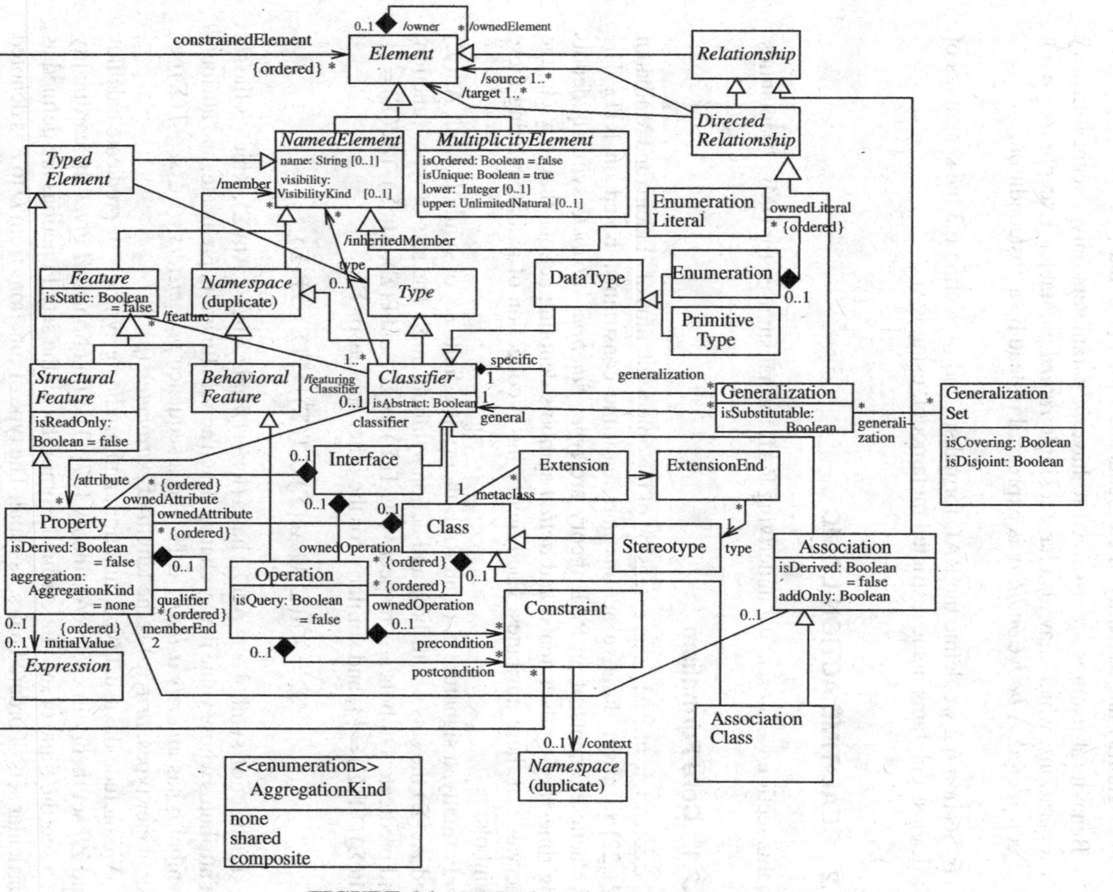

FIGURE 6.1 UML class diagram metamodel.

- Attributes always have multiplicities 1..1:

$$attribute \rightarrow notEmpty()\ implies\ attribute.lower = 1\ and\ attribute.upper = 1$$

- Navigability and visibility of elements are not represented.
- Behavioral features are assumed to have *in* parameters only, except for query operations, which may also have a single *return* parameter. Exceptions are not considered. A *bodyCondition* is expressed instead by a postcondition.

In Section 6.2 we define the RAL formalism and in Section 6.3 the semantics of UML class diagrams in the restricted metamodel, using RAL.

6.2 REAL-TIME ACTION LOGIC

In this section we present the underlying RAL formalism used for UML 2 semantics.

6.2.1 Core Formalism

The core logic of RAL is an extension of the object calculus of Fiadeiro and Maibaum [21,22] to cover durative actions and real-time constraints, based on RTL. The syntactic elements of an RAL theory are *type*, *function*, *attribute* symbols denoting time-varying data items, and *action* symbols denoting actions that may change the value of these attributes. Each theory has a collection of axioms relating these symbols.[1]

Formally, a signature Σ of an RAL theory is a finite set of symbols, with $\mathrm{Att}(\Sigma)$ and $\mathrm{Ac}(\Sigma)$ the sets of attribute and action symbols in Σ. The sets of type, function, and predicate symbols are, respectively, $\mathrm{T}(\Sigma)$, $\mathrm{F}(\Sigma)$, and $\mathrm{P}(\Sigma)$. $\mathrm{Att}(\Sigma) \cap \mathrm{Ac}(\Sigma) = \{\}$, $\mathrm{Att}(\Sigma) \cap \mathrm{T}(\Sigma) = \{\}$, and similarly for the other subsets of Σ:

$$\Sigma = \mathrm{Att}(\Sigma) \cup \mathrm{Ac}(\Sigma) \cup \mathrm{T}(\Sigma) \cup \mathrm{F}(\Sigma) \cup \mathrm{P}(\Sigma)$$

Each action symbol $\alpha \in \mathrm{Ac}(\Sigma)$ has a *(write) frame* $\mathcal{F}(\alpha) \subseteq \mathrm{Att}(\Sigma)$, which is the set of attributes whose value it may change. Each action, function, predicate, and attribute symbol p has an *arity* $arity(p) \in \mathbb{N}$, and a sequence $parameters(p) \in seq(\mathrm{T}(\Sigma))$ of parameter types. $arity(p)$ is the length of $parameters(p)$.

We include the usual type, function, and predicate symbols of predicate calculus and ZF set theory in each RAL theory [57]. The function *card* gives the cardinality of a set (the finite or infinite cardinal isomorphic to the set). Functions are defined as particular sets of ordered pairs, as usual. The type of functions from D to R is denoted $D \rightarrow R$. The range of a function f is denoted $\mathrm{ran}(f)$ and the domain is $\mathrm{dom}(f)$. The types $\mathbb{N}$, $\mathbb{Z}$, $\mathbb{R}$ and $\mathbb{S}$ (of strings) will usually be assumed to exist in $\mathrm{T}(\Sigma)$ with the usual axioms. A "universal type" corresponding to *OclAny* [66] could also be added.

[1] Theories are also termed *modules* in the following.

We also assume that there is a type *TIME* of times, with $\mathbb{N} \subseteq TIME$. *TIME* is totally ordered by a relation $<$, with least element 0, and satisfying the axioms of a totally ordered ring with addition $+$ and unit 0, and multiplication operation $*$ with unit 1. We will usually assume that there is an attribute $now : TIME$.

For each action α there are TIME-valued function symbols $\leftarrow(\alpha, i)$, $\rightarrow(\alpha, i)$, $\uparrow(\alpha, i)$, and $\downarrow(\alpha, i)$, where the parameter i ranges over $\mathbb{N}_1$. These correspond to the RTL event occurrence operators for operation events and have the following meanings:

1. $\leftarrow(\alpha, i)$ is the time of the invocation that created the ith instance of α. Equivalently, it is the send time of the ith invocation instance of α, since we enumerate these instances in the order of their creation.
2. $\rightarrow(\alpha, i)$ is the time that the ith instance of α is received (by the specific target object).
3. $\uparrow(\alpha, i)$ is the activation time of the ith invocation instance of α.
4. $\downarrow(\alpha, i)$ is the termination time of the ith invocation instance of α.

The parameters of these functions are those of α plus $i : \mathbb{N}_1$. Figure 6.2 shows a simple example of these times, used as annotations on a sequence diagram.

In UML terms, (α, i) can be considered as an instance of the behavior denoted by α, considered as a class [62, Sec. 13]. The times $\leftarrow(\alpha, i)$, $\rightarrow(\alpha, i)$, $\uparrow(\alpha, i)$, $\downarrow(\alpha, i)$ are the times of events associated with this instance (*MessageEvent*, *CallEvent*, and *ExecutionEvent*s, respectively). The semantics also relates directly to the concept of a *stimulus* in the UML profile for performance and time [40,63].

Local attributes of (α, i) are written as $(\alpha, i).att$ and are represented as attributes of the module, with parameters those of α, plus i, plus any defined for *att* itself. These attributes can represent local variables of α or denote the identity $(\alpha, i).sender$ of the sender of the request.

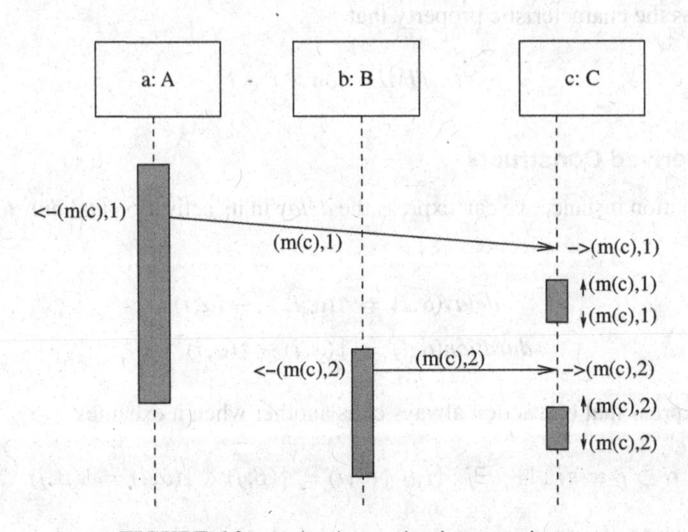

FIGURE 6.2 Action invocation instance times.

Notice that the $\leftarrow, \rightarrow, \uparrow, \downarrow$ times can be undefined (equivalently, equal to a non-finite time ∞ larger than any finite element of *TIME*, with the $\leftarrow, \rightarrow, \uparrow, \downarrow$ functions defined as ranging over $TIME^{\infty} = TIME \cup \{\infty\}$):

- $\leftarrow(\alpha, i)$ undefined means that no more than $i-1$ instances of α are created in the model. $\leftarrow(\alpha, j)$ is then undefined for $j > i$, and the times $\rightarrow(\alpha, i)$, $\uparrow(\alpha, i)$, $\downarrow(\alpha, i)$ are also undefined.
- $\leftarrow(\alpha, i)$ can be defined, with $\rightarrow(\alpha, i)$ undefined, meaning that the message is never received at its target object (a *lost* message in terms of UML interactions). In this case, $\uparrow(\alpha, i)$ and $\downarrow(\alpha, i)$ are also undefined.
- $\leftarrow(\alpha, i)$ and $\rightarrow(\alpha, i)$ can be defined with $\uparrow(\alpha, i)$ undefined, meaning that the message is received but is indefinitely delayed in being scheduled for execution. In this case, $\downarrow(\alpha, i)$ is also undefined.
- $\leftarrow(\alpha, i)$, $\rightarrow(\alpha, i)$, and $\uparrow(\alpha, i)$ can be defined with $\downarrow(\alpha, i)$ undefined, meaning that the invocation starts execution but does not terminate.

We can denote by $\overline{\alpha}$ the set of $i : \mathbb{N}_1$ such that $\leftarrow(\alpha, i)$ is defined. This is the set of invocation instances of α created in the model.

In the following we usually only consider cases of actions where all the times are defined. A quantification $\forall i : \mathbb{N}_1 \cdot P(\uparrow(\alpha, i))$ is taken to mean "for all i such that $\uparrow(\alpha, i)$ is defined, $P(\uparrow(\alpha, i))$" and similarly for the other invocation times.

The only other elements of the core language are predicates of the form $\varphi \circledcirc t$ "φ holds at time $t : TIME$," where φ is a predicate; and terms of the form $e \circledast t$ "the value of term e at time $t : TIME$." Otherwise, terms and formulas are constructed as for classical predicate calculus with equality and with connectives $\wedge, \vee, \Rightarrow, \neg, \forall$, and $\exists$. As usual, $\forall x \cdot x \in T \Rightarrow \varphi$ is abbreviated to $\forall x : T \cdot \varphi$. The connectives $\circledcirc$ and $\circledast$ bind more closely than any other binary operators. Thus, $x = y \circledast t$ means that $x = (y \circledast t)$.

now has the characteristic property that

$$\forall t : TIME \cdot now \circledast t = t$$

6.2.2 Derived Constructs

For each action instance we can express the *delay* in its activation and *duration* of its execution:

$$\begin{aligned} delay(\alpha, i) &= \uparrow(\alpha, i) - \rightarrow(\alpha, i) \\ duration(\alpha, i) &= \downarrow(\alpha, i) - \uparrow(\alpha, i) \end{aligned}$$

We can express that one action always calls another when it executes

$$\alpha \supset \beta \equiv \forall i : \mathbb{N}_1 \cdot \exists j : \mathbb{N}_1 \cdot \uparrow(\alpha, i) = \uparrow(\beta, j) \wedge \downarrow(\alpha, i) = \downarrow(\beta, j)$$

"α calls β." This is also used to express that α is defined by a (composite) action β.

The RTL event-occurrence operators $\clubsuit(\varphi := true, i)$ "the ith time that φ becomes true" and $\clubsuit(\varphi := false, i)$ "the ith time that φ becomes false" can also be defined.

Some important properties of $\supset$ are that it is transitive:

$$(\alpha \supset \beta) \wedge (\beta \supset \gamma) \Rightarrow (\alpha \supset \gamma)$$

and that statement constructs such as; and *if then else* (Section 6.2.8) are monotonic with respect to it:

$$(\alpha_1 \supset \alpha_2) \wedge (\beta_1 \supset \beta_2) \Rightarrow (\alpha_1 ; \beta_1 \ \supset \ \alpha_2 ; \beta_2)$$

and

$$(\alpha_1 \supset \alpha_2) \wedge (\beta_1 \supset \beta_2) \Rightarrow \textit{if } E \textit{ then } \alpha_1 \textit{ else } \beta_1 \ \supset \ \textit{if } E \textit{ then } \alpha_2 \textit{ else } \beta_2$$

In UML terms the input pool of messages of an object *obj* received and waiting to be processed are all those $m(obj, x), i$ instances of operations of *obj* for which $\rightarrow(m(obj, x), i) \leq now$ and $\uparrow(m(obj, x), i) > now$. x are the data input parameter values of the invocation of m.

We can define counters $\#req(\alpha)$, $\#act(\alpha)$, $\#fin(\alpha)$, and $\#snd(\alpha)$ for requests, activations, terminations, and invocations of action α:

1. $\#req(\alpha) \circledast t = card(\{j : \mathbb{N}_1 | \rightarrow(\alpha, j) \leq t\})$ (the number of distinct request events for α that have occurred so far)
2. $\#act(\alpha) \circledast t = card(\{j : \mathbb{N}_1 | \uparrow(\alpha, j) \leq t\})$
3. $\#fin(\alpha) \circledast t = card(\{j : \mathbb{N}_1 | \downarrow(\alpha, j) \leq t\})$
4. $\#snd(\alpha) \circledast t = card(\{j : \mathbb{N}_1 | \leftarrow(\alpha, j) \leq t\})$

The number of currently executing instances of α (at a time t) is therefore

$$\#active(\alpha) \circledast t = \#act(\alpha) \circledast t - \#fin(\alpha) \circledast t$$

while the number waiting to be activated is

$$\#waiting(\alpha) \circledast t = \#req(\alpha) \circledast t - \#act(\alpha) \circledast t$$

Using these counters, we can express a wide range of mutual exclusion, synchronization, and prioritization properties. For example, a set S of actions are *fully mutually exclusive*, $fmutex(S)$ if at most one instance of these actions can be executing at any time:

$$\forall t : TIME \cdot (\#active(\alpha_1) + \cdots + \#active(\alpha_n) \leq 1) \circledcirc t$$

where $S = \{\alpha_1, \ldots, \alpha_n\}$. In particular, if (the behavior of) an operation m is not reentrant, $fmutex(\{m\})$ holds. Properties such as absence of deadlock and starvation can also be expressed.

The operators $\bigcirc$ ("next"), $\Box$ ("always in the future"), and $\diamond$ ("eventually") of linear temporal logic can be defined in terms of the activation times of execution instances. For example, $\Box\phi$ ("ϕ holds at all future instants") is interpreted as meaning "ϕ holds at all future activation times of an action of the system":

$$
\begin{aligned}
(\Box_S \phi) \circledcirc t \equiv\ & \forall i : \mathbb{N}_1 \cdot \uparrow(\alpha_1, i) \geq t \Rightarrow \phi \circledcirc \uparrow(\alpha_1, i) \wedge \cdots \wedge \\
& \forall i : \mathbb{N}_1 \cdot \uparrow(\alpha_n, i) \geq t \Rightarrow \phi \circledcirc \uparrow(\alpha_n, i)
\end{aligned}
$$

where the set of actions is $S = \{\alpha_1, \ldots, \alpha_n\}$.

The motivation for this definition is that in a concurrent environment, invariant properties of a module must be true at all time points where the state of a system can be *observed*. At the specification level the effects of operations are defined by comparing the state at initiation of the operation to the state at termination. So states at the initiation and termination of operations are the critical "observable" points.

Similarly, we define $\bigcirc_S\phi$ and $\diamond_S\phi$. We usually drop the subscript S where it is clear from the context.

There are corresponding temporal operators which refer to *all* times:

$$(\Box^{\tau} \varphi) \circledcirc t \equiv \forall s : \mathit{TIME} \cdot s \geq t \Rightarrow \varphi \circledcirc s$$

Finally, the weakest precondition operator, $[\alpha]P$ "every execution of α establishes P" of B [1] and modal action logic [73] can be defined, where P may contain terms of the form $e@pre$, denoting the value of expression e at the initiation of α:

$$([\alpha]P) \circledcirc t \equiv \forall i : \mathbb{N}_1 \cdot \uparrow(\alpha, i) = t \Rightarrow P[e \circledast \uparrow(\alpha, i)/e@pre] \circledcirc \downarrow(\alpha, i)$$

$E[ex/v]$ denotes the substitution of expression(s) ex for identifier(s) v in E. In this substitution each pre-state expression $e@pre$ in P is replaced by the value $e \circledast \uparrow(\alpha, i)$ of e at initiation of α.

The [] operator can be used to express properties of action invocations concisely without requiring reference to the index of these invocations. It also provides a general way of expressing the effect of actions. Notice that $[\alpha]\mathit{false}$ means that executions of α started at the current time do not terminate.

6.2.3 Axioms of RAL

We take the axioms of classical predicate logic with equality in this language, with the following modifications.

The predicate logic axiom $\forall$-elimination:

$$(\forall v : T \cdot \varphi) \Rightarrow \varphi[e/v]$$

is valid only if e is free for the variable v in φ, and the substitution does not introduce new occurrences of attributes within modal operators ($\circledast$ and $\circledcirc$ in the core language) in φ. Similarly, the equality axiom

$$e_1 = e_2 \Rightarrow (\varphi[e_1/v] \equiv \varphi[e_2/v])$$

is asserted only when e_1 and e_2 are free for the variable v in φ, and all free occurrences of v in φ are outside the scope of a modal operator:

$$(\Box^{\tau}(e_1 = e_2)) \circledcirc 0 \Rightarrow (\varphi[e_1/v] \equiv \varphi[e_2/v])$$

for any formula φ, where e_1 and e_2 are terms free for the variable v in φ.

If v_i is a variable not free in the terms e or t, then

$$\exists v_i \cdot (v_i = e) \circledcirc t$$

The equality axiom

$$e = e$$

is valid for all terms e.

Variables act as logical constants over time:

$$\forall v_i : X \cdot \forall t : TIME \cdot v_i = v_i \circledast t$$

The core logical axioms assumed are

$$(C1) : \forall i : \mathbb{N}_1 \cdot \leftarrow(\alpha, i) \leq \leftarrow(\alpha, i+1)$$

for each action α. This expresses that the index i identifies an invocation instance of α by the order in which the request for the execution is sent:

$$(C2) : \forall i : \mathbb{N}_1 \cdot \leftarrow(\alpha, i) \leq \rightarrow(\alpha, i) \leq \uparrow(\alpha, i) \leq \downarrow(\alpha, i)$$

for each action α. "Each invocation instance must be sent before it is requested, requested before it can activate, and must activate before it can terminate".

This axiom does not require that executions initiate in the order of their requests, or are received in the order of their sending. These additional properties can be asserted by a constraint if required.

The *compactness* condition is that for all $p \in \mathbb{N}$ there are only finitely many $i : \mathbb{N}_1$ and $x : X$ such that $\uparrow(\alpha(x), i) < p$ for each action α. Similar conditions are required for the $\rightarrow$, $\leftarrow$, and $\downarrow$ times.

The *frame* axioms express that attributes of a module M can only change in value over intervals in which an action of M executes—these axioms are a form of *locality* property in the sense of Fiadeiro and Maibaum [22]:

For each attribute $att \in \mathrm{Att}(\Sigma)$, where Σ is the signature of M, let $\alpha_1, \ldots, \alpha_n$ be all the actions $\alpha \in \mathrm{Ac}(\Sigma)$ which have $att \in \mathcal{F}(\alpha)$. Then $Frame_{att}$ is the axiom

$$\begin{array}{l} \forall t1, t2 : TIME \cdot \\ \quad t1 < t2 \wedge att \circledast t1 \neq att \circledast t2 \Rightarrow \\ \quad\quad \exists t : TIME \cdot t1 \leq t < t2 \wedge \\ \quad\quad\quad ((\#active(\alpha_1) > 0) \circledcirc t \vee \cdots \vee (\#active(\alpha_n) > 0) \circledcirc t) \end{array}$$

In words: "If the value of *att* changes from $t1$ to $t2$, there must be an action with *att* in its write frame which executes in that interval".[2]

These axioms are particularly relevant when defining the meaning of subclassing. They are used to define a class as being an "open" or "extendible" type in the sense of Simons [74]: New behavior and data can be added to a class but must preserve the behavior of the superclass.

($C3$): *Axioms for* $\circledcirc$: for all $t : TIME$:

$$
\begin{aligned}
(\varphi \circledcirc s) \circledcirc t &\equiv \varphi \circledcirc (s \circledast t) \\
(\varphi \wedge \phi) \circledcirc t &\equiv \varphi \circledcirc t \wedge \phi \circledcirc t \\
(\varphi \vee \phi) \circledcirc t &\equiv \varphi \circledcirc t \vee \phi \circledcirc t \\
(\varphi \Rightarrow \phi) \circledcirc t &\equiv (\varphi \circledcirc t \Rightarrow \phi \circledcirc t) \\
(\neg \varphi) \circledcirc t &\equiv \neg (\varphi \circledcirc t) \\
(\forall v : T \cdot \varphi) \circledcirc t &\equiv \forall v : T \cdot (\varphi \circledcirc t) \\
(\exists v : T \cdot \varphi) \circledcirc t &\equiv \exists v : T \cdot (\varphi \circledcirc t)
\end{aligned}
$$

In the last two cases, v must not be free in t.

($C4$): *Axioms for* $\circledast$:

$$\varphi \circledcirc t \equiv \varphi^{*t}$$

where φ contains no modal operators, and φ^{*t} is φ with each outermost term e occurring in a subformula replaced by $e \circledast t$, where $t : TIME$ has no free variables.

Also ($C5$):

$$g(e_1, \ldots, e_n) \circledast t = g(e_1 \circledast t, \ldots, e_n \circledast t)$$

for each $g \in \mathrm{F}(\Sigma)$ of arity n, $t : TIME$.

$C3$, $C4$, and $C5$ are essential to prove the completeness of the RAL formalism with respect to its denotational semantics [37].

The usual concept of inference, denoted by $\vdash$, is taken. The inference rules are those of classical predicate calculus: modus ponens and $\forall$-introduction. In addition, there is the rule of $\Box^{\tau}$-introduction: From

$$\Gamma \vdash \varphi$$

derive

$$\Gamma \vdash \forall t : TIME \cdot \varphi \circledcirc t$$

6.2.4 Theory Refinement and Composition

RAL supports modular specification to decompose a system into analyzable parts. We use this to structure the UML semantics into theories at the three levels of objects,

[2] When α_i has parameters $x_i : X_i$, we use $(\exists x_i : X_i \cdot \#active(\alpha_i(x_i)) > 0) \circledcirc t$ in the conclusion.

classes, and subsystems (submodels). The principal way in which theories can be combined is via morphisms between the theories.

6.2.5 Theory Morphisms

Let M and M' be two theories with signatures Σ and Σ', respectively.

A *signature morphism* $\sigma : \Sigma \to \Sigma'$ must map attribute symbols to attribute symbols, action symbols to action symbols, and so on, and preserve the arities of these symbols:

$$\sigma(\!|\mathrm{Att}(\Sigma)|\!) \subseteq \mathrm{Att}(\Sigma')$$

$$\sigma(\!|\mathrm{Ac}(\Sigma)|\!) \subseteq \mathrm{Ac}(\Sigma')$$

$$\sigma(\!|\mathrm{T}(\Sigma)|\!) \subseteq \mathrm{T}(\Sigma')$$

$$\sigma(\!|\mathrm{P}(\Sigma)|\!) \subseteq \mathrm{P}(\Sigma')$$

$$\sigma(\!|\mathrm{F}(\Sigma)|\!) \subseteq \mathrm{F}(\Sigma')$$

with the arity in Σ' of $\sigma(f)$ being the same as $arity(f)$ in Σ for each $f \in \mathrm{F}(\Sigma) \cup \mathrm{P}(\Sigma) \cup \mathrm{Ac}(\Sigma) \cup \mathrm{Att}(\Sigma)$, and with parameter types also translated via σ for corresponding function, predicate, attribute, and action symbols in the two theories.

Normally, σ maps the standard types *TIME*, $\mathbb{N}$, and so on, in M to the corresponding types in M'.

For each action symbol $\alpha \in \mathrm{Ac}(\Sigma)$,

$$\mathcal{F}(\sigma(\alpha)) \subseteq \sigma(\!|\mathcal{F}(\alpha)|\!)$$

In other words, the frame of an action may become more restrictive in M'.

σ can be extended to general terms and formulas of M in the usual way, so that $\sigma(t)$ is a term of M' if t is a term of M, and so on.

σ is a *theory morphism* if

$$M \vdash \varphi \Rightarrow M' \vdash \sigma(\varphi)$$

for each formula φ of M.

In particular, this means that the frame axiom for each attribute *att* of M must be true in interpreted form in M':

$$\begin{aligned}
&\forall t1, t2 : \mathit{TIME} \cdot \\
&\qquad t1 < t2 \wedge \sigma(\mathit{att}) \circledast t1 \neq \sigma(\mathit{att}) \circledast t2 \Rightarrow \\
&\qquad\quad \exists t : \mathit{TIME} \cdot t1 \leq t < t2 \wedge \\
&\qquad\qquad ((\#\mathit{active}(\sigma(\alpha_1)) > 0) \circledcirc t \vee \cdots \vee (\#\mathit{active}(\sigma(\alpha_n)) > 0) \circledcirc t)
\end{aligned}$$

where the α_i are all the actions of M with *att* in their write frame. In other words, (the interpretation of) *att* can only change value over intervals where (the interpretation of) one of its updating actions of M is executing. But this means that every new action

$$\beta \in \mathrm{Ac}(\Sigma') \setminus \sigma(\!|\mathrm{Ac}(\Sigma)|\!)$$

which has $\sigma(att)$ in $\mathcal{F}(\beta)$ coexecutes with (or calls) one of the $\sigma(\alpha_i)$.

This form of encapsulation of data is similar to that found in languages such as B [1], or in the subtyping definition of Liskov and Wing [55]: Only the actions declared in the same module as a particular data item can write that data directly. Actions of other modules must invoke these actions in order to change the data. This enables simpler proof of invariant properties of a class, by induction on the invocations of operations that may affect the invariant.

6.2.6 Class and Instance Theories

In an object-oriented system, we may have theories $\mathcal{I}_C$ representing a *typical instance* (or *object*) of a class C, and a theory Γ_C representing the class itself (including all its current instances) [8].

RAL attributes will represent UML instance scope and class scope attributes, roles (association ends), and query operations (collectively referred to as *data features*), and RAL actions will represent instance and class scope update operations. An instance theory $\mathcal{I}_C$ will have an attribute $att : X'$ for each declared attribute $att : X$ in the text of a UML class C for each query operation of C and for each opposite association end of an association attached to C. X' is a semantic type corresponding to X. There will be an action $\alpha(X')$ for each update operation with input parameter type X.

In instance theories, instance-level properties can be proved, independent of object identity. In the class theory these properties then become available as theorems about all objects of the class.

We represent class scope (static) features in the instance theories, since these features are available at the instance level. Their special property is that their values are always identical in every instance, this follows since there is a single semantic representation of the static feature.

In the class theory Γ_C, there will be a type $@C$ of possible instances of C and an attribute

$$\overline{C} : \mathbb{F}(@C)$$

representing the set of currently existing instances, together with actions $kill_C(@C)$ and $create_C(@C)$ to delete and add elements to this set. $\overline{C}$ corresponds to $C.allInstances()$ in OCL [65].

Every element of $\overline{C}$ will have an associated value for each data feature $f : X$ declared in the class. An additional parameter of type $@C$ representing the object is added to each (instance scope) attribute $att : X'$ and action $\alpha(X')$ of $\mathcal{I}_C$ to produce a parameterized attribute or action of Γ_C:

$$att(@C) : X'$$

$$\alpha(@C, X')$$

For a in $@C$ we usually write $att(a)$ as $a.att$ and $\alpha(a, x)$ as $a.\alpha(x)$ for consistency with standard OO notation.

Attributes or actions that represent class scope (static) features do not gain the additional parameter.

This general construction is termed an *A-morphism* [21], where A is the set of object identifiers/references, and this involves a modified form of signature morphism $\sigma : \Sigma \to \Sigma'$ in which

$$\begin{aligned} arity(\sigma(att)) &= arity(att) + 1 \\ arity(\sigma(\alpha)) &= arity(\alpha) + 1 \end{aligned}$$

where $att \in \mathrm{Att}(\Sigma)$ and $\alpha \in \mathrm{Ac}(\Sigma)$ are of instance scope. The new parameter has type $A \in \mathrm{T}(\Sigma')$ and is the first parameter of $\sigma(att)$ or $\sigma(\alpha)$ in the second theory. Otherwise, σ is as defined previously.

The analogy of a theory morphism in this case is that

$$M \vdash \varphi \Rightarrow M' \vdash \forall a : A \cdot a.\sigma(\varphi)$$

where $a.\psi$ is ψ with a substituted into each new parameter slot created by the morphism.

We construct the class theory Γ_C as a combination of $\mathcal{I}_C$ via a $@C$-morphism, and a generic *class manager* theory M via a theory morphism μ:

$$\begin{aligned} @X &\longmapsto @C \\ \overline{X} &\longmapsto \overline{C} \\ create_X &\longmapsto create_C \\ kill_X &\longmapsto kill_C \end{aligned}$$

Figure 6.3 shows this structure.

M has type symbol $@X$, attribute $\overline{X} : \mathbb{F}(@X)$, actions $create_X(@X)$ and $kill_X(@X)$, and axioms

$$\begin{aligned} (\overline{X} &= \{\}) \circledcirc 0 \\ \forall a : @X \cdot [create_X(a)](\overline{X} &= \overline{X}@pre \cup \{a\}) \\ \forall a : @X \cdot [kill_X(a)](\overline{X} &= \overline{X}@pre - \{a\}) \end{aligned}$$

The frames of $kill_X$ and $create_X$ are both $\{\overline{X}\}$.

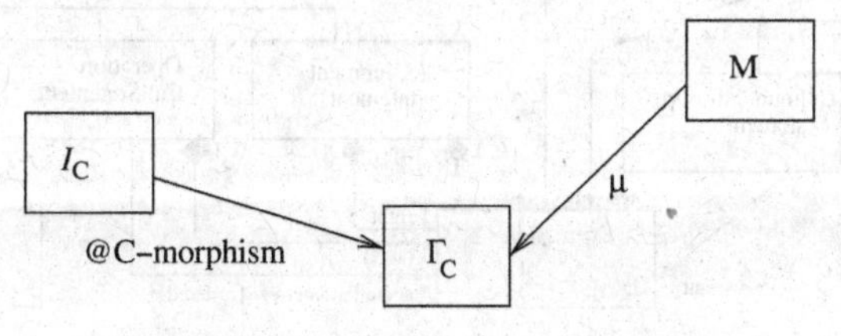

FIGURE 6.3 Class theory construction.

6.2.7 Time Variables

In the specification of real-time or hybrid systems, two types of attributes can be identified:

1. Discrete data, corresponding to discrete data in the real world, or discretized approximations of continuous data
2. Continuous data, or "time variables"

Both can be represented by RAL attributes. However, whereas discrete variables are conventional variables of a computational system, time variables represent physical quantities and may vary as arbitrary functions of time. The prime example of a time variable, included in every instance theory, is the attribute *now* : *TIME*, which satisfies the axiom

$$\forall t : TIME \cdot now \circledast t = t$$

6.2.8 Composite and Procedural Actions

We introduce a small procedural language (Figure 6.4) to allow procedural-style definitions of behavior for UML operations. Normally, $\leftarrow(S,i) = \rightarrow(S,i) = \uparrow(S,i)$ is assumed for such composed actions S, since they are normally invoked by the same object on which they execute.

Assignment $t_1 := t_2$ can be defined as the action $\alpha_{t_1:=t_2}$, where t_1 is an attribute symbol, the write frame of this action is $\{t_1\}$, and

$$\forall i : \mathbb{N}_1 \cdot t_1 \circledast \downarrow(\alpha_{t_1:=t_2}, i) = t_2 \circledast \uparrow(\alpha_{t_1:=t_2}, i)$$

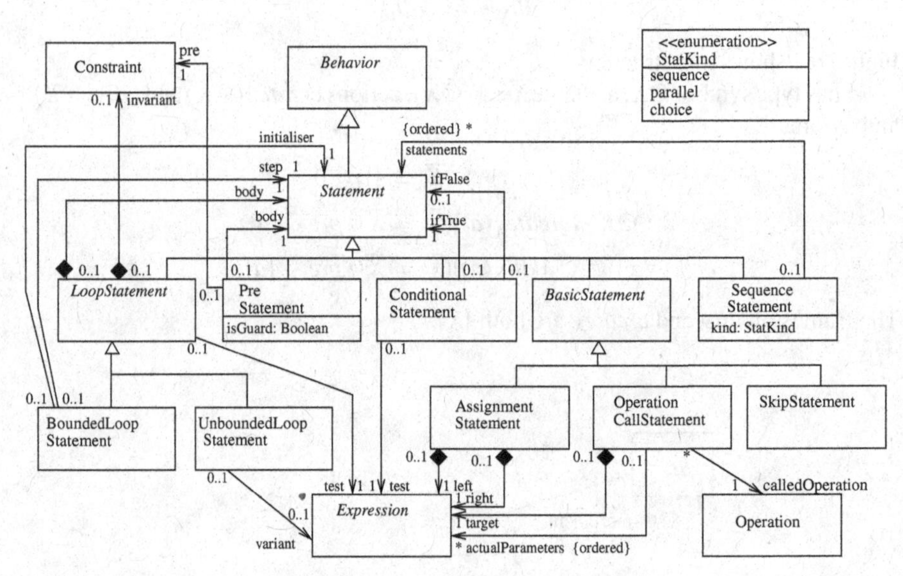

FIGURE 6.4 Statement metamodel.

For formulas P without time variables, occurrences of modal operators or *@pre*, this means that

$$([\alpha_{t_1:=t_2}]P) \circledcirc t \equiv P[t_2/t_1] \circledcirc t$$

as usual for assignment, if no other action coexecutes with this action.

Similarly, sequential composition ; and parallel composition || of actions can be expressed as derived combinators:

$$\forall i : \mathbb{N}_1 \cdot \exists j,k : \mathbb{N}_1 \cdot \uparrow(\alpha;\beta,i) = \uparrow(\alpha,j) \wedge \downarrow(\alpha;\beta,i) = \downarrow(\beta,k) \wedge \uparrow(\beta,k) = \downarrow(\alpha,j)$$

and

$$\forall j,k : \mathbb{N}_1 \cdot \uparrow(\beta,k) = \downarrow(\alpha,j) \Rightarrow \exists i : \mathbb{N}_1 \cdot \uparrow(\alpha;\beta,i) = \uparrow(\alpha,j) \wedge \downarrow(\alpha;\beta,i) = \downarrow(\beta,k)$$

These two conditions yield the usual axiom that $[\alpha;\beta]\varphi \equiv [\alpha][\beta]\varphi$ for φ without occurrences of *@pre*.

For parallel $\gamma = \alpha || \beta$ ((i.e.), a *SequenceStatement* with *kind* = *parallel*):

$$\forall i : \mathbb{N}_1 \cdot \exists j,k : \mathbb{N}_1 \cdot$$
$$\uparrow(\gamma,i) = \uparrow(\alpha,j) \wedge \uparrow(\gamma,i) = \uparrow(\beta,k) \wedge \downarrow(\gamma,i) = \downarrow(\beta,k) \wedge \downarrow(\gamma,i) = \downarrow(\alpha,j)$$

and

$$\forall j,k : \mathbb{N}_1 \cdot \uparrow(\beta,k) = \uparrow(\alpha,j) \wedge \downarrow(\beta,k) = \downarrow(\alpha,j) \Rightarrow$$
$$\exists i : \mathbb{N}_1 \cdot \uparrow(\gamma,i) = \uparrow(\alpha,j) \wedge \downarrow(\gamma,i) = \downarrow(\alpha,j)$$

The usual property,

$$(P_1 \Rightarrow [\alpha]Q_1) \wedge (P_2 \Rightarrow [\beta]Q_2) \Rightarrow (P_1 \wedge P_2 \Rightarrow [\gamma](Q_1 \wedge Q_2))$$

can be derived. The ; and || composite actions have as write frames the union of the write frames of their component actions.

Unguarded choice $\alpha = \text{S1}[]\ \text{S2}$ is represented by a *SequenceStatement* with *kind* = *choice*. This is defined to have

$$\textit{forall } i : \mathbb{N}_1 \cdot \exists j : \mathbb{N}_1 \cdot \uparrow(\alpha,i) = \uparrow(\text{S1},j) \wedge \downarrow(\alpha,i) = \downarrow(\text{S1},j) \vee$$
$$\exists j : \mathbb{N}_1 \cdot \uparrow(\alpha,i) = \uparrow(\text{S2},j) \wedge \downarrow(\alpha,i) = \downarrow(\text{S2},j)$$

together with the dual properties that every instance of S1 is an instance of α, and every instance of S2 is an instance of α.

Conditional actions α representing *if E then* S_1 *else* S_2 are defined to have the properties

$$\forall i : \mathbb{N}_1 \cdot E \circledcirc \uparrow(\alpha,i) \Rightarrow \exists j : \mathbb{N}_1 \cdot \uparrow(\alpha,i) = \uparrow(S_1,j) \wedge \downarrow(\alpha,i) = \downarrow(S_1,j)$$

and

$$\forall i : \mathbb{N}_1 \cdot \neg E \circledcirc \uparrow(\alpha, i) \Rightarrow \exists j : \mathbb{N}_1 \cdot \uparrow(\alpha, i) = \uparrow(S_2, j) \land \downarrow(\alpha, i) = \downarrow(S_2, j)$$

Occurrences of *if E then* S_1 *else* S_2 are either occurrences of S_1 if E holds at commencement of this action, or occurrences of S_2, if $\neg E$ holds. This action has as write frame the union of those of S_1 and S_2.

Occurrences of *while E do S* are a sequence of occurrences $(S, i_1), \ldots, (S, i_n)$ of S, where E holds at the commencement of each of these actions and where E fails to hold at termination of (S, i_n). The *while* action has the same write frame as S. Bounded loops can be defined in terms of unbounded loops.

Preconditioned actions β: *pre Pre then S* are defined to have

$$\forall i : \mathbb{N}_1 \cdot Pre \circledcirc \uparrow(\beta, i) \Rightarrow \exists j : \mathbb{N}_1 \cdot \uparrow(\beta, i) = \uparrow(S, j) \land \downarrow(\beta, i) = \downarrow(S, j)$$

and

$$\forall i : \mathbb{N}_1 \cdot Pre \circledcirc \uparrow(S, i) \Rightarrow \exists j : \mathbb{N}_1 \cdot \uparrow(\beta, j) = \uparrow(S, i) \land \downarrow(\beta, j) = \downarrow(S, i)$$

A *guard* has, in addition, the property that *Pre* always holds at the start of β:

$$\forall i : \mathbb{N}_1 \cdot Pre \circledcirc \uparrow(\beta, i)$$

The relationship

$$S_1 \ \textit{invokes}\ S_2$$

between composed actions that S_1 contains (syntactically) an invocation of S_2 is defined inductively by *S invokes S*, and that

$$S_1 \ \textit{invokes}\ S_2 \Rightarrow C(S_1) \ \textit{invokes}\ S_2$$

for any construct C of actions: sequence, parallel, conditional, loop, pre.

6.3 SEMANTICS OF CLASS DIAGRAMS

The semantics of a class diagram model M is constructed in a modular fashion [7] from *instance theories* $\mathcal{I}_C$ of typical instances of classes C of the model, and *class theories* Γ_C of these classes, and *subsystem theories* Γ_S of subsystems S of the model. These are composed together to define a theory Γ_M of the complete model. In the following sections we show how these theories are constructed incrementally from the elements of a class diagram.

6.3.1 Types

A model may define enumerated types T as enumerations of enumeration literals $val_1, \ldots, val_n$. That is, T is an instance of the *Enumeration* metatype, and

$$T.ownedLiteral = Sequence\{val_1, \ldots, val_n\}$$

These types are represented in a theory Γ_T with no action symbols and with a type symbol T defined as the appropriate finite set:

$$(ETD): \qquad T = \{val_1, \ldots, val_n\}$$

The val_i are defined as distinct constants of Γ_T (attributes that are not in the write frame of any action).

The primitive types *Integer*, *Real*, and *Boolean* are interpreted by the corresponding mathematical data types $\mathbb{Z}$, $\mathbb{R}$, and $\mathbb{B} = \{TRUE, FALSE\}$. *String* is interpreted as the type $\mathbb{S}$ of sequences of characters. $\mathbb{B}$ and $\mathbb{S}$ are disjoint from $\mathbb{R}$ and from any enumerated type. All enumerated types are also disjoint from $\mathbb{R}$, $\mathbb{B}$, and $\mathbb{S}$.

6.3.2 Data Features

If classifier C declares attributes $att_1 : T_1, \ldots, att_n : T_n$, that is,

$$C.ownedAttribute = Sequence\{att_1, \ldots, att_n\}$$

with each $att_i : Property$ having $att_i.type = T_i$, then $\mathcal{I}_C$ has corresponding semantic attributes $att_1 : T_1', \ldots, att_n : T_n'$ where T' is the semantic interpretation of type T.

If an enumerated type T is used in an attribute declaration, $\mathcal{I}_C$ is defined to extend the theory Γ_T.

If there is an association from C to a classifier D (Figure 6.5), $r : Association$ with $r.memberEnd = Sequence\{p_1, p_2\}$ and $p_1.type = C$, $p_2.type = D$, any role p_2 at the D association end is represented in $\mathcal{I}_C$ as an attribute

$$(RTD): \quad p_2 : DT$$

where DT is a type built from the type symbol $@D$ representing the type of possible instances of D. Table 6.1 shows the different cases of possible multiplicities M of *role* and the corresponding DT type, and any additional axiom included in $\mathcal{I}_C$.

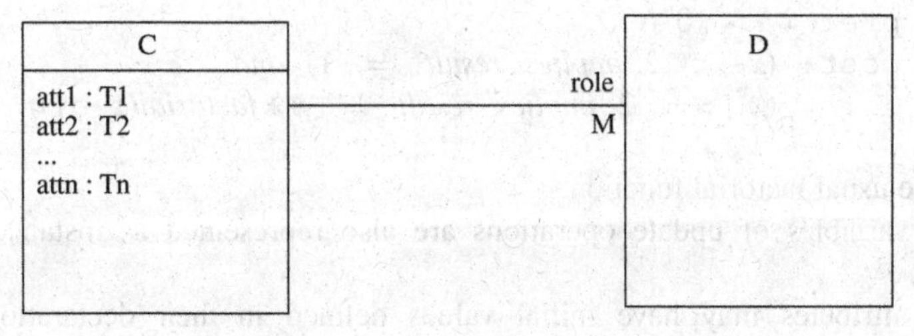

FIGURE 6.5 Classifier definitions in UML.

TABLE 6.1 Representation of Role Multiplicities

Multiplicity M	Semantic Type DT	Axiom
1	$@D$	
a..b	$\mathbb{F}(@D)$	$a \leq card(p_2) \wedge card(p_2) \leq b$
a	$\mathbb{F}(@D)$	$a = card(p_2)$
a..*	$\mathbb{F}(@D)$	$a \leq card(p_2)$
*	$\mathbb{F}(@D)$	

When the D association end is $\{ordered\}$, the sequence type $seq(@D)$ is used instead of $\mathbb{F}(@D)$.

In $\mathcal{I}_C$ we also include a Boolean attribute $exists_C : \mathbb{B}$, which indicates if *self* currently exists as a valid object (i.e., if creation has occurred more recently than deletion).

Query operations $f(p_1 : PT_1, \ldots, p_n : PT_n) : RT$ of C (i.e., f in $C.ownedOperation$ with $f.isQuery = true$) are also represented as (constant) attributes

$$(FTD): \quad f(p_1 : PT_1', \ldots, p_n : PT_n') : RT'$$

of $\mathcal{I}_C$, where T' denotes the semantic representation of type T.

The definition of f is assumed to be given by a pre-/postcondition pair in which the *result* parameter is used in the postcondition to denote the intended value of the query:

$$\begin{aligned} &f(p: \ PT): \ RT \\ &\quad \texttt{pre:} \ Pre_f \\ &\quad \texttt{post:} \ Post_f \end{aligned}$$

This definition is expressed semantically by the axiom

$$(FDef): \quad exists_C = TRUE \Rightarrow (\forall p : PT' \cdot Pre_f' \Rightarrow Post_f'[f(p)/result])$$

For example:

```
factorial(x : Integer) : Integer
pre: x > 0
post: (x < 2 implies result = 1) and
      (x >= 2 implies result = x * factorial(x - 1))
```

defines the usual factorial function.

Local variables of update operations are also represented as instance theory attributes.

UML attributes may have initial values defined in their declarations (i.e., $att.initialValue : Expression$). These values are defined using pure literal values without any feature occurrences. The collection of all such initializations $att_i = e_i$ are grouped together into a single new action $init_C$, defined as

$$(InitDef): \qquad init_C \supset att_1 := e'_1 \mid\mid \cdots \mid\mid att_n := e'_n \mid\mid exists_C := TRUE$$

This has write frame $\{att_1, \ldots, att_n, exists_C\}$.

This action will in turn be invoked by the $create_C(a)$ action of the class theory (Section 6.3.8).

A $terminate_C$ action destroys the object:

$$(TermDef): \qquad terminate_C \supset exists_C := FALSE$$

Its write frame is $\{exists_C\}$.

6.3.3 Operations

For each modifiable attribute $att : T$ of a class C there is assumed to be an operation $setatt(attx : T)$ which has the effect $post : att = attx$. It has a write frame including att, but may need to modify other attributes in addition (to maintain invariants). *frozen* attributes do not have such operations. Similarly, for each modifiable rolename *role* on the opposite end of an association incident to C, there is a *setrole* operation, and *addrole* and *removerole* operations if *role* is not of multiplicity 1 (*removerole* is omitted if *role* is addOnly). These operations all have a standard definition: for example,

$addrole(rolex \; : \; D)$
  pre: $(role \rightarrow including(rolex)) \rightarrow size() \;\leq\; b$
  post: $role \;=\; role@pre \rightarrow including(rolex)$

in the case of an unordered role of maximum cardinality b. All of these operations are represented as corresponding actions of $\mathcal{I}_C$.

If feature f has private visibility, so should its associated operations, and similarly, the operations of protected and public features should have the same visibility as their features. Any other class that modifies a feature of C should do so by invoking its *set* operation or *add*/*remove* operations. This ensures the validity of the frame axiom of C.

User-defined update operations of C are also represented by actions of $\mathcal{I}_C$, with the same arity and set of input parameters. The declaration

$m(x_1 : \; X_1, \; \ldots, \; x_n : \; X_n)$
  pre: Pre_m
  post: $Post_m$

yields an action symbol $m(X'_1, \ldots, X'_n)$ of $\mathcal{I}_C$ and the axiom (OpD):

$$\forall i : \mathbb{N}_1; x_1 : X'_1; \ldots; x_n : X'_n$$
$$(exists_C = TRUE \wedge Pre'_m) \circledcirc \uparrow(m(x_1, \ldots, x_n), i) \Rightarrow$$
$$Post'_m[att \circledast \uparrow(m(x_1, \ldots, x_n), i)/att@pre] \circledcirc \downarrow(m(x_1, \ldots, x_n), i)$$

In other words, if the precondition holds at the commencement of an execution of $m(x_1, \ldots, x_n)$, the postcondition holds at termination, with each *att@pre* expression interpreted as the value of *att* at commencement.

This is the usual concept of precondition, in which no properties of the execution of the operation can be deduced if it is executed outside its precondition. This definition is used in languages such as B and Eiffel [57]. Alternative possible semantics are skip/ignore semantics (the operation is executed but has no effect if the precondition fails) and blocking semantics (the operation blocks its caller and does not execute until the precondition becomes true).

UML does not specify which interpretation of a precondition should be used: "The behaviour of an invocation of an operation when a precondition is not satisfied is a semantic variation point" [62, p. 107] and "... corresponds semantically to a precondition violation, for which no predefined behaviour is defined in UML" [62, p. 534].

The semantics of a precondition as a permission guard is stated [65, Sec. 12.7]: "The precondition must evaluate to true whenever the operation starts executing." Instead, our semantics uses the most general assumption that it may be possible for an operation to be executed when its precondition fails, but that no guarantee then can be made about its behavior (an implementation may throw an exception, or skip, or block, for example). A separate proof obligation requires that callers ensure that the precondition is true at the point where they make the call.

The *write frame* of an operation is the set of modifiable (nonfrozen) attributes or roles *att* that it may change. This is calculated as the set of those attributes *att* which occur in one of two forms:

1. In prestate form *att@pre* in $Post_m$.
2. In a *writable modality* in $Post_m$, that is, in a subformula $att = exp$, $att \rightarrow includes(exp)$, $att \rightarrow excludes(exp)$, $att \rightarrow excludesAll(exp)$ (except for addOnly roles *att* in these last two cases), $att \rightarrow includesAll(exp)$, and where *exp* does not involve *att* except in the form *att@pre*.

The *in* parameters of an operation cannot be modified in its postcondition.

If an update operation is defined by a procedural code using the metamodel of Figure 6.4:

$$m(x : X)$$
$$\texttt{pre } Pre_m \texttt{ then } Code_m$$

this is also represented by an action symbol $m(X')$ of $\mathcal{I}_C$ with write frame calculated from the form of $Code_m$ as for composite actions in Section 6.2.8

In either case, we assume that the operation definition is *complete*: Any change to an attribute that is required to take place as a result of the operation is defined explicitly in its postcondition or code: for example, changes to the value of a derived attribute resulting from a direct update of one of its defining features.

$Code_m$ can be interpreted as an RAL composite action $Code'_m$ in $\mathcal{I}_C$, and the effect of m expressed by the axiom

$$(OpP): \quad \forall x : X' \cdot m(x) \supset (pre\ exists_C = true \wedge Pre'_m\ then\ Code'_m)$$

In other words, if $m(x)$ is invoked when the object exists and the precondition holds, we are guaranteed to get the behavior specified by $Code_m$.

If $Code_m$ itself involves operation calls $a.n(e)$ for $a : D$, or a collection a of D objects, these are interpreted in $Code'_m$ as actions $invoke_n(a', e')$ with empty write frames. Similarly, a creation invocation $new_D(a)$ is interpreted as the action $create\_invoke_D(a')$ with an empty write frame. These operations have no effect on the local state but will be linked with the behaviors they invoke in subsystem theories (Section 6.3.9).

Inconsistency between operation postconditions and class invariants can be detected by internal consistency checking using a proof tool such as B [6]. Although the semantics presented here can represent update operations defined in a self or mutually recursive manner, these cannot be translated to B for semantic analysis, since B does not permit such operations. However, query operations can be defined recursively; these are translated as recursive functions (constant data) in B.

6.3.4 Expression Semantics

In this section we define the mathematical interpretation of OCL in our semantics. For primitive literal expressions e: numbers, strings, Booleans, and elements of enumerations, the semantic denotation e' of e corresponds directly to e (Table 6.2). If v and w are two distinct enumeration literals (of the same or different enumerations), their semantic denotations satisfy $v' \neq w'$. If v and w are syntactically the same but belong to two distinct enumerations, $v' \neq w'$. Otherwise, $v' = w'$. The UML superstructure leaves this semantic aspect undefined [62, Sec. 7.3.16].

Also, for any enumeration literal v, $v' \notin \mathbb{R}$, $v' \notin \mathbb{B}$, $v' \notin \mathbb{S}$, and $v' \notin @C$ for any class C.

We consider only two kinds of collections (sets and sequences), and restrict these to consist only of elements of a single type, as in UML OCL 2.0 [65]. This type

TABLE 6.2 Semantic Mapping for Primitive Literals

OCL Term e	Semantics e'
number n	n
true	*TRUE*
false	*FALSE*
String "t"	Sequence denoted "t" consisting of characters of t in left to right order
val from enumeration T	Representation of $T :: val$

can be either a numeric type, Boolean type, string type, a particular enumeration, or a particular class. Apart from elements of subclasses of a common superclass, mixtures of elements of different types are not allowed.

Collection literal expressions have a direct interpretation: A set literal $Set\{e_1, \ldots, e_n\}$ is interpreted by the mathematical set $\{e'_1, \ldots, e'_n\}$. This has type $\mathbb{F}(T)$, where T is the semantic representation of the common type of the elements of the set. A sequence literal $Sequence\{e_1, \ldots, e_n\}$ is interpreted by the mathematical sequence s of length n, which has $s(1) = e'_1, \ldots, s(n) = e'_n$. This is also written as $[e'_1, \ldots, e'_n]$. The typing of s is a sequence $1..n \rightarrow T$, where T is the semantic representation of the common type of the elements.

An identifier *var* denoting an attribute or role name of a class C is represented by the corresponding RAL attribute *var* in $\mathcal{I}_C$.

Numeric operators such as *, +, /, − are represented as corresponding function symbols of arity 2 on $\mathbb{R}$. The definitions of UML OCL 2.0 [65] are used; likewise for *abs*, *floor*, >, <, <=, >=, *div*, and *mod*. The logical operators are interpreted by the corresponding semantic operators: *and* by $\wedge$, *or* by $\vee$, *not* by $\neg$, and *implies* by $\Rightarrow$.

size, =, and + (*concat*) are defined on strings as in UML OCL 2.0 [65]. Equality of strings means that they have the same characters in the same order (as in sequence equality). Similarly, the Boolean operators *or*, *and*, *not*, and *implies* are defined according to the usual truth tables on $\mathbb{B}$.

Operators on a collection considered as a single object (such as its size) are written following an arrow symbol from the collection: for example,

$$Set\{1, 5, 6\} \rightarrow size()$$

is 3. *max* and *min* apply to nonempty sets of elements (numerics or strings) comparable by $\leq$. For a nonempty set s, $(s \rightarrow max())'$ is the unique element x of s' such that

$$y \in s' \Rightarrow y \leq x$$

Similarly, $(s \rightarrow min())'$ is the unique element z of s' such that

$$y \in s' \Rightarrow z \leq y$$

On collections, the operators *includes*, *excludes*, *includesAll*, *excludesAll*, and *size* are given the usual definitions of membership, nonmembership, subset, disjointness, and cardinality. Table 6.3 shows some examples of interpretations of collection operators.

The operators *union* and *intersection* are defined in terms of their mathematical counterparts (Table 6.4); *union* on sequences is defined to be the same as concatenation, as in UML OCL 2.0 [66].

Sequence-specific operations are defined in Table 6.5. *including* for a sequence is defined as *append*. $s \rightarrow excluding(x)$ for sequence s is defined as $s \rightarrow select(self \neq x)$ (see Table 6.8).

Table 6.6 shows the semantics of navigation expressions on single objects.

TABLE 6.3 Semantic Mapping for Collection Operations

OCL Term e	Condition	Semantics e'
$s \rightarrow size()$	collection s	cardinality $card(s')$
$s \rightarrow includes(x)$	set s	$x' \in s'$
$s \rightarrow excludes(x)$	set s	$x' \notin s'$
$s \rightarrow includes(x)$	sequence s	$x' \in \text{ran}(s')$
$s \rightarrow excludes(x)$	sequence s	$x' \notin \text{ran}(s')$
$s \rightarrow asSet()$	s set	s'
	s sequence	$\text{ran}(s')$
$s \rightarrow includesAll(t)$	sets s and t	$t' \subseteq s'$
	sequences s and t	$\text{ran}(t') \subseteq \text{ran}(s')$
$s \rightarrow excludesAll(t)$	sets s and t	$s' \cap t' = \{\}$
	sequences s and t	$\text{ran}(s') \cap \text{ran}(t') = \{\}$
$s \rightarrow sum()$	set s	sum of elements of s'
	sequence s, $card(s') = n$	$s'(1) + \cdots + s'(n)$

TABLE 6.4 Semantic Mapping for Collection Construction Operations

OCL Term e	Condition	Semantics e'
$s \rightarrow union(t)$	s and t sets	$s' \cup t'$
	s and t sequences	$s' \frown t'$
$s \rightarrow intersection(t)$	s and t sets	$s' \cap t'$
$s \rightarrow excluding(t)$	s a set	$s' - \{t'\}$
$s \rightarrow including(t)$	s a set	$s' \cup \{t'\}$

TABLE 6.5 Semantic Mapping for Sequence Operations

OCL Term e	Condition	Semantics e'
$s = t$	s and t sequences	$s' = t'$ as maps
$s \rightarrow first()$	nonempty sequence s	$s'(1)$
$s \rightarrow last()$	nonempty sequence s	$s'(card(s'))$
$s \rightarrow front()$	nonempty sequence or string s	subsequence $[s'(1), \ldots, s'(card(s') - 1)]$ of s'
$s \rightarrow tail()$	nonempty sequence or string s	subsequence $[s'(2), \ldots, s'(card(s'))]$ of s'
$s \rightarrow sort()$	sequence s	reordering of s' such that elements are in nondescending $<$ order
$s \rightarrow reverse()$	sequence s, $n = card(s')$	$\{i \mapsto s'(n - i + 1) \mid i \in \text{dom}(s')\}$
$s \rightarrow append(x)$	sequence s	$s' \frown [x']$
$s \rightarrow prepend(x)$	sequence s	$[x'] \frown s'$
$s \rightarrow subSequence(i,j)$	sequence s	subsequence $[s'(i), \ldots, s'(j)]$ of s'

TABLE 6.6 Semantic Mapping for Navigation Expressions on Objects

OCL Term e	Condition	Semantics e'
$obj.att$	attribute att	$att(obj')$
$obj.role$	1-multiplicity role	$role(obj')$
	unordered collection-valued role	set $role(obj')$
	ordered collection-valued role	sequence $role(obj')$

TABLE 6.7 Semantics of Navigation Expressions on Collections

OCL Term e	Condition	Semantics e'
$objs \rightarrow collect(e)$	$objs$ unordered	$\{x.e' \mid x \in objs'\}$
	$objs$ ordered	$\{i \mapsto (objs'(i)).e' \mid i \in \text{dom}(objs')\}$
$objs \rightarrow at(i)$	$objs$ ordered	$objs'(i')$
$objs.att$	$objs$ unordered	$\{att(obj) \mid obj \in objs'\}$
	$objs$ ordered	$\{i \mapsto att(objs'(i)) \mid i \in \text{dom}(objs')\}$
$objs.role$ $role$ 1-multiplicity	$objs$ unordered $objs$ ordered	$\{role(obj) \mid obj \in objs'\}$ $\{i \mapsto role(objs'(i)) \mid i \in \text{dom}(objs')\}$
$objs.role$ $role$ not 1-multiplicity	$objs$ unordered and $role$ unordered	$\bigcup(\{role(obj) \mid obj \in objs'\})$
$objs.role$ $role$ not 1-multiplicity	$objs$ unordered and $role$ ordered	$\bigcup(\{\text{ran}(role(obj)) \mid obj \in objs'\})$
$objs.role$ $role$ not 1-multiplicity	$objs$ ordered and $role$ unordered	$\bigcup(\{role(objs'(i)) \mid i \in \text{dom}(objs')\})$
$objs.role$ $role$ not 1-multiplicity	$objs$ and $role$ ordered	$conc(\{i \mapsto role(objs'(i)) \mid i \in \text{dom}(objs')\})$
$C.allInstances()$		$\overline{C}$
$C \rightarrow size()$		$card(\overline{C})$

Table 6.7 shows the semantics of navigation expressions that start from sets of objects. In the case of $objs \rightarrow collect(e)$, e is an expression that can be evaluated on each element x of $objs$. The result is the collection of the values $x.e$.

In Table 6.7 $conc(seqs)$ is a distributed concatenation of the sequences in $seqs$. Navigations involving query operations are treated in a similar way to those with attributes or roles.

Select expressions evaluate to sets or sequences, depending on the collection they operate over (Table 6.8). Their first argument must denote a finite set or sequence. $contract(m)$ turns a map $m : 1..n \mapsto T$ into a sequence sq by removing gaps in the index set, maintaining the same order of elements. For example, $contract(\{2 \mapsto a, 3 \mapsto b, 7 \mapsto c\})$ is $[a, b, c]$.

The notation $a.P$ denotes the class version of P with a substituted into each new parameter slot; for example, $a.(att > 10)$ is $att(a) > 10$. $a.self$ is a.

TABLE 6.8 Semantic Mapping for Select Expressions

OCL Term e	Condition	Semantics e'
$objs \rightarrow select(P)$	set $objs$	$\{x \mid x \in objs' \wedge x.P'\}$
	sequence $objs$	$contract(\{i \mapsto x \mid (i \mapsto x) \in objs' \wedge x.P'\})$

In a similar way we could define the semantics of collection operators for bags and ordered sets.

6.3.5 Invariants

The following are proof obligations for consistency of a class, which a developer must ensure, for example, by specifying that additional actions execute when the initialization takes place or when some update operation takes place.

The invariant Inv_C of a class must be established by the initialization

$$(InitInv): \quad [init_C]Inv'_C$$

The invariant Inv_C must hold at the initiation and termination of every update operation:

$$\begin{aligned}(PInv): \quad & \Box_S(exists_C = TRUE \Rightarrow Inv'_C) \wedge \\ & \forall x_1 : X_1 \cdot [\alpha_1(x_1)](exists_C = TRUE \Rightarrow Inv'_C) \wedge \cdots \wedge \\ & \forall x_n : X_n \cdot [\alpha_n(x_n)](exists_C = TRUE \Rightarrow Inv'_C)\end{aligned}$$

where $S = \{\alpha_1, \ldots, \alpha_n\}$ is the set of actions representing the update operations of C, which have corresponding parameters $x_1 : X_1$, and so on.

Because of the frame axioms, these two requirements ensure that the semantics of an invariant in UML [65, Sec. 12] are valid: "The invariant must be true for each instance of the classifier at any moment in time. Only when the instance is executing an operation, this does not need to evaluate to true" (Section 7.3.3 of the UML OCL 2.0 [65] incorrectly omits the qualification).

6.3.6 Nested Classes

A class C may have a set of nested classifiers (a specialization of the *ownedMember* role of *Element*), which are regarded as parts of C: If C is removed from a model, so are these classifiers. For semantic purposes we simply consider these classes as additional classes within the model, as if they had been declared in the outer level of the model, but with each of their names qualified by C's name.

6.3.7 Inheritance

If class C inherits from class D (i.e., $C = g.specific$ and $D = g.general$ for some g : *Generalization*), then $\mathcal{I}_C$ incorporates $\mathcal{I}_D$; similarly if a behaviored classifier

C implements an interface D. In addition, there are axioms linking the creation, destruction, and existence of objects of C and D:

$$(OIAx): \qquad exists_C = TRUE \Rightarrow exists_D = TRUE$$

$$init_C \supset init_D$$

$$terminate_D \supset terminate_C$$

These correspond to the relationship $\overline{C} \subseteq \overline{D}$ in the class theory and express the semantics "each instance of the specific classifier is also an instance of the general classifier" [63, p. 74].

This model of inheritance also has the consequence that "any constraint applying to instances of the general classifier also applies to instances of the specific classifier" [63, p. 74]. In particular, semantic data features $att(d :@D)$ of $\mathcal{I}_D$ can be supplied with arguments of type $@C$ in $\mathcal{I}_C$.

Despite the transitive nature of this concept of generalization, it is not the case that UML generalization is transitive: It is possible for

$$a = g1.general \wedge b = g1.specific \wedge b = g2.general \wedge c = g2.specific$$

for classes a, b, and c and generalizations $g1$ and $g2$ without there being any generalization between a and c.

Similar issues apply to interface realization, which also uses the "satisfaction of all constraints" condition when comparing a classifier to an interface that it is implementing [62, p. 88].

There are two points in UML 2 where relaxation of the "all constraints of the general class should be satisfied in the specific" condition appears:

1. Attributes may have default values for their initialization [62, p. 52]. If these defaults differ in a subclass and superclass, the semantics of the classes will also differ. In our semantics any initialization performed in the superclass cannot be varied by the subclass. There are no defaults.
2. Similarly, static features are permitted to change their values in subclasses [62, p. 72]. This can be modeled by considering such redefinition as the declaration of a new static feature, with a name qualified by the name of the redefining class, and semantically unrelated to the feature it replaces.

We use the "one object" view of specialization [26]: Even though an object may be classified by many classifiers (related in an inheritance hierarchy), it is represented as the same semantic element in each. Its identity cannot change. It is, however, possible for an object to move from one subclass of a class to another subclass (dynamic classification) by the occurrence of *create* and *kill* actions of these subclasses on the object.

The axioms *OIAx* and *OpD* together imply that if an operation is defined both in the superclass and subclass, both sets of the pre and post specifications apply when it is used on an object of the subclass ($exists_C$ and $exists_D$ both true). A semantic variation in which the subclass postcondition is allowed to override and contradict the superclass postcondition could be considered, since this is common practice in OO programming (cf. the redefinition of *bodyCondition* on page 107 of UCL OCL 2.0 [62]). However, the subclass would not then be substitutable with regard to the superclass.

6.3.8 Class Theory of *C*

In the class theory Γ_C of a class C we define the (finite) set $\overline{C}$ of existing objects of C as an attribute of type $\mathbb{F}(@C)$, where $@C$ is the type of all possible instances of C. Initialization of a C object is carried out at object creation; termination takes place at object destruction:

$$(CI): \quad \forall a : @C \cdot create_C(a) \supset init_C(a)$$

$$\forall a : @C \cdot kill_C(a) \supset terminate_C(a)$$

The constant $self(@C) : @C$ is defined as a constant attribute (i.e., an attribute that is not in the write frame of any action). *self* is the identity function:

$$(SelfD): \quad \forall a : @C \cdot self(a) = a$$

$exists_C$ expresses that an object exists:

$$(ExistsD): \quad \forall a : @C \cdot (exists_C(a) = TRUE) \equiv (a \in \overline{C})$$

If an attribute *att* of C has an attached {*identity*} constraint, the axiom

$$(IdenD): \quad \forall a1, a2 : \overline{C} \; \cdot \; att(a1) = att(a2) \;\Rightarrow\; a1 = a2$$

is included in Γ_C; similarly if there is a group of attributes which together form a compound primary key (a single identity constraint is attached to all elements of the group).

6.3.9 Subsystem Theories

If class C uses class D as a supplier (i.e., there is an association directed from C to D), Γ_D and Γ_C are combined in the theory Γ_S of the subsystem of D and C together with their linking association, and we connect the actions denoting calls with the actual operations invoked:

$$(RSC): \quad \forall a : @D \cdot invoke_n(a, e) \supset a.n(e)$$

and

$$(RCC): \quad \forall a : @D \cdot create\_invoke_D(a) \supset create_D(a)$$

TABLE 6.9 Additional Axioms for Associations

Association	Additional Axioms
$A_* -^r_* B$	$\forall a : \overline{A} \cdot r(a) \in \mathbb{F}(\overline{B})$
$A_{0..1} -^r_* B$	$\forall a : \overline{A} \cdot r(a) \in \mathbb{F}(\overline{B})$
	$\forall a1, a2 : \overline{A} \cdot r(a1) \cap r(a2) \neq \{\} \Rightarrow a1 = a2$
$A_1 -^r_* B$	$\forall a : \overline{A} \cdot r(a) \in \mathbb{F}(\overline{B})$
	$\forall a1, a2 : \overline{A} \cdot r(a1) \cap r(a2) \neq \{\} \Rightarrow a1 = a2$
	$\forall b : \overline{B} \cdot \exists a : \overline{A} \cdot b \in r(a)$
$A_* -^r_1 B$	$\forall a : \overline{A} \cdot r(a) \in \overline{B}$
$A_{0..1} -^r_1 B$	$\forall a : \overline{A} \cdot r(a) \in \overline{B}$
	$\forall a1, a2 : \overline{A} \cdot r(a1) = r(a2) \Rightarrow a1 = a2$
$A_1 -^r_1 B$	$\forall a : \overline{A} \cdot r(a) \in \overline{B}$
	$\forall a1, a2 : \overline{A} \cdot r(a1) = r(a2) \Rightarrow a1 = a2$
	$\forall b : \overline{B} \cdot \exists a : \overline{A} \cdot b = r(a)$

TABLE 6.10 Axioms for Association Constraints

Association	Additional Axiom
$A_* -^r_* B$	$\forall a : \overline{A}; b : \overline{B} \cdot b \in r(a) \Rightarrow a.(b.Inv)$
$A_{0..1} -^r_* B$	the same
$A_1 -^r_* B$	the same
$A_* -^r_1 B$	$\forall a : \overline{A} \cdot a.(r(a).Inv)$
$A_{0..1} -^r_1 B$	the same
$A_1 -^r_1 B$	the same

These model synchronous invocations with no communication delays between client and supplier. The properties could be generalized to deal with distributed systems: for example, by asserting

$$\forall i : \mathbb{N}_1 \cdot \exists j : \mathbb{N}_1 \cdot \uparrow(invoke_n(a, e), i) = \leftarrow(n(a, e), j)$$

and that $invoke_n(a, e)$ terminates when a result message is received from a for this request.

When $invoke_n(objs, e)$ is used with a set $objs$ of objects, it is interpreted as a concurrent invocation of each of the individual object operations:

$$(MRSC): \quad invoke_n(objs, e) \supset \|_{a:objs} n(a, e)$$

Additional axioms may be required in Γ_S to define the properties of the association from C to D, depending on its multiplicity at the C end (Table 6.9).

If a constraint *Inv* is attached to the association between a class A and a supplier class B, an axiom expressing its meaning is included in Γ_S, depending on the form of association (Table 6.10). *Inv* may involve features of both A and B. The notation

TABLE 6.11 Axioms for Bidirectional Associations

Association	Additional Axiom
$A_{*}^{ar}\__{*}^{br}B$	$\forall a : \overline{A}; b : \overline{B} \cdot a \in ar(b) \equiv b \in br(a)$
$A_{1}^{ar}\__{*}^{br}B$	$\forall a : \overline{A}; b : \overline{B} \cdot a = ar(b) \equiv b \in br(a)$
$A_{*}^{ar}\__{1}^{br}B$	$\forall a : \overline{A}; b : \overline{B} \cdot a \in ar(b) \equiv b = br(a)$
$A_{1}^{ar}\__{1}^{br}B$	$\forall a : \overline{A}; b : \overline{B} \cdot a = ar(b) \equiv b = br(a)$

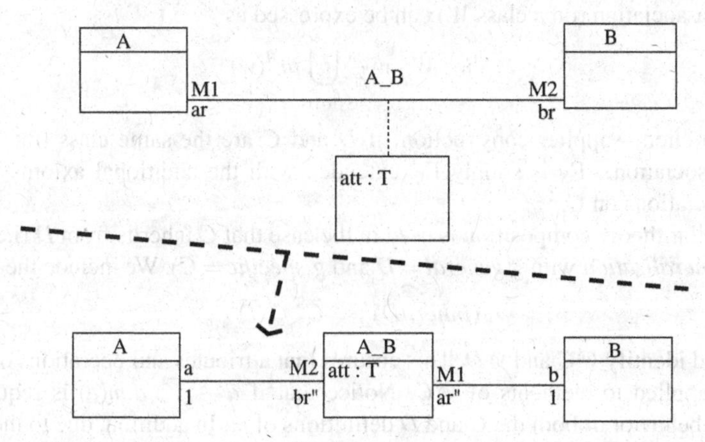

FIGURE 6.6 Transformation of association classes to associations.

a.(*b*.*Inv*) means that *b* is substituted into all new @*B* parameter slots in the class version of *Inv*, and *a* into all new @*A* parameter slots.

In the case of bidirectional associations, there are properties relating the two directions (Table 6.11). The case of 0..1 multiplicity at an association end produces the same axioms as for $*$.

The semantics of other forms of association between classes can also be expressed in this semantics, by transforming them into simpler constructs. Association classes are modeled as a class plus associations (Figure 6.6). The new axiom

$$(AssocClass) : \quad \forall r1, r2 : \overline{A\_B} \cdot a(r1) = a(r2) \land b(r1) = b(r2) \Rightarrow r1 = r2$$

holds in such a subsystem.

Qualified associations can also be modeled by introducing a new intermediate class. We can also formalize the two key properties of composite aggregations [62, p. 43]. The deletion propagation property of a composition (Figure 6.7) is expressed by

$$\forall w : \overline{W} \cdot kill_W(w) \supset ||_{p \in pr(w)} kill_P(p)$$

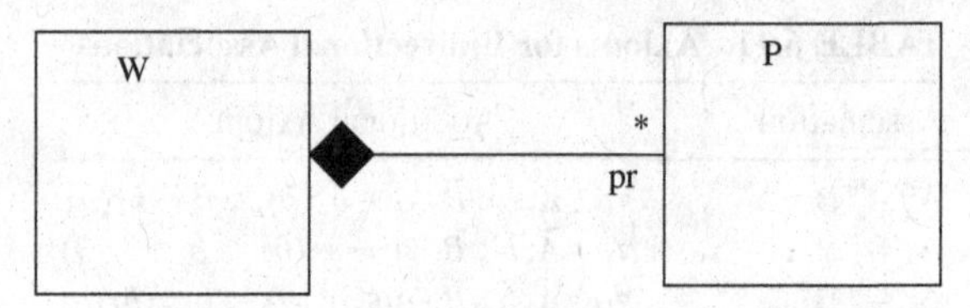

FIGURE 6.7 Composite aggregation association.

The property that there are no object-level loops in the extent of a composite that is a self-association (on a class W) can be expressed as

$$\forall w : \overline{W} \cdot w \notin \bigcup_{n:\mathbb{N}_1} pr^n(w)$$

In the client–supplier construction, if D and C are the same class (the case of a self-association), Γ_S is simply Γ_C extended with the additional axioms for any self-associations on C.

A similar theory composition is used in the case that C inherits from D (i.e., there is g : *Generalization* with $g.general = D$ and $g.specific = C$). We include the axioms

$$(InheritD): \quad \overline{C} \subseteq \overline{D}$$

in Γ_S, and identify $@C$ and $@D$. This ensures that attributes and operations of D can also be applied to elements of $@C$. Notice that if $a \in \overline{C}$, $a.m(e)$ is required to obey the behavior of both the C and D definitions of m. In addition, due to the frame axioms, operations of the subclass can modify data of the superclass only by invoking (coexecuting with) update operations of the superclass which have that data in their frames. This condition ensures the subtyping principle of Liskov and Wing [54].

In addition, if a class A is a superclass of classes $A_1, \ldots, A_n$, these classes should all be represented in a single subsystem whose theory extends Γ_A and each Γ_{A_i}. If A is {*abstract*}, the axiom

$$(AbsD): \quad \overline{A} = \overline{A_1} \cup \cdots \cup \overline{A_n}$$

is added to this subsystem theory.

In the general case of several inheritance relationships, all classes concerned are represented in a single subsystem theory; only the classes C without superclasses are represented by a type $@C$. When forming the theory of a system involving both inheritance and associations, the inheritance construction should be applied to form a composed subsystem theory before the clientship construction.

The notion of a generalization set in UML 2 places constraints on the possible elements of a group of subclasses of a particular class. If gs : *GeneralizationSet* has $gs.generalization = gset$, the elements (g : *Generalization*) of $gset$ have the same value sp of $g.general$, and the subclasses $gset.specific$ of sp are constrained as follows:

- If $gs.isCovering = true$, all elements of sp must be elements of at least one subclass in $gset.specific$:

$$\overline{Sp} = \overline{Sb_1} \cup \cdots \cup \overline{Sb_n}$$

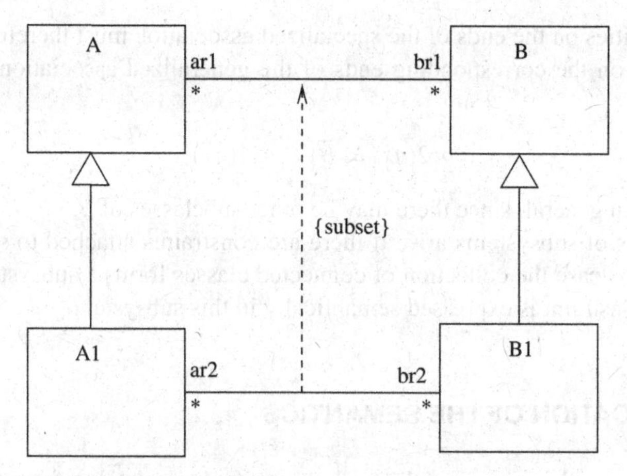

FIGURE 6.8 Specialization of associations.

- If $gs.isDisjoint = true$, the subclasses have no element in common:

$$\overline{Sb_1} \cap \cdots \cap \overline{Sb_n} = \{\}$$

The latter condition appears to be the intended interpretation of disjointness [62, p. 77]; however a more useful property is pairwise disjointness:

$$\overline{Sb_i} \cap \overline{Sb_j} = \{\}$$

for each $i \neq j$. This, together with the covering property, would then express that the subclasses form a partition of the superclass.

One association can be a specialization of another (i.e., there may be $r1, r2 : Association$ and $g : Generalization$ such that $r1 = g.general$ and $r2 = g.specific$).

In this case the corresponding elements of $ms1 = r1.memberEnd$ and $ms2 = r2.memberEnd$ must also be equal or related by generalizations:

$$\begin{aligned} ms1 \rightarrow at(1) \;&=\; ms2 \rightarrow at(1) \;\vee \\ &\exists g1 : \; Generalization \;\cdot \\ &g1.general \;=\; ms1 \rightarrow at(1).type \;\wedge\; g1.specific \;=\; ms2 \rightarrow at(1).type \end{aligned}$$

and similarly for the second element of the member ends.

In this situation the rolenames of $r2$ are asserted to be subsets of the corresponding rolenames of $r1$ (Figure 6.8); that is,

$$bx : \overline{B1} \Rightarrow ar2(bx) \subseteq ar1(bx)$$

and

$$ax : \overline{A1} \Rightarrow br2(ax) \subseteq br1(ax)$$

The multiplicities on the ends of the specialized association must therefore be $\leq$ the multiplicities on the corresponding ends of the generalized association. Equations such as

$$br2(ax) = \overline{B1} \cap br1(ax)$$

will not hold in general, since there may be other subclasses of B.

Other cases of subsystems arise if there are constraints attached to sets of associations. In this case the collection of connected classes forms a subsystem, and the association constraint is expressed semantically in this subsystem.

6.4 APPLICATION OF THE SEMANTICS

The semantics has been used as the basis of verified translations from UML to the formal specification language B and to the SMV model checker [2]. These translations enable checks on the consistency of UML models, and animation of the models. However, in both cases there are restrictions on the models which can be analyzed: For B it is not possible to have cycles in the operation calling relationship except for query operations defined by recursion. Other forms of recursion or callbacks cannot be translated. For translation to SMV it is necessary that all classes have a maximum cardinality.

The semantics has also been used to justify a number of model transformations, as described in Chapter 14.

6.5 RELATED WORK

Other work on UML class diagram semantics has used the following approaches:

1. Expression of UML semantics in a semantic representation outside UML, using denotational [11,19,26,52,72], operational [17], axiomatic [36], or category-theoretic [75] semantics.
2. Metamodeling, representing UML semantics in terms of a small-core UML notation together with OCL [15]. This is the approach used in the UML 2 infrastructure and superstructure documents, although in these many of the semantic definitions are informally expressed and not formalized in OCL (in some cases OCL is unable to express the definitions).

Denotational semantics (e.g., [11,19,72]) are very useful as an underpinning for axiomatic semantics; however, they can be very complex and difficult to understand and implement directly, or to tailor to different semantic variation points of UML. For this reason we prefer to give an axiomatic semantics, which is closely linked to notations used for proof and semantic analysis (in classical mathematical and logical notation, or in B).

In comparison to the system model defined by the UML semantics project [11], we use a more abstract and general semantic representation, avoiding low-level details of data storage and behavior mechanisms.

In general, the strategy of restricting to a subset of UML is necessary, since some of its notations, such as activities, have unclear semantics. However, the subset should itself be a useful part of UML, so that the results of semantic analysis can be expressed in a comprehensible manner to software developers. Translating interactions to state machines, or flattening state machines, should be avoided for this reason. Our semantics can represent directly the semantics of interactions [49] and unflattened state machines [53].

As pointed out by Naumenko and Wegmann [59], the self-referential metamodeling approach can result in a semantics that fails to provide a consistent interpretation for the terms of UML. Instead, we have taken the first approach and given a semantics of an essential core of UML in a formalism that is entirely independent of UML and based on well-established mathematical logic and set theory. In decomposing the semantics of UML models into theories linked by morphisms, we are also using a category-theoretic approach.

An approach closely related to ours is the formalization of UML and OCL in PVS [35]. This deals with a restricted subset of class diagrams (association ends have maximum multiplicity 1). The expression of the semantics in PVS can be complex and difficult to relate to the UML source models, but automated proof can be applied as with model checking.

Our semantics represents the *extension* of a class C as a element $\overline{C}$ of the semantics but does not represent the *intension* of C [60] as an element within the semantics. Instead, this is represented as the theory $\mathcal{I}_C$. This means that the semantics of concepts such as *leaf* and *root* classes and operations cannot be expressed in our semantics. *private* and *public* modalities of features are also not represented. However, the correctness of models with regard to such constraints can be checked effectively by diagram editing and syntax-level analysis tools, so the inability to represent such concepts in our semantics does not impair the verifiability of UML models.

6.6 CONCLUSIONS

In this chapter we have shown that an axiomatic approach can be used to give a comprehensive semantics to UML class diagram notation in a way that is consistent with the informal semantics expressed in the UML standard. Elements of class diagram notation, such as qualified associations and associations of higher arity, which have not been covered explicitly here, can be expressed in the subset of the notation which has been assigned a semantics, so they can be given a semantics by transformation.

REFERENCES

1. J.-R. Abrial. *The B Book: Assigning Programs to Meanings*. Cambridge University Press, New York, 1996.

2. K. Androutsopoulos. Verification of reactive system specifications using model checking. Ph.D. dissertation, King's College, London, 2004.
3. G. Aruchamy and A. Mo Kim Cheng. *Translating Real-Time UML Timing Constraints into Real-Time Logic Formulas*. Technical Report UH-CS-06-07. University of Houston, Houston, TX, 2006.
4. D. Bämer et al. Role object. In *Pattern Languages of Program Design*. Addison-Wesley, Reading, MA, 2000.
5. C. Batini, S. Ceri, and S. Navathe. *Conceptual Database Design: An Entity-Relationship Approach*. Benjamin-Cummings, Redwood City, CA, 1992.
6. B-Core. *The BToolkit*. B-Core UK Ltd., Harwell, UK, 2005.
7. J. C. Bicarregui, K. C. Lano, and T. S. E. Maibaum. Objects, associations and subsystems: a hierarchical approach to encapsulation. In *ECOOP'97*. Lecture Notes in Computer Science, vol. 1241, Springer-Verlag, New York, pp. 324–343, 1997.
8. J. C. Bicarregui, K. C. Lano, and T. S. E. Maibaum. Towards a compositional interpretation of object diagrams. In *Proceedings of the IFIP TC2 Working Conference on Algorithmic Languages and Calculi*, Feb. 1997.
9. M. Blaha and W. Premerlani. A catalog of object model transformations. Presented at the 3rd Working Conference on Reverse Engineering, Monterey, CA, 1996.
10. G. Booch, M. Engel, and B. Young. *Object Oriented Analysis and Design with Applications*. Addison-Wesley, Reading, MA, 2007.
11. M. Broy, M. Cengarle, and B. Rumpe. *Towards a System Model for UML*. UML Semantics Project Document 06.06.04, System Model Part 1, 2006.
12. J. M. Chiaradia and C. Pons. Improving the OCL semantics definition by applying dynamic meta modelling and design patterns. In *OCL for (Meta-) Models in Multiple Application Domains*. TUD-FI06-04, 2006.
13. F. Chauvel, and J-M. Jézéquel. Code generation from UML models with semantic variation points. In *MoDELS 2005*. Leacture Notes in Computer Science, vol. 3713. Springer-Verlag, New York, 2005.
14. S. Cook and J. Daniels. *Designing Object Systems: Object-Oriented Modelling with Syntropy*. Prentice Hall, Upper Saddle River, NJ, 1994.
15. T. Clark, A. Evans, S. Kent, and P. Sammut. The MMF approach to engineering object-oriented design languages. In *Workshop on Language Descriptions, Tools and Applications (LDTA)*, 2001.
16. J. Crupi, D. Alur, and D. Malks. *Core J2EE Patterns*. Prentice Hall, Upper Saddle River, NJ, 2001.
17. W. Damm, B. Josko, A. Pnueli, and A. Votintseva. A discrete-time UML semantics for concurrency and communication in safety-critical applications. *Science of Computer Programming*, 55:81–115, 2005.
18. H. Dierks. Comparing model-checking and logical reasoning for real-time systems. In *Workshop Proceedings ESSLLI'98*, pp. 13–22, 1998.
19. A. Evans and S. Kent. Core meta-modelling semantics of UML: the pUML approach. In *UML'99*, pp. 140–155, 1999.
20. H. Fecher, J. Schonborn, M. Kyas, and W.-P. de Roever. 29 new unclarities in the semantics of UML 2.0 state machines. In *Formal Methods and Software Engineering; ICFEM 2005*.

Lecture Notes in Computer Science, vol. 3785, pp. 52–65. Springer-Verlag, New York, 2005.

21. J. Fiadeiro and T. Maibaum. Describing, structuring and implementing objects. In *Foundations of Object Oriented Languages*. Lecture Notes in Computer Science, vol. 489. Springer-Verlag, New York, 1991.
22. J. Fiadeiro and T Maibaum. Sometimes "tomorrow" is "sometime." In *Temporal Logic*. Lecture Notes in Artificial Intelligence, vol. 827, pp. 48–66. Springer-Verlag, New York, 1994.
23. M. Fowler. *Refactoring: Improving the Design of Existing Code*. Addison-Wesley, Reading, MA, 2000.
24. E. Gamma, R. Helm, R. Johnson, and J. Vlissides. *Design Patterns: Elements of Reusable Object-Oriented Software*. Addison-Wesley, Reading, MA, 1995.
25. M. Glinz. Problems and deficiencies of UML as a requirements specification language. In *Proceedings of the 10th International Workshop on Software Specification and Design (IWSSD-10)*, pp. 11–22, 2000.
26. M. Gogolla, O. Radfelder, and M. Richters. *A UML Semantics FAQ: The View from Bremen*. University of Bremen, Bremen, Germany, 1999.
27. S. Goldsack, K. Lano, and A. Sanchez. Transforming continuous into discrete specifications with VDM^{++}. In *IEE C8 Colloquium Digest on Hybrid Control for Real-Time Systems*. IEE, London, 1996.
28. S. Graf, I. Ober, and I. Ober. Timed annotations with UML. In *SVERTS'03*, 2003.
29. M. Grand. *Patterns in Java*, vol. 1. Wiley, New York, 1998.
30. D. Gries. *The Science of Programming*. Springer-Verlag, New York, 1981.
31. D. Harel and A. Naamad. The STATEMATE semantics of statecharts. *ACM Transactions on Software Engineering and Methodology*, 5(4):293–333, Oct. 1996.
32. C. A. R. Hoare. An axiomatic basis for computer programming. *Communications of the ACM*, 12(10):576–585, 1969.
33. A. Knapp and J. Wuttke, Model-checking of UML 2.0 interactions. In *Proceedings of the 5th International Workshop on Critical Systems Development Using Modelling Languages (CSDUML)*. Telenor Report 20/2006, 2006.
34. F. Jahanian and A. K. Mok. Safety analysis of timing properties in real-time systems. *IEEE Transactions on Software Engineering*, 12:890–904, Sept. 1986.
35. M. Kyas, H. Fecher, F. de Boer, J. Jacob, J. Hooman, M. van der Kwaag, T. Arons, and H. Kugler. Formalizing UML models and OCL constraints in PVS. In *SFEDL'04*, 2004.
36. L. Lamport. *The Temporal Logic of Actions*. Technical Report 79. Digital Equipment Corporation, Systems Research Center, Palos Alto, CA, Dec. 1991.
37. K. Lano. Logical specification of reactive and real-time systems. *Journal of Logic and Computation*, 8(5):679–711, 1998.
38. K. Lano. UML to B: formal verification of object-oriented models. In *IFM '04*, 2004.
39. K. Lano and K. Androutsopolous. Automated synthesis of high-integrity systems using model-driven development. In *Proceedings of the 5th International Workshop on Critical Systems Development Using Modeling Languages (CSDUML)*. Telenor Report 20/2006, 2006.

40. K. Lano, K. Androutsopolous, and D. Clark. Concurrency specification in UML-RSDS. In *MARTES'06, MoDELS Conference*, 2006.
41. K. Lano, D. Clark, and K. Androutsopolous. From implicit specifications to explicit designs in reactive system development. In *IFM'02*, 2002.
42. K. Lano, D. Clark, K. Androutsopolous, and P. Kan. Invariant-based synthesis of fault-tolerant systems. In *FTRTFT*. Springer-Verlag, New York, 2000.
43. K. Lano, D. Clark, and K. Androutsopoulos. RSDS: a subset of UML with precise semantics. *L'Objet*, 9(4):53–73, 2003.
44. K. Lano. Transformational program analysis. *Journal of Software Testing Verification and Reliability*, 4:155–189, 1994.
45. K. Lano. Constraint-driven development. *Information and Software Technology*, 50: 406–423, 2008.
46. K. Lano. Formalising design patterns as model transformations, Chapter VIII in T. Taibi, ed., *Design Pattern Formalisation Techniques*. IGI Publishing, Hershey, PA, 2007.
47. K. Lano and D. Clark. Direct semantics of extended state machines. In *TOOLS'07*, 2007.
48. K Lano. A compositional semantics of UML-RSDS. *SoSyM*, 8(1): 85–116, Feb. 2009.
49. K. Lano. Formal specification using interaction diagrams. In *Proceedings of the 5th IEEE International Conference on Software Engineering and Formal Methods*, pp. 293–304, 2007.
50. King's College London. UML RSDS toolset, 2007. http://www.dcs.kcl.ac.uk/staff/kcl/umlrsds.
51. K. Lano. Catalogue of model transformations. http://www.dcs.kcl.ac.uk/staff/kcl/tcat.pdf, 2007.
52. K. Lano and A. Evans. Rigorous development in UML. In *FASE'99*. Lecture Notes in Computer Science, vol. 1577, pp. 129–144. Springer-Verlag, New York, 1999.
53. K. Lano and D. Clark. Semantics and refinement of behaviour state machines, In *Proceedings of the 10th International Conference on Enterprise Information Systems* (*ICEIS 2008*), 2008.
54. B. Liskov and J. Wing. Specifications and their use in defining subtypes. In *ZUM'95 Proceedings*. Lecture Notes in Computer Science, vol. 967. Springer-Verlag, New York, 1995.
55. S. Markovic and T. Baar. Refactoring OCL annotated UML class diagrams. In *MoDELS 2005 Proceedings*, Lecture Notes in Computer Science, vol. 3713. Springer-Verlag, New York, 2005.
56. B. Meyer. *Object-Oriented Software Construction*. Prentice Hall, Upper Saddle River, NJ, 1997.
57. J. D. Monk. *Mathematical Logic*. Springer-Verlag, New York, 1976.
58. C. Morgan. *Programming from Specifications*. Springer-Verlag, New York, 1990.
59. A. Naumenko and A. Wegmann. Triune continuum paradigm and problems of UML semantics. http://icwww.epfl.ch/publications/documents/IC_TECH_REPORT_200344.pdf, 2003.
60. OMG. Model-driven architecture. http://www.omg.org/mda/, 2007.
61. OMG. *UML Superstructure, Version 2.0*. OMG Document Formal/05-07-04. Object Management Group, Needham, MA, 2005.

62. OMG. *UML Superstructure, Version 2.1.1*. OMG Document Formal/2007-02-03. Object Management Group, Needham, MA, 2007.
63. OMG. UML profile for schedulability, performance and time, version 1.1. http://www.omg.org/, 2005.
64. OMG. *UML Profile for Modeling and Analysis of Real-Time and Embedded Systems*. OMG Document 08-06-08. Object Management Group, Needham, MA, 2008.
65. OMG. *UML OCL 2.0 Specification*. Final/06-05-01. Object Management Group, Needham, MA, 2006.
66. OMG, *Query/View/Transformation Specification*. Technical Report ptc/05-11-01, Object Management Group, Needham, MA, 2005.
67. D. Schmidt and C. Cranor. Half-sync/half-async: an architectural pattern for efficient and well-structured concurrent I/O. In *Proceedings of the 2nd Annual Conference on the Pattern Languages of Programs*, Monticello, IL, pp. 1–10, Sept. 1995.
68. C. Snook and M. Butler, U2B: a tool for translating UML-B models into B. Chapter 6 in J. Mermet, ed., *UML-B Specification for Proven Embedded Systems Design*. Springer-Verlag, New York, 2004.
69. G. Sunyé, A. Le Guennec, and J. M. Jézéquel. Design patterns application in UML. In *ECOOP 2000*, Lecture Notes in Computer Science, vol. 1850, pp. 44–62. Springer-Verlag, New York, 2000.
70. J. S. Ostroff. *Temporal Logic for Real-Time Systems*. Wiley, New York, 1989.
71. A. Pnueli. Applications of temporal logic to the specification and verification of reactive systems: a survey of current trends. In *Current Trends in Concurrency*. Lecture Notes in Computer Science, vol. 224. Springer-Verlag, New York, 1986.
72. M. Richters. OCL semantics. Annex A of [65], 2005.
73. M. Ryan, J. Fiadeiro, and T. S. E. Maibaum. Sharing actions and attributes in modal action logic. In *Proceedings of the International Conference on Theoretical Aspects of Computer Science (TACS'91)*. Springer-Verlag, New York, 1991.
74. A. Simons. The theory of classification: 8, Classification and inheritance. *Journal of Object Technology*, 2(4):55–64, July–Aug. 2003.
75. J. Smith, S. DeLoach, M. Kokar, and K. Baclawski. Category theoretic approaches of representing precise UML semantics. In *Proceedings of the ECOOP Workshop on Defining Precise Semantics for UML*, 2000.
76. J. Rumbaugh, M. Blaha, W. Lorensen, F. Eddy, and W. Premerlani. *Object-Oriented Modeling and Design*. Prentice Hall, Upper Saddle River, NJ, 1994.
77. UML 2 Semantics Project. http://www.cs.queensu.ca/~stl/internal/uml2/bibtex/ref_uml2semantics.html, 2008.
78. L. Tratt Model transformations and tool integration. *SoSyM*, 8(2): 85–116, May 2005.
79. F. Wagner. *Modeling Software with Finite State Machines: A Practical Approach*. Auerbach Publications, Boca Raton, FL, 2006.

CHAPTER 7

OBJECT CONSTRAINT LANGUAGE: METAMODELING SEMANTICS

ANNEKE KLEPPE
Independent Consultant, The Netherlands

7.1 INTRODUCTION

In this chapter we explain the semantics defined in Section 10 of the Object Constraint Language (OCL) specification [1]. This standard is freely available; therefore, we do not describe the semantics in full. Instead, we give the reader some insights into the reasoning behind these semantics as well as the formalism used to express them. As such, this material serves as an introduction to Section 10 of the OCL standard.

The semantics is described here using a technique that was later called metamodeling semantics [2]. Because this is a new and fairly unfamiliar formalism, this manner of describing semantics is explained as well. Basically, in metamodeling semantics not only the abstract syntax of the language, but also the semantic domain is specified using a model. The actual semantic mapping is described as the relationship (defined using associations) between the two models. The semantic domain model of the OCL is explained as is its relationship with the OCL abstract syntax model or metamodel.

OCL is the OMG standard for specifying expressions that add vital information to object-oriented models and other object-modeling artifacts. These expressions can have the following types:

- Invariants, which state a fact that must always be true for a given object.
- Pre- and postconditions, which state a fact that must be true before and after execution of an operation, respectively.
- Body expressions, which indicate how the result of a query operation must be calculated.
- Initial value expressions, which indicate the initial value of an attribute or association end.

UML 2 Semantics and Applications. Edited by Kevin Lano

The first two expression types indicate a required situation; therefore, the value of these expressions will always be of the Boolean type. The latter two expression types indicate a value and may be of any type.

OCL is a side-effect-free language; evaluation or execution of its expressions may not alter the system state. An expression is merely an indication of a value; in no way is it an indication of how parts of the system are executed. Therefore, I prefer the use of the term *evaluation* of an OCL expression to *execution*.

Given the side-effect-free nature of OCL, the semantics of OCL can be brought down to a single question: What is the resulting value of evaluating an OCL expression? To answer this question, we must have a clear notion of what is meant by *value*. Thus, the most important elements of the OCL semantic domain are the values: in other words, the instances of the OCL types.

The semantics of OCL are described using a formalism that was later called *metamodeling semantics* [2]. Because this is a new and fairly unfamiliar formalism, it is explained in Section 7.2. In Section 7.3 we explain the first part of the OCL semantic domain model, of which values are the key ingredient. Section 7.4 covers the second part of the OCL semantic domain, which describes evaluations of OCL expressions. The chapter concludes with Section 7.5, which includes a short summary.

7.2 METAMODELING SEMANTICS

In the OCL specification the semantics are described using a new formalism, which is based on metamodeling. In this section we explain this formalism briefly. Furthermore, we describe the underlying definition of semantics as well as the way that metamodeling semantics fits this definition. Furthermore, we define the term *mogram*.

7.2.1 What Is Semantics?

Semantics is just another word for *meaning*, so actually the question in the title is: What is meaning? To answer it, we have to turn to philosophy. In 1923, Ogden and Richards, two leading linguists and philosophers of their time, wrote the book *The Meaning of Meaning* [3]. They state that there is a triangular relationship among ideas (concepts), the real world, and linguistic symbols such as words, often referred to as the *meaning triangle*. An example is shown in Figure 7.1, which depicts the triangular relationship using the example of a larch tree.

The meaning triangle explains that every person links a real-world item to a word (linguistic symbol) through a mental concept. Similarly, a word can be linked to a real-world item via a concept. Imagine that you hear or read the word *tricycle* and see a three-wheeled vehicle either in real life or in a photograph. At that moment you build a mental image connecting the word and the real-world item.

An important understanding of Ogden and Richards is that ideas (concepts) exist only in a person's mind. In fact, they state that ultimately every person understands the world around him or her in his or her own particular manner, a manner that no other person is able to copy, because that understanding of a new concept is fed by (based on) all other concepts that this person acquired previously. For example, the

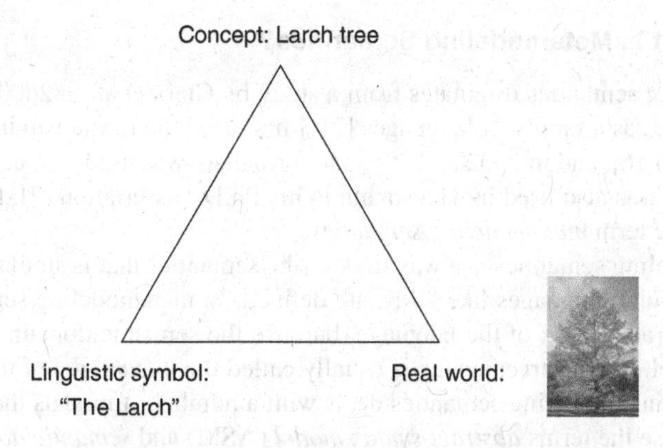

FIGURE 7.1 Ogden and Richards' meaning triangle.

concept "tricycle" can be explained as a three-wheeled bicycle only when you know what a bicycle is. A person who has no understanding of bicycles will still not grasp this concept. Thus, one concept builds on another. As no person has exactly the same knowledge as another person, each person's understanding of the world will be different. In fact, Ogden and Richards state that communication, which is understanding of each other's linguistic utterances, is fundamentally crippled. Therefore, my definition of semantics is the following.

Definition 7.2.1 (Semantics Description) A *description of the semantics* of a language L is a means to communicate an (subjective) understanding of the linguistic utterances of L to another person or persons.

Definition 7.2.1 is based on the common understanding that a language is a set of linguistic utterances; it originates from formal language theory (see, e.g., [4]). To make absolutely clear that Definition 7.2.1 as well as metamodeling semantics can be used not only for modeling languages but for any language, I introduced the term *mogram* [5] to replace *linguistic utterance*. A mogram can be either a model or a program, a database schema or a query, an XML file, or any other thing written in a software language.

Following the meaning triangle, a semantics description of a language consists of (1) a description of the real-world concepts, and (2) a description of the relationship between every mogram of that language and the real-world concepts. The first part of a semantics description is usually called the *semantic domain*; the second is called the *semantic mapping*. The semantic domain describes the right-hand corner of the meaning triangle, providing an understanding of the "real world." In other words, the semantic domain provides us with the mental concepts mentioned in the upper corner of the semantic triangle. The left-hand corner of the meaning triangle is provided by the language's abstract syntax. The semantic mapping is a description of how a human being should relate the abstract syntax to the semantic domain. In the next section we look at how metamodeling semantics provides the two parts of a semantics description.

7.2.2 What Is Metamodeling Semantics?

Metamodeling semantics originates from a study by Clark et al. in 2000 of the definition of UML as a family of languages [2]. I first used the formalism in a technical report in 2001 [6], and in 2002 and 2003 the formalism was used to specify the OCL semantics. It was also used by Hausmann in his Ph.D. dissertation [7]. Engels et al. [8] coined the term *metamodeling semantics*.

Metamodeling semantics is a way to describe semantics that is similar to the way in which popular languages like UML are defined. In metamodeling semantics, not only the abstract syntax of the language, but also the semantic domain, is specified using a model. The abstract syntax is usually called the *metamodel* of the language, but because metamodeling semantics deals with a number of models that define the language, I use the terms *abstract syntax model* (ASM) and *semantic domain model* (SDM) (see Figure 7.2 for their position in the meaning triangle). Both ASM and SDM are metamodels in the sense that both state information about the mograms of the language. The ASM states whether a mogram has a statically valid structure; the SDM states the possible meanings of a mogram.

Because both ASM and SDM are models, we have to be aware of the two levels at which the meaning triangle occurs (see Figure 7.3): the model level and the instance level. The ASM and SDM reside at the model level; the mogram and the part of the

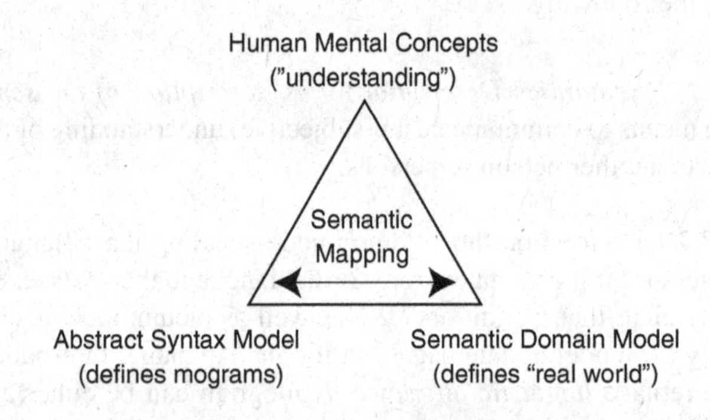

FIGURE 7.2 Metamodeling semantics.

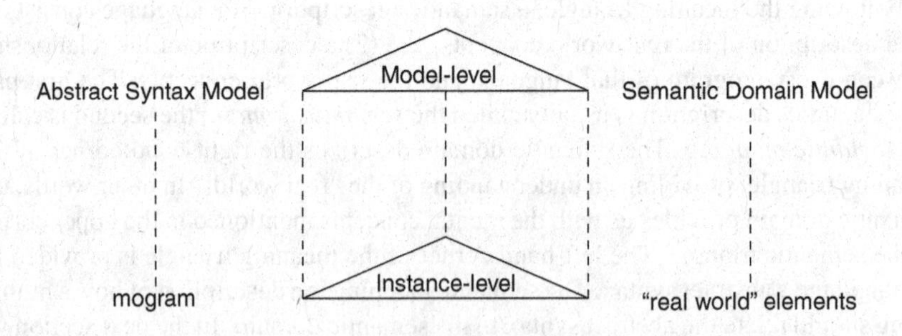

FIGURE 7.3 Metamodeling semantics has two levels.

real world that represents the mogram's meaning reside at the instance level. Just as the mogram is an instance of the ASM, the elements of the real world are instances of the SDM.

As an example of an SDM, consider the semantic domain of the OCL, which consists of values and evaluations of expressions. In the SDM both values and evaluations are modeled as metaclasses; the actual values and evaluations are instances of these metaclasses.

In metamodeling semantics, the semantic mapping is given by associating each metaclass in the ASM with one or more metaclasses in the SDM. Each association between an ASM metaclass and an SDM metaclass states that the meaning of an instance of the ASM metaclass is an instance of the SDM metaclass. For example, in Figure 7.4 the metaclass OclExpression from the ASM is associated with the metaclass OclExpEval from the SDM, stating that the meaning of an OCL expression is given by an evaluation of this expression. The metaclass Classifier from the ASM is associated with the metaclass Value, stating that the meaning of a classifier is given by a set of values.

Of course, the associations in the semantic mapping are restricted by constraints. The constraints specify which instance of the ASM metaclass is linked to which instance of the SDM metaclass. In the example in Figure 7.4, each OclExpEval instance defined in the SDM has a property `resultValue` of type Value, which holds the actual value of the expression being evaluated. Similarly, each OclExpression instance defined in the ASM has a property `type` of type Classifier, which indicates the type of the expression. The semantic mapping states that there is an association between Value and Classifier as well as between OclExpEval and OclExpression. This combination of associations is restricted by the following constraint,

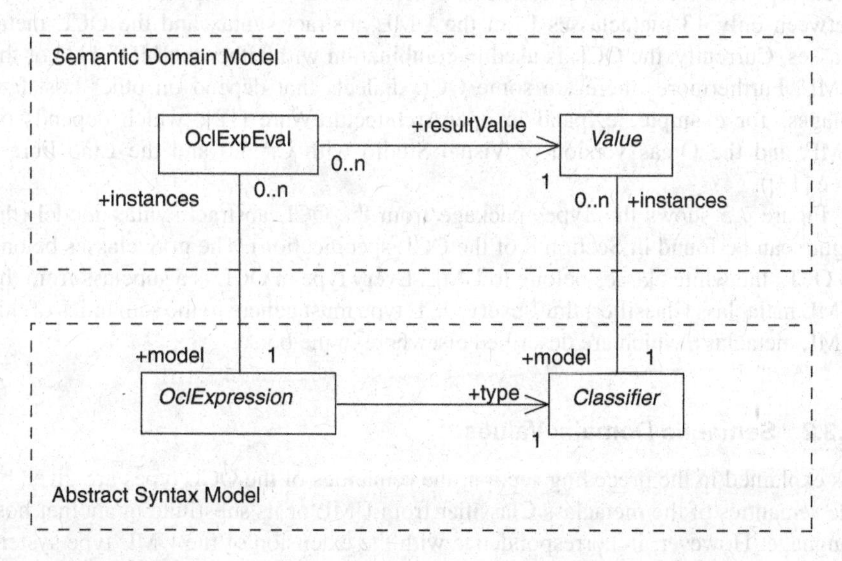

FIGURE 7.4 General associations between some ASM and SDM classes.

which states that the result value of the evaluation of an OCL expression must be an instance of the type of that expression:

```
context OclExpEval
inv: resultValue.isInstanceOf( model.type )
```

7.3 OCL SEMANTICS: TYPES AND VALUES

The OCL semantic domain is divided into two parts: values and evaluations. In this section we describe the first part of the semantics domain. It explains the relationship between OCL types and UML types and defines the semantics of OCL types.

7.3.1 OCL and Its Host Language

OCL is a special language in the sense that it is not a stand-alone language. OCL can only be used in cooperation with another language that provides a type system. Each of the types provided by this host language can be used in any OCL expression and can be the type of any OCL expression. Therefore, part of OCL semantics is the semantics of the host language. That is, to understand the semantics of OCL, one must understand the semantics of the type system provided by the host language.

OCL was created to be the constraint language for UML [9,10]; thus, UML is the dedicated host language, but combinations with other host languages are feasible. For this purpose the interface between OCL and its host language has deliberately been kept to a minimum: It consists of associations and inheritance relationships between only 13 metaclasses from the UML abstract syntax and the OCL metaclasses. Currently, the OCL is used in combination with either the MOF [11] or the UML. Furthermore, there are some OCL dialects that depend on other host languages: for example, eXpand in openArchitectureWare [12], which depends on EMF, and the Orcas version of Visual Studio with C# 3.0 and the Linq library (see [13]).

Figure 7.5 shows the Types package from the OCL abstract syntax model (the figure can be found in Section 8 of the OCL specification). The gray classes belong to OCL; the white classes belong to UML. Every type in OCL is a subclass from the UML metaclass Classifier; thus, every OCL type must adhere to the semantics of this UML metaclass, which are described elsewhere in the book.

7.3.2 Semantic Domain: Values

As explained in the preceding section, the semantics of the OCL types are given by the semantics of the metaclass Classifier from UML or its substitute in another host language. However, in correspondence with the extension of the UML type system in the Types package in the OCL ASM, the semantics of the Classifier must also be

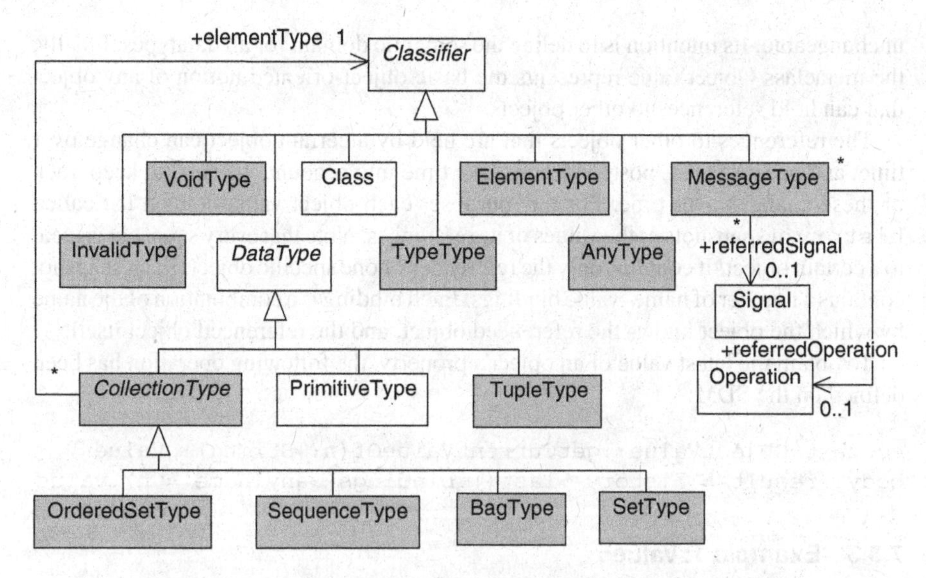

FIGURE 7.5 Types package from the OCL abstract syntax model.

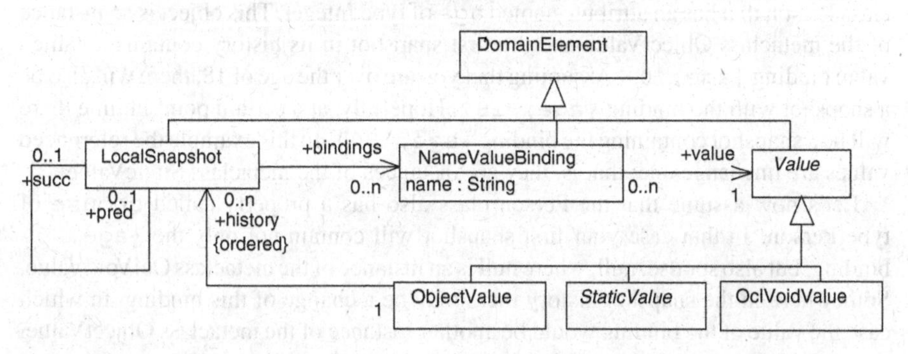

FIGURE 7.6 Values package from the OCL semantic domain model.

extended. The semantics of OCL must specify, for example, the meaning of the OCL CollectionType and TupleType metaclasses.

The basis for the semantics of the OCL types is the assumption that OCL is always used in combination with a host language that adheres to the object-oriented ideas of values being objects that can hold references to other objects. This basic idea is captured in the Values package in the SDM, which is shown in Figure 7.6. Every element in the SDM inherits from the metaclass DomainElement, just as every metaclass in the ASM inherits from ModelElement.

As shown in Figure 7.6, the abstract metaclass Value has three subclasses: ObjectValue, StaticValue, and OclVoidValue. OclVoidValue is the representation of the undefined value (null, void, OclUndefined). Its intention is to define the semantic domain for the OclVoid type. The metaclass StaticValue represents all values that are unchangeable. Its intention is to define the semantic domain for all datatypes. Finally, the metaclass ObjectValue represents the basic object-oriented notion of any object that can hold references to other objects.

The references to other objects that are held by a certain object can change over time, and because OCL postconditions take time into account, we need to keep track of these changes over time. For this purpose, each object value holds a list called `history` of snapshots of the values of its references. Note that every snapshot is local to a certain object: It contains only the references of one specific object. Each snapshot contains a number of name–value bindings. Each binding is a combination of the name by which the object knows the referenced object, and the referenced object itself.

To obtain the latest value of an object's property, the following operation has been defined on the SDM:

```
context ObjectValue::getCurrentValueOf(n: String): Value
body: result = history->last().bindings->any(name = n).value
```

7.3.3 Example 1: Values

As an example of how to interpret the Values package, think of yourself as an object of class Person that has an attribute named `age` of type Integer. This object is an instance of the metaclass ObjectValue and the first snapshot in its history contains a name–value binding `{age, 0}`. Assuming that you are over the age of 18, there will also be a snapshot with the binding `{age, 18}`. Hopefully, at a certain point in time there will be a snapshot containing the binding `{age, 90}`. In this example the referenced values are unchangeable; that is, they are instances of the metaclass StaticValue.

Let's now assume that the Person class also has a property called `spouse` of type Person. In that case your first snapshot will contain not only the `{age, 0}` binding, but also spouse, null, where null is an instance of the metaclass OclVoidValue. Somewhere in the snapshot history there may be a change of this binding, in which case the value of the binding would be another instance of the metaclass ObjectValue. Thus, the instances of ObjectValue form the expected graph of objects as nodes and references as edges.

To obtain the latest value of your spouse property, the following (meta) operation call must be executed:

```
YOU.getCurrentValueOf('spouse')
```

To obtain your latest spouse's age we need the following (meta)operation call:

```
YOU.getCurrentValueOf('spouse').getCurrentValueOf('age')
```

7.3.4 Example 2: OCL Set Values

In Section 7.3.2 I have stated the intention of the metaclasses ObjectValue, Static Value, and OclVoidValue, which is to serve as the semantic domain for certain metaclasses from the ASM. These intentions have been formalized for each abstract syntax metaclass in the Types package in the form of associations and well-formedness rules. All of these can be found in the OCL specification. In this section only one example is explained, that of the OCL Set type.

Informally, the meaning of the OCL Set type can be stated as: The OCL Set type defines values each of which is unchangeable over time and each of which holds a number of other values that must be unique within the set value. More formally, this means that each set value is an instance of the SDM metaclass StaticValue, but this is not enough because set values hold other values. Therefore, the SDM metaclass SetTypeValue was introduced. It inherits its collection nature from the metaclass CollectionValue, which is a subclass of StaticValue (see Figure 7.7).

A collection value is a list of values. In the metamodel, this list of values is shown as an association from CollectionValue to Element. Element instances function as a holder for a single part of a tuple value or collection value. An element has an index number and a value.[1] The purpose of the index number is to identify uniquely the position of each element within the enclosing collection when it is used as an element of a sequence or ordered set. Note that each collection has an implicit identity that is different from the identity of each of its elements.

With this knowledge we are able to define the uniqueness of the set's elements by the following constraint:

```
context SetTypeValue
inv: self.element->isUnique(e : Element | e.value)
```

7.3.5 Mapping OCL Types to Values

Once the ASM and SDM are specified in detail, the semantic mapping is relatively simple. The semantic mapping is described in the AS-Domain package (see Section 10.4 of the OCL specification). The package contains no extra metaclasses, only a large number of associations between ASM metaclasses and SDM metaclasses and a number of well-formedness rules defined on these associations. Looking again at the OCL Set type, the semantic mapping is given by the association between the ASM metaclass SetType and the SDM metaclass SetTypeValue as shown in Fig. 7.7. There are no well-formedness rules defined on this association.

7.4 OCL SEMANTICS: EXPRESSIONS AND EVALUATIONS

As stated in Section 7.3, the OCL semantic domain is divided into two parts: values and evaluations. In this section we explain the second part, the evaluations, thus defining the semantics of OCL expressions.

7.4.1 Semantic Domain: Evaluations and Their Context

The Evaluations package in the SDM provides the elements that represent a "calculation" of the result of an OCL expression. Figure 7.8 shows the most important

[1] A minor correction to the OCL specification is required. The class Element should also have a name attribute. The name is used when the instance is part of a tuple value.

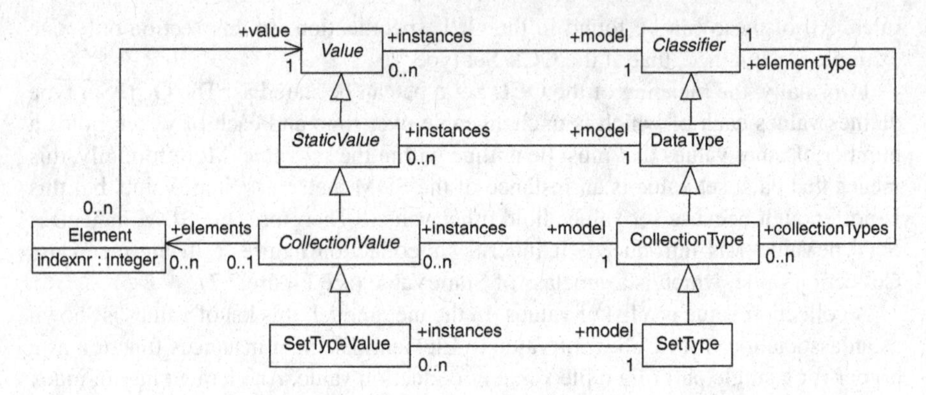

FIGURE 7.7 Semantic mapping of the OCL Set type.

element in this package: OclExpEval, the class that represents any evaluation of an OCL expression. The value that results from an evaluation is represented by the property `resultValue` of type Value. One could rightly state that the complete OCL semantics is dedicated to describing the value of this property, thus answering the question stated in the introduction: What is the resulting value of evaluating an OCL expression?

7.4.1.1 Bindings To be able to determine the value of the property `resultValue`, all variables in the expression need to be bound. Similar to the binding of object values and their references, this binding is represented by a set of instances of the class NameValueBinding. Figure 7.8 shows three different sets of

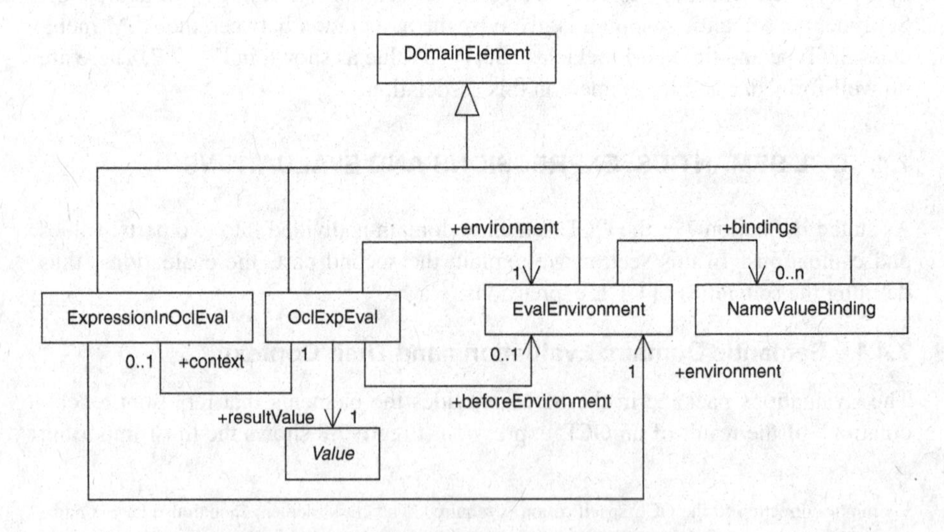

FIGURE 7.8 Evaluations package from the SDM.

bindings for one OclExpEval: `environment`, `beforeEnvironment`, and—via ExpressionInOclEval—`context.environment`. The first contains the bindings that are visible for this evaluation and the names by which they can be referenced. A second set of bindings contains all bindings that were present at precondition time. These are used only when the expression to be evaluated is a postcondition. The third is a constant set of bindings that are given by the context in which the expression is used. Note that because an expression can be part of a larger expression, names may become invisible for the inner expression; that is, they are not included in its environment set of bindings. Still, for every subexpression the context set of bindings is the same.

For example, focus on the subexpression `child.age < self.age` in the following postcondition:

```
context Person::adoptChild(child : Person)
pre: child.age < 18 and self.age > 18
post: self.children->includes( child ) and
 self.children->forAll( child | child.age < self.age )
```

The subexpression's context bindings contain a single object: namely, the object that has executed the operation `adoptChild`, named `self` of type Person. Using the metaoperation `getCurrentValueOf` defined above, we can obtain the values for its properties `age` and `children`, and for each of its children we can obtain the value of the child's properties.

The subexpression's precondition bindings differ from the context bindings because the set property `children` is still unchanged. It does not yet contain the new child. The expression's precondition bindings contain (a copy of) the self object, whose `history` property remains unchanged. Furthermore, the expression's precondition bindings contain a binding of the name `child` to the value of the operation's parameter as it was at precondition time.

The postcondition bindings for the given subexpression are the same as the context bindings combined with a binding for the name `child`, not to the value of the operation's parameter at postcondition time but to one of the elements of the set `self.children`. The declaration of the variable `child` within the forAll loop hides the operation's parameter.

7.4.1.2 *Passing Bindings and Results Through the Tree* Expressions and subexpressions are structured as trees, of which the top is always an ExpressionInOcl instance (defined in Section 12 of the OCL specification). A simple way of thinking about evaluations is that they form a similar tree. In this tree the environment set of bindings is passed down from the top of the tree to the bottom, sometimes changing for a certain subexpression. The result value is calculated on the leaves and then passed upward to the top, while at every node the result value of that subexpression is calculated based on the result values of its branches. A well-formedness rule ensures that the result value of the evaluation of an OCL expression is an instance of the type of that expression:

```
context OclExpEval
inv: resultValue.isInstanceOf( model.type )
```

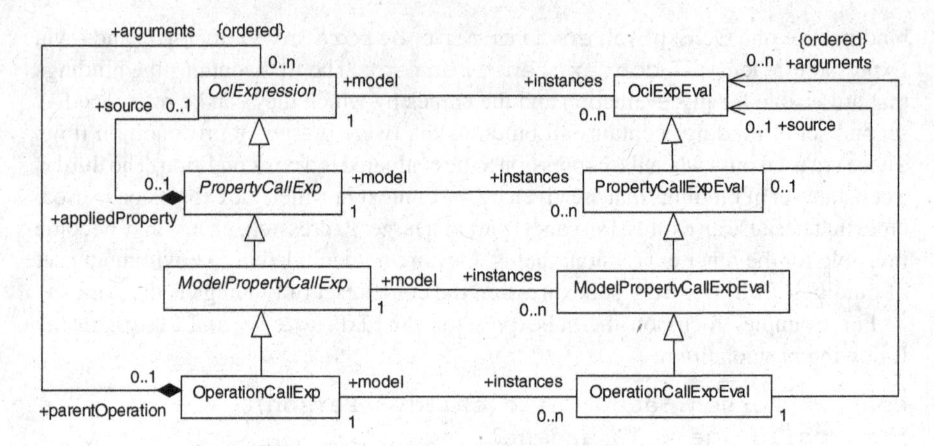

FIGURE 7.9 Semantic mapping of OCL expressions.

7.4.2 Mapping Expressions to Evaluations

The semantic mapping of expressions to evaluations is described in the AS-Domain package (see Section 10.4 of the OCL specification), as is the semantic mapping of types to values. Figure 7.9 shows the associations that constitute the semantic mapping for the abstract syntax metaclass OperationCallExp, which represent an operation call. Well-formedness rules are put in place to ensure the correct configuration of evaluations; for instance:

```
context PropertyCallExpEval
inv: source.model = model.source
```

The result value of an operation call expression is a complicated thing, because of the existence of out and in/out parameters. If the operation has no out or in/out parameters, its result value will have the type given by the Operation being called; else the type will be a tuple containing all out or in/out parameters and the result value. This is specified by the following well-formedness rule.

```
context OperationCallEval inv:
let outparameters : Set( Parameter )  =
  referredOperation.parameter->select( p |
      p.kind = ParameterDirectionKind::in/out or
      p.kind = ParameterDirectionKind::out)
  in
    if outparameters->isEmpty()
    then resultValue.model = model.referredOperation.parameter
      ->select(kind = ParameterDirectionKind::result).type
    else resultValue.model.oclIsType( TupleType ) and
      outparameters->forAll( p |
        resultValue.model.attribute->exists( a |
          a.name = p.name and a.type = p.type ))
    endif
```

As explained, the definition of the semantics of the operation call expression, (i.e., the rule that gives the result value) depends on the definition of operation call execution in the UML semantics. This is part of the UML infrastructure specification and is not defined in the OCL specification.

7.4.3 Example 3: A Let Expression

The following let expression defines an invariant on the Person class which states that the age of the spouse of a person must be over 18 and must not be equal to the age of the person him- or herself.

```
context Person
inv: let spouse-age: Integer = self.spouse.age
  in spouse-age <> self.age and spouse-age >= 18
```

This expression can be structured as shown in Figure 7.10. To evaluate this expression, the context must provide the value bindings for the self variable and the properties of the self object. These bindings are available to every subexpression. The binding of the name `spouse-age` to a particular value is present in the environment of the subexpression in the in-part of the let clause and its subexpressions, but not to the subexpression `self.spouse.age`. This is a general rule and is defined in the semantics by the following well-formedness rule:[2]

```
context LetExpEval
inv: in.environment = self.environment ->add(
    NameValueBinding( variable, initExpression.resultValue ))
```

The result of the expression is determined from the leaves of the tree. For instance, the value of the subexpression `self.age` is given by a call to the additional operation

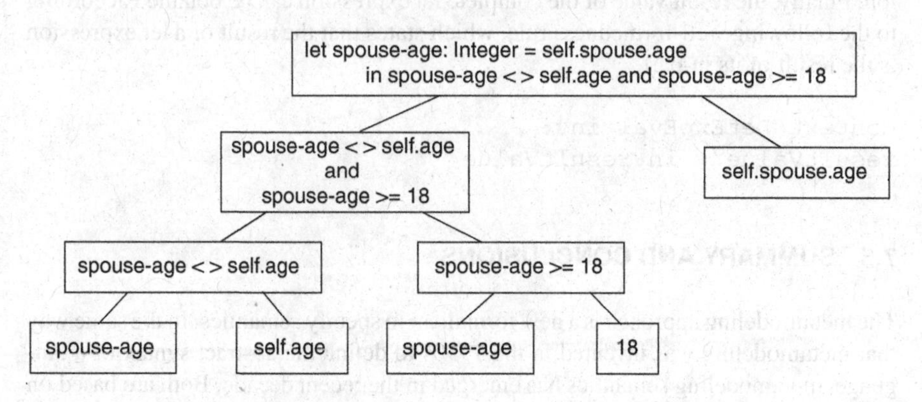

FIGURE 7.10 Let expression structured as a tree.

[2] This rule is evidence of a second minor revision of the OCL specification. In the specification the new name value binding is created as NameValueBinding(variable.varName, variable.initExpression.result-Value). The rule in this chapter is a correction thereof.

mentioned in Section 7.3.2, which is defined in the semantics in the well-formedness rule for AttributeCallExpEval:

```
context AttributeCallExpEval inv:
resultValue =
  if source.resultValue->isOclType(ObjectValue)
  then source.resultValue->asOclType(ObjectValue)
    .getCurrentValueOf(referredAttribute.name)
  else -- must be a tuple value
    source.resultValue->asOclType( TupleValue )
    .getValueOf(referredAttribute.name)
endif
```

Note that thc source property of an AttributeCallExpEval is an OclExpEval instance. In this example the result value of the source will be the self object. The if-statement in the well-formedness rule is present to distinguish between the evaluation of a property of an object and a property of a tuple value. Once the result values of subexpressions `self.age` and `spouse-age` have been determined, the values can be used to determine the result value of the subexpression `spouse-age <> self.age`. This subexpression is an instance of the ASM metaclass OperationCallExp and is evaluated by an OperationCallExpEval. Here again, the fact that OCL is not a stand-alone language emerges. The semantics of an operation call must be provided by the host language and is therefore not included in the OCL specification. The OCL semantics assumes that the OperationCallExpEval obtains the correct result value. However, the OCL semantics do state that the environments for the arguments of an OperationCallExpEval are equal to the environment of the OperationCallExpEval itself. The result values of the other subexpressions are determined in the same fashion. Finally, the result value of the complete let expression can be obtained according to the following well-formedness rule, which states that the result of a let expression is the result of its in-part.

```
context LetExpEval inv:
resultValue = in.resultValue
```

7.5 SUMMARY AND CONCLUSIONS

The metamodeling approach is a new formalism to specify semantics. In the same way that metamodeling was invented in the 1990s to define the abstract syntax of a language, metamodeling semantics has emerged in the recent decade. Both are based on creating a model that provides metainformation on the mogram or linguistic utterance.

The abstract syntax model defines the rules to determine whether a given mogram is a valid element of the language. The semantic domain model provides the possible values of the mogram, where the word *values* must be understood in a very broad sense. The semantic mapping is given by associating the metaclasses in the abstract syntax model with the metaclasses in the semantic domain model. Part of the semantic mapping are constraints that restrict these associations.

The OCL semantics provided in Section 10 of the standard are written using the metamodeling formalism. The semantic domain model is divided into two parts, values and evaluations. Each OCL expression type is associated with a specific evaluation type, which in turn is restricted by specific constraints. The value that results from an evaluation can be considered to be the heart of the semantics of the expression. This value is represented by a property called `resultValue` of an evaluation. Well-formedness rules specify how this property is calculated.

The metamodeling formalism for specifying the OCL semantics was preferred over a purely mathematical approach (Appendix A in [14], written by Mark Richters) because the metamodeling formalism is close to the formalisms known to users of UML and readers of the UML and OCL specifications. However, it is still a young and not very widely explored formalism. Further research is necessary to determine the full possibilities of the metamodeling formalism.

REFERENCES

1. OMG. *OCL 2.0 Specification.* Technical Report Formal/06-05-01. Object Management Group, Needham, MA, 2006.
2. T. Clark, A. Evans, S. Kent, S. Brodsky, and S. Cook. *A Feasibility Study in Rearchitecting UML as a Family of Languages Using a Precise OO Meta-Modeling Approach.* Technical Report. Clark, Evans, Kent and IBM, Sept. 2000.
3. C. K. Ogden and I. A. Richards, eds. *The Meaning of Meaning: A Study of the Influence of Language upon Thought and of the Science of Symbolism*, reissue edition. Harcourt, New York, June 1989. First published in 1923.
4. J. E. Hopcroft and J. D. Ullman. *Introduction to Automata Theory, Languages and Computation.* Addison-Wesley, Reading, MA, 1979.
5. A. Kleppe. *Software Language Engineering: Creating Domain-Specific Languages Using Metamodels.* Addison-Wesley Longman, Boston, Jan. 2009.
6. A. Kleppe and J. Warmer. *Unification of Static and Dynamic Semantics of UML.* Technical Report K-01. Klasse Objecten, July 2001.
7. J. H. Hausmann. Dynamic meta modeling: a semantics description technique for visual modeling languages. Ph.D. dissertation, University of Paderborn, Tönning, Lübeck und Marburg, Germany, Oct. 2005.
8. G. Engels, J. H. Hausmann, R. Heckel, and S. Sauer. Dynamic meta modeling: a graphical approach to the operational semantics of behavioral diagrams in UML. In A. Evans, S. Kent, and B. Selic, eds., *Proceedings of UML 2000: The Unified Modeling Language, Advancing the Standard, 3rd International Conference*, York, UK, October 2–6, 2000, Lecture Notes in Computer Science, vol. 1939, pp. 323–337. Springer-Verlag, New York, 2000.
9. OMG. *Unified Modeling Language (UML): Infrastructure.* Technical Report ptc/04-10-14. Object Management Group, Needham, MA, 2004.
10. OMG. *Unified Modeling Language (UML): Superstructure.* Technical Report Formal/05-07-04. Object Management Group, Needham, MA, 2005.

11. OMG. *Meta Object Facility (MOF) Core Specification, Version 2.0*. Technical Report Formal/06-01-01. Object Management Group, Needham, MA, 2006.
12. openArchitectureWare. http://www.openarchitectureware.org/, 2008.
13. D. Akehurst, G. Howells, M. Scheidgen, and K. McDonald-Maier. C# 3.0 makes OCL redundant! In *Ocl4All: Modelling Systems with OCL*. Electronic Communications of the EASST, vol. 9. European Association of Software Science and Technology, Nashville, TN, 2007.
14. OMG. *OCL 2.0 Final Adopted Specification*. Technical Report ptc/03-1014. Object Management Group, Needham, MA, 2003.

CHAPTER 8

AXIOMATIC SEMANTICS OF STATE MACHINES

KEVIN LANO and DAVID CLARK
Department of Computer Science, King's College London, London, UK

8.1 INTRODUCTION

In this chapter we provide an axiomatic semantics of UML 2 state machine notation by translating this notation into the RAL formalism introduced in Chapter 6. Initially, we consider "flat" state machines without state hierarchies, then extend the semantics to include nested and concurrent states and compound transitions. The semantics is used to resolve issues of ambiguity with the informal definitions of transition priority and history states in the UML documents.

Figure 8.1 shows the state machine metamodel which we consider initially. Notice that *Behavior* inherits from *Class*, so particular kinds of behavior, such as state machines or interactions, can have local (owned) attributes and can be instantiated and specialized. We represent behavior instances by invocation instances (α, i) of the semantic action α representing the behavior (described in Chapter 6): This is reasonable since there is always only a finite number of such instances in any system execution, so they can be enumerated in order of their creation.

In this model, *Parameter* also inherits from *TypedElement* and *MultiplicityElement*. State machines can have entry actions to states, and state invariants. Behavior state machine transitions are written with the syntax

$$s \longrightarrow_{ev[G]/acts} t$$

where s is the source state, t the target state, ev a trigger event (an operation call), G a guard condition, and $acts$ a list of actions $objs.op(p)$ to be performed on supplier objects or on the *self* object. Protocol transitions have a postcondition in place of the actions. The trigger, guard, and actions/postcondition can all be omitted. The default guard is *true*.

UML 2 Semantics and Applications. Edited by Kevin Lano

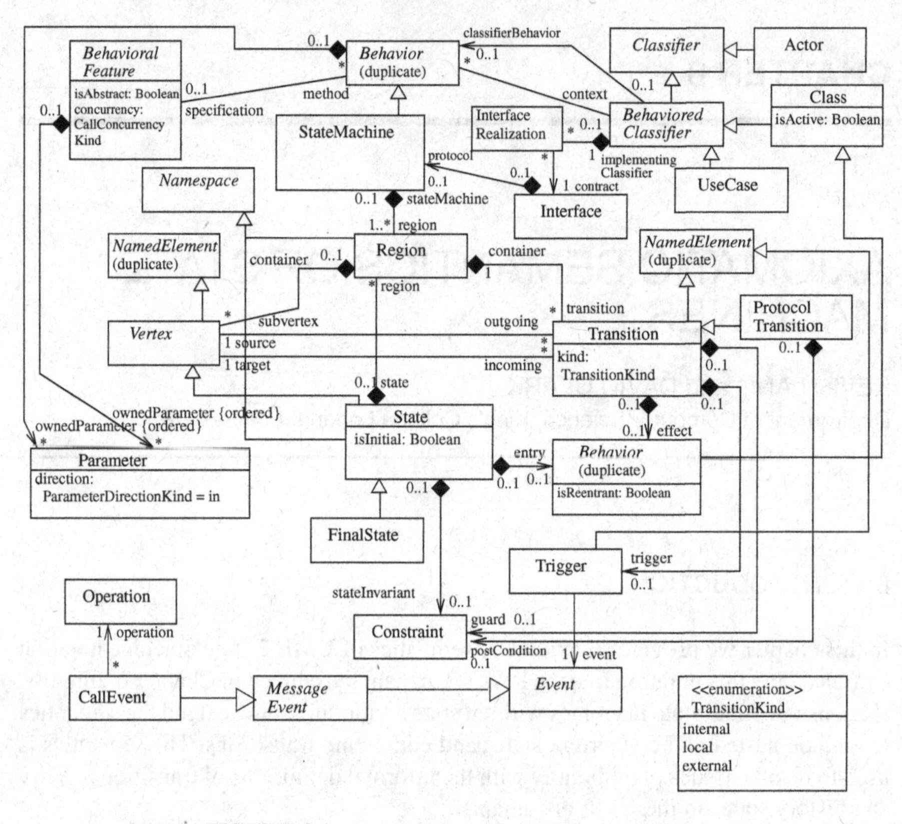

FIGURE 8.1 Restricted state machine metamodel.

The following restrictions apply compared to UML 2 state machines:

- Only state machines that consist only of basic (noncomposite) states are used. Concurrent composite states are not permitted except at the top level of the system specification:

$$region \rightarrow size() = 1$$

  is an invariant of *StateMachine* in Figure 8.1.
- There are no pseudostates such as history states. Initial states are represented by the *isInitial* attribute of *State*.
- If a state machine describes the behavior of objects of a class, all the triggers of its transitions are call events of operations of this class:

$$\begin{aligned} & specification \rightarrow isEmpty() \quad implies \\ & \quad region.transition \rightarrow forAll(trigger \rightarrow size() \; = \; 1) \quad and \\ & \quad region.transition.trigger.event \rightarrow forAll(oclIsTypeOf(CallEvent)) \quad and \\ & \quad context.feature \rightarrow includesAll(region.transition.trigger.event.operation) \end{aligned}$$

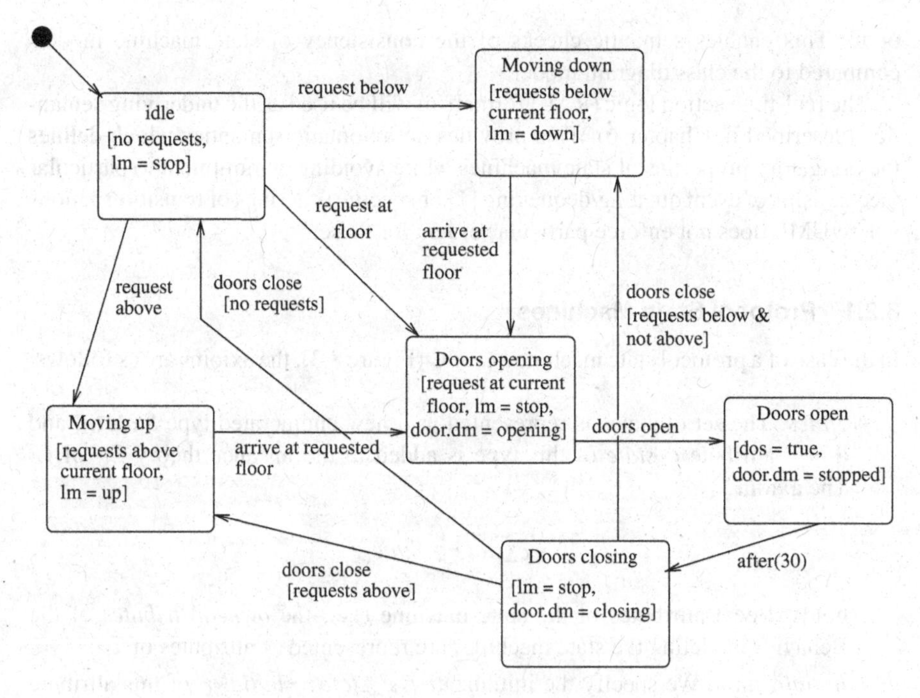

FIGURE 8.2 Lift state machine.

Active classes can also have timeout triggers in their state machine.

- If a state machine describes the behavior of an operation, its transitions have no triggers (they are triggered by completion events of their source states [49, p. 570]):

$$specification \rightarrow notEmpty() \ implies \ region.transition.trigger = Set\{\}$$

A simple example of a protocol state machine for a class could be that for a lift (Figure 8.2).

8.2 STATE MACHINE SEMANTICS

We consider initially the metamodel of Figure 8.1. This incorporates both protocol and behavior state machines, and also permits behavior state machines to have state invariants, which is a generalization of UML behavior state machine notation. We consider this to be useful because behavior state machines may describe algorithms, and therefore state invariants are useful to define loop invariants or other intermediate pre- and postconditions.

We define the semantics of protocol and behavior state machines for a class C by incorporating their semantics into theories representing the class diagram semantics of C. This enables semantic checks of the consistency of state machine models compared to the class diagram model.

The real-time action logic (RAL) formalism will be used as the underlying semantics (described in Chapter 6). This provides an axiomatic semantics which defines the obligatory properties of state machines while avoiding commitment to particular mechanisms of event queuing/dequeuing [1] or specific orderings of transition actions where UML does not enforce particular orders for these.

8.2.1 Protocol State Machines

In the case of a protocol state machine SC of C (Figure 8.3), the axioms are as follows:

- *States*. The set of states is represented as a new enumerated type $State_{SC}$, and a new attribute *c_state* of this type is added to the instance theory $\mathcal{I}_C$ of C. The axiom

$$c\_state \in State_{SC}$$

  holds. Local attributes of the state machine (i.e., the *ownedAttributes* of the Behavior modeling the state machine) are represented as attributes of $\mathcal{I}_C$.
- *Initialization*. We specify the initialization $c\_state := initial_{SC}$ of this attribute to the initial state of SC. This initialization is invoked by $init_C$ ("When an instance of a behaviored classifier is created, its classifier behavior is invoked" [49, p. 434]).
- *Transitions*. Each transition *tr* from a state *src* to a state *trg*, triggered by $m(x)$, with guard G and postcondition *Post*, is represented as an additional pre- or postspecification of m [49, p. 535],

$$(c\_state = src \wedge G')$$

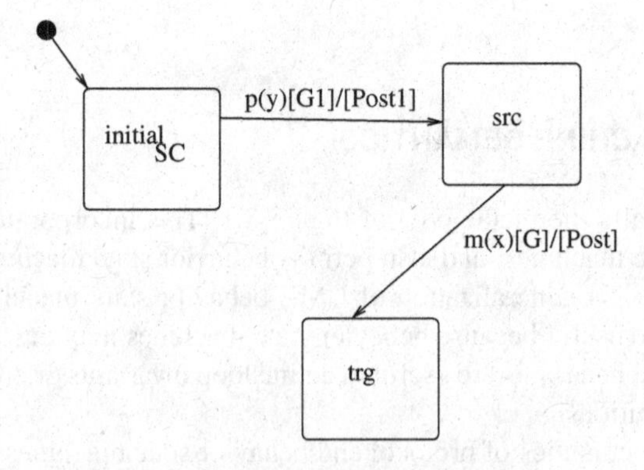

FIGURE 8.3 Protocol state machine example.

as an additional disjunct of the semantic representation of the precondition of $m(x)$, and

$$(c\_state = src \wedge G')@pre \Rightarrow (c\_state = trg \wedge Post')$$

as an additional conjunct of the postcondition. G' is the semantic interpretation of G, as in Chapter 6. Axiom (*OpD*) of Chapter 6 applies with these extended conditions. The write frame of m is extended to include *c_state* and any attributes or roles in a writable modality in *Post*. Only operations with at least one transition in the state machine have *c_state* in their write frame—other operations are assumed not to change the state [49, p. 536].

- *StateInv*. State invariants Inv_s have the semantics

$$exists_C = TRUE \wedge c\_state = s \Rightarrow Inv'_s$$

An alternative modeling approach would be to use actions to represent individual transitions [30].

In the UML documents there is an apparent inconsistency regarding the time at which guards are evaluated: "the guard is evaluated before the transition is triggered" [49, p. 571], "the [guard] expression is evaluated at the moment the transition attached to the guard is attempted" [51, Sec. 12.11], and another, similar statement [49, p. 568]. The latter corresponds correctly with the equivalence of transition guards and preconditions (for protocol state machines) and with our semantic interpretation. In practical implementation, the guard may be evaluated before the transition is selected and starts executing; however, its truth value should not change over this interval.

8.2.2 Behavior State Machines

In the case of a behavior state machine *SC* of a class *C*, transitions have an action that executes when the transition is taken, instead of a postcondition. The transition actions *acts* are sequences

$$obj_1.op_1(e_1); \ldots; obj_n.op_n(e_n)$$

of operation calls on supplier objects, sets of supplier objects, or on the *self* object. These can be represented as composite actions *acts'* in RAL:

$$obj'_1.op_1(e'_1); \ldots; obj'_n.op_n(e'_n)$$

where obj'_i and e'_j are interpretations of these expressions in RAL. In addition to state invariants, there may be entry actions to states.

The axiomatic representation of a behavior state machine is:

- *States*. The set of states is represented as a new enumerated type $State_{SC}$.
- *Initialization*. A new attribute *c_state* of this type is added to $\mathcal{I}_C$, together with the initialization $c\_state := initial_{SC}$ of this attribute to the initial state of *SC*.

An entry action $entry_{initial_{SC}}$ coexecutes with this update, if specified. Local attributes of the state machine are represented as attributes of $\mathcal{I}_C$.

- *Transitions*. The transitions t_i, $i : 1..k$, from states src_i to states trg_i, triggered by $m(x)$, with guard G_i and actions $acts_i$, are represented as an additional operational specification $Code_m$ of m:

$$(BSCOpP): \quad \alpha(x) \supset Code_m$$

where $Code_m$ is the action

```
if (exists_C = TRUE ∧ c_state = src_1 ∧ G'_1)
then acts'_1; c_state := trg_1
else if ....
else if (exists_C = TRUE ∧ c_state = src_k ∧ G'_k)
then acts'_k; c_state := trg_k
```

where α represents m, and any entry action of trg_i is included at the end of the $acts_i$ sequence.

If there is already an existing procedural definition D_m of m in the class C, the complete definition of each case in the definition of m is D'_m; $acts'_j$; $c\_state := trg_j$ [49, p. 436]; we assume that an existing pre- or postspecification should, however, always refer to the entire span of execution of m.

- *Invariants*. The axioms (*StateInv*).

The semantics defined here corresponds to the usual "run to completion" semantics of UML state machines: a transition completes execution only when all of its (synchronously) generated actions do so [49, p. 562].

A behavior state machine *SC* attached to an operation *op* defines an explicit algorithm for *op*. It is formalized as follows:

- *States*. The set of states is represented as a new enumerated type $State_{SC}$.
- *Initialization*. A new attribute *op_state* of this type is added to $\mathcal{I}_C$ as a local variable of *op*, together with the initialization $op\_state := initial_{SC}$ of this attribute to the initial state of *SC*. Local attributes of the state machine are represented as local variables of *op*.
- *Transitions*. The state machine yields the operational definition

$$(BSCOpM): \quad op(p) \supset pre\ exists_C = TRUE\ then\ Code_{op}$$

where $Code_{op}$ is

```
entry'_initial_SC;
op_state := initial_SC;
while op_state ≠ terms_1 ∧ ... ∧
      op_state ≠ terms_m
```

```
do
  if op_state = src1 ∧ G'1
  then
    act'1; entry'trg1; op_state := trg1;
  else if ...
  else if op_state = srck ∧ G'k
  then
    act'k; entry'trgk; op_state := trgk;
```

where the $terms_i$ are all the terminal (final) states of SC (i.e., states with no outgoing transitions), and the transitions of SC are $src_1 \rightarrow_{[G_1]/act_1} trg_1$ up to $src_k \rightarrow_{[G_k]/act_k} trg_k$.

Entry actions of a state must complete before the state machine is considered to enter the state properly ("Before commencing a run-to-completion step, a state machine is in a stable state configuration with all entry ... activities completed" [49, p. 561]. An entry action will often be used to ensure that the state invariant holds.

- *Invariants*. The loop invariant of the *while* loop above is

$$(op\_state = s_1 \Rightarrow Inv'_{s_1}) \wedge \cdots \wedge (op\_state = s_n \Rightarrow Inv'_{s_n})$$

where s_1 to s_n are all the states of SC. This expresses that the local data of the particular execution instance of *op* is in a consistent state, satisfying a particular state invariant, when no transition or entry action is occurring.

8.2.3 Semantic Profiles for State Machine Semantics

The UML semantics for protocol state machines does not specify whether transition guards are preconditions (sufficient conditions for valid execution of the actions of the transition and entering the target state) or are permission guards (necessary conditions for the transition to take place). In addition, the meaning of an omitted transition for an operation is left open: It may mean that execution of the operation in that case is not permitted, is undefined in its effect, or has no effect.

Our semantics assumes only the minimal properties given in [49]:

1. If a logical case is missing for the transitions triggered by an operation, leaving a particular state, the state machine gives no information about the effect of executing the operation in that state, and such an execution may not be possible [49, p. 534].
2. Operations that do not appear on the state machine are assumed to be state-insensitive in their behavior, and not to modify the state [49, p. 536].

To express the concept of a guard as permission for an operation to execute, additional specification notation is needed. A clause $guard : G$ could be added as a new form of constraint to an operation $op(x : X)$. The clause would have the semantics

$$(OpG): \quad \forall x : X \cdot \forall i : \mathbb{N}_1 \cdot G' \circledcirc \uparrow(op(x), i)$$

Alternatively, we could define the disjunction G of guards of the transitions leaving a particular state s and triggered by op as constituting a permission guard for op on that state (similar to the semantics of op being deferred in that state):

$$(PreAsGuard): \quad \forall x : X \cdot \forall i : \mathbb{N}_1 \cdot (c\_state = s \Rightarrow G') \circledcirc \uparrow(op(x), i)$$

The third alternative is that the operation is a "skip" for these missing cases, as in behavior state machines [49, p. 561] (*SkipCase*):

$$\forall x : X \cdot \forall i : \mathbb{N}_1 \cdot (c\_state = s \wedge \neg G') \circledcirc \uparrow(op(x), i) \Rightarrow (c\_state = s) \circledcirc \downarrow(op(x), i)$$

op is permitted to take place if G fails in state s, but then it does not change the state.

These three alternatives form three "semantic profiles" which are alternative extensions of the basic semantics. Each constitutes possible extra notations and additional axioms. Developers should indicate which semantics they are adopting and record this together with the models.

8.3 EXTENDED STATE MACHINES

In this section we consider a larger subset of UML state machine notation, including additional features of composite states, deferred events, compound transitions (modeled semantically as transitions with sets of sources and targets), history states, and final states. Figure 8.4 shows the metamodel for such extended behavior models. We consider first, transitions with postconditions instead of actions, and do not consider entry, exit, or do actions. In Section 8.6 we address these further aspects.

A *basic state* is a state with $region \rightarrow size() = 0$; other states are *composite states*. A composite state with one region is termed an OR state, and a composite state with more than one region is termed an AND state. The default initial state of an OR state or region s is denoted $initial_s$.

In addition to the UML constraints on the metamodel:

1. We require that regions and OR states always have a unique initial pseudostate, a unique default initial state, and at most one final state.
2. We require that default transitions from history states target a top-level substate of the container of the history state. The target state cannot be a pseudostate.
3. Similarly, the default transition from an initial state must target a normal state in the same composite state at the same level as the initial pseudostate.

The notation $s \sqsubseteq s'$ means that $s = s'$ or s is a (recursive) substate of s'.

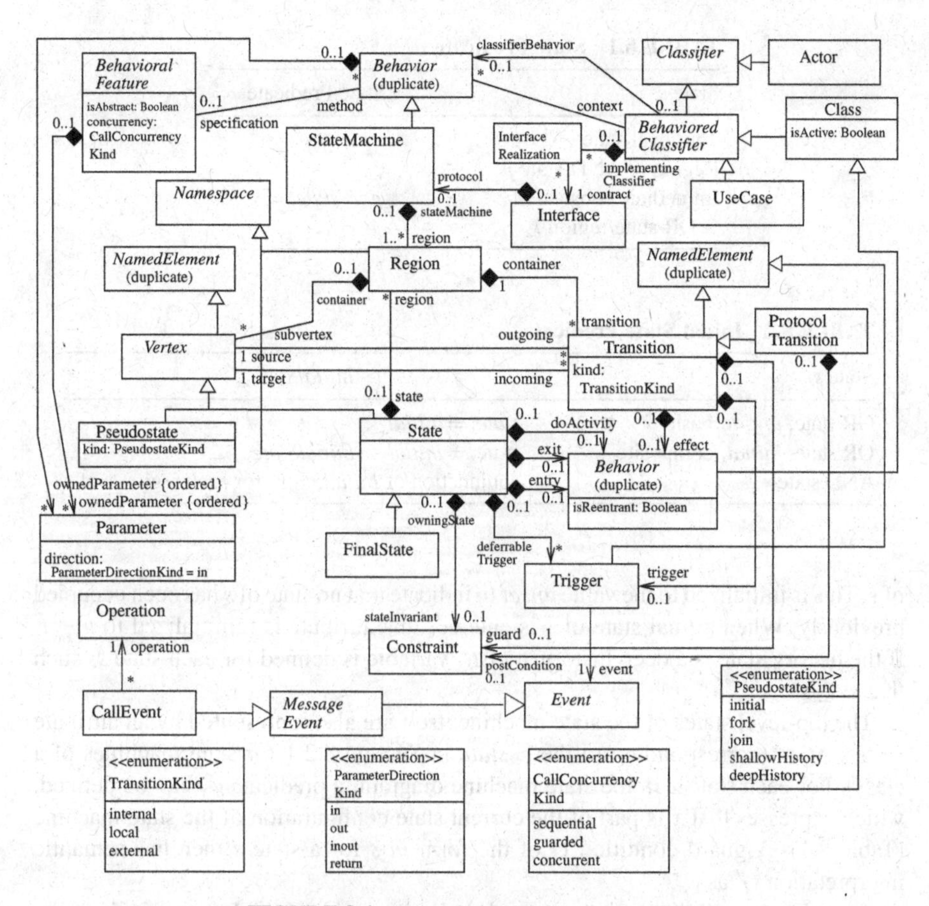

FIGURE 8.4 Extended behavior metamodel.

Normally, if one region r of an AND state has a final state, so should all regions of the AND state; otherwise, a completion event from the AND state can never be triggered by reaching the final state of r.

8.4 SEMANTICS FOR EXTENDED STATE MACHINES

We extend the semantics given to flat state machines to state machines with OR and AND composite states, compound transitions, and history and final states. For each OR state s in the state machine, we define a state attribute $state_s : State_s$, where $State_s$ represents the set of normal states (including final states) contained directly in s. Regions of an AND state are also represented by a type and an attribute in the same manner (so must be named). Each such OR state/region has a default initial state $initial_s$, and each $state_s$ is initialized to this value. If a final state is present, it is denoted by $final_s$. If s has a history pseudostate as a direct substate, an attribute $last_s : State_s \cup \{unset\}$ is also introduced, to record the last active top-level substate

TABLE 8.1 State Predicate

State s	State Predicate φ_s
Top-level state	$state = s$
Region of AND-state p	φ_p
Immediate substate of OR state/region r	$\varphi_r \wedge state_r = s$

TABLE 8.2 Initial State Predicate

State s	$InitialState_s$
OR state, $initial_s$ basic	$state_s = initial_s$
OR state, $initial_s$ composite	$state_s = initial_s \wedge InitialState_{initial_s}$
AND state	conjunction of $InitialState_r$ for each region r of s

of s. This is initialized to the value *unset* to indicate that no state of s has been occupied previously. When a final state of s is entered, this attribute is reinitialized to *unset*. If the history state is a deep history, a $last_{ss}$ variable is defined for each state ss such that $ss \sqsubseteq s$.

The top-level states of the state machine itself are also represented by an attribute $state : State$ (corresponding to the *c_state* in Section 8.2.1 for state machines of a class). For each state x in the state machine diagram, a predicate φ_x can be defined, which expresses that x is part of the current state configuration of the state machine (Table 8.1). A guard condition G of the form *in* s for a state s then has semantic interpretation G' as φ_s.

A predicate $InitialState_s$ expresses that the (recursive) initial state of s is occupied (Table 8.2). Using these predicates, the state-changing behavior of transitions can be expressed as pre- and postconditions. The *enabling condition* $enc(tr, s)$ of a transition tr

$$s \rightarrow_{op[G]/Post} t$$

from state s is $\varphi_s \wedge G'$, conjoined with $\neg(\varphi_{ss} \wedge G'_1)$ for each different transition tr' from a state ss, $ss \neq s$, $ss \sqsubseteq s$, for the same trigger event:

$$ss \rightarrow_{op[G_1]/Post'} tt$$

This expresses that tr is enabled only if higher-priority transitions for the same event are not enabled.

The precondition for operation op derived from a transition tr triggered by op is then the conjunction

$$enc(tr) = \wedge_{s \in sources(tr)} enc(tr, s)$$

of the $enc(tr, s)$ for each explicit source s of tr.

TABLE 8.3 Target State Predicate

State t	$Target_{tr}$
composite state	$InitialState_t$
basic nonhistory state	φ_t
shallow history state in OR-state/region p with direct substates $\{s_1, \ldots, s_m\}$	$(last_p@pre = unset \Rightarrow Target_{tr_0}) \wedge (last_p@pre = s_1 \Rightarrow Target_{tr_1}) \wedge \ldots \wedge (last_p@pre = s_m \Rightarrow Target_{tr_m})$
deep history state in OR-state/region p	$(last_p@pre = unset \Rightarrow Target_{tr_0}) \wedge (last_p@pre \neq unset \Rightarrow LastState_p)$
final state $final_p$	$Target_{tf}$

TABLE 8.4 Last State Predicate

State s	$LastState_s$
OR state, $last_s$ basic	$states_s = last_s$
OR state, $last_s$ composite	$states_s = last_s \wedge LastState_{last_s}$
AND state	conjunction of $LastState_r$ for each region r of s

The enabling condition is a critical semantic aspect that can be defined in different ways to produce different semantic profiles for state machines. We could use an alternative definition $enc'(tr)$, which is the conjunction of $enc(tr, s)$ for each *explicit and implicit* source s of tr. Implicit sources are those AND state regions that contain no explicit source of tr but will be exited when it takes place.

For the postcondition, there are several cases. A predicate $Target_{tr}$ expresses which state(s) are entered directly because of a transition tr with target t (Table 8.3).

In the third and fourth cases, tr_0 is a transition identical to tr except that it is targeted at the default history state of p. In the third case, tr_i is a transition identical to tr except that its target is s_i, the substate of p equal to $last_p$. The difference between shallow and deep history is that in the former, composite substates of the last active state will be entered at their initial state, while with deep history they are entered at their last active state, defined by the predicate $LastState_p$ (Table 8.4). In the final case, tf is a transition composed from tr followed by any completion-triggered transitions triggered by reaching t, from p or (recursively) from superstates of p. For transitions with multiple targets, the conjunction of the *Target* predicate for each target is taken.

In addition to the postcondition describing the direct target, the transition may also cause other states to be reinitialized. After taking account of the effect of history and final states, for each AND composite state x, if transition tr causes x to be entered, then all the regions of x that do not contain an actual target of tr must be reinitialized. This additional effect (which may apply to several AND compositions) is expressed by a predicate $ReInit_{tr}$.

The complete postcondition of tr is the conjunction Π_{tr} of its explicit postcondition, its target state predicate(s), and $ReInit_{tr}$. The axioms regarding states and initialization in Section 8.2.1 can therefore be restated using the $state_r$ variables for each OR state and region r. The axiom dealing with transitions applies with the pre- and postconditions derived from each transition as described above;

$$enc(tr)$$

is added as an additional disjunct of the semantic representation of the precondition of $op(x)$, for each transition tr triggered by $op(x)$, and

$$enc(tr)@pre \Rightarrow \Pi_{tr}$$

is added as an additional conjunct of the postcondition. This definition allows several transitions triggered by op to execute together, provided that they do not conflict.

The axiom StateInv in Section 8.2.1 holds in the form

$$\varphi_s \Rightarrow Inv_s$$

for each state s.

Other elements of UML state machine notation can also be given a semantics:

1. If event e is deferred in state s, which also has a set of explicit transitions $tr_i : s_i \rightarrow_{e[G_i]/Post_i} t_i$ for e, where $s_i \sqsubseteq s$, this means that e cannot be consumed unless one of these transitions is enabled:

$$\forall i : \mathbb{N}_1 \cdot (\varphi_s \Rightarrow enc(tr_1) \vee \cdots \vee enc(tr_n)) \circledcirc \uparrow(e, i)$$

This is in accordance with the semantics of UML superstructure version 2.1.1 [49], whereby substates that accept an event override superstates that defer it.

2. Internal transitions $\rightarrow_{e[G]/Post}$ of state s are expressed as pre- and postconditions of e with the form $\varphi_s \wedge G'$ and $(\varphi_s \wedge G')@pre \Rightarrow \varphi_s \wedge Post'$.
3. Timeout transitions $src \rightarrow_{after(T)} trg$ are given a semantics by defining that they are fired as soon as φ_{src} has been true for duration T:

$$duration(\varphi_{src}) \geq T$$

where $duration(P)$ is defined as

$$duration(P) \circledast t = max(\{0\} \cup \{x : TIME \mid \forall y : TIME \cdot y \in [t - x, t] \Rightarrow P \circledcirc y\})$$

4. If an operation of class C has a method (behavior) with $isReentrant = false$, the action α representing the operation cannot coexecute with itself:

$$\#active(\alpha) \leq 1$$

is an axiom of $\mathcal{I}_C$.

The semantic definition for behavior state machines is similar except that we define the sequence of actions executed by a transition in addition to the target state predicate (Section 8.6).

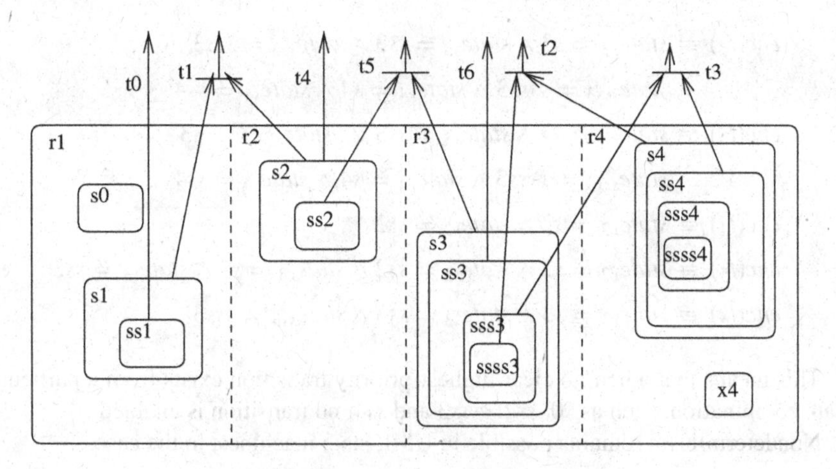

FIGURE 8.5 Priority examples [7].

8.5 SOLUTIONS FOR SEMANTIC PROBLEMS

Many of the semantic problems identified by Fecher et al. [7] remain in the UML 2 state machine notation definitions [49]. In particular, the definitions of transition priority have not been improved and remain ambiguous: "The priority of joined transitions is based on the priority of the transition with the most transitively nested source state" [49, p. 562]. Page 563 of [49] gives an algorithm for calculating the fired set of transitions when an event occurs involves starting from "innermost nested simple states" [49, p. 563], but it does not resolve cases such as Figure 8.5. We assume that all the transitions are triggered by the same event and have *true* guards.

Our semantics defines solutions to the problems of ambiguity and imprecision of UML identified by Fecher et al. [7] for transition priority and history states. For priority the semantics implies that a transition t has priority over another t' in state s if t is enabled in this state and t' is not.

For history states, the semantics means that the history of an OR state/region is always unset by entering a final state [49, p. 551], and that this history is independent of the history of any other state in the model.

8.5.1 Transition Priorities

We define that transition t has priority over transition t' (which has the same trigger) in a state s if

$$\varphi_s \implies enc(t) \land \neg\, enc(t')$$

In the example of Figure 8.5, we have

$$enc(t_0) \equiv state_{r1} = s1 \land state_{s1} = ss1$$
$$enc(t_1) \equiv state_{r1} = s1 \land state_{s1} \neq ss1 \land state_{r2} = s2 \land state_{s2} \neq ss2$$

$$enc(t_2) \equiv state_{r3} = s3 \wedge state_{s3} = ss3 \wedge state_{ss3} = sss3 \wedge$$
$$state_{sss3} = ssss3 \wedge state_{r4} = s4 \wedge state_{s4} \neq ss4$$
$$enc(t_3) \equiv state_{r3} = s3 \wedge state_{s3} = ss3 \wedge state_{ss3} = sss3 \wedge$$
$$state_{sss3} \neq ssss3 \wedge state_{r4} = s4 \wedge state_{s4} = ss4$$
$$enc(t_4) \equiv state_{r2} = s2 \wedge state_{s2} \neq ss2$$
$$enc(t_5) \equiv state_{r2} = s2 \wedge state_{s2} = ss2 \wedge state_{r3} = s3 \wedge state_{s3} \neq ss3$$
$$enc(t_6) \equiv state_{r3} = s3 \wedge state_{s3} = ss3 \wedge state_{ss3} \neq sss3$$

This means that when no clear highest-priority transition exists from a particular state combination, such as $s0$, $ss2$, $ssss3$ and $ss4$, no transition is enabled.

Nondeterminism remains possible in UML state machines, in the cases:

1. Two transitions with the same priority can be enabled at the same time from the same state (e.g., t_0 and t_4 and t_6 are all enabled in the states $ss1$, $s2$, $ss3$, and $x4$).
2. The order of entry actions to orthogonal regions, exit actions from orthogonal regions, and actions on transitions executed in orthogonal regions as part of the same event reaction are undefined [49, p.551].
3. The choice of enabled transitions exiting a choice point is not defined [49, p. 538].

The first indicates a potential inconsistency in a state machine model and should be eliminated: It can be checked statically, since the enabling conditions (omitting transition guards) consist only of equalities and inequalities over finite sets. The second can be modeled using the parallel execution operator $\|$. The third indicates an ambiguous model, which should be made unambiguous by refining the conditions concerned.

If we take the stronger definition of enabling, enc', from Section 8.4, then many cases of transitions that conflict under the *enc* definition no longer conflict. t_0, for example, has the implicit source $r2$, which is disabled if t_4 is enabled. However, this definition is further from the visual representation, since it requires determination of the (possibly nonobvious) implicit sources of transitions.

8.5.2 History States

There is some ambiguity in the UML documents regarding the meaning of history states. Consider the statement "*deepHistory* represents the most recent active configuration of the composite state that directly contains this pseudostate (e.g., the state configuration that was active when the composite state was last exited)" [49, p. 537]. This suggests a semantics where "most recent active" means "the state from which the composite state was last exited." But the document says, instead, that deep history can be defined even if no exit from the composite state has taken place [49, p. 543].

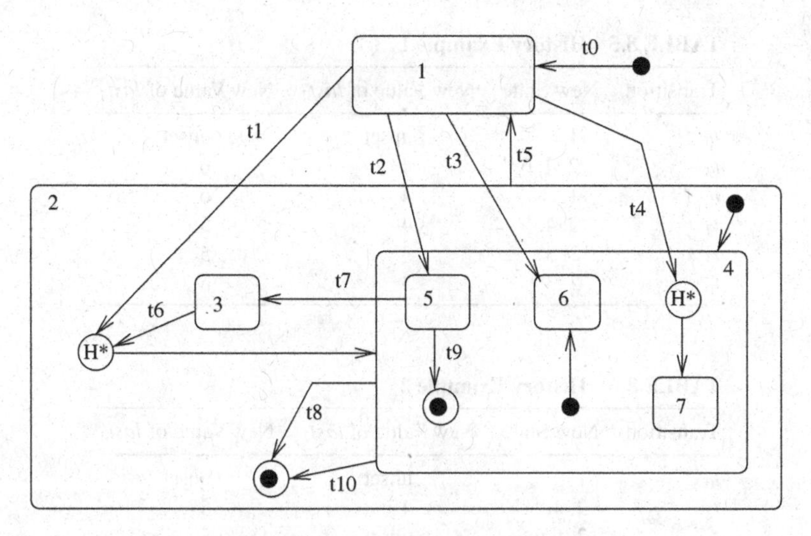

FIGURE 8.6 Example of history states.

We assume that "most recent active" means "most recently active before the transition to the history state," regardless of whether the transition came from inside or outside the composite state.

Our semantics also resolves the problems of history states described by Fecher et al. [7]. Figure 8.6 illustrates the problems identified by these authors. The problems are:

1. It is not clear if default transitions from history states must go to normal states (not pseudostates or final states). We have enforced this restriction.
2. The notion of "last active" state is ambiguous; it is not clear if this can include final states of composite states (see Table 8.7). We enforce that final states cannot be considered as being last active states; instead, entry to a final state resets the record of the last active state in the composite state. The reason for this decision is that we consider final states have meaning only as a signal that the containing state has completed its activity.
3. Do history states of nested states affect deep history entry to these states? We prescribe that they do not, only the last active states of these states determine the target of a deep history entry to a state already visited (see Table 8.5).
4. Does the reset of the last active state in a composite state p on entry to p's final state also reset the records of last active state in its substates? We prescribe that it does not, the reset only applies to p (see Table 8.6).

Tables 8.5 to 8.7 illustrate the effect of our semantics in some scenarios of Figure 8.6. We assume that all transitions have different triggers and that only t_8 has a completion event trigger.

TABLE 8.5 History Example 1

Transition	New State	New Value of $last_2$	New Value of $last_4$
t_0	1	unset	unset
t_3	2, 4, 6	4	6
t_5	1	4	6
t_2	2, 4, 5	4	5
t_7	2, 3	3	5
t_6	2, 3	3	5

TABLE 8.6 History Example 2

Transition	New State	New Value of $last_2$	New Value of $last_4$
t_0	1	unset	unset
t_2	2, 4, 5	4	5
t_{10}	2, $final_2$	unset	5
t_5	1	unset	5
t_4	2, 4, 5	4	5

TABLE 8.7 History Example 3

Transition	New State	New Value of $last_2$	New Value of $last_4$
t_0	1	unset	unset
t_2	2, 4, 5	4	5
t_9	2, $final_2$	unset	unset
t_5	1	unset	unset
t_1	2, 4, 6	4	6

8.6 STRUCTURED BEHAVIOR STATE MACHINES

In this section we consider transitions with actions as well as entry, exit, and do actions for states. The semantics for structured behavior state machines defines the sequence of actions caused by the firing of a transition, in addition to the target state predicate. In general, these actions are all the actions caused by exiting the source state(s), followed by explicit actions on the transition, followed by the actions caused by entering the target state(s) [49, p. 527], although page 548 of the document seems to contradict this by instead stating that exit actions are executed after transition actions, however.

Transitions may consist of multiple segments joined by pseudostates such as join, fork, and choice. Only one trigger is allowed on such a compound transition, although multiple guard conditions and actions may exist along it. We represent such transitions as single transitions with possibly multiple sources and targets. Two sources of a

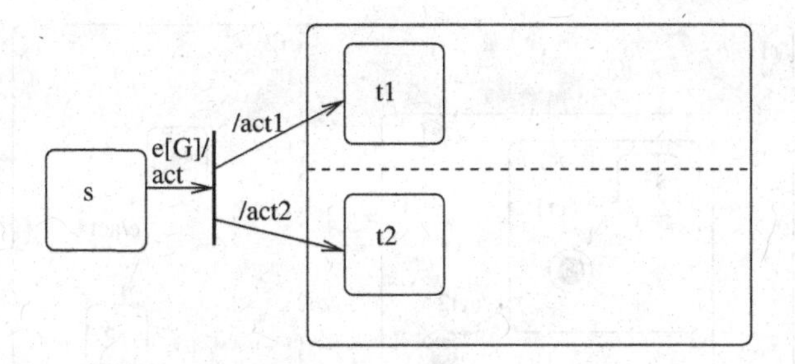

FIGURE 8.7 Removing compound transitions.

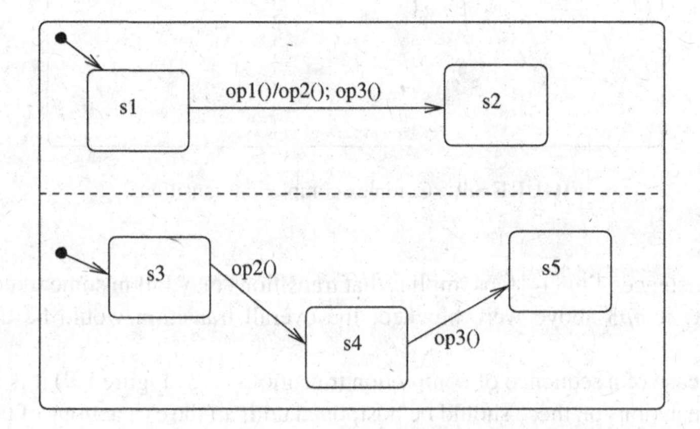

FIGURE 8.8 Microsteps in UML state machines

transition cannot be related by $\sqsubseteq$, and their closest common containing state/region must be an AND state, and similarly for target states. A fork with incoming action *act* and outgoing actions act_1 upto act_n is considered to have combined action

$$act;\ (act_1 \| \cdots \| act_n)$$

(Figure 8.7), and similarly for joins. A dynamic choice point is simply represented by a new basic state. Static choice points require the creation of new transitions, one for each path starting from the choice point. The condition for this path is added to the condition of the resulting transition.

Although UML state machines do not have an explicit notion of "microstep" as in other statechart formalisms [2], the definition of transition execution in UML superstructure 2.1.1 [49, pp. 562, 572] suggests that individual steps within a compound transition do indeed constitute microsteps. In Figure 8.8, the system, if started in states $s1$ and $s3$, will execute $op2$ and then $op3$ in two steps in response to a request for $op1$, so that the successive actions

$$op1();\ exit_{s1};\ op2();\ exit_{s3};\ entry_{s4};\ op3();\ exit_{s4};\ entry_{s5};\ entry_{s2}$$

take place.

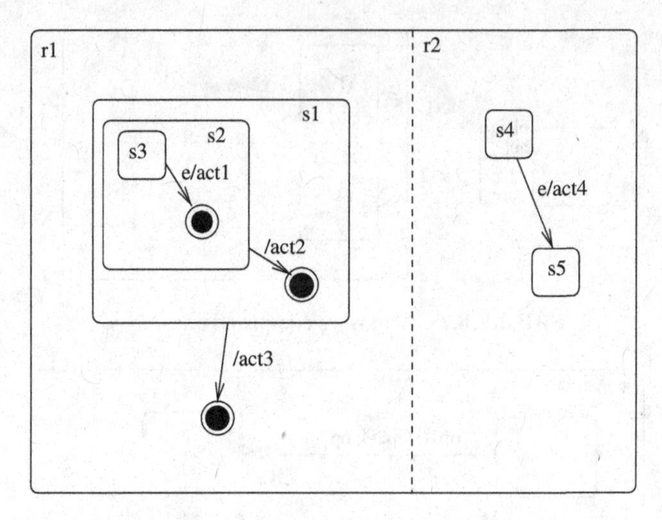

FIGURE 8.9 Complex completion transitions.

The existence of microsteps implies that transitions may fail in some intermediate state (e.g., if *op*3 above were blocked, the overall transition would be unable to proceed).

In the case of a sequence of completion transitions (e.g., Figure 8.9) it is not clear that all the actions on these should be postponed until all the exit actions of the exited states have been performed [49, p. 572]; however, we will assume that this is the case. Hence, in this example, execution of the two *e*-triggered transitions in the same step leads from the state configuration $\{s3, s2, s1, s4\}$ to the configuration $\{final_{r1}, s5\}$, and the sequence

$$((exit'_{s3};\ exit'_{s2};\ exit'_{s1}) \| exit'_{s4});\ ((act1';\ act2';\ act3') \|\ act'_4);\ entry'_{s5}$$

of actions is performed as a result of this behavior.

Table 8.3 is used to compute the actual target state(s) in the case that history states or completion transitions are involved in a transition behavior. The sequence of actions resulting in such cases is given by sequential composition of the actions on each individual transition when these are ordered sequentially. For transitions that execute in two different regions of the same AND state, their actions are combined by parallel composition.

A transition *tr* causes a state or region *s* to be entered (explicitly) if *tr* has *s* as an explicit target, or it has a target contained in *s*, and some source not contained in or equal to *s*. It causes a region *r* of an AND state *p* to be entered implicitly (at its initial state) if *p* or another region of *p* is entered explicitly because of *tr* and there is no explicit target of *tr* in *r*. When an OR state *s* is entered, its initial state is entered implicitly unless there is an explicit target of *tr* within *s*. Internal transitions of a state do not cause any state entry or exit.

TABLE 8.8 Entry Actions for a Transition

State s	Entry Actions $Entry_{s,tr}$
Basic state	$entry'_s$
OR state/region: one direct substate trg is explicitly entered	$entry'_s; Entry_{trg,tr}$
OR state/region: implicitly entered or explicit target	$entry'_s; init'_s; Entry_{initial_s,tr}$
AND state with regions $r1, \ldots, rn$	$entry'_s; (Entry_{r1,tr} \| \cdots \| Entry_{rn,tr})$

TABLE 8.9 Exit Actions for a Transition

State s	Exit Actions $Exit_{s,tr}$
Basic state	$exit'_s$
OR state/region exited: one direct substate src is exited explicitly	$Exit_{src,tr}; exit'_s$
Region exited implicitly	$Exit_{state_s,tr}; exit'_s$
OR state; some target is not $\sqsubseteq s$	$Exit_{state_s,tr}; exit'_s$
AND state with regions $r1, \ldots, rn$	$(Exit_{r1,tr} \| \ldots \| Exit_{rn,tr}); exit'_s$

Table 8.8 defines the complete semantic action executed when a state s is entered (having first taken into account the effects of history states and completion transitions, as described in Table 8.3). $init_s$ is the action on the default initial transition of s, in the third case (see [49, p. 551]). The parallel combinator $\|$ is used in this definition because UML 2 does not prescribe any relative ordering of the combined actions [49, p. 551].

A transition with a source in one region of an AND state and a target in a different region causes the AND state to be exited and entered. A transition tr causes a region r of an AND state p to be implicitly exited (from its current state, $state_r$) if p or another region of p is exited because of tr and there is no explicit source of tr in r. An OR state s will be exited if there is a tr source equal to s or within s and a target outside s. If an OR state p is a source of tr, the currently occupied substate $state_p$ of p will be exited unless all targets of tr are contained in or equal to this substate. p is not exited if all targets of tr are contained in p [49, p. 570]. An external self-transition on a state (drawn outside the state boundary) causes exit and entry of the state.

Table 8.9 defines of the complete action executed when a state s is exited. The definitions of *main source* and *main target* of a transition given in UML superstructure

2.1.1 [49, p. 571] are used: The main source of a transition is a maximal state that is exited because of the transition, and the main target is a maximal state that is entered because of the transition. In the case of transitions between regions of the same AND state p, the main source and target are both p: Exit and entry of the complete AND state is carried out.

The following axiom on transitions defines the behavior of an operation resulting from all the transitions for it. We assume that the operations invoked from these transitions do not trigger any transition that conflicts with any of these transitions; that is, these operations can only trigger events in regions orthogonal to all the transitions triggered by the original operation call, as in the example of Figure 8.8.

If the transitions triggered by $op(x)$ are tr_i, $i : 1..k$, with actions $acts_i$, the behavior of $op(x)$ is defined as a composite action $Code_{op}$:

$$\|_{j:1..k}(\textit{if } enc(tr_j) \textit{ then } Exit_j;\ acts'_j;\ Entry_j)$$

where each of the $Exit_j$ is an exit action $Exit_{ms_j,tr_j}$ from the main source ms_j of tr_j (Table 8.9), and $Entry_j$, entry action $Entry_{mt_j,tr_j}$ to the main target mt_j of tr_j (Table 8.8).

This definition chooses a maximal set of enabled transitions to execute at each step [49, p. 563]. If no transition is enabled, a skip is performed (in accordance with the UML semantics of behavior state machines [49, p. 561]).

If we know that the $enc(tr_j)$ are mutually exclusive, this can be simplified to

```
if enc(tr1)
then Exit'1; acts'1; Entry'1
else if ....
else if enc(trk)
then Exit'k; acts'k; Entry'k
```

because $(\textit{if } E_1 \textit{ then } C_1) \| (\textit{if } E_2 \textit{ then } C_2)$ is equivalent to

$$\textit{if } E_1 \wedge E_2 \textit{ then } C_1 \| C_2 \textit{ else } (\textit{if } E_1 \textit{ then } C_1 \textit{ else if } E_2 \textit{ then } C_2)$$

For each transition tr triggered by an operation $op(x)$, the pre- and postbehavior due to tr is

$$\forall i : \mathbb{N}_1 \cdot enc(tr) \circledcirc \uparrow(op(x), i) \implies \Pi_{tr} \circledcirc \downarrow(op(x), i)$$

The complexity of the exit and entry definitions suggests that some simplification of UML state machine notation should be made. Figure 8.10 illustrates some of the situations that may arise.

In example (a), the transition does not exit s, so its main source is $s1$. s is entered, at its initial state, however, so the main target is s.

In example (b), the actual source of the local transition tr is $state_s$, the current state of s, so this is the main source (assuming that it is not $s1$). s itself is not exited (according to [49, pp. 570 and 577]). $s1$ is entered, so it is the main target.

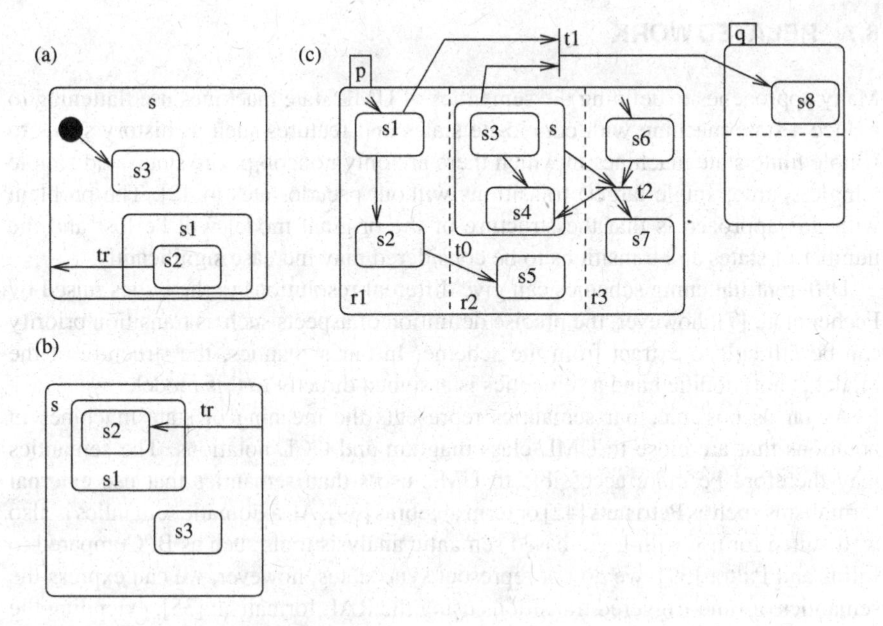

FIGURE 8.10 Complex entry and exit.

A self-transition that exits and enters a state must be drawn on the outside of the state boundary.

In example (c), transitions $t0$ and $t2$ both have main source and target p. For $t1$ the main source is p, the main target is q.

We also need to define the effect of do-actions. These can execute only while their state is occupied:

$$\#active(do'_s) > 0 \implies \varphi_s$$

and they initiate execution at the point where their state is entered [49, p. 548]:

$$\forall i : \mathbb{N}_1 \cdot \uparrow(do'_s, i) = \clubsuit(\varphi_s := true, i)$$

Axiom (StateInv) holds in the form

$$\varphi_s \implies Inv'_s$$

for each state s.

The semantics of behavior state machines attached to operations is generalized to structured state machines in the same way.

The semantics above can be used to give meaning to models that extend the UML 2 standard (e.g., where there are transitions that cross from one region of an AND state to another [49, p. 572]).

8.7 RELATED WORK

Many approaches to defining the semantics of UML state machines use flattening to reduce a state machine with composite states and features such as history states to simple finite state machines in which there are only noncomposite states and simple (single source, single target) transitions without pseudostates [4,42]. The problem with this approach is that the structure of the original model will be lost and the number of states and transitions to be considered may increase significantly.

Different flattening schemes can give different resolutions to the issues raised by Fecher et al. [7]; however, the precise definition of aspects such as transition priority can be difficult to extract from the scheme. In our semantics, the structure of the model is not modified and a semantics is assigned directly to this model.

As far as possible, our semantics represents the meaning of state machines in notations that are close to UML class diagram and OCL notations. The semantics may therefore be more accessible to UML users than semantics that use external formalisms such as Petri nets [42] or term algebras [39]. An axiomatic semantics is also well suited for use with logic-based semantic analysis tools such as B. Compared to Lilius and Paltor [39], we do not represent sync states, however, we can express the semantics of time-triggered transitions using the RAL formalism [35], extending the work of Lilius and Paltor.

The approach by Le et al. [59] is close to ours, but translates directly into B from statecharts instead of utilizing an underlying axiomatic semantics. Elements of UML state machine notation, such as time triggers, which require a temporal logic semantics, are not handled by this approach.

8.8 SUMMARY

We have given an axiomatic semantics for state machines based on the informal UML semantics. Areas where the informal semantics are unclear or ambiguous have been resolved, and precise "semantic profiles" have been given to the three semantic variations permitted in UML, for the case in which no transition exists from a state for a given trigger event that may occur in that state.

REFERENCES

1. F. Chauvel and J.-M. Jezequel. Code generation from UML models with semantic variation points. In *MoDELS 2005*. Lecture Notes in Computer Science, vol. 3713. Springer Verlag, New York, 2005.
2. M. Crane and J. Dingel. UML vs Classical vs Rhapsody statecharts: not all models are created equal. In *MoDELS 2005*, Lecture Notes in Computer Science, vol. 3713. Springer-Verlag, New York, 2005.
3. J. Crupi, D. Alur, and D. Malks. *Core J2EE Patterns*. Prentice Hall, Upper Saddle River, NJ, 2001.

4. W. Damm, B. Josko, A. Pnueli, and A. Votintseva. A discrete-time UML semantics for concurrency and communication in safety-critical applications. *Science of Computer Programming*, 55:81–115, 2005.
5. H Dierks. Comparing model-checking and logical reasoning for real-time systems. In *Workshop Proceedings, ESSLLI'98*, pp. 13–22, 1998.
6. A. Evans and S. Kent, Core meta-modelling semantics of UML: the pUML approach. In *UML '99*, pp. 140–155, 1999.
7. H. Fecher, J. Schonborn, M. Kyas, and W.-P. de Roever. 29 new unclarities in the semantics of UML 2.0 state machines. In *Formal Methods and Software Engineering (ICFEM 2005)*. vol. 3785, Lecture Notes in Computer Science, pp. 52–65. Springer-Verlag, New York, 2005.
8. J. Fiadeiro and T. Maibaum. Describing, structuring and implementing objects. In *Foundations of Object Oriented Languages*. Lecture Notes in Computer Science, vol. 489. Springer-Verlag, New York, 1991.
9. J. Fiadeiro and T. Maibaum. Sometimes "tomorrow" is "sometime." In *Temporal Logic*. Lecture Notes in Artificial Intelligence, vol. 827, pp. 48–66. Springer-Verlag, New York, 1994.
10. M. Fowler. *Refactoring: Improving the Design of Existing Code*. Addison-Wesley, Reading, MA, 2000.
11. E. Gamma, R. Helm, R. Johnson, and J. Vlissides. *Design Patterns: Elements of Reusable Object-Oriented Software*. Addison-Wesley, Reading, MA, 1995.
12. M. Glinz. Problems and deficiencies of UML as a requirements specification language. In *Proceedings of the 10th International Workshop on Software Specification and Design (IWSSD-10)*, pp. 11–22, 2000.
13. M. Gogolla, O. Radfelder, and M. Richters. *A UML Semantics FAQ: The View from Bremen*. University of Bremen, Bremen, Germany, 1999.
14. S. Goldsack, K. Lano, and A. Sanchez. Transforming continuous into discrete specifications with VDM^{++}. In *IEE C8 Colloquium Digest on Hybrid Control for Real-Time Systems*. IEE, London, 1996.
15. S. Graf, I. Ober, and I. Ober. Timed annotations with UML. In *SVERTS'03*, 2003.
16. M.Grand. *Patterns in Java*, Vol. 1. Wiley, New York, 1998.
17. D. Gries. *The Science of Programming*, Springer-Verlag, New York, 1981.
18. D. Harel and A. Naamad. The STATEMATE semantics of statecharts. *ACM Transactions on Software Engineering and Methodology*, 5(4):293–333, October 1996.
19. C. A. R. Hoare. An axiomatic basis for computer programming. *Communications of the ACM*, 12(10): 576–585, Oct. 1969.
20. A. Knapp and J. Wuttke, Model-checking of UML 2.0 interactions. In *Proceedings of the 5th International Workshop on Critical Systems Development Using Modelling Languages (CSDUML)*. Telenor Report 20/2006, 2006.
21. F. Jahanian and A. K. Mok. Safety analysis of timing properties in real-time systems. *IEEE Transactions on Software Engineering*, 12:890–904, Sept. 1986.
22. A. Knapp and J. Wuttke. Model checking of UML 2.0 interactions. In *5th International Workshop CSDUML*, 2006.
23. M. Kyas, H. Fecher, F. de Boer, J. Jacob, J. Hooman, M. van der Kwaag, T. Arons, and H. Kugler. Formalizing UML models and OCL constraints in PVS. In *SFEDL '04*, 2004.

24. K. Lano. Logical specification of reactive and real-time systems. *Journal of Logic and Computation*, 8(5):679–711, 1998.
25. K. Lano. UML to B: formal verification of object-oriented models. In *IFM'04*, 2004.
26. K. Lano and K. Androutsopolous. Automated synthesis of high-integrity systems using model-driven development. In *5th International Workshop CSDUML*, 2006.
27. K. Lano, K. Androutsopolous, and D. Clark. Concurrency specification in UML-RSDS. In *MARTES'06, MoDELS Conference*, 2006.
28. K. Lano, D. Clark, and K. Androutsopolous. From implicit specifications to explicit designs in reactive system development. In *IFM'02*, 2002.
29. K. Lano, D. Clark, K. Androutsopolous, and P. Kan. Invariant-based synthesis of fault-tolerant systems. In *FTRTFT*. Springer-Verlag, New York, 2000.
30. K. Lano, D. Clark, and K. Androutsopoulos. RSDS: a subset of UML with precise semantics. *L'Objet*, 9(4):53–73, 2003.
31. K. Lano. Transformational program analysis. *Journal of Software Testing Verification and Reliability*, 4:155–189, 1994.
32. K. Lano. Constraint-driven development. *Information and Software Technology*, 50:406–423, 2008.
33. K. Lano. Formalising design patterns as model transformations. Chapter VIII in T. Taibi, ed., *Design Pattern Formalisation Techniques*. IGI Publishing, Hershey, PA, 2007.
34. K. Lano and D. Clark. Direct semantics of extended state machines. In *TOOLS'07*, 2007.
35. K. Lano. A compositional semantics of UML-RSDS. *SoSyM*, 8(1): 85–116, Feb. 2009.
36. King's College London. UML RSDS toolset, 2007. http://www.dcs.kcl.ac.uk/staff/kcl/umlrsds.
37. K. Lano. Catalogue of model transformations. http://www.dcs.kcl.ac.uk/staff/kcl/tcat.pdf, 2007.
38. K. Lano and A. Evans. Rigorous development in UML. In *FASE'99*, Lecture Notes in Computer Science, vol. 1577, pp. 129–144. Springer-Verlag, New York, 1999.
39. J. Lilius and I. Paltor. *The Semantics of UML State Machines*. TUCS Technical Report 273. Turku Centre for Computer Science, Turku, Finland, 1999.
40. B. Liskov and J. Wing. Specifications and their use in defining subtypes. In *ZUM'95 Proceedings*. Lecture Notes in Computer Science, vol. 967. Springer-Verlag, New York, 1995.
41. S. Markovic and T. Baar. *Refactoring OCL Annotated UML Class Diagrams*, *MoDELS 2005 Proceedings*. Lecture Notes in Computer Science, vol. 3713. Springer-Verlag, New York, 2005.
42. J. Merseguer, J. Campos, S. Bernardi, and S. Donatelli. A compositional semantics for UML state machines aimed at performance evaluation. In M. Silva, A. Giua, and J. M. Colom, eds., *Proceedings of the 6 International Workshop on Discrete Event Systems (WODES 2002)*, 2002.
43. B. Meyer. *Object-Oriented Software Construction*. Prentice Hall, Upper Saddle River, NJ, 1997.
44. J. D. Monk. *Mathematical Logic*. Springer-Verlag, New York, 1976.
45. C. Morgan. *Programming from Specifications*. Springer-Verlag, New York, 1990.

46. A. Naumenko and A. Wegmann. Triune continuum paradigm and problems of UML semantics. http://icwww.epfl.ch/publications/documents/ IC_TECH_REPORT_200344.pdf, 2003.
47. OMG. Model-driven architecture. http://www.omg.org/mda/, 2007.
48. OMG. *UML Superstructure, Version 2.0*. OMG Document Formal/05-07-04. Object Management Group, Needham, MA, 2005.
49. OMG. *UML Superstructure, Version 2.1.1*. OMG Document Formal/2007-02-03. Object Management Group, Needham, MA, 2007.
50. OMG, UML profile for schedulability, performance and time, version 1.1. http://www.omg.org/, 2005.
51. OMG. *UML OCL 2.0 Specification*. Final/06-05-01. Object Management Group, Needham, MA, 2006.
52. OMG. *Query/view/transformation specification*. Technical Report ptc/05-11-01. Object Management Group, Needham, MA, 2005.
53. D. Schmidt and C. Cranor. Half-sync/half-async: an architectural pattern for efficient and well-structured concurrent I/O. In *Proceedings of the 2nd Annual Conference on the Pattern Languages of Programs*, Monticello, IL, pp. 1–10, Sept. 1995.
54. C. Snook and M. Butler. U2B: A tool for translating UML-B models into B. Chapter 6, in J. Mermet, ed., *UML-B Specification for Proven Embedded Systems Design*. Springer-Verlag, New York, 2004.
55. J. S. Ostroff. *Temporal Logic for Real-Time Systems*. Wiley, New York, 1989.
56. A. Pnueli. Applications of temporal logic to the specification and verification of reactive systems: a survey of current trends. In *Current Trends in Concurrency*. Lecture Notes in Computer Science, vol. 224. Springer-Verlag, New York, 1986.
57. M. Richters. OCL semantics. Annex A of [34], 2005.
58. M. Ryan, J. Fiadeiro, and T. S. E. Maibaum. Sharing actions and attributes in modal action logic. In *Proceedings of the International Conference on Theoretical Aspects of Computer Science (TACS '91)*. Springer-Verlag, New York, 1991.
59. D. Le, E. Sekerinski, and S. West, Statechart verification with iState. *FM'06*. Lecture Notes in Computer Science, vol. 4085. Springer-Verlag, New York, 2006.
60. A. Simons. The theory of classification: 8. Classification and inheritance. *Journal of Object Technology*, 2(4):55–64, July–Aug. 2003.
61. J. Smith, S. DeLoach, M. Kokar, and K. Baclawski. Category theoretic approaches of representing precise UML semantics. In *Proceedings of the ECOOP Workshop on Defining Precise Semantics for UML*, 2000.
62. J. Rumbaugh, M. Blaha, W. Lorensen, F. Eddy, and W. Premerlani. *Object-Oriented Modeling and Design*. Prentice Hall, Upper Saddle River, NJ, 1994.
63. UML 2 Semantics Project. http://www.cs.queensu.ca/~stl/internal/uml2/bibtex/ref_uml2semantics.html, 2008.
64. L. Tratt. Model transformations and tool integration. *SoSyM*, 4(2):112–122, May 2005.
65. F. Wagner. *Modeling Software with Finite State Machines: A Practical Approach*. Auerbach Publications, Boca Raton, FL, 2006.

CHAPTER 9

INTERACTIONS

MARÍA VICTORIA CENGARLE
Institut für Informatik, Technische Universität München, München, Germany

ALEXANDER KNAPP and HERIBERT MÜHLBERGER
Institut für Informatik, Universität Augsburg, Augsburg, Germany

9.1 INTRODUCTION

UML interactions describe possible message exchanges between system instances. The UML 2 [45] offers a powerful interaction language, which, besides integrating such standard operations as sequential, parallel, and iterative composition of interactions, provides means to specify recursive and negative behavior (i.e., behavior forbidden in system implementations).

The current UML 2 language for interactions is a complete overhaul of the interaction language of earlier versions. The UML 1 dialect was, on the one hand, based on the interaction diagrams of OOSE's [31], on the abstract, visual programming languages used by Fusion [13] and Syntropy [15], and also on ITU's message sequence charts (MSCs [30]). On the other hand, in the form of collaborations, it was also enriched with notions from role modeling in OORam [2]. Quite some effort has been spent on providing UML 1 sequence and collaboration diagrams with a formal semantics (see, e.g., [19,21,34,47]), thus making them amenable for use in formally based software development. However, it was realized that the language showed some defects in expressivity for more complex software engineering purposes, in particular with respect to modular modeling, describing alternatives, and combining interactions in different ways.

The UML 2 interaction language countered the deficiencies in expressivity of its previous version by incorporating and adapting many constructs of MSCs [30]. Additionally, means were introduced for distinguishing behavior that an implementing system should show and behavior that the system must not show, which was inspired by live sequence charts (LSCs [16]) and from software testing notions

UML 2 Semantics and Applications. Edited by Kevin Lano

and notations [54]. The increase in expressivity, and also in complexity, of the UML 2 interaction language spurred new efforts in providing it with a formal semantics [12,20,23,36,39,40,43,49,50]. In particular, the division of behaviors into being positive or valid for a system, negative or invalid, and finally, being inconclusive if it is neither positive nor negative, has received much attention. All these types of behavior are described by a single interaction, but it has not been clear how the different types are to be combined and how they interact [12,36,49].

In the present chapter we provide and discuss the formal semantics for UML 2 interactions following the UML specification [45] as closely as possible and also integrating the existing research results on the semantics of interactions. First, an interleaved, trace-based, denotational semantics is detailed which is built in several steps. The presentation starts from simple, basic interactions that are similar to what was present in UML 1. It is then extended by considering different message types, executions, combinations of interactions, and constraints. Finally, high-level interactions are integrated. A discussion of some alternative proposals to a formal semantics follows. In particular, an operational approach and a truly concurrent approach with event structures are considered. UML 2 interactions are related briefly with MSCs and LSCs. Finally, an overview of some notions of implementation and refinement of interactions and their role in verification and animation are given.

9.2 TRACE-BASED SEMANTICS

A trace-based formal semantics for UML 2 interactions is developed. According to the UML 2 specification document, an interaction describes *valid* (or *positive*) and *invalid* (or *negative*) traces of event occurrences. The union of the two sets of valid and invalid traces need not cover the entire universe of traces. A trace that is neither valid nor invalid for an interaction is said to be *inconclusive* for the interaction. Moreover, the semantics that we propose allows traces that are both valid and invalid for the same interaction. Hence, our semantics is based on a four-valued logic.

In developing the semantics, we proceed in a step-by-step manner, beginning with the core language constructs for describing basic interactions and then moving on to different communication types, combined fragments (including negation), constraints, and high-level interactions. For a start, however, in the following subsection we give a brief review of some mathematical concepts necessary to define appropriate semantic domains.

9.2.1 Pomsets

The formal semantics that we propose for UML 2 interactions employs partially ordered, labeled multisets which were introduced by Pratt [48] for modeling concurrency.

A *labeled partial order* (abbreviated lpo) $(X, \leq_X, \lambda_X)$ consists of a set X, a partial order $\leq_X$ on X (i.e., a relation on X that is reflexive, antisymmetric, and transitive), and a labeling function λ_X on X. An isomorphism between two lpos $(X, \leq_X, \lambda_X)$ and $(Y, \leq_Y, \lambda_Y)$ is a one-to-one mapping φ from X onto Y which is monotonic with respect to $\leq_X$ and $\leq_Y$, whose inverse mapping is also monotonic and which is label preserving [i.e., $\lambda_X(x) = \lambda_Y(\varphi(x))$ for all $x \in X$]. A *partially ordered, labeled multiset*, or *pomset* is the isomorphism class of an lpo, denoted $[(X, \leq_X, \lambda_X)]$.

A pomset p is said to be *finite* if for some (and hence, for all) $(X, \leq_X, \lambda_X) \in p$ the basic set X is finite. A pomset $p = [(X, \leq_X, \lambda_X)]$ is said to be *finitary* if for all $x \in X$ the set $\{x' \in X \mid x' \leq_X x\}$ is finite. A pomset p is said to be *linear* or *a trace* if for some $(X, \leq_X, \lambda_X) \in p$ the ordering $\leq_X$ is total on X. Let $\asymp$ be a binary, symmetric relation on labels. A pomset $p = [(X, \leq_X, \lambda_X)]$ is said to be $\asymp$*-linear* if it holds that $\forall x_1, x_2 \in X.\ \lambda_X(x_1) \asymp \lambda_X(x_2) \Rightarrow x_1 \leq_X x_2 \vee x_2 \leq_X x_1$. A pomset q is said to be *an extension* of a pomset p if there are two representatives $(X, \leq_X, \lambda_X) \in p$ and $(Y, \leq_Y, \lambda_Y) \in q$ such that $X = Y$ and $\leq_X \subseteq \leq_Y$ and $\lambda_X = \lambda_Y$. A pomset q is said to be a *linearization* of a pomset p if q is a linear extension of p. A pomset q is said to be a $\asymp$*-linearization* of a pomset p if q is a $\asymp$-linear extension of p. The set of all linearizations or $\asymp$-linearizations of p is denoted by $p\downarrow$ and $p\asymp\downarrow$, respectively. A function f that maps labels to labels is lifted to pomsets by defining $f([(X, \leq_X, \lambda_X)]) = [(X, \leq_X, f \circ \lambda_X)]$. Given a pomset $p = [(X, \leq_X, \lambda_X)]$ and a Boolean predicate π on labels, we define the *restriction* of p with respect to π by $p\restriction\pi = [(X', \leq_X \cap (X' \times X'), \lambda_X\restriction X')]$ with $X' = \{x \in X \mid \pi(\lambda_X(x))\}$.

The *empty* pomset, represented by $(\emptyset, \emptyset, \emptyset)$, is denoted by ε. Let $p = [(X, \leq_X, \lambda_X)]$ and $q = [(Y, \leq_Y, \lambda_Y)]$ be pomsets such that $X \cap Y = \emptyset$. The *concurrence* of p and q, written as $p \parallel q$, is given by $[(X \cup Y, \leq_X \cup \leq_Y, \lambda_X \cup \lambda_Y)]$. The *concatenation* of p and q, written as $p\,;q$, is given by $[(X \cup Y, \leq_X \cup \leq_Y \cup (X \times Y), \lambda_X \cup \lambda_Y)]$. Given a binary, symmetric relation $\asymp$ on labels, the $\asymp$*-concatenation* of p and q, written as $p\,;_\asymp q$, is given by $[(X \cup Y, (\leq_X \cup \leq_Y \cup \{(x, y) \in X \times Y \mid \lambda_X(x) \asymp \lambda_Y(y)\})^*, \lambda_X \cup \lambda_Y)]$. It is easy to ascertain that these definitions do not depend on the choice of representatives. Note that concatenation and $\asymp$-concatenation are associative, and concurrence is associative and commutative.

A *process* is a set of pomsets. An n-ary function f that maps pomsets to pomsets is lifted to processes $P_1, \ldots, P_n$ by defining

$$f(P_1, \ldots, P_n) = \{f(p_1, \ldots, p_n) \mid p_1 \in P_1, \ldots, p_n \in P_n\}$$

(e.g., $P_1 \asymp P_2 = \{p_1 \asymp p_2 \mid p_1 \in P_1 \wedge p_2 \in P_2\}$). For an n-ary function f that maps pomsets to processes, the image elements of the lifting of f are "flattened" [i.e., $f(P_1, \ldots, P_n) = \bigcup\{f(p_1, \ldots, p_n) \mid p_1 \in P_1, \ldots, p_n \in P_n\}$]. For instance, $P\downarrow = \bigcup\{p\downarrow \mid p \in P\}$. Furthermore, we define the *n-fold* $\asymp$*-iteration* of a process P, written $P^{(n)}$, as follows: $P^{(0)} = \{\varepsilon\}$ and $P^{(n+1)} = P \asymp P^{(n)}$.

9.2.2 Core Language

9.2.2.1 *Basic Interactions* The sample basic interaction ex1 in Figure 9.1(a) specifies two instances x and y, which exchange messages a and b. The dispatch of a message (depicted by the arrow tail) and the arrival of a message (arrowhead) on the lifeline of an instance (dashed line) are called *event occurrences* or, more precisely, *message event occurrences*. The pictorial representation of a basic interaction carries the intuitive meaning of a partially ordered set of event occurrences: The dispatch of a message occurs before the arrival of the same message, and the event occurrences

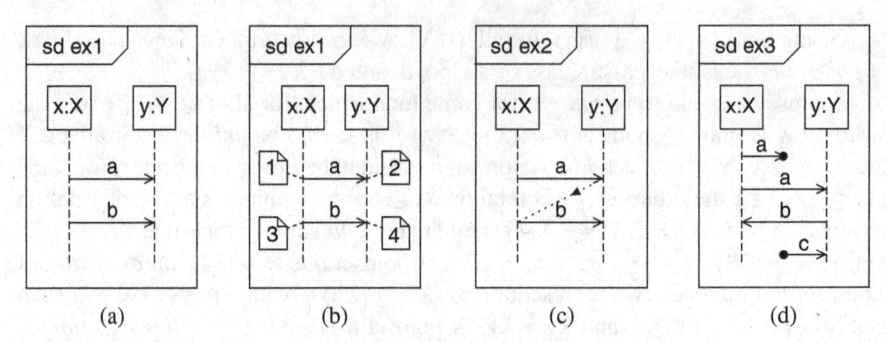

FIGURE 9.1 Basic interaction diagram (a), with labeled event occurrences (b), with an additional general ordering (c), and with lost and found messages (d).

on the lifeline of an instance are ordered from top to bottom. Thus, if we symbolize the dispatch of a from x by 1, the arrival of a at y by 2, the dispatch of b from x by 3, and the arrival of b at y by 4 [see Figure 9.1(b)], the interaction ex1 defines two valid traces: 1234 and 1324. All other traces are inconclusive for this interaction.

Additional ordering relations between event occurrences can be specified by means of general orderings. Interaction ex2, shown in Figure 9.1(c), is essentially equal to interaction ex1, except that a general ordering is added (depicted by a dotted line with an arrowhead placed somewhere in the middle of the dotted line). The general ordering in ex2 specifies that the arrival of message a has to occur before the dispatch of message b. Hence, only the trace 1234 remains valid for interaction ex2, whereas the trace 1324 is inconclusive. Finally, messages can get lost (depicted by a small black circle at the arrow end of the lost message) and messages can also be found (depicted by a small black circle at the arrow tail of the found message) [see Figure 9.1(d)]. We interpret a found message as a message whose origin lies outside the scope of the description.

9.2.2.2 Metamodel Figure 9.2 shows the fragment of the UML 2 metamodel that comprises the core language constructs for describing basic interactions. Metaclass Interaction is a subclass both of Behavior (from BasicBehaviors) and of Interaction-Fragment, the latter being an abstract notion of the most general interaction unit. An Interaction owns a set of Lifelines, a set of Messages, and an ordered set of InteractionFragments.

A Lifeline represents a system instance which participates in the Interaction. The mechanism by means of which these system instances are specified is not self-explanatory because it is interwoven with the concept of the context classifier of the Interaction (see BasicBehaviors::Behavior::context). Syntactically, a Lifeline references an instance of a concrete subclass of ConnectableElement (from InternalStructures). There are two such concrete subclasses specified in the package CompositeStructures, namely Property and Port. We discuss only the former here: A Property (from InternalStructures) is a specification of a set S of instances that are owned by a containing classifier instance. In the simplest case, this "containing classifier" coincides with the context classifier of the Interaction. If the Property concerned is multivalued (i.e., S may contain more than one instance), the Lifeline

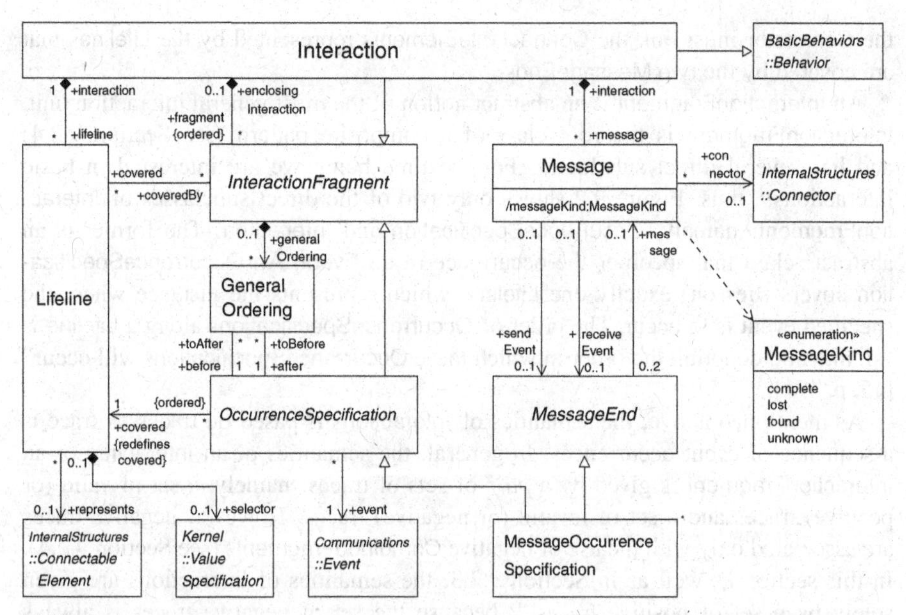

FIGURE 9.2 Fragment of the UML 2 metamodel that comprises the core language constructs for describing basic interactions.

may have an expression (the selector) that specifies which particular instance of S is represented by the Lifeline. If the selector is omitted, this means that an arbitrary representative of the multivalued Property is chosen. As already mentioned, Lifelines are depicted by vertical dashed lines. The left Lifeline of Interaction ex1, for instance, references a nonmultivalued Property named x which is typed by a Class named X; see Figure 9.1(a).

A Message defines a particular communication between Lifelines of an Interaction. A Message may, and usually does, associate two MessageEnds that are referenced by sendEvent and receiveEvent. A MessageEnd can either be a MessageOccurrenceSpecification or a Gate. The former specifies a message event occurrence, as mentioned above; Gates are dealt with in Sections 9.2.4 and 9.2.6. Message has a derived attribute messageKind whose value (complete, lost, found, or unknown) depends on the presence or absence of the MessageEnds. If both MessageEnds are present, messageKind is complete [see, e.g., message a in Figure 9.1(a)]. If only sendEvent or only receiveEvent is present, messageKind has the values lost and found, respectively [see message a (first dispatch) and message c in Figure 9.1(d), respectively]. If both MessageEnds are absent, which preferably should not occur, then messageKind is unknown. Message has also a second attribute called messageSort, which specifies the type of communication action used to generate the message. The present section deals with asynchronous communication only (i.e., messageSort is asynchCall or asynchSignal); synchronous communication is treated in Section 9.2.3. A Message may specify a Connector on which the Message is sent. If both MessageEnds of a Message are specified as MessageOccurrenceSpecifications, the Connector must link the ConnectableElements represented by the Lifelines that are covered by the two MessageEnds.

An InteractionFragment is an abstract notion of the most general interaction unit. InteractionFragment is the root class of a composite pattern (see Section 9.2.4) and has several direct subclasses. For the time being we are interested in basic interactions;[1] thus, Figure 9.2 shows only two of the direct subclasses of InteractionFragment: namely, OccurrenceSpecification and Interaction. The former is an abstract[2] class that specifies the occurrence of an Event. An OccurrenceSpecification covers (lies on) exactly one Lifeline, which represents the instance where the specified event is to occur. The order of OccurrenceSpecifications along a Lifeline is "significant, denoting the order in which these OccurrenceSpecifications will occur" [45, p. 491].[3]

As mentioned above, the semantics of Interactions is based on traces. A trace is a sequence of event occurrences. In general, the semantics of an Interaction or an InteractionFragment is given by a *pair* of sets of traces: namely, a set of valid (or positive) traces and a set of invalid (or negative) traces. However, negative traces are associated only with the use of negative CombinedFragments (see Section 9.2.4). In this section as well as in Section 9.2.3, the semantics of interactions are given solely by a set of positive traces P because the set of negative traces is always empty.

The UML specification document [45, p. 497] describes the semantics of an OccurrenceSpecification to be "just the trace of that single OccurrenceSpecification," thereby identifying an event that occurs in a (semantic) trace with its specifying (syntactic) OccurrenceSpecification. Although this identification is a legitimate approach, we prefer to consider an OccurrenceSpecification o as a *syntactic* unit which specifies (an occurrence of) a semantic event e, although this "event" is not only given by the Event that is referenced by o but also contains information about the role that o plays in the interaction, in particular, which Lifeline l is covered by o. Actually, e contains the same information as o. Bearing this in mind, we declare that an OccurrenceSpecification has only one trace, which consists of only one occurrence of the event e that is specified by the OccurrenceSpecification (i.e., $P = \{e\}$).

[1] A *basic interaction* is defined as an Interaction that does not own CombinedFragments. For the purposes of this section, however, a basic interaction is simply an Interaction whose constituent InteractionFragments are all OccurrenceSpecifications.

[2] Three class diagrams of the UML specification document [45] (the diagrams on pp. 460, 461, and 462) treat OccurrenceSpecification as an abstract class. In contrast, the class diagram (p. 463) as well as the specification text treat OccurrenceSpecification as a concrete class. We have decided to regard the metaclass OccurrenceSpecification as abstract.

[3] The authors of the present chapter are not absolutely certain of the necessity of the order designator at the nonnavigable end of the association between OccurrenceSpecification and Lifeline (see Figure 9.2). In our opinion, the order designator is redundant because the order of OccurrenceSpecifications along a Lifeline is completely specified by weak sequencing of the InteractionFragments that are owned by an Interaction.

The semantics of a basic interaction is specified as follows: Let I be an Interaction that owns pairwise distinct[4] OccurrenceSpecifications $o_1, \ldots, o_n$ (in this order) with positive trace sets $\{e_1\}, \ldots, \{e_n\}$, respectively. A binary, temporal relation $\rightarrow$ on $O = \{o_i | i = 1, \ldots, n\}$ is defined such that for all $i, j \in \{1, \ldots, n\}$, $o_i \rightarrow o_j$ if, and only if, at least one of the following conditions is satisfied:

1. o_i and o_j are referenced by a Message (with messageKind = complete) via sendEvent and receiveEvent, respectively.
2. o_i and o_j are referenced by a GeneralOrdering via before and after, respectively.
3. o_i and o_j cover the same Lifeline and $i < j$ (i.e., o_i lies above o_j).

The semantics of I can then be specified as the set of all traces $e_{\pi^{-1}(1)}\dot{e}_{\pi^{-1}(n)}$ with a permutation π on $\{1, \ldots, n\}$ such that for all $i, j \in \{1, \ldots, n\}$, $o_i \rightarrow o_j$ implies that $\pi(i) < \pi(j)$. Quite evidently, such a permutation π can exist only if $(O, \rightarrow)$ is a directed acyclic graph, with emphasis on *acyclic*. Calling $(O, \rightarrow)$ the *specification graph* of basic interaction I, we end up with the following constraint: *The specification graph of a basic interaction must not have (directed) cycles.*[5]

9.2.2.3 Example By instantiating the metamodel, we obtain the instance diagram in Figure 9.3, which is (a part of) the abstract syntax of the basic interaction ex1 in Figure 9.1(a). For reasons of readability, the model elements for message b are omitted. We assume that the collaboration C in Figure 9.4(a) underlies[6] the interaction ex1. Furthermore, we assume that the connector named "channel," which is part of C, is typed with association A of the class diagram in Figure 9.4(b).

9.2.2.4 Semantics We define a formal semantics of basic interactions by first mapping the metamodel in Figure 9.2 to an appropriate domain of pomsets and then defining valid traces as linearizations of these pomsets. For this purpose we assume

[4] In terms of object identity.

[5] Note that this constraint, albeit necessary, is not specified by the UML specification document. However, the idea of this constraint underlies several passages in the specification text, such as the following notation instruction: "A message is shown as a line from the sender message end to the receiver message end. The line must be such that every line fragment is either horizontal or downwards when traversed from send event to receive event" [45, p. 493].

[6] An Interaction is an *emergent* behavior. Emergent behavior results from the interaction of one or more participant objects. If the participating objects are parts of a larger composite object, an emerging behavior can be seen as indirectly describing the behavior of the container object also (cf. [45, p. 419]). In this case, the container object serves as a (pseudo-)execution context of the emergent behavior. The question arises from which metaclass a container object has to be selected if it is supposed to serve as a pseudoexecution context of an interaction of system instances contained in the container object. Since the object has to be referenced by Behavior::context it has to be selected as a BehavioredClassifier (from BasicBehaviors) Since the object contains system instances that are represented by ConnectableElements, it has to be selected as a StructuredClassifier (from InternalStructures). Consequently, the object must be an instance of a metaclass which is a specialization of both BehavioredClassifier and StructuredClassifier. Metaclass Collaboration (from Collaborations) meets these requirements.

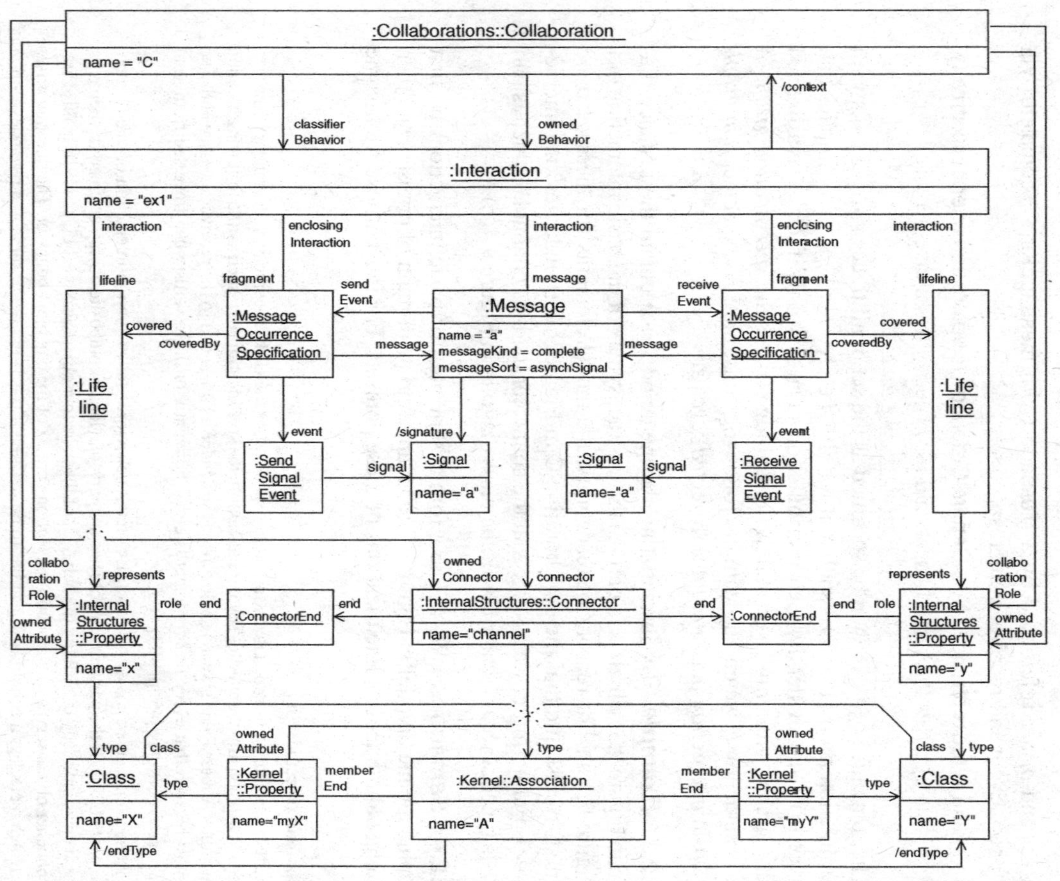

FIGURE 9.3 Fragment of the abstract syntax of basic interaction ex1 in Figure 9.1(a), with the collaboration C in Figure 9.4(a) serving as a (pseudo-)execution context of interaction ex1.

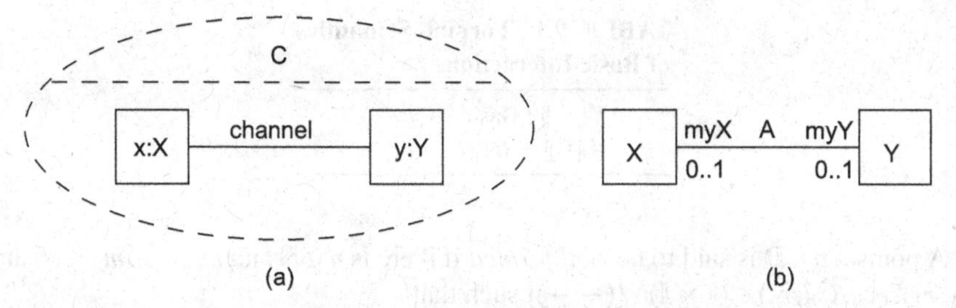

FIGURE 9.4 Underlying Collaboration C (a) of interaction ex1 and a class diagram (b) containing an association A for the purpose of typing the Connector "channel" in C and in Figure 9.3.

two primitive domains for instances $\mathbb{I}$ and messages $\mathbb{M}$. Metavariables s, r, l range over $\mathbb{I}$ and m ranges over $\mathbb{M}$. Using $\hat{s}, \hat{r} \in \hat{\mathbb{I}} ::= l \mid -$, the domain of *(message) events* $\mathbb{E}$ is defined as follows:

$$\begin{aligned} e \in \mathbb{E} ::= & \ \mathsf{snd}(s, \hat{r}, m) \\ & \mid \mathsf{rcv}(\hat{s}, r, m) \end{aligned}$$

An event of the form $\mathsf{snd}(s,r,m)$ or $\mathsf{rcv}(s,r,m)$ represents the dispatch and arrival of a message m (with messageKind = complete) from *sender* instance s to *receiver* instance r, respectively. An event of the form $\mathsf{snd}(s,-,m)$ represents the dispatch of a message m (with messageKind = lost) from sender instance s. An event of the form $\mathsf{rcv}(-,r,m)$ represents the arrival of a message m (with messageKind = found) at receiver instance r. We define:

$$\begin{aligned} &\alpha : \mathbb{E} \longrightarrow \wp(\mathbb{I}) && \mu : \mathbb{E} \longrightarrow \mathbb{M} \\ &\alpha(\mathsf{snd}(s, \hat{r}, m)) = \{s\} && \mu(\mathsf{snd}(s, \hat{r}, m)) = m \\ &\alpha(\mathsf{rcv}(\hat{s}, r, m)) = \{r\} && \mu(\mathsf{rcv}(\hat{s}, r, m)) = m \end{aligned}$$

If $\alpha(e) = \{l\}$, the instance l is said to be *active* for event e. Since we identify instances with their representing lifelines, we call α the lifeline function. If instance l is active for event e, we also say that e *lies on* lifeline l. We define a binary, symmetric *conflict* relation $\asymp \subseteq \mathbb{E} \times \mathbb{E}$ as follows: $e_1 \asymp e_2$ if, and only if, $\alpha(e_1) \cap \alpha(e_2) \neq \emptyset$. Hence, two events are in conflict if, and only if, they lie on the same lifeline.

The domain $\mathbb{D}$ comprises all finitary pomsets $[(O, \leq_O, \lambda_O)]$ such that $\mathrm{ran}\,(\lambda_O) \subseteq \mathbb{E}$, with $\mathrm{ran}\,(\lambda_O)$ denoting the range of λ_O. An element $o \in O$ of the basic set of a representative $(O, \leq_O, \lambda_O)$ of a pomset $p \in \mathbb{D}$ denotes an *occurrence* of event $\lambda_O(o)$. A pomset $p \in \mathbb{D}$ is said to be *locally linear* if it is $\asymp$-linear. We define $\mathbb{P} = \{p \in \mathbb{D} \mid p \text{ is locally linear}\}$ and $\mathbb{T} = \{p \in \mathbb{D} \mid p \text{ is a trace}\}$. Clearly, $\mathbb{T} \subseteq \mathbb{P} \subseteq \mathbb{D}$ and $\varepsilon \in \mathbb{T}$. By identifying a pomset $[(\{o\}, \leq_{\{o\}}, \lambda_{\{o\}})]$ with event $\lambda_{\{o\}}(o)$ we can regard $\mathbb{E}$ as a subset of $\mathbb{T}$. Given n events $e_1, e_2, \ldots, e_n \in \mathbb{E}$ with $n \geq 1$, we also write the finite trace $e_1 \,;\, e_2 \,;\, \ldots \,;\, e_n$ as $e_1 e_2 \cdots e_n$.

TABLE 9.1 Formal Semantics of Basic Interactions

$$\mathcal{P}[\![-]\!] : \text{Basic} \rightarrow \wp(\mathbb{T})$$
$$\mathcal{P}[\![\text{B}]\!] = B{\downarrow}$$

A pomset $p \in \mathbb{D}$ is said to be *well formed* if there is $n \in \mathbb{N}$ and $m_1, \ldots, m_n \in \mathbb{M}$ and $(\hat{s}_1, \hat{r}_1), \ldots, (\hat{s}_n, \hat{r}_n) \in (\hat{\mathbb{I}} \times \hat{\mathbb{I}}) \setminus \{(-,-)\}$ such that[7]

$$p \in (M(\hat{s}_1, \hat{r}_1, m_1) \parallel \cdots \parallel M(\hat{s}_n, \hat{r}_n, m_n)) \asymp{\downarrow}$$

where $M(\hat{s}, \hat{r}, m)$ is defined as follows: $M(s, r, m) = \mathsf{snd}(s, r, m) ; \mathsf{rcv}(s, r, m)$, $M(s, -, m) = \mathsf{snd}(s, -, m)$, and $M(-, r, m) = \mathsf{rcv}(-, r, m)$. Well-formed pomsets are obviously finite and locally linear.

For the purpose of developing our semantics, basic interactions are given syntactically by well formed pomsets. We define Basic $= \{B \in \mathbb{P} \mid B \text{ is well formed}\}$ and use B as a metavariable that ranges over Basic. The formal semantics of basic interactions is given by a semantic function $\mathcal{P}[\![-]\!]$ which maps basic interactions to sets of positive (valid) traces (see Table 9.1). As mentioned above, basic interactions do not have negative traces.

The question remains how the metamodel in Figure 9.2 is to be mapped into the new (syntactic) domain Basic: Let I be a basic interaction and $(O, \rightarrow)$ the specification graph of I; see Section 9.2.2.2. Since $(O, \rightarrow)$ is an acyclic graph, the O-reflexive-transitive closure of $\rightarrow$ is a partial order on O; we define $\leq_O$ by $\rightarrow^*$. Basic interaction I is then mapped to $[(O, \leq_O, \lambda_O)]$, where λ_O is a labeling function $O \rightarrow \mathbb{E}$, whose definition is straightforward; in particular, synchronous messages (see Section 9.2.3) and coregions (see [45]) can be dealt with easily. The only interesting issue in defining λ_O is how a Message M is to be mapped to a message identificator $m \in \mathbb{M}$. One possibility would be to use the Message M itself (i.e., the object identificator). However, we define m as the set of any information that is conveyed by the message and can be used by the receiver to distinguish between two messages coming from the same sender. In particular, m comprises the name of M, arguments, and any kind of message content. Note that the resulting mapping of the metamodel into Basic is not injective (see Figure 9.5). A receiver instance cannot determine the order in which it receives two completely identical messages.

9.2.3 Synchronous and Asynchronous Messages

9.2.3.1 Communication Types The sample interaction ex4 in Figure 9.6 models the establishing of a connection between a client instance x and a server instance y and the subsequent processing of a client request by an instance z that has been created by y for this very purpose. Unlike the previous examples, which used only asynchronous communication (depicted by open arrowheads), interaction ex4

[7] The concurrence of $n = 0$ pomsets is defined by the empty pomset ε.

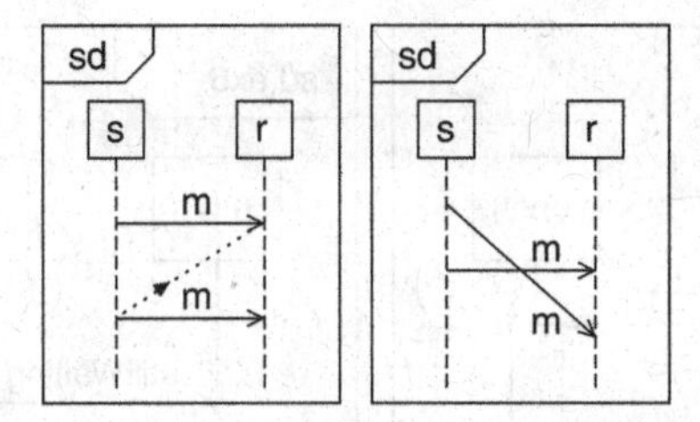

FIGURE 9.5 Two structurally distinct basic interaction diagrams that are both mapped to the same element snd(s, r, m) snd(s, r, m) rcv(s, r, m) rcv(s, r, m) $\in$ Basic.

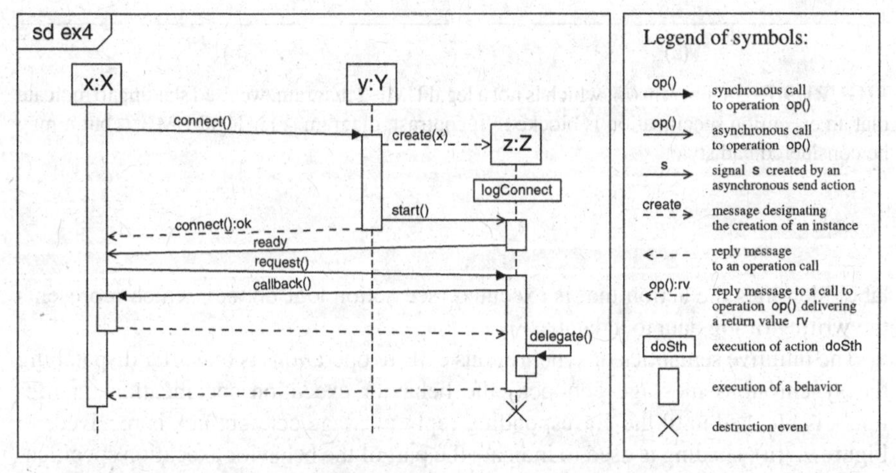

FIGURE 9.6 Sample interaction diagram that uses different types of communication.

also specifies messages reflecting *synchronous calls to operations* (depicted by filled arrowheads). These messages are connect(), request(), callback(), and delegate(). A synchronous call to an operation typically results in a reply message, which is shown graphically by a dashed line. Reply message connect():ok, for instance, delivers a return value ok, indicating that a connection with the server has been established successfully. Messages start() and ready represent an asynchronous call to an operation and a signal, respectively. Message create(x) designates the creation of a new instance z, with the argument x informing z what its communication partner is. The ╳ at the bottom of the lifeline of z depicts a *destruction event* that represents the destruction of instance z.

An *execution specification* (also known as *activation bar* or *focus of control*) is a notation that can appear on a lifeline to indicate the time during which an instance is *active* (i.e., executes a behavior or performs an action). In the case of a behavior, the execution specification is called a *behavior execution specification*, which is depicted by a thin rectangle that covers a part of a lifeline (e.g., instance x is active right from the start). In the case of an action, the execution specification is called an *action execution specification*, which is depicted by a wider, labeled rectangle, where the

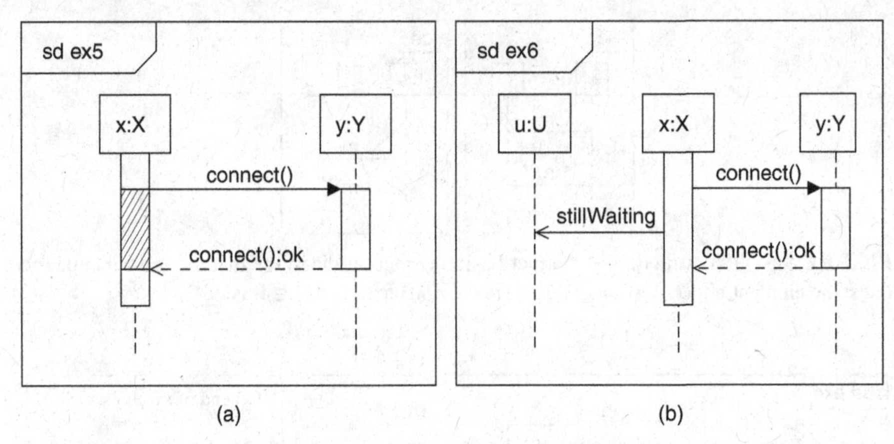

FIGURE 9.7 In diagram (a), which is not a legal UML 2 diagram, we used shading to indicate that an execution specification is blocked. In contrast, diagram (b) is legal UML 2, but it may be considered bad style.

label identifies the action that is executed (see action logConnect, which represents the writing of log data to a database).

The intuitive semantics of synchronous calls to operations is that after dispatching the synchronous message connect() the behavior execution specification on lifeline x is blocked until the corresponding reply message connect():ok is received. In Figure 9.7(a), shading is used to indicate the part of the behavior execution specification on lifeline x that is blocked by message connect(). Note that this form of shading is not a legal UML 2 notation, although it has actually been used in the literature (see, e.g., [51]). Regardless of how a blocked execution specification is depicted, the question arises whether message arrows may depart from positions on a lifeline where the lifeline is covered by a blocked execution specification; see, for example, message stillWaiting in Figure 9.7(b), which informs a user u that client x is still waiting for a reply message from server y. At first sight, from a sequential operational point of view, the dispatch of message stillWaiting would be unimplementable because the behavior execution specification on lifeline x is blocked by the synchronous message connect(). This view on synchronous messages, although legitimate, is by no means mandatory, because one and the same execution specification may represent behavior that emerges from several concurrent subbehaviors (e.g., parallel regions of a state machine). Even if one of the concurrent subbehaviors is blocked by a synchronous call, the other subbehaviors can still be active and send messages (although this may be considered bad style).

9.2.3.2 Metamodel Figure 9.8 shows the fragment of the UML 2 metamodel that is relevant to the new language constructs introduced by Figure 9.6. Model elements that have already appeared in our previous metamodel diagrams are shaded.

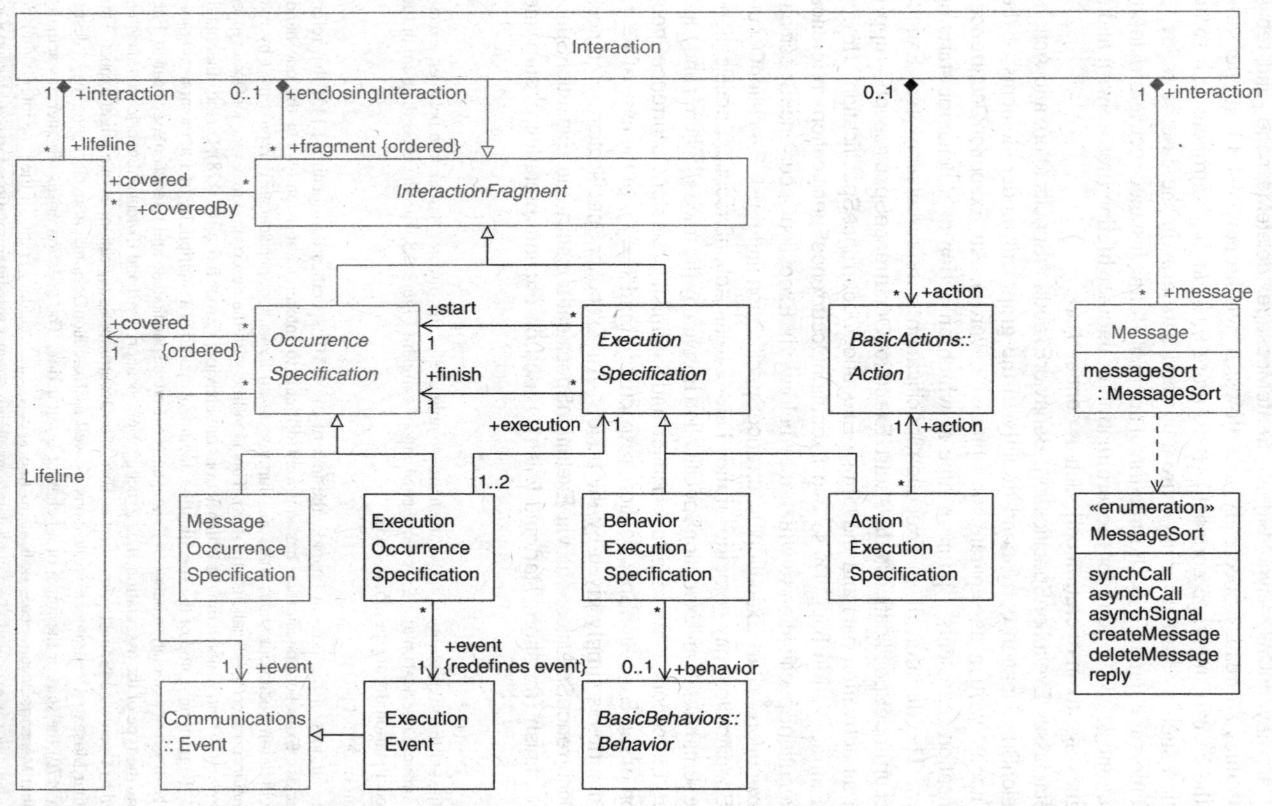

FIGURE 9.8 Fragment of the UML 2 metamodel that is relevant to different communication types and execution specification bars.

Attribute Message::messageSort specifies the type of communication action that was used to generate a message. It has the enumeration type MessageSort with values synchCall, asynchCall, asynchSignal, createMessage, deleteMessage, and reply. These values are read, respectively, as follows: A synchronous call to an operation as in the case of message connect() (see Figure 9.6); an asynchronous call to an operation such as start(); an asynchronous send action as in the case of ready; a pseudomessage standing for the creation of another lifeline instance such as create(x); a pseudomessage standing for the termination of another lifeline (not shown); and a reply message to an operation call such as connect():ok.

Metaclasses ExecutionSpecification, BehaviorExecutionSpecification, and ActionExecutionSpecification correspond directly to the graphical model elements of the same name (written as separate, uncapitalized words). An ExecutionOccurrenceSpecification represents a point in time at which an action or a behavior starts or finishes. The duration of an ExecutionSpecification is represented by two ExecutionOccurrenceSpecifications: the "start ExecutionOccurrenceSpecification" (upper end of an activation bar) and the "finish ExecutionOccurrenceSpecification" (lower end of an activation bar). These two ExecutionOccurrenceSpecifications reference the ExecutionSpecification to which they belong via ExecutionOccurrenceSpecification::execution.[8] Start ExecutionOccurrenceSpecification and finish ExecutionOccurrenceSpecification may coincide[9] if they belong to an ActionExecutionSpecification.

The semantics of an ExecutionSpecification is given by the trace sf where s and f are the start ExecutionOccurrenceSpecification and the finish ExecutionOccurrenceSpecification of the ExecutionSpecification, respectively (and $s \neq f$). In the case of $s = f$, the semantics is simply given by the trace s. An ExecutionSpecification references two OccurrenceSpecifications via ExecutionSpecification::start and ExecutionSpecification::finish (for short: start and finish). Based on our interpretation,[10] start and

[8] We adjusted the multiplicity value at the nonnavigable end of the directed association between ExecutionOccurrenceSpecification and ExecutionSpecification; compare Figure 9.8 with the class diagram of the UML specification document [45, p. 463].

[9] In terms of object identity.

[10] To the authors of the present chapter, the text of the UML specification document [45] that refers to metaclass ExecutionSpecification has appeared difficult to interpret consistently. On the one hand, the specification document states that "the duration of an ExecutionSpecification is represented by two ExecutionOccurrenceSpecifications" (p. 478). This is in line with the description of ExecutionOccurrenceSpecifications as "moments in time at which actions or behaviors start or finish" (p. 478). On the other hand, the class diagram on p. 463 of the specification document specifies a multiplicity of 1 at the nonnavigable end of the directed association between ExecutionOccurrenceSpecification and ExecutionSpecification. Furthermore, the type of the association ends ExecutionSpecification::start and ExecutionSpecification::finish is specified as OccurrenceSpecification—not as ExecutionOccurrenceSpecification, as one might expect. This means that MessageOccurrenceSpecifications as well as ExecutionOccurrenceSpecifications may "designate" (p. 479) the start or the finish of a behavior or an action. The question arises whether this actually means that MessageOccurrenceSpecifications may specify the boundary points of the time interval during which a behavior is executed. Two considerations weigh against this interpretation. First, a MessageOccurrenceSpecification cannot reference an ExecutionSpecification. Second, even if the arrival of a message causes execution of a behavior, typically some time elapses between the arrival of the message and the start of the execution.

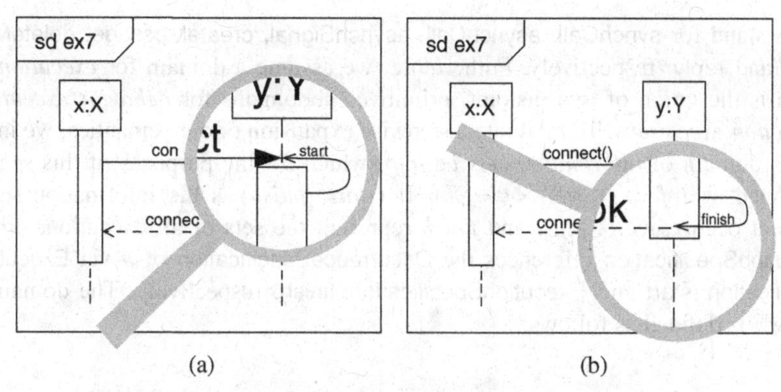

FIGURE 9.9 Suggested interpretation of (a) start and (b) finish.

finish generally do *not* coincide with s and f, respectively. Instead, start references an OccurrenceSpecification which lies so closely above s that the time interval between start and s is smaller than the resolution limit of the diagram. Typically start is a MessageOccurrenceSpecification of an incoming Message which causes the specified behavior to start [see Figure 9.9(a)]. Association end finish has a similar meaning: It references an OccurrenceSpecification which lies so closely above f that the time interval between finish and f is smaller than the resolution limit of the diagram. Typically, finish is a MessageOccurrenceSpecification of an outgoing reply message with a return value [see Figure 9.9(b)]. The authors of the present chapter want to point out that the meaning of start and finish which is conveyed by Figure 9.9 is just a *suggestion* for a consistent interpretation of the UML specification text. We further wish to stress that UML interactions do not imply statements about causality. They merely deal with temporal relationships.

A few notes about delete messages and destruction events are necessary. Since DestructionEvent is a specialization of Event – and not of ExecutionEvent – and since ExecutionOccurrenceSpecification::event redefines OccurrenceSpecification::event, a DestructionEvent cannot be referenced by an ExecutionOccurrenceSpecification. Since we decided[11] to regard the metaclass OccurrenceSpecification as abstract, a DestructionEvent can only be referenced by a MessageOccurrenceSpecification. This means that a destruction event cannot occur separately on a lifeline (as it is depicted, for example, in Figure 9.6). Actually, a message head is supposed to point at the destruction event. A delete message lends itself to this purpose. Whenever an instance decides to destruct itself, it has to send itself a delete message.[12]

9.2.3.3 Semantics We define a domain $MSort = \{$sc, ac, as, cm, dm, r$\}$ that corresponds directly to enumeration type MessageSort. The values listed between the

[11] For a (very) short discussion of this question, see footnote 2.

[12] As a matter of fact, this pseudocommunication has little to do with actual processes in a runtime environment.

braces stand for synchCall, asynchCall, asynchSignal, createMessage, deleteMessage, and reply, respectively. Futhermore, we assume a domain for *executions* $\mathbb{X}$ which is the union of two disjoint, primitive subdomains for *behavior executions* and *action executions*. To facilitate a stepwise expansion of our semantics, we introduce a domain of *information sets* $i \in Info$, which for the purposes of this section is defined as $Info = \wp_{\text{fin}}(\mathbb{X}) \times \wp_{\text{fin}}(\mathbb{X})$. If $(start, finish)$ is the information set of an event occurrence o, *start* and *finish* represent the sets of all executions whose ExecutionSpecification references the OccurrenceSpecification of o via ExecutionSpecification::start and ExecutionSpecification::finish, respectively. The domain of *events* $\mathbb{E}$ is defined as follows:

$$
\begin{aligned}
e \in \mathbb{E} ::= \; & \mathsf{snd}(s, \hat{r}, m, ms, i) \\
\mid \; & \mathsf{rcv}(\hat{s}, r, m, ms, i) \\
\mid \; & \mathsf{exec}(l, x, i)
\end{aligned}
$$

An occurrence of an event of the form $\mathsf{snd}(s, \hat{r}, m, ms, (start, finish))$ means:

1. In the case of $\hat{r} = r$: Dispatch of a message m (with messageKind $=$ complete and messageSort $= ms$) from sender instance s to receiver instance r.
2. In the case of $\hat{r} = -$: Dispatch of a message m (with messageKind $=$ lost and messageSort $= ms$) from sender instance s.

An occurrence of an event of the form $\mathsf{rcv}(\hat{s}, r, m, ms, (start, finish))$ means:

3. In the case of $\hat{s} = s$: Arrival of a message m (with messageKind $=$ complete and messageSort $= ms$) from sender instance s at receiver instance r.
4. In the case of $\hat{s} = -$: Arrival of a message m (with messageKind $=$ found and messageSort $= ms$) at receiver instance r.

Finally, an occurrence of an event of the form $\mathsf{exec}(l, x, (start, finish))$ means:

5. If x is a behavior execution, the occurrence denotes an (upper or lower) boundary point of the time interval during which the behavior is executed by instance l.
6. If x is an action execution, the occurrence denotes the (idealized) point in time at which the action is performed by instance l.

Using $\hat{m} \in \hat{\mathbb{M}} ::= m \mid -$, the lifeline function α and the message function μ are redefined as follows:

$$
\begin{aligned}
&\alpha : \mathbb{E} \longrightarrow \wp(\mathbb{I}) && \mu : \mathbb{E} \longrightarrow \hat{\mathbb{M}} \\
&\alpha(\mathsf{snd}(s, \hat{r}, m, ms, i)) = \{s\} && \mu(\mathsf{snd}(s, \hat{r}, m, ms, i)) = m \\
&\alpha(\mathsf{rcv}(\hat{s}, r, m, ms, i)) = \{r\} && \mu(\mathsf{rcv}(\hat{s}, r, m, ms, i)) = m \\
&\alpha(\mathsf{exec}(l, x, i)) = \{l\} && \mu(\mathsf{exec}(l, x, i)) = -
\end{aligned}
$$

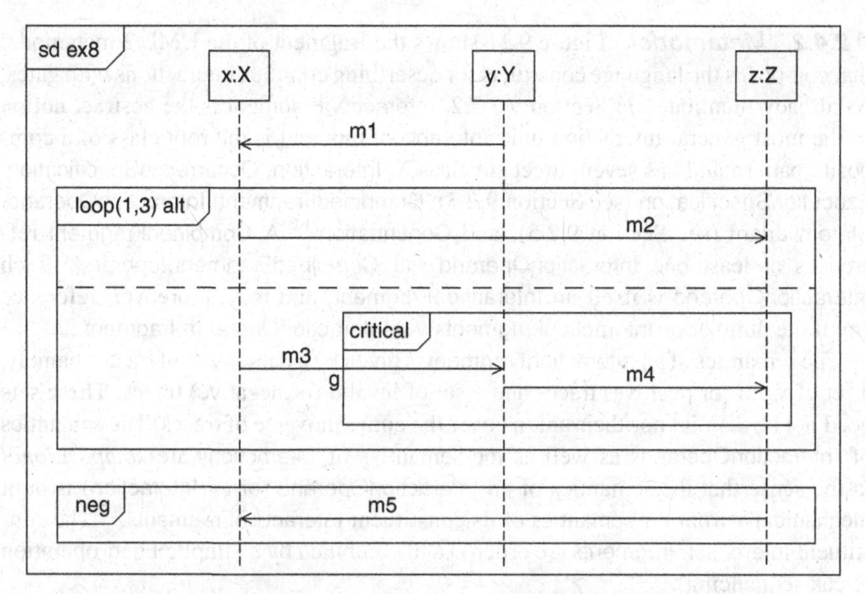

FIGURE 9.10 Sample interaction diagram using combined fragments.

9.2.4 Combined Fragments

9.2.4.1 Complex Interactions All interaction diagrams that have been discussed in previous sections are basic interaction diagrams. In the present section, we turn to *complex interactions*, which are characterized by the presence of *combined fragments*. A combined fragment defines an expression of interaction fragments. It is depicted by a solid-outline rectangle, in which an *interaction operator* is specified in a pentagon in the upper left-hand corner of the rectangle (pentagon descriptor). If the arity of this operator is greater than 1, the *interaction operands* are separated from each other graphically by dashed horizontal lines. More than one operator may be specified in the pentagon descriptor. This is shorthand for nesting combined fragments.

In addition to message m1, the sample interaction ex8 in Figure 9.10 specifies four combined fragments of kind loop(1,3), alt, critical, and neg.[13] The combined fragment with operator kind loop(1,3) has only one operand, which is a combined fragment with operator kind alt. The latter, in turn, has two operands: (1) a basic interaction consisting of message m2, and (2) a combined fragment of type critical together with a message m3 which enters the combined fragment via a *combined fragment gate* named g. No notation is specified for gates. They are merely points on the frame of a combined fragment. However, they may have explicit names.

[13] We postpone an explanation of the semantics of these operators to the following section.

9.2.4.2 Metamodel Figure 9.11 shows the fragment of the UML 2 metamodel that comprises the language constructs for describing complex interactions with gates. As already mentioned in Section 9.2.2.2, InteractionFragment is the abstract notion of the most general interaction unit. InteractionFragment is the root class of a composite pattern and has seven direct subclasses: Interaction, OccurrenceSpecification, ExecutionSpecification (see Section 9.2.3), CombinedFragment, InteractionOperand, StateInvariant (see Section 9.2.5), and Continuation.[14] A CombinedFragment references at least one InteractionOperand via CombinedFragment::operand. Each InteractionOperand is itself an InteractionFragment, and may, moreover, reference any finite number of InteractionFragments via InteractionOperand::fragment.

The semantics of an InteractionFragment is given by a pair of sets of traces: namely, a set of valid (or positive) traces and a set of invalid (or negative) traces. These sets need not be disjoint nor their union cover the entire universe of traces. The semantics of InteractionOperands as well as the semantics of Interactions are *compositional* in the sense that the semantics of an InteractionOperand (or an Interaction) is built mechanically from the semantics of its constituent InteractionFragments.[15] The constituent InteractionFragments are ordered and combined by an implicit seq-operation (weak sequencing).

Given an ordered set of traces $t_1 = e_{1,1}e_{1,2}\dots e_{1,l_1}, \dots, t_n = e_{n,1}e_{n,2}\dots e_{n,l_n}$, the *weak sequencing of* $t_1, \dots, t_n$ is defined by the set of all traces $e_{\pi(1)}e_{\pi(2)}\cdots e_{\pi(l)}$, where $l = l_1 + \cdots + l_n$, and π is a bijection (i.e., a one-to-one and onto mapping), $\pi : \{1, 2, \dots, l\} \to \{(1,1), \dots, (1, l_1), \dots, (n, 1), \dots, (n, l_n)\}$, $i \mapsto (\pi_1(i), \pi_2(i))$ such that for all $1 \leq i < j \leq l$, the following conditions hold:

1. If $e_{\pi(i)}$ and $e_{\pi(j)}$ lie on the same lifeline, then $\pi_1(i) \leq \pi_1(j)$.
2. If $\pi_1(i) = \pi_1(j)$, then $\pi_2(i) < \pi_2(j)$.

The semantics of a CombinedFragment depends on the value of its attribute interactionOperator. This attribute has the enumeration type InteractionOperatorKind with the values strict, seq, par, loop, alt, ignore, neg, assert, critical, break, opt, and consider. A description of the semantics of these operators can be found in the UML specification document 2.1.2 [45, pp. 468–470].[16] We restrict ourselves to citing some defining phrases in Table 9.2, and refer to our formal semantics in Section 9.2.4.4 for the rest.

9.2.4.3 Abstract (Term) Syntax We assume a primitive domain for *gates* $\mathbb{G}$ and use g as a metavariable that ranges over $\mathbb{G}$. The domains $\mathbb{I}_G$ and $\hat{\mathbb{I}}_G$ are defined by $r_G, s_G \in \mathbb{I}_G ::= l \mid g$ and by $\hat{r}_G, \hat{s}_G \in \hat{\mathbb{I}}_G ::= l \mid g \mid -$, respectively. The definition of the

[14] A Continuation allows the concatenation of branches in alternatives; as it is a mere syntactic entity, it is not covered in this chapter.

[15] See UML specification document 2.1.2 [45, pp. 482, 486].

[16] These three pages are a veritable wellspring of hermeneutical problems.

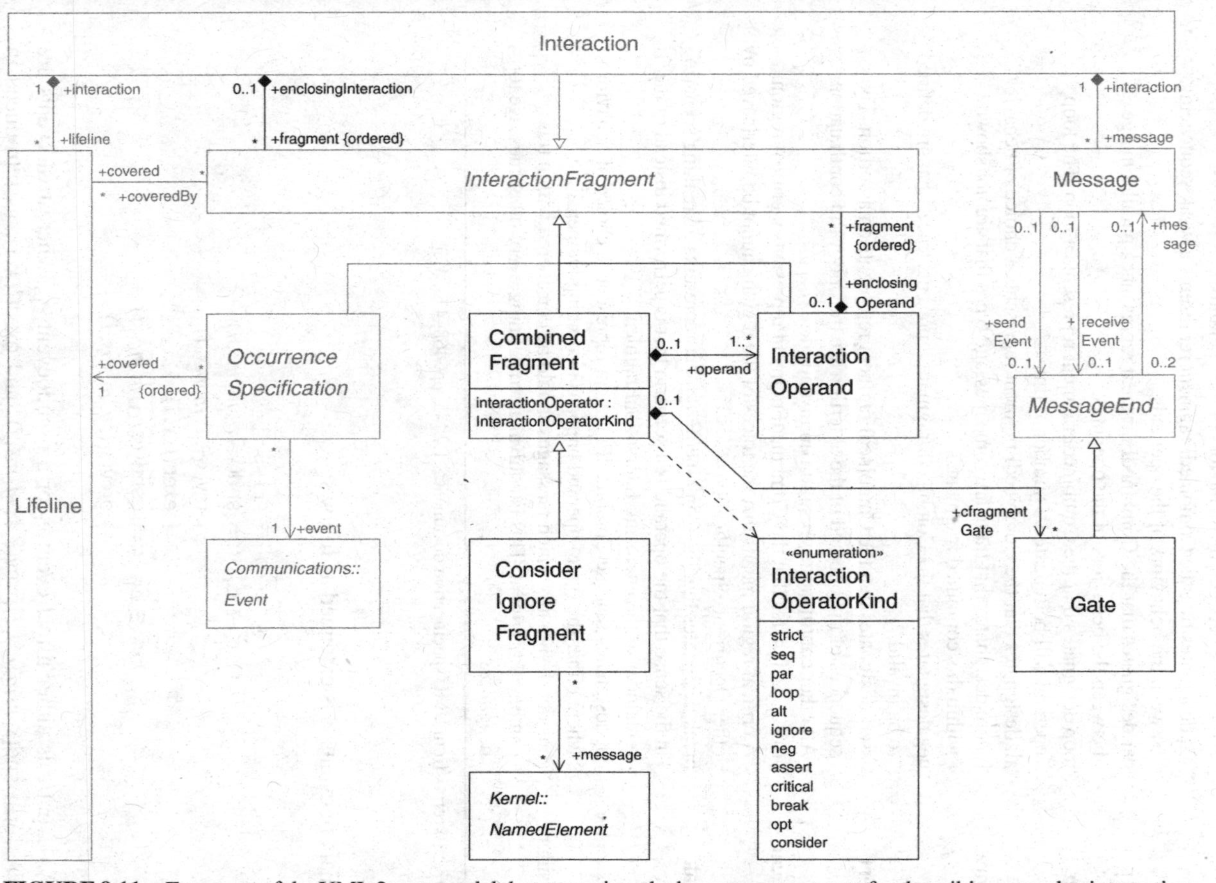

FIGURE 9.11 Fragment of the UML 2 metamodel that comprises the language constructs for describing complex interactions with gates.

TABLE 9.2 Semantics of Interaction Operators in Combined Fragments

strict	"strict designates [read means] that the CombinedFragment represents a strict sequencing between the behaviors of the operands."
seq	"seq designates that the CombinedFragment represents a weak sequencing between the behaviors of the operands."
par	"par designates that the CombinedFragment represents a parallel merge between the behaviors of the operands."
loop	"loop designates that the CombinedFragment represents a loop. The loop operand will be repeated a number of times."
alt	"alt designates that the CombinedFragment represents a choice of behavior."
ignore	"ignore designates that there are some message types that are not shown within this combined fragment."
neg	"neg designates that the CombinedFragment represents traces that are defined to be invalid."
assert	"assert designates that the CombinedFragment represents an assertion. The sequences of the operand of the assertion are the only valid continuations. All other continuations result in an invalid trace."
critical	"critical designates that the CombinedFragment represents a critical region. A critical region means that the traces of the region cannot be interleaved by other OccurrenceSpecifications."
break	"break designates that the CombinedFragment represents a breaking scenario in the sense that the operand is a scenario that is performed instead of the remainder of the enclosing InteractionFragment."
opt	"opt designates that the CombinedFragment represents a choice of behavior where either the (sole) operand happens or nothing happens."
consider	"consider designates which messages should be considered within this combined fragment. This is equivalent to defining every other message to be *ignores*."

Source: Excerpts from UML specification document 2.1.2 [45, pp. 468–470, 473].

domain of events $\mathbb{E}$ is extended as follows:

$$
\begin{aligned}
e \in \mathbb{E} \; &::= \; e_{\mathrm{r}} \mid e_{\mathrm{p}} \\
e_{\mathrm{r}} \in \mathbb{E}_{\mathrm{r}} \; &::= \; \mathsf{snd}(s, \hat{r}_{\mathrm{G}}, m, ms, i) \\
&\quad\mid \mathsf{rcv}(\hat{s}_{\mathrm{G}}, r, m, ms, i) \\
&\quad\mid \mathsf{exec}(l, x, i) \\
e_{\mathrm{p}} \in \mathbb{E}_{\mathrm{p}} \; &::= \; \mathsf{gsnd}(g, r_{\mathrm{G}}, m, ms, i) \\
&\quad\mid \mathsf{grcv}(s_{\mathrm{G}}, g, m, ms, i)
\end{aligned}
$$

An event e is either a real event e_{r} or a pseudoevent e_{p}, where real events are of the form $\mathsf{snd}(s, \hat{r}, m, ms, i)$, $\mathsf{rcv}(\hat{s}, r, m, ms, i)$, and $\mathsf{exec}(l, x, i)$, as introduced in Section 9.2.3.3. Now, a real event of the form $\mathsf{snd}(s, g, m, ms, i)$ represents the dispatch of a message m (with $\mathsf{messageKind} = \mathsf{complete}$ and $\mathsf{messageSort} = ms$) from sender instance s to gate g. Similarly, a real event of the form $\mathsf{rcv}(g, r, m, ms, i)$ represents the arrival of a message m (with $\mathsf{messageKind} = \mathsf{complete}$ and $\mathsf{messageSort} = ms$)

TABLE 9.3 Abstract Syntax of Interaction Terms

$$
\begin{array}{rcl}
T \in \text{IFragment} & ::= & B_q \\
& | & CF \\
& | & O \\
CF \in \text{CFragment} & ::= & \mathsf{strict}_q(O_1, O_2) \\
& | & \mathsf{seq}_q(O_1, O_2) \\
& | & \mathsf{par}_q(O_1, O_2) \\
& | & \mathsf{loop}_q(m, \hat{n}, O) \\
& | & \mathsf{alt}_q(O_1, O_2) \\
& | & \mathsf{ignore}_q(M, O) \\
& | & \mathsf{neg}_q(O) \\
& | & \mathsf{assert}_q(O) \\
& | & \mathsf{critical}_q(O) \\
& | & \mathsf{break}_q(O_1, O_2) \\
O \in \text{IOperand} & ::= & T
\end{array}
$$

from gate g at receiver instance r. A pseudoevent of the form $\mathsf{grcv}(s_G, g, m, ms, i)$ occurs whenever a message m coming from sender s_G enters (i.e., arrives at) a gate g. A pseudoevent of the form $\mathsf{gsnd}(g, r_G, m, ms, i)$ occurs whenever a message m has passed through a gate g and leaves the gate on the other side in the direction of r_G. The definitions of the lifeline function α and the message function μ are extended as follows:

$$
\begin{array}{llll}
\alpha : \mathbb{E} \to \wp(\mathbb{I}_G) & & \mu : \mathbb{E} \to \hat{\mathbb{M}} & \\
\alpha(\mathsf{snd}(s, \hat{r}, m, ms, i)) & = \{s\} & \mu(\mathsf{snd}(s, \hat{r}, m, ms, i)) & = m \\
\alpha(\mathsf{rcv}(\hat{s}, r, m, ms, i)) & = \{r\} & \mu(\mathsf{rcv}(\hat{s}, r, m, ms, i)) & = m \\
\alpha(\mathsf{exec}(l, x, i)) & = \{l\} & \mu(\mathsf{exec}(l, x, i)) & = - \\
\alpha(\mathsf{gsnd}(g, r_G, m, ms, i)) & = \{g\} & \mu(\mathsf{gsnd}(g, r_G, m, ms, i)) & = m \\
\alpha(\mathsf{grcv}(s_G, g, m, ms, i)) & = \{g\} & \mu(\mathsf{grcv}(s_G, g, m, ms, i)) & = m
\end{array}
$$

The definition of the conflict relation $\asymp$ given in Section 9.2.2 remains unchanged. Note that we consider gate identifiers g as a form of pseudolifelines.

The abstract syntax of interactions is given by the grammar in Table 9.3. Therein, T ranges over terms representing interaction fragments (*terms* for short), B ranges over terms representing basic interactions (*basic terms* or *leaf terms* for short), CF ranges over terms representing combined fragments (*combined terms* for short), O ranges over terms representing interaction operands,[17] m ranges over natural numbers, $\hat{n}$ ranges over natural numbers or ∞, and M ranges over $\wp_{\text{fin}}(\mathbb{M})$. The occurrences of metavariable q that adorn each operator symbol constitute a numbering schema that allows us to identify each basic term uniquely and each loop-operator inside a term. For this purpose we define the domain of paths by $q \in \text{Path} ::= \epsilon \mid q\,n$, $n \in \{1, 2\}$, with 1 denoting a left (or sole) operand and with 2 denoting a right operand. The concatenation of two paths q, q' is written $q.q'$. Each operator symbol inside a term is annotated

[17] In Section 9.2.5, constraints (i.e., guard expressions) are added to the syntax of these terms.

with a unique path identifier q (see Table 9.3). The function top : IFragment $\rightarrow$ Path ("topmost operator path") maps a term T to the path q with the topmost (or outermost) operator of T is annotated. We inductively define a unary predicate "is well numbered" on terms as follows:

1. B_q is well numbered.
2. If T is a well-numbered term and $uop \in \{\mathsf{loop}, \mathsf{ignore}, \mathsf{neg}, \mathsf{assert}, \mathsf{critical}\}$, and if there is a path r such that $\mathrm{top}(T) = q.1.r$, then $uop_q(T)$ is a well-numbered term.
3. If T_1 and T_2 are well-numbered terms and $bop \in \{\mathsf{strict}, \mathsf{seq}, \mathsf{par}, \mathsf{alt}, \mathsf{break}\}$, and if there are paths r_1 and r_2 such that $\mathrm{top}(T_1) = q.1.r_1$ and $\mathrm{top}(T_2) = q.2.r_2$, then $bop_q(T_1, T_2)$ is a well-numbered term.

In the following, we always use terms with the implicit understanding that these terms are well numbered. Furthermore, we use the name Empty for the term that represents the empty (basic) interaction; Empty is given by $[(\emptyset, \emptyset, \emptyset)]$. $\mathsf{opt}(T)$ abbreviates $\mathsf{alt}\,(\mathsf{Empty}, T)$, and $\mathsf{consider}\,(M, T)$ abbreviates $\mathsf{ignore}\,(\mathbb{M} \setminus M, T)$.

9.2.4.4 Intermediate Semantics We define a formal semantics of complex interactions by employing a two-step approach: First, we compositionally define two semantic functions $\mathcal{P}_{\mathrm{i}}[\![-]\!], \mathcal{N}_{\mathrm{i}}[\![-]\!]$: IFragment $\rightarrow \wp(\mathbb{T})$, which map interaction terms to sets of positive and negative traces, respectively. The pair $(\mathcal{P}_{\mathrm{i}}[\![T]\!], \mathcal{N}_{\mathrm{i}}[\![T]\!])$ is said to be the *intermediate semantics* of a term T. In a second step, filtering functions $\wp(\mathbb{T}) \rightarrow \wp(\mathbb{T})$ are employed to map the intermediate semantics to the (definitive) semantics. Pseudoevents and gate identifiers may occur in the intermediate semantics, but they do not occur in the (definitive) semantics.

Both specification of the formal semantics of critical regions that occur in the body of a loop and of the handling of gates require event occurrences to be equipped with additional semantic information. For this purpose, we redefine the domain of information sets as follows:

$$Info = \wp_{\mathrm{fin}}(\mathbb{X}) \times \wp_{\mathrm{fin}}(\mathbb{X}) \times \wp_{\mathrm{fin}}(\mathrm{Path}) \times [\mathrm{Path} \rightarrow \mathbb{N}] \times \mathrm{Path}$$

Let (*start*, *finish*, *region*, *loop*, *basic*) be the information set of an event occurrence o. Then *region* is the set of all paths that identify critical-operators whose operands contain the syntactic specification of o. The function *loop* maps a path that identifies a loop-operator to the iteration number of the loop to which the event occurrence o belongs. *loop* is a partial function, with $loop(q) = 0$ meaning "*loop* is not defined at q" because either q does not identify a loop-operator or the operand of the loop-operator does not contain the syntactic specification of o. The path *basic* identifies the basic term that contains the syntactic specification of o. The meanings of *start* and *finish* remain unchanged (see Section 9.2.3).

Let $q \in \mathrm{Path}$ and $n \in \mathbb{N}$. Moreover, let f_q, $g_{q,n}$, and h_q denote three functions $\mathbb{E} \rightarrow \mathbb{E}$, which are defined as follows. If $e \in \mathbb{E}$ is an event with information set

$i = (start, finish, region, loop, basic)$, then $f_q(e)$ is the event that is obtained from e by substituting $(start, finish, region \cup \{q\}, loop, basic)$ for i; $g_{q,n}(e)$ is obtained from e by substituting $(start, finish, region, loop[q \mapsto n], basic)$ for i; and $h_q(e)$ is obtained from e by substituting $(start, finish, region, loop, q)$ for i. We lift f_q, $g_{q,n}$, and h_q to pomsets (see Section 9.2.1), and for each $p \in \mathbb{D}$ we let $(p)_q$ be defined by $f_q(p)$, $p[q \mapsto n]$ be defined by $g_{q,n}(p)$, and $[p]_q$ be defined by $h_q(p)$. Furthermore, we define the *n-fold iteration* of a process $P \subseteq \mathbb{D}$ with respect to q, written $P_q^{(n)}$, as follows: $P_q^{(0)} = \{\varepsilon\}$ and $P_q^{(n+1)} = P[q \mapsto n+1] ;_{\approx} P_q^{(n)}$.

Let $M \subseteq \mathbb{M}$ be a set of messages. On pomsets in $\mathbb{D}$, the filtering relation $mfilter(M) : \mathbb{D} \to \wp(\mathbb{D})$ removes some elements of p whose labels show a message in M. More precisely, we first define $mfilter(M)$ on event-labeled sets as follows. Let O be a set and $\lambda : O \to \mathbb{E}$ a labeling function. Then $O' \in mfilter(M)(O, \lambda)$ if $O' \subseteq O$ and $\mu(\lambda(o)) \in M$ for any $o \in O \setminus O'$. For an event-labeled partial order $(O, \leq_O, \lambda_O)$, we set $(O', \leq_O \cap (O' \times O'), \lambda_O \lceil O') \in mfilter(M)(O, \leq_O, \lambda_O)$ if $O' \in mfilter(M)(O, \lambda_O)$. Finally, we extend these definitions to event-labeled pomsets $p \in \mathbb{D}$ by setting $p \in mfilter(M)([(O, \leq_O, \lambda_O)])$ if there is $(O', \leq_{O'}, \lambda_{O'}) \in mfilter(M)(O, \leq_O, \lambda_O)$ such that $p = [(O', \leq_{O'}, \lambda_{O'})]$. The relation $mfilter(M)$ obviously is well defined. Given a pomset $p \in \mathbb{D}$, by $mfilter(M)^{-1}(p)$ we denote $\{q \in \mathbb{D} \mid p \in mfilter(M)(q)\}$. This "inverse relation" is lifted to processes in the usual way (see Section 9.2.1). Given a process $P \subseteq \mathbb{D}$, we write $P\langle M \rangle$ for $mfilter(M)^{-1}(P)$. Furthermore, we define $\lhd(P)$ to be the prefix closure of P.

The intermediate semantics of complex interactions is given by a pair of semantic functions $\mathcal{P}_{\mathrm{i}}[\![-]\!]$ and $\mathcal{N}_{\mathrm{i}}[\![-]\!]$ that map interaction terms to sets of positive and negative traces, respectively; see Tables 9.4 and 9.5. These sets constitute an intermediate semantics since their traces may contain pseudoevents as well as gate identifiers.

The semantics of the positive fragment of the language closely follows the textual description of the specification (see Table 9.2). Indeed, the literature [12,36,49] shows a broad consensus on the semantics of this fragment. On the contrary, for the negative fragment the specification leaves room for different interpretations, and consequently diverging proposals have been made (see also [27]). In line with Kobro Runde et al. [36], we have adopted the view that a trace is negative for an interaction fragment whenever it has exhaustively traversed a negative subfragment. Only assert is an exception to this rationale, since, following the specification, it makes negative everything that is not explicitly positive.

9.2.4.5 Filtering Let $\mathbb{T}_{\mathrm{r}}$ be the set of all traces of occurrences of real events that do not contain gate identifiers. We define a filter $\mathcal{F}_{\mathrm{gate}} : \wp(\mathbb{T}) \to \wp(\mathbb{T}_{\mathrm{r}})$. This filter (1) removes all pseudoevents from a trace, (2) replaces all gate identifiers in events of the form $\mathsf{snd}(s, g, m, ms, i)$ and $\mathsf{rcv}(g, r, m, ms, i)$ with the lifelines of the actual receiver and the actual sender of the message, respectively, and (3) discards the trace if the actual sender or the actual receiver of a message cannot be determined or if the trace is malformed for some other reason. This "gate filter" works as follows. Let $P \subseteq \mathbb{T}$ be a process consisting of traces. For each trace $t \in P$, the following rewriting rule (R)

TABLE 9.4 Intermediate Semantics of Complex Interactions (Positive Fragment)

$\mathcal{P}_{\mathrm{i}}[\![-]\!] : \mathrm{IFragment} \to \wp(\mathbb{T})$	
$\mathcal{P}_{\mathrm{i}}[\![B_q]\!]$	$= [B{\downarrow}]_q$
$\mathcal{P}_{\mathrm{i}}[\![\mathsf{strict}_q(O_1, O_2)]\!]$	$= \mathcal{P}_{\mathrm{i}}[\![O_1]\!] \,;\, \mathcal{P}_{\mathrm{i}}[\![O_2]\!]$
$\mathcal{P}_{\mathrm{i}}[\![\mathsf{seq}_q(O_1, O_2)]\!]$	$= (\mathcal{P}_{\mathrm{i}}[\![O_1]\!] \,;_{\asymp}\, \mathcal{P}_{\mathrm{i}}[\![O_2]\!]){\downarrow}$
$\mathcal{P}_{\mathrm{i}}[\![\mathsf{par}_q(O_1, O_2)]\!]$	$= (\mathcal{P}_{\mathrm{i}}[\![O_1]\!] \parallel \mathcal{P}_{\mathrm{i}}[\![O_2]\!]){\downarrow}$
$\mathcal{P}_{\mathrm{i}}[\![\mathsf{loop}_q(m, \hat{n}, O)]\!]$	$= \bigcup_{m \leq i < \hat{n}+1} ((\mathcal{P}_{\mathrm{i}}[\![O]\!])^{(i)}_q){\downarrow}$
$\mathcal{P}_{\mathrm{i}}[\![\mathsf{alt}_q(O_1, O_2)]\!]$	$= \mathcal{P}_{\mathrm{i}}[\![O_1]\!] \cup \mathcal{P}_{\mathrm{i}}[\![O_2]\!]$
$\mathcal{P}_{\mathrm{i}}[\![\mathsf{ignore}_q(M, O)]\!]$	$= (\mathcal{P}_{\mathrm{i}}[\![O]\!]\langle M \rangle){\downarrow}$
$\mathcal{P}_{\mathrm{i}}[\![\mathsf{neg}_q(O)]\!]$	$= \{\varepsilon\}$
$\mathcal{P}_{\mathrm{i}}[\![\mathsf{assert}_q(O)]\!]$	$= \mathcal{P}_{\mathrm{i}}[\![O]\!]$
$\mathcal{P}_{\mathrm{i}}[\![\mathsf{critical}_q(O)]\!]$	$= (\mathcal{P}_{\mathrm{i}}[\![O]\!])_q$
$\mathcal{P}_{\mathrm{i}}[\![\mathsf{break}_q(O_1, O_2)]\!]$	$= \mathcal{P}_{\mathrm{i}}[\![O_1]\!] \cup (\lhd(\mathcal{P}_{\mathrm{i}}[\![O_1]\!]) \,;_{\asymp}\, \mathcal{P}_{\mathrm{i}}[\![O_2]\!]){\downarrow}$

TABLE 9.5 Intermediate Semantics of Complex Interactions (Negative Fragment)

$\mathcal{N}_{\mathrm{i}}[\![-]\!] : \mathrm{IFragment} \to \wp(\mathbb{T})$	
$\mathcal{N}_{\mathrm{i}}[\![B_q]\!]$	$= \emptyset$
$\mathcal{N}_{\mathrm{i}}[\![\mathsf{strict}_q(O_1, O_2)]\!]$	$= (\mathcal{P}_{\mathrm{i}}[\![O_1]\!] \,;\, \mathcal{N}_{\mathrm{i}}[\![O_2]\!]) \cup (\mathcal{N}_{\mathrm{i}}[\![O_1]\!] \,;\, \mathcal{P}_{\mathrm{i}}[\![O_2]\!])$ $\cup (\mathcal{N}_{\mathrm{i}}[\![O_1]\!] \,;\, \mathcal{N}_{\mathrm{i}}[\![O_2]\!])$
$\mathcal{N}_{\mathrm{i}}[\![\mathsf{seq}_q(O_1, O_2)]\!]$	$= (\mathcal{P}_{\mathrm{i}}[\![O_1]\!] \,;_{\asymp}\, \mathcal{N}_{\mathrm{i}}[\![O_2]\!]){\downarrow} \cup (\mathcal{N}_{\mathrm{i}}[\![O_1]\!] \,;_{\asymp}\, \mathcal{P}_{\mathrm{i}}[\![O_2]\!]){\downarrow}$ $\cup (\mathcal{N}_{\mathrm{i}}[\![O_1]\!] \,;_{\asymp}\, \mathcal{N}_{\mathrm{i}}[\![O_2]\!]){\downarrow}$
$\mathcal{N}_{\mathrm{i}}[\![\mathsf{par}_q(O_1, O_2)]\!]$	$= (\mathcal{P}_{\mathrm{i}}[\![O_1]\!] \parallel \mathcal{N}_{\mathrm{i}}[\![O_2]\!]){\downarrow} \cup (\mathcal{N}_{\mathrm{i}}[\![O_1]\!] \parallel \mathcal{P}_{\mathrm{i}}[\![O_2]\!]){\downarrow}$ $\cup (\mathcal{N}_{\mathrm{i}}[\![O_1]\!] \parallel \mathcal{N}_{\mathrm{i}}[\![O_2]\!]){\downarrow}$
$\mathcal{N}_{\mathrm{i}}[\![\mathsf{loop}_q(m, \hat{n}, O)]\!]$	$= \bigcup_{m \leq i < \hat{n}+1} ((\mathcal{P}_{\mathrm{i}}[\![O]\!] \cup \mathcal{N}_{\mathrm{i}}[\![O]\!])^{(i)}_q){\downarrow} \setminus ((\mathcal{P}_{\mathrm{i}}[\![O]\!])^{(i)}_q){\downarrow}$
$\mathcal{N}_{\mathrm{i}}[\![\mathsf{alt}_q(O_1, O_2)]\!]$	$= \mathcal{N}_{\mathrm{i}}[\![O_1]\!] \cup \mathcal{N}_{\mathrm{i}}[\![O_2]\!]$
$\mathcal{N}_{\mathrm{i}}[\![\mathsf{ignore}_q(M, O)]\!]$	$= (\mathcal{N}_{\mathrm{i}}[\![O]\!]\langle M \rangle){\downarrow}$
$\mathcal{N}_{\mathrm{i}}[\![\mathsf{neg}_q(O)]\!]$	$= \mathcal{P}_{\mathrm{i}}[\![O]\!] \cup \mathcal{N}_{\mathrm{i}}[\![O]\!]$
$\mathcal{N}_{\mathrm{i}}[\![\mathsf{assert}_q(O)]\!]$	$= (\mathbb{T} \setminus \mathcal{P}_{\mathrm{i}}[\![O]\!]) \cup \mathcal{N}_{\mathrm{i}}[\![O]\!]$
$\mathcal{N}_{\mathrm{i}}[\![\mathsf{critical}_q(O)]\!]$	$= (\mathcal{N}_{\mathrm{i}}[\![O]\!])_q$
$\mathcal{N}_{\mathrm{i}}[\![\mathsf{break}_q(O_1, O_2)]\!]$	$= \mathcal{N}_{\mathrm{i}}[\![O_1]\!] \cup (\lhd(\mathcal{P}_{\mathrm{i}}[\![O_1]\!]) \,;_{\asymp}\, \mathcal{N}_{\mathrm{i}}[\![O_2]\!]){\downarrow}$ $\cup (\lhd(\mathcal{N}_{\mathrm{i}}[\![O_1]\!]) \,;_{\asymp}\, \mathcal{P}_{\mathrm{i}}[\![O_2]\!]){\downarrow}$ $\cup (\lhd(\mathcal{N}_{\mathrm{i}}[\![O_1]\!]) \,;_{\asymp}\, \mathcal{N}_{\mathrm{i}}[\![O_2]\!]){\downarrow}$

is iteratively applied to t as long as the rule matches:

$$(R) \qquad t_1\, a\, t_2\, b\, t_3\, c\, t_4\, d\, t_5 \;\longrightarrow\; t_1\, a'\, t_2\, t_3\, t_4\, d'\, t_5$$

$$\begin{aligned}
\text{where } a &= \mathsf{snd}(s, g, m, ms, (\mathit{start}, \mathit{finish}, \mathit{region}, \mathit{loop}, q)),\\
b &= \mathsf{grcv}(s, g, m, ms, (_, _, _, _, q)),\\
c &= \mathsf{gsnd}(g, l_{\mathrm{G}}, m, ms, (_, _, _, _, q')),\\
d &= k(g, l_{\mathrm{G}}, m, ms, (\mathit{start}', \mathit{finish}', \mathit{region}', \mathit{loop}', q'))\\
a' &= \mathsf{snd}(s, l_{\mathrm{G}}, m, ms, (\mathit{start}, \mathit{finish}, \mathit{region}, \mathit{loop}, q)),\\
d' &= k(s, l_{\mathrm{G}}, m, ms, (\mathit{start}', \mathit{finish}', \mathit{region}', \mathit{loop}', q')),
\end{aligned}$$

TABLE 9.6 Semantics of Complex Interactions

$\mathcal{P}[\![-]\!], \mathcal{N}[\![-]\!]$: IFragment $\longrightarrow \wp(\mathbb{T}_r)$		
$\mathcal{P}[\![-]\!]$	$=$	$\mathcal{F}_{crit} \circ \mathcal{F}_{gate} \circ \mathcal{P}_i[\![-]\!]$
$\mathcal{N}[\![-]\!]$	$=$	$\mathcal{F}_{crit} \circ \mathcal{F}_{gate} \circ \mathcal{N}_i[\![-]\!]$

with (($k=$ rcv and $l_G \in \mathbb{I}$) or ($k=$ grcv and $l_G \in \mathbb{G}$)), and $t_1, t_2, t_3, t_4 \in \mathbb{T}$ do not contain a, b, c, d, respectively. If the resulting trace is an element of $\mathbb{T}_r$ (i.e., if it does not contain pseudoevents or gate identifiers), the trace is retained as an element of $\mathcal{F}_{gate}(P)$; otherwise, the trace is discarded.

A filter $\mathcal{F}_{crit} : \wp(\mathbb{T}_r) \to \wp(\mathbb{T}_r)$ is required to prevent traces from violating atomicity constraints specified by critical-constructs. For the purpose of defining this filter, let $\varrho : \mathbb{E} \to \wp_{fin}(\text{Path})$ and $\ell : \mathbb{E} \to [\text{Path} \to \mathbb{N}]$ be two functions that map an event e to the third and fourth components of the information set of e, respectively. For each path q, the set $\text{prefix}(q) = \{q' \mid \exists q''.\, q = q'q''\}$ contains all prefixes of q; in particular, $q \in \text{prefix}(q)$. We say that a (finite) trace $t = e_1 e_2 \cdots e_n \in \mathbb{T}_r$ *preserves atomicity* if for all $1 \le i \le j \le k \le n$ and for all $q \in \text{Path}$, $q \in \varrho(e_j)$ and $\ell(e_i)\restriction \text{prefix}(q) = \ell(e_j)\restriction \text{prefix}(q)$ whenever $q \in \varrho(e_i) \cap \varrho(e_k)$ and $\ell(e_i)\restriction \text{prefix}(q) = \ell(e_k)\restriction \text{prefix}(q)$. Given a process $P \subseteq \mathbb{T}_r$, we define $\mathcal{F}_{crit}(P)$ by $\{t \in P \mid t \text{ preserves atomicity}\}$.

9.2.4.6 Semantics The semantics of complex interactions is given by a pair of semantic functions $\mathcal{P}[\![-]\!]$ and $\mathcal{N}[\![-]\!]$ that map terms to sets of positive and negative traces of occurrences of real events, respectively (see Table 9.6). Therein, $\mathcal{P}_i[\![-]\!]$ and $\mathcal{N}_i[\![-]\!]$ are the semantic functions defined in Tables 9.4 and 9.5, respectively. The filtering functions $\mathcal{F}_{gate}$ and $\mathcal{F}_{crit}$ are defined in Section 9.2.4.5.

9.2.5 Constraints

9.2.5.1 Guards and State Invariants The sample interaction ex9 in Figure 9.12 illustrates the use of guards and state invariants. The combined fragment of type alt which is contained in ex9 has two guarded operands: The first (upper) operand has the guard z.p >= 1; the second (lower) operand has an else-guard. These guards have the following meanings:

1. If the upper operand is chosen and the dispatch of m2 occurs before the dispatch of m3, the Boolean expression z.p >= 1 has to be true with respect to the global state of the system that exists directly before the dispatch of m2.
2. If the upper operand is chosen and the dispatch of m3 occurs before the dispatch of m2, the Boolean expression z.p >= 1 has to be true with respect to the global state that exists directly before the dispatch of m3.
3. If the lower operand is chosen, the Boolean expression z.p >= 1 has to be false with respect to the global state directly before the dispatch of m4.

The state invariant 2 > z.p >= 0 on the lifeline of z is evaluated in the global state of the system that exists directly before the next event occurs on the same lifeline

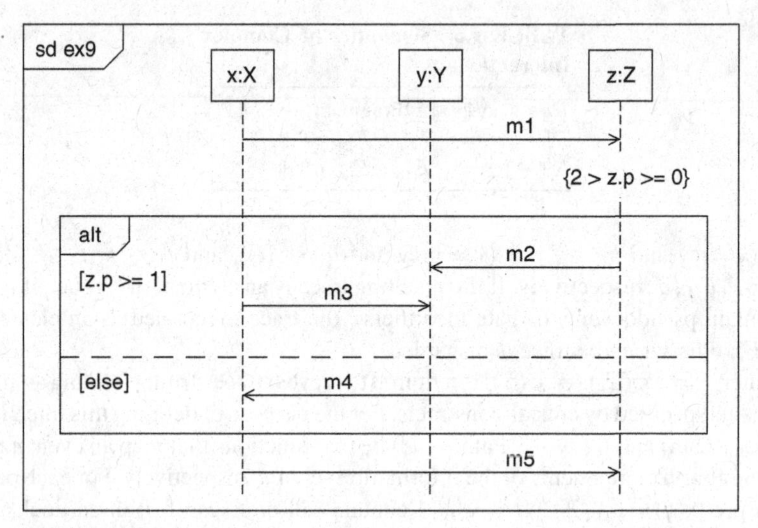

FIGURE 9.12 Sample interaction diagram using guards and state invariants.

after the state invariant. This may be the dispatch of m2, the dispatch of m4, or the arrival of m5.

9.2.5.2 Metamodel Figure 9.13 shows the fragment of the UML 2 metamodel that is relevant to guards and state invariants. Considering the class diagram, an

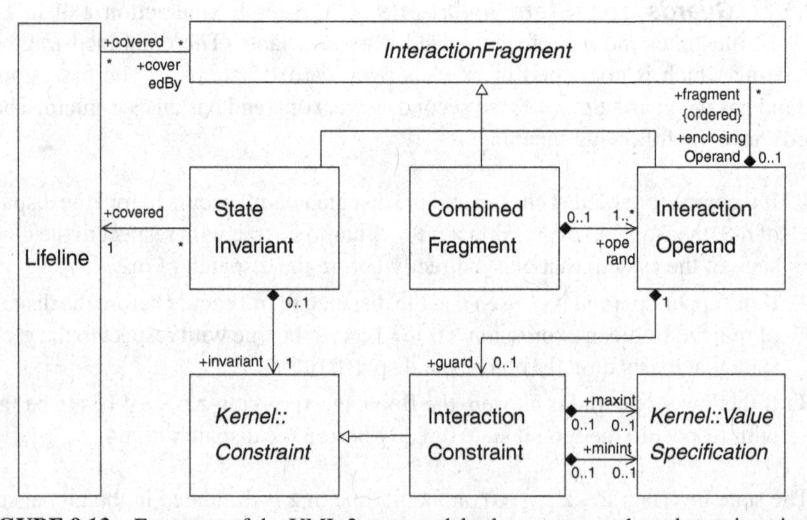

FIGURE 9.13 Fragment of the UML 2 metamodel relevant to guards and state invariants.

InteractionConstraint may be assigned only to an InteractionOperand (as a whole).[18] We therefore recommend placing a guard anywhere in the frame of an interaction operand.

9.2.5.3 *Abstract Syntax* We assume a domain of constraints $C \in \text{Constraint}$ whose syntax is left unspecified, except for the requirement that the domain contains the logical connectives $\vee$, $\neg$, and the logical expression true. Interaction operands are equipped with these constraints as follows (see Table 9.3):

$$O \in \text{IOperand} ::= [C]T$$

The constraint C that occurs in an interaction operand $[C]T$ acts as a guard for T. If an InteractionOperand (for fragments represented by T) does not specify a guard, the InteractionOperand is translated into our term syntax as $[\mathsf{true}]T$. A CombinedFragment of type $k \in \{\mathsf{strict}, \mathsf{seq}, \mathsf{par}\}$ with more than two InteractionOperands is translated using the following syntactic transformation:

$$\begin{aligned} & k([C_1]T_1, \ldots, [C_n]T_n) \\ & = k([C_1]T_1, [\mathsf{true}]k([C_2]T_2, \ldots, [\mathsf{true}]k([C_{n-1}]T_{n-1}, [C_n]T_n)\ldots)) \end{aligned}$$

A CombinedFragment of type alt with $n \geq 0$ InteractionOperands is interpreted as $\mathsf{alt}\,([C_1]T_1, \ldots, [C_n]T_n, [\neg(C_1 \vee \cdots \vee C_n)]\mathsf{Empty})$.[19] If $n \geq 2$, the latter is translated using the syntactic transformation given above. A CombinedFragment of type loop with operand $[C]T$, lower bound m, and upper bound $\hat{n}$ is translated using the following syntactic transformation:[20]

$$\mathsf{loop}\,(m, \hat{n}, [C]T) = \underbrace{\mathsf{seq}(T, \ldots, \mathsf{seq}}_{m \text{ times}}\,(T, \mathsf{loop}\,(0, \hat{n} - m, [C]T))\ldots)$$

Furthermore, a new sort of pseudoevent is introduced, which represents a state invariant C lying on lifeline l (see Section 9.2.4.3):

$$e_p \in \mathbb{E}_p \ ::= \ \ldots \mid \mathsf{stateinv}\,(l, C, i)$$

We define $\alpha(\mathsf{stateinv}(l, C, i))$ by $\{l\}$, and $\mu(\mathsf{stateinv}(l, C, i))$ by $-$.

[18] However, several passages in the UML specification document indicate that an InteractionConstraint is—at least graphically—assigned to a particular lifeline: namely, "the lifeline where the first event occurrence [of the interaction operand] will occur" [45, p. 484]. In addition, there is a formal constraint specifying that a "guard must be placed directly prior to (above) the OccurrenceSpecification that will become the first OccurrenceSpecification within this InteractionOperand" [45, p. 486]. Since the minimum of a partial order of event occurrences is, in general, not determined uniquely, the quoted passages of the specification document appear ill-formed to the authors of the present chapter.

[19] UML specification document 2.1.2 [45, p. 468] states that if "none of the operands [of a combined fragment of kind alt] has a guard that evaluates to true, [...] the remainder of the enclosing Interaction-Fragment is executed." This means that the set of positive traces of such an alt-fragment is $\{\varepsilon\}$ (and not $\emptyset$).

[20] UML specification document 2.1.2 [45, p. 470] states that "a loop will iterate minimum 'minint' number of times [...]. After the minimum number of iterations have executed and the Boolean expression is false the loop will terminate." In our opinion, this means that the Boolean expression is not to be evaluated during the first 'minint' iterations.

9.2.5.4 Semantics Let Σ be the set of all global states of the overall system. We assume a semantic function $\mathcal{C}[\![-]\!]$: Constraint $\rightarrow (\Sigma \rightarrow \{tt, ff\})$ which maps a constraint and a global state to a Boolean value.[21] Furthermore, we assume that $\mathcal{C}[\![-]\!]$ interprets $C_1 \vee C_2$, $\neg C$, and true in the canonical way.

A pair $(\sigma, e) \in \Sigma \times \mathbb{E}$ is said to be a *stateful event*. We define $\underline{\mathbb{E}}$ by $\Sigma \times \mathbb{E}$ and use $\underline{e}$ as a metavariable that ranges over $\underline{\mathbb{E}}$. The lifeline function α, the message function μ, and the functions ϱ and ℓ (see Section 9.2.4.5) are defined on stateful events (σ, e) by applying the respective functions to the second component e. Two stateful events $\underline{e}_1$ and $\underline{e}_2$ are in conflict, written $\underline{e}_1 \asymp \underline{e}_2$, if $\alpha(\underline{e}_1) \cap \alpha(\underline{e}_2) \neq \emptyset$. The domains of $\underline{\mathbb{E}}$-labeled pomsets $\underline{\mathbb{D}}$, $\underline{\mathbb{P}}$, and $\underline{\mathbb{T}}$ correspond directly to $\mathbb{D}$, $\mathbb{P}$, and $\mathbb{T}$, respectively. For each (σ, e) that occurs in a trace $\underline{t} \in \underline{\mathbb{T}}$, the state σ denotes the global state of the overall system *directly before* the event e occurs. If the occurrence of e depends on whether a certain constraint C evaluates to tt in the state σ, the evaluation of C (to tt) and the event e occur *atomically*.

A compositional definition of the semantics of interaction operands $[C]T$—namely, the one whose term T produces an empty trace ε—requires a refined definition of events:

$$e \in \mathbb{E} \ ::= \ e_{\mathrm{r}} \mid e_{\mathrm{p}} \mid \varepsilon(i)$$

Therein, e_{r} and e_{p} range over real events and pseudoevents, respectively, as they are defined in Section 9.2.4.3. A stateful event $(\sigma, \varepsilon(i))$ is said to be a *state marker*. A state marker is a special form of pseudoevent that occurs only in traces, but not in syntactic terms. We set $\alpha(\sigma, \varepsilon(i)) = \emptyset$ (i.e., a state marker does not conflict with any event). An occurrence of a state marker $(\sigma, \varepsilon(i))$ in a trace $\underline{t} \in \underline{\mathbb{T}}$ indicates that the state of the system at this point of the trace is σ. A state marker $(\sigma, \varepsilon(i))$ is inserted in a trace automatically whenever the constraint C of an interaction operand $[C]T$ is evaluated in a state σ, the result of the evaluation is tt, and the term T produces an empty trace.[22]

For each $C \in$ Constraint, we define a filter $\mathcal{F}_C : \wp(\underline{\mathbb{T}}) \rightarrow \wp(\underline{\mathbb{T}})$ which (1) discards each nonempty trace that starts with a stateful event (σ, e) such that C is false in σ, and (2) replaces the empty trace ε (if any) with the set of all state markers $(\sigma, \varepsilon(\emptyset))$ such that C is true in σ. The symbol $\emptyset$ denotes an information set with an empty *region* component and a totally undefined *loop* component. Formally, we define

$$\begin{aligned}\mathcal{F}_C(P) = & \{\underline{t} \in P \mid \exists \sigma \in \Sigma, e \in \mathbb{E}, \underline{t}' \in \underline{\mathbb{T}}. \underline{t} = (\sigma, e)\underline{t}' \wedge \mathcal{C}[\![C]\!]\sigma = tt\} \\ & \cup \{(\sigma, \varepsilon(\emptyset)) \mid \varepsilon \in P \wedge \sigma \in \Sigma \wedge \mathcal{C}[\![C]\!]\sigma = tt\}\end{aligned}$$

[21] The proposal by Calegari García et al. [9] uses OCL/RT, an extension of OCL for real time (see [11,44]), which in fact is based on a three-valued logic.

[22] The latter is indicated by the symbol ε in the state marker.

TABLE 9.7 Intermediate Semantics of Interactions with Constraints (Positive Fragment)[a]

$$\mathcal{P}_{\mathrm{i}}[\![-]\!] : \mathrm{IFragment} \to \wp(\mathbb{T})$$
$$\mathcal{P}_{\mathrm{i}}[\![B_q]\!] = \Sigma([B\downarrow]_q)$$
$$\mathcal{P}_{\mathrm{i}}[\![[C]T]\!] = \mathcal{F}_C(\mathcal{P}_{\mathrm{i}}[\![T]\!])$$

[a]Only clauses differing from Table 9.4 are shown.

TABLE 9.8 Intermediate Semantics of Interactions with Constraints (Negative Fragment)[a]

$$\mathcal{N}_{\mathrm{i}}[\![-]\!] : \mathrm{IFragment} \to \wp(\mathbb{T})$$
$$\mathcal{N}_{\mathrm{i}}[\![\mathsf{assert}_q(O)]\!] = \mathbb{T} \setminus \mathcal{P}_{\mathrm{i}}[\![O]\!]$$
$$\mathcal{N}_{\mathrm{i}}[\![[C]T]\!] = \mathcal{F}_{\neg C}(\mathcal{P}_{\mathrm{i}}[\![T]\!]) \cup \mathcal{N}_{\mathrm{i}}[\![T]\!]$$

[a]Only clauses differing from Table 9.5 are shown.

A mapping $\Sigma(-)$ is defined that transforms an $\mathbb{E}$-labeled pomset $p \in \mathbb{D}$ into a set of $\underline{\mathbb{E}}$-labeled pomsets, thereby pairing off the labels e of p with all possible combinations of states $\sigma \in \Sigma$, that is, $\Sigma(\varepsilon) = \{\varepsilon\}$ and $\Sigma(p) = \{[(O, \leq_O, \lambda'_O)] \mid \exists \sigma_O : O \to \Sigma.\lambda'_O = (\sigma_O, \lambda_O)\}$ for each $p = [(O, \leq_O, \lambda_O)] \in \mathbb{D} \setminus \{\varepsilon\}$.

The intermediate semantics of interactions with constraints is given by a pair of semantic functions $\mathcal{P}_{\mathrm{i}}[\![-]\!]$ and $\mathcal{N}_{\mathrm{i}}[\![-]\!]$ that map interaction terms to sets of positive and negative traces, respectively (see Tables 9.7 and 9.8).[23]

9.2.6 High-Level Interactions

9.2.6.1 References to Interactions The sample interaction ex10 shown in Figure 9.14(a) references another interaction ex11 shown in Figure 9.14(b) in a ref. Intuitively, the referenced interaction is expanded into the place where it is referred to. In fact, the UML specification also allows to use arguments for formal parameters of interactions; we do not handle parameters in this chapter.

9.2.6.2 Metamodel Figure 9.15 shows the fragment of the UML 2 metamodel that is relevant to high-level interactions. An InteractionUse refers to an Interaction via refersTo. The InteractionUse must cover all Lifelines of the enclosing Interaction that appear within the referred Interaction. An InteractionUse has an ordered set of arguments that must correspond to the parameters of the referred Interaction. Furthermore, an InteractionUse has a set of actualGates that must match the formalGates of

[23] The set of traces positively associated with a constrained interaction coincides with the definition by Calegari García et al. [9]. On the contrary, the set of traces negatively associated with a constrained interaction does not; in that work, $\mathcal{N}_{\mathrm{i}}[\![[C]T]\!] = \mathcal{F}_{\neg C}(\mathbb{T}) \cup \mathcal{N}_{\mathrm{i}}[\![T]\!]$.

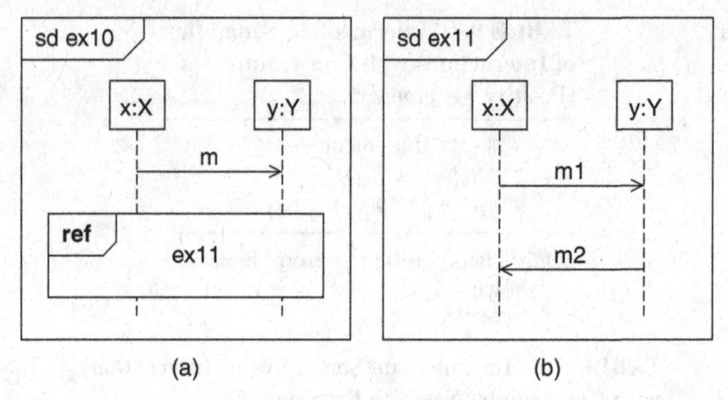

FIGURE 9.14 (a) Sample interaction diagram ex10 using references to (b) another interaction (ex11).

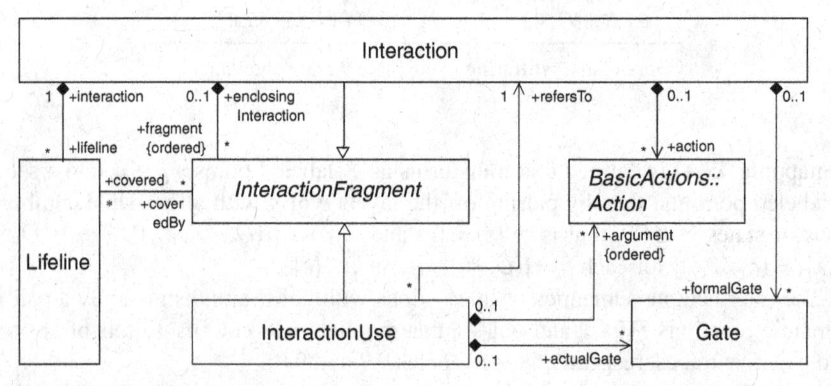

FIGURE 9.15 Fragment of the UML 2 metamodel relevant to high-level interactions.

the referred Interaction. Since parameters and gates are mere syntactic constructs, we do not handle them in our formal semantics.

9.2.6.3 Semantics Let us assume a syntactic category Name of *names*. The abstract syntax of interactions is given by the grammar in Table 9.9. An *interaction environment* ν is a set of interactions $\mathsf{sd}\,(n, T)$ where all interactions in ν have a different name n.

Let $q \in$ Path. A function $f_q : \mathbb{E} \to \mathbb{E}$ is defined as follows: If $e \in \mathbb{E}$ is an event with information set $i = (\mathit{start}, \mathit{finish}, \mathit{region}, \mathit{loop}, \mathit{basic})$, then $f_q(e)$ is the event that is obtained from e by substituting $(\mathit{start}, \mathit{finish}, \mathit{region}', \mathit{loop}', \mathit{basic}')$ for i, with basic',

TABLE 9.9 Abstract Syntax of High-Level Interaction Terms

$n \in$ Name	
$S \in$ Interaction	$::= \mathsf{sd}(n, T)$
$T \in$ IFragment	$::= \ldots \mid \mathsf{ref}(n)$

TABLE 9.10 Intermediate Semantics of High-Level Interactions (Positive Fragment)[a]

$\mathcal{P}_\mathrm{i}[\![-]\!] : \text{Interaction} \to (\text{IEnvironment} \to \wp(\mathbb{T}))$
$\mathcal{P}_\mathrm{i}[\![\mathsf{ref}_q(n)]\!]\nu = (\mathcal{P}_\mathrm{i}[\![T]\!]\nu)_q.\ \mathit{if}\ \mathsf{sd}(n,T) \in \nu$

[a]Only clauses differing from Table 9.4 are shown.

TABLE 9.11 Intermediate Semantics of High-Level Interactions (Negative Fragment)[a]

$\mathcal{N}_\mathrm{i}[\![-]\!] : \text{Interaction} \to (\text{IEnvironment} \to \wp(\mathbb{T}))$
$\mathcal{N}_\mathrm{i}[\![\mathsf{ref}_q(n)]\!]\nu = (\mathcal{N}_\mathrm{i}[\![T]\!]\nu)_q.\ \mathit{if}\ \mathsf{sd}(n,T) \in \nu$

[a]Only clauses differing from Table 9.5 are shown.

region', and *loop'* being defined as $q.basic$, $\{q.q' \mid q' \in region\}$, and

$$loop'(q'') := \begin{cases} loop(q') & \text{if } q'' = q.q' \\ 0 & \text{otherwise} \end{cases}$$

respectively. The function $f'_q : \mathbb{E} \to \mathbb{E}$ is defined on stateful events (σ, e) by applying the function f_q to the second component e. We lift f'_q to pomsets (see Section 9.2.1). For each $p \in \mathbb{D}$ we define $(p)_q.$ by $f'_q(p)$.

The intermediate semantics of high-level interactions is given by a pair of semantic functions $\mathcal{P}_\mathrm{i}[\![-]\!]$ and $\mathcal{N}_\mathrm{i}[\![-]\!]$ which map interaction terms to sets of positive and negative traces, respectively (see Tables 9.10 and 9.11).

It appears that the specification treats interaction uses by macro expansion ("The InteractionUse is a shorthand for copying the contents of the referred Interaction where the InteractionUse is" [45, p. 487]). If also (mutually) recursive interactions are to be handled, some notion of fixpoint in constructing the semantics has to be involved. The semantic functions $\mathcal{P}_\mathrm{i}[\![-]\!]$ and $\mathcal{N}_\mathrm{i}[\![-]\!]$ can be rendered as a monotonic $F : \wp(\mathbb{T}) \times \wp(\mathbb{T}) \to \wp(\mathbb{T}) \times \wp(\mathbb{T})$, where $\wp(\mathbb{T}) \times \wp(\mathbb{T})$ is equipped with the ordering $(X_1, X_2) \subseteq (X'_1, X'_2)$ if, and only if, $X_1 \subseteq X'_1$ and $X_2 \subseteq X'_2$; thus, we are assured that the least and the greatest fixpoint exist. If the least fixpoint is chosen, only finite (stateful) traces can be produced; if the greatest fixpoint is chosen, infinite (stateful) traces are also possible.

9.3 ALTERNATIVE SEMANTICS

9.3.1 Operational Semantics

An operational semantics for a part of the positive fragment of the term language of UML interactions is defined. The reduced syntax of the term language is given in Table 9.12. Therein, B ranges over Basic (as defined in Section 9.2.2) and p ranges over Path (see Section 9.2.4).

TABLE 9.12 Reduced Syntax of Interaction Terms

$T \in$ IFragment	::=	B_q
	|	$\mathsf{strict}_q(T_1, T_2)$
	|	$\mathsf{seq}_q(T_1, T_2)$
	|	$\mathsf{par}_q(T_1, T_2)$
	|	$\mathsf{loop}_q(T)$
	|	$\mathsf{alt}_q(T_1, T_2)$

9.3.1.1 Domains and Restriction Functions We define the domain $\mathbb{E}_\tau$ of events and the *silent event* τ as $\mathbb{E} \cup \{\tau\}$. The domain $\mathbb{D}_\tau$ comprises all finitary pomsets labeled with events from $\mathbb{E}_\tau$. We define $\alpha(\tau) = \emptyset$ (i.e., the silent event does not conflict with any event). The domains $\mathbb{P}_\tau$ and $\mathbb{T}_\tau$ comprise all pomsets $p \in \mathbb{D}_\iota$ such that p is locally linear and a trace, respectively. We extend the lifeline function α to pomsets $p = [(O, \leq_O, \lambda_O)] \in \mathbb{D}_\tau$ by $\alpha(p) = \bigcup_{o \in O} \alpha(\lambda_O(o))$. Given a process $P \subseteq \mathbb{D}_\tau$, we set $\alpha(P) = \bigcup_{p \in P} \alpha(p)$. On processes in $\wp(\mathbb{D}_\tau)$ and for a set of lifelines L, the *restriction* function $restr(L) : \wp(\mathbb{D}_\tau) \to \wp(\mathbb{D}_\tau)$ removes all those pomsets from a process which show an event that lies on a lifeline of L [i.e., $restr(L)(P) = \{p \in P \mid \alpha(p) \cap L = \emptyset\}$]. We also write $P[L]$ for $restr(L)(P)$.

Transition rules regarding the construct $\mathsf{seq}_q(T_1, T_2)$ can only be correct (with respect to the denotational semantics) if it is guaranteed that after execution of an event e of the term T_2, no event e' of T_1 is executed that conflicts with e. If a non-deterministic choice construct (alt or loop) occurs in term T_1, it may happen that both traces containing events conflicting with e (type 1) and traces not containing such events (type 2) occur in the positive evaluation set of T_1. The desired completeness of the transition rules necessitates retaining traces of type 2, even though traces of type 1 have to be discarded. One possible solution to this problem is based on a syntactic transformation $\mathrm{R}_L : \mathrm{Term} \to \mathrm{Term}$ such that $\mathcal{P}[\![\mathrm{R}_L(T)]\!] = \mathcal{P}[\![T]\!][L]$, where Term is an appropriate extension of the language IFragment and L is a set of lifelines. Typically, this "syntactic restriction function" is defined by $\mathrm{R}_L(T) = \mathsf{restr}(L, T)$, where $\mathsf{restr}(L, T)$ is a language extension whose denotational semantics is given by $\mathcal{P}[\![\mathsf{restr}(L, T)]\!] = \mathcal{P}[\![T]\!][L]$ and whose operational semantics is given by the following rule:

$$\text{(restr)} \quad \frac{T \xrightarrow{\bar{e}} T'}{\mathsf{restr}(L, T) \xrightarrow{\bar{e}} \mathsf{restr}(L, T')} \quad \text{if } \alpha(\bar{e}) \cap L = \emptyset$$

However, we choose a slightly different approach using a language extension None whose denotational semantics is given by $\mathcal{D}[\![\mathsf{None}]\!] = \emptyset$. The operational semantics is given simply by the fact that there is no rule for None. The definition of the syntactic restriction function R_L is shown in Table 9.13. Therein, *uop* is a unary operator and *bop* is a binary operator. By induction on the structure of $T \in$ Term, it can easily be shown that $\mathcal{P}[\![\mathrm{R}_L(T)]\!] = \mathcal{P}[\![T]\!][L]$.

TABLE 9.13 Syntactic Restriction Function (for $L \subseteq \mathbb{I}$)

$$
\begin{array}{lcl}
\mathrm{R}_L : \mathrm{Term} \longrightarrow \mathrm{Term} & & \\
\mathrm{R}_L(\mathsf{None}_q) & = & \mathsf{None}_q \\
\mathrm{R}_L(B_q) & = & \begin{cases} B_q & \mathit{if}\ \alpha(B) \cap L = \emptyset \\ \mathsf{None}_q & \text{otherwise} \end{cases} \\
\mathrm{R}_L(uop_q(T)) & = & uop_q(\mathrm{R}_L(T)) \\
\mathrm{R}_L(bop_q(T_1, T_2)) & = & bop_q(\mathrm{R}_L(T_1), \mathrm{R}_L(T_2))
\end{array}
$$

Furthermore, we introduce a function ren : Path $\times \{1,2\} \times$ Term $\longrightarrow$ Term, which is defined as follows:

$$
\begin{array}{ll}
\mathrm{ren}(p, n, const) & = const \\
\mathrm{ren}(p, n, uop_q(T)) & = \begin{cases} uop_{p.n.q'}(\mathrm{ren}(p, n, T)) & \text{if } q = p.q' \\ uop_q(T) & \text{otherwise} \end{cases} \\
\mathrm{ren}(p, n, bop_q(T_1, T_2)) & = \begin{cases} bop_{p.n.q'}(\mathrm{ren}(p, n, T_1), \\ \qquad \mathrm{ren}(p, n, T_2)) & \text{if } q = p.q' \\ bop_q(T_1, T_2) & \text{otherwise} \end{cases}
\end{array}
$$

We also write ${}_{p.n}T$ for $\mathrm{ren}(p, n, T)$.

9.3.1.2 *Transition System*

A configuration of our operational small-step semantics is a term $T \in \mathrm{Term}$. The only terminal configuration is Empty, which is defined by ε. Transitions are of the form $T \xrightarrow{\bar{e}} T'$ with $T, T' \in \mathrm{Term}$, $T \neq \mathsf{Empty}$, and $\bar{e} \in \mathbb{E}_\tau$. The rules for the transition relation are shown in Table 9.14. In these rules the variously decorated metavariables range as follows: T over Term, e over $\mathbb{E}$, and $\bar{e}$ over $\mathbb{E}_\tau$. Given a locally linear pomset B, Min (B) is defined as the set of all events of B that are minimal with respect to the ordering of B. $B \setminus \{e\}$ is obtained from B by removing the (unique) occurrence of e.

9.3.2 Event Structures

An alternative definition of the formal semantics of UML 2.0 interactions is given by Küster Filipe [39,40]. The language is enriched with OCL constraints (see also [10]) as well as locations and temperature as defined for LSCs (see [16]). These additions serve the needs of expressing liveness properties such as progress of a lifeline or the requirement that a sent message may or must be received. The approach concentrates on positive behavior; that is, it does not consider negative traces as in the semantics defined above. Then Küster Filipe [40] purposely disregards some interaction building operators: neg since forbidden behavior can be expressed by a false state invariant appended to the interaction modeling that behavior, and assert since mandatory behavior can be indicated by a hot interaction fragment. The presentation is, moreover, simplified by the omission of loop and strict, which can be integrated. In other words, only alt, par, and seq are considered. The operator alt can have more than

TABLE 9.14 Operational Semantics of Interactions (Part of Positive Fragment)

(basic) $B_q \xrightarrow{e} (B \setminus \{e\})_q \quad \text{if } e \in \mathrm{Min}\,(B)$

(strict¹) $$\frac{T_1 \xrightarrow{\bar{e}} T_1'}{\mathsf{strict}_q(T_1, T_2) \xrightarrow{\bar{e}} \mathsf{strict}_q(T_1', T_2)}$$

(strict²) $\mathsf{strict}_q(\mathsf{Empty}_{q'}, T_2) \xrightarrow{\tau} T_2$

(seq¹) $$\frac{T_1 \xrightarrow{\bar{e}} T_1'}{\mathsf{seq}_q(T_1, T_2) \xrightarrow{\bar{e}} \mathsf{seq}_q(T_1', T_2)}$$

(seq²) $\mathsf{seq}_q(\mathsf{Empty}_{q'}, T_2) \xrightarrow{\tau} T_2$

(seq³) $$\frac{T_2 \xrightarrow{\bar{e}} T_2'}{\mathsf{seq}_q(T_1, T_2) \xrightarrow{\bar{e}} \mathsf{seq}_q(\mathrm{R}_{\alpha(\bar{e})}(T_1), T_2')}$$

(par¹) $$\frac{T_1 \xrightarrow{\bar{e}} T_1'}{\mathsf{par}_q(T_1, T_2) \xrightarrow{\bar{e}} \mathsf{par}_q(T_1', T_2)}$$

(par²) $$\frac{T_2 \xrightarrow{\bar{e}} T_2'}{\mathsf{par}_q(T_1, T_2) \xrightarrow{\bar{e}} \mathsf{par}_q(T_1, T_2')}$$

(par³) $\mathsf{par}_q(\mathsf{Empty}_{q'}, T_2) \xrightarrow{\tau} T_2$

(par⁴) $\mathsf{par}_q(T_1, \mathsf{Empty}_{q'}) \xrightarrow{\tau} T_1$

(loop¹) $\mathsf{loop}_q(T) \xrightarrow{\tau} \mathsf{Empty}_q$

(loop²) $\mathsf{loop}_q(T) \xrightarrow{\tau} \mathsf{seq}_q(T, \mathsf{loop}_{q.2}({}_{q.2}T))$

(alt¹) $\mathsf{alt}_q(T_1, T_2) \xrightarrow{\tau} T_1$

(alt²) $\mathsf{alt}_q(T_1, T_2) \xrightarrow{\tau} T_2$

two operands, each of them must be accompanied by a precondition, and at most one of them is executed. The semantic domain is that of labeled event structures, a true-concurrent model that naturally captures alternative and parallel behavior (see [55]). Labeled event structures are nothing but labeled pomsets (see [48]) equipped with a binary conflict relation. The abstract syntax for interactions is considerably more involved than the one given above; in return, there is a relatively easy way to define, given an interaction term, the conditions on a labeled event structure that, on the one hand, satisfy the interaction and, on the other, may possibly lose cold messages. Besides this logic for interobject communication, Küster Filipe [40] defines a *home logic* for the description of intraobject behavior.

Küster Filipe expands her semantics by including the ref operator [39]. This operator references an interaction fragment which appears in a different diagram. This fragment is called an *interaction use*. By means of ref, interactions can be decomposed or, put the other way, defined hierarchically and reused. Furthermore, ref allows the decomposition of lifelines, whose messages can trespass the diagram boundaries through gates. Lifeline decomposition can be used for modeling components whose internals are hidden or unknown. Küster Filipe addresses refinement by means of a categorical construction over two categories of labeled event structures [39]. In this setting, refinement consists of solving references to interactions and gates. This definition aims at formal reasoning and verification of complex scenario-based interobject behavioral models; these matters have not been worked out yet.

This semantics over event structures, restricted to the simplest operators, is comparable to the positive semantics presented in the sections above. Beyond the core constructs, the proposals seem to diverge, as different language fragments and extensions are considered in each case.

9.3.3 Other Formalisms: MSCs and LSCs

The language of message sequence charts (MSCs [30]) is designed to describe the interaction between a number of independent message-passing instances. MSC is a graphical scenario language, equipped with a formal semantics (see [24,25,32,41], to name a few) and nevertheless of practical use. MSC captures interobject communication patterns typically emerging from use cases, and is easily used in conjunction with other methods and notations. An MSC basic diagram usually contains an MSC heading, a representation for one or more instances, possibly a condition, input and output events including perhaps messages to the environment, and in some cases instance terminations. An MSC diagram may refer to another one, and messages arising from a referred diagram exit this diagram through a gate. The MSC language became more sophisticated, allowing, besides higher-order diagrams, alternatives and restrictive conditions, general ordering, inline expressions, data, time, object orientation, remote method calls, and so on.

Although widely used in industry, MSCs are expressively weak, as they permit only the specification of sample scenarios that are based semantically simply on the notion of partial order of events. MSCs allegedly turn from existential into universal specification of behavior as the requirements evolve to a more formal and/or specific design (see [7]). In particular, the language of MSCs leaves a number of questions open like, such as specification of mandatory behavior, safety and liveness properties, and activation time.

Live sequence charts (LSCs, [16]) increase the expressive power of MSCs by the addition of constructs that allow the specification of liveness properties. LSCs impose a clear distinction between possible and mandatory behavior and at both the global and local levels.

As with basic MSCs, the elementary building blocks of an LSC are instances and messages. Instances are depicted by an instance head, a lifeline, and possibly an instance end. Messages are represented by arrows connecting lifelines. There are two types of messages, synchronous and asynchronous. The former are associated with horizontal arrows (→), the latter with slanted arrows with half stick heads (↘). LSCs allow the specification of time constraints either in the form of an MSC-style timer or in interval notation. Mandatory behavior is specified by universal charts, possible scenarios by an existential chart. Along lifelines a number of locations are identified: for example, the point depicting the arrival of a message. Locations, messages, and conditions have a temperature, hot or cold. Hot locations enforce progress (i.e., the instance must move beyond the location), whereas at cold locations the instance need not move farther. Hot messages imply that the message, if sent, will be received, whereas cold messages may be lost. Hot conditions must be met; cold conditions that fail to hold imply that the chart is to be exited.

An LSC consists, in general, of a pre-chart and a chart. The live interpretation of such an LSC requires that the behavior specified by the chart *must* be exhibited by a system whenever the system has shown the behavior specified by the pre-chart. Live elements, called *hot* (indicating that progress is enforced), make it possible to define forbidden scenarios. Mandatory and possible conditions, invariants, and other finesses, such as simultaneous regions and coregions, activation, and quantification may also be specified.

The formal semantics of LSCs is based on the concept of timed Büchi automata (see [7]). The acceptance criterion for Büchi automata takes the infiniteness of the words into account. Timed Büchi automata also take the occurrence times of the letters of words into account.

The language of LSCs is thus much more expressive than that of MSCs or of UML 2.0 interactions. Consequently, LSCs require a more involved domain for the definition of a formal semantics. Complexity and expressive power of LSCs have been studied by a number of people (see, e.g., [6,17,28]). Additionally, Harel and Maoz [27] treat the constructs assert and neg not as operators but as modalities, give an interpretation of them into LSCs, and define a UML 2.0 profile for the positive fragment of the language of interactions that includes those modalities; the resulting language is called modal sequence diagrams (MSDs).

9.4 IMPLEMENTATION AND REFINEMENT

The trace-based semantics of the preceding section assigns a pair of sets of traces to each interaction: positive and negative traces. This semantics has been developed by following the UML 2 specification as closely as possible. However, the specification does not tell under which circumstances a given system can be said to be complying with an interaction, or, put differently, when a system is an implementation of an interaction. Moreover, it would be rather useful to also have a notion of refinement for interactions.

9.4.1 Implementation

For discussing possible notions of implementation we take a system abstractly to be a set of traces over stateful events $\mathbb{E}$ (see Section 9.2.5.4); that is, we assume that implementations and the interpretation of interactions are grounded in a common semantic domain. For concrete systems this representation in terms of traces may be, at least partially, achieved by appropriate instrumentation in order to monitor their particular stateful event occurrences.

As a first possible notion of implementation [12], we say that a system $I \subseteq \mathbb{T}$ *implements* an interaction S, written as $I \models S$, if $I \cap \mathcal{P}[\![S]\!] \neq \emptyset$ and $I \cap \mathcal{N}[\![S]\!] = \emptyset$, (i.e., if I shows at least one positive trace and does not show any negative trace). The definition is sensible, since it can easily be verified by induction that in the trace-based semantics each interaction shows at least one positive trace.[24] Another possibility [36] is to require a system simply not to show any negative traces but

[24] When an interaction operator such as "refuse" [36] is introduced, which does not show positive traces, the implementation relation $\models$ may be weakened as follows: $I \models S$ if $\mathcal{P}[\![S]\!] \neq \emptyset$, $I \cap \mathcal{P}[\![S]\!] \neq \emptyset$, and $I \cap \mathcal{N}[\![S]\!] = \emptyset$.

to be indifferent to positive and inconclusive traces. This notion of implementation assumes that an assert is used to rule out inconclusive traces.

Either definition allows us to handle *interaction formulas*, introducing boolean connectives for interactions. Writing $S_1 \wedge S_2$ for "interaction S_1 *and* interaction S_2 must hold," then $I \models S_1 \wedge S_2$ amounts to $I \models S_1$ and $I \models S_2$ in the classical sense [i.e., $I \cap (\mathcal{P}[\![S_1]\!] \cap \mathcal{P}[\![S_2]\!]) \neq \emptyset$ and $I \cap (\mathcal{N}[\![S_1]\!] \cup \mathcal{N}[\![S_2]\!]) = \emptyset$]. Similarly, writing $\neg S$ for "interaction S must *not* hold," then $I \models \neg S$, again interpreted classically, amounts to $I \cap \mathcal{P}[\![S]\!] = \emptyset$ or $I \cap \mathcal{N}[\![S]\!] \neq \emptyset$. Note that $I \models \neg S$ and $I \models \mathsf{neg}(T)$ [with $S = \mathsf{sd}(n, T)$] are quite different. We can also introduce an *or* connective $S_1 \vee S_2$ as an abbreviation for $\neg((\neg S_1) \wedge (\neg S_2))$, and again $I \models S_1 \vee S_2$ is quite different from $I \models \mathsf{alt}(T_1, T_2)$ [with $S_1 = \mathsf{sd}(n_1, T_1)$, $S_2 = \mathsf{sd}(n_2, T_2)$].

However, a single interaction or a set of interactions to be interpreted conjunctively rarely are used to describe an entire system. Generally, interactions are employed for describing particular situations of communication and interaction, and these situations may come up only once in awhile in a system and need not cover its complete behavior. This can be expressed in interactions by surrounding the interaction fragment describing such a partial behavior by ignore or consider. But what is left open is the possibility of identifying when a given interaction has to be obeyed during system execution and when it is not relevant, that is, being able to define a *precondition* under which an interaction takes effect (see the discussion on LSCs in Section 9.3.3). Let us write $S_1 \rhd S_2$ to mean informally: If interaction S_1 occurs in an implementation, then S_2 has to occur afterward. This amounts formally to defining $I \models S_1 \rhd S_2$ to hold if for all $t_1 \in \mathbb{T}$ and $t_2 \in \mathbb{T}$ with $t_1 \,;_{\bowtie}\, t_2 \in I$, if $\{t_1\} \models S_1$, then $\{t_2\} \models S_2$.

9.4.2 Refinement

Refinement is a well-known concept in computer science. Given any specification formalism, be it a model or a program, *refinement* refers to the verifiable transformation of an abstract (high-level) word into a concrete (low-level) word of that language. Refinement can also cross language boundaries and relate a specification with a program; in this case the relation is sometimes called *implementation*. The emphasis here is put on the verifiability of the transformation. For this purpose, a formal semantics is indispensable.

An implementation relation between interaction diagrams (or interaction terms) and sets of traces supplies the natural basis for the definition of refinement: An interaction S' refines an interaction S, denoted by $S \rightsquigarrow S'$ if any implementation of S' is also an implementation of S (see [12]). Obviously, this refinement relation is reflexive, transitive, and antisymmetric (i.e., a partial order). This definition is the classical, model-theoretic notion; other possibilities are conceivable, like syntactical transformation of terms such that some conditions hold (e.g., the transformation rules are semantics preserving or semantics narrowing).

On the one hand, $S \rightsquigarrow S'$ if $I \models S'$ implies that $I \models S$. On the other, $I \models S$ if $I \cap \mathcal{P}[\![S]\!] \neq \emptyset$ and $I \cap \mathcal{N}[\![S]\!] = \emptyset$. Therefore, refinement is verifiable.

Notice that if associated with S' there are more positive traces and fewer negative traces than with S (i.e., if $\mathcal{P}[\![S]\!] \subseteq \mathcal{P}[\![S']\!]$ and $\mathcal{N}[\![S']\!] \subseteq \mathcal{N}[\![S]\!]$), then $S \rightsquigarrow S'$. This is not necessarily the only possibility. The verification of refinement via computing the sets of positive and negative traces can become very cumbersome. More interesting than this type of mathematical gymnastics with pairs of pairs of arbitrarily big trace sets is an inference system that allows the derivation of pairs of interaction terms in the refinement relation. Unfortunately, the interaction-building operators do not possess very useful properties in combination with a notion of refinement based on model inclusion. For instance, in general they are not monotonic: that is $S_1 \rightsquigarrow S'_1$ does not imply $op(S_1, \ldots) \rightsquigarrow op(S'_1, \ldots)$ for every operator op. In some cases an inference is possible; a number of rules is given by Calegari García et al. [9,12].

A different notion of refinement in terms of reduction of uncertainty is given by Störrle: Two interactions are in the refinement relation when the sets of positive and negative traces of the abstract interaction, respectively, are included in the sets of positive and negative traces of the concrete interaction (see [49,50]). This definition requires disjointness of the sets of positive and negative traces associated with an arbitrary interaction.

In contrast, Kobro Runde et al. [36] require disambiguation of inconclusive traces and/or narrowing of the set of positive traces, thus reducing underspecification. This work includes an enlightening discussion on the differences between underspecification, object of disambiguation by refinement, and inherent nondeterminism, which is not to be removed from the abstract specification. The approach is part of STAIRS [37], a framework for stepwise development based on refinement of interaction specifications. Some interaction-building operators are not monotonic with respect to this notion of refinement, as discussed by Oldevik and Haugen [46]. Lund [43] presents a trace generation algorithm which to a great extent conforms[25] with the denotational semantics for interactions defined in STAIRS, as well as algorithms for test generation and test execution. Therein, trace generation and refinement à la STAIRS are used to devise a method for refinement verification.

9.5 VERIFICATION AND VALIDATION

As descriptions of emergent behaviors, interactions lend themselves to be seen as properties of a system that have to be verified. This view is also reflected by the notions of implementation in Section 9.4.1. On the other hand, interactions may also be interpreted as executable, high-level specifications, which should be used for validation in system development.

9.5.1 Model Checking

To verify that a particular interaction is indeed satisfied by a given system, research has concentrated mostly on the fully automatic technique of model checking. Interactions

[25] The operational semantics for seq does not take into account possible interleavings of events in the two operands [see rule (seq^3_G) in Table 9.14].

are turned into logical, temporal formulas or directly to some kind of automata that then can be run against the system.

Model checking of MSCs and LSCs has been studied in great detail (see [5,7, 33,42]). For UML interactions based on this previous work, a translation of a fragment of interactions into interaction automata has been developed [35]. The language fragment handles basic interactions and the operators seq, par, strict, ignore, as well as state invariants; loop is restricted to containing only basic interactions, as otherwise the model-checking problem becomes undecidable [1]. The interaction automata, interpreted as Büchi automata, are checked against instrumented UML state machines using the model translation tool Hugo/RT and the model checker Spin.

A similar goal is followed by Charmy [3]. The focus of Charmy is on architectural descriptions and verification of their consistency. The semantics of interactions, given by translation rules, however, deviates from the one presented here; currently, combined fragments are not supported.

9.5.2 Animation

The most outstanding example of interaction animation is the Play Engine (see [29]). The tool implements an extension of LSCs and supports two techniques. The first, called *play-in*, allows the intended system to be supplied with scenario-based behavior specificatons using a graphical user interface. The second, called *play-out*, permits execution or animation of the behavior specified. These two techniques combined constitute the play-in/play-out methodology.

The Play Engine can be used in more than one phase of system development: for instance, for requirements elicitation and for prototyping and testing. The authors also propose use of the Play Engine to program reactivity, which is based on interobject communication and thus closer to the way in which systems and their behavior are conceived. This is only possible because the language of LSCs was extended with symbolic instances and allows a message to cause a change of state in the destination instance. In this way, an instance can react to incoming messages also according to its internal state.

The animation, or play-out, is highly nontrivial. The scenarios specified may be very sophisticated, including the above-mentioned symbolic instances and state changes caused by message processing as well as the entire paraphernalia of LSCs, such as time and forbidden elements, may and must conditions, hot and cold messages, and universal and existential charts.

The semantics of the LSCs extension is not given just in the form of a tool. The Play Engine is accompanied by an operational semantics given as a transition system whose definition is based on the concepts of object-oriented system modeling and cut of a chart. There are two types of transitions, steps and supersteps. A superstep is a sequence of steps, and a step is an event carried out by the system in response to the input by the user. Once a stimulus has arrived, and due to underspecification and/or nondeterminism, more than one superstep may be enabled. Some of these enabled supersteps may, however, lead to an inconsistent system state that violates a constraint. The smart play-out mechanism of the Play Engine uses formal analysis methods, mainly model checking, to find a correct superstep if one exists, or to prove that a correct superstep does not exist. Complex case studies have been carried out using the Play Engine, such as the one reported by Combes et al. [14].

Apart from the Play Engine there are other tools, like Rhapsody (see [4]) and Unistep (see [52]), that support interaction animation. Because these tools are only commercially available, details on the respective realizations are not public.

A further animation of interactions was reported by Burd et al. [8], focusing on comprehensibility of interactions. An experiment was carried out which from a pedagogical point of view, showed that the number of misinterpretations considerably declines when users are in front of an animated interaction instead of a static representation. Animated interactions are also employed for requirements testing in the spirit of control flow analysis (see [23]).

Some other approaches translate interactions into a formalism susceptible to animation. Fernandes et al. [20] translate interactions, possibly including the operators opt, alt, par, and loop, and the interaction fragment ref, into colored Petri nets, which are then animated. In a similar manner, a set of MSCs can be translated into a statechart (see [26,38]) which is susceptible to animation (see, e.g., [4,18,53]).

REFERENCES

1. R. Alur and M. Yannakakis. Model checking of message sequence charts. In J. C. M. Baeten and S. Mauw, eds., *10th International Conference on Concurrency Theory* (*CONCUR'99, Proceedings*), Lecture Notes in Computer Science, vol. 1664, pp. 114–129. Springer-Verlag, New York, 1999.
2. E. P. Andersen. Conceptual modeling of objects: a role modeling approach. Ph.D. dissertation, Universitetet i Oslo, Oslo, Norway, 1997.
3. M. Autili, P. Inverardi, and P. Pelliccione. A scenario based notation for specifying temporal properties. In *5th International Workshop on Scenarios and State Machines: Models, Algorithms, and Tools* (*SCESM'06, Proceedings*), pp. 21–27. ACM Press, New York, 2006.
4. R. Boldt. Model-driven architecture, embedded developers and Telelogic Rhapsody. http://www.telelogic.com/download/get_file.cfm?id=4890, Oct. 2008. Accessed Nov. 28, 2008.
5. Y. Bontemps and P. Heymans. Turning high-level live sequence charts into automata. In *ICSE Workshop on Scenarios and State-Machines: Models, Algorithms and Tools* (*SCESM'02, Proceedings*), Orlando, FL, 2002.
6. Y. Bontemps and P.Y. Schobbens. The computational complexity of scenario-based agent verification and design. *Journal of Applied Logic*, 5(2):252–276, 2007.
7. M. Brill, W. Damm, J. Klose, B. Westphal, and H. Wittke. Live sequence charts: an introduction to lines, arrows, and strange boxes in the context of formal verification. In H. Ehrig, W. Damm, J. Desel, M. Große-Rhode, W. Reif, E. Schnieder, and E. Westkämper, eds., *Integration of Software Specification Techniques for Applications in Engineering, Priority Program SoftSpez of the German Research Foundation* (*DFG*), *Final Report*. Lecture Notes in Computer Science, vol. 3147, pp. 374–399. Springer-Verlag, New York, 2004.

8. E. Burd, D. Overy, and A. Wheetman. Evaluating using animation to improve understanding of sequence diagrams. In *10th International Workshop on Program Comprehension (IWPC'02, Proceedings)*, pp. 107–113. IEEE Computer Society, Los Alamitos, CA, 2002.
9. D. Calegari García, M. V. Cengarle, and N. Szasz. UML 2.0 interactions with OCL/RT constraints. In *Forum on Specification and Design Languages (FDL'08, Proceedings)*, pp. 167–172. IEEE, New York, 2008.
10. A. Cavarra and J. Küster Filipe. Combining sequence diagrams and OCL for liveness. *Electronic Notes in Theoretical Computer Science*, 115:19–38, 2005.
11. M. V. Cengarle and A. Knapp. Towards OCL/RT. In L.-H. Eriksson and P. Lindsay, eds., *International Symposium of Formal Methods Europe (FME'02, Proceedings)*, Lecture Notes in Computer Science, vol. 2391, pp. 390–409. Springer-Verlag, New York, 2002.
12. M. V. Cengarle and A. Knapp. UML 2.0 interactions: semantics and refinement. In J. Jürjens, E. B. Fernandez, R. France, and B. Rumpe, eds., *3rd International Workshop on Critical Systems Development with UML (CSDUML'04, Proceedings)*, Technical Report TUM-I0415, pp. 85–99. Institut für Informatik, Technische Universität München, Munich, Germany, 2004.
13. D. Coleman, P. Arnold, S. Bodoff, C. Dollin, H. Gilchrist, F. Hayes, and P. Jeremaes. *Object-Oriented Development: The Fusion Method.* Object-Oriented Series. Prentice Hall, Upper Saddle River, NJ, 1994.
14. P. Combes, D. Harel, and H. Kugler. Modeling and verification of a telecommunication application using live sequence charts and the play-engine tool. *Software and Systems Modeling*, 7(2):157–175, 2008.
15. S. Cook and J. Daniels. *Designing Object Systems: Object-Oriented Modelling with Syntropy*. Object-Oriented Series. Prentice Hall, Upper Saddle River, NJ, 1994.
16. W. Damm and D. Harel. LSCs: breathing life into message sequence charts. *Formal Methods in System Design*, 19(1):45–80, 2001.
17. W. Damm, T. Toben, and B. Westphal. On the expressive power of live sequence charts. In T. W. Reps, M. Sagiv, and J. Bauer, eds., *Program Analysis and Compilation: Theory and Practice—Essays Dedicated to Reinhard Wilhelm on the Occasion of His 60th Birthday*, Lecture Notes in Computer Science, vol. 4444, pp. 225–246. Springer-Verlag, New York, 2007.
18. B. P. Douglass, D. Harel, and M. Trakhtenbrot. Statecharts in use: structured analysis and object-orientation. In F. Vaandrager and G. Rozenberg, eds., *Lectures on Embedded Systems*, Lecture Notes in Computer Science, vol. 1494, pp. 368–394. Springer-Verlag, New York, 1998.
19. G. Engels, R. Hücking, S. Sauer, and A. Wagner. UML collaboration diagrams and their transformation to Java. In France and Rumpe [22, pp. 473–488].
20. J. Fernandes, S. Tjell, J. B. Jørgensen, and Ó. Ribeiro. Designing tool support for translating use cases and UML 2.0 sequence diagrams into a coloured Petri net. In *6th International Workshop on Scenarios and State Machines (SCESM'07, Proceedings)*, p. 2, Washington, DC, 2007. IEEE Computer Society, Los Alamitos, CA, 2007.
21. T. Firley, M. Huhn, K. Diethers, T. Gehrke, and U. Goltz. Timed sequence diagrams and tool-based analysis: a case study. In France and Rumpe [22, pp. 645–660].
22. R. France and B. Rumpe, eds. *2nd International Conference on the Unified Modeling Language (UML'99, Proceedings)*, Lecture Notes in Computer Science, vol. 1723. Springer-Verlag, New York, 1999.

23. V. Garousi, L. Briand, and Y. Labiche. Control flow analysis of UML 2.0 sequence diagrams. In A. Hartman and D. Kreische, eds., *Model Driven Architecture—Foundations and Applications* (*ECMDA-FA'05, Proceedings*), Lecture Notes in Computer Science, vol. 3748, pp. 160–174. Springer-Verlag, New York, 2005.
24. T. Gehrke. An algebraic semantics for an abstract language with intra-object-concurrency. In D. Pritchard and J. Reeve, eds., *4th International Conference on Parallel Processing* (*Euro-Par'98, Proceedings*), Lecture Notes in Computer Science, vol. 1470, pp. 733–737. Springer-Verlag, New York, 1998.
25. P. Graubmann, E. Rudolph, and J. Grabowski. Towards a Petri net based semantics definition for message sequence charts. In O. Færgemand and A. Sarma, eds., *6th SDL Forum: Using Objects* (*SDL'93, Proceedings*). North-Holland, Amsterdam, 1993.
26. D. Harel, H. Kugler, and A. Pnueli. Synthesis revisited: generating statechart models from scenario-based requirements. In H.-J. Kreowski, U. Montanari, F. Orejas, G. Rozenberg, and G. Taentzer, eds., *Formal Methods in Software and Systems Modeling: Essays Dedicated to Hartmut Ehrig, on the Occasion of His 60th Birthday*. Lecture Notes in Computer Science, vol. 3393, pp. 309–324. Springer-Verlag, New York, 2005.
27. D. Harel and S. Maoz. Assert and negate revisited: modal semantics for UML sequence diagrams. *Software and System Modeling*, 7(2):237–252, 2008.
28. D. Harel, S. Maoz, and I. Segall. Some results on the expressive power and complexity of LSCs. In A. Avron, N. Dershowitz, and A. Rabinovich, eds., *Pillars of Computer Science: Essays Dedicated to Boris* (*Boaz*) *Trakhtenbrot on the Occasion of His 85th Birthday*. Lecture Notes in Computer Science, vol. 4800, pp. 351–366. Springer-Verlag, New York, 2008.
29. D. Harel and R. Marelly. *Come, Let's Play: Scenario-Based Programming Using LSCs and the Play-Engine*. Springer-Verlag, New York, 2003.
30. ITU. *Message Sequence Chart* (*MSC*). Recommendation Z.120, ITU-TS. International Telecommunication Union, Geneva, 1996 (revised 2003).
31. I. Jacobson, M. Christerson, P. Jonsson, and G. Övergaard. *Object-Oriented Software Engineering: A Use Case Driven Approach*, 4th ed., Addison-Wesley, Wokingham, UK, 1993.
32. J.-P. Katoen and L. Lambert. Pomsets for MSC. In H. König and P. Langendörfer, eds., *Formale Beschreibungstechniken für verteilte Systeme* (*8th GI/ITG-Fachgespräch, Proceedings*), pp. 197–207. Shaker, Aachen, 1998.
33. J. Klose and H. Wittke. An automata based interpretation of live sequence charts. In T. Margaria and W. Yi, eds., *7th International Conference on Tools and Algorithms for the Construction and Analysis of Systems* (*TACAS'01, Proceedings*). Lecture Notes in Computer Science, vol. 2031, pp. 512–527. Springer-Verlag, New York, 2001.
34. A. Knapp. A formal semantics for UML interactions. In France and Rumpe [22, pp. 116–130].
35. A. Knapp and J. Wuttke. Model checking of UML 2.0 interactions. In T. Kühne, ed., *Models in Software Engineering, Workshops and Symposia at MoDELS 2006, Reports and Revised Selected Papers*, Lecture Notes in Computer Science, vol. 4364, pp. 42–51. Springer-Verlag, New York, 2007.
36. R. Kobro Runde, Ø. Haugen, and K. Stølen. Refining UML interactions with underspecification and nondeterminism. *Nordic Journal of Computing*, 12(2):157–188, 2005.

37. R. Kobro Runde, Ø. Haugen, and K. Stølen. The pragmatics of STAIRS. In F. de Boer, M. Bonsangue, S. Graf, and W.-P. de Roever, eds., *5th International Symposium on Formal Methods for Components and Objects* (*FMCO'06, Proceedings*). Lecture Notes in Computer Science, vol. 4111, pp. 88–114. Springer-Verlag, New York, 2006.

38. I. Krüger, R. Grosu, P. Scholz, and M. Broy. From MSCs to statecharts. In F. Rammig, ed., *International Workshop on Distributed and Parallel Embedded Systems* (*DIPES'98, Proceedings*). IFIP Conference Proceedings, vol. 155, pp. 61–71. Kluwer Academic, Norwell, MA, 1999.

39. J. Küster Filipe. Decomposing interactions. In M. Johnson and V. Vene, eds., *11th International Conference on Algebraic Methodology and Software Technology* (*AMAST'06, Proceedings*), Lecture Notes in Computer Science, vol. 4019, pp. 189–203. Springer-Verlag, New York, 2006.

40. J. Küster Filipe. Modelling concurrent interactions. *Theoretical Computer Science*, 351(2):203–220, 2006.

41. A. Letichevsky, J. Kapitonova, V. Kotlyarov, V. Volkov, A. Letichevsky, Jr., and T. Weigert. Semantics of message sequence charts. In A. Prinz, R. Reed, and J. Reed, eds., *12th International SDL Forum* (*SDL'05: Model Driven Systems Design, Proceedings*). Lecture Notes in Computer Science, vol. 3530, pp. 117–132. Springer-Verlag, New York, 2005.

42. S. Leue and P. Ladkin. Implementing and verifying MSC specifications using Promela/XSpin. In J.-C. Gregoire, G. J. Holzmann, and D. Peled, eds., *2nd International Workshop on SPIN Verification System* (*SPIN'96, Proceedings*). Discrete Mathematics and Theoretical Computer Science, vol. 32, pp. 65–89. American Mathematical Society, Providence, RI, 1997.

43. M. S. Lund. Operational analysis of sequence diagram specifications. Ph.D. dissertation, Universitetet i Oslo, Oslo, Norway, 2007.

44. OMG. Object constraint language, version 2.0. http://www.omg.org/spec/OCL/2.0/, May 2006. Accessed Dec. 11, 2008.

45. OMG. Unified modeling language: superstructure, version 2.1.2. http://www.omg.org/docs/formal/07-11-02,pdf, Nov. 2007. Accessed Nov. 11, 2008.

46. J. Oldevik and Ø. Haugen. Semantics preservation of sequence diagram aspects. In I. Schieferdecker and A. Hartman, eds., *4th European Conference on Model Driven Architecture, Foundations and Applications* (*ECMDA-FA'08, Proceedings*). Lecture Notes in Computer Science, vol. 5095, pp. 215–230. Springer-Verlag, New York, 2008.

47. G. Övergaard. A formal approach to collaborations in the unified modeling language. In France and Rumpe [22, pp. 99–115].

48. V. R. Pratt. Modelling concurrency with partial orders. *International Journal of Parallel Programming*, 15(1):33–71, 1986.

49. H. Störrle. Assert, negate and refinement in UML-2 interactions. In J. Jürjens, B. Rumpe, R. France, and E. B. Fernandez, eds., *2nd International Workshop on Critical Systems Development with UML* (*CSDUML'03, Proceedings*). Technical Report TUM-I0323, pp. 79–93. Institut für Informatik, Technische Universität München, Munich, Germany, 2003.

50. H. Störrle. *Trace Semantics of UML 2.0 Interactions*. Technical Report 0409. Institut für Informatik, Ludwig-Maximilians-Universität München, Munich, Germany, 2004.

51. H. Störrle. *UML 2.0 für Studenten*. Pearson, Munich, Germany, 2005.

52. Sysoft. Unistep: animation of UML sequence diagram. Technical Report, 2008. http://www.sysoft-fr.com/en/unistep/unistep_webDemoUmlSeq.asp. Accessed Nov. 28, 2008.
53. Sysoft. Unistep: animation of UML statechart. Technical Report, 2008. http://www.sysoft-fr.com/en/unistep/unistep_webDemoUmlState.asp. Accessed Dec. 4, 2008.
54. C. Willcock, T. Deiß, S. Tobies, S. Keil, F. Engler, and S. Schulz. *An Introduction to TTCN-3*. Wiley, Hoboken, NJ, 2005.
55. G. Winskel and M. Nielsen. Models for concurrency. In *Handbook of Logic in Computer Science, vol. 4, Semantic Modelling*, pp. 1–148. Oxford Science, Oxford, UK, 1995.

CHAPTER 10

CO-ALGEBRAIC SEMANTIC FRAMEWORK FOR REASONING ABOUT INTERACTION DESIGNS

SUN MENG
CWI, Amsterdam, The Netherlands

LUÍS S. BARBOSA
Department of Informatics, Minho University, Braga, Portugal

10.1 INTRODUCTION

The aphorism *modeling is for reasoning*, which even if in an implicit way, underlies most research in formal methods, sums up the fundamental interconnection between *modeling* and *calculation*. The former is understood as the ability to choose the right abstractions for a problem domain. The latter concerns the need to express such abstractions in a framework whose mathematical structure is sufficiently rich to enable rigorous reasoning either to establish models' properties or to transform models toward effective implementations.

Recalling such an interconnection seems particularly appropriate with respect to the formalization attempts of UML 2.0. The number and diversity of diagrams expressing a UML model makes it difficult to base its semantics on a single framework. On the other hand, some of the formalizations proposed in the literature are essentially descriptive and difficult to use.

There are at least two levels at which the contribution of a formal semantics for the UML is deeply needed. One concerns model composition (their operators and the laws that govern their behavior), the other model *refactoring* (i.e., model transformations that preserve external behavior while improving their internal structure).

In this chapter we introduce a new, co-algebraic semantics for UML 2.0 interaction models represented, as usual, by *sequence diagrams*. The semantics proposed was partially sketched by Meng and Barbosa [25]. Moreover, a set of operators for such

UML 2 Semantics and Applications. Edited by Kevin Lano

diagrams, described informally in UML superstructure 2.1.1 [30], is formally characterized, settling the bases for a calculus to reason about them. Finally, we discuss how both composition and refactoring laws for sequence diagrams can be dealt with within the proposed framework. This extends previous work by the authors in seeking a unifying co-algebraic semantics for UML, as reported in [4,41,42]. Those references introduced a semantics for class diagrams, use cases, and statecharts based on co-algebras [38] taken as a suitable mathematical structure for expressing the behavior of state-based systems. A similar approach is taken here for sequence diagrams. In all cases, the co-algebraic point of view puts forward a well-defined notion of behavior, as equivalence classes for the bisimilarity relation induced by the particular functor used, upon which properties of UML models can be formulated and checked.

Although the emphasis is placed on the formalization of sequence diagrams, this chapter also intends to be an almost tutorial introduction to the use of co-algebraic techniques in semantics. Main concepts and tools are introduced in Section 10.2, with a UML class diagram acting as a running example.

Mathematically, co-algebras are the formal duals of algebras, exactly in the sense that makes *observation* and *construction* symmetric notions. Differently from familiar, inductive data types, which are completely defined by a set of constructors, the sort of computational structures that co-algebras can describe admits only behavioral characterizations, as we will see soon. Typical examples of such structures are *processes*, *transition systems*, *objects*, *streamlike structures* used in lazy programming languages, "infinite" or *non-well-founded objects* arising in semantics, and as we want to argue in this chapter, *interaction models* among software systems, as seen from the point of view of the working, model-based software architect.

The remainder of this chapter is organized as follows. In Section 10.2 we introduce co-algebras and related notions of behavior and bisimulation. This is applied later to the construction of a semantic model for sequence diagrams in Section 10.3 and construction of their combinators in Section 10.4. Section 10.5 illustrates how UML 2.0 diagram annotations (such as typical neg or critical tags) can be incorporated within the model. Finally, Section 10.6 covers semantics "in action," illustrating its use to prove properties of combinators and detailing the corresponding proof techniques. Some pointers for current and future work are collected in Section 10.7.

10.2 WHY CO-ALGEBRAS?

10.2.1 Classes and Co-algebras

Our starting point is that any useful semantic framework for UML descriptions should be able to address two factors:

- Diagram *composition*, defining and investigating operators and laws that govern the behavior of the underlying models
- Diagram *refactoring*, in the sense of the original definition of this term given by Opdyke almost two decades ago, understood as "the process of changing a

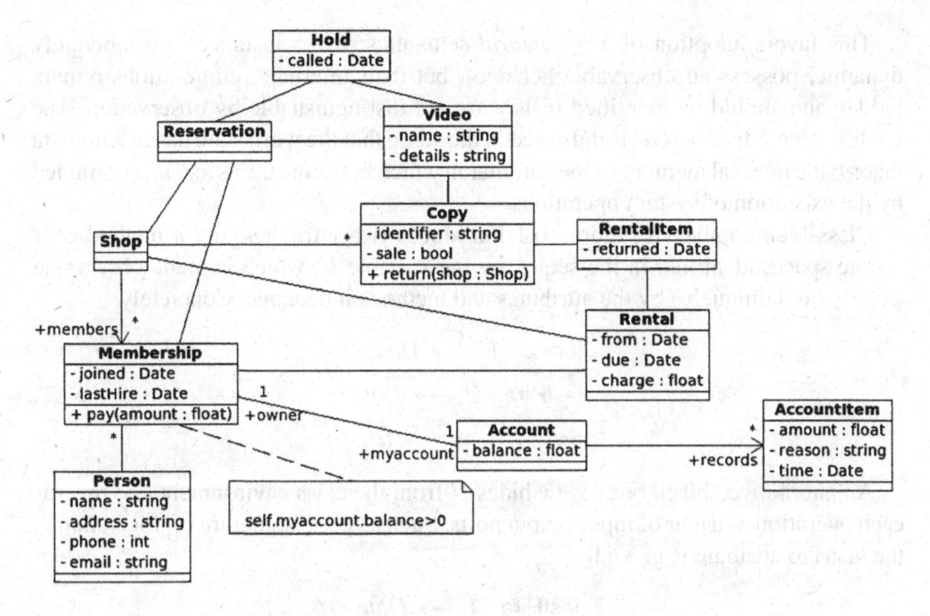

FIGURE 10.1 An example class diagram.

software system in such a way that it does not alter the external behavior of the code, yet improves its internal structure" [31].

In both cases a precise notion of *behavior* and a calculational approach to *behavioral equivalence* and *refinement* is the key issue. Actually, such notions are at the kernel of co-algebra theory [15,38], often suitably called the *mathematics of dynamic systems*. In particular, co-algebra theory provides a standard notion of systems' behavior in terms of the bisimilarity relation induced by the signature functor, a technical way to capture a suitable notion of system's interface. As explained below, refinement, will correspond to the ability of a diagram to simulate another in a quite precise way.

Experience seems to validate our claim that co-algebra theory may provide an expressive and powerful framework for studying the semantics of UML diagrams, as widely documented [4,25,41,42]. Thus, before delving into the details of a semantics for interaction designs, this section should be read as a tutorial introduction to the co-algebraic framework for the working systems' architect. Our running example to introduce the main ideas and notation is a fragment of the class diagram depicted in Figure 10.1, corresponding to a simplified model of a video rental e-business.

The model is certainly self-explanatory. In any case we focus only on class Membership. The aim of a class declaration is to introduce a signature of attributes and methods. As a representation of object families, a class can actually be regarded as a specification of *state-based* structures, encompassing the following basic elements:

- The presence of an *internal state space* that evolves and persists in time
- The possibility of *interaction* with other class instances through well-defined interfaces and during the overall computation

This favors adoption of a *behavioral* semantics: Class instances are inherently dynamic, possess an observable behavior, but their internal configurations remain hidden and should be identified if they are not distinguishable by observation. The qualificative "state-based" is thus used in the sense that the word state has in automata theory: the internal memory of the automaton which both constrains and is constrained by the execution of system operations.

Class Membership in Figure 10.1 introduces two attributes and a method over a state space, identified in the sequel by the variable U, which is made observable exactly (and uniquely) by the attributes and methods it declares. Concretely,

$$\mathsf{joined} : U \longrightarrow \mathit{Date}$$

$$\mathsf{lastHire} : U \longrightarrow \mathit{Date}$$

$$\mathsf{pay} : U \times \mathbb{R} \longrightarrow U$$

An alternative "black box" view hides U from the class environment and regards each operation as a pair of input/output ports. Such a "port" signature of, for example, the lastHire attribute is given by

$$\mathsf{lastHire} : \mathbf{1} \longrightarrow \mathit{Date}$$

where **1** stands for the nullary (or unit) datatype (i.e., a representation of the singleton set). The intuition is that lastHire is activated with the simple pushing of a 'button' (its argument being the class instance private state space), whose effect is the production of a *Date* value in the corresponding output port. Similarly, typing pay as

$$\mathsf{pay} : \mathbb{R} \longrightarrow \mathbf{1}$$

means that an external argument is required on activation but no visible output is produced, but for a trivial indication of successful termination. Such "port" signatures are grouped together in the layout below, in which all occurrences of **1** are dropped:

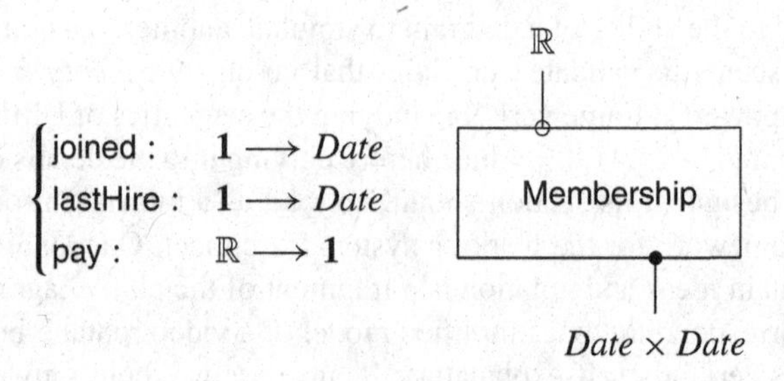

This setup represents the class input interface (in the upper part) and its output interface (in the lower part). The behavior of class Membership instances is given solely in terms of these interface types. Let us detail how and why, making the state space explicit once again. Note that the three declarations can be grouped into one through a *split* construction:

$$\langle \mathsf{joined}, \mathsf{lastHire}, \overline{\mathsf{pay}} \rangle : U \longrightarrow \mathit{Date} \times \mathit{Date} \times U^{\mathbb{R}} \tag{10.1}$$

where the notation $\overline{\mathsf{pay}}$ denotes the *currying* of pay.[1] Therefore, we write

$$[\![\mathsf{Membership}]\!] = \langle \mathsf{joined}, \mathsf{lastHire}, \overline{\mathsf{pay}} \rangle \tag{10.2}$$

That is, the semantics of each instance of class Membership is given by the function (10.1), which describes how it reacts to input stimuli, makes its attributes available, and changes state (i.e., as a *co-algebra* $U \longrightarrow \mathsf{T}U$ for datatype transformer $\mathsf{T}X = Date \times Date \times U^{\mathbb{R}}$), as explained in the sequel.

The basic insight in co-algebraic modeling is that for an arbitrary T, a state-based system can be represented by a function

$$p : U \longrightarrow \mathsf{T}U \tag{10.3}$$

For every state $u \in U$, the function p describes the observable effects of an elementary step in the evolution of the system (i.e., a state transition). The possible outcomes of such a step are captured by the notation $\mathsf{T}U$. Technically, T is a *functor*.[2] Intuitively, it is a *shape* for the observations allowed.

Let us consider a few possible alternatives for T. An extreme case is the "opaque" shape $\mathsf{T} = \mathbf{1}$: no matter what one tries to observe through it, the outcome is always the same. A slightly more interesting case is $\mathsf{T} = \mathbf{2}$, which has the ability to classify states into two different classes (say, "black" and "white") and therefore to identify *subsets* of U. Should an arbitrary set O be chosen, the possible observations become more discriminating. Naturally, the same "universe" can be observed through different attributes, and furthermore, such observations can be carried out in parallel, as in, for example, $\mathsf{T} = O \times O'$.

The case of a "transparent" T (i.e., $\mathsf{T}U = U$) is not particularly useful: Any function $p : U \longrightarrow U$ is a co-algebra for T. But this also means that by using p, the values in the state space U can indeed be modified. On the other hand, the absence of attributes makes any meaningful observation impossible. More interesting, however, are interfaces able to model, for example, computational *partiality* ($\mathsf{T}U = U + \mathbf{1}$) or *nondeterminism* ($\mathsf{T}U = \mathscr{P}U$) for $\mathscr{P}U$ the finite powerset of U or *input triggering* ($\mathsf{T}U = U^I$), among many others. Technically:

[1] To emphasize the dependency of the possible observations X from the input, we resort to the standard mathematical notation X^I for functional dependency instead of the equivalent $I \to X$ more familiar in computing.

[2] Note that our semantic constructions "live" in a space of typed functions, something one could model as a graph with sets as nodes and set-theoretic functions as arrows. As functions (with the right types) can be composed and, for each set S, one may single out a function id_s (the identity on S) acting as the neutral element for composition, this working universe has the structure of a (partial) monoid (i.e., a category). In this setting a *functor* is simply a function T over this universe which preserves the graph and monoidal structure (i.e., for each function $f : A \longrightarrow B$, $\mathsf{T}f$ is typed as $\mathsf{T}A \longrightarrow \mathsf{T}B$) and verifies

$$\mathsf{Tid}_X = \mathsf{id}_{\mathsf{T}X} \quad \text{and} \quad \mathsf{T}(f \cdot g) = \mathsf{T}f \cdot \mathsf{T}g$$

As with most conceptual structures used in mathematics and computer science, this notion is borrowed from category theory [22], where it can be appreciated in its full genericity.

Definition 10.2.1 The pair $\langle U, p : U \longrightarrow \mathsf{T}U\rangle$ constitutes a *co-algebra* for functor T over *carrier* U. A *morphism* connecting two such co-algebras is a function between their carriers making the following diagram commute:

$$\begin{array}{ccc} U & \xrightarrow{p} & \mathsf{T}U \\ {\scriptstyle h}\downarrow & & \downarrow{\scriptstyle \mathsf{T}h} \\ U' & \xrightarrow[p']{} & \mathsf{T}U' \end{array} \tag{10.4}$$

T co-algebras and the corresponding morphisms form a category whose composition and identities are inherited from Set, the usual category of sets and functions.

Back to our class diagram, note that, in general, the semantics $[\![c]\!]$ of a class c is given by a specification of a co-algebra

$$\langle \mathsf{at}, \overline{\mathsf{m}}\rangle : U \longrightarrow A \times U^I \tag{10.5}$$

where A is the attribute domain (*Date* $\times$ *Date* in the example above), and each method accepts a parameter, of type I ($\mathbb{R}$, above), and delivers a state change, that is, a co-algebra for the functor[3]

$$\mathsf{T} : X \longrightarrow A \times X^I \tag{10.6}$$

Typically, I is a *sum* type, aggregating the input–output parameters of each method declared. In its turn, A is usually a *product* type joining all attribute outputs in a way that emphasizes that each of them is available independent of the others, and therefore is always able to be accessed in parallel.

10.2.2 Behavior and Bisimulation

By now one may ask what a convenient functor for co-algebraic models of software system interactions would be and what notion of system behavior such a choice would enforce. These questions are discussed in detail in Section 10.3. For the moment, however, let us stick to a few variants of an elementary, deterministic model in order to introduce the basic ideas of co-algebraic modeling applied to software systems.

The simplest model one could think of is that of systems inspected by an *attribute* $\mathsf{at} : U \longrightarrow O$ and reacting (deterministically) to a *method* (or *action*) $\mathsf{m} : U \longrightarrow U$ with no external influence (but for, say, pushing a button). Those two functions can be "glued" together leading to the co-algebra

$$p = \langle \mathsf{at}, \mathsf{m}\rangle : U \longrightarrow O \times U \tag{10.7}$$

Successive observations of (or experiments with) system p reveals its behavioral patterns.

[3] In the general case, we should also consider methods producing visible outputs, in which case the relevant functor becomes $\mathsf{T} : X \longrightarrow A \times (O \times X)^I$, where O is the method output type, which was trivially $\mathbf{1}$ in the Membership example; see the article by Meng and Barbosa [25] for details.

For each state value $u \in U$, the *behavior* of p at u (more precisely, *from* u onward)—represented by $[\![(p)]\!]\ u$ — is an *infinite* sequence of values of type O computed by observing the successive state configurations, that is,

$$[\![(p)]\!]\ u = \langle \mathsf{at}\ u,\ \mathsf{at}\,(\mathsf{m}\ u),\ \mathsf{at}\,(\mathsf{m}\,(\mathsf{m}\ u)), \ldots \rangle \tag{10.8}$$

Thus, the space of *all* behaviors for this sort of system is the set of *streams* (infinite sequences) of O (i.e., O^ω).

Bringing *input* information into the scene leads to a mild sophistication of this model. The result is known as a *Moore transducer*, a classical notion in automata theory [28], where each state is associated to an output symbol. Generalizations of Moore machines play a fundamental role in the semantics of UML diagrams. The semantics of classes, as discussed above, is an example. As we will see in Section 10.3, the semantics of sequence diagrams is another. Thus, it pays to take them as our running example in the sequel.

Consider, then, an elementary Moore transducer

$$p = \langle \mathsf{at}, \overline{\mathsf{m}} \rangle : U \longrightarrow A \times U^I \tag{10.9}$$

Its dynamics can be decomposed in the following transition relations:

$$u \xrightarrow{i}_p u' \Leftrightarrow \overline{\mathsf{m}}\, u\, i = u' \tag{10.10}$$

$$u \downarrow_p b \Leftrightarrow \mathsf{at}\, u = b \tag{10.11}$$

On the other hand, the *behavior* of p at (from) a state $u \in U$ is revealed by successive observations (experiments) triggered on the input of different values $i \in I$:

$$[\![(p)]\!] u = \langle \mathsf{at}\, u,\ \mathsf{at}\,(\overline{\mathsf{m}}\, u\, i_0),\ \mathsf{at}\,(\overline{\mathsf{m}}\,(\overline{\mathsf{m}}\, u\, i_0)\, i_1), \ldots \rangle \tag{10.12}$$

or, in a recursive definition,

$$[\![(p)]\!] u\ \mathsf{nil} \ = \ \mathsf{at}\, u \tag{10.13}$$

$$[\![(p)]\!] u\,(i : t) \ = \ [\![(p)]\!]\,(\overline{\mathsf{m}}\, u\, i)\, t \tag{10.14}$$

Behaviors of Moore transducers organize themselves into *tree*-like structures, because they depend on the sequences of input processed. Such trees, whose arcs are labeled with I values and nodes with A values, can be represented by functions from sequences of input type I to the attribute type A. In other words, the space of behaviors of Moore machines (on I and A) is the set A^{I^*}.

Instantiating diagram (10.4) for functor (10.6) defines a morphism $h : \langle \mathsf{at}, \overline{\mathsf{m}} \rangle \longrightarrow \langle \mathsf{at}', \overline{\mathsf{m}}' \rangle$ as a function connecting their state spaces, which satisfies the following equations:

$$\mathsf{at}' \cdot h = \mathsf{at} \tag{10.15}$$

$$\overline{\mathsf{m}}' \cdot (h \times \mathsf{id}) = h \cdot \overline{\mathsf{m}} \tag{10.16}$$

Clearly:

Lemma 10.2.1 *Morphisms preserve attributes and transitions.*

Proof:

$$
\begin{array}{ll}
 & u \xrightarrow{i}_p u' \quad \text{and} \quad u \downarrow_p a \\
\Leftrightarrow & \quad \{\text{definition}\} \\
 & \mathsf{m}(u, i) = u' \quad \text{and} \quad \mathsf{at}\, u = a \\
\Leftrightarrow & \quad \{\text{Liebniz}\} \\
 & h\, \mathsf{m}(u, i) = h\, u' \quad \text{and} \quad \mathsf{at}\, u = a \\
\Leftrightarrow & \quad \{h \text{ is a morphism}\} \\
 & \mathsf{m}'(h\, u, i) = h\, u' \quad \text{and} \quad \mathsf{at}'\, h\, u = a \\
\Leftrightarrow & \quad \{\text{definition}\} \\
 & h u \xrightarrow{i}_q h\, u' \quad \text{and} \quad h\, u \downarrow_q a
\end{array}
$$

□

Observe now that set A^{I^*} of behaviors can itself be equipped with the structure of a Moore machine as well. Actually, define

$$\omega = \langle \overline{\mathsf{m}}_\omega, \mathsf{at}_\omega \rangle : A^{I^*} \longrightarrow A \times (A^{I^*})^I \tag{10.17}$$

where

$$
\begin{array}{ll}
\mathsf{at}_\omega f = f\ \mathsf{nil} & \text{(i.e., the attribute value before any input is received)} \\
\overline{\mathsf{m}}_\omega f\, i = \lambda\, s \cdot f\,(i : s) & \text{(i.e., every input determines its evolution)}
\end{array}
$$

Note that a state in ω is a function f. Therefore, the attribute is computed by function application, whereas the method gives a new function that reacts to a sequence s of inputs exactly as f would react to the appending of i to s.

Having turned the set of observations A^{I^*} into a co-algebra itself, it is not surprising that every state of a machine p can be mapped into its behaviors in a "well-behaved" way. In other words:

Lemma 10.2.2 *The behavior* $[\![(p)]\!]$ *of a co-algebra* p *can be singled out as a* morphism *from* p *to* ω.

Proof: For $[\![(p)]\!] : p \longrightarrow \omega$, we check the corresponding instances of conditions (10.15) and (10.16):

$$\mathsf{at}_\omega \cdot [\![(p)]\!] = \mathsf{at} \quad \text{and} \quad \mathsf{m}_\omega \cdot ([\![(p)]\!] \times \mathsf{id}) = [\![(p)]\!] \cdot \mathsf{m} \tag{10.18}$$

Thus,

$$
\begin{aligned}
& \mathsf{at}_\omega \cdot [\![(p)]\!] = \mathsf{at} \\
\Leftrightarrow \quad & \{\text{introduction of variables}\} \\
& \mathsf{at}_\omega([\![(p)]\!]\, u) = \mathsf{at}\, u \\
\Leftrightarrow \quad & \{\text{definition of } \mathsf{at}_\omega\} \\
& ([\![(p)]\!]\, u)\mathsf{nil} = \mathsf{at}\, u \\
\Leftrightarrow \quad & \{\text{definition of } [\![(p)]\!]\} \\
& \mathsf{true}
\end{aligned}
$$

and similarly,

$$
\begin{aligned}
& \mathsf{m}_\omega \cdot ([\![(p)]\!] \times \mathsf{id}) = [\![(p)]\!] \cdot \mathsf{m} \\
\Leftrightarrow \quad & \{\text{introduction of variables and application}\} \\
& \mathsf{m}_\omega([\![(p)]\!]\, u, i) = [\![(p)]\!]\, \mathsf{m}\,(u, i) \\
\Leftrightarrow \quad & \{\text{definition of } \mathsf{m}_\omega\} \\
& \lambda\, s \cdot ([\![(p)]\!]\, u)\,(i : s) = [\![(p)]\!]\, \mathsf{m}\,(u, i) \\
\Leftrightarrow \quad & \{\text{introduction of variables and application}\} \\
& ([\![(p)]\!] u)(i : t) = ([\![(p)]\!]\, \mathsf{m}\,(u, i))\, t \\
\Leftrightarrow \quad & \{\text{definition of } [\![(p)]\!]\} \\
& \mathsf{true}
\end{aligned}
$$

□

Note that a fundamental result on co-algebra morphisms is behavior *preservation*. Formally, given two co-algebras p and q and a morphism $h : p \longrightarrow q$ between them,

$$[\![(p)]\!] u = [\![(q)]\!] hu \tag{10.19}$$

This leads to a precise and generic notion of *behavior*: any two states generate the same behaviour if they can be identified by a co-algebra morphism.

By induction on I^*, it can be proved that there is always a morphism $[\![(p)]\!]$ from any p to ω and, as morphisms preserve behavior, such a morphism is *unique*. This makes ω a very special Moore co-algebra: It is the only such co-algebra to which, from any other one, there is one and only one morphism. We say that ω is the *final* Moore machine. *Finality* is an example of a *universal* property[4] which, up to isomorphism, provides a complete characterization of ω.

[4] Because, roughly speaking, it singles out an entity (ω) among a family of "similar" entities to which every other member of the family can be *reduced* or *traced back*. The study of *universal* properties is the "essence" of category theory.

Actually, suppose that finality is shared by two Moore co-algebras, ω and ω'. The *existence* component of the property gives rise to two morphisms h and h' connecting both machines in reverse directions. On the other hand, *uniqueness* implies that $h \cdot h' = \mathsf{id}$ and $h' \cdot h = \mathsf{id}$, thus establishing h and h' as isomorphisms. These two aspects of *finality* provide both a *definition* scheme and a *proof* principle upon which co-algebraic reasoning is based. In general:

Definition 10.2.2 Whenever the *space of behaviors* of a class of T co-algebras can be turned into a T co-algebra itself (written as $\omega_{\mathsf{T}} : \nu_{\mathsf{T}} \longrightarrow \mathsf{T}\nu_{\mathsf{T}}$), this is the *final* co-algebra: From any other T co-algebra p there is a unique morphism $[\![(p)]\!]$ making the following diagram commute:

$$\begin{array}{ccc} \nu_{\mathsf{T}} & \xrightarrow{\omega_{\mathsf{T}}} & \mathsf{T}\nu_{\mathsf{T}} \\ {\scriptstyle [\![(p)]\!]}\uparrow & & \uparrow{\scriptstyle \mathsf{T}[\![(p)]\!]} \\ U & \xrightarrow{p} & \mathsf{T}U \end{array}$$

The universal property is, equivalently, captured by the following law:

$$k = [\![(p)]\!] \Leftrightarrow \omega_{\mathsf{T}} \cdot k = \mathsf{T}k \cdot p \tag{10.20}$$

Morphism $[\![(p)]\!]$ applied to a state value u gives, of course, the (observable) behavior of a sequence of p transitions starting at u. It is called the *coinductive extension* of p [44] or the *anamorphism* generated by p [23]. Co-algebra p is referred to as its *gene*. In this context, equation (10.20) is the basic tool for calculating with behaviors. Being an *universal* property, it asserts, for each *gene* co-algebra p, the *existence* and *uniqueness* of its coinductive extension $[\![(p)]\!]$.

As we have already remarked, the *existence* part of this universal property provides a *definition* principle for functions to spaces of behaviors (technically, carriers of final co-algebras). This is called definition by *co-recursion* and boils down to equipping the source of the function to be defined with a co-algebra to capture the "one-step" dynamics in the behavior-generation process. This is exactly the way that component combinators will be defined in Section 10.4. Then the corresponding anamorphism gives the rest. The *uniqueness* part, on the other hand, entails a powerful *proof* principle: *coinduction*.

Behavioral equivalence can also be defined in terms of anamorphisms:

Definition 10.2.3 Two states u and v in the carriers of coalgebras $\langle U, p\rangle$ and $\langle V, q\rangle$, respectively, are *behaviorally equivalent*, represented by $u \sim v$, iff $[(p)]\ u = [(q)]\ v$.

Therefore, the final co-algebra can be characterized alternatively as a co-algebra whose carrier is composed by all equivalence classes of behavioral equivalence.

By equality (10.19), a somewhat simpler way of establishing *behavioral equivalence*, which has the advantage of not depending on the existence of final co-algebras, is to look for a morphism h such that one of the states is the h-image of the other. Once conjectured, h determines a relation $R \subseteq U \times V$ such that

$$\langle u, v \rangle \in R \Rightarrow u \sim v \tag{10.21}$$

Such a relation is, of course, the *graph* of h (*i.e.*, $\{\langle x, h\,x \rangle \mid x \in U\}$). Can this idea be generalized? More precisely, what properties must a relation R have so that one can conclude $u \sim v$ simply by checking whether $\langle u, v \rangle$ is in R? Such a relation can be characterized and is called a T-*bisimulation*. Formally,

Definition 10.2.4 A (T)-*bisimulation* relating co-algebras p and q is a relation over their carriers which is *closed* for their dynamics, that is,

$$(x, y) \in R \Rightarrow (p\,x, q\,y) \in \mathsf{T}R \tag{10.22}$$

Getting rid of variables, (10.22) becomes the following inequality in the language of the (pointfree) calculus of binary relations [2]:

$$R \subseteq p^{\circ} \cdot (\mathsf{T}R) \cdot q \tag{10.23}$$

where p° stands for the relational converse of p. Applying the *shunting* rule of the calculus on p°, this simplifies to

$$p \cdot R \subseteq (\mathsf{T}R) \cdot q \tag{10.24}$$

Informally, two states of a T co-algebra (or of two different T co-algebras) are related by a bisimulation if their observation produces equal results and this is maintained along all possible transitions (i.e., each one can mimic the other's evolution). Originally, the notion was introduced in a functional formulation by Segerberg [39] and in a relational one by van Benthem [7]. Park's landmark paper [32] made bisimulation a basic tool in the context of process calculi. Later, Aczel and Mendler [1] gave a categorical definition which applies not only to the type of transition systems underlying the operational semantics of process calculi, but also to arbitrary co-algebras. Bisimulation *acquired a shape*: the shape of the chosen observation interface T.

10.2.3 Properties and Invariants

Co-algebra theory also provides a way to express and reason about properties of systems. For example, to give semantics to the whole of a UML class diagram, such as the one depicted in Figure 10.1, both *constraints* and *associations* must be taken into account. The former are typically attached to class specifications and their semantic effect is to constrain what co-algebras count as valid implementations for the class. Such is the case, for example, of constraint

$$\mathsf{balance} > 0$$

attached to class Membership in our running example. Associations can also be interpreted as constraints, with respect to the subdiagram formed by the relevant associated classes, as discussed by Barbosa and Meng [4].

In general, constraints are predicates that are supposed to be preserved along the system lifetime. Formally, they are incorporated in the semantics as *invariants*. Following the approach recently proposed in by Barbosa et al. [5], such predicates, once encoded as coreflexive relations, that is, fragments of the identity, according to

$$y \; \Phi_P \; x \;\equiv\; y = x \wedge P\,x$$

can be specified as *invariants* for a co-algebra q as follows:

$$q \cdot \Phi_P \;\subseteq \mathsf{T}\,\Phi_P \cdot q \tag{10.25}$$

When reasoning about diagram transformations such as refactoring, constraints entail *proof obligations*. For example,

$$[\![\mathsf{balance} > 0]\!] = [\![\mathsf{Membership}]\!] \cdot \Phi_{\mathsf{balance}>0} \subseteq \mathsf{T}\,\Phi_{\mathsf{balance}>0} \cdot [\![\mathsf{Membership}]\!]$$

needs to be discarded whenever justifying a refactoring involving class Membership.

10.2.4 Discussion

Only recently, co-algebra theory emerged as a common framework to describe state-based dynamical systems. Its study, along the lines of universal algebra, was initiated by Rutten [36,38]. There are a number of tutorials and lecture notes (see, e.g., [10,15,19]) to which the interested reader can be referred to. The proceedings of the Coalgebraic Methods in Computer Science workshop series, initiated in 1998, document current research ranging from the study of concrete co-algebras over different base categories [27,44] to the development of Set-independent (i.e., purely categorical) presentations of co-algebra theory (see, among others, [9,33,44]), from co-algebraic logic (e.g., [20,29]) to applications. Application examples range from automata [37] to objects [13,34], from process semantics [3,21,45] to hybrid transition systems [12]. Jacobs and his group, following earlier work by Reichel [11,34], have coined the term *co-algebraic specification* [14,16,35] to denote a style of axiomatic specification involving equations up to bisimilarity acting as constraints on the observable behavior.

10.3 A SEMANTICS FOR UML SEQUENCE DIAGRAMS

Graphically, a UML sequence diagram has two dimensions: a horizontal dimension representing the participants in the scenario, and a vertical dimension representing

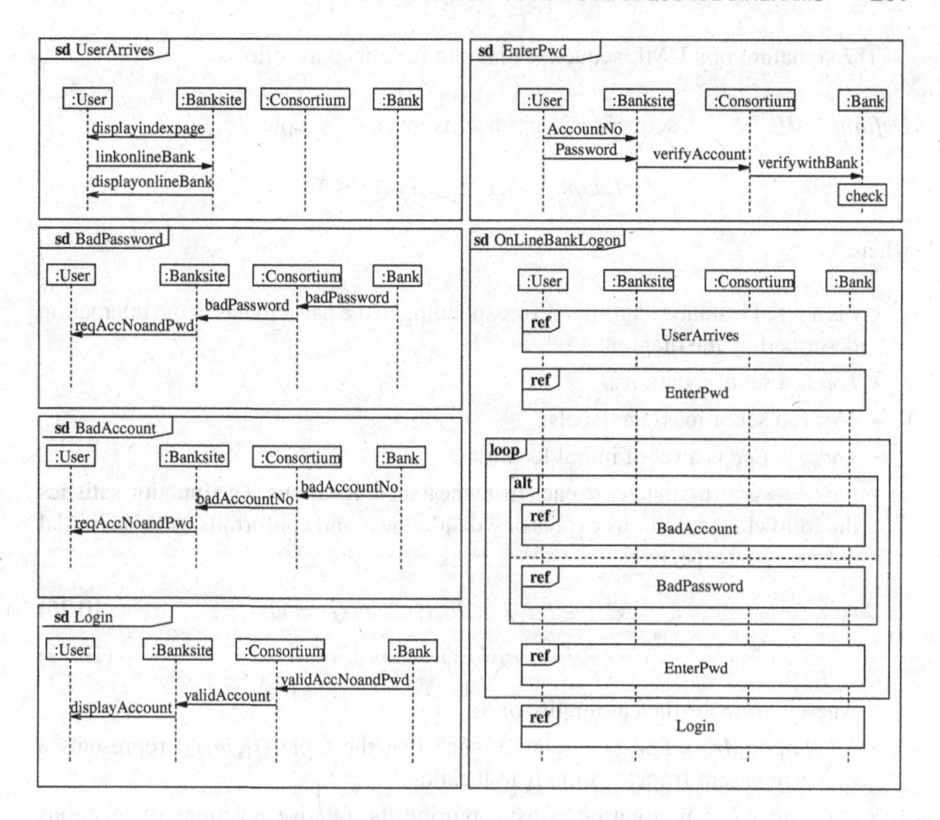

FIGURE 10.2 Annotated sequence diagram.

time. Participants evolve along *lifelines*, represented by vertical dashed lines. Interactions between participants are shown as horizontal arrows called *messages*. A message is a communication between two participants, and specifies both the type of communication (synchronous or asynchronous) and the associated sending and receiving event occurrences. Events situated on the same lifeline are ordered in time from the top down.

Figure 10.2 shows sequence diagrams that describe the interactions in the login phase of an online banking scenario. A UML SD is represented as a rectangular frame labeled by the keyword **sd** followed by the interaction name. The vertical lines in the SD represent lifelines for the individual participants in the interaction. Different SDs can be combined to describe complex scenarios; details are discussed in Section 10.4.

A message defines a particular communication between lifelines of an interaction. It can be either asynchronous or synchronous. Additionally, there are two special types of messages, *lost* and *found*, with the obvious meaning, which are described by a small black circle at the arrowhead, or origin, respectively.

The signature of a UML sequence diagram is defined as follows:

Definition 10.3.1 A sequence diagram *sd* is given by a tuple

$$(I, Loc, Mes, Loc_{ini}, loc, E, \leq)$$

where:

- I is a set of instance identifiers corresponding to the participants in the interaction described by the diagram.
- *Loc* is a set of locations.
- *Mes* is a set of message labels.
- $Loc_{ini} \subseteq Loc$ is a set of initial locations.
- $loc : I \to 2^{Loc}$ associates to each instance a set of locations. The function satisfies the following conditions expressing disjointness and conformity with the initial constraints, respectively,

$$\forall i, j \in I, i \neq j \cdot loc(i) \cap loc(j) = \emptyset \tag{10.26}$$

$$\forall i \in I \cdot card(loc(i) \cap Loc_{ini}) = 1 \tag{10.27}$$

  where $card(S)$ is the cardinality of S.
- $E \subseteq Loc \times Mes \times Loc$ is a relation such that the tuple (l_1, m, l_2) represents a message m sent from location l_1 to location l_2.
- $\leq \subseteq Loc \times Loc$ is a partial order capturing the relative positions of locations within each of the diagram lifelines.

Note that, in general, for an edge to represent a communication between participants in a sequence diagram, its source and target locations cannot be the same; that is, the following property is assumed:

$$\forall (l_1, m, l_2) \in E \cdot l_1 \neq l_2 \tag{10.28}$$

On the other hand, *local events*, which by definition are relative to a unique participant, are represented by reflexive edges at a particular location [e.g., (l, a, l)].

Within this model function, $next : Loc \to Loc$ returns locations of a particular participant and the next location in a particular lifeline,

$$next(l) = l' \text{ iff } \exists i \in I \cdot l, l' \in loc(i) \wedge l < l' \wedge \forall l'' \in loc(i) \cdot l < l'' \Rightarrow l' \leq l''$$

Let l_1, l_2 range over *Loc*, and Σ_m be the set of communication events relative to messages exchanged in a sequence diagram *sd*. Such events have one of the following forms:

1. $\langle l_1 \odot\!\!\rightarrow l_2, m \rangle$—$l_1$ sends asynchronously message m to l_2.
2. $\langle l_1 \leftarrow\!\!\odot l_2, m \rangle$—$l_1$ receives asynchronously message m from l_2.

3. $\langle l_1 \boxdot\!\!\rightarrow l_2, m\rangle$—$l_1$ sends synchronously message m to l_2.
4. $\langle l_1 \leftarrow\!\!\boxdot\, l_2, m\rangle$—$l_1$ receives synchronously message m from l_2.

Note that a *lost*, represented by $\bullet\!\!-$ (respectively, a *found*, represented by $-\!\!\bullet$) message corresponds to an asynchronous sending (respectively, receiving) event to (from) an unknown location. The type of an arbitrary event $e \in \Sigma_m$,

$$type(e) \in \{\odot\!\!\rightarrow, \leftarrow\!\!\odot, \boxdot\!\!\rightarrow, \leftarrow\!\!\boxdot, \bullet\!\!-, -\!\!\bullet\}$$

denotes the type of the event (respectively, sent/received/lost/found an asynchronous message, and sent/received a synchronous message). Since sending and receiving a synchronous message (i.e., events $e = \langle l_1 \boxdot\!\!\rightarrow l_2, m\rangle$ and $\overline{e} = \langle l_2 \leftarrow\!\!\boxdot\, l_1, m\rangle$, respectively) happen simultaneously, we resort to notation $\langle e, \overline{e}\rangle$ to denote the occurrence of such a pair of events. Finally, let Σ_τ denote the set of local actions in a sequence diagram. Such actions have the form $\langle l \circlearrowleft a\rangle$, which means local action a happens at location l. We use $\overline{\Sigma}$ as an abbreviation of $\Sigma_m \cup \Sigma_\tau$. The set of all event occurrences in a sequence diagram is denoted by Σ and defined as

$$\Sigma = \overline{\Sigma} \setminus \{e \mid type(e) = \boxdot\!\!\rightarrow \vee\, type(e) = \leftarrow\!\!\boxdot\} \cup \{\langle e, \overline{e}\rangle \mid type(e) = \boxdot\!\!\rightarrow\} \quad (10.29)$$

For any event $e \in \overline{\Sigma}$, the location at which e happens is defined by $\pi(e) = l$ iff $e = \langle l(\cdots)\rangle$. This notation generalizes to a set of events $\Sigma' \subseteq \overline{\Sigma}$ as

$$\pi\Sigma' = \{\pi(e) \mid e \in \Sigma'\}$$

and $\pi(\langle e, \overline{e}\rangle) = \{\pi(e), \pi(\overline{e})\}$.

A *configuration* for a sequence diagram denotes a global state, joining together all participants' local states. For every configuration, there is a set of active events that may happen.

Definition 10.3.2 A configuration G of a sequence diagram is a tuple of participants' local states (locations).

Suppose that C denotes the set of all possible configurations, and let function $\epsilon : C \longrightarrow \mathscr{P}(\overline{\Sigma})$ return the set of active events on a given configuration. A configuration G is called *final* if $\epsilon(G) = \emptyset$. For a configuration G and event e, $\pi(e) \in G$ means that $\pi(e)$ is a location in G.

In this context, the semantics of a sequence diagram *sd* can be given by a split of two functions over C:

$$\langle \epsilon, \overline{\alpha}\rangle \quad (10.30)$$

where ϵ was defined above and $\overline{\alpha} : C \longrightarrow C^{\Sigma}$ captures the diagram's state transition relation triggered by event occurrence. The pair

$$(C, \langle \epsilon, \overline{\alpha}\rangle) \quad (10.31)$$

together with an *initial* configuration c_0 (i.e., a tuple of initial locations, one per diagram column), is a pointed co-algebra for the functor

$$\mathsf{T}X = \mathscr{P}\overline{\Sigma} \times X^{\Sigma} \tag{10.32}$$

The set of enabled events is recorded as a state attribute.

A fundamental observation is that (10.32) is an instance of a functor (10.5). Therefore, the semantics of a sequence diagram can be regarded as yet another instance of a Moore transducer.

One of the advantages of this semantics is to make explicit that a set of enabled events is present in the initial state (i.e., before any interaction occurs). Another advantage is the quite simple form taken by the carrier of the corresponding final co-algebra, as discussed in Section 10.2.2:

$$\nu = \mathscr{P}\overline{\Sigma}^{\Sigma^*} \tag{10.33}$$

(i.e., a function that relates each Σ traces to the set of enabled events upon completion of its execution). As the empty trace $\langle\,\rangle$ is a valid trace, one can talk of an initial set of enabled events. To capture the intended semantics for sequence diagrams, this is defined as

$$\epsilon(c_0) = \{e \mid \pi(e) \in Loc_{ini} \wedge type(e) \neq \leftarrow\!\odot\} \tag{10.34}$$

Finally, note there is a well-formedness condition on T co-algebras suitable as models of sequence diagrams: In a given state $s \in G$, only events enabled in s can be triggered. Formally,

$$\langle \forall e, s \;:\; e \in \overline{\Sigma}, g \in G \;:\; e \notin \epsilon(s) \Rightarrow \alpha(s, e) = s\rangle \tag{10.35}$$

Clearly, if at a given state $s \in G$ the set of enabled events becomes empty [i.e., $\epsilon(s) = \emptyset$], the diagram will remain indefinitely in the same state.

To define functions ϵ and α, we proceed by enumerating all possible transition schemes. First, note that if an event e is not active in a configuration G [i.e., either $e \notin \epsilon(G)$ or $\pi(e) \notin G$], it will not be executed until by some other event occurrence, e is added to the set of active events. This case is captured by a trivial transition

$$\alpha(G, e) = G$$

and

$$\epsilon(\alpha(G, e)) = \epsilon(G)$$

When a local action a happens at location $l \in loc(i)$, the current location of participant i is changed to $next(l)$. Thus, for $e = \langle l \circlearrowright a\rangle$ where $l \in G$,

$$\alpha(G, e) = G[next(l)/l]$$

and

$$\epsilon(\alpha(G,e)) = \epsilon(G) \setminus \{e\} \cup \{e' \mid \pi(e') = next(l) \wedge type(e') \neq ?\leftarrow\})$$

Events modeling sending and receiving of a synchronous message occur simultaneously (i.e., in an atomic, noninterruptible way): No other event can occur in between. So if the current configuration is G and both the sending event $e = \langle l_1 \boxdot\!\!\rightarrow l_2, m\rangle$ and the corresponding receiving event $\overline{e} = \langle l_2 \leftarrow\!\!\boxdot\, l_1, m\rangle$ are active [i.e., $e \in \epsilon(G), \overline{e} \in \epsilon(G)$], we have

$$\alpha(G, \langle e, \overline{e}\rangle) = G[next(l_1)/l_1, next(l_2)/l_2]$$

and

$$\epsilon(\alpha(G, \langle e, \overline{e}\rangle)) = \epsilon(G) \setminus \{e, \overline{e}\} \cup \left\{ e' \mid \bigvee_{k=1,2} \pi(e') = next(l_k) \wedge type(e') \neq \leftarrow\!\!\odot \right\}$$

For asynchronous messages, however, when the sending event occurs, the location of the sender will be updated to the next location in its lifeline, while locations of the other participants will remain unchanged. The sending event is therefore removed from the set of active events. On the other hand, the corresponding receiving event will be added to such set. Furthermore, the events at the next location of the sender's lifeline will become active in the new configuration. If $e = \langle l_1 \odot\!\!\rightarrow l_2, m\rangle$ is active in configuration (G), we have

$$\alpha(G, e) = G[next(l_1)/l_1]$$

and

$$\epsilon(\alpha(G,e)) = \epsilon(G) \setminus \{e\} \cup \{\langle l_2 \leftarrow\!\!\odot\, l_1, m\rangle\} \cup \{e' \mid \pi(e') = next(l_1) \wedge type(e') \neq \leftarrow\!\!\odot\}$$

Dually, when an asynchronous message is received, the receiver will change to the next location in its lifeline, while locations of all other participants remain unchanged. Formally, if $e = \langle l_1 \leftarrow\!\!\odot l_2, m\rangle$ is active in configuration G, we have

$$\alpha(G, e) = G[next(l_1)/l_1],$$

and

$$\epsilon(\alpha(G,e)) = \epsilon(G) \setminus \{e\} \cup \{e' \mid \pi(e') = next(l_1) \wedge type(e') \neq \leftarrow\!\!\odot\}$$

The case of a lost message, represented by event $e = \langle l \bullet\!\!-, m\rangle$, is similar to the asynchronous communication: The sender updates its location and e is removed from the set of active events. However, no corresponding receiving event becomes active. Similarly, for a found message, when a receiving event $e = \langle l -\!\!\bullet, m\rangle$ occurs, only the location of the receiver is updated and e is removed from the set of active events. Both cases are therefore handled by

$$\alpha(G, e) = G[next(l)/l]$$

and

$$\epsilon(\alpha(G,e)) = \epsilon(G) \setminus \{e\} \cup \{e' \mid \pi(e') = next(l) \wedge type(e') \neq \leftarrow\odot\}$$

assuming that the corresponding events are enabled in configuration G.

10.4 NEW SEQUENCE DIAGRAMS FROM OLD

In the preceding section the semantics of an arbitrary sequence diagram *sd* was defined by a pointed co-algebra

$$[\![sd]\!] = (C, \langle \epsilon, \overline{\alpha} \rangle : C \to \mathscr{P}(\overline{\Sigma}) \times C^{\Sigma}, c_0) \tag{10.36}$$

over the set C of *sd* configurations.

UML 2.0 sequence diagrams may contain subinteractions called *interaction fragments* that can be structured and combined using a number of *interaction operators*. Although the semantics of an interaction fragment depends on the set of operators available, the precise definition of such a set is still an open topic in UML modeling. Recently, the UML superstructure specification [30] proposed one such set and gave an informal characterization of the associated behaviors as follows:

- The operator **alt** offers a choice of behavior alternatives represented by its two operands. The chosen *sd* must have an explicit or implicit guard expression that evaluates to true at this point in the interaction.
- The operator **opt** designates a choice between its (sole) operand or an idle behavior.
- The operator **par** stands for the parallel merge of the behaviors of the *sd* acting as its operands. Event occurrences in the different operands can be interleaved in any way as long as the ordering imposed inside each *sd* is preserved.
- The operator **seq** represents a weak sequencing between the behaviors of the operands (i.e., the ordering of event occurrences within each of the operands is maintained in the result), whereas event occurrences on different lifelines in different operands may come in any order. Event occurrences on the same lifeline in different operands are ordered in such a way that an event occurrence of the first operand comes before that of the second operand.
- The operator **strict** represents a strict sequencing of the behaviors: All events in the first operand are made to occur before any event in the second.
- The **loop** operator specifies an iteration of sequential composition: The execution of its operand repeats itself on completion.

The denotation of these operators in the envisaged semantic model formalizes an algebra for *building new sequence diagrams from old*.

In the sequel, we assume, for $sd_i = (I_i, Loc_i, Mes_i, Loc^i_{ini}, loc_i, E_i, \leq_i)$, that

$$[\![sd_i]\!] = (C_i, \langle \epsilon_i, \overline{\alpha_i} \rangle : C_i \to \mathscr{P}(\overline{\Sigma}_i) \times C_i^{\Sigma_i}, c^i_0)$$

where for any $G \in C_i$ which denotes the tuple of local states of participants in sd_i, $\Sigma_A^i = \epsilon_i(G)$ returns the set of events that are active in G. Moreover, we let $\epsilon_i(c_0^i) = \Sigma_0^i$. For a tuple of elements $t = (e_1, e_2, \ldots, e_m)$, we use the projection function π_i, for $i = 1, \ldots, m$, to return the ith element e_i. With such notational conventions we are prepared to give the semantics of operators for combining interaction fragments.

Choice: $\mathbf{alt}(sd_1, sd_2)$ Denoting an alternative form of aggregation of sequence diagrams, it is required that $c_1^0 = c_2^0$, and that all events in both Σ_0^1 and Σ_0^2 become active in the initial configuration c_0. Therefore, $c_0 = c_1^0$ and $C = \{c_0\} \cup (C_1 \setminus \{c_0^1\}) \cup (C_2 \setminus \{c_0^2\})$. Formally,[5]

$$[\![\mathbf{alt}(sd_1, sd_2)]\!] = (C, \overline{\langle \mathbf{alt}(\epsilon_1, \epsilon_2), \mathbf{alt}(\alpha_1, \alpha_2) \rangle}, c_0)$$

with

$$\mathbf{alt}(\epsilon_1, \epsilon_2)(x) = \begin{cases} x = c_0 \Rightarrow & \Sigma_0^1 \cup \Sigma_0^2 \\ x \in C_1 \setminus \{c_0^1\} \Rightarrow & \epsilon_1(x) \\ x \in C_2 \setminus \{c_0^2\} \Rightarrow & \epsilon_2(x) \end{cases}$$

$$\mathbf{alt}(\alpha_1, \alpha_2)(x, e) = \begin{cases} x = c_0 \wedge e \in \Sigma_i \Rightarrow & \alpha_i(c_0^i, e) \text{ for } i = 1, 2 \\ x \in C_1 \setminus \{c_0^1\} \wedge e \in \Sigma_1 \Rightarrow & \alpha_1(x, e) \\ x \in C_2 \setminus \{c_0^2\} \wedge e \in \Sigma_2 \Rightarrow & \alpha_2(x, e) \\ \text{otherwise} & x \end{cases}$$

where x is a configuration in C, and e is an event in either Σ_1 or Σ_2.

Option: $\mathbf{opt}(sd_1)$ The purpose of $\mathbf{opt}(sd_1)$ is to offer an alternative between an empty scenario (in which "nothing happens") and the activation of its (sole) operand, sd_1. To formalize its meaning, we need to introduce a new event—*skip*—into the set of events to capture the absence of effective behavior. Then

$$[\![\mathbf{opt}(sd_1)]\!] = (C, \overline{\langle \mathbf{opt}(\epsilon_1), \mathbf{opt}(\alpha_1) \rangle}, c_0)$$

where $C = C_1$ and $c_0 = c_0^1$. The transition structure is defined as

$$\mathbf{opt}(\epsilon_1)(x) = \begin{cases} x = c_0 \Rightarrow & \epsilon_1(x) \cup \{skip\} \\ \text{otherwise} & \epsilon_1(x) \end{cases}$$

$$\mathbf{opt}(\alpha_1)(x, e) = \begin{cases} x \neq c_0 \wedge e \in \Sigma_1 \Rightarrow & \alpha_1(x, e) \\ x = c_0 \wedge e = skip \Rightarrow & \mathbf{let}\ x' = c_0^1\ \mathbf{in}\ \epsilon x' = \emptyset \Rightarrow x' \\ x = c_0 \wedge e \in \Sigma_1 \Rightarrow & \alpha_1(c_0, e) \\ \text{otherwise} & x \end{cases}$$

[5] To avoid an excessive notational burden, we use the same syntax for the combinator over sequence diagrams and its denotation in the semantics proposed.

Parallel: $\mathbf{par}(sd_1, sd_2)$ As one would expect, the state space for parallel composition is a Cartesian product [i.e., $C = C_1 \times C_2$, with $c_0 = (c_0^1, c_0^2)$]. Then,

$$[\![\mathbf{par}(sd_1, sd_2)]\!] = (C, \langle \mathbf{par}(\epsilon_1, \epsilon_2), \overline{\mathbf{par}(\alpha_1, \alpha_2)} \rangle, c_0)$$

where the transition structure is defined as

$$\mathbf{par}(\epsilon_1, \epsilon_2)(x) = \epsilon_1(\pi_1 x) \cup \epsilon_2(\pi_2 x)$$

$$\mathbf{par}(\alpha_1, \alpha_2)(x, e) = \begin{cases} e \in \Sigma_1 \Rightarrow & \textbf{let } x' = \alpha_1(\pi_1 x, e) \textbf{ in } (x', \pi_2 x) \\ e \in \Sigma_2 \Rightarrow & \textbf{let } x' = \alpha_2(\pi_2 x, e) \textbf{ in } (\pi_1 x, x') \\ \text{otherwise} & x \end{cases}$$

Strict sequential composition: $\mathbf{strict}(sd_1, sd_2)$ The transition structure in

$$[\![\mathbf{strict}(sd_1, sd_2)]\!] = (C, \langle \mathbf{strict}(\epsilon_1, \epsilon_2), \overline{\mathbf{strict}(\alpha_1, \alpha_2)} \rangle, c_0)$$

is defined over $C = C_1 \cup C_2 \setminus \{c \mid c \in C_1 \wedge \epsilon_1(c) = \emptyset\}$ and $c_0 = c_0^1$ as follows

$$\mathbf{strict}(\epsilon_1, \epsilon_2)(x) = \begin{cases} x \in C_1 \wedge \epsilon_1(x) \neq \emptyset & \Rightarrow \epsilon_1(x) \\ x \in C_2 & \Rightarrow \epsilon_2(x) \end{cases}$$

$$\mathbf{strict}(\alpha_1, \alpha_2)(x, e) = \begin{cases} x \in C_1 \Rightarrow & \textbf{let } x' = \alpha_1(x, e) \textbf{ in } \epsilon_1 x' = \emptyset \Rightarrow c_0^2 \\ & \qquad \text{otherwise } x' \\ \text{otherwise} & \alpha_2(x, e) \end{cases}$$

Weak sequential composition: $\mathbf{seq}(sd_1, sd_2)$ The case for weak sequential composition $\mathbf{seq}(sd_1, sd_2)$ for $sd_i, i = 1, 2$ is a bit more demanding because its definition depends on whether the operands share a number of lifelines. If such is the case, that is, if an identifier, say s, exists in $I_1 \cap I_2$, all the event occurrences on s in sd_1 should happen before those on s in sd_2. However, any other events on lifelines out of the scope of both sd_1 and sd_2 may occur in any order. Note that if the operands involve disjoint sets of participants, the weak sequencing reduces to a parallel merge.

Assume an identifier s such that $I_1 \cap I_2 = \{s\}$, and function loc_1 and loc_2 assigning locations to instances in sd_1 and sd_2, respectively. Let $loc(s) = loc_1(s) \cup loc_2(s)$. Furthermore, and without loss of generality, let $C_1 = loc_1(s) \times L$ and $C_2 = loc_2(s) \times K$ be the set of configurations for sd_1 and sd_2, respectively, where $L = \prod_{i \in I_1 \setminus \{s\}} loc_1(i)$ and $K = \prod_{j \in I_2 \setminus \{s\}} loc_2(j)$. Then define

$$[\![\mathbf{seq}(sd_1, sd_2)]\!] = (C, \langle \mathbf{seq}(\epsilon_1, \epsilon_2), \overline{\mathbf{seq}(\alpha_1, \alpha_2)} \rangle, c_0)$$

with $C = loc(s) \times L \times K$ and $c_0 = (\langle \pi_1, \pi_2 \rangle c_0^1, \pi_3 c_0^2)$. We use ϵ as an abbreviation for $\mathbf{seq}(\epsilon_1, \epsilon_2)$, and for any $G \in C$,

$$\epsilon(G) = \bigcup_{(a_i, \pi_{i+1} G) \in C_i, i=1,2} \epsilon_i((a_i, \pi_{i+1} G)) \setminus \{e \mid \pi(e) \in loc(s) \wedge \pi(e) \neq \pi_1(G)\}$$

where $a_i \in loc_i(s), i = 1, 2$ are two locations such that

$$(a_1, \pi_2 G) \in C_1 \wedge (a_2, \pi_3 G) \in C_2 \wedge (\pi_1 G = a_1 \vee \pi_1 G = a_2)$$

The transition structure is given by

$$
\begin{array}{l}
\mathbf{seq}(\alpha_1, \alpha_2)(x, e) = \\
\qquad \mathbf{let}\ \{s\} = I_1 \cap I_2 \\
\qquad\qquad \begin{cases}
\pi(e) \cap loc(s) \neq \emptyset \Rightarrow \\
\quad \begin{cases}
\pi e(x) \cap loc_1(s) \neq \emptyset \Rightarrow \\
\quad \mathbf{let}\ x' = \alpha_1(\langle \pi_1, \pi_2 \rangle x, e),\ c_0^2 = (l, t)\ \mathbf{in} \\
\quad \begin{cases}
\forall l' \in loc_1(s).l' \leq \pi(e) \cap loc_1(s) \Rightarrow & (l, \pi_2 x', \pi_3 x) \\
\text{otherwise} & (\pi_1 x', \pi_2 x', \pi_3 x)
\end{cases} \\
\pi e(x) \cap loc_2(s) \neq \emptyset \Rightarrow \\
\quad \mathbf{let}\ x' = \alpha_2(\langle \pi_1, \pi_3 \rangle x, e)\ \mathbf{in}\ (\pi_1 x', \pi_2 x, \pi_2 x')
\end{cases} \\
\pi(e) \cap loc(s) = \emptyset \Rightarrow \\
\quad \begin{cases}
e \in \Sigma_1 \Rightarrow \\
\quad \mathbf{let}\ x' = \alpha_1(\langle \pi_1, \pi_2 \rangle x, e)\ \mathbf{in}\ (\pi_1 x', \pi_2 x', \pi_3 x) \\
e \in \Sigma_2 \Rightarrow \\
\quad \mathbf{let}\ x' = \alpha_2(\langle \pi_1, \pi_3 \rangle x, e)\ \mathbf{in}\ (\pi_1 x', \pi_2 x, \pi_2 x')
\end{cases}
\end{cases}
\end{array}
$$

The definition can easily be generalized to an arbitrary number of shared lifelines in sd_1 and sd_2.

On the other hand, if $I_1 \cap I_2 = \emptyset$, the definition of the transition structure reduces to the second branch of the case structure. By redefining the projection functions (since there is no s in the configurations), we can find that

$$\mathbf{seq}(sd_1, sd_2) = \mathbf{par}(sd_1, sd_2) \tag{10.37}$$

Furthermore, whenever $I_1 = I_2$, we have

$$\mathbf{seq}(sd_1, sd_2) = \mathbf{strict}(sd_1, sd_2) \tag{10.38}$$

The equalities above are in fact *bisimulation* equations between the corresponding denotations; for example, for equation (10.37),

$$[\![\mathbf{seq}(sd_1, sd_2)]\!] \sim [\![\mathbf{par}(sd_1, sd_2)]\!]$$

as such is the notion of equality in a co-algebraic setting.

They are, therefore, the first illustration of a *calculus* of sequence diagrams made possible by the semantic definition. The issue is discussed further in Section 10.6.

Loop: $\mathbf{loop}(sd_1)$. Finally, the semantics of the iteration combinator is given by

$$[\![\mathbf{loop}(sd_1)]\!] = (C, \langle \mathbf{loop}(\epsilon_1), \overline{\mathbf{loop}(\alpha_1)} \rangle, c_0)$$

over $C = C_1$ and $c_0 = c_0^1$, and with the following transition structure:

$$\mathbf{loop}(\epsilon_1)(x) = \epsilon_1(x)$$

$$\mathbf{loop}(\alpha_1)(x,e) = \begin{cases} e \in \mathbf{loop}(\epsilon_1)(x) \Rightarrow & \mathbf{let}\ x' = \alpha_1(x,e)\ \mathbf{in} \\ & \quad \mathbf{loop}(\epsilon_1)(x') = \emptyset \Rightarrow c_0 \\ & \quad \text{otherwise } x' \\ \text{otherwise} & x \end{cases}$$

10.5 COERCIONS AND DESIGNS

The description of a sequence diagram in UML 2.0 can also be annotated with some sort of coercion that restricts or expands the underlying possible behaviors. In the UML tradition, such conditions are themselves specified as sequence diagrams (instead of, say, through formulas in a logic). An example is depicted in Figure 10.3. Note that although annotations such as critical or alt are syntactically similar, their intended semantics is completely different: The former stands for a behavioral restriction in the diagram, the latter for a composition operator. Annotated diagrams will also be called *designs*.

In this section we show how such coercions can be accommodated in our semantic framework. To be concise, we consider only the following, most common cases of possible coercions on a diagram *sd*:

- Annotation neg, parametric on a sequence diagram p, which restricts the behavior of *sd* to exclude all interactions specified by p. It is required that the set of events Σ_p of p is a subset of the corresponding set Σ in *sd*. In the example of Figure 10.3, a neg rules out a sequence of confirmation message followed immediately by the production of a receipt.
- Annotation critical, parametric on a sequence diagram p, which requires that all interactions specified by p occur without interruption or interference of other events in *sd*. Such is the case of pin validation in the example of Figure 10.3.
- Annotation ignore, parametric on a message m, which abstracts away the behavior of *sd* of any occurrence of m.

We have already claimed that an advantage of adopting a co-algebraic framework for diagram semantics is that once the functor is fixed, a canonical characterisation of behavior pops out as the carrier of the final coalgebra. As discussed above, for T given by (10.32), behaviors are elements of $\mathscr{P}\overline{\Sigma}^{\Sigma^*}$. Thus, we may define the semantics of an annotated diagram *sd* as a pair

$$\langle [\![sd]\!], \beta(sd) \rangle \tag{10.39}$$

where $[\![sd]\!]$ denotes the semantics of *sd*, as in (10.36), and ignoring any annotation, and $\beta(sd)$ is the behavior of the annotated diagram. The latter is, typically, but not

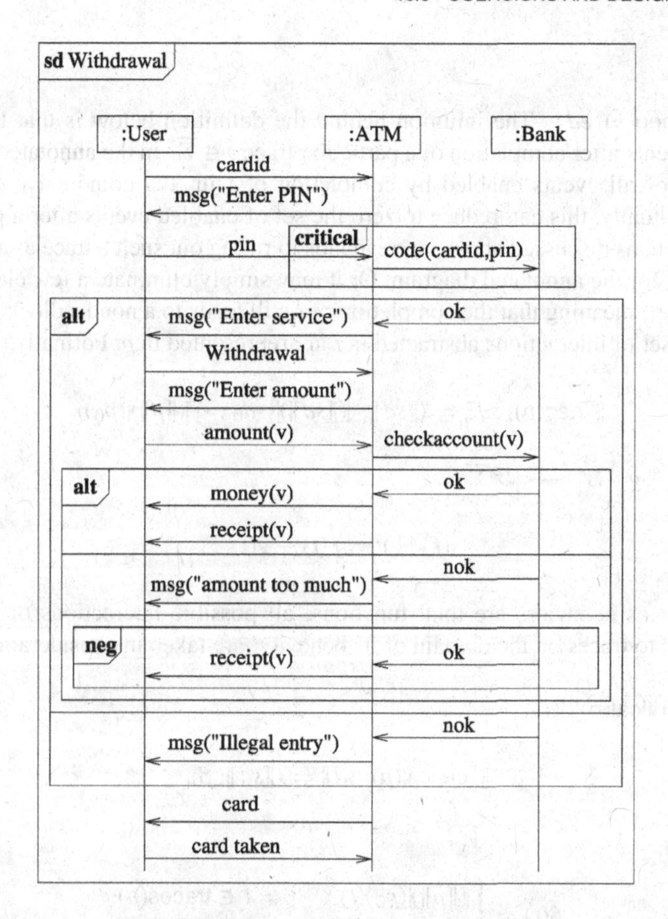

FIGURE 10.3 Annotated sequence diagram.

always, a restriction of the behavior of $[\![sd]\!]$. This, on the other hand, is, as you may recall, canonically given as the coinductive extension of co-algebra $[\![sd]\!]$ applied to the initial configuration of sd, denoted here by sd_0 [i.e., $[\!([\![sd]\!])\!](sd_0)$]. For the sake of uniformity, we can also present the semantics of a nonannotated diagram as a pair

$$\langle [\![sd]\!], [\!([\![sd]\!])\!](sd_0) \rangle \tag{10.40}$$

We shall now define the semantics of the three sorts of designs discussed here. In all cases consider annotations over a diagram sd with sd_0 as the initial configuration.

Also note that in the final model ν, we can rule out all sequences of events that lead to empty sets of observations (i.e., of enabled events). This entails the definition of the following function to compute the (allowed) traces of a sequence diagram sd with initial configuration sd_0:

$$\text{traces} = \{t \in \Sigma^* \mid [\!([\![sd]\!])\!](sd_0)(t) \neq \emptyset\} \tag{10.41}$$

Thus:

Design: $\langle \mathsf{neg}(p) \rangle\ sd$. The intuition behind the definition below is that the set of enabled events after completion of a particular trace $t \in \overline{\Sigma}^*$ in the annotated diagram is purged of all events enabled by completion of t in (the coinductive extension of) p. Eventually, this can reduce to zero the set of enabled events after a particular trace, which, as discussed above, corresponds to ruling out such a trace as a possible interaction for the annotated diagram. Or it may simply eliminate a few elements of the event set, meaning that the completion of t still leads to a nondeadlocked state if only a subset of interactions abstracted in t are represented in p. Formally,

$$[\![\langle \mathsf{neg}(p) \rangle\ sd]\!] = \langle [\![sd]\!],\ [\!([\![sd]\!])\!](sd_0) \lhd [\!([\![p]\!])\!](p_0) \rangle \tag{10.42}$$

where, for $f, g : \Sigma^* \longrightarrow \mathscr{P}\overline{\Sigma}$,

$$(f \lhd g)t = f(t) - g(t) \tag{10.43}$$

Notice that as behaviors are total functions, all possible interactions of p, which correspond to traces on the domain of its behavior, are taken in consideration.

Design: $\langle \mathsf{critical}(p) \rangle\ sd$.

$$[\![\langle \mathsf{critical}(p) \rangle\ sd]\!] = \langle [\![sd]\!], \beta \rangle \tag{10.44}$$

where

$$\beta(t) = \begin{cases} [\!([\![p]\!])\!](p_0)(t) & \Leftarrow t \in \mathsf{traces}(p) \\ [\!([\![sd]\!])\!](sd_0)(t) & \Leftarrow \mathsf{otherwise} \end{cases} \tag{10.45}$$

Notice that as *all* traces in p are taken into consideration and that the prefix of a trace is also a trace, the dynamics of p will always override that of the original sd whenever the latter involves events in the former. For example, suppose that sd allows trace $\langle a, z, b \rangle$, but p has $\langle a, b \rangle$ as the unique trace starting with event a, thus forcing it to occur with no interruption in the annotated diagram. Clearly, event z is enabled in sd after a [i.e., $z \in [\!([\![sd]\!])\!]\ sd_0(\langle a \rangle)$], but such is not the case in p, where $[\!([\![p]\!])\!]\ p_0(\langle a \rangle) = \{b\}$. Therefore, traces $\langle a, z \rangle$ and $\langle a, z, b \rangle$ are not allowed in the semantics of the annotated diagram.

Design: $\langle \mathsf{ignore}(m) \rangle\ sd$. In this design, the annotation is parametric on a single message $m \in \Sigma_{sd}$ which is supposed to be ignored in any interaction specified by sd. The behavior of this design will thus be defined over $\Sigma_{sd} - \{m\}$: For each original trace t ending in m, the enabled events of t and of its maximal prefix are joined together. Formally,

$$[\![\langle \mathsf{ignore}(m) \rangle\ sd]\!] = \langle [\![sd]\!], \gamma \rangle \tag{10.46}$$

where

$$\gamma(t) = [\![[\![p]\!]]\!](p_0)(t) \cup [\![[\![p]\!]]\!](p_0)(t \frown \langle m \rangle) \tag{10.47}$$

The following result shows that compositional reasoning is still possible when dealing with annotated diagrams:

Lemma 10.5.1 *Annotations always sum up: that is, the design resulting from composing two other designs with θ corresponds to the composition of the underlying diagrams with θ to which both coercions are added afterward. Formally,*

$$(\langle \mathsf{coer}_1(p) \rangle \, sd_1) \, \theta \, (\langle \mathsf{coer}_2(q) \rangle \, sd_2) \;=\; \langle \mathsf{coer}_1(p) \rangle \, \langle \mathsf{coer}_2(q) \rangle \, (sd_1 \, \theta \, sd_2)$$

for coer *ranging over* neg, critical, *and* ignore.

Proof: Let θ be any of the sequence diagrams operators characterized in Section 10.4. As annotations in a sequence diagram affect only disjoint subdiagrams, it is trivial to check from the semantics of neg, critical, and ignore that restrictions act over disjoint sets of events. Thus, their effects manifest themselves cumulatively. □

10.6 A CALCULUS FOR INTERACTIONS

10.6.1 Toward a Calculus of Diagram Composition

Equations (10.37) and (10.38) were our first examples of properties that establish, under suitable conditions, equality of behavior between expressions denoting arbitrary compositions of UML sequence diagrams. As mentioned there, such equalities are, in fact, bisimulation equations relating the co-algebras that represent the diagrams' semantics.

For functor T given by (10.32), the bisimulation definition (10.2.4) boils down to

$$(c, d) \in R \Rightarrow \forall_{e \in \Sigma} \cdot \epsilon(c) = \varepsilon(d) \wedge (\phi(c, e), \varphi(d, e)) \in R \tag{10.48}$$

for every pair of configurations (c, d), where $\alpha = \langle \epsilon, \phi \rangle$ and $\beta = \langle \varepsilon, \varphi \rangle$. This provides a rather simple way of testing behavioral equivalence for (the denotations of) UML sequence diagrams.

Not surprisingly, some simple proofs, which proceed by the construction of a witnessing bisimulation, establish a number of algebraic laws relating different composition patterns. For example:

Lemma 10.6.1 *Operators* **alt**, **par**, *and* **strict** *are associative. Formally,*

$$\textbf{tensor}(\textbf{tensor}(sd_1, sd_2), sd_3) = \textbf{tensor}(sd_1, \textbf{tensor}(sd_2, sd_3)) \tag{10.49}$$

for **tensor = alt, par, strict.**

Proof: Let us consider the case for **alt**, that is,

$$[\![\textbf{alt}(\textbf{alt}(sd_1, sd_2), sd_3)]\!] \sim [\![\textbf{alt}(sd_1, \textbf{alt}(sd_2, sd_3))]\!]$$

The set of configurations for both sides of this equation is $C = \{c_0\} \cup \bigcup_{1 \le i \le 3} (C_i \setminus \{c_0^i\})$, and the initial configuration, also in both cases, is c_0. Let $\epsilon_i(c_0^i) = \Sigma_0^i$ for $i = 1, 2, 3$. For any $x \in C$ and event e, one gets, according to the definition,

$$\begin{aligned}
&\textbf{alt}\ (\textbf{alt}(\epsilon_1, \epsilon_2), \epsilon_3)(x) \\
&= \begin{cases} x = c_0 \Rightarrow & \bigcup_{1 \le i \le 3} \Sigma_0^i \\ x \in C_1 \setminus \{c_0^1\} \Rightarrow & \epsilon_1(x) \\ x \in C_2 \setminus \{c_0^2\} \Rightarrow & \epsilon_2(x) \\ x \in C_3 \setminus \{c_0^3\} \Rightarrow & \epsilon_3(x) \end{cases} \\
&= \textbf{alt}(\epsilon_1, \textbf{alt}(\epsilon_2, \epsilon_3))(x) \\
&\textbf{alt}\ (\textbf{alt}(\alpha_1, \alpha_2), \alpha_3)(x, e) \\
&= \begin{cases} x = c_0 \wedge e \in \Sigma_i \Rightarrow & \alpha_i(c_0^i, e) \text{ for } i = 1, 2, 3 \\ x \in C_1 \setminus \{c_0^1\} \wedge e \in \Sigma_1 \Rightarrow & \alpha_1(x, e) \\ x \in C_2 \setminus \{c_0^2\} \wedge e \in \Sigma_2 \Rightarrow & \alpha_2(x, e) \\ x \in C_3 \setminus \{c_0^3\} \wedge e \in \Sigma_3 \Rightarrow & \alpha_3(x, e) \\ \text{otherwise} & x \end{cases} \\
&= \textbf{alt}(\alpha_1, \textbf{alt}(\alpha_2, \alpha_3))(x, e)
\end{aligned}$$

□

Similarly:

Lemma 10.6.2 *Operators* **alt** and **par** are commutative. Formally,

$$\textbf{tensor}(sd_1, sd_2) = \textbf{tensor}(sd_2, sd_1) \tag{10.50}$$

for **tensor** = **alt**, **par**.

Proof: Again our task is to verify the bisimulation equation

$$[\![\textbf{par}(sd_1, sd_2)]\!] \sim [\![\textbf{par}(sd_2, sd_1)]\!]$$

The sets of configurations for $[\![\textbf{par}(sd_1, sd_2)]\!]$ and $[\![\textbf{par}(sd_2, sd_1)]\!]$ are $C = C_1 \times C_2$ and $D = C_2 \times C_1$, respectively, where G_i is a configuration of sd_i for $i = 1, 2$. Define $h : C \to D$ as $h = \langle \pi_2, \pi_1 \rangle$. To prove the bisimulation equation, we only need to show that h is a co-algebra morphism, that is, to prove that the equations

$$\begin{aligned}
\textbf{par}(\epsilon_1, \epsilon_2)(x) &= \textbf{par}(\epsilon_2, \epsilon_1)(h(x)) \\
h \cdot \textbf{par}(\alpha_1, \alpha_2)(x, e) &= \textbf{par}(\alpha_2, \alpha_1)(h(x), e)
\end{aligned}$$

are satisfied for any configuration x and event e. According to the definition of **par**,

$$
\begin{aligned}
&\mathbf{par}(\epsilon_2,\epsilon_1)(h(x))\\
&\quad= \mathbf{par}(\epsilon_2,\epsilon_1)(\langle\pi_2,\pi_1\rangle x)\\
&\quad= \epsilon_2(\pi_1\cdot\langle\pi_2,\pi_1\rangle x)\cup\epsilon_1(\pi_2\cdot\langle\pi_2,\pi_1\rangle x)\\
&\quad= \epsilon_2(\pi_2 x)\cup\epsilon_1(\pi_1 x)\\
&\quad=' \epsilon_1(\pi_1 x)\cup\epsilon_2(\pi_2 x)\\
&\quad= \mathbf{par}(\epsilon_1,\epsilon_2)(x)
\end{aligned}
$$

and for $e \in \Sigma_1$,

$$
\begin{aligned}
&\mathbf{par}(\alpha_2,\alpha_1)(h(x),e)\\
&\quad= \mathbf{par}(\alpha_2,\alpha_1)(\langle\pi_2,\pi_1\rangle(x),e)\\
&\quad= \mathbf{let}\ x' = \alpha_1(\pi_2\cdot\langle\pi_2,\pi_1\rangle x,e)\ \mathbf{in}\ (\pi_1\cdot\langle\pi_2,\pi_1\rangle x,x')\\
&\quad= (\pi_2 x,\alpha_1(\pi_1 x,e))\\
&\quad= \langle\pi_2,\pi_1\rangle\cdot(\alpha_1(\pi_1 x,e),\pi_2 x)\\
&\quad= h\cdot\mathbf{par}(\alpha_1,\alpha_2)(x,e)
\end{aligned}
$$

Similarly, for $e \in \Sigma_2$, we also get $\mathbf{par}(\alpha_2,\alpha_1)(h(x),e) = h\cdot\mathbf{par}(\alpha_1,\alpha_2)(x,e)$. And for $e \notin \Sigma_1\cup\Sigma_2$, the result is obvious: $h(x) = h(x)$. The proof is complete, noting that $h(c_0^1) = c_0^2$. □

Notice how in this second proof a quite handy technique of coinductive reasoning was used: To establish bisimilarity it is enough to define a co-algebra morphism connecting the two co-algebras. Such a technique is based on the fact that co-algebra morphisms entail bisimulation, a direct consequence of (10.19).

Following a similar strategy, one can prove, for example, idempotence results, reductions, and in particular, distribution of strict sequential and parallel composition over choice. Formally,

$$\mathbf{alt}(sd,sd) = \mathbf{sd} \tag{10.51}$$

$$\mathbf{alt}(sd,\emptyset_{I_{sd}}) = \mathbf{opt} \tag{10.52}$$

$$\mathbf{strict}(\mathbf{alt}(sd_1,sd_2),sd_3) = \mathbf{alt}(\mathbf{strict}(sd_1,sd_3),\mathbf{strict}(sd_2,sd_3)) \tag{10.53}$$

$$\mathbf{strict}(sd_1,\mathbf{alt}(sd_2,sd_3)) = \mathbf{alt}(\mathbf{strict}(sd_1,sd_2),\mathbf{strict}(sd_1,sd_3)) \tag{10.54}$$

$$\mathbf{par}(\mathbf{alt}(sd_1,sd_2),sd_3) = \mathbf{alt}(\mathbf{par}(sd_1,sd_3),\mathbf{par}(sd_2,sd_3)) \tag{10.55}$$

$$\mathbf{par}(sd_1,\mathbf{alt}(sd_2,sd_3)) = \mathbf{alt}(\mathbf{par}(sd_1,sd_2),\mathbf{par}(sd_1,sd_3)) \tag{10.56}$$

In equation (10.52) we use $\emptyset_{I_{sd}}$ to denote the empty sequence diagram with the same set of participants as sd, but no events. Suppose that $sd = (I, Loc, Mes, Loc_{ini}, loc, E, \leq)$: then $\emptyset_{I_{sd}} = (I, Loc_{ini}, \emptyset, Loc_{ini}, \{i \mapsto l_0^i\}, \emptyset, =)$.

10.6.2 Refactoring

Just as Section 10.6.1 was intended to illustrate how a calculus of UML sequence diagrams can emerge from the proposed semantics, we focus now on another application mentioned in Section 10.1: *refactoring*. Again we shall not be exhaustive, but rather, suggest possible steps in this direction.

Introduced by Opdyke [31] in the context of OO programming, refactoring has been widely used in modern software development processes such as the rational unified process [18] and eXtreme Programming [6] to support iterative software development and improve the quality of software artifacts. In [8] it is defined as "the process of changing a software system in such a way that it does not alter the external behavior of the code, yet improves its internal structure." Later, interest in research shifted from the code level to model refactoring [40,43,46].

In any case, typical refactoring laws are supposed to preserve behavior, and therefore they boil down to bisimulation equations such as the ones considered above. Well-known examples are laws expressing fine-grained refactoring steps, such as adding, removing, and moving elements in sequence diagrams. For example:

Lemma 10.6.3 *A new lifeline can be introduced into a sequence diagram.*

Proof: Suppose that $sd = (I, Loc, Mes, Loc_{ini}, loc, E, \leq)$ is a sequence diagram. Adding a new lifeline to *sd* means that a new instance identifier i is added to I. Since there is no message exchange between i and other participants in the diagram, it has only one location, the initial location l_0^i. So the resulting diagram is $sd' = (I \cup \{i\}, Loc \cup \{l_0^i\}, Mes, Loc_{ini} \cup \{l_0^i\}, loc, E, \leq)$. If G is a configuration for *sd*, then $\langle G, l_0^i \rangle$ is a configuration for sd'. Let $h = \pi_1 \times \mathsf{id}$. This morphism maps every configuration of sd' to a configuration of *sd* and forms a co-algebra morphism between them, which justifies the law. □

A similar argument justifies the dual law for removing lifelines:

Lemma 10.6.4 *A lifeline that does not interact with other participants and has no local actions can be removed from a sequence diagram.*

Other refactoring laws, however, require preservation of behavior in a weaker sense. Such is the case, for example, of refactorings involving the split of a lifeline into a set of independent lifelines representing sections of noninterfering execution and enforcing time constraints by specific message exchange.

In the semantic framework discussed here, such weak preservation of behavior corresponds to relating (denotations of) sequence diagrams by *refinement* instead of bisimilarity. Refinement for co-algebras has been studied by Meng and Barbosa in [24,26]. In brief, the idea is to relax the co-algebra morphism condition in (10.3) by

$$\mathsf{T}h \cdot p \leq p' \cdot h \tag{10.57}$$

where $\leq$ is called *refinement preorder* [24]. Function h is said to be a *forward morphism* which is intended to preserve transitions from the source co-algebra but fails to reflect them back. Relation $\leq$, for functor T given in (10.32), is a preorder on functions from events to configurations. A possible example requires one of the diagrams to possess less active events than the other in related configurations, as captured by the following (in)equations:

$$\epsilon_1(G_1) \subseteq \epsilon_2(h(G_1))$$

$$h \cdot \alpha_1(G_1, e) = \alpha_2(h(G_1), e)$$

The existence of a forward morphism connecting two (co-algebraic denotations of) sequence diagrams witnesses a refinement situation represented by preorder $\preccurlyeq$. With respect to this preorder, designs discussed in Section 10.5 can be related to the original diagram by *forward* refinement. In particular:

Lemma 10.6.5

$$\langle \mathsf{neg}(p) \rangle\, sd \preccurlyeq sd \tag{10.58}$$

$$\langle \mathsf{critical}(p) \rangle sd \preccurlyeq sd \tag{10.59}$$

$$sd \preccurlyeq \langle \mathsf{ignore}(m) \rangle sd \tag{10.60}$$

In the references cited above, forward morphisms are shown to compose and enjoy a number of calculational properties. In particular, they are powerful enough (more exactly, weak enough!) to capture a great number of refactoring situations for sequence diagrams, as refinement results.

10.7 CONCLUDING REMARKS

This chapter introduced a co-algebraic semantic framework for UML 2.0 sequence diagrams, including the formalization of the recently proposed set of combinators for such diagrams. It was also illustrated how coinductive techniques can be used to prove properties of UML designs and develop a theory of sequence diagram composition and refactoring. This piece of research is in line with our previous work on co-algebraic semantics for other UML models [4,41,42] and can be regarded as part of a major attempt to give a precise semantics to UML descriptions. Several proposals for formalizing UML 2.0 sequence diagrams are known. Among them, we are particularly interested in approaches, such as that of Knapp and Wuttke [17], which are also based on translating sequence diagrams to a language of automata, therefore entailing, even if implicitly, a co-algebraic perspective. A proper comparison with the approach proposed in this chapter is in inorder.

For future work, we single out as a main open issue the need for a detailed classification of possible refactoring patterns and their formalization in this framework.

Refactoring by (co-algebraic) refinement, as pointed out in Section 10.6, is also an open field for further research.

REFERENCES

1. P. Aczel and N. Mendler. A final coalgebra theorem. In D. Pitt, D. Rydeheard, P. Dybjer, A. Pitts, and A. Poigne, eds., *Proceedings on Category Theory and Computer Science*. Lecture Notes in Computer Science, vol. 389, pp. 357–365. Springer-Verlag, New York, 1988.
2. R. C. Backhouse and P. F. Hoogendijk. Elements of a relational theory of datatypes. In B. Möller, H. Partsch, and S. Schuman, eds., *Formal Program Development*. Lecture Notes in Computer Science, vol. 755, pp. 7–42. Springer-Verlag, New York, 1993.
3. L. S. Barbosa. Process calculi à la Bird-Meertens. In *CMCS'01*, Genova, Italy, Apr. 2001. Electronic Notes in Theoretical Computer Science Elsevier, Amsterdam, vol. 44.4, pp. 47–66.
4. L. S. Barbosa and S. Meng. UML model refactoring as refinement: a coalgebraic perspective. In G. Ciobanu and E. Nicolae Todoran, eds., *Proceedings of GlobalComp at 10th SYNASC*, Sept. 26–29, 2008, Timisoara, Romania. IEEE Computer Society, Los Alamitos, CA, 2008.
5. L. S. Barbosa, J. N. Oliveira, and A. M. Silva. Calculating invariants as coreflexive bisimulations. In J. Meseguer and G. Rosu, eds., *Algebraic Methodology and Software Technology: Proceedings of the 12th International Conference* (*AMAST 2008*), Urbana, IL, July 28–31, 2008, Lecture Notes in Computer Science, vol. 5140, pp. 83–89. Springer-Verlag, New York, 2008.
6. K. Beck. *Extreme Programming Explained: Embrace Change*, 2nd ed. Addison-Wesley, Reading, MA, 2004.
7. J. van Benthem. Modal correspondence theory. Ph.D. dissertation, University of Amsterdam, 1976.
8. M. Fowler. *Refactoring: Improving the Design of Existing Code*. Addison-Wesley, Reading, MA, 1999.
9. H. P. Gumm and T. Schroeder. Covarieties and *complete covarieties. In B. Jacobs, L. Moss, H. Reichel*, and J. Rutten, eds., *CMCS'98. Electronic Notes in Theoretical Computer Science,* vol. 11. Elsevier, Amsterdam, Mar. 1998.
10. H. P. Gumm. *Elements of the General Theory of Coalgebras*. Technical Report. Lecture Notes for LUTACS'99, South Africa, 1999.
11. U. Hensel and H. Reichel. Defining equations in terminal coalgebras. In E. Astesiano, G. Reggio, and A. Tarlecki, eds., *Recent Trends in Data Type Specification*. Lecture Notes in Computer Science, vol. 906, pp. 307–318. Springer-Verlag, New York, 1995.
12. B. Jacobs. Object-oriented hybrid systems of coalgebras plus monoid actions. In M. Wirsing and M. Nivat, eds., *Algebraic Methodology and Software Technology* (*AMAST*). Lecture Notes in Computer Science, vol. 1101, pp. 520–535. Springer-Verlag, New York, 1996.
13. B. Jacobs. Objects and classes, co-algebraically. In C. Lengauer, B. Freitag, C.B. Jones and H.-J. Schek, eds., *Object-Orientation with Parallelism and Persistence*, pp. 83–103. Kluwer Academic, Norwell, MA, 1996.

14. B. Jacobs. Behaviour-refinement of coalgebraic specifications with coinductive correctness proofs. In *TAPSOFT'97: Theory and Practice of Software Development*. Lecture Notes in Computer Science, vol. 1214, pp. 787–802. Springer-Verlag, New York, 1997.
15. B. Jacobs and J. Rutten. A tutorial on (co)algebras and (co)induction. *EATCS Bulletin*, 62:222–159, 1997.
16. B. Jacobs. Exercises in coalgebraic specification. In R. Backhouse, R. Crole, and J. Gibbons, eds., *Algebraic and Coalgebraic Methods in the Mathematics of Program Construction*. Lecture Notes in Computer Science, vol. 2297, pp. 237–280. Springer-Verlag, New York, 2002.
17. A. Knapp and J. Wuttke. Model checking of UML 2.0 interactions. In T. Kühne, ed., *Models in Software Engineering: Workshops and Symposia at MoDELS 2006, Genoa, Italy, Oct. 1–6, 2006: Reports and Revised Selected Papers*. Lecture Notes in Computer Science, vol. 4364, pp. 42–51. Springer-Verlag, New York, 2007.
18. P. Kruchten. *The Rational Unified Process: An Introduction*, 3rd ed. Addison-Wesley, Reading, MA, 2003.
19. A. Kurz. *Coalgebras and Modal Logic*. Technical Report. Lecture Notes for ESSLLII'2001, Helsinki, Finland, 2001.
20. A. Kurz. Logics for coalgebras and applications to computer science. Ph.D. dissertation. Fakultat fur Mathematik, Ludwig-Maximilians Universität Muenchen, Munich, Germany, 2001.
21. M. Lenisa. Themes in final semantics. Ph.D. dissertation. Universita de Pisa-Udine, Udine, Italy, 1998.
22. S. MacLane. *Categories for the Working Mathematician*. Springer-Verlag, New York, 1971.
23. E. Meijer, M. Fokkinga, and R. Paterson. Functional programming with bananas, lenses, envelopes and barbed wire. In J. Hughes, ed., *Proceedings of the 1991 ACM Conference on Functional Programming Languages and Computer Architecture*. Lecture Notes in Computer Science, vol. 423, pp. 124–144. Springer-Verlag, New York, 1991.
24. S. Meng and L. S. Barbosa. Components as coalgebras: the refinement dimension. *Theoretical Computer Science*, 351:276–294, 2006.
25. S. Meng and L. S. Barbosa. A coalgebraic semantic framework for reasoning about UML sequence diagrams. In H. Zhu, ed., *Proceedings of the 8th International Conference on Quality Software* (*QSIC 2008*), *12–13 August 2008, Oxford, UK*, pp. 17–26. IEEE Computer Society, Los Alamitos, CA, 2008.
26. S. Meng and L. S. Barbosa. On refinement of generic state-based software components. In C. Rattray, S. Maharaj, and C. Shankland, eds., *Proceedings of AMAST'04*. Lecture Notes in Computer Science, vol. 3116, pp. 506–520. Springer-Verlag, New York, 2004.
27. L. Monteiro. Observation systems. In H. Reichel, ed., *CMCS'00: Workshop on Coalgebraic Methods in Computer Science*. ENTCS, vol. 33. Elsevier, Amsterdam, 2000.
28. E. F. Moore. Gedanken experiments on sequential machines. In *Automata Studies*, pp. 129–153. Princeton University Press, Princeton, NJ, 1966.
29. L. Moss. Coalgebraic logic. *Annals of Pure and Applied Logic*, 96 (1–3): 277–317, 1999.
30. OMG. Unified modeling language: superstructure, version 2.1.1, 2007. http://www.uml.org/.

31. W. F. Opdyke. *Refactoring: a program restructuring aid in designing object-oriented application frameworks*. Ph.D. dissertation, University of Illinois at Urbana–Champaign, 1992.

32. D. Park. Concurrency and automata on infinite sequences. Lecture Notes in Computer Science, vol. 104, pp. 561–572. Springer-Verlag, New York, 1981.

33. J. Power and H. Watanabe. An axiomatics for categories of coalgebras. In B. Jacobs, L. Moss, H. Reichel, and J. Rutten, eds., *CMCS'98*, Electronic Notes in Theoretical Computer Science, vol. 11. Elsevier, Amsterdam, Mar. 1998.

34. H. Reichel. An approach to object semantics based on terminal co-algebras. *Mathematical Structures in Computer Science*, 5:129–152, 1995.

35. J. Rothe, B. Jacobs, and H. Tews. The coalgebraic class specification language CCSL. *Journal of Universal Computer Science*, 7(2), 2001.

36. J. Rutten. A calculus of transition systems (towards universal co-algebra). In A. Ponse, M. de Rijke, and Y. Venema, eds., *Modal Logic and Process Algebra: A Bisimulation Perspective*. CSLI Lecture Notes, vol. 53, pp. 231–256. CSLI Publications, Stanford, CA, 1995.

37. J. Rutten. Automata and coinduction (an exercise in coalgebra). In *Proceedings of CONCUR'98*, Lecture Notes in Computer Science, vol. 1466, pp. 194–218. Springer-Verlag, New York, 1998.

38. J. Rutten. Universal coalgebra: a theory of systems. *Theoretical Computer Science*, 249(1):3–80, 2000. (Revised version of CWI Technical Report CS-R9652, 1996.)

39. K. Segerberg. An essay in classical modal logic. *Filosofiska Studier*, 13, 1971.

40. R. Van Der Straeten, V. Jonckers, and T. Mens. Supporting model refactoring through behaviour inheritance consistencies. In T. Baar et al., eds., *UML 2004*. Lecture Notes in Computer Science, vol. 3273, pp. 305–319. Springer-Verlag, New York, 2004.

41. M. Sun, B. K. Aichernig, L. S. Barbosa, and Z. Naixiao. A coalgebraic semantic framework for component based development in UML. In L. Birkedal, ed., *Proceedings of the International Conference on Category Theory and Computer Science* (*CTCS'04*). Electronic Notes in Theoretical Computer Science, vol. 122, pp. 229–245. Elsevier, Amsterdam, 2005.

42. M. Sun, Z. Naixiao, and L. S. Barbosa. On semantics and refinement of UML statecharts: a coalgebraic view. In J. Cuellar and Z. Liu, eds., *Proceedings of the 2nd IEEE International Conference on Software Engineering and Formal Methods*, pp. 164–173, Beijing, China, Sept. 2004. IEEE Computer Society, Los Alamitos, CA, 2004.

43. G. Sunyé, D. Pollet, Y. Le Traon, and J.-M. Jézéquel. Refactoring UML Models. In M. Gogolla and C. Kobryn, eds., *Proceedings of UML 2001*. Lecture Notes in Computer Science, vol. 2185, pp. 134–148. Springer-Verlag, New York, 2001.

44. D. Turi and J. Rutten. On the foundations of final coalgebra semantics: non-well-founded sets, partial orders, metric spaces. *Mathematical Structures in Computer Science*, 8(5):481–540, 1998.

45. U. Wolter. A coalgebraic introduction to CSP. In *Proceedings of CMCS'99*, Electronic Notes in Theoretical Computer Science, vol. 19. Elsevier, Armsterdam, 1999.

46. A. Zawlocki, G. Marczyński, and P. Kosiuczenko. Property preserving redesign of specifications. In J. L. Fiadeiro et al., eds., *CALCO 2005*. Lecture Notes in Computer Science, vol. 3629, pp. 439–455. Springer-Verlag, New York, 1998.

CHAPTER 11

SEMANTICS OF ACTIVITY DIAGRAMS

KEVIN LANO
Department of Computer Science, King's College London, London, UK

11.1 INTRODUCTION

UML activity diagrams define behavior as structured collections of individual actions such as operation invocations, assignments, and other state-modifying or state-enquiry processing steps. Actions can be connected by control or data flows within an activity. Activities can be used to define the behavior of objects or of operations, as an alternative to state machines. They can also be used to define more general forms of behavior, such as workflows of organizational tasks.

The UML 2 activity diagram notation is subdivided into five subnotations, which define subsets of the complete notation:

- *Fundamental activities:* defines the notion of an *Activity* as a container of nodes, which include actions.
- *Basic activities:* defines control sequencing and data flow between actions.
- *Intermediate activities:* defines activity diagrams with concurrent control and data flow and decisions. It is similar to Petri nets with queuing. It builds on the basic level.
- *Complete activities:* adds edge weights and streaming concepts to intermediate activities.
- *Structured activities:* adds traditional control flow constructs of loops, sequencing, and conditionals to the fundamental level.

Two further levels, complete structured activities and extra structured activities, build on both the structured and basic activity sublanguages.

In this chapter we are concerned primarily with structured activities. We consider two alternative approaches to defining a semantics for these: (1) by transforming them

UML 2 Semantics and Applications. Edited by Kevin Lano

to the state machine notation; and (2) by defining them in terms of semantic actions. The first approach has the advantage of relating one UML model to another and of being easily comprehensible to users of UML; however, it does not cover all possible cases of activity diagrams. The second is more complex and further from UML notation; however, it is comprehensive. We describe the two approaches in parallel.

11.2 SEMANTICS OF STRUCTURED ACTIVITIES

Figure 11.1 shows the metamodel of structured activity diagrams. The basis of the semantic mapping to state machines will be to interpret actions as basic (unstructured) states and activities as composite states containing the states that represent the component actions of the activity.

For each *Activity* A, we define a class C_A that will act as a context for A if A does not already have a *context* class, and a new state machine S_A defining the classifier behavior of C_A. C_A must be linked to any class used within A as data or as a supplier.

For each Action instance *ac* in *A.node*, we define a basic state *st* of S_A whose entry action *st.entry* carries out the behavior defined by *ac* (the entry action is used, instead of the do activity of the state, since the behavior should be noninterruptible). An InitialNode is mapped to an initial state, and an ActivityFinalNode is mapped to a final state. Figure 11.2 shows the mapping of sequence, conditional, and loop nodes.

A SequenceNode instance *sn* with sequence $sn.executableNode = ss$ of component nodes maps to an OR composite state *st* which has $st.region = Set\{r\}$, and $r.subvertex = sts \rightarrow union(Set\{ini, fin\})$, with each element of *sts* representing one element of *ss*. The states *sts* are connected in sequence by transitions in the order defined by *ss*. *ini* is an initial pseudostate, with a transition to the state representing $ss \rightarrow at(1)$, and *fin* is a final pseudostate.

A ConditionalNode instance *cn* with a single clause: $cn.clause = cls \rightarrow at(1)$, where *cls* is a sequence of *Clause* objects linked in a linear chain by *predecessorClause/successorClause* links, maps to an OR composite state *st* which has $st.region = Set\{r\}$, and $r.subvertex = sts \rightarrow union(tsts) \rightarrow union(Set\{ini, fin\})$, with each *tsts* element representing a corresponding element of *cls.test* (assuming that there is one test for each clause) and each element of *sts* representing the corresponding element of *cls.body* (to be executed if the test is true). $sts \rightarrow size() = tsts \rightarrow size()$. The states *sts* are the targets of transitions from the corresponding *tsts*, which are taken if the test evaluates to true: otherwise, control flow goes to the state representing the successor clause. *ini* is an initial pseudostate, with a transition to the state representing the first clause.

The mapping for (simplified) LoopNodes is similar. A state is introduced for each of the *setupPart*, *test*, and *bodyParts* of the loop, with transitions connecting these either into a while or until-loop structure, depending on the value of *isTestedFirst*.

The semantics in terms of actions defines a theory Γ_A for A, with action symbols for A and each ExecutableNode within A. The theory will import Γ_X for each class X used by A as data or as a supplier, and will contain attributes for each Variable in *A.variable*.

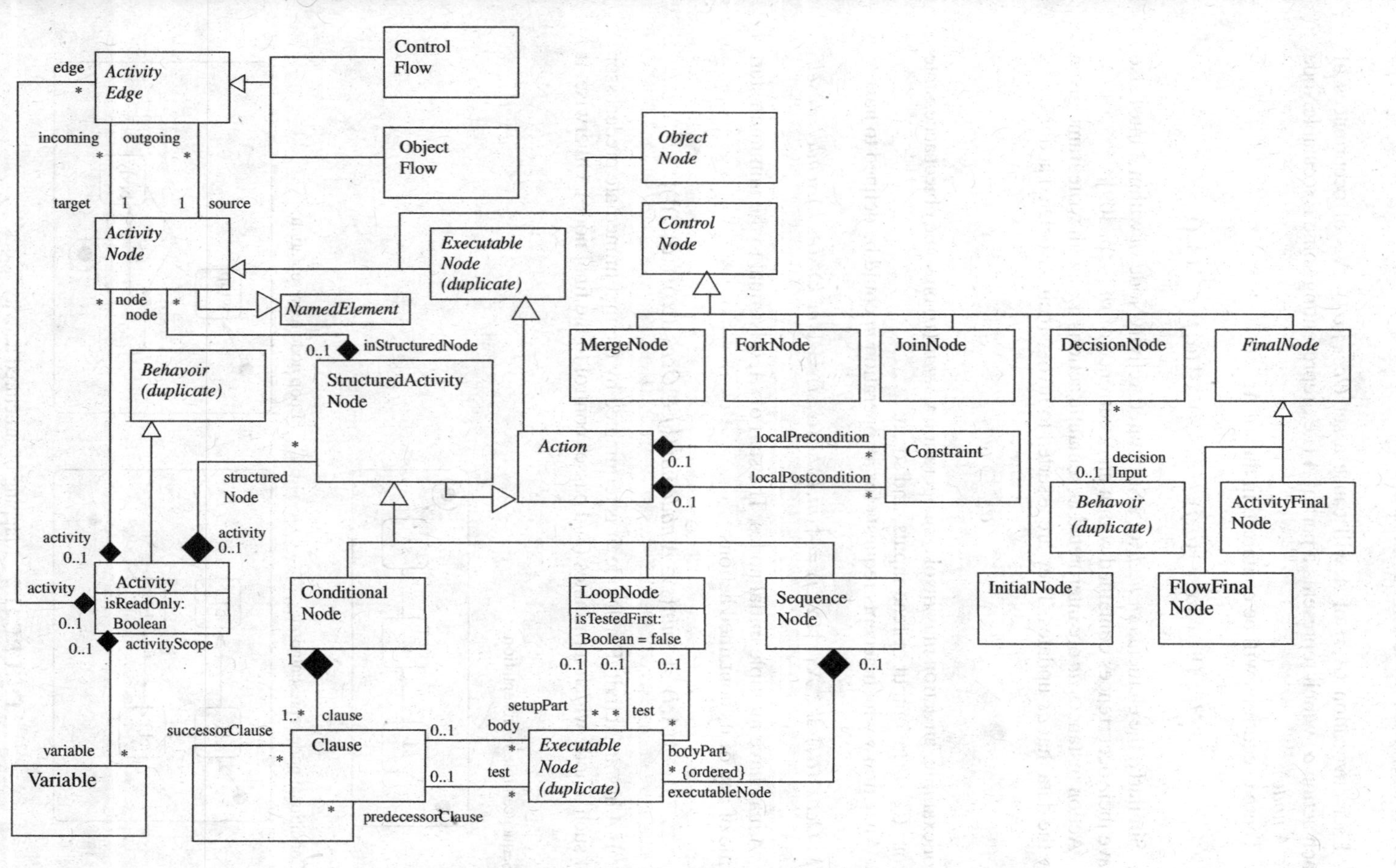

FIGURE 11.1 Metamodel of structured activities.

Each invocation (A, i) of A will cause a set $Occ_{A,i}(\alpha) \subseteq \mathcal{N}_1$ of occurrences of each action α, which represents a part of A (i.e., representing some ExecutableNode $s \in A.node$).

These executions will be contained in that of A:

$$\forall j : Occ_{A,i}(\alpha) \cdot \uparrow(\alpha, j) \geq \uparrow(A, i) \wedge \downarrow(\alpha, j) \leq \downarrow(A, i)$$

Similarly, the elements *sn.node* of a StructuredActivityNode *sn* within A must also have their occurrences contained within an occurrence of *sn* [4, p. 409].

Action instances *ac* are interpreted as semantic actions α_{ac}, with write frame given by the data that *ac* updates. They are asserted to invoke their associated actions:

$$\alpha_{ac} \supset acts'$$

For example, an action may invoke an operation $x.setatt(v)$ on some object accessible from C_A, write output or read inputs, and so on.

An action s which accepts requests for an operation m could be defined to have

$$\forall j : Occ_{A,i}(\alpha_s) \cdot \exists k : \mathcal{N}_1 \cdot \uparrow(\alpha_s, j) = \uparrow(m, k) \wedge \downarrow(\alpha_s, j) = \downarrow(m, k) \wedge (m, k).sender \neq self$$

A may have multiple initial nodes. The start of (A, i) is equal to the minimum start time of any of its contained actions:

$$\uparrow(A, i) \; = \; min\{s \in A.node | min(\{j \in Occ_{A,i}(\alpha_s) | \uparrow(\alpha_s, j)\})\}$$

If A has an ActivityFinalNode, it is terminated by the first immediate predecessor of such a node which terminates (and passes control to the final node). Otherwise, it

Sequence node representation:

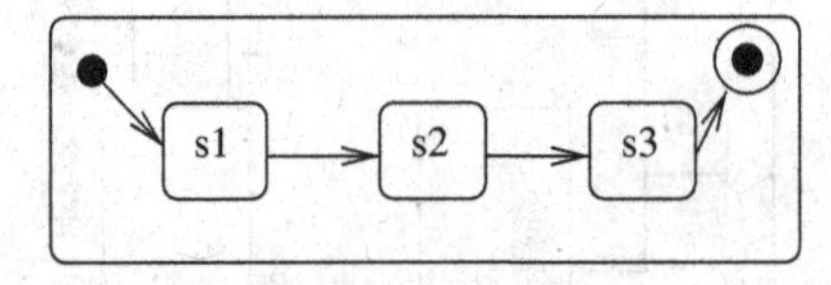

Conditional node representation:

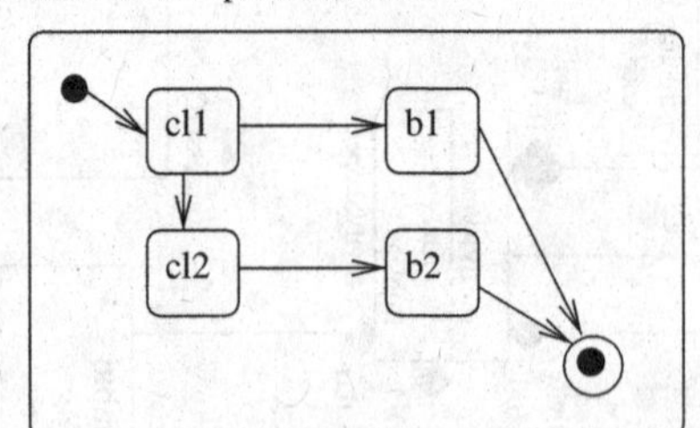

Loop node representation:

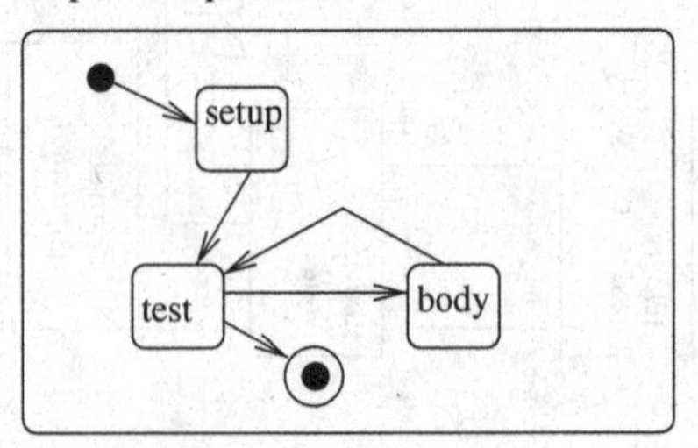

FIGURE 11.2 Mapping of structured activity nodes.

is terminated when all its actions have terminated:

$$\downarrow(A, i) = max\{s \in A.node | max(\{j \in Occ_{A,i}(\alpha_s) | \downarrow(\alpha_s, j)\})\}$$

FlowFinal nodes do not have a semantic representation.

Sequence, conditional, and loop nodes are mapped to corresponding structured semantic actions (Figure 6.4): for example, to $\alpha_{ss1}; \alpha_{ss2}$ for a sequence node with two executable nodes, and to structured actions of the form

$test1;$
$if\ \ result1 \ = \ true$
$then\ \ b1$
$else$
  $test2;$
  $if\ \ result2 \ = \ true$
  $then\ \ b2$

in the case of a conditional node as considered in Figure 11.2; similarly for loop nodes.

11.3 SEMANTICS OF INTERMEDIATE ACTIVITIES

The mappings can be extended to model control flows between activities. In the mapping to state machines these are simply represented as transitions between the corresponding states; however, this only handles cases where fork and join nodes are paired in a structured manner, and similarly for merge and decision nodes. Cases where a single node participates in two separate activity flows (Figure 11.3) cannot be mapped directly to state machines.

Control nodes of the form fork and join are modeled by defining new AND composite states introduced to contain the groups of states that are linked by a fork/join pair in parallel flows: For each separate parallel flow defined by a fork node, a separate region of the new AND state is used to contain the states representing the nodes of the flow (Figure 11.4 shows a complex example). AND states are defined for flows starting from the fork/join pairs of largest scope, and then working inward from these. Decision nodes are mapped to dynamic choice pseudostates, and hence to new basic states. Merge nodes are also mapped to new basic or final states.

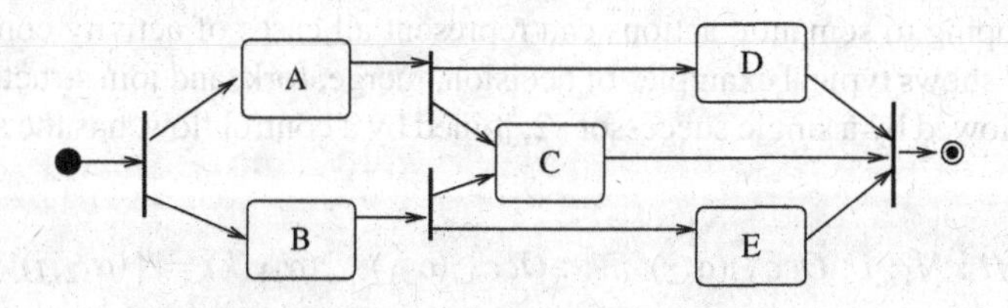

FIGURE 11.3 Unstructured parallel control flows.

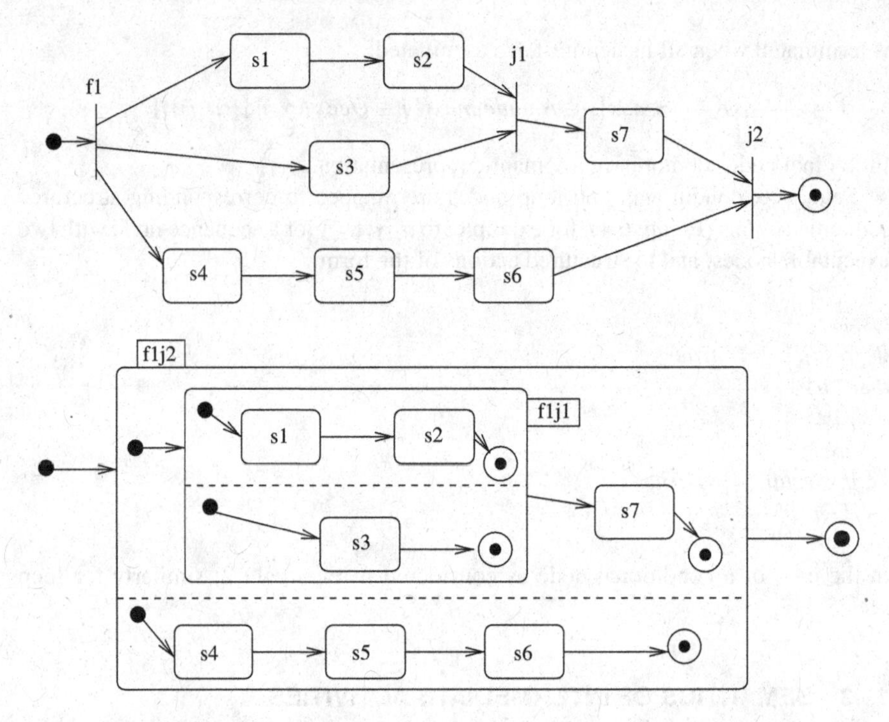

FIGURE 11.4 Representing parallel control flows in a state machine.

In addition, the concept of a *localPrecondition* and *localPostcondition* of an action can be expressed: the *localPostcondition* can be defined as the state invariant of the state representing the action (it must be established by the entry action of the state). *localPrecondition* is expressed as a precondition of the entry action, using the *pre* statement form of Figure 6.4: The precondition must be established by each transition to the state.

As an example of the mapping, Figure 11.5 shows a structured activity diagram with fork and join, decision/merge, and sequence nodes.

A version of the workflow in Figure 11.5, expressed in state machine notation, is shown in Figure 11.6. All the transitions are triggered by completion of the processing of their source state. In the AND composite state, this means that the processing of both regions of this state must be completed (they have both reached their final states) before the transition to *Release Fix* can occur.

The mapping to semantic actions can represent all cases of activity control flow. Figure 11.7 shows typical examples of decision, merge, fork, and join structures. One node $s1$ followed by a single successor $s2$, joined by a control flow, has the semantics

$$\forall i : \mathcal{N}_1; j : Occ_{A,i}(\alpha_{s2}) \cdot \exists k : Occ_{A,i}(\alpha_{s1}) \cdot \downarrow(\alpha_{s1}, k) = \uparrow(\alpha_{s2}, j)$$

$$\forall i : \mathcal{N}_1; j : Occ_{A,i}(\alpha_{s1}) \cdot \exists k : Occ_{A,i}(\alpha_{s2}) \cdot \downarrow(\alpha_{s1}, j) = \uparrow(\alpha_{s2}, k)$$

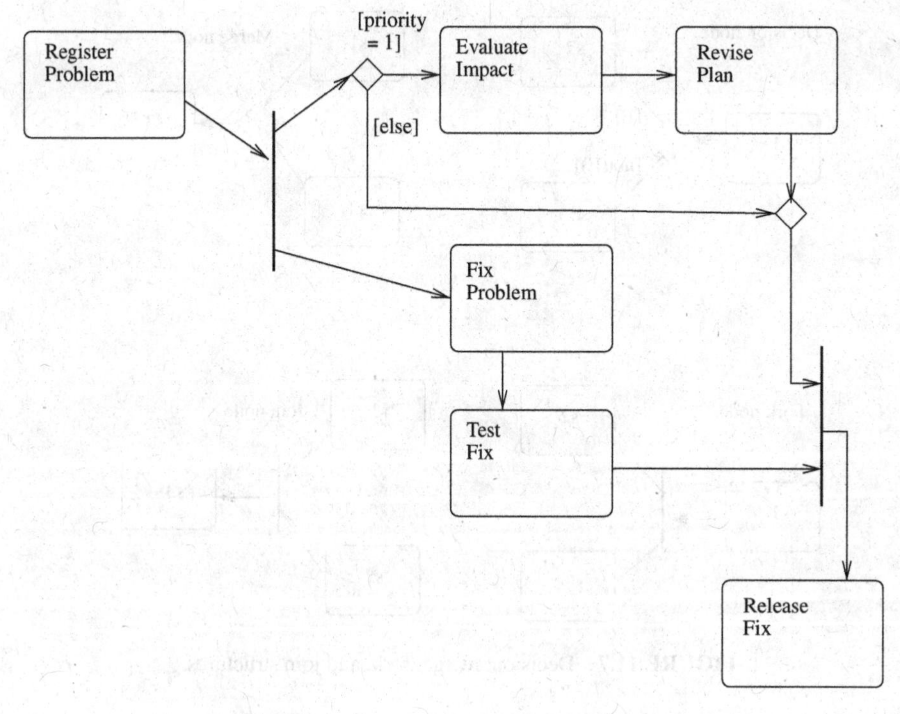

FIGURE 11.5 Handling problem workflow.

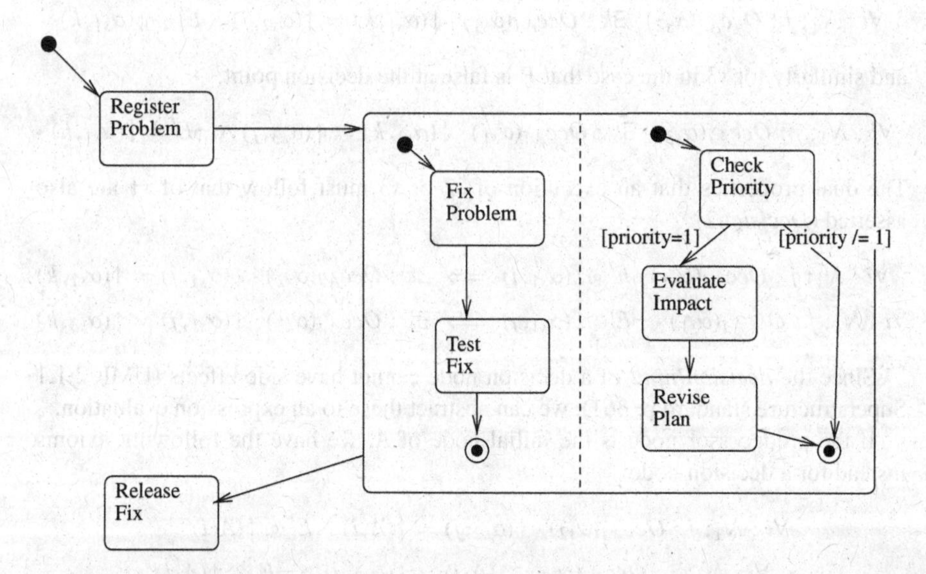

FIGURE 11.6 Handling problem workflow as a state machine.

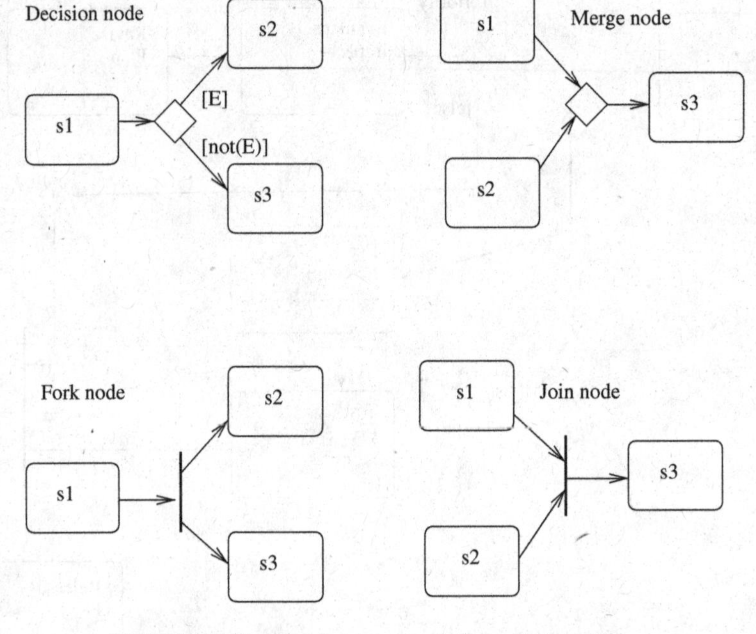

FIGURE 11.7 Decision, merge, fork, and join structures.

A decision node with predecessor (*incoming*) node $s1$ and successors (*outgoing*) nodes $s2$ and $s3$ and condition E has the semantics (*Decision*1)

$$\forall i : \mathcal{N}_1; j : Occ_{A,i}(\alpha_{s2}) \cdot \exists k : Occ_{A,i}(\alpha_{s1}) \cdot \downarrow(\alpha_{s1}, k) = \uparrow(\alpha_{s2}, j) \wedge E' \circledcirc \downarrow(\alpha_{s1}, k)$$

and similarly for $s3$ in the case that E is false at the decision point:

$$\forall i : \mathcal{N}_1; j : Occ_{A,i}(\alpha_{s3}) \cdot \exists k : Occ_{A,i}(\alpha_{s1}) \cdot \downarrow(\alpha_{s1}, k) = \uparrow(\alpha_{s3}, j) \wedge \neg E' \circledcirc \downarrow(\alpha_{s1}, k)$$

The dual properties that an execution of $s2$ or $s3$ must follow that of $s1$ are also asserted (*Decision*2):

$$\forall i : \mathcal{N}_1; j : Occ_{A,i}(\alpha_{s1}) \cdot E' \circledcirc \downarrow(\alpha_{s1}, j) \implies \exists k : Occ_{A,i}(\alpha_{s2}) \cdot \downarrow(\alpha_{s1}, j) = \uparrow(\alpha_{s2}, k)$$
$$\forall i : \mathcal{N}_1; j : Occ_{A,i}(\alpha_{s1}) \cdot \neg E' \circledcirc \downarrow(\alpha_{s1}, j) \implies \exists k : Occ_{A,i}(\alpha_{s3}) \cdot \downarrow(\alpha_{s1}, j) = \uparrow(\alpha_{s3}, k)$$

Since the *decisionInput* of a decision node cannot have side effects (UML 2.1.1 Superstructure standard p. 361), we can abstract these to an expression evaluation.

If the predecessor node is the initial node of A, we have the following axioms instead for a decision node:

$$\forall i : \mathcal{N}_1; j : Occ_{A,i}(\alpha_{s2}) \cdot \uparrow(\alpha_{s2}, j) = \uparrow(A, i) \wedge E' \circledcirc \uparrow(A, i)$$
$$\forall i : \mathcal{N}_1; j : Occ_{A,i}(\alpha_{s3}) \cdot \uparrow(A, i) = \uparrow(\alpha_{s3}, j) \wedge \neg E' \circledcirc \uparrow(A, i)$$

with corresponding dual properties.

A fork node with predecessor $s1$ and successors $s2$ and $s3$ initiates execution of both (*Fork*1)

$$\forall i : \mathcal{N}_1; j : Occ_{A,i}(\alpha_{s2}) \cdot \exists k : Occ_{A,i}(\alpha_{s1}) \cdot \downarrow(\alpha_{s1}, k) = \uparrow(\alpha_{s2}, j)$$

$$\forall i : \mathcal{N}_1; j : Occ_{A,i}(\alpha_{s3}) \cdot \exists k : Occ_{A,i}(\alpha_{s1}) \cdot \downarrow(\alpha_{s1}, k) = \uparrow(\alpha_{s3}, j)$$

Again the dual properties are asserted (*Fork*2):

$$\forall i : \mathcal{N}_1; j : Occ_{A,i}(\alpha_{s1}) \cdot \exists k : Occ_{A,i}(\alpha_{s2}) \cdot \downarrow(\alpha_{s1}, j) = \uparrow(\alpha_{s2}, k)$$
$$\forall i : \mathcal{N}_1; j : Occ_{A,i}(\alpha_{s1}) \cdot \exists k : Occ_{A,i}(\alpha_{s3}) \cdot \downarrow(\alpha_{s1}, j) = \uparrow(\alpha_{s3}, k)$$

If $s1$ is the initial node of A, we have

$$\forall i : \mathcal{N}_1; j : Occ_{A,i}(\alpha_{s2}) \cdot \uparrow(A, i) = \uparrow(\alpha_{s2}, j)$$
$$\forall i : \mathcal{N}_1; j : Occ_{A,i}(\alpha_{s3}) \cdot \uparrow(A, i) = \uparrow(\alpha_{s3}, j)$$

Again the dual properties are asserted.

A merge node with predecessors $s1$ and $s2$ and successor $s3$ launches an execution of $s3$ whenever either $s1$ or $s2$ terminates (*Merge*1):

$$\begin{aligned} &\forall i : \mathcal{N}_1; j : Occ_{A,i}(\alpha_{s3}) \cdot \\ &\exists k : Occ_{A,i}(\alpha_{s1}) \cdot \downarrow(\alpha_{s1}, k) = \uparrow(\alpha_{s3}, j) \vee \\ &\exists k : Occ_{A,i}(\alpha_{s2}) \cdot \downarrow(\alpha_{s2}, k) = \uparrow(\alpha_{s3}, j) \end{aligned}$$

with the dual properties (*Merge*2)

$$\forall i : \mathcal{N}_1; j : Occ_{A,i}(\alpha_{s1}) \cdot \exists k : Occ_{A,i}(\alpha_{s3}) \cdot \downarrow(\alpha_{s1}, j) = \uparrow(\alpha_{s3}, k)$$
$$\forall i : \mathcal{N}_1; j : Occ_{A,i}(\alpha_{s2}) \cdot \exists k : Occ_{A,i}(\alpha_{s3}) \cdot \downarrow(\alpha_{s2}, j) = \uparrow(\alpha_{s3}, k)$$

A join node of this form instead requires that both its predecessors have terminated (*Join*1)

$$\begin{aligned} &\forall i : \mathcal{N}_1; j : Occ_{A,i}(\alpha_{s3}) \cdot \exists k : Occ_{A,i}(\alpha_{s1}); l : Occ_{A,i}(\alpha_{s2}) \\ &\quad \cdot max(\downarrow(\alpha_{s1}, k), \downarrow(\alpha_{s2}, l)) = \uparrow(\alpha_{s3}, j) \end{aligned}$$

and (*Join*2)

$$\begin{aligned} &\forall i : \mathcal{N}_1; j : Occ_{A,i}(\alpha_{s1}); k : Occ_{A,i}(\alpha_{s2}) \cdot \exists l : Occ_{A,i}(\alpha_{s3}) \\ &\quad \cdot max(\downarrow(\alpha_{s1}, j), \downarrow(\alpha_{s2}, k)) = \uparrow(\alpha_{s3}, l) \end{aligned}$$

The number of control tokens at the input to the join from $s1$ is the number of terminations of α_{s1}, less the number of activations of α_{s3}:

$$tokens_{A,i}(s1) = \#fin_{A,i}(\alpha_{s1}) - \#act_{A,i}(\alpha_{s3})$$

where $\#act_{A,i}(\alpha)$ only counts event occurrences from $Occ_{A,i}(\alpha)$, and similarly for $\#fin$.

The default semantics of the join in UML superstructure 2.1.1 [4] requires that there are control tokens at both inputs to the join before the successor action can activate (*Join*3):

$$\forall i : \mathcal{N}_1; j : Occ_{A,i}(\alpha_{s3}) \cdot (tokens_{A,i}(s1) > 0 \wedge tokens_{A,i}(s2) > 0) \circledcirc \uparrow(\alpha_{s3}, j)$$

Additional or alternative join conditions [4, pp. 382–384] can also be represented. For example, if instead, repeated occurrences of a control token at one input should be merged, we could define

$$\begin{aligned} mtokens_{A,i}(s1) &= card(\{j : Occ_{A,i}(\alpha_{s1}) | \downarrow(\alpha_s, j) < now \wedge \\ &\neg\exists k : Occ_{A,i}(\alpha_{s3}) \cdot \downarrow(\alpha_{s1}, j) \leq \uparrow(\alpha_{s3}, k) < now\}) \end{aligned}$$

and use this in place of *tokens* in the axiom above.

11.4 DATA FLOW SEMANTICS

The main extension of activity diagrams over state machines is the possibility of data flow between actions, whereby data (typically, objects) are queued at the inputs of actions and consumed when the action is enabled to execute. The action may produce data outputs for use by other actions. Data flow can be modeled by the use of explicit variables holding collections of data items (tokens). Each object node (data store) in the activity diagram is also represented by an explicit variable holding the set of tokens at that node. A weight on an object flow from an object node to an action indicates how many instances are required to be present at the object node before the action can activate: The action will then consume these instances.

Figure 11.8 shows how an activity node s that waits for a condition G to become true is expressed as a state machine. In the mapping to semantic actions, it is instead modeled by the requirement

$$\forall i : \mathcal{N}_1; j : Occ_{A,i}(\alpha_s) \cdot G' \circledcirc \uparrow(\alpha_s, j)$$

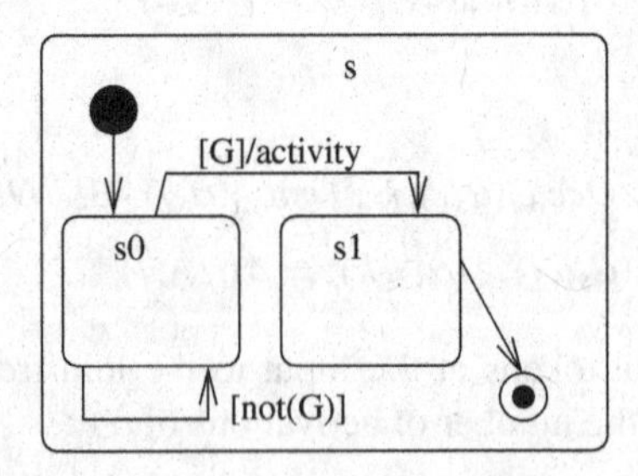

FIGURE 11.8 Activity waiting for a condition.

11.5 SEMANTIC ANALYSIS

The semantics can be used to analyze properties of the activity diagram—in particular:

- If an activity node is unreachable from the initial node.
- If the postcondition of one activity contradicts the precondition of an immediately following activity.
- If the branch conditions of a decision node are consistent and complete.

These map via the translation to corresponding state machine properties and so can be verified using state machine tools. In addition, tools for animation of state machines could be used to animate the activity diagram via the translation. Similarly, proof tools for RTL can be used to analyze the interpretation of activities as semantic actions.

Activity extension is referred to in UML superstructure 2.1.1 [4, Chap. 12] but is not defined. A concept of activity diagram refinement could be derived from refinement of the corresponding state machines. For example, replacing an action executable node by a structured activity. This corresponds to decomposition of a basic state into a composite state, which is a refinement [4, p. 563]. Similarly, adding a new parallel stream of activity nodes to an activity corresponds to a state machine refinement, adding a new orthogonal region to an AND state. Refinement can also be defined using theory extension of the corresponding theories of the activities, using the second semantics.

For example, we can show that a merge node can be replaced by explicit duplication of its successor node as a refinement transformation (Figure 11.9). The theory interpretation ζ is that α_{s3} is interpreted by the choice $\alpha_{s4}[]\alpha_{s5}$. α_{s4} and α_{s5} are defined to call the same actions as α_{s3}.

$\zeta(Merge1)$ holds in the new model since every execution of $\zeta(\alpha_{s3})$ is either one of α_{s4} and is preceded by an execution of α_{s1}, or is one of α_{s5} and is preceded by one of α_{s2}. $\zeta(Merge2)$ holds in the new model since every execution of α_{s1} is followed by one of α_{s4} and hence by one of $\zeta(\alpha_{s3})$, and every execution of α_{s2} is followed by one of α_{s5} and hence by one of $\zeta(\alpha_{s3})$.

We can also use reasoning using the compactness principle (Chapter 6) to show that if an occurrence of an activity produces an unbounded set of action occurrences, it cannot terminate (e.g., Figure 11.10).

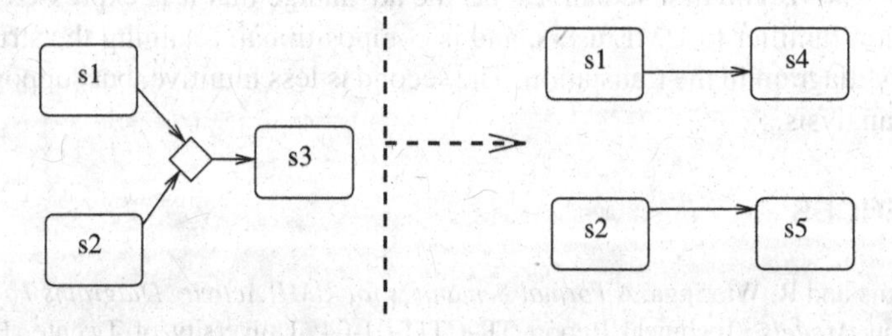

FIGURE 11.9 Remove merge node.

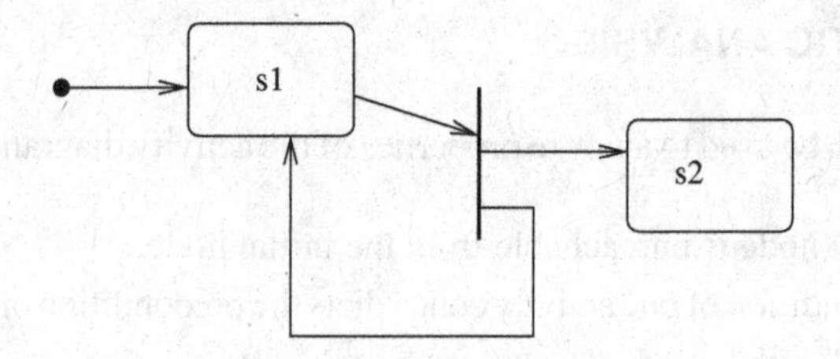

FIGURE 11.10 Unbounded activity.

The addition of invariants to all activities (*local Postcondition* acts as such an invariant for actions) would enable reasoning about the effect and correctness of activities. Such invariants can be expressed as state invariants in translation of the activity diagram to a state machine.

11.6 RELATED WORK

UML 2 activities have similarities to Petri nets, so it appears natural to provide them with a semantics in terms of this formalism, as is done by Storrle and Hausmann [5]. However, other notations of UML cannot easily be related to Petri nets, so restricting the scope for analysis. Petri nets have also been considered inappropriate for modeling activities for workflows because of their lack of capability for reactiveness [1]. Other formalisms, such as the π-calculus, have also been used for activity diagram semantics [2]. These are more complex than activity diagrams, and we consider it more appropriate and useful to express activities in terms of simpler constructs within the UML itself, taking advantage of the considerable overlap between the concepts of activities and state machines.

A semantics in terms of semantic actions allows the semantics of activities to be related to that of class diagrams (Chapter 6), state machines (Chapter 8), and sequence diagrams [3].

11.7 SUMMARY

In this chapter we have shown how a large subset of the UML 2 activity diagram notation can be expressed in terms of state machines and semantic actions, and hence can be provided with a semantics by means of the axiomatic semantics defined in Chapters 4 and 6. The first semantics has the advantage that it is expressed in terms of a notation familier to UML users, and is compositional, retaining the structure of the activity diagram in the translation. The second is less intuitive, but supports direct semantic analysis.

REFERENCES

1. R. Eshuis and R. Wieringa, *A Formal Semantics for UML Activity Diagrams Formalising Workflow Models*. Technical Report TR-CTIT-01-04. University of Twente, Enschede, The Netherlands, 2001.

2. J. Kuster, J. Koehler, J. Novatnack, and K. Ryndina. *A Classification of UML 2 Activity Diagrams*. Technical Report 3673. IBM ZRL, 2006.
3. K. Lano. Formal specification using interaction diagrams. In *SEFM'07 Proceedings*, 2007.
4. OMG. *UML Superstructure Version 2.1.1*. OMG Document Formal/2007-02-03. Object Management Group, Needham, MA, 2007.
5. H. Storrle and J. Hausmann. Towards a formal semantics of UML 2.0 activities. In *Software Engineering*. LNI, vol. 64, ACTA Press, Innsbruck, Austria, 2005.

CHAPTER 12

VERIFICATION OF UML MODELS

KEVIN LANO
Department of Computer Science, King's College London, London, UK

12.1 INTRODUCTION

In this chapter we describe conditions for the completeness and consistency of UML models, both with respect to individual models and between several models of the same system.

The correctness of a UML model generally concerns four types of properties:

1. *Consistency*. A model is inconsistent if there are contradictions present in the model, which mean that no situation can ever satisfy it. In UML it is necessary to consider both the consistency of an individual model (such as a class diagram) and the consistency of this model when compared with other models that describe other aspects of the same system (e.g., state machine models).
2. *Completeness*. A model is incomplete if there are missing elements of the system, such as cases of behavior or missing subclasses, which should be present to give an adequate specification.
3. *Validation*. Validation checks that the model formalizes the requirements correctly.
4. *Quality*. The model must satisfy certain quality criteria, which will make it more amenable to refinement, analysis, and adaption [10].

A wide range of techniques can be used to perform these checks, such as:

- Inspection (structured examination) of the model by one or more reviewer(s), who should not have been involved in the creation of the model.
- Translation of the model to the notation of a *proof tool* [76], which will support the proving of theorems about the model.

UML 2 Semantics and Applications. Edited by Kevin Lano

- *Animation* of the model, to examine how situations can be constructed that satisfy the model and how these evolve as determined by the model [26]. Animation corresponds to testing, at the specification level, and can include symbolic execution of the specification.
- Translation to the notation of a *model checker* tool [2], which allows an automated exploration of a large number of sequences of behavior of the model, as a form of automated animation.

Proof can be used to identify incompleteness or inconsistency in a model: For example, all operations of a class should preserve the invariant constraints of the class, and an initialization operation should establish these constraints. If the proof of these conditions fails, it identifies possible inconsistency between operation postconditions and the class invariants, or incompleteness in the specification of the operations (e.g., that some cases of behavior have been omitted). Proof can also be used to check that validation properties (formalized conditions which are expected to hold for the system) are true.

Animation may also reveal inconsistency and incompleteness, as different test scenarios for the system are "executed" using its specification. Some animation tools can show the value (true or false) of each invariant in each state, so identifying inconsistencies. The main use of animation is in validation, showing that the behavior of the system is as intended in each test case scenario.

Model checking is used primarily to validate that certain required properties hold in a model. If the properties do not hold, counterexample traces of the history of the system are generated, which identify how the property can be violated.

12.2 CLASS DIAGRAMS

The following are common errors in defining class diagrams:

- Misuse of the notation (e.g., confusing the notations for attributes and operations)
- Incorrect modeling choices, such as using inheritance incorrectly to model a situation that should be modeled by an association, or viceversa
- Unnecessary duplication, such as defining the same attributes in both a class and its subclasses, or defining a feature of a class as both an association end owned by the class and as an attribute of the class
- Incompleteness, such as defining an abstract class that has no concrete subclass: Such a class will not be able to be used in a program
- Inconsistency in modeling, such as defining a *setatt* operation for a frozen attribute *att*
- Semantic inconsistency, such as defining a postcondition of an operation that is inconsistent with the invariant of the class

At the design level there are errors of modeling that affect the quality of the design, rather than its correctness, and so may make implementation, testing, or maintenance unduly expensive or error-prone [10]; for example:

- Circular dependency between classes
- Abstract class inheriting from concrete class
- Parent class accessing features of a child class
- Operations with excessive numbers of parameters
- Concrete base class of an inheritance tree

12.2.1 Syntactic Correctness of Class Diagrams

The incorrect use of class diagram notations can be detected by tools that enforce the UML metamodels, preventing the creation of incorrect models.

Some checks that should be made include the following:

- Two different classes must have different names within the same namespace.
- Two different enumerated types should not have same-named elements, and the values within a single enumerated type should be distinct.
- If an attribute is declared in a class, it should not be declared in any subclass (it is inherited and does not need to be redeclared).
- No cycles are possible in the inheritance relationship.
- If an operation is declared in both a class and a subclass of the class, these declarations should be consistent: with the same input and output types, and the postcondition of the subclass version should imply the postcondition of the superclass version.
- If an association end is defined for both a superclass and a subclass, the multiplicity restrictions on the subclass version cannot be less restrictive than on the superclass version. The opposite association end for the subclass version must be attached to the same class as for the superclass version, or to a subclass of it (i.e., the type of the role at that end cannot be enlarged in the subclass). If a role is ordered for the superclass, it should also be ordered for the subclass, and viceversa.
- A class containing an abstract operation must itself be abstract.
- An interface cannot inherit from a class.
- An abstract class must have a concrete subclass (direct or indirect).
- Expressions in constraints should be type correct (e.g., if an operation is defined to have an *Integer* result, a postcondition $result = 2.5$ is an error).

Many of these errors can be detected automatically by a diagram-editor tool and users warned whenever they try to save a model containing such flaws.

Incorrect choice of modeling elements can be detected by carrying out reviews of the models by other developers and by comparison with the system requirements.

12.2.2 Semantic Correctness of Class Diagrams

The semantic correctness of a class consists of the following conditions:

1. There is some possible object of the class; that is, it is possible to give values to its structural (data) features which satisfy the typing constraints of these features and all constraints in the model that depend on these features, in particular the class invariants. The invariants of superclasses of the class are also considered to apply to the class itself (Chapter 6), so these must be logically consistent with its own constraints.
2. Any initial or default values assigned to the data features of the class must satisfy all the applicable constraints (considered in condition 1).
3. The constraints themselves must be well defined. Any conditions necessary for the valid execution of an operation should be specified in its precondition.
4. The precondition and postcondition of each operation must be consistent with the class invariant.
5. If an explicit code definition $Code_{op}$ is given for an operation *op*, this must satisfy the pre- and postspecifications of the operation.

Semantic inconsistency violating the first condition can arise if two conflicting requirements are formalized without their inconsistency being recognized; in this case the requirements must be amended. For example, the model of Figure 12.1 is inconsistent: It is impossible to instantiate the class *A* with even a single element *ax* because then (via associations *A_B* and *B_C*) there must be 15 elements of *C* attached to this *A* instance, but this violates the property that there are exactly 10 times as many *C* instances as *A* instances, because of the *A_C* association.

Violation of the third condition can result if insufficient preconditions are given for an operation; for example,

```
density(m: Real, vol: Real): Real
post: result = m/vol
```

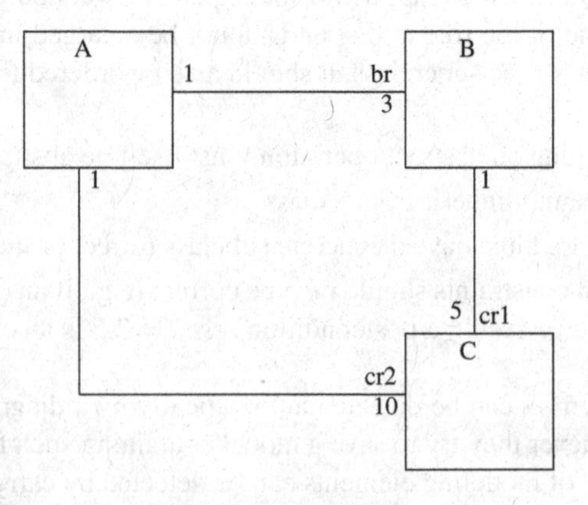

FIGURE 12.1 Inconsistent model.

is ill defined when $vol = 0$. The operation should be corrected to

```
density(m: Real, vol: Real): Real
pre: vol > 0
post: result = m/vol
```

We can formalise the consistency conditions by using the notion of weakest precondition of an update behavior. The notation $[Code]P$ means that the operation or program statements *Code* always establish the predicate P. *Code* can be a statement using the syntax described by the metamodel of Figure 6.4 or some other behavior specification language. $[Code]P$ is called the "weakest precondition" of *Code* with respect to P. The formula $R \implies [Code]P$ means that if R is true when *Code* starts to execute, P will be true when *Code* terminates.

The consistency rules of a class can be expressed precisely using this concept, as follows:

1. The class invariant must be satisfiable; that is, there must exist at least one combination of attribute/role values of C in which Inv_C is true:

$$\exists v_1 : T_1; \ldots; v_n : T_n; rv_1 : DT_1; \ldots; rv_m : DT_m \cdot Inv_C[v/att, rv/role]$$

   where the $att_i : T_i$ are the attributes (including inherited attributes) of C and the $role_j : DT_j$ represent the roles of C and its ancestors. This also confirms that the explicit invariant of C is consistent with superclass invariants, because these are all conjoined to form the complete class invariant of C.
2. The initialization of a class always establishes the invariant:

$$[init_C]Inv_C$$

   where $init_C$ is the code defining the constructor of C.
3. Definedness obligations: The invariant of a class should always be well defined (not contain applications of functions to elements outside their domain, such as division by zero), and the precondition of an operation should ensure that the postcondition or code definition of this operation is well defined.
4. The precondition and postcondition of each operation must be consistent with the class invariant.
5. If an explicit code definition $Code_{op}$ is given for an operation op, this must satisfy the pre- and postspecification of the operation

$$Inv_C \wedge Pre_{op} \implies [Code_{op}]Post_{op}$$

Incompleteness can arise if the data of a class or the effect of an operation omit cases that are required. For example, in the lift system (Chapter 2) the class invariants of *Lift* are incomplete, since they only determine the value of *lm*, the lift motor, in one case (the motor is always off if the doors are not closed):

$$door.dcs = false \;\; implies \;\; lm = stop$$

Further analysis of the system identifies constraints that determine when the motor should be set to *up* or *down*:

$$dest > fps \; and \; door.dcs = true \;\; implies \;\; lm = up$$
$$dest < fps \; and \; door.dcs = true \;\; implies \;\; lm = down$$

However, there is still incompleteness since the disjunction of the antecedents of these rules is

$$(dest > fps \; or \; dest < fps) \; and \; door.dcs = true \; or \; door.dcs = false$$

and the negation of this is

$$dest = fps \; and \; door.dcs = true$$

which is a possible state to which the system should respond. Therefore, we need an additional rule with this condition as its antecedent:

$$dest = fps \; and \; door.dcs = true \;\; implies \;\; lm = stop$$

The following two principles can be defined to detect if a set of constraints are complete:

1. For each attribute *att* that represents an output of the system (such as an actuator in a reactive control system), some constraint should define its value. *att* will occur on the succedent of such constraints and normally not in the antecedent.
2. The collection of constraints that define the value of *att* should cover all possible conditions that could arise in the system: The disjunction of the antecedents of the constraints defining *att* should be *true* or should be provable from other constraints of the system. In particular, each possible combination of input values (such as sensor attributes) should be considered.

The *Door* class invariant is also incomplete, as no constraint defines when the door motor should be opening or closing. Similarly, constraints are needed to set the lights, for example,

$$lightsets{\rightarrow}forAll(lights{\rightarrow}at(fps).lit = true)$$

Other data incompleteness in this example concerns the size of *lightsets* and the possible range of values of *fps* and *dest*.

Another form of incompleteness is *underspecification* of operations. For example, an operation to add a new student to a course could be specified as

```
addStudent(s: Student)
post:  courselist->includes(s.name)
```

where *courselist* is the list of names of students on the course. The operation does require that the name of the student be placed in the courselist, but the operation permits *courselist* to change in any other way, even to remove all other student names from the list.

A more explicit and complete specification would be

```
addStudent(s: Student)
post:   courselist = courselist@pre->append(s.name)
```

A check on the completeness of an operation is that

$$(Pre_{op} \wedge Inv_C)@pre \wedge Post_{op} \implies Inv_C$$

"If the operation precondition and class invariant hold at the start of the operation, and its postcondition holds at the operation termination, the class invariant should also hold."

For example, if an operation is defined to have postcondition $x > x@pre$, and the class invariant is $x > 0$, the completeness check is

$$(x > 0)@pre \wedge x > x@pre \implies x > 0$$

which is clearly true.

However, if the postcondition was, instead,

$$x = x@pre + y$$

where y is a numeric input parameter of the operation, we would also need a precondition $y \geq 0$ to guarantee the invariant after the operation.

In many cases a complete definition of an operation can be generated automatically from an incomplete definition by using the class invariants. This permits us to use simple but incomplete definitions of operations initially (e.g., in a CIM), and then to include the full definition when a PIM is produced.

If the CIM postcondition of an operation has the form

$$(E_1 \; implies \; att_1 = v_1 \; and \; ... \; and \; att_m = v_m) \; and \; ... \; and$$
$$(E_k \; implies \; att_1 = v_{(k-1)m+1} \; and \; ... \; and \; att_m = v_{km})$$

where the att_i are some (not all) of the attributes of the class, and an invariant of the class is *A implies B*, where *A* or *B* contain some of these attributes, an additional postcondition

$$E_j \; and \; A[v_{(j-1)m+1}/att_1, ..., v_{jm}/att_m] \; implies \; B[v_{(j-1)m+1}/att_1, ..., v_{jm}/att_m]$$

should be added to the original postcondition, for $j = 1, ..., k$.

This process of adding extra postconditions to make an operation complete may also identify cases of inconsistency between the effect of the operation and the class invariants; in this case, additional preconditions may be needed to prevent the operation from being invoked in situations that could produce inconsistency.

Particular care is required when associations are modified from one end, because the other end of the association will usually also need to be modified to maintain the inverse relationship between the ends and any multiplicity constraints on the ends.

For example, if there is a 1-* association between classes *A* and *B*, with roles *ar* at the *A* end and *br* at the *B* end, a postcondition

```
removebr(ax: A, bx: B)
pre: bx : ax.br
post:  ax.br = (ax.br)@pre->excluding(bx)
```

contradicts that *bx.ar* must always be an element of *A* (since *bx* has been removed from *ax.br*, *bx.ar* cannot be *ax*): the postcondition must be extended either to delete *bx* from *B*, or to assign a new *A* value to *bx.ar*.

Similarly, if there is a composition aggregation from a class *W* to a class *P*, deletion of an element of *W* will also require deletion of its attached *P* objects.

12.2.3 Verification Techniques

Verification of class diagrams can be carried out by translating the model into the notation of a formal analysis tool and carrying out proof, animation, or other analysis using this tool. The B language has been used for class diagram analysis [38,76] because its semantic base is consistent with many concepts of UML, and its tool support is among the best available for any formal method. However, the structural mismatch between the object-based structuring of B and the object-oriented structure of UML means that analysis of global properties of large modules may be infeasible by this technique. It is most useful for demonstrating local consistency of individual classes and detecting incompleteness of operations (inadequate preconditions or postconditions).

The use of a translation to a different language requires that the translation preserves the semantic meaning of the UML model in the new language, and that (ideally) the analysis results obtained are reexpressed in terms of the UML model. Provided that the translation is semantically *sound*, that is,

$$M1 \vdash_{UML} \psi \implies M2 \vdash_{F} \zeta(\psi)$$

for each ψ, where $M1$ is the original UML model, $M2$ its translation in the new formalism F, and ζ the interpretation of UML constraints in F, then contradictions in the starting model will give rise to contradictions in the translation:

$$M1 \vdash_{UML} P \; and \; not(P)$$

means that also

$$M2 \vdash_{F} \zeta(P \; and \; not(P))$$

and ζ will respect logical operators, so the consequent formula also has the form of a contradiction. This implies that inconsistencies in $M1$ can in principle be detected by analysis in $M2$, and that proof of consistency in $M2$ ensures that of $M1$.

General-purpose theorem provers such as SPASS [75] or PVS can be used to analyze UML models using such a translation, as in Chapter 5.

Analysis tools for UML that operate on the models without translation are also available. The USE (UML-based specification environment) tool provides [26] type checking, syntax checking, animation, and theorem-proving capabilities for OCL constraints, relative to a given class diagram model. The KeY system [1] also provides checks on the consistency of constraints and checks that constraints hold in a proposed implementation. The UML2Web tools [47] generate Java implementations from OCL constraints, and these implementations are correct by construction relative to the constraints.

12.3 STATE MACHINE DIAGRAMS

Common errors in the definition of state machines include:

- Unreachable states within a state machine model—states for which there is no possible path of transitions from the initial state to the state, so it can never be occupied. This may arise because of mistakes made in defining guard conditions or the direction of transitions.
- Failure to define a unique initial state for a state machine, or for composite states/regions.
- Invalid use of transitions: for example, direct transitions from one region of a composite state to another (Figure 12.2).
- Unstructured control flow in behavior state machines for operations, such as loop structures with multiple entry and exit points.
- State invariants that contradict the guards of transitions exiting the state, so that these transitions can never be enabled.
- State invariants that contradict the postconditions of transitions entering the state.
- State invariants that contradict an invariant of a superstate of the state, meaning that it can never be occupied.

Because of the complexity of state machine semantics, it is more difficult to detect such errors for state machine models by manual inspection, and some automated analysis, such as model checking, may be necessary.

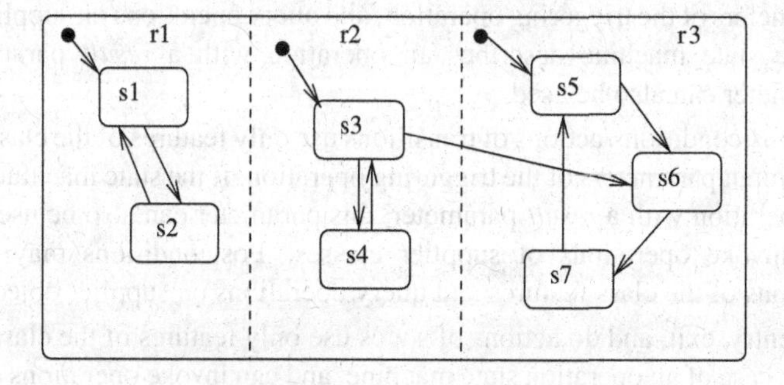

FIGURE 12.2 Invalid transition.

The use of constructs such as history states and event deferral, which have complex semantics, should be limited as far as possible, in order to improve the analyzability of a model. In addition, situations where the behavior of a model depends on the order of execution of actions on the initial transitions of different regions of an AND composite state should be avoided, since UML does not specify the order in which these should be executed; similarly for exit behavior of an AND state.

12.3.1 Syntactic Correctness of State Machines

Syntactic correctness conditions on state machines include:

- The states within a state machine model should have distinct names.
- If a transition has multiple sources, these must be in different regions of an AND state: They cannot be in the same region/OR state; similarly for multiple targets of a transition.
- States cannot overlap, except for a state and its substates, which must be entirely contained within it.
- States should always be named, and have distinct names within each composite state and at the top level of a state machine.
- OR states/regions must have an initial state.
- Transitions in protocol state machines and behavior state machines for objects should have triggers, which are either timeout triggers or update operations of the object.
- Transitions in behavior state machines for operations can have completion (implicit) triggers or timeout triggers.

Syntactic consistency of a state machine with respect to a class diagram means that:

1. All operations appearing as triggers on the transitions of a state machine for a class *C* are update operations of that class (or of an ancestor of the class), and have the same parameters and parameter types in both diagrams.
2. The guards of transitions use only features of the class, together with input parameters of the triggering operation, and query operations on supplier objects. If the state machine describes an operation with a *result* parameter, this parameter can also be used.
3. The postconditions/actions of transitions use only features of the class, together with input parameters of the triggering operation. If the state machine describes an operation with a *result* parameter, this parameter can also be used. Actions can invoke operations of supplier classes. Postconditions may use *@pre* versions of the class features and query operations on supplier objects.
4. The entry, exit, and do actions of states use only features of the class, or *result* in the case of an operation state machine, and can invoke operations of supplier classes.

All syntactic conditions can be checked and enforced by diagram editors for state machines.

12.3.2 Semantic Correctness of State Machines

Semantic correctness conditions for state machines include internal consistency, completeness, and consistency with other UML models of the same system, especially class diagrams.

The following conditions should be satisfied:

- *Consistency*. Two transitions with the same source state and trigger event should have nonoverlapping guards; it should not be possible for the guards to be true at the same time.
- *Completeness*. The disjunction of the guards of the transitions leaving one state, triggered by the same event, should be implied by the source state invariant.
- The invariant of an (abstract) OR state/region must be consistent with the disjunction of the invariants of its direct substates. The invariant of an AND state must be consistent with the conjunction of the invariants of its regions.

There may be internal inconsistency in state machine diagrams due to conflicting transitions: When two transitions with the same source state are both enabled to occur at the same time, so that contradictory behaviors are defined.

Incompleteness may arise because of missing transitions if the adopted semantics for a state machine is that missing cases of behavior indicate undefined behavior in that case. Even if missing cases are taken to mean that an implicit skip (no state change) occurs, the situation should be checked to ensure that this behavior is what was intended.

A state machine may also be inconsistent with a class diagram, for example, the invariant of a state may be inconsistent with the class invariant of the class that owns the state machine.

Figure 12.3 shows an example of internal inconsistency: If $x = y$ and the state is s, both transitions for *op* are enabled, and the result state cannot be determined.

Figure 12.4 shows an example of incompleteness: If $x = y$ and the state is s, no transition for *op* is enabled, and its behavior in this case is not defined (the situation is the same as a missing precondition, for protocol state machines), or is an implicit skip (no state change).

An example of inconsistency between a class invariant and an operation postcondition expressed by a state machine is when a class C has an invariant

$$br \rightarrow size() \leq n$$

limiting the size of a role *br*, but an operation $op(x)$ has an unguarded transition with postcondition $br = br@pre \rightarrow including(x)$. This can contradict the invariant if $br@pre \rightarrow size()$ is n and x is not already in this set.

To avoid this conflict, a guard $br \rightarrow size() < n$ should be added to the transition.

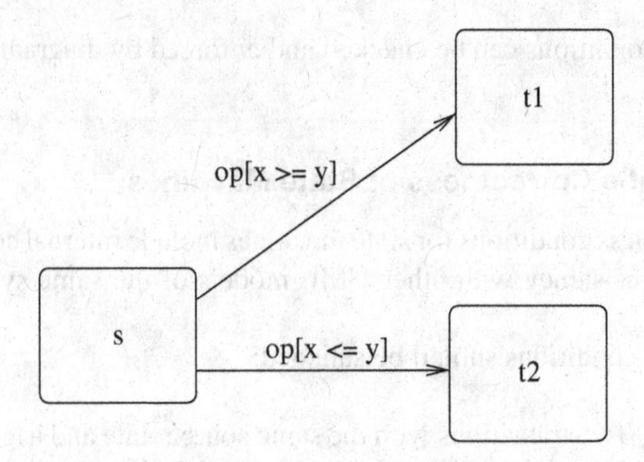

FIGURE 12.3 Inconsistent state machine.

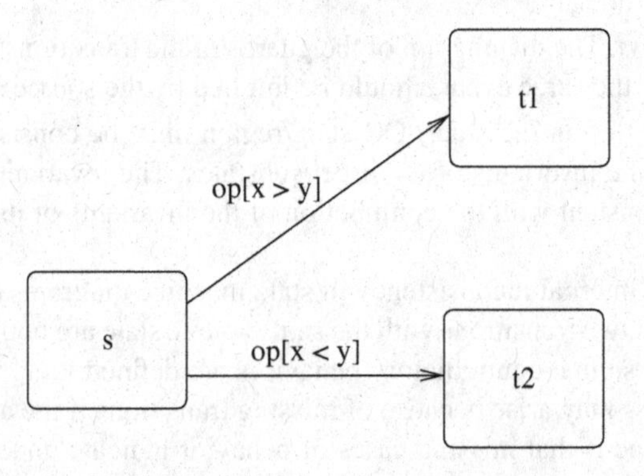

FIGURE 12.4 Incomplete state machine.

The correctness conditions for state machines can be expressed precisely as follows:

1. The consistency requirement for a state machine for a class C is that there cannot be two different transitions from the same state triggered by the same operation whose guards are both true at the same time:

$$c\_state = s \wedge G_1 \implies \neg G_2$$

for the guards G_1 and G_2 of any two transitions for the same operation $op(x : X)$ from state s. More generally, $enc(tr1)$ and $enc(tr2)$ for two transitions triggered by the same event can both be true only if the main source of $tr1$ is in an orthogonal region to the main source of $tr2$.

2. The state machine is *complete* if for any operation *op* which has at least one transition in the state machine, for each state s from which there is a transition for *op*, the disjunction of the guards on the transitions for *op* from s is equivalent to *true* (or to the invariant of the source state s, if there is one):

$$Inv_s \implies (G_1 \vee \cdots \vee G_m)$$

This makes the behavior of *op* completely explicit in all cases, with no difference between the three alternative state machine semantics, since there are no cases of undefined behavior/implicit skips/implicit blocking.

3. There should exist possible data values that satisfy both the invariant of an OR state/region r and the invariants of its direct substates $s1$, ..., sn:

$$\exists v : T \cdot Inv_r \wedge (Inv_{s1} \vee \cdots \vee Inv_{sn})$$

Similarly for an AND state s and its regions $r1$, ..., rm:

$$\exists v : T \cdot Inv_s \wedge (Inv_{r1} \wedge \cdots \wedge Inv_{rm})$$

4. If an explicit algorithm is provided for an operation *op* by a behavior state machine, this algorithm $Code_{op}$ must satisfy the pre- and postconstraints given for the operation:

$$Pre_{op} \implies [Code_{op}]Post_{op}$$

The initial state should usually satisfy Pre_{op} and the final states should satisfy $Post_{op}$. If $Code_{op}$ includes calls of other operations, the preconditions of these operations should be true at the point of call.

5. The actions of each state machine transition should establish the invariant of the target state, if any:

$$Inv_s \wedge G \implies [op(x); exit_s; acts; entry_t]Inv_t$$

for a transition $s \rightarrow_{op(x)[G]/acts} t$ of a behavior state machine for an object. For protocol state machines, the postcondition of a transition should be consistent with the invariant of its target state.

6. The do-action of a state should preserve its invariant:

$$Inv_s \implies [do_s]Inv_s$$

The same is true for any internal transitions of the state.

12.3.3 Algorithm Correctness

Reasoning using weakest preconditions ([ ]) can also be used to prove the correctness of algorithms defined in a behavior state machine for an operation. For example, considering the algorithm of Figure 12.5 for computing the quotient and remainder of one positive integer y when divided by another x, we have:

1. The initialization establishes the loop invariant:

$$[q := 0; r := y](y = q * x + r \wedge r \geq 0)$$

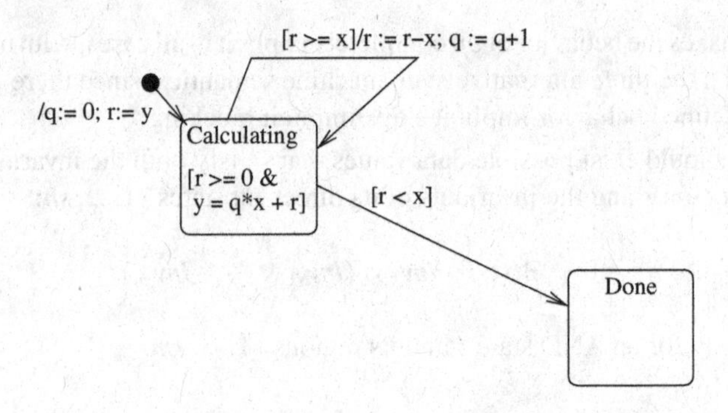

FIGURE 12.5 Specification of a quotient remainder loop.

2. The loop invariant is maintained by the self-transition on the loop state:

$$(y = q * x + r \land r \geq 0) \land r \geq x \implies [r := r - x; q := q + 1]$$
$$(y = q * x + r \land r \geq 0)$$

   The conclusion holds because the new value of r is $r - x$, which is nonnegative due to the guard $r \geq x$.

3. When the final state is reached, the postcondition of the operation is true:

$$r < x \land y = q * x + r \land r \geq 0$$

   defining q and r as the quotient and remainder.

The attribute q holds the value of the quotient, and r the remainder. At termination of the loop $r < x$ holds, so together with the loop invariant, we know that q and r are the correct quotient and remainder. For example, if y is 33 and x is 4, the final value of q is 8 and of r is 1.

In general, we can use induction over a behavior state machine to establish that a property holds in each state. If a state machine has states s_1, ..., s_n, and these have proposed invariants Inv_1, ..., Inv_n, these invariants are valid if:

1. For each initial transition $\rightarrow_{[G]/acts}\ s_k$ to an initial state s_k,

$$G \implies [acts; entry_{s_k}]Inv_k$$

2. For any transition $s_i \rightarrow_{op(x)[G]/acts}\ s_j$,

$$Inv_i \land G \implies [op(x); exit_{s_i}; acts; entry_{s_j}]Inv_j$$

3. For any transition $s_i \rightarrow_{[G]/acts}\ s_j$,

$$Inv_i \land G \implies [exit_{s_i}; acts; entry_{s_j}]Inv_j$$

4. For do actions of a state s_k,

$$Inv_k \implies [do_{s_k}]Inv_k$$

Similarly for internal transitions of the state.

In Figure 12.5 we can therefore deduce that

$$r \geq 0 \wedge y = q * x + r \wedge r < x$$

is an invariant of *Done*.

Having established that the Inv_j are valid in their states, we can deduce that any property I that is implied by all of these invariants is true in every state:

$$Inv_1 \vee \cdots \vee Inv_n \implies I$$

Termination of a loop in an algorithm can be proved by identifying a loop variant, a nonnegative integer quantity which always decreases when any path from the loop state to itself is taken. For example, in Figure 12.5, the quantity r is such a value. It decreases each time the self-transition is taken, which means that this transition can be taken only a finite number of times (as r is never increased by any transition), and therefore the algorithm must terminate.

12.3.4 Verification Techniques

Many tools exist for state machine definition and syntactic analysis. Verification of semantic properties can be carried out by translation to a notation such as B [38] or Petri nets [69] for which animation and proof tools exist. Established commercial tools exist for the classical statechart notation and the Rhapsody object-oriented version of statecharts. However, the syntax and semantics of these notations differ significantly from that of UML state machines, which limits the usefulness of such tools [14].

Automated model checking can be achieved by translating UML state machines to the notations of tools such as SPIN [22] or SMV [2]. One disadvantage of model checking is that the state space of the system must be finite. An alternative is symbolic execution or interactive theorem proving [7].

A novel verification technique for state machines is state machine slicing [11,35]. This adapts the concepts of program slicing to state machines, in order to simplify the state machines, removing all elements that do not contribute to the value of selected data items at a particular state. So far the technique applies only to state machines without composite states.

12.4 SEQUENCE DIAGRAMS

Syntactic correctness conditions for sequence diagrams include:

- The endpoint of a message must be at the same or lower vertical level as its source.

- Lifelines must have distinct names within a single sequence diagram.
- Conditions P attached to a lifeline must be evaluable on the object cx of the lifeline (i.e., $cx.P$ is well defined); similarly for conditions on messages with cx as their starting point (parameters of the operation of the message can also be used in the message condition).

A semantic correctness condition is that there should be no traces which are both permitted and excluded by the same diagram.

Sequence diagrams can be checked for consistency with class diagrams and state machine models by identifying if the execution scenarios they describe are permitted by the other models.

Each lifeline in a sequence diagram must be an instance of a class in the class diagram or an instance of an agent in the use case diagram.

If a message m is sent from object $ax : A$ to object $bx : B$ in a sequence diagram, (1) m must be an operation of B or of one of its ancestors, with parameter types including the parameter values of m, and (2) there must be a series of navigable associations from ax to bx.

For each message m sent from object $ax : A$ to object $bx : B$ in a sequence diagram I, it should be checked that there is a transition in the state machine for A which includes an operation invocation $bs.m$ in its generations, where bs is a set of B objects or an individual B object. That is, there exists transition tr with actions $acts$ such that

$$acts\ invokes\ bx.m$$

States and conditions specified in the sequence diagram must be consistent with the state machine states at corresponding time points.

Alternatively, such a message send could be defined in the class diagram as part of the operation definitions of A.

More generally, a sequence of message sends from ax in a sequence diagram should be checked for consistency by identifying if there is a path in the state machine model for the class of ax that can give rise to this behavior, with the same order of message sends.

Conditions required to be true at time points or intervals on a lifeline for $ax : A$ must be consistent with the class invariant of A if they include times at which ax is not executing any operation.

12.4.1 Completeness

Completeness checks include:

- There is at least one sequence diagram describing each use case of the system.
- Each valid variation of behavior of each use case should be shown in some sequence diagram: in particular, each case of execution of an extension to a primary use case.

- Each explicitly forbidden behavior of a use case should be shown on an interaction diagram marked as negated.
- For each state machine transition that invokes operations, there is some sequence diagram containing this message send.

12.4.2 Validation

Validation checks can be carried out by animation of sequence diagrams, to identify if expected properties hold, or by proof, using reasoning tools for real-time logic (RTL) such as SDRTL [3].

A subset of RTL that uses only linear inequalities between event occurrence times is decidable, permitting automated validation. We could express many real-time constraints in this subset, *pathRTL* [57], which consists of inequations

$$e1 +/- constant \leq e2$$

where the ei are times $@(event, j)$ of occurrences of events.

12.5 SUMMARY

In this chapter we have defined concepts of model correctness, completeness, quality, consistency, and validity for UML class diagrams, state machines, and interactions, and have described techniques for verification of these properties.

REFERENCES

1. W. Ahrendt, T. Baar, B. Beckert, M. Giese, E. Habermalz, R. Hahnle, W. Menzel, and P. H. Schmitt. *The KeY Approach: Integrating Object Oriented Design and Formal Verification*. Technical Report 2000/4. Karlsruhe, Germany, Department of Computer Science, University of Karlsruhe, Jan. 2000.
2. K. Androutsopoulos. Verification of reactive system specifications using model checking. Ph.D. dissertation, King's College, London, 2004.
3. S. Andrei, W. Chin, A. Cheng, and M. Lupu. Incremental automatic debugging of real-time systems based on satisfiability counting. Presented at the IEEE-CS Real-Time and Embedded Technology and Applications Symposium, San Francisco, Mar. 2005.
4. G. Aruchamy and A. Mo Kim Cheng. *Translating Real-Time UML Timing Constraints into Real-Time Logic Formulas*. Technical Report UH-CS-06-07. University of Houston, Houston, TX, 2006.
5. D. Bämer et al. *Role Object: Pattern Languages of Program Design*. Addison-Wesley, Reading, MA, 2000.
6. C. Batini, S. Ceri, and S. Navathe. *Conceptual Database Design: An Entity-Relationship Approach*. Benjamin-Cummings, Redwood City, CA, 1992.
7. S. Bäumler, M. Balser, W. Reif, A. Thums, and A. Knapp. *Interactive verification of UML state machines*. Presented at ICFEM 2004.

8. M. Blaha and W. Premerlani. A catalog of object model transformations. Presented at the 3rd Working Conference on Reverse Engineering, Monterey, CA, 1996.
9. G. Booch, M. Engel, and B. Young. *Object Oriented Analysis and Design with Applications*. Addison-Wesley, Reading, MA, 2007.
10. B. Cheng, R. Stephenson, and B. Berenbach. Lessons learned from automated analysis of industrial UML class models. In *MoDELS 2005*. Lecture Notes in Computer Science, vol. 3713. Springer-Verlag, New York, 2005.
11. D. Clark. Amorphous slicing for EFSMs. Presented at PLID '08, 2008.
12. S. Cook and J. Daniels. *Designing Object Systems: Object-Oriented Modelling with Syntropy*. Prentice Hall, Upper Saddle River, NJ, Sept. 1994.
13. T. Clark, A. Evans, S. Kent, and P. Sammut. The MMF approach to engineering object-oriented design languages. Presented at the Workshop on Language Descriptions, Tools and Applications (LDTA), 2001.
14. M. Crane and J. Dingel. UML vs Classical vs Rhapsody statecharts: not all models are created equal. *MoDELS 2005*. Lecture Notes in Computer Science, vol. 3713. Springer-Verlag, New York, 2005.
15. W. Damm, B. Josko, A. Pnueli, and A. Votintseva. A discrete-time UML semantics for concurrency and communication in safety-critical applications. *Science of Computer Programming*, 55:81–115, 2005.
16. H. Dierks. Comparing model-checking and logical reasoning for real-time systems. In *Workshop Proceedings, ESSLLI '98*, pp. 13–22, 1998.
17. A. Evans and S. Kent. Core meta-modelling semantics of UML: the pUML approach. In *UML'99*, pp. 140–155, 1999.
18. H. Fecher, J. Schonborn, M. Kyas, and W.-P. de Roever. 29 new unclarities in the semantics of UML 2.0 state machines. In *Formal Methods and Software Engineering (ICFEM 2005)*. vol. 3785, pp. 52–65. Springer-Verlag, New York, 2005.
19. J. Fiadeiro and T. Maibaum. Describing, structuring and implementing objects. In *Foundations of Object Oriented Languages*. Lecture Notes in Computer Science, vol. 489. Springer-Verlag, New York, 1991.
20. J. Fiadeiro and T. Maibaum. Sometimes "tomorrow" is "sometime." In *Temporal Logic*. Lecture Notes in Artificial Intelligence, vol. 827, pp. 48–66. Springer-Verlag, New York, 1994.
21. M. Fowler. *Refactoring: Improving the Design of Existing Code*. Addison-Wesley, Reading, MA, 2000.
22. G. Holzmann. The model checker SPIN. *IEEE Transactions on Software Engineering*, 23(5): 279–295, 1997.
23. E. Gamma, R. Helm, R. Johnson, and J. Vlissides. *Design Patterns: Elements of Reusable Object-Oriented Software*. Addison-Wesley, Reading, MA, 1995.
24. M. Glinz. Problems and deficiencies of UML as a requirements specification language. In *Proceedings of the 10th International Workshop on Software Specification and Design (IWSSD-10)*, pp. 11–22, 2000.
25. M. Gogolla, O. Radfelder, and M. Richters. *A UML Semantics FAQ: The View from Bremen*. University of Bremen, Bremen, Germany, 1999.
26. H. Bauerdick, M. Gogolla, and F. Gutsche. *Detecting OCL Traps in the UML 2.0 Superstructure*. (*UML 2004*). Lecture Notes in Computer Science, vol. 3273. Springer-Verlag, New York, 2004.

27. S. Goldsack, K. Lano, and A. Sanchez. Transforming continuous into discrete specifications with VDM++. In *IEE C8 Colloquium Digest on Hybrid Control for Real-Time Systems*. IEE, London, 1996.
28. S. Graf, I. Ober, and I. Ober. Timed annotations with UML. In *SVERTS '03*, 2003.
29. M. Grand. *Patterns in Java*, Vol. 1. Wiley, New York, 1998.
30. D. Gries. *The Science of Programming*, Springer-Verlag, New York, 1981.
31. D. Harel and A. Naamad. The STATEMATE semantics of statecharts. *ACM Transactions on Software Engineering and Methodology*, 5(4):293–333, Oct. 1996.
32. C. A. R. Hoare. An axiomatic basis for computer programming. *Communications of the ACM*, 12(10): 576–585, 1969.
33. A. Knapp and J. Wuttke. Model-checking of UML 2.0 interactions. In *Proceedings of the 5th International Workshop on Critical Systems Development Using Modelling Languages (CSDUML)*. Telenor Report 20/2006, 2006.
34. F. Jahanian and A. K. Mok. Safety analysis of timing properties in real-time systems. *IEEE Transactions on Software Engineering*, 12:890–904, 1986.
35. B. Korel, I. Singh, L. Tahat, and B. Vaysburg. Slicing of state-based models. In *19th International Conference on Software Maintenance*, p. 34, 2003.
36. M. Kyas, H. Fecher, F. de Boer, J. Jacob, J. Hooman, M. van der Kwaag, T. Arons, and H Kugler. Formalizing UML models and OCL constraints in PVS. In *SFEDL '04*, 2004.
37. K. Lano. Logical specification of reactive and real-time systems. *Journal of Logic and Computation*, 8(5):679–711, 1998.
38. K. Lano. UML to B: formal verification of object-oriented models. In *IFM '04*, 2004.
39. K. Lano and K. Androutsopolous. Automated synthesis of high-integrity systems using model-driven development. Presented at the 5th International Workshop CSDUML, 2006.
40. K. Lano, K. Androutsopolous, and D. Clark. Concurrency specification in UML-RSDS. In *MARTES'06, MoDELS Conference*, 2006.
41. K. Lano, D. Clark, and K. Androutsopolous. From implicit specifications to explicit designs in reactive system development. In *IFM'02*, 2002.
42. K. Lano, D. Clark, K. Androutsopolous, and P. Kan. Invariant-based synthesis of fault-tolerant systems. In *FTRTFT*. Springer-Verlag, New York, 2000.
43. K. Lano, D. Clark, and K. Androutsopoulos. RSDS: A subset of UML with precise semantics. *L'Objet*, 9(4):53–73, 2003.
44. K. Lano. Transformational program analysis. *Journal of Software Testing Verification and Reliability*, 4:155–189, 1994.
45. K. Lano. Constraint-driven development. *Information and Software Technology*, 50: 406–423, 2008.
46. K. Lano. Formalising design patterns as model transformations. Chapter 7 in T. Taibi, ed., *Design Pattern Formalisation Techniques*. IGI Publishing, Hershey, PA, 2007.
47. K. Lano. A compositional semantics of UML-RSDS. *SoSyM*, 8(1): 85–116, Feb. 2009.
48. K. Lano and D. Clark. Direct semantics of extended state machines. In *TOOLS'07*, 2007.
49. King's College London. UML RSDS toolset, 2007. http://www.dcs.kcl.ac.uk/staff/kcl/umlrsds.
50. K. Lano. Catalogue of model transformations. http://www.dcs.kcl.ac.uk/staff/kcl/tcat.pdf, 2007.

51. K. Lano and A. Evans. Rigorous development in UML. In *FASE'99*. Lecture Notes in Computer Science, vol. 1577. pp. 129–144. Springer-Verlag, New York, 1999.
52. B. Liskov and J. Wing. Specifications and their use in defining subtypes. In *ZUM'95 Proceedings*. Lecture Notes in Computer Science, vol. 967. Springer-Verlag, New York, 1995.
53. S. Markovic and T. Baar. Refactoring OCL annotated UML class diagrams. *MoDELS 2005 Proceedings*. Lecture Notes in Computer Science, vol. 3713. Springer-Verlag, New York, 2005.
54. B. Meyer. *Object-Oriented Software Construction*. Prentice Hall, Upper Saddle River, NJ, 1997.
55. F. Jahanian and A. K. Mok. Safety analysis of timing properties in real-time systems. *IEEE Transactions on Software Engineering*, 12:890–904, Sept. 1986.
56. J. D. Monk. *Mathematical Logic*. Springer-Verlag, New York, 1976.
57. C. Morgan. *Programming from Specifications*. Springer-Verlag, New York, 1990.
58. A. Naumenko and A. Wegmann. Triune continuum paradigm and problems of UML semantics. http://icwww.epfl.ch/publications/documents/ IC_TECH_REPORT_200344.pdf, 2003.
59. OMG. Model-driven architecture. http://www.omg.org/mda/, 2007.
60. OMG. *UML Superstructure, Version 2.0*. OMG Document Formal/05-07-04. Object Management Group, Needham, MA, 2005.
61. OMG. *UML Superstructure, Version 2.1.1*. OMG Document Formal/2007-02-03. Object Management Group, Needham, MA, 2007.
62. OMG. UML profile for schedulability, performance and time, version 1.1. http://www.omg.org/, 2005.
63. OMG. *UML OCL 2.0 Specification*. Final/06-05-01. Object Management Group, Needham, MA, 2006.
64. OMG. *Query/View/Transformation Specification*. Technical Report ptc/05-11-01. Object Management Group, Needham, MA, 2005.
65. D. Schmidt and C. Cranor. Half-sync/half-async: an architectural pattern for efficient and well-structured concurrent I/O. In *Proceedings of the 2nd Annual Conference on the Pattern Languages of Programs*, Monticello, IL, pp. 1–10, Sept. 1995.
66. C. Snook and M. Butler. U2B: a tool for translating UML-B models into B. Chapter 6 in J. Mermet, ed., *UML-B Specification for Proven Embedded Systems Design*. Springer-Verlag, New York, 2004.
67. G. Sunyé, A. Le Guennec, and J. M. Jézéquel. Design patterns application in UML. In *ECOOP 2000*. Lecture Notes in Computer Science, vol. 1850, pp. 44–62. Springer-Verlag, New York, 2000.
68. J. S. Ostroff. *Temporal Logic for Real-Time Systems*. Wiley, New York, 1989.
69. A. Pataricza. Semi-decisions in the validation of dependable systems. In *Proceedings of DSN 2001: International IEEE Conference on Dependable Systems and Networks*, pp. 114–115. IEEE Press, New York, 2001.
70. A. Pnueli. Applications of temporal logic to the specification and verification of reactive systems: a survey of current trends. In *Current Trends in Concurrency*. Lecture Notes in Computer Science, vol. 224. Springer-Verlag, New York, 1986.
71. M. Richters. OCL semantics. Annex A of [63], 2005.

72. M. Ryan, J. Fiadeiro, and T. S. E. Maibaum. Sharing actions and attributes in modal action logic. In *Proceedings of the International Conference on Theoretical Aspects of Computer Science (TACS '91)*. Springer-Verlag, New York, 1991.
73. A. Simons. The theory of classification: 8. Classification and inheritance. *Journal of Object Technology*, 2(4):55–64, July–Aug. 2003.
74. J. Smith, S. DeLoach, M. Kokar, and K. Baclawski. Category theoretic approaches of representing precise UML semantics. In *Proceedings of the ECOOP Workshop on Defining Precise Semantics for UML*, 2000.
75. SPASS theorem prover. http://www.spass-prover.org/, 2008.
76. C. Snook and M. Butler. U2B: a tool for translating UML-B models into B. Chapter 6 in J. Mermet, ed., *UML-B Specification for Proven Embedded Systems Design*. Springer-Verlag, New York, 2004.
77. UML 2 Semantics Project. http://www.cs.queensu.ca/~stl/internal/uml2/bibtex/ref_uml2 semantics.html, 2008.
78. L. Tratt. Model transformations and tool integration. *SoSyM*, 4(2): 112–122, May 2005.
79. F. Wagner. *Modeling Software with Finite State Machines: A Practical Approach*. Auerbach Publications, Boca Raton, FL, 2006.

CHAPTER 13

DESIGN VERIFICATION WITH STATE INVARIANTS

EMIL SEKERINSKI
Department of Computing and Software, McMaster University, Hamilton, Ontario, Canada

13.1 INTRODUCTION

This chapter is focused on statically verifying the design expressed by a statechart. Statecharts extend finite state machines with *clustering*, expressed by XOR states, with *concurrency*, expressed by AND states, and with *broadcast communication*. Both XOR and AND states structure the states hierarchically: If a chart is in an XOR state, it must be in exactly one of its children; if the chart is in an AND state, it must be in all of its children. Transitions between states can assign to and depend on global variables of arbitrary types, thus lifting the restriction to a finite number of states; the statechart states partition the combined state of the chart and the variables into *modes*. These extensions of finite state machines are meant to allow the requirements of embedded systems to be expressed directly [6].

Statecharts are appealing to practitioners, as the underlying formalism of finite state machines is well understood, as the visual designs are "easy to communicate to domain experts," and as statecharts can be executed directly through interpretation or compilation. With their inclusion in UML, statecharts are used for object-oriented design.

Statecharts on their own do not immediately lead to opportunities for verifying the safety of the design: If an event is received and no transition on that event can take place, it is ignored. There is no intrinsic notion that an error occurs or an invalid state is reached for a given sequence of events. This reflects the requirement that embedded systems have to be robust and be prepared for arbitrary behavior of their environment.

In this chapter we explore design verification through *state invariants*. These are conditions that are attached to individual states and specify what has to hold in that state. If a state S has invariant I attached to it, every incoming transition must ensure

UML 2 Semantics and Applications. Edited by Kevin Lano

that I holds. Dually, every outgoing transition can assume that I holds initially. This gives a method for checking a chart against an annotation consisting of invariants attached to states in the state hierarchy. Intuitively, state invariants document the "purpose" of states. In UML, state invariants can be attached to behavioral state machines and protocol state machines [18].

Consider the TV control example in Figure 13.1. The activity is partitioned into two states, the Basic state *Standby* and the AND state *Working*. When in *Working* state, the chart is in both *Picture* and *Sound* XOR states. Within *Picture* the chart is in one of the basic states *WarmingUp* and *Displaying*; within *Sound* the system is in one of the basic states *Waiting*, *On*, and *Off*. The invariant of *Working* is that whenever *Picture* is in *Displaying*, *Sound* must not be in *Waiting* (i.e., must be in *On* or *Off*). The invariant of *Sound* states that the sound level *lev* must be between 1 and 10. The event *power* causes the chart to flip between *Standby* and *Working*, no matter which substates of *Working* the chart is in. The transition on the event *warm* broadcasts the event *soundOn*. The transition on the events *down* can be taken only if $lev > 1$ and, when taken, will decrement *lev*. The transition on *power* to *Working* sets *Picture* and *Sound* to the default initial states *WarmingUp* and *Waiting* sets *lev* to 5.

State invariants can express the *safety* of an embedded system or *consistency* of a software system. Compared to writing an equivalent combined invariant as a single global predicate, state invariants allow a potentially large invariant to be decomposed into parts that are in visual proximity to affected transitions, making complex invariants more comprehensible. State invariants allow for shorter invariant expressions, as *state tests* are implicit to the state to which an invariant is attached.

The interpretation of XOR and AND states carries over to state invariants: If a chart is in an XOR state, its invariant and the invariant of exactly one of its children have to hold; if the chart is in an AND state, its invariant and the invariants of all its children have to hold. As a consequence, the attached invariant of a state is *inherited* by all its children and thus all its descendants. Dually, the children of a state contribute to a *synthesized* invariant that is passed on to their parent and thus all their ancestors.

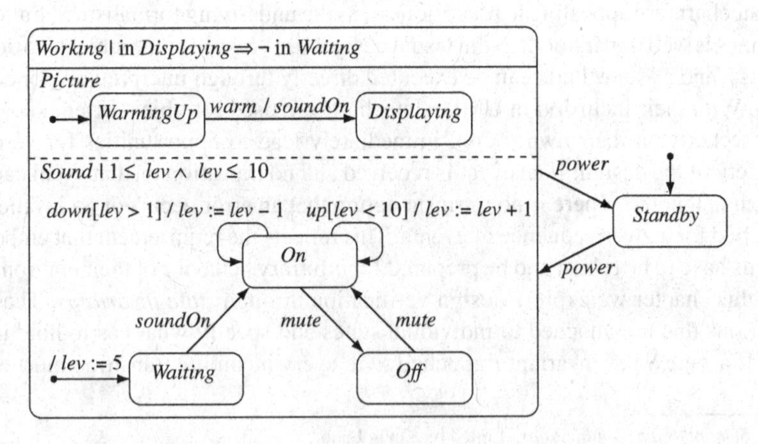

FIGURE 13.1 Statechart with invariants for a TV set.

The conjunction of the attached invariant, the inherited invariant, and the synthesized invariant of a state is called the *accumulated invariant*. A contribution of this chapter is to define accumulation formally and to justify it (Section 13.6).

State invariants can be used for verifying a design by testing or by static verification. The use for testing is conceptually simple: After each transition the accumulated invariant of the target states have to be checked; more precisely, for all leaf states in which the chart ends up, the attached invariant of those states as well as the attached invariant of all their ancestors have to hold. To check this at runtime, the evaluation of invariants has to be sufficiently efficient. Here we consider static verification and do not impose restrictions on the composition of invariants.

Static verification proceeds by generating a number of *verification conditions* from the annotated chart and then showing that these hold. The verification conditions depend on the definition of a transition, which in the presence of broadcasting can have different interpretations. The interpretation taken here is that all transitions resulting from broadcasts are to be taken simultaneously with the initiating transition, which we call *simultaneous broadcasting*. Thus, if in the chart of Figure 13.1 the event *warm* is received when the chart is initially in *WarmingUp* and *Waiting*, the transitions on *warm* and *soundOn* are taken simultaneously and the invariant of *Working* is preserved.

Simultaneous broadcasting can be formalized using *parallel composition* of statements. The B method subsumes an extension of guarded commands by parallel composition [1]. A number of approaches define statecharts by translation to the B method [9–11,13,15,17,20,24]. The (bounded) nondeterminism of guarded commands allows nondeterminism in the choice of transitions to be reflected. As the B method also supports proofs of invariants, such a translation leads to a method for proving preservation of accumulated invariants, to be precise with one verification condition per event. The second contribution of this chapter is a procedure that instead generates several smaller, "more local" verification conditions per event and justifies this in terms of the straightforward generation (Section 13.7). Automated theorem provers are more effective at proving or disproving many small conditions than a few large ones. Thus, the prospect is that state invariants not only make it easier to specify correctness conditions for statecharts but also make it easier to verify them.

The original interpretation of broadcasting leads to a sequence of internal *microsteps*. In the example above this implies that first the transition on *warm* is taken, resulting in *Picture* being in *Displaying* and *Sound* remaining in *Waiting*, hence violating the invariant $\mathsf{in}\,Displaying \Rightarrow \neg\,\mathsf{in}\,Waiting$. Thus, the transition on *soundOn* would be taken in a configuration when the accumulated invariant of its source state does not hold. As the transition on *soundOn* follows immediately, this violation is not observable from outside. This interpretation necessitates that the invariant be relaxed to the following one, where $\mathsf{gen}\,E$ means that event E has been generated and is awaiting processing:

$$Working \mid \mathsf{in}\,Displaying \Rightarrow (\neg\,\mathsf{in}\,Waiting) \vee (\mathsf{in}\,Waiting \wedge \mathsf{gen}\,soundOn)$$

The set of generated events needs to be kept in a global variable and determines the next microstep in a loop that is executed as long as the set is not empty. A verification method that attempts to be complete needs to allow this sequence to be referred to in invariants, such as through the function gen above. Simultaneous broadcasting does not need such a set and allows events to be interpreted as operations (procedures). While microsteps allow the same transition to be taken repeatedly within a macrostep, potentially leading to nontermination, simultaneous broadcasting forbids this. As intermediate states are not present with simultaneous broadcasting, it is more abstract than sequencing microsteps. An implementation of simultaneous broadcasting would still need to introduce intermediate states following the refinement rules of parallel composition [1].

Nondeterminism arises in statecharts if more than one transition is enabled. Classical statecharts [4,7,19] and UML statecharts [18] resolve nondeterminism that can arise due to transitions on different levels differently: Classical statecharts give priority to outer transitions, as this facilitates zooming in and out of complex states; UML statecharts give priority to inner transition, as an inner state can "override" the behavior of an outer state. As a third contribution of this chapter, we study the consequences of resolving this nondeterminism either way for invariant verification and code generation (Section 13.8).

The final contribution of this chapter is a discussion on when and how to use state invariants (Section 13.9). After preliminaries (Section 13.2), we first define the (syntactic) statechart structure (Section 13.3), the meaning of statecharts in term of configurations and operations (Section 13.4), and the meaning of state invariants (Section 13.5).

Formal verification of statecharts has been studied extensively (e.g., in [3,5,8,12, 14,16]; see [2] for a survey on model-checking approaches. These approaches specify invariants globally rather than attaching them to states. However, they allow more general temporal properties than the invariants that we consider here.

This line of work emerged from an attempt to generate comprehensible code from statecharts, as a way of cross-checking the statechart design [22,23]. Compared to the approach there, a preprocessing step that leads to normalized statecharts is eliminated, as this step became awkward in an interactive tool. Here the translation scheme is described more abstractly and the well-formedness criteria are revised and justified. In this chapter we revise and extend our earlier approach to verification condition generation [21].

13.2 PRELIMINARIES

We use *generalized program statements* to define the meaning of an event. Generalized statements subsume those that may appear in a body of a transition. We are interested in models that are sufficiently abstract that transition bodies do not contain loops and recursion but may contain conditionals. To simplify matters, we assume that the evaluation of expressions is always defined.

A (generalized) statement P is defined by a pair, a *predicate* or *Boolean expression* $[P]$ relating the initial and final states, and a list αP of *variables* that are assigned in P (Table 13.1). The initial and final states are referred to by unprimed and primed

TABLE 13.1 Definition of Statements

P	$[P]$	αP	Side Condition
skip	true	$\emptyset$	
stop	false	$\emptyset$	
$xv := ev$	$xv' = ev$	xv	
$g \rightarrow Q$	$g \wedge [Q]$	αQ	
$Q \,[]\, R$	$[Q] \wedge xv' = xv \vee$ $[R] \wedge yv' = yv$	$\alpha Q \cup \alpha R$	$xv = \alpha R - \alpha Q$ $yv = \alpha Q - \alpha R$
$Q \parallel R$	$[Q] \wedge [R]$	$\alpha Q \cup \alpha R$	$\alpha Q \cap \alpha R = \emptyset$
$Q\,;R$	$\exists xv'' \,.\, [Q][xv' \backslash xv''] \wedge$ $[R][xv \backslash xv'']$	$\alpha Q \cup \alpha R$	$xv = \alpha Q \cap \alpha R$

variables. Let g be a Boolean expression, xv a list of unique variables, ev a list of expressions of the same length as xv, and Q and R statements. The statement skip can always be executed and does not change any variables. The statement stop can never be executed (i.e., is always disabled). The multiple assignment $xv := ev$ assigns the values of ev simultaneously to the variables xv. The guarded statement $g \rightarrow Q$ blocks if g does not hold, otherwise is as Q. The *nondeterministic choice* $Q \,[]\, R$ selects either operand that is enabled: If both are enabled, their choice is arbitrary; if neither is enabled, $Q \,[]\, R$ blocks. The *parallel* or *independent* composition $Q \parallel R$ is well defined only if the variables assigned to in Q and R are disjoint. However, Q and R may read the variables assigned by the other; in that case, their initial value is read. The parallel composition is executed in one atomic step, without interleaving. Parallel composition is a generalization of multiple assignment in the sense that $(x, y := e, f) = (x := e \parallel y := f)$. The *sequential composition* $Q\,;R$ joins the final variables of Q with the initial variables of R formally expressed by renaming: $e[xv \backslash ev]$ stands for expression e with each occurrence of a variable of xv replaced by the corresponding expression in ev. Sequential composition is always well defined. The *conditional statement* is defined in terms of the above:

$$\text{if } g \text{ then } Q \;\widehat{=}\; (g \rightarrow Q) \,[]\, (\neg g \rightarrow \text{skip})$$
$$\text{if } g \text{ then } Q \text{ else } R \;\widehat{=}\; (g \rightarrow Q) \,[]\, (\neg g \rightarrow R)$$

The *enabledness domain* en P is the domain of the relation of statement P:

$$\text{en } P = \exists xv' \,.\, [P] \quad \text{where } xv = \alpha P$$

For example, en skip = true and en stop = false. The *prioritizing composition* $P \,/\!/\, Q$ is like P if P is enabled; otherwise, it is like Q:

$$P \,/\!/\, Q \;\widehat{=}\; P \,[]\, \neg \text{ en } P \rightarrow Q$$

As nondeterministic choice and parallel composition are associative and commutative, they can be generalized to choice over a finite number of alternatives, $[]\; i \in s \,.\, P$ and to a parallel composition of a finite number of statements, $\| \, i \in s \, . \, P$, where s is a finite set. The correctness assertion $\{p\}\ Q\ \{r\}$ states that under precondition p statement Q terminates with postcondition r:

$$\{p\}\ Q\ \{r\} \mathrel{\widehat{=}} \forall xv' \, . \, p \wedge [Q] \Rightarrow r[xv \backslash xv'] \quad \text{where } xv = \alpha\, Q$$

The common verification rules for statements hold; for example:

$$\begin{aligned}
\{p\}\ xv := ev\ \{r\} &\equiv p \Rightarrow r[xv \backslash ev]\\
\{p\}\ g \rightarrow Q\ \{r\} &\equiv \{p \wedge g\}\ Q\ \{r\}\\
\{p\}\ Q \mathbin{[\,]} R\ \{r\} &\equiv \{p\}\ Q\ \{r\} \wedge \{p\}\ R\ \{r\}\\
\{p\}\ Q \mathbin{/\!/} R\ \{r\} &\equiv \{p\}\ Q\ \{r\} \wedge \{p \wedge \neg\, \mathsf{en}\ Q\}\ R\ \{r\}\\
\{p\}\ Q \,;\, R\ \{r\} &\equiv \exists q \, . \, \{p\}\ Q\ \{q\} \wedge \{q\}\ R\ \{r\}
\end{aligned}$$

13.3 STATECHART STRUCTURE

A statechart $\mathcal{S}$ is a structure (*Basic*, *AND*, *XOR*, *Root*, *parent*, *Event*, *Transition*, *default*) with a number of constraints on the components, which we visit in turn. The finite sets *Basic*, *AND*, and *XOR* are mutually disjoint sets of states. We let $Composite = AND \cup XOR$ be the set of composite states and $State = Basic \cup Composite$ be the set of all states. Among the XOR states is a distinguished root state, $Root \in XOR$.

The partial function (or functional relation) $parent : State \nrightarrow State$ maps every element of *State* except *Root* to a composite state, $\mathsf{dom}\ parent = State - \{Root\}$ and $\mathsf{ran}\ parent = Composite$. All states form a tree that is rooted in *Root*, formally $Root \in parent^*[\{s\}]$ for any $s \in State$, where r^* is the transitive and reflexive closure of relation r and $r[S]$ is the image of the set S under r. We let the relation *children* be the inverse of *parent* (i.e., $children = parent^{-1}$). The children of an AND state are said to be *concurrent*; the children of an XOR state are said to be *exclusive*. The children of an AND state must be XOR states.

The finite set *Event* is that of event names. The elements of the finite set *Transition* are tuples t, represented as $ss \xrightarrow{t:E[g]/B} ts$, where $ss = source(t) \subseteq State$ is the set of source states, $ts = target(t) \subseteq State$ is the set of target states, $E = event(t) \in Event$ is the transition event, $guard(t) = g$ is a Boolean chart expression, the transition guard, and $body(t) = B$ is a chart statement, the transition body. The state *Root* must not be the source or target of any transition, $Root \notin source(t)$ and $Root \notin target(t)$ for any $t \in Transition$. All transitions must have at least one source state and one target state, $source(t) \neq \{\}$ and $target(t) \neq \{\}$ for any $t \in Transition$.

The partial function $default : XOR \nrightarrow Transition$ maps XOR states to default transitions. The source of a default transition of an XOR state s, if defined, is s itself, $source(default(s)) = \{s\}$. A fat dot inside the source state is used to visualize the source of a default transition. Certain XOR states are "required to have a default transition": A default transition must be defined for the root state and any XOR state that is the target of some transition (default or regular) or that is being entered implicitly, as it has an AND ancestor that is being entered; this will be made precise shortly. The default transition of a state s, if defined, must go to a descendant of s [i.e., $target(default(s)) \subseteq children^+[\{s\}]$, where r^+ is the transitive closure of relation r].

Chart expressions are composed of program variables, the state tests in $S_1, \ldots, S_m$, where S_i is any state except *Root*, and functions *fn* applied to zero or more arguments (functions with zero arguments being constants). We assume that the functions include common Boolean, arithmetic, and relational operators.

$$Ex ::= v \mid \text{in}\, S_1, \ldots, S_m \mid fn(Ex_1, \ldots, Ex_n)$$

Chart statements are the skip statement, the multiple assignment, the broadcast E, with $E \in Event$, the parallel composition, and the conditional:

$$St ::= \text{skip} \mid v_1, \ldots, v_m := Ex_1, \ldots, Ex_m \mid E \mid St \parallel St \mid \text{if}\, Ex\, \text{then}\, St[\text{else}\, St]$$

In charts, we allow the specifications of the transition name t:, the transition guard $[g]$, and the transition body $/B$ to be left out. If a transition guard is missing, it is assumed to be true. If a transition body is missing, it is assumed to be skip. The event and guard of a default transition do not play any role and are always left out.

The *closest common ancestor* $cca(ss)$ of a set ss of states is the state that is a proper ancestor of each state in ss and all other common ancestors are also its ancestor. We write $x\ r\ y$ for the pair (x, y) belonging to relation r.

$$c = cca(ss) \equiv c \in parent^+[ss] \wedge (\forall a \in State\ .\ a \in parent^+[ss] \Rightarrow a\, parent^*\, c)$$

The closest common ancestor exists and is unique for any nonempty set of states that does not include the root state. States r, s are *orthogonal*, written $r \perp s$, if their closest common ancestor is an AND state and neither is an ancestor of the other. A set ss of states is called orthogonal, written $\perp ss$, if every pair of distinct states of ss is orthogonal. For any transition, both its source and target states must be orthogonal, $\perp source(t)$ and $\perp target(t)$ for all $t \in Transition$. This concludes the definition of the statechart structure.

For example, in Figure 13.2, states X and Z are orthogonal, as their closest common ancestor, V, is an AND state and neither is an ancestor of the other. States X and T are not orthogonal, as their closest common ancestor, S, is an XOR state. States W and X

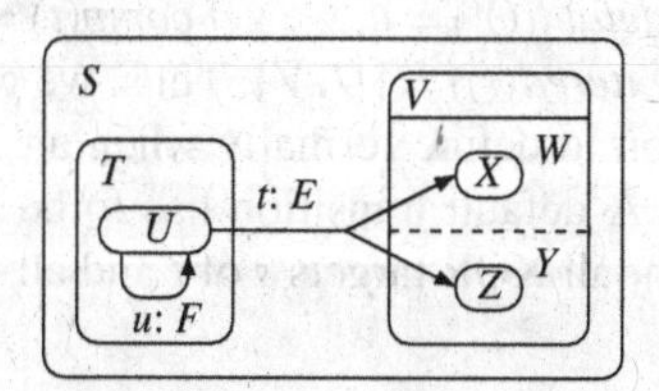

FIGURE 13.2 Self-transition and interlevel transition.

are not orthogonal, as W is an ancestor of X, although their closest common ancestor, V, is an XOR state.

We continue with several useful definitions. The *scope* of a transition is the state closest to the root through which the transition passes:

$$scope(t) \mathrel{\widehat{=}} cca(source(t) \cup target(t))$$

The *path* from state s to a set ss of descendants of s is the set of those states that are descendants of s and ancestors of states in ss, excluding s but including the states of ss:

$$path(s, ss) \mathrel{\widehat{=}} children^{+}[\{s\}] \cap parent^{*}[ss]$$

The states *entered* by a transition are all the states on the path from the scope of the transition to its targets. The states *exited* by a transition are all the states on the path from the scope of the transition to its sources:

$$\begin{aligned} entered(t) &\mathrel{\widehat{=}} path(scope(t), target(t)) \\ exited(t) &\mathrel{\widehat{=}} path(scope(t), source(t)) \end{aligned}$$

Figure 13.2 defines $source(t) = \{U\}$ and $target(t) = \{X, Z\}$. The scope of t is the closest common ancestor of $\{U, X, Z\}$, which is S, thus $entered(t) = \{V, W, X, Y, Z\}$ and $exited(t) = \{U, T\}$. We also have that $source(u) = \{U\} = target(u)$. The scope of u is the closest common ancestor of $\{U\}$, which is T, thus $entered(u) = \{U\} = exited(u)$.

Given a state set ss, the *implicit children* are those children of AND states of ss that are not in ss. If a chart is in ss, it is also in all its implicit children:

$$imp(ss) \mathrel{\widehat{=}} children[ss \cap AND] - ss$$

The *completion* of a transition t is the set of all transitions that are taken when t is taken: It adds all default transitions of XOR targets of t and all default transitions of implicit targets of t.

$$comp(t) \mathrel{\widehat{=}} \{t\} \cup \left(\bigcup s \in (target(t) \cap XOR) \cup imp(entered(t))\ .\ comp(default(s))\right)$$

In Figure 13.3(a) we have that $target(t) = \{U\}$, an XOR state, $default(U) = u$, and therefore $comp(t) = \{t, u\}$. In (b) we have that $entered(t) = \{T, U, V, W, X\}$ and $imp(entered(t)) = \{Y\}$. As $default(Y) = u$, we get $comp(t) = \{t, u\}$. In (c) we have that $entered(t) = \{T\}$ and $imp(entered(t)) = \{U, V\}$. Thus, we get $comp(t) = \{t, u, v\}$.

We are now in a position to define formally when an XOR state is "required to have a default transition": A default transition has to be defined for the root state, $Root \in \mathrm{dom}\ default$, and for all XOR targets s of t and all implicit targets $imp(t)$, for all transitions t, formally:

$$\forall t \in Transition\ .\ (target(t) \cap XOR) \cup imp(entered(t)) \subseteq \mathrm{dom}\ default$$

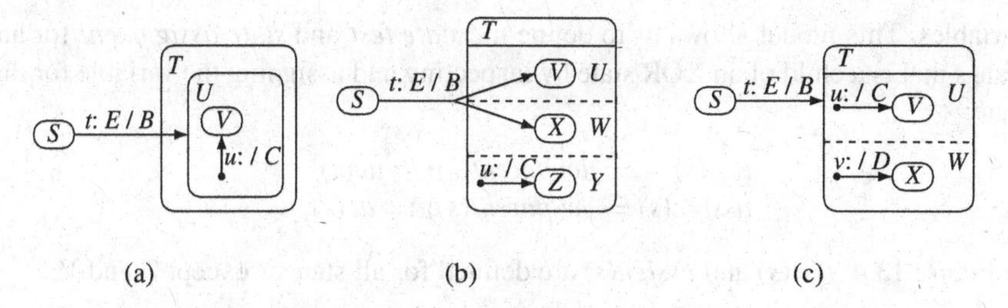

FIGURE 13.3 Transition completion.

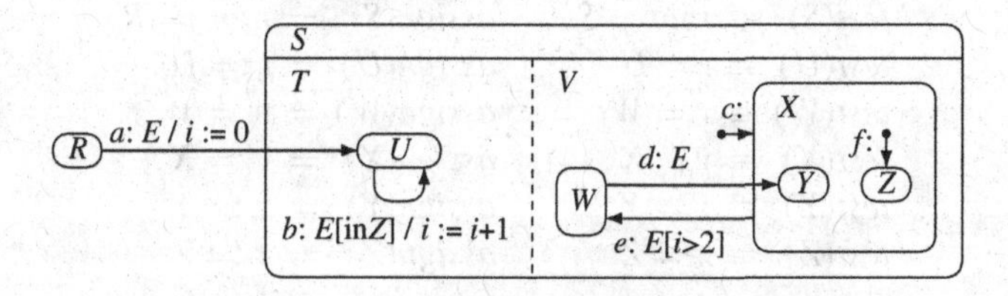

FIGURE 13.4 State hierarchy with transitions.

With this restriction on statecharts, *comp*(t) is well defined for any transition t, as in the definition s in *default*(s) ranges over XOR states are required to have a default transition. Furthermore, the recursion terminates as the level (i.e., the distance to the root) of the scope of the parameter t increases with each call, and the depth of every statechart is bounded.

13.4 CONFIGURATIONS AND OPERATIONS

The "state" of a statechart $\mathcal{S}$ is given by its *configuration* of states and by the state of its global variables. A configuration can be defined as a maximal set of statechart states such that (1) it contains the root state, (2) for any XOR state it contains exactly one of its children, and (3) for any AND state it contains all of its children [7,19]. We use here a different model that makes it easier to explain independent (concurrent) updates of a configuration [20]. For every XOR state s, including *Root*, a variable $lc(s)$, ranging over $uc(c)$ for every child c of s, is declared. We interpret $lc(s)$ and $uc(s)$ to be the state s starting with a lowercase or an uppercase letter. For the statechart of Figure 13.4 we get

$$root : \{R, S\} \qquad t : \{U\} \qquad v : \{W, X\} \qquad x : \{Y, Z\}$$

Note the use of X as a value of variable v and the use of x as a variable. Formally, it is sufficient to assume that lc and uc are injective functions with disjoint ranges. The function *var* is defined to map the variable names to the set of possible values [e.g., $var(root) = \{R, S\}$]. Thus, *var* defines the set of possible configurations. We assume that these variables and their values are distinct from the global program variables. This model allows us to define the *state test* and *state assignment* for any state s that is a child of an XOR state by inspecting and assigning the variable for that state:

$$\begin{aligned} test(s) &\mathrel{\widehat{=}} lc(parent(s)) = uc(s) \\ assign(s) &\mathrel{\widehat{=}} lc(parent(s)) := uc(s) \end{aligned}$$

In Figure 13.4, $test(s)$ and $assign(s)$ are defined for all states s except T and V:

$$\begin{array}{llll} test(R) & \equiv root = R & assign(R) & = root := R \\ test(S) & \equiv root = S & assign(S) & = root := R \\ test(U) & \equiv t = U & assign(U) & = t := U \\ test(W) & \equiv v = W & assign(W) & = v := W \\ test(X) & \equiv v = X & assign(X) & = v := X \\ test(Y) & \equiv x = Y & assign(Y) & = x := Y \\ test(Z) & \equiv x = Z & assign(Z) & = x := Z \end{array}$$

All other operations on configurations are expressed in terms of *test* and *assign*. The predicate $in(ss)$ tests if the current state is in the set ss; similarly, $goto(ss)$ sets the current state to ss.

$$\begin{aligned} in(ss) &\mathrel{\widehat{=}} \bigwedge s \in ss \cap children[XOR] \;.\; test(s) \\ goto(ss) &\mathrel{\widehat{=}} \parallel s \in ss \cap children[XOR] \;.\; assign(s) \end{aligned}$$

The statement $goto(ss)$ is well defined if the states of ss are not exclusive. For example, in Figure 13.4, $goto(\{U, X\})$ and $goto(\{X, Y\})$ are well defined, but $goto(\{Y, Z\})$ is not.

The *trigger* of a transition t is a predicate that checks if the transition guard holds and if the system is in all source states; only all exited states are tested. The *effect* of a statement t is to execute the body of t, to go to the states entered by t, and to repeat this for all transitions of the completion of t.

$$\begin{aligned} trigger(t) &\mathrel{\widehat{=}} in(exited(t)) \wedge guard(t) \\ effect(t) &\mathrel{\widehat{=}} \parallel u \in comp(t) \;.\; body(u) \parallel goto(entered(u)) \end{aligned}$$

We allow ourselves to confuse the chart expression $guard(t)$ with its meaning as an expression and chart statement $body(u)$ with its meaning as a statement, whereby a broadcast of E occurring in a transition body is defined by $op(E)$, to be made precise further below, and a state test in $S_1, \ldots, S_n$ occurring in the guard or body of transition t, written $\mathsf{in}_t\, S_1, \ldots, S_n$, is defined as testing being in $S_1, \ldots, S_n$ relative to being in $source(t)$:

$$\mathsf{in}_t S_1, \ldots, S_n \mathrel{\widehat{=}} in(parent^*[\{S_1, \ldots, S_n\}] - parent^*[source(t)])$$

The *goto* statement of $effect(t)$ is always well defined as entered states are not exclusive. For Figure 13.4, noting that $comp(a) = \{a, c, f\}$, $comp(b) = \{b\}$, and

$body(c) = \text{skip} = body(f)$, we get

$$
\begin{aligned}
trigger(a) &\equiv in(\{R\}) \wedge true \\
&\equiv test(R) \\
effect(a) &= body(a) \parallel goto(\{S,T,U\}) \parallel goto(\{X\}) \parallel goto(\{Z\}) \\
&= i := 0 \parallel assign(S) \parallel assign(U) \parallel assign(X) \parallel assign(Z) \\
trigger(b) &\equiv in(\{U\}) \wedge \text{in}_b\, Z \\
&\equiv test(U) \wedge test(X) \wedge test(Z) \\
effect(b) &= body(b) \parallel goto(\{U\}) \\
&= i := i+1 \parallel assign(U)
\end{aligned}
$$

The simplification carried out above is that $\text{skip} \parallel P = P$ for any statement P.

The *operation* of an event E is a statement that captures the joint effect of all transitions in a chart on E. For brevity, let $Trans(E,s)$ stand for the set of transitions on event E with scope s:

$$Trans(E,s) \mathrel{\widehat{=}} \{t \in Transition \mid event(t) = E \wedge scope(t) = s\}$$

The operation $op(E)$ is defined by recursively visiting all transitions on E, starting with those on the outermost scope, *Root*. In case there is a choice between transitions with the same scope, one is selected arbitrarily. In case there is a choice between transitions on different scopes, transitions on outer scopes are given priority. All transitions on the same event in concurrent states are taken in parallel. Of all transitions in an exclusive state, at most one can be taken.

$$
\begin{aligned}
op(E) &\mathrel{\widehat{=}} scopeop(E, Root) \\
scopeop(E,s) &\mathrel{\widehat{=}} ([]\ t \in Trans(E,s)\ .\ trigger(t) \rightarrow effect(t)) \mathbin{/\!/} childop(E,s) \\
childop(E,s) &\mathrel{\widehat{=}} \text{case } s \text{ of} \\
&\qquad Basic : \text{skip} \\
&\qquad XOR : []\ c \in children[\{s\}]\ .\ test(c) \rightarrow scopeop(E,c) \\
&\qquad AND : \parallel c \in children[\{s\}]\ .\ scopeop(E,c) \\
&\quad \text{end}
\end{aligned}
$$

Figure 13.5 gives two examples. In Figure 13.4 there is one event, E, with four transitions. With simplifications we get

$$
\begin{aligned}
op(E) = {} & test(R) \rightarrow i := 0 \parallel assign(S) \parallel assign(U) \parallel assign(X) \parallel assign(Z) \\
& \mathbin{/\!/} (\, test(R) \rightarrow \text{skip} \\
& \quad []\ test(S) \rightarrow \\
& \qquad (\, (test(U) \wedge test(X) \wedge test(Z) \rightarrow i := i+1 \parallel assign(U)) \\
& \qquad\quad \mathbin{/\!/} \text{skip} \\
& \qquad \parallel (\, test(W) \rightarrow assign(X) \parallel assign(Y) \\
& \qquad\quad []\ test(X) \wedge i > 2 \rightarrow assign(W)) \\
& \qquad\quad \mathbin{/\!/} \text{skip}\,))
\end{aligned}
$$

The simplifications are that choice over the empty range is stop, $[]\ i \in \{\}\,.\,P = \text{stop}$, that parallel composition over the empty range is skip, $\parallel i \in \{\}\,.\,P = \text{skip}$, that

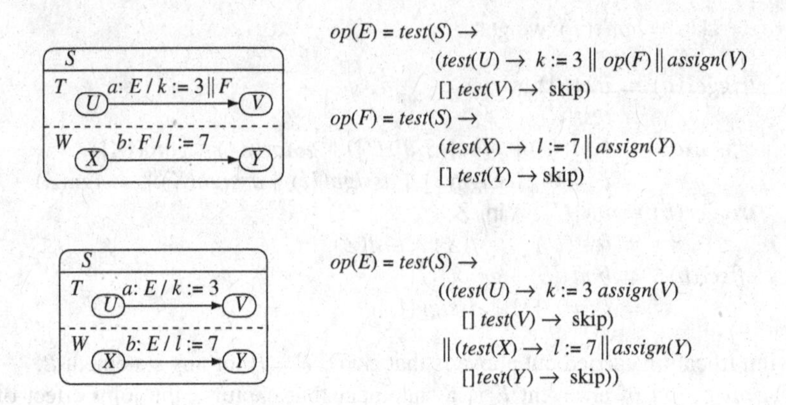

FIGURE 13.5 Concurrent transitions and broadcasting.

skip $\parallel P = P$, that stop $[]\ P = P$, that stop $/\!/\ P = P$, that $g \to P\ []\ h \to P = g \vee h \to P$, and that $true \to P = P$.

The *semantics* of statechart S is defined by the pair of functions *var* and *op*, with *var* defining the possible configurations and *op* defining for each event a (possibly nondeterministic) statement operating on the configuration.

13.4.1 Well-Definedness

The definition of *op* restricts the statecharts to which a meaning can be given. These restrictions arise due to the use of parallel composition, which requires that operands assign to distinct variables, and due to possible recursion in the definition of *op*, which results from broadcasting. The following two conditions are sufficient and necessary:

1. $effect(t)$ must be well defined for all transitions t.
2. $effect(t) \parallel effect(u)$ must be well defined for all t, u such that $event(t) = event(u)$ and $scope(t) \perp scope(u)$.

The first condition excludes transition bodies such as $k := 3 \parallel k := 7$ and the charts of Figure 13.6: In (a), the broadcast of F results in two parallel assignments to k. In (b), as the completion of a includes b, the effect of a again includes two parallel assignments to k. In (c), transition a leads to $assign(T) \parallel assign(U)$, which would result in parallel assignments to the same state variable, as is the case in (d) and (e). In (f), transition a leads to transitions c and b being taken, which results in $assign(V) \parallel assign(W)$. More generally, this condition prohibits any direct or indirect recursion among events, as these lead to parallel assignments to the same state variable.

The second condition excludes charts of Figure 13.7: In (a), on event E, both transitions a and b would be taken, resulting in parallel assignments to k. In (b), on event E, event F would be broadcast twice, resulting in $assign(Z) \parallel assign(Z)$.

Condition 1 ensures that *scopeop* is well defined, provided that *childop* is well defined. Condition 2 ensures that *childop* is well defined, provided that *scopeop* is

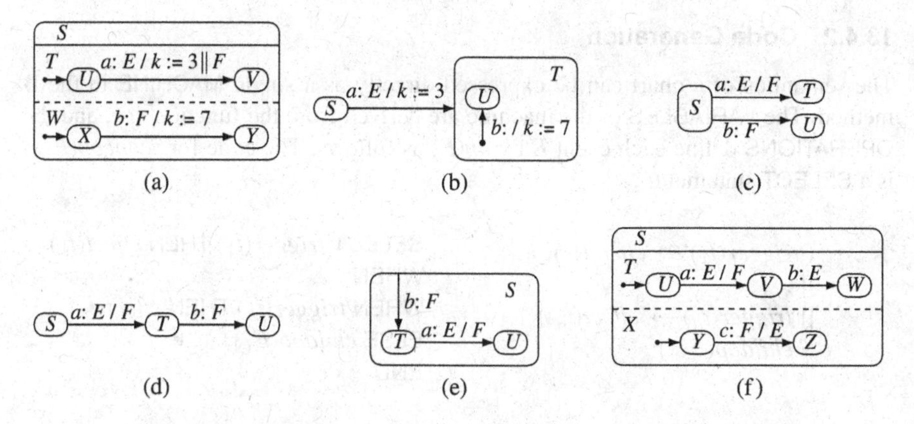

FIGURE 13.6 Violations of well-definedness condition 1.

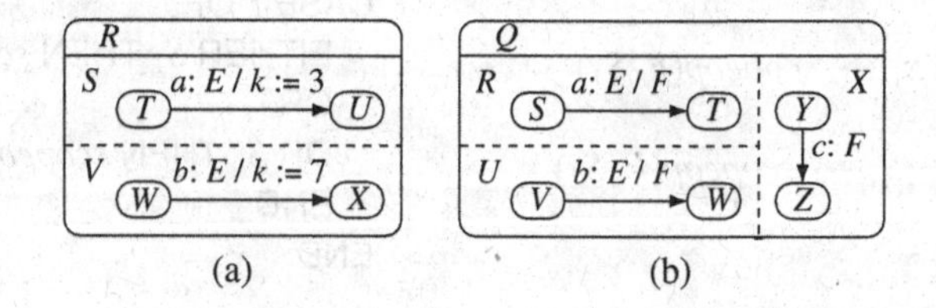

FIGURE 13.7 Violations of well-definedness condition 2.

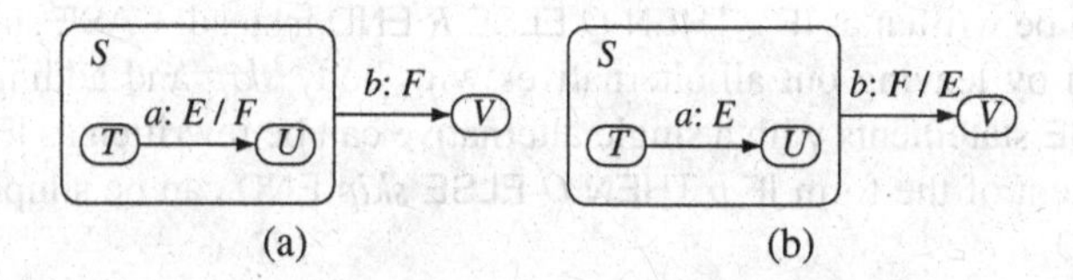

FIGURE 13.8 Violations of well-definedness condition 3.

well defined. Condition 1 also disallows any direct or indirect recursion among event operations. Hence, these two conditions are sufficient and necessary. We nevertheless consider a third condition:

3. If the body of transition t contains a broadcast of event E and u is a transition on E, then t and u must be within concurrent states [i.e., $scope(t) \perp scope(u)$].

In Figure 13.8(a), if the chart is in S and T, on event E both transitions a and b would be taken, as the effect of a is $assign(V) \parallel assign(U)$. Similarly, in (b) on F both transitions would be taken. In both cases the chart does not end up being in the targets of transitions taken due to broadcasting of events with transitions at outer levels. The condition above restricts broadcasting to events with transitions only in concurrent states.

13.4.2 Code Generation

The semantics of a chart can be expressed directly as a single MACHINE in the B method. The VARIABLES of the machine are derived from the function *var*, and the OPERATIONS define each event E by $op(E)$ as follows. The code for $scopeop(E, s)$ is a SELECT statement:

$(\, trigger(t_1) \rightarrow effect(t_1)$	SELECT $trigger(t_1)$ THEN $effect(t_1)$
$[] \ldots$	WHEN ...
$[]\; trigger(t_n) \rightarrow effect(t_n))$	WHEN $trigger(t_n)$ THEN $effect(t_n)$
$/\!/\; childop(E, s)$	ELSE $childop(E, s)$
	END

The code for $childop(E, s)$, for an XOR state s, is a CASE statement:

	CASE r OF
$(r = S_1 \rightarrow scopeop(E, S_1)$	EITHER S_1 THEN $scopeop(E, S_1)$
$[] \ldots$	OR...
$[]\; r = S_n \rightarrow scopeop(E, S_n)\,)$	OR S_n THEN $scopeop(E, S_n)$
	END
	END

The code generated can be simplified further. If there is only a single transition on a level for an event, the code generated is of the form SELECT g THEN Q ELSE R END and can be written as IF g THEN Q ELSE R END instead. CASE statements can be simplified by leaving out all alternatives with body *skip* and adding ELSE *skip* instead. CASE statements with a single alternative can be rewritten as IF statements. An IF statement of the form IF b THEN Q ELSE *skip* END can be simplified to IF g THEN Q END.

Figure 13.9 gives the code of the TV example as generated by the iState tool [23]. The code generated preserves the broadcasting structure by calling the operation of the broadcast event rather than inlining it. As the B method does not allow calls of operations within the same machine, this is expressed in terms of auxiliary DEFINITIONS. The B method also requires that all variables be initialized. In case the value of a state variable is initially irrelevant, a nondeterministic assignment is generated.

For generating an executable implementation, the SELECT statement needs to be refined by an IF statement in which the guards are evaluated in some arbitrary order. An implementation of parallel composition by sequential composition requires in general that copies of the involved state variables and global variables are made such that their initial values are available to all statements of the parallel composition. If there is no dependency on the initial values, these copies are not needed. For example, in Figure 13.9 all parallel compositions can be implemented by sequential compositions in any order. In principle the elimination of parallel composition can be automated.

```
MACHINE TV

SETS
    ROOT = {Standby, Working};
    PICTURE = {Displaying, WarmingUp};
    SOUND = {Waiting, On, Off}

VARIABLES
    root,
    picture,
    sound,
    lev

INVARIANT
    root : ROOT ∧
    picture : PICTURE ∧
    sound : SOUND ∧
    lev : INTEGER

INITIALISATION
    root := Standby
    ||
    picture :∈ PICTURE
    ||
    sound :∈ SOUND
    ||
    lev :∈ INTEGER


DEFINITIONS
DEF_soundOn ==
    IF (root = Working) THEN
        IF (sound = Waiting) THEN
            sound := On
        END
    END


OPERATIONS
mute =
    IF (root = Working) THEN
        CASE sound OF
            EITHER Off THEN
                sound := On
            OR On THEN
                sound := Off
            OR Waiting THEN
                skip
            END
        END
    END
;
power =
    CASE root OF
        EITHER Working THEN
            root := Standby
        OR Standby THEN
            lev := 5
            ||
            root := Working
            ||
            picture := WarmingUp
            ||
            sound := Waiting
        END
    END
;
up =
    IF (root=Working) THEN
        IF (sound = On) THEN
            IF (lev < 10) THEN
                lev := (lev+ 1)
                ||
                sound := On
            END
        END
    END
;
down =
    IF (root = Working) THEN
        IF (sound = On) THEN
            IF (lev > 1) THEN
                lev := (lev - 1)
                ||
                sound := On
            END
        END
    END
;
soundOn =
    DEF_soundOn
;
warm =
    IF (root = Working) THEN
        IF (picture = WarmingUp) THEN
            DEF sound On
            ||
            picture := Displaying
        END
    END

END
```

FIGURE 13.9 B code of TV example.

13.5 STATE INVARIANT VERIFICATION

A statechart with invariants I, or *invariantchart* for short, is a statechart structure with two additional components, *inv* and *Gobal*. The function *inv* maps every state to a Boolean chart expression, the *state invariant*. Attaching chart expression I to state S, visually $S \mid I$, defines $inv(S)$ to be I. If no invariant is attached, $inv(S)$ is assumed to be true. Typically, we allow a richer set of Boolean expressions in invariants than in guards, although we do not make such a distinction here. The set *Global* is a nonempty subset of *Event*, the set of *global* events; all other events are *local*. The intention is that only transitions on global events need to establish the invariants. Transitions on local events can occur only as part of a transition on a global event, but not on their own. The global events are the interface through which the environment asks the system for a response.

We allow ourselves to confuse a chart expression attached to a state with its meaning as an expression, whereby a state test in $S_1, \ldots, S_n$ occurring in I attached to S, indicated by writing $\mathsf{in}_S\, S_1, \ldots, S_n$, is defined as testing being in $S_1, \ldots, S_n$ relative to being in S:

$$\mathsf{in}_S S_1, \ldots, S_n \mathrel{\hat{=}} in(parent^*[\{S_1, \ldots, S_n\}] - parent^*[\{S\}])$$

The *chart invariant* is defined by recursively visiting all attached invariants, starting with that attached to *Root*. In case a state is an XOR state, the invariant attached to some child has to hold as well. In case the state is an AND state, the invariant attached to each child has to hold as well.

$$\begin{aligned}
chartinv &\mathrel{\hat{=}} scopeinv(Root) \\
scopeinv(s) &\mathrel{\hat{=}} inv(s) \wedge childinv(s) \\
childinv(s) &\mathrel{\hat{=}} \mathsf{case}\ s\ \mathsf{of} \\
&\qquad Basic : \mathsf{true} \\
&\qquad XOR : \bigvee c \in children[\{s\}] \,.\, test(c) \wedge scopeinv(c) \\
&\qquad AND : \bigwedge c \in children[\{s\}] \,.\, scopeinv(c) \\
&\quad \mathsf{end}
\end{aligned}$$

Chart S is *correct* if the default transition of *Root* establishes the chart invariant and all operations of global events preserve the chart invariant:

$$\begin{aligned}
&(a)\ \{\mathsf{true}\}\ default(Root)\ \{chartinv\} \\
&(b)\ \forall E \in Global \,.\, \{chartinv\}\ op(E)\ \{chartinv\}
\end{aligned}$$

For the TV example, we define $Global = \{power, warm, down, up, mute\}$, which makes *soundOn* the only local event, and have

$$\begin{aligned}
inv(Working) &\equiv test(Displaying) \Rightarrow \neg test(Waiting) \\
inv(Sound) &\equiv 1 \le lev \wedge lev \le 10
\end{aligned}$$

For all other states, including *Root*, the attached invariant is true. It follows that *scopeinv*(*s*) for all Basic states *s* of the chart is true; for the other states we get

$$\begin{aligned}
scopeinv(Picture) &\equiv test(WarmingUp) \vee test(Displaying)\\
scopeinv(Sound) &\equiv inv(Sound) \wedge (test(Waiting) \vee test(On) \vee test(Off))\\
scopeinv(Working) &\equiv inv(Working) \wedge scopeinv(Picture) \wedge scopeinv(Sound)\\
scopeinv(Root) &\equiv test(Standby) \vee (test(Working) \wedge scopeinv(Working))
\end{aligned}$$

The last line defines the chart invariant. The B method allows this invariant to be expressed in the INVARIANT section:

```
INVARIANT
  (root = Standby) ∨
  (root = Working ∧
    (picture = Displaying ⇒ ¬(sound = Waiting)) ∧
    (1 ≤ lev ∧ lev ≤ 10))
```

This leads to five correctness conditions, one for each event *power*, *warm*, *down*, *up*, and *mute*, plus one for the initialization. The B tools generate these conditions and allow them to be proven automatically or interactively.

The invariant above has been simplified. The definition of *chartinv* would generate predicates such as $picture = WarmingUp \vee picture = Displaying$ that arise from the XOR case in *childinv*(*Picture*). Such tautologies can be eliminated during generation with the following reformulation:

$$\begin{aligned}
&childinv(s) \equiv \text{case } s \text{ of}\\
&\qquad Basic : \text{true}\\
&\qquad XOR : \textstyle\bigwedge c \in children[\{s\}] \,.\, test(c) \Rightarrow scopeinv(c)\\
&\qquad AND : \textstyle\bigwedge c \in children[\{s\}] \,.\, scopeinv(c)\\
&\quad \text{end}
\end{aligned}$$

Now, if *scopeinv*(*c*) is true (which it is for every Basic state *c* without attached invariant), $test(c) \Rightarrow scopeinv(c)$ is immediately true. If this is the case for all children *c* of *s*, *childinv*(*s*) is immediately true.

13.6 ACCUMULATED INVARIANTS

The observation underlying a more targeted verification condition generation is that sometimes it is sufficient to consider correctness of individual transitions rather than that of an event operation, and that parts of the chart invariant may be irrelevant for the correctness of transitions. To start with, let the *base* of a state set *ss* be *ss* together with the implicit children of all ancestors of *ss*. That is, the base of *ss* adds to *ss* all children of AND ancestors that are not ancestors of *ss* (i.e., the "AND uncles"). The *(upward) closure* of state set *ss* is the set of all ancestors of the base of *ss*, including *ss*. That is, it is the set of states in which a chart must be if it is in *ss*.

$$\begin{aligned} base(ss) &\mathrel{\widehat{=}} ss \cup imp(parent^{+}[ss]) \\ closure(ss) &\mathrel{\widehat{=}} parent^{*}[base(ss)] \end{aligned}$$

If a chart is in state set *ss*, (1) it has to be in all ancestors of *ss*, (2) the attached invariants of all states of the closure of *ss* have to hold, and (3) the child invariants for all states of the base of *ss* have to hold. The invariant constructed in this way is called the *accumulated invariant* of *ss*.

$$\begin{aligned} accinv(ss) \mathrel{\widehat{=}} & \; in(parent^{*}[ss]) \wedge \\ & \left(\bigwedge s \in closure(ss) \, . \, inv(s)\right) \wedge \\ & \left(\bigwedge s \in base(ss) \, . \, childinv(s)\right) \end{aligned}$$

The invariants that originate from the descendants of the base are the *synthesized* invariants; those that originate from ancestors of the base are the *inherited* invariants. For example, in Figure 13.10 we have

$$\begin{aligned} base(\{X\}) &= \{T, X\} \\ closure(\{X\}) &= \{Root, S, T, W, X\} \\ accinv(\{X\}) &= test(S) \wedge test(X) \wedge \\ & \quad inv(Root) \wedge inv(S) \wedge inv(T) \wedge inv(W) \wedge inv(X) \wedge \\ & \quad ((test(U) \wedge inv(U)) \vee (test(V) \wedge inv(V))) \end{aligned}$$

That is, the invariants of *Root*, *S*, and *T* are inherited in *S* and the invariants of *U* and *V* are synthesized for *X*. The following property justifies accumulation: If a chart is in state set *ss*, the chart invariant is reduced to the accumulated invariant of *ss*.

Theorem 13.6.1 *For any nonempty state set ss,*

$$chartinv \wedge in(parent^{*}[ss]) \equiv accinv(ss)$$

Rather than proving this theorem directly, we prove a more general one, but first state a lemma about how the accumulated invariant of a state relates to the accumulated invariant of its parent.

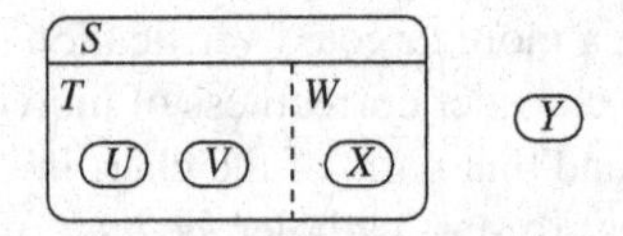

FIGURE 13.10 State hierarchy.

Lemma 13.6.1 *For any state s except Root:*

$$accinv(\{parent(s)\}) \wedge test(s) \equiv accinv(\{s\}) \quad \text{if } parent(s) \in XOR \qquad \text{(a)}$$
$$accinv(\{parent(s)\}) \equiv accinv(\{s\}) \quad \text{if } parent(s) \in AND \qquad \text{(b)}$$

We omit the proof. The following theorem states how the accumulated invariant of a state relates to the accumulated invariant of a set of descendants.

Theorem 13.6.2 *For any state s and any nonempty state set ss with $ss \subseteq children^*[\{s\}]$:*

$$accinv(\{s\}) \wedge in(path(s, ss)) \equiv accinv(ss)$$

Proof: The proof proceeds by induction over the maximal distance between s and ss, under the assumption that $ss \subseteq children^*[\{s\}]$. Let r^n be relation r composed n times, formally $r^0[p] = p$ and $r^{n+1}[p] = r[r^n[p]]$. Defining

$$p(s, ss) \mathrel{\widehat{=}} accinv(\{s\}) \wedge in(path(s, ss)) \equiv accinv(ss)$$

we show that $p(s, ss)$ holds for $s \in \bigcup i \in [0..n] \,.\, parent^i[ss]$ by induction over n. In the base case, $n = 0$ implies that $ss = \{s\}$; hence, $p(s, ss)$ follows immediately. For the induction step, suppose that $p(s, ss)$ holds for all $s \in \bigcup i \in [0..n] \,.\, parent^i[ss]$. We show that $p(parent(s), ss)$ holds:

$$accinv(\{parent(s)\}) \wedge in(path(parent(s), ss)) \equiv accinv(ss)$$
$\equiv$ ⟨from the definitions of *in* and *path*⟩
$$accinv(\{parent(s)\}) \wedge in(s) \wedge in(path(s, ss)) \equiv accinv(ss)$$
$\equiv$ ⟨case $parent(s) \in XOR$ and Lemma (a), case $parent(s) \in AND$ and (b)⟩
$$accinv(\{s\}) \wedge in(path(s, ss)) \equiv accinv(ss)$$

Hence, $p(s, ss)$ holds for $s \in parent[parent^n[ss]] = parent^{n+1}[ss]$. With the induction assumption it follows that $p(s, ss)$ holds for $s \in \bigcup i \in [0..n+1] \,.\, parent^i[ss]$, which completes the induction step and allows us to conclude that $p(s, ss)$ holds for $s \in \bigcup i \in nat \,.\, parent^i[ss]$. The theorem follows by noting that $parent^*[ss] = \bigcup i \in nat \,.\, parent^i[ss]$ and that $s \in parent^*[ss]$ follows from the assumption $ss \subseteq children^*[\{s\}]$. □

Theorem 13.6.1 follows from Theorem 13.6.2 by taking $s = Root$ and observing that $chartinv \equiv accinv(Root)$.

For the TV chart we note that, for example,

$$\begin{array}{ll} base(Standby) = \{Standby\} & closure(Standby) = \{Root, Standby\} \\ base(Working) = \{Working\} & closure(Working) = \{Working, Standby\} \\ base(On) = \{Picture, On\} & closure(On) = \{Root, Working, Picture, Sound, On\} \\ base(Off) = \{Picture, Off\} & closure(Off) = \{Root, Working, Picture, Sound, Off\} \end{array}$$

and we obtain the following accumulated invariants:

$$\begin{array}{lll} accinv(\{Standby\}) & \equiv & test(Standby) \\ accinv(\{Working\}) & \equiv & test(Working) \wedge (test(Displaying) \Rightarrow \neg test(Waiting)) \\ & & \wedge\, 1 \leq lev \wedge lev \leq 10 \\ accinv(\{On\}) & \equiv & test(Working) \wedge test(On) \wedge (test(Displaying) \\ & & \Rightarrow \neg test(Waiting)) \wedge 1 \leq lev \wedge lev \leq 10 \\ accinv(\{Off\}) & \equiv & test(Working) \wedge test(Off) \wedge (test(Displaying) \\ & & \Rightarrow \neg test(Waiting)) \wedge 1 \leq lev \wedge lev \leq 10 \end{array}$$

13.7 VERIFICATION CONDITION GENERATION

The *source invariant* of a transition is the accumulated invariant of its source states. The *target invariant* of transition t consists of the accumulated invariant of its target states; if target states are composite states or if states are implicitly entered by t, the accumulated invariant of the targets of the completion of t have to be added:

$$\begin{array}{ll} sourceinv(t) & \widehat{=}\ accinv(source(t)) \\ targetinv(t) & \widehat{=}\ accinv\left(\bigcup u \in comp(t)\ .\ target(u)\right) \end{array}$$

We are now prepared to present an alternative way of checking the correctness of a chart. The idea is to visit all transitions, starting with those that have the root state as their scope, and then to descend to all children. The correctness condition of transition t is, in the simplest case,

$$\{sourceinv(t) \wedge guard(t)\}\ effect(t)\ \{targetinv(t)\}$$

In two cases this correctness assertion is not adequate. First, when t is taken simultaneously with other transitions, other target invariants have to be established and other source invariants can be assumed. Second, when an ancestor of $scope(t)$ has other transitions on $event(t)$, these transitions have priority. In the recursive definition below, the conjunction of the negations of all triggers on E of one scope, expressed as $\bigwedge t \in Trans(E, s)\ .\ \neg trigger(t)$, is "assumed" when visiting the children:

$$\begin{array}{ll} correct(E) & \widehat{=}\ scopecorrect(E, Root) \\ scopecorrect(E, s) & \widehat{=}\ \left(\bigwedge t \in Trans(E, s)\right. \\ & \qquad \left.\ .\ \{sourceinv(t) \wedge guard(t)\}\ effect(t)\ \{targetinv(t)\}\right) \\ & \quad \wedge \left(\left(\bigwedge t \in Trans(E, s)\ .\ \neg trigger(t)\right) \Rightarrow childcorrect(E, s)\right) \end{array}$$

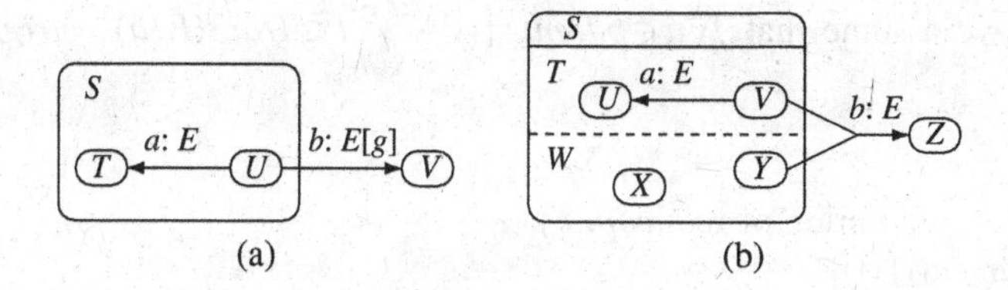

FIGURE 13.11 Transitions with different priorities.

$$childcorrect(E, s) \mathrel{\widehat{=}} \text{case } s \text{ of}$$
$$Basic : \text{true}$$
$$XOR : \bigwedge c \in children[\{s\}] \,.\, scopecorr(E, c)$$
$$AND : \{accinv(\{s\})\}\ childop(E, s)\ \{accinv(\{s\})\}$$
$$\text{end}$$

Figure 13.11 illustrates the consequence of priorities on preconditions. We note that $\neg trigger(t) \equiv \neg in(exited(t)) \vee \neg guard(t)$. In (a), transition b has priority over a; hence a is taken only if g does not hold, as $\neg guard(b)$ is part of the precondition of the correctness assertion for a. In general, for any predicates q, p, and r and statement Q,

$$g \Rightarrow \{p\}\ Q\ \{r\} \equiv \{g \wedge p\}\ Q\ \{r\}$$

In (b), transition a is taken only if T is in V and W is not in Y as $\neg in(exited(b))$ is part of the precondition of the correctness assertion for a.

Theorem 13.7.1 *For any $E \in Global$:*

$$\{chartinv\}\ op(E)\ \{chartinv\} \equiv correct(E)$$

Rather than proving this theorem directly, we prove a more general one: If we consider only transitions at scope s or below, then $\{accinv(\{s\})\}\ scopeop(E, s)\ \{accinv(\{s\})\}$ and $scopecorrect(E, s)$ are equivalent:

Theorem 13.7.2 *For any state s:*

$$\{accinv(\{s\})\}\ scopeop(E, s)\ \{accinv(\{s\})\} \equiv scopecorrect(E, s)$$

Proof: The proof proceeds by induction over the structure of charts. Defining

$$p(s) \mathrel{\widehat{=}} \{accinv(\{s\})\}\ scopeop(E, s)\ \{accinv(\{s\})\} \equiv scopecorrect(E, s)$$

the base case is that $p(s)$ holds for Basic or AND state s and the induction step is that $p(s)$ holds for XOR state s provided that $p(c)$ holds for all children c of s. To start with, we assume that $\bigwedge a \in parent^{+}[\{s\}] \,.\, \bigwedge t \in Trans(E,a) \,.\, \neg trigger(t)$ and simplify:

$$
\begin{array}{ll}
& p(s) \\
\equiv & \quad \langle \text{definition of } scopeop, \, /\!/ \rangle \\
& \{accinv(\{s\})\} \\
& \quad ([]\ t \in Trans(E,s) \,.\, trigger(t) \to effect(t))\ [] \\
& \quad \big((\bigwedge t \in Trans(E,s) \,.\, \neg trigger(t)\big) \to childop(E,s)\big) \\
& \{accinv(\{s\})\} \\
& \equiv \\
& scopecorrect(E,s) \\
\equiv & \quad \langle \text{verification rules for } [], \to, \text{definition of } trigger, scopecorrect \rangle \\
& \big(\bigwedge t \in Trans(E,s) \,. \\
& \quad \{accinv(\{s\}) \wedge in(exited(t)) \wedge guard(t)\}\ effect(t)\ \{accinv(\{s\})\}\big) \wedge \\
& \big((\bigwedge t \in Trans(E,s) \,.\, \neg trigger(t)\big) \Rightarrow \\
& \quad \{accinv(\{s\})\}\ childop(E,s)\ \{accinv(\{s\})\} \\
& \equiv \\
& \big(\bigwedge t \in Trans(E,s) \,. \\
& \quad \{sourceinv(t) \wedge guard(t)\}\ effect(t)\ \{targetinv(t)\}\big) \wedge \\
& \big((\bigwedge t \in Trans(E,s) \,.\, \neg trigger(t)\big) \Rightarrow childcorrect(E,s)\big) \\
\Leftarrow & \quad \langle \text{by Theorem 2: } accinv(\{s\}) \wedge in(exited(t)) \equiv sourceinv(t), (*) \rangle \\
& \big((\bigwedge t \in Trans(E,s) \,.\, \neg trigger(t)\big) \Rightarrow \\
& \quad \{accinv(\{s\})\}\ childop(E,s)\ \{accinv(\{s\})\} \\
& \equiv \\
& \big((\bigwedge t \in Trans(E,s) \,.\, \neg trigger(t)\big) \Rightarrow childcorrect(E,s)\big) \\
\Leftarrow & \quad \langle \text{logic} \rangle \\
& \{accinv(\{s\})\}\ childop(E,s)\ \{accinv(\{s\})\} \ \equiv\ childcorrect(E,s)
\end{array}
$$

In the step (*) we use that $effect(t)$ does indeed establish $\bigwedge u \in comp(t) \,.\, in(entered(u))$, which is given by the definition of $effect(t)$, and does preserve $accinv(\{s\})$, which is guaranteed by well-formedness condition 3. Hence, $\bigwedge u \in comp(t) \,.\, in(entered(u))$ can be conjoined to the postcondition $accinv(\{s\})$. It is then straightforward to show that by Theorem 13.6.2 and the definition of $comp(t)$:

$$accinv(\{s\}) \wedge \Big(\bigwedge u \in comp(t) \,.\, in(entered(u))\Big) \equiv targetinv(t)$$

We continue the proof with a case analysis. If $s \in Basic$, $childop(E,s)$ simplifies to skip and $childcorrect(E,s)$ simplifies to true; hence, the last line follows immediately. If $s \in AND$, $childcorrect(E,s)$ is equivalent to $\{accinv(\{s\})\}\ childop(E,s)\ \{accinv(\{s\})\}$; hence, the last line follows immediately. If $s \in XOR$, we continue:

$$
\begin{array}{ll}
& \{accinv(\{s\})\}\ []\ c \in children[\{s\}] \,.\, test(c) \to scopeop(E,c)\ \{accinv(\{s\})\} \\
& \equiv \\
& \big(\bigwedge c \in children[\{s\}] \,.\, scopecorr(E,c)\big) \\
\Leftarrow & \quad \langle \text{verification rules for } [], \to \rangle
\end{array}
$$

$$(\bigwedge c \in children[\{s\}] \, . \, \{accinv(\{s\}) \wedge test(c)\} \; scopeop(E,c) \; \{accinv(\{s\})\})$$
$$\equiv$$
$$(\bigwedge c \in children[\{s\}] \, . \, scopecorr(E,c))$$
$$\Leftarrow \quad \langle \text{logic, by Theorem 2: } accinv(\{s\}) \wedge test(c) \equiv accinv(\{c\}), (^{**})\rangle$$
$$\bigwedge c \in children[\{s\}] \, . \; \{accinv(\{c\})\} \; scopeop(E,c) \; \{accinv(\{c\})\}) \equiv scopecorr(E,c)$$

In the step (**) we use the fact that $scopeop(E,c)$ preserves $accinv(\{c\})$, which is guaranteed by well-formedness condition 3. The last line is exactly the induction assumption. This concludes the induction step and the case analysis. □

Theorem 13.7.1 follows by taking $s = Root$ and observing that $chartinv \equiv accinv(Root)$.

The recursion of *scopecorrect* stops when a Basic state or an AND state are encountered. The condition for an AND child (second last line of *childcorrect*) is equivalent to:

$$\{accinv(\{s\})\} \parallel c \in children[\{s\}] \, . \, scopeop(E,c) \, \{accinv(\{s\})\} \qquad (*)$$

In general, $\{p\} \; Q \parallel R \; \{r\}$ cannot be split into one condition for Q and one for R, as can be seen for $\{k = l\} \; k := 7 \parallel l := 7 \; \{k = l\}$. Figure 13.12(a) illustrates that the correctness of b and d cannot be shown individually.

For the TV chart we have that

$$\begin{aligned} op(soundOn) = (&test(Working) \rightarrow \\ &\quad (test(Waiting) \rightarrow assign(On) \\ &\quad [] \; test(On) \rightarrow \mathsf{skip} \\ &\quad [] \; test(Off) \rightarrow \mathsf{skip}) \\ &[] \; test(Standby) \rightarrow \mathsf{skip}) \end{aligned}$$

and get the following correctness assertions, with some simplifications:

$$\begin{aligned} correct(power) \equiv \; &\{accinv(\{Standby\})\} \\ &\quad assign(Working) \parallel assign(WarmingUp) \parallel \\ &\quad assign(Waiting) \parallel lev := 5 \\ &\{accinv(\{Working\})\} \end{aligned}$$

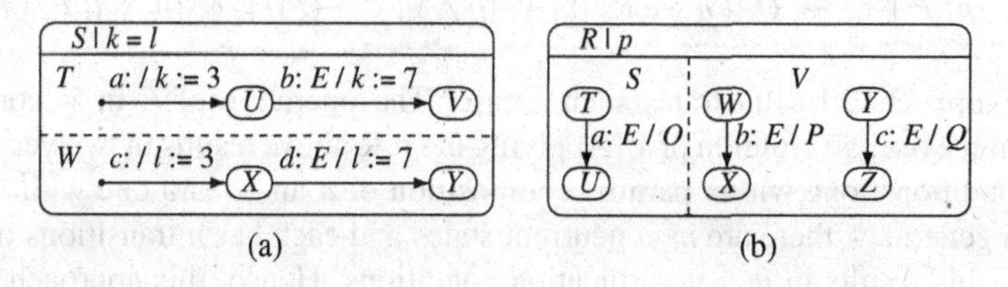

FIGURE 13.12 Concurrent transitions and invariants.

$$
\begin{array}{lll}
 & \wedge & \\
 & \{accinv(\{Working\})\} & \\
 & \quad assign(Standby) & \\
 & \{accinv(\{Standby\})\} & \\
correct(warm) & \equiv \{accinv(\{Working\})\} & \\
 & \quad test(WarmingUp) \rightarrow op(soundOn) \parallel assign(Displaying) & \\
 & \{accinv(\{Working\})\} & \\
correct(down) & \equiv \{accinv(\{Working\})\} & \\
 & \quad test(On) \rightarrow lev := lev - 1 \parallel assign(On) & \\
 & \{accinv(\{Working\})\} & \\
correct(up) & \equiv \{accinv(\{Working\})\} & \\
 & \quad test(On) \rightarrow lev := lev + 1 \parallel assign(On) & \\
 & \{accinv(\{Working\})\} & \\
correct(mute) & \equiv \{accinv(\{Working\})\} & \\
 & \quad (\, test(On) \rightarrow assign(Off) & \\
 & \quad [\,]\ test(Off) \rightarrow assign(On)) & \\
 & \{accinv(\{Working\})\} &
\end{array}
$$

The simplifications carried out are that verification conditions of the form $\{p\}\, Q \mathbin{/\!/} \mathsf{skip}$ $\{p\}$ are replaced by $\{p\}\ Q\ \{p\}$.

In the design of embedded systems, physical components are typically modeled by concurrent states on outer levels. For such designs, the possibility for generating targeted verification conditions by *scopecorrect* is limited, as the recursion stops as soon as an AND state is encountered. Still, special cases exist:

1. If only one concurrent state contains transitions on event E, the parallel composition in (*) disappears, resulting in

$$\{accinv(\{s\})\}\ scopeop(E, s)\ \{accinv(\{s\})\}$$

   Theorem 13.7.2 can now be used to continue decomposing the verification conditions according to *scopecorrect*.

2. Further splitting of the verification condition is possible according to the structure of $scopeop(E, c)$. If an operand of the parallel composition contains a nondeterministic choice with guards, we can use the fact that $\parallel$ distributes over $[\,]$:

$$\{p\}\ P \parallel (g \rightarrow Q\ [\,]\ h \rightarrow R)\ \{r\} \equiv \{p \wedge g\}\ P \parallel Q\ \{r\}\ \wedge\ \{p \wedge h\}\ P \parallel R\ \{r\}$$

   Figure 13.12(b) illustrates such a case: The operation of E in V contains a choice over all children of V. Applying the rule above results in two verification conditions, one with a parallel composition of a and b and one with a and c. In general, if there are m concurrent states and each has n transitions on event E, this results in $m \times n$ verification conditions. Hence, this approach has the potential of generating a possibly large number of smaller conditions.

3. The distributivity of $\|$ over $[]$ can also be applied for bodies containing conditional statements, as if g then Q else $R = (g \rightarrow Q)\ []\ (\neg g \rightarrow R)$. Hence, for each transition the number of proof conditions involving that transition double with each conditional statement that it contains.

For the TV example we note transitions on *warm*, *down*, *up*, *mute* occur only in one concurrent state and apply rule 1 above. As *warm* broadcasts *soundOn*, we apply rule 2 as well.

$$
\begin{array}{lll}
correct(warm) & \equiv & \{accinv(\{WarmingUp\})\} \\
& & \quad test(WarmingUp) \rightarrow test(Working) \rightarrow \\
& & \qquad test(Waiting) \rightarrow assign(On) \parallel assign(Displaying) \\
& & \{accinv(\{Displaying\})\} \\
& & \wedge \\
& & \{accinv(\{WarmingUp\})\} \\
& & \quad test(WarmingUp) \rightarrow test(Working) \rightarrow test(On) \rightarrow \\
& & \qquad assign(Displaying) \\
& & \{accinv(\{Displaying\})\} \\
& & \wedge \\
& & \{accinv(\{WarmingUp\})\} \\
& & \quad test(WarmingUp) \rightarrow test(Working) \rightarrow test(Off) \rightarrow \\
& & \qquad assign(Displaying) \\
& & \{accinv(\{Displaying\})\} \\
correct(down) & \equiv & \{accinv(\{On\})\}\ lev := lev - 1 \parallel assign(On)\ \{accinv(\{On\})\} \\
correct(up) & \equiv & \{accinv(\{On\})\}\ lev := lev + 1 \parallel assign(On)\ \{accinv(\{On\})\} \\
correct(mute) & \equiv & \{accinv(\{On\})\}\ assign(Off)\ \{accinv(\{Off\})\} \\
& & \wedge \\
& & \{accinv(\{Off\})\}\ assign(On))\ \{accinv(\{On\})\}
\end{array}
$$

The two verification conditions for *power* are unchanged. Thus, this results in nine verification conditions, compared to the original five, plus one for the initialization.

The proof conditions are now of the form $\{p\}\ Q_1 \parallel \cdots \parallel Q_n\ \{r\}$, where each Q_i is a multiple assignment statement, assigning to state variables or to global variables. Using the fact that $(x := e \parallel y := f) = (x, y := e, f)$, these can be merged into a single multiple assignment. The verification rule for assignments then yields a plain predicate that can be passed to a theorem prover.

13.8 PRIORITY AMONG TRANSITIONS

UML statecharts differ from the interpretation above in giving transitions with inner scope priority over transitions with outer scope [18]. Thus, in Figure 13.13(a) transition a has priority over transition b, as $\neg guard(a)$ is part of the precondition of the correctness assertion for b. In (b), transition b is taken only if T is not in U or V is not in X, as $\neg in(exited(a))$ is part of the precondition of the correctness assertion

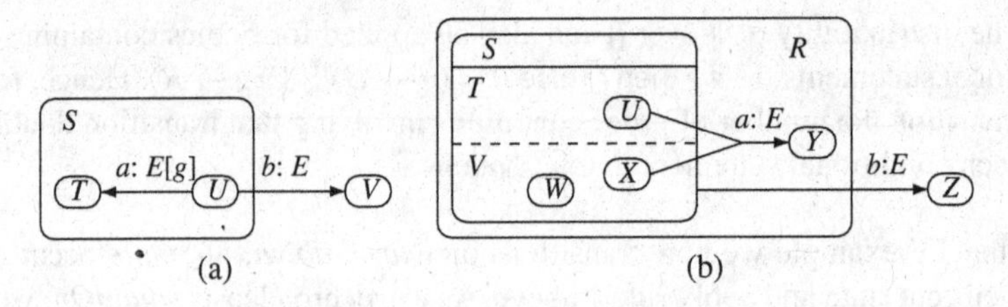

FIGURE 13.13 Transitions with different priorities.

for b. In this interpretation, the notion of a chart invariant remains the same, but *op* and *correct* have to be adapted. Let $\underline{Trans}(E,s)$ be the set of all transitions on E with scope below s:

$$\underline{Trans}(E,s) \mathrel{\widehat{=}} \{t \in Transition \mid event(t) = E \wedge scope(t) \in children^{+}[\{s\}]\}$$

The operation $\underline{op}(E)$ allows a transition to be taken only if no other transition with lower scope is enabled. Formally, all transitions on scope s are guarded by $\bigwedge t \in \underline{Trans}(E,s) \,.\, \neg trigger(t)$. The choice among transitions with the same scope is arbitrary.

$$\begin{aligned}
&\underline{op}(E) && \mathrel{\widehat{=}} \underline{scopeop}(E, Root)\\
&\underline{scopeop}(E,s) && \mathrel{\widehat{=}} \big((\bigwedge t \in \underline{Trans}(E,s) \,.\, \neg trigger(t)) \rightarrow\\
& && \qquad [] \; t \in Trans(E,s) \,.\, trigger(t) \rightarrow effect(t)\big)\\
& && \quad /\!/ \; \underline{childop}(E,s)\\
&\underline{childop}(E,s) && \mathrel{\widehat{=}} \textsf{case } s \textsf{ of}\\
& && \qquad Basic : \textsf{skip}\\
& && \qquad XOR : [] \; c \in children[\{s\}] \,.\, test(c) \rightarrow \underline{scopeop}(E,c)\\
& && \qquad AND : \| \; c \in children[\{s\}] \,.\, \underline{scopeop}(E,c)\\
& && \quad \textsf{end}
\end{aligned}$$

The verification conditions reflect this by assuming that $\bigwedge t \in \underline{Trans}(E,s) \,.\, \neg trigger(t)$ holds for transitions with scope s:

$$\begin{aligned}
&\underline{correct}(E) && \mathrel{\widehat{=}} \underline{scopecorrect}(E, Root)\\
&\underline{scopecorrect}(E,s) && \mathrel{\widehat{=}} \big((\bigwedge t \in \underline{Trans}(E,s) \,.\, \neg trigger(t)) \implies\\
& && \qquad (\bigwedge t \in Trans(E,s) \,.\\
& && \qquad\quad \{sourceinv(t) \wedge guard(t)\}\; effect(t)\; \{targetinv(t)\})) \wedge\\
& && \quad \underline{childcorrect}(E,s)\big)\\
&\underline{childcorrect}(E,s) && \mathrel{\widehat{=}} \textsf{case } s \textsf{ of}\\
& && \qquad Basic : \textsf{true}\\
& && \qquad XOR : \bigwedge c \in children[\{s\}] \,.\, \underline{scopecorrect}(E,c)\\
& && \qquad AND : \{accinv(\{s\})\}\; \underline{childop}(E,s)\; \{accinv(\{s\})\}\\
& && \quad \textsf{end}
\end{aligned}$$

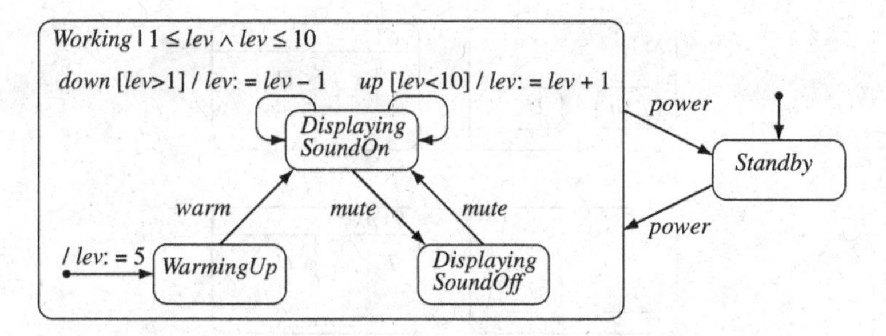

FIGURE 13.14 Alternative state structure for a TV set.

Without proof we claim that the preservation of the chart invariant by $\underline{op}(E)$ can be verified by $\underline{correct}(E)$:

Theorem 13.8.1 *For any E ∈ Global:*

$$\{chartinv\}\ \underline{op}(E)\ \{chartinv\} \equiv \underline{correct}(E)$$

The verification conditions from $\underline{correct}(E)$ are similar in complexity to those from *correct*(E). However, if $\underline{op}(E)$ were used directly for code generation, the resulting code would be more complex: As in the recursive definition, transitions on outer scopes are visited first; the triggers of all transitions of lower scopes on that event need to be evaluated before these are visited, where they are reevaluated.

13.9 CONCLUSIONS

Having an effective mechanism for verifying invariants begs the question of when and how to use invariants. Sometimes the need for an invariant can be avoided altogether. Figure 13.14 gives a chart that is equivalent to that of Figure 13.1 but avoids the invariant originally attached to *Working* by restructuring the states of *Working*. If one were not able to express and check invariants, one might prefer the restructured one, on the grounds that by its mere structure it cannot lead to an invalid configuration. However, the structure of concurrent states of the original chart reflects the structure of the components of the application better, and one would believe that it is easier to design, comprehend, and maintain. We could also avoid the invariant $1 \leq lev \wedge lev \leq 10$ by having 10 distinct *On* states, one for each level. Such a design would be awkward at best and impossible if the range of variables were unbounded. In the presence of global variables, invariants cannot be avoided through restructuring. After all, we get confidence in a design by having descriptions with some redundancy—here by state transitions and by invariants—and checking their consistency. By removing the possibility for these checks through a "clever" design, the design will not be more trustworthy.

We define two chart annotations to be *equivalent* if the resulting chart invariants are equivalent, meaning that they lead to the same correctness conditions. Figure 13.15

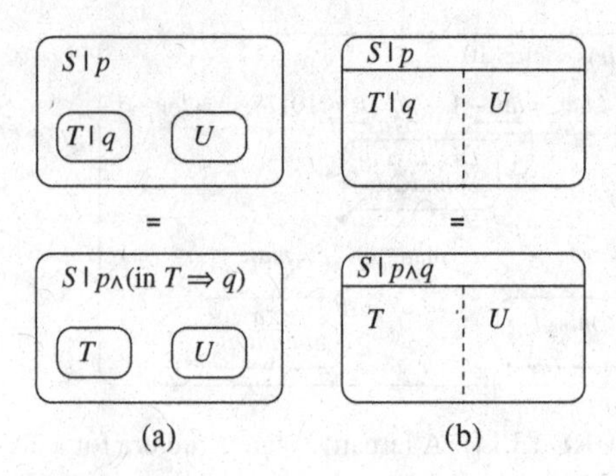

FIGURE 13.15 Equivalent annotations.

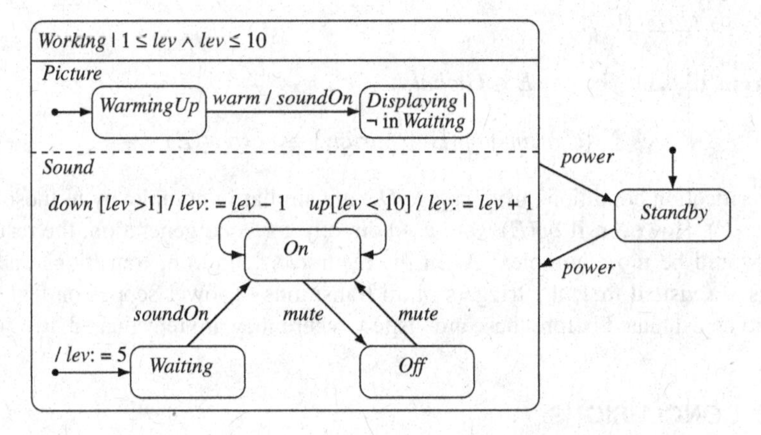

FIGURE 13.16 Alternative annotation for a TV set.

illustrates two sets of equivalent chart annotations. Used as transformation rules, these two equivalencies allow all invariants to be moved up to *Root*. This design freedom leads to a question as to where best to attach invariants. Figure 13.16 provides an annotation that is equivalent to that of Figure 13.1. The original invariant of *Sound* is now attached to *Working*. However, only transitions within *Sound* are relevant for this invariant: The invariant is above the scope of all affected transitions. In Figure 13.16, the original invariant of *Working* has been moved to *Displaying*. Although this shortens the invariant expression by leaving out the state tests, some relevant transitions are now in a concurrent state, making the dependency less visual. These two observations motivate the following rule: *Invariants should be attached exactly to the scope of all relevant transitions.* Figure 13.1 follows this rule. We summarize the main points of the approach:

1. Configurations are defined by state variables, and each event is defined as one operation for all transitions on that event. This disallows Boolean combinations of events as in classical statecharts, but is in line with UML statecharts.

2. An operation of an event is defined by a "recursive descent" of the state hierarchy. This favors giving priority to transitions on outer levels over transitions on inner levels. This definition also serves as a scheme for code generation.
3. The state variables and event operations are mapped to one module (MACHINE in the B method).
4. All transitions on an event are taken simultaneously rather than in a sequence of microsteps. For this, all transitions taken simultaneously must be conflict-free. In our experience this excludes some statecharts that would be of questionable design.
5. Invariants can be attached to basic and composite states. The chart invariant is derived from the attached invariants. All event operations have to preserve the chart invariant.
6. The default transition of the root state has to establish the chart invariant; default transitions are also used for establishing a local invariant. For this, default transitions need to have a body.
7. Local verification conditions are computed from the accumulated invariant of the source and target states. The justification of the local verification conditions is in terms of the chart invariant.

An alternative to mapping the state variables and event operations to a single module is to distribute them by certain design criteria among several modules with an acyclic or tree dependency structure [10]. With invariants distributed among modules as well, this also leads to more local verification conditions, but in a different way than through accumulated invariants. Entry and exit actions, history states, and transitions with segments remain future work.

Acknowledgments

The author is indebted to Kevin Lano for his patience and his help. Dai Tri Man Le suggested the term *accumulated invariant*. Daniel Zingaro pointed out several errors.

REFERENCES

1. J.-R. Abrial. *The B Book: Assigning Programs to Meaning*. Cambridge University Press, New York, 1996.
2. P. Bhaduri and S. Ramesh. *Model Checking of Statechart Models: Survey and Research Directions*. Technical Report cs.SE/0407038, arXiv, July 2004.
3. E. Clarke and W. Heinle. *Modular Translation of Statecharts to SMV*. Technical Report CMU-CS-00-XXX. School of Computer Science, Carnegie Mellon University, Pittsburgh, PA, August 2000.
4. W. Damm, B. Jasko, H. Hungar, and A. Pnueli. A compositional real-time semantics of STATEMATE designs. In W.-P. de Roever, H. Langmaack, and A. Pnueli, eds., *Compositionality: The Significant Difference*, Bad Malente, Germany, 1998. Lecture Notes in Computer Science, vol. 1536, pp. 186–238. Springer-Verlag, New York, 1998.

5. N. Day and J. Joyce. The semantics of statecharts in HOL. In J. Joyce and C.-J. Seger, eds., *Higher Order Logic Theorem Proving and Its Applications*, Vancouver, British Columbia, Canada, 1994. Lecture Notes in Computer Science, vol. 780, pp. 338–351. Springer-Verlag, New York, 1994.
6. D. Harel. Statecharts: a visual formalism for complex systems. *Science of Computer Programming*, 8:231–274, 1987.
7. D. Harel and A. Naamad. The STATEMATE semantics of statecharts. *ACM Transactions on Software Engineering and Methodology*, 5(5):293–333, 1996.
8. A. Knapp, S. Merz, and C. Rauh. Model checking timed UML state machines and collaborations. In W. Damm and E.-R. Olderog, eds., *Formal Techniques in Real-Time and Fault-Tolerant Systems*, Oldenburg, Germany, 2002. Lecture Notes in Computer Science, vol. 2469, pp. 395–416. Springer-Verlag, New York, 2002.
9. R. Laleau and A. Mammar. An overview of a method and its support tool for generating B specifications from UML notations. In *15th IEEE International Conference on Automated Software Engineering (ASE 2000)*, Grenoble, France. IEEE Computer Society Press, Los Alamitos, CA, 2000.
10. K. Lano, K. Androutsopoulos, and P. Kan. Structuring reactive systems in B AMN. In *3rd IEEE International Conference on Formal Engineering Methods*, York, UK. IEEE Computer Society Press, Los Alamitos, CA, 2000.
11. K. Lano and D. Clark. Direct semantics of extended state machines. *Journal of Object Technology*, 6(9):35–51, 2007.
12. D. Latella, I. Majzik, and M. Massink. Automatic verification of a behavioural subset of UML statechart diagrams using the SPIN model-checker. *Formal Aspects of Computing*, 11(6):637–664, 1999.
13. H. Ledang and J. Souquières. Contributions for modelling UML state-charts in B. In *Integrated Formal Methods, Third International Conference, IFM '2002*, Turku, Finland, May 2002. Lecture Notes in Computer Science, vol. 2335, pp. 109–127. Springer-Verlag, New York, 2002.
14. J. Lilius and I. P. Paltor. Formalising UML state machines for model checking. In R. France and B. Rumpe, eds., *UML '99: The Unified Modeling Language Beyond the Standard*, Fort Collins, CO, 1999. Lecture Notes in Computer Science, vol. 1723, pp. 430–445. Springer-Verlag, New York, 1999.
15. E. Meyer and J. Souquières. A systematic approach to transform OMT diagrams to a B specification. In J. Wing, J. Woodcock, and J. Davies, eds., *World Congress on Formal Methods in the Development of Computing Systems, FM'99*, Toulouse, France, Sept. 1999. Lecture Notes in Computer Science, vol. 1708, pp. 875—895. Springer-Verlag, New York, 1999.
16. E. Mikk, Y. Lakhnech, M. Siegel, and G. J. Holzmann. Implementing statecharts in Promela/Spin. In *Second IEEE Workshop on Industrial-Strength Formal Specification Techniques*, Boca Raton, FL, 1998. IEEE Computer Society Press, Los Alamitos, CA, 1998.
17. H. P. Nguyen. Dérivation de spécifications formelles B à partir de spécifications semi-formelles. Doctoral dissertation, INIST-CNRS, 1998.
18. OMG. Unified modeling language, superstructure, v2.1.2. http://www.omg.org/spec/UML/2.1.2/Superstructure/PDF, 2007.

19. A. Pnueli and M. Shalev. What is in a step: on the semantics of statecharts. In T. Ito and A. Meyer, eds., *Proceedings of the 1st International Conference on Theoretical Aspects of Computer Software* (*TACS '91*), Sendai, Japan, 1991. Lecture Notes in Computer Science, vol. 526, pp. 244–264. Springer-Verlag, New York, 1991.
20. E. Sekerinski. Graphical design of reactive systems. In D. Bert, ed., *2nd International B Conference*, Montpellier, France, 1998. Lecture Notes in Computer Science, vol. 1393, pp. 182–197. Springer-Verlag, New York, 1998.
21. E. Sekerinski. Verifying statecharts with state invariants. In K. Breitman, J. Woodcock, R. Sterritt, and M. Hinchey, eds., *ICECCS '08–13th IEEE International Conference on Engineering of Complex Computer Systems*, pp. 7–14, Belfast, Northern Ireland, Mar. 2008. IEEE Computer Society Press, Los Alamitos, CA.
22. E. Sekerinski and R. Zurob. iState: a statechart translator. In M. Gogolla and C. Kobryn, eds., *UML 2001: The Unified Modeling Language, 4th International Conference*. Toronto, Ontario, Canada, 2001. Lecture Notes in Computer Science, vol. 2185, pp. 376–390. Springer-Verlag, New York, 2001.
23. E. Sekerinski and R. Zurob. Translating statecharts to B. In M. Butler, L. Petre, and K. Sere, eds., *Third International Conference on Integrated Formal Methods*, Turku, Finland, 2002. Lecture Notes in Computer Science, vol. 2335, pp. 128–144, Springer-Verlag, New York, 2002.
24. D. Snook and M. Butler. UML-B: formal modeling and design aided by UML. *ACM Transactions on Software Engineering and Methodology*, 15(1):92–122, 2006.

CHAPTER 14

MODEL TRANSFORMATION SPECIFICATION AND VERIFICATION

Kevin Lano
Department of Computer Science, King's College London, London, UK

14.1 INTRODUCTION

Model transformations are becoming increasingly important in software development, particularly as part of model-driven development. In this chapter we consider different techniques for the specification of transformations, based on the semantics of class diagrams and state machines, and formally describe several UML class and state machine model transformations.

Model transformations are mappings of one software engineering model into another, semantically related model. The models usually considered are constructed using graphical languages such as the unified modeling language (UML) [34]. Ideally, transformations should be specified so that they can be applied systematically to all models that satisfy certain conditions, to produce a correct result.

The concepts of model-driven architecture (MDA) [33] and model-driven development (MDD) use model transformations as a central element, principally to transform high-level models [such as platform-Independent models (PIMs)] toward more implementation-oriented models [platform-specific models (PSMs)], but also to improve the quality of models at a particular level of abstraction. As part of the MDA, a standard for queries, views, and transformations (QVT) was developed [36], and different notations for specifying and implementing model transformations were defined. QVT has been used for the specification of model transformations [4] and model semantics [5]. However, issues of demonstrating the consistency and correctness of transformations specified using QVT remain, and efficient implementation of transformations to avoid unnecessary rework if changes are made to part of the starting model is also an open problem [43].

Another important use of transformations is for the analysis and verification of models, by translating them into a representation that supports these techniques.

UML 2 Semantics and Applications. Edited by Kevin Lano

Translations of UML to B [27,39], SMV [1], finite state machines [20], Petri nets, and many other formalisms have been defined for this purpose. Although this form of reexpression transformation is not the main subject of this chapter, the concepts of correctness defined in Section 14.3.3 also apply to these transformations.

Previous work on the classification of model transformations has focused on the implementation of transformations as sets of rules or algorithms [14,43]. In this chapter we separate the specification and implementation of model transformations and classify transformations based on their purpose and their effect on models.

In Section 14.2 we summarize the various categories of model transformation, in Section 14.3 present techniques for the specification of transformations, in Section 14.4 present some widely used refinement transformations, in Section 14.5 present quality improvement transformations, in Section 14.6 present design pattern–based transformations, and in Section 14.7 present enhancement transformations.

14.2 CATEGORIES OF MODEL TRANSFORMATION

Following a workshop on model-driven development, the following classifications of model transformation approaches were defined [30]:

- The languages on which the transformation operates: that is, program-level versus model-level transformations, endogenous (source and target language are the same) versus exogenous (different source and target languages), horizontal (transformation does not change abstraction level) versus vertical (source and target models are at different abstraction levels), and which technology is used to support the transformation (e.g., XML versus MDA).
- The level of automation and complexity of the transformation, and the semantic correctness of the transformation.

Criteria for the effectiveness of a transformation language and tool were also proposed, including the ability to compose transformations and to demonstrate syntactic and semantic correctness.

In this chapter we focus on semantically based criteria to classify transformations, in particular the criteria of abstraction level and semantic relation between the source and target models. These criteria will be used as classification features, following the approach of Mens et al. [14] for the classification of model transformation implementations. The following two features of a model transformation from a source model M_1 to a target model M_2 are therefore considered as significant for classifying its purpose and use:

1. If M_2 is at the same abstraction level as M_1, at a lower abstraction level (e.g., is a PSM relative to M_1 as a PIM), or at a higher abstraction level.
2. If M_2 is an extension of M_1, if the semantics of M_2 is stronger than the semantics of M_1 (but M_2 is not simply an extension of M_1), if the semantics of the models are equivalent, or if the semantics of M_2 is weaker than that of M_1.

TABLE 14.1 Transformation Categories

	Same Abstraction Level	M_2 Lower	M_2 Higher
M_2 is extension of M_1	Enhancement		
M_2 semantically stronger	Specialization	Refinement	
M_2, M_1 equivalent	Reexpression/ quality improvement	Refinement/ Reexpression	Abstraction
M_2 semantically weaker	Generalization	—	Abstraction

Table 14.1 shows the possible combinations of these feature values. Using these features, model transformations can be classified in the following general categories:

- *Refinements:* transformations used to refine a model toward an implementation: for example, PIM-to-PSM transformations in the MDA. They may remove certain constructs or structures, such as multiple inheritance, from a model and represent them instead by constructs that are available in a particular implementation platform. The semantics and language of the model may be changed, but all the properties of the original model should be true in the new model, via some interpretation.
- *Specializations of a model:* strengthen the logical properties of a model at one level of abstraction. Some implementations that satisfy the original model will not satisfy the new model. *Generalization* is the inverse of specialization.
- *Quality improvements:* transformations that usually operate on the same language, do not change the abstraction level of a model, and preserve its semantics (under a suitable interpretation) but improve its structure and organization (e.g., by factoring out duplicated elements).
- *Enhancements:* elaborate or extend a model at the same level of abstraction in the same language by adding new elements while not restricting the existing elements.
- *Reexpressions:* translate a model in one language into its nearest equivalent in a different language. This is useful for reengineering, migration, validation, and tool integration. Code generation (e.g., from a UML Java PSM to Java) can also be considered to be in this category.
- *Abstractions:* the inverse of refinement transformations. These can be useful for reverse engineering (e.g., from a PSM to a PIM).

Design patterns can be considered as transformations from a starting model (without the pattern) to a target model that conforms to the pattern. These are usually refinements or quality improvements; for example, the template method [18] can be regarded as a quality improvement transformation.

14.3 SPECIFICATION OF MODEL TRANSFORMATIONS

14.3.1 Model Transformation Semantics

Transformations can be defined as relations between models. The models may be in the same or in different modeling languages. Let $\mathcal{L}_1$ and $\mathcal{L}_2$ be the languages concerned (in the case of UML these will typically be defined as metamodels which are subsets of the UML metamodels or variants of them, e.g., metamodels of older versions of UML). A transformation τ then describes which models M_1 of $\mathcal{L}_1$ correspond to (transform to) which models M_2 of $\mathcal{L}_2$.

Let $Models_{\mathcal{L}}$ be the set of models that interpret the language (metamodel) $\mathcal{L}$. The elements of $Models_{\mathcal{L}}$ are all structures M which have interpretations $M.T$ for each data type T of M, including a set $M.E$ (of object identifiers) for each metaclass E of $\mathcal{L}$, and functions

$$f_M : M.E \rightarrow M.T$$

for each metafeature f: T specified for instances of E in $\mathcal{L}$. The structures M should contain no other additional elements not specified in $\mathcal{L}$, and should satisfy any logical properties defined for $\mathcal{L}$. We may simply write M: $\mathcal{L}$ instead of M: $Models_{\mathcal{L}}$. $f_M(e)$ is usually written as $e.f_M$.

A model transformation τ from language $\mathcal{L}_1$ to language $\mathcal{L}_2$ can therefore be expressed as a relation

$$Rel_\tau : Models_{\mathcal{L}_1} \leftrightarrow Models_{\mathcal{L}_2}$$

For example, consider the minimal language $\mathcal{L}$ of Figure 14.1. Models M of this language consist of collections $M.Entity$ of entities; each $e : M.Entity$ has $e.name_M$: $M.String$.

Consider a reexpression transformation $\tau(p$: $M.String)$ on this language, which prefixes a particular string p to each entity name in the model. We could define this first on an individual entity of the source model:

$$\begin{array}{l} Rel_{\tau(p,e)}(M1, M2) \quad \equiv \\ \quad M1.Entity \;=\; M2.Entity \;\; \wedge \\ \quad e :\; M1.Entity \;\; \wedge \\ \quad e.name_{M2} \;=\; p \;+\; \text{``\_''} \;+\; e.name_{M1} \;\; \wedge \\ \quad \forall e' :\; M1.Entity \cdot e' \neq e \;\; \Longrightarrow \;\; e'.name_{M2} \;=\; e'.name_{M1} \end{array}$$

This transforms one entity of $M1$ into the form required.

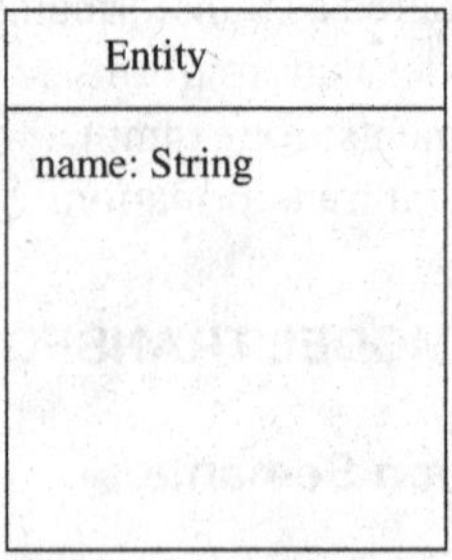

Entity
name: String

FIGURE 14.1 Basic metamodel $\mathcal{L}$.

A relation that transforms all the entities in one step is

$$\begin{array}{l} Rel_{\tau(p)}(M1, M2) \quad \equiv \\ \quad M1.Entity \;=\; M2.Entity \;\wedge \\ \quad \forall e : M1.Entity \cdot e.name_{M2} = p + \text{"\_"} + e.name_{M1} \end{array}$$

Relations that represent transformations are normally:

- *Functions*. The relation maps each source model to a unique target model.
- *Irreflexive*. They do not map all models to themselves.
- *Nontransitive*. Iterating the transformation produces different results.

Sequential composition $\tau;\sigma$ of transformations corresponds to relational composition of their representing relations. Transformations can also be combined using conditional expressions:

$$\textit{if } E \textit{ then } \tau \textit{ else } \sigma$$

where E can be evaluated in the source model and by union (disjunction): $\tau \cup \sigma$, provided that the resulting relation remains functional.

In general, it may be that only some models in $\mathcal{L}_1$ can have a transformation τ applied to them validly, termed the *applicability condition* of τ. It is defined as

$$\mathrm{dom}(Rel_\tau) = \{M : Models_{\mathcal{L}_1} | \exists M' : Models_{\mathcal{L}_2} \cdot Rel_\tau(M, M')\}$$

In the case of the example transformation above, the applicability condition is *true*: It can always be applied to any model of $\mathcal{L}$.

A transformation is *invertible* if it can be applied in the reverse direction. The reversed transformation τ^{-1} is represented by the inverse Rel_τ^{-1} relation, which is only defined on the domain

$$\mathrm{ran}(Rel_\tau) = \{M : Models_{\mathcal{L}_2} | \exists M' : Models_{\mathcal{L}_1} \cdot Rel_\tau(M', M)\}$$

The reversed relation may not be functional, since there may be many different models of $\mathcal{L}_1$ that map to the same model of $\mathcal{L}_2$.

In the example above, the inverse relation is functional and well defined on $\mathrm{ran}(Rel_\tau)$; this transformation removes the $p +$ "_" prefix from names.

Another important property of a transformation is *monotonicity*: A transformation is monotonic if extensions of the source model transform into extensions of the target model. That is, given a model M_1' that extends a model M_1 by enlarging entity type interpretations and feature interpretations: $M_1'.E \supseteq M_1.E$ for each metaclass E and $f_{M_1'} \supseteq f_{M_1}$ for each metafeature f, M_1' transforms to a model M_2', which is an extension of the transformation M_2 of M_1.

The example above is monotonic.

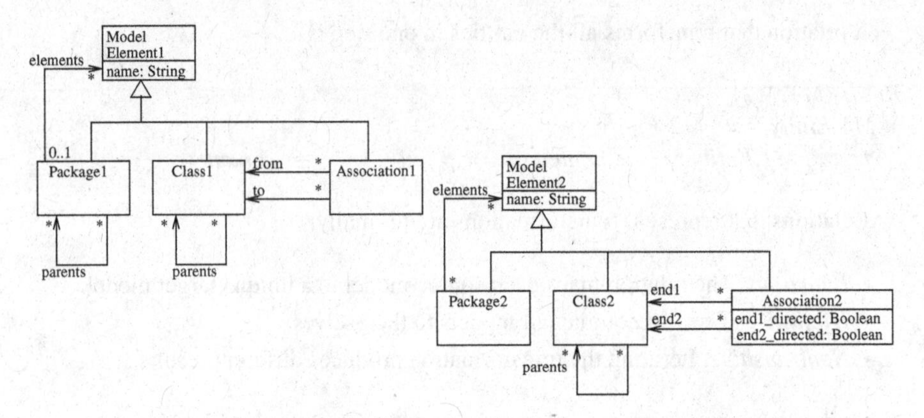

FIGURE 14.2 Metamodels $\mathcal{L}_1$ and $\mathcal{L}_2$.

The formalism we have introduced here permits ternary or higher-multiplicity transformations: for example, a transformation

$$union : \mathcal{L} \times \mathcal{L} \leftrightarrow \mathcal{L}$$

which produces a union of two models. In this chapter we consider only binary transformations.

Another example of a transformation, shown in Figure 14.2, is based on a reexpression transformation of Tratt [43]. On the left-hand side is a metamodel for the language $\mathcal{L}_1$, in which packages can be inherited by other packages, but associations are restricted to being unidirectional. On the right-hand side is a metamodel for the language $\mathcal{L}_2$, in which packages cannot be inherited by other packages, but associations can be unidirectional, bidirectional, and undirected.

If τ is being used to construct a new model $M2$ of $\mathcal{L}_2$ from a model $M1$ of $\mathcal{L}_1$, we can define Rel_τ as

$$
\begin{array}{l}
\quad M2.Class2 \;=\; M1.Class1 \\
\quad M2.Association2 \;=\; M1.Association1 \\
\quad M2.ModelElement2 \;=\; M1.ModelElement1 \\
\quad M2.Package2 \;=\; M1.Package1 \\
\forall a\colon\ M2.Association2 \;\cdot \\
\quad a.name_{M2} \;=\; a.name_{M1} \\
\quad a.end1\_directed_{M2} \;=\; false \\
\quad a.end2\_directed_{M2} \;=\; true \\
\quad a.from_{M1} \;=\; a.end1_{M2} \\
\quad a.to_{M1} \;=\; a.end2_{M2} \\
\forall p\colon\ M2.Package2 \;\cdot \\
\quad p.name_{M2} \;=\; p.name_{M1} \\
\quad p.elements_{M2} \;=\; p.elements_{M1} \;\cup\; \bigcup \{p1\colon\ p.parents_{M1} \mid p1.elements_{M2}\} \\
\forall c\colon\ M2.Class2 \;\cdot
\end{array}
$$

$$c.name_{M2} = c.name_{M1}$$
$$c.parents_{M2} = c.parents_{M1}$$

Provided that $parents_{M1}$ is noncyclic, this defines a relationship between the respective sets of models of $\mathcal{L}_1$ and $\mathcal{L}_2$. The packages in the new model do not have parent packages; instead, all the elements that were present in themselves or any of their parents (recursively) are now included directly in themselves. The $\mathcal{L}_1$ expressions *parents* and *elements* on packages do not have an interpretation in $\mathcal{L}_2$.

This transformation is invertible, but has restricted application on $\mathcal{L}_2$ because undirected and bidirectional associations in $\mathcal{L}_2$ have no representation in $\mathcal{L}_1$. The inverse relation is nonfunctional since different arrangements of $\mathcal{L}_1$ packages can produce the same $\mathcal{L}_2$ packages.

14.3.2 Approaches for Transformation Specification

The definition of model transformations by imperative rules was the main specification approach prior to the OMG's QVT initiative. These approaches defined graph transformation steps, or term rewriting rules, to specify *how* the transformation should be performed [13]. An alternative approach abstracts from the implementation of the transformation and instead, expresses *what* relation between languages is intended by the transformation [2]. In practice, some combination of these two approaches is necessary, with the relational specification approach supplemented by strategies for efficient implementation of the transformation relations.

The QVT standard [36] adopts such a hybrid approach, providing a declarative *Relations* language to specify transformations as relations and an imperative *Operational Mappings* language to specify transformation implementations. The Relations language includes a graphical notation to describe transformations using metaobject models. Figure 14.3 shows an example for the transformation τ. The left-hand-side object model describes to which elements the transformation should be applied; the right-hand side shows the effect of the transformation. A *when* clause on the LHS can define additional applicability conditions using OCL. A *where* clause defines further properties between the left- and right-hand sides which the transformation should establish, in this case that the association end classes are translated by *Class1ToClass2* (i.e., some one-to-one mapping from *Class1* to *Class2*).

C denotes that the left-hand side (LHS) model is checked but not modified by the transformation; *E* denotes that the right-hand side (RHS) model is modified if necessary to enforce the transformation relationship between the models.

This representation specifies a mathematical relationship between the set of models of language $L1$ and the set of models of $L2$, defining how models $m1 : L1$ (LHS) correspond to models $m2 : L2$ (RHS) when they are in the relation.

An alternative specification notation is to use sets of constraints directly in a language such as OCL to specify the LHS and RHS as predicates. For example, the LHS of the example above could be defined as

$$a1 : Association1$$

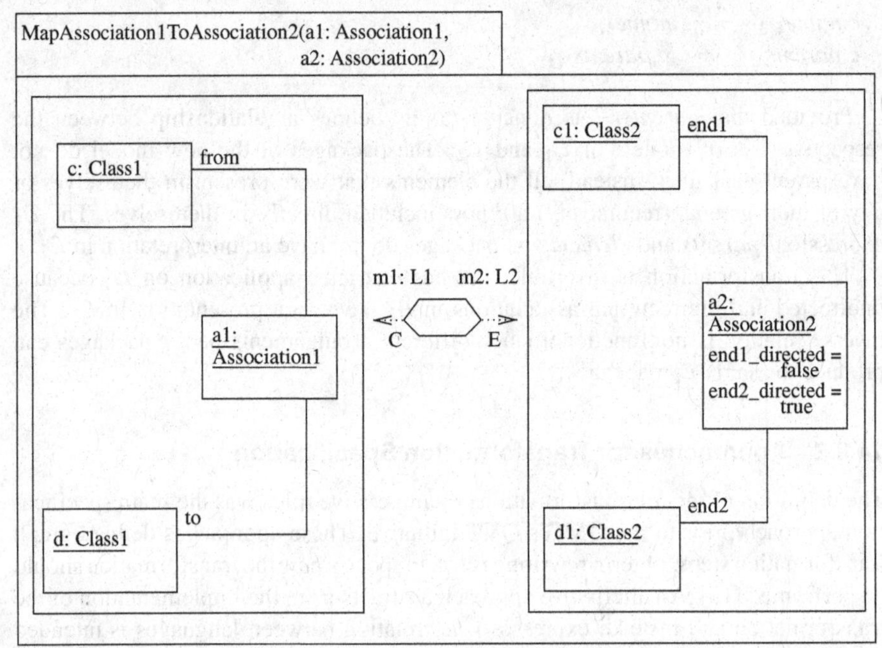

FIGURE 14.3 Transformation specification in QVT.

and the RHS as

$$\begin{aligned}
&a2 : Association2 \\
&a2.name \;=\; a1.name \\
&MapClass1ToClass2(a1.from, a2.end1) \\
&MapClass1ToClass2(a1.to, a2.end2) \\
&a2.end1_directed \;=\; false \\
&a2.end2_directed \;=\; true
\end{aligned}$$

These predicates can be used to define transformations as relations as follows. From a pair L, R of predicates over models, we can derive the relation Rel_τ as

$$Rel_\tau(M1, M2) \equiv M1.L \wedge (M1, M2).R$$

where expressions of the form $e@pre$ in R are evaluated using $M1$. Elements x: T which are defined in R but do not occur in L are assumed to be created by the transformation, and are added to $M2.T$. Any free variables of the combined predicate become parameters of the transformation.

Metaclasses and features that do not occur in L or R are assumed unchanged by the transformation except when these need to change to ensure constraints of $\mathcal{L}_2$.

In particular, we assume that opposite association end properties are modified appropriately when one end is changed explicitly [25]; for example, if a one–many association with ends $r1$ (one) and $r2$ (many) has

$$x.r1 = y$$

specified in R, implicitly this also results in $y.r2$ being extended by x. If an object of $M1$ is deleted, it must be removed from any role set in $M2$, and any part objects of it must also be removed. For example, if a state s is deleted, so must be its state invariant and entry and exit actions, and it must be removed from the *subvertex* set of any containing region. Outgoing and ingoing transitions of s must be assigned different sources or targets or be deleted, in order to maintain the UML 2 metamodel constraints for state machines.

For convenience we usually specify transformations by such pairs of constraints in this chapter, with diagrams (at the model level) used additionally to describe the transformation step informally. The L predicate acts like a precondition of the transformation, considered as a metalevel operation on models, and the R predicate as a postcondition of this operation.

Logical operators such as conjunction and universal quantification can be applied to transformations based on their definition by predicates. If transformation τ from $\mathcal{L}_1$ to $\mathcal{L}_2$ is defined by predicates $L1$ and $R1$, and transformation σ from $\mathcal{L}_1$ to $\mathcal{L}_2$ by predicates $L2$ and $R2$, the transformation τ *and* σ, which applies both transformations simultaneously, is specified by the predicates $L1 \vee L2$, $(L1@pre \implies R1) \wedge (L2@pre \implies R2)$.

Similarly, a universal quantification can be applied to parameterized transformations. If $\tau(a : A)$ is a transformation from $\mathcal{L}_1$ to $\mathcal{L}_2$ defined by predicates L and R, a transformation $\forall a : A \cdot \tau(a)$ is defined by predicates $\exists a : A \cdot L$ and $\forall a : A \cdot (L@pre \implies R)$.

The transformation of Figure 14.2 can be constructed using these operators, from separate transformations on packages and associations.

14.3.3 Model Transformation Correctness

The following notions of transformation correctness have been defined [44]:

- *Syntactic correctness*. The transformation always produces syntactically well-formed models of the target language from valid models of the source language.
- *Termination*. The transformation (defined imperatively) terminates on each source model.
- *Uniqueness/confluence*. The transformation produces a unique result from a given starting model.
- *Semantic correctness*. For each property of the source model that should be preserved (correctness properties), the target model satisfies the property, under a fixed interpretation of the source language into the target language.

In our relational setting, we can define these criteria precisely as follows for a model transformation τ from $\mathcal{L}_1$ to $\mathcal{L}_2$:

Syntactic correctness. For each model that conforms to (is a model in the language) $\mathcal{L}_1$, and to which the transformation can be applied, the transformed model conforms to $\mathcal{L}_2$:

$$\forall M1 : \mathcal{L}_1;\ M2 \cdot Rel_\tau(M1, M2) \implies M2 : \mathcal{L}_2$$

Termination (definedness). The applicability condition of Rel_τ is *true*: Its domain is the complete collection of models of $\mathcal{L}_1$.

Uniqueness. Rel_τ is functional.

Semantic correctness. With respect to the semantics of $\mathcal{L}_1$ and $\mathcal{L}_2$ being used, if a model $M1$ of $\mathcal{L}_1$ is transformed to a model $M2$ of $\mathcal{L}_2$, each model-level property φ of $M1$ true under the $\mathcal{L}_1$ semantics is also true, under the interpretation ζ on expressions induced by τ, in $M2$ under the $\mathcal{L}_2$ semantics:

$$\forall M1 : \mathcal{L}_1;\ M2 : \mathcal{L}_2 \cdot Rel_\tau(M1, M2) \wedge M1 \models \varphi \implies M2 \models \zeta(\varphi)$$

The final property should be expected for refinement, specialization, enhancement, quality improvement, and design pattern transformations. For abstractions it will instead be the case that all $M2$ properties should be valid in $M1$. For reexpression transformations there may be cases where $M1$ properties cannot be expressed in $M2$ (ζ will be a partial interpretation), but all expressible properties should be preserved from $M1$ to $M2$.

Semantic correctness means that Figure 14.4 commutes: Each formula $\varphi \in \Gamma_1$ has

$$\Gamma_2 \vdash \zeta(\varphi)$$

where Γ_1 is the semantics of M_1 under *Sem*1 (e.g., a set of formulas in a language such as OCL characterizing its meaning), and Γ_2 is the semantics of M_2 under *Sem*2. Only model-level properties (properties that can be expressed at the M1 level in terms of the UML four-layer metamodel [35]) should be considered; metamodel-level properties (M2-level) will usually be invalidated by any metamodel change.

Notice that if τ and σ are semantically correct, so is their composition $\tau;\sigma$ if the composition of the interpretations is used.

In the case of the prefixing transformation $\tau(p)$ on the language of Figure 14.1, a unique names property is preserved by τ: If the constraint

$$e1 : \mathit{Entity\ and\ } e2 \mathit{: Entity\ and\ } e1.\mathit{name} = e2.\mathit{name\ implies\ } e1 = e2$$

is added to the language, this is true in interpreted form, since name_{M1} is interpreted by name_{M2} with the prefix removed.

An often-neglected consideration is that not only the graphical elements of models change under a transformation, but also its constraints may need to change, in order to be correct interpretations in the new model of the constraint in the source model.

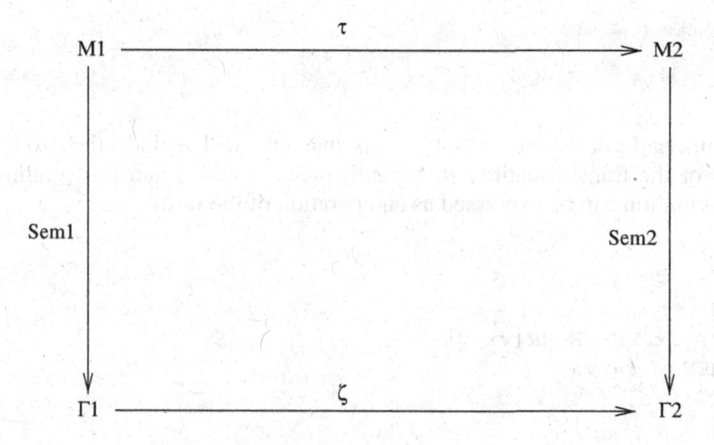

FIGURE 14.4 Transformation correctness.

For example, a constraint *from* = *to* defining a self-association in $\mathcal{L}_1$ from Figure 14.2 would need to be transformed to *end*1 = *end*2 in $\mathcal{L}_2$.

In general, a constraint φ should be transformed to $\zeta(\varphi)$ or to a predicate that implies this. Markovic and Baar [4] consider the issue of when constraints need to change as a result of a class diagram transformation, but does not investigate the semantic correctness of the combined transformation. In this chapter we specify the ζ interpretation for particular transformations and demonstrate the correctness of the transformations with respect to this.

Varro and Pataricza [44] define a model-checking technique for testing that a transformation preserves selected properties, on a model-per-model basis, but does not provide a means to verify transformations on a global basis. By considering transformations as operations on metamodels, specified by pre- and postconditions, we can in principle apply standard verification techniques to prove these operations correct (e.g., by translation into the language of a proof tool such as B) [22].

For example, the name prefixing transformation can be expressed in B as follows:

```
MACHINE L1L2
SETS ENTITY
VARIABLES entities, name1, name2
INVARIANT
  entities <: ENTITY &
  name1 : entities --> STRING &
  name2 : entities --> STRING &
  !(e1,e2).(e1 : entities & e2 : entities & name1(e1) = name1(e2) => e1 = e2) &
  !(e1,e2).(e1 : entities & e2 : entities & name2(e1) = name2(e2) => e1 = e2)
INITIALISATION entities := {} || name1 := {} || name2 := {}
OPERATIONS
  tau(p) =
  PRE p: STRING
  THEN
    ANY name2x WHERE name2x : entities --> STRING &
      !ex.(ex: entities => name2x(ex) = p + "_" + name1(ex))
```

```
      THEN name2 := name2x
      END
    END
  END
```

The internal consistency proof of this machine will include the proof of correctness of the transformation. In general, precondition L and postcondition R of a transformation can be expressed as an operation of the form

```
op(p) =
PRE p: PT & LL
THEN
  ANY vx WHERE RR[vx/v]
  THEN v := vx
  END
END
```

where LL and RR express L and R in B notation. The metamodel data of $\mathcal{L}_1$ and $\mathcal{L}_2$ can be separated into different machines and then combined into a machine that defines the transformation, similar to the approach used by Akehurst and Kent [2].

Additional correctness properties can also be considered, to specify that there is no conflict between two model transformations which can both be applied to a particular model, and that the result of an individual transformation applied repeatedly to a model does not depend on the order in which it is applied.

It is often the case that groups of related transformations are used together to transform a model. For example, the transformations to form a relational database schema from a class diagram (introduce primary and foreign keys, remove inheritance, many–many associations, and association classes), described in Section 14.4, would normally be used in this way. For such groups, the property of *consistency* is important: It should not be the case that two transformations in the group can both be applied to the same model and produce different results.

If a group fails to satisfy this property (e.g., as is the case for the "introduce primary keys" and "amalgamate classes" transformations), a definite order of application or priority scheme must be defined to remove such conflicts. In this case the ordering could be:

1. Eliminate inheritance (removing multiple inheritance, then single inheritance).
2. Introduce primary keys.
3. Eliminate many–many associations and association classes (the primary keys of the classes at the association ends can be used together as a compound key of the intermediate class).
4. Implement many–one associations by foreign keys.

This defines an algorithm, which may be expressed as a behavior state machine (Figure 14.5). The correctness of this algorithm can be shown by defining suitable state invariants and loop variants.

Consistency is also an issue for individual transformations, if the transformation could be applied in two different (possibly overlapping) regions of a model so that the

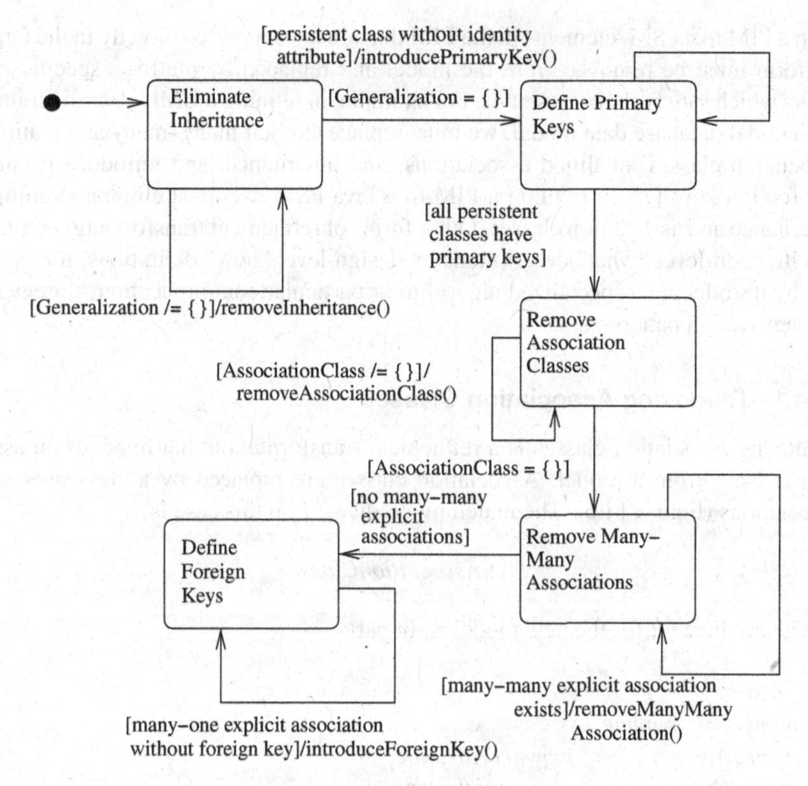

FIGURE 14.5 Transformation algorithm.

result of performing the transformation on one region, and then the second, is different from that when the regions are chosen in the reverse order. The *removeInheritance*() transformation is an example of this.

In the following sections we provide a catalog of several UML transformations in each of the categories described in Section 14.2, taken from published papers, books, or tool descriptions. Each transformation is described, with a brief reference to its purpose, effect, and provenance. For selected transformations of particular significance, we also give a precise semantic definition of the transformation and a semantic analysis of its correctness.

For design patterns, enhancements, specializations, and quality improvements, the transformations usually operate within a single language (i.e., $\mathcal{L}_1 = \mathcal{L}_2$). For refinements, abstractions, and reexpressions, the source and target languages may be different.

14.4 REFINEMENT TRANSFORMATIONS

Refinement transformations have the general aim of refining a model to a more implementation-oriented version. In the context of the MDA, this means transforming a computation-independent model (CIM) to a PIM, or a PIM to a PSM. In moving from a PIM to a PSM, elements in the PIM that are not supported directly in the target platform must be removed from the model and replaced by platform-specific elements which satisfy their semantics. For example, in refining a UML class diagram to a relational database data model, we must replace explicit many–many associations, association classes, qualified associations, and inheritance, and introduce primary and foreign keys [7]. In refining a PIM to a Java PSM, we must eliminate multiple inheritance and association classes. Other forms of refinement transformation replace specification-level "what" descriptions by design-level "how" definitions: for example, by introducing a specialized algorithm or particular communication strategy (as in many design patterns).

14.4.1 Removing Association Classes

Removing association classes is a refinement transformation that removes an association class from a model. Association classes are replaced by a class plus new associations (Figure 14.6). The matching predicate L in this case is

$$r : AssociationClass$$

The predicate R for the new model is, in part:

$$\begin{aligned}
&c : Class \\
&c.name = r.name \\
&c.ownedAttribute = r.ownedAttribute \\
&c.ownedOperation = r.ownedOperation \\
&c.generalization = r.generalization \\
&c.specialization = r.specialization
\end{aligned}$$

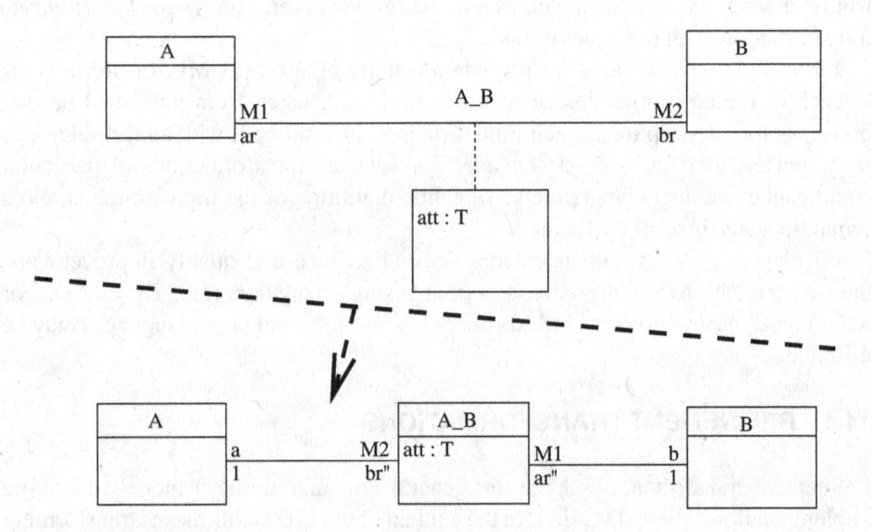

FIGURE 14.6 Transformation of association classes to associations.

$$\begin{array}{l}
Element.allInstances() \rightarrow excludes(r) \\
a1,\ a2\ :\ Association \\
e11,\ e12,\ e21,\ e22\ :\ Property \\
a1.memberEnd\ =\ Sequence\{\ e11,\ e12\ \} \\
a2.memberEnd\ =\ Sequence\{\ e21,\ e22\ \} \\
e11.type\ =\ r.memberEnd \rightarrow at(1).type \\
e22.type\ =\ r.memberEnd \rightarrow at(2).type \\
e12.type\ =\ c \\
e21.type\ =\ c
\end{array}$$

This defines a new class c which has a copy of r's features, defines that r itself is removed from the model, and that there are two new associations $a1$ and $a2$ which link c to the original end classes of r.

A new constraint Inv_{A_B},

$$r1 : A\_B \ and \ r2 : A\_B \ and \ r1.a = r2.a \ and \ r1.b = r2.b \ implies \ r1 = r2$$

is introduced into the resulting model, replacing the corresponding property of the association class.

The original role ar in Figure 14.6 is implemented by the composition $ar''.a$; br is implemented similarly by $br''.b$. Attributes $(ax, bx).att$ of elements of the association class are implemented by $cx.att$, where cx: A_B is the unique element of this class with $cx.a = ax$ and $cx.b = bx$. In other words, ζ is the interpretation

$$\begin{array}{l}
ar \ \longmapsto \ ar''.a \\
br \ \longmapsto \ br''.b \\
(ax, bx).f \ \longmapsto \ cx.f \ where \ cx : \ A_B \ and \ cx.a \ = \ ax \ and \ cx.b \ = \ bx
\end{array}$$

for any feature f of the association class. Associations connected to the association class remain connected to A_B in the new model without changing their multiplicities or names. The invariant Inv_{A_B} is the same as that of the original association class (note that the ends named a and b are present implicitly in the original model as navigable ends from the association class to A and B). The pre- and post conditions of operations of the association class remain unchanged in A_B.

The multiplicities $M1$ and $M2$ can be any multiplicities allowed in the modeling language. The uniqueness property defined above ensures that the interpretation of the multiplicity properties hold in the new model (e.g., $br''.b$ satisfies $M2$ if br does).

In addition, the mutual inverse property of the opposite ends of the association is preserved:

$$ax : A \ and \ bx : B \ implies \ (ax : bx.ar \ \equiv \ bx : ax.br)$$

is true in interpreted form:

$$ax : A \ and \ bx : B \ implies \ (ax : bx.ar''.a \ \equiv \ bx : ax.br''.b)$$

since

$$ax : bx.ar''.a$$

implies that $ax = cx.a$ for some $cx : bx.ar''$, so $cx : ax.br''$ by the opposite ends property for a and br''. But also $bx = cx.b$ by the opposite ends property for ar'' and b, and therefore $bx : ax.br''.b$ as required. Likewise for the opposite direction. Semantic correctness therefore follows. This transformation is T20 in a paper by Blaha and Premerlani [8]. A similar transformation, "Remove qualified association" [27], refines away qualified associations by introducing a new intermediate class.

14.4.2 Amalgamating Subclasses into a Superclass

Amalgamating subclasses into a superclass is a refinement transformation that amalgamates all features of all subclasses of a class C into C itself, together with an additional flag attribute to indicate to which class the current object really belongs. It is one strategy for representing a class hierarchy in a relational database.

The matching condition L is

$$\begin{aligned} &c : \ Class \\ &c.generalization \ = \ Set\{\} \\ &c.specialization \rightarrow notEmpty() \end{aligned}$$

In addition, to remove possible inconsistency in application, each direct or indirect subclass of c must have no superclass from outside the collection of direct or indirect subclasses of c. An example of the transformation is shown in Figure 14.7. To ensure semantic correctness, constraints of the subclasses must be reexpressed as constraints of the amalgamated class, using the flag attribute, as illustrated in Figure 14.7.

The transformation can be applied in a series of steps, which each move one direct subclass d of c up to c, together with the associations connected to d. For each subclass removed, a new element is added to the enumerated type for the flag attribute.

The interpretation ζ maps features $B :: f$ of subclasses into the corresponding new features $A :: f$ of the superclass. For class types it maps each subclass B of A to the set

$$A.allInstances() \rightarrow collect(flag = isB)$$

The new invariant of the superclass is therefore

$$(flag = isA \ implies \ Inv_A) \ and \ \ldots \ and \ (flag = isB \ implies \ Inv_B)$$

where each subclass of A is included in the conjunction.

The precondition of an operation m defined in some subclasses of A is expressed as

$$\begin{aligned} &(flag = isB1 \ or \ \ldots \ or \ flag = isBn) \ and \\ &(flag = isB1 \ implies \ Pre_{m,B1}) \ and \ \ldots \ and \\ &(flag = isBn \ implies \ Pre_{m,Bn}) \end{aligned}$$

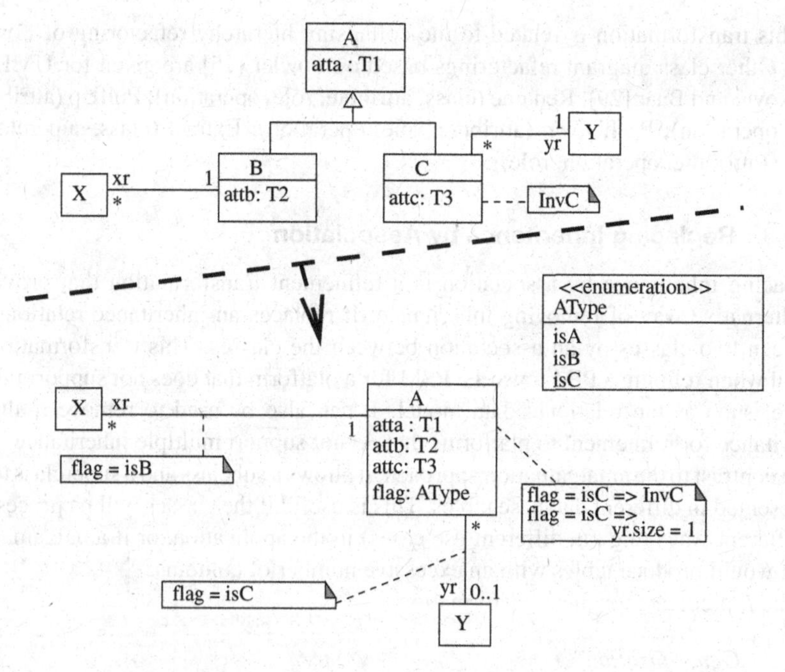

FIGURE 14.7 Amalgamating subclass transformation.

where the Bi are the subclasses—possibly including the original superclass—which have a valid definition of m (it is defined in Bi or in one of its ancestors), and $Pre_{m,Bi}$ is the precondition of m in Bi.

The postcondition of m is expressed in the superclass as

$$(flag \;=\; isB1 \; and \; (Pre_{m,B1})@pre \; implies \; Post_{m,B1}) \; and \; \ldots \; and$$
$$(flag \;=\; isBn \; and \; (Pre_{m,Bn})@pre \; implies \; Post_{m,Bn})$$

where $Post_{m,Bi}$ is the postcondition of m in Bi.

An association end on a subclass B is lifted to an association end with the same name, multiplicity, and other properties, attached to the superclass. The opposite end (e.g., xr) of the association will have multiplicity $*$ if the original end had multiplicity $m..M$. A constraint

$$flag = isB \;\; implies \;\; xr \rightarrow size() \geq m \; and \; xr \rightarrow size() \leq M$$

is added to ensure that the original multiplicity is provable for objects of A that represent instances of B.

The state machine of A is formed as a superstate of the individual state machines of its subclasses, each of which is represented as a separate state machine. The initial transition is directed to enter the subclass state machine corresponding to the value of the flag attribute initialization.

This transformation is related to the collapsing hierarchy refactoring of Fowler [15]. Other class diagram refactorings based on Fowler [15] are given for UML by Markovic and Baar [29]: Rename (class, attribute, role, operation); PullUp (attribute, role, operation); PushDown (attribute, role, operation); Extract (class, superclass); Move (attribute, operation, role).

14.4.3 Replacing Inheritance by Association

Replacing inheritance by association is a refinement transformation that provides an alternative way of removing inheritance. It replaces an inheritance relationship between two classes by an association between the classes. This transformation is useful when refining a PIM toward a PSM for a platform that does not support inheritance, such as the relational data model. It can also be used to remove multiple inheritance for refinement to platforms that do not support multiple inheritance.

In contrast to the amalgamation approach, it allows a subclass and a superclass to be represented in different database tables. This is useful if the classes will be processed in different ways (e.g., in different use cases) in the application, or if amalgamating them would produce tables with an excessive number of columns.

The L predicate for this transformation is

$$
\begin{aligned}
&g : Generalization\\
&c1 : Class\\
&c2 : Class\\
&c1 = g.general\\
&c2 = g.specific
\end{aligned}
$$

The R predicate is

$$
\begin{aligned}
&a : Association\\
&r1,\ r2 : Property\\
&a.memberEnd = Sequence\{r1,\ r2\}\\
&r1.classifier = c1\\
&r2.classifier = c2\\
&r1.type = c2\\
&r2.type = c1\\
&Element.allInstances()\rightarrow excludes(g)
\end{aligned}
$$

and $r1$ is defined to have 0..1 multiplicity and $r2$ to have 1 multiplicity. g is deleted from the new model.

Figure 14.8 shows the metamodel fragment for this transformation. The transformation is invertible and monotone. However, not all 0..1 to 1 associations can be validly converted into inheritances: The classes at the ends of the association must be different, and the class at the 1 end must represent conceptually a generalization of the other class. If both classes have primary keys, these should be the same.

Figure 14.9 shows an application of this transformation. The inheritance of B on A is replaced by a 0..1 to 1 association from B to A.

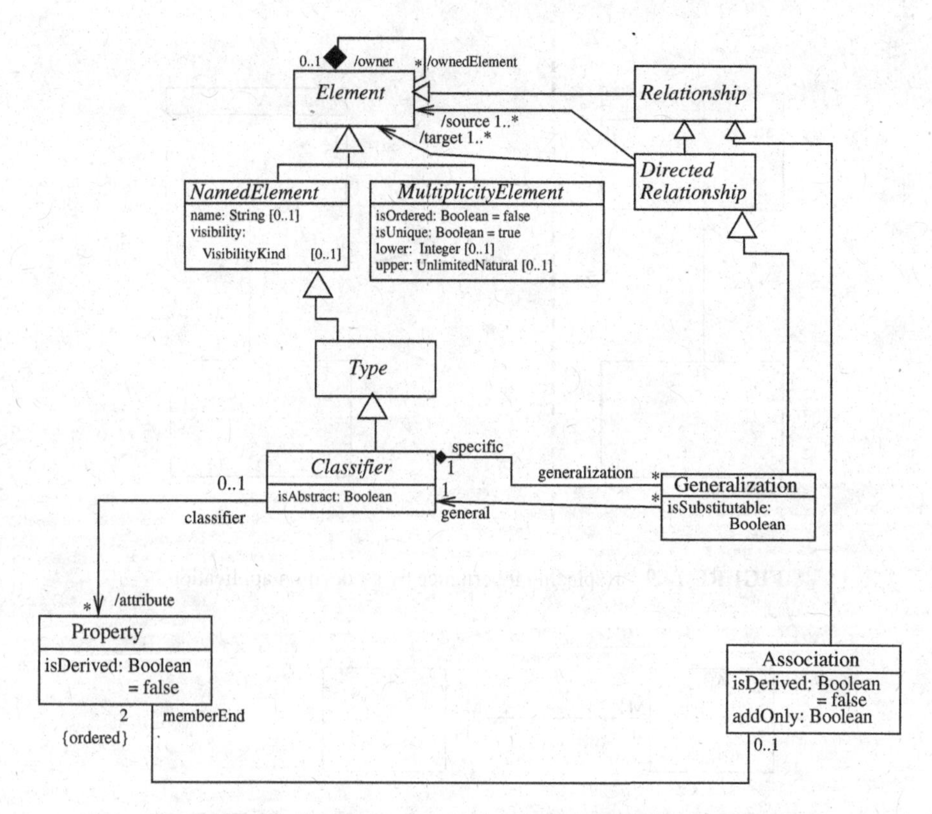

FIGURE 14.8 Replacing inheritance by association transformation.

To ensure semantic correctness, any expression in the original model that has B (or a subclass of B) as a contextual classifier, and which uses a feature f inherited from A, must be modified in the new model to use $ar.f$ instead. That is, the interpretation ζ maps f in the original model to $ar.f$ in the new model.

The transformation is used in by Grand [18] to improve the quality of models where inheritance would be misapplied, such as situations of dynamic and multiple roles. It is related to the Role pattern of Bämer et al. [3].

14.4.4 Removing Many–Many Associations

Removing many–many associations is a refinement transformation that replaces a many–many association with a new class and two many–one associations. Explicit many–many associations cannot be implemented directly using foreign keys in a relational database—an intermediary table would be needed instead. This transformation is the object-oriented equivalent of introducing such a table.

The transformation is shown in Figure 14.10 The L constraint is

$r : Association$
$r.stereotypeNames \rightarrow includes(\text{``}explicit\text{''})$

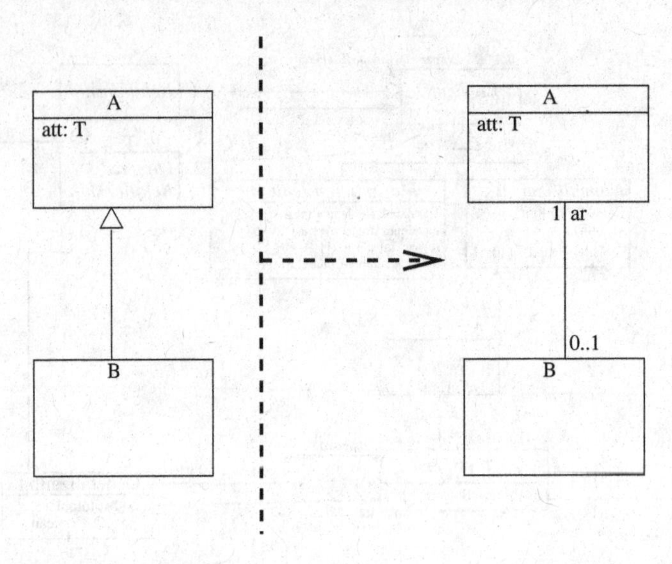

FIGURE 14.9 Replacing inheritance by association application.

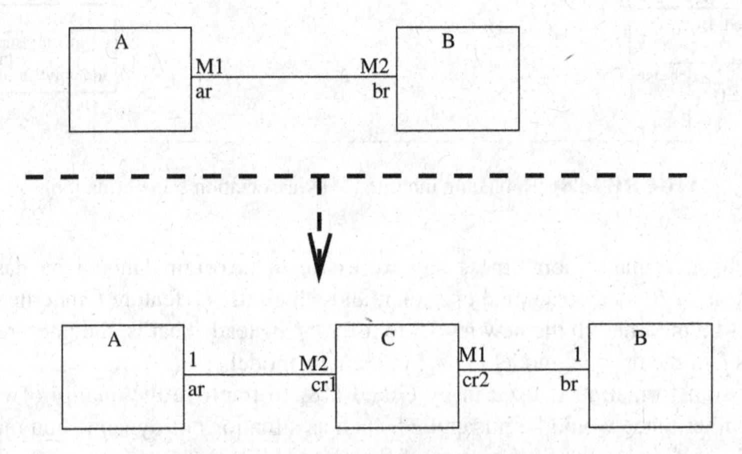

FIGURE 14.10 Removing a many–many association.

$$r.memberEnd{\rightarrow}at(1).upper \quad > \quad 1$$
$$r.memberEnd{\rightarrow}at(2).upper \quad > \quad 1$$

m.stereotypeNames gives the set of names of stereotypes attached to a model element *m*.

The new class must link exactly those objects that were connected by the original association and must not duplicate such links:

$$c1 : C \ and \ c2 : C \ and \ c1.ar = c2.ar \ and \ c1.br = c2.br \ \ implies \ \ c1 = c2$$

In addition, any constraint with contextual classifier A or a subclass of A, which refers to br, must replace this reference by $cr1.br$ in the new model, and similarly for navigations from B to A. ζ is

$$ar \longmapsto cr2.ar, \quad br \longmapsto cr1.br$$

14.4.5 Introducing a Primary Key

Introducing a primary key is a refinement transformation that applies to any persistent class. If the class does not already have a primary key (in the sense of a relational database table primary key), it introduces a new identity attribute (an attribute that always has a different value in different objects), usually of Integer or String type, for this class, together with extensions of the constructor of the class, and a new *get* method, to allow initialization and read access of this attribute.

This is an essential step for implementation of a data model in a relational database. L in this case is

$$\begin{array}{l} c \;:\; Class \\ c.stereotypeNames \rightarrow includes(\text{``persistent''}) \\ c.ownedAttribute.stereotypeNames \rightarrow excludes(\text{``identity''}) \\ c.feature.name \rightarrow excludes(c.name \;+\; \text{``Id''}) \end{array}$$

using the metamodel of UML 2 [34].

L will be true for any model element c that is a persistent class without an identity attribute. For such elements the transformation defined by R will be applied to create a new model from the old, in which a new identity attribute is added to the class selected:

$$\begin{array}{l} a \;:\; Property \\ a.name \;=\; c.name \;+\; \text{``Id''} \\ a.stereotypeNames \;=\; Set\{\ \text{``identity''}\ \} \\ c.ownedAttribute \;= \\ \quad (c.ownedAttribute)@pre \;+\; Sequence\{\ a\ \} \\ a.classifier \;=\; c \\ a.type \;=\; IntegerType \end{array}$$

Because a occurs in R but not in L, it is assumed that it is created by the transformation. We could write $a.oclIsNew()$ to make this explicit. An example of this transformation is shown in Figure 14.11.

To ensure semantic correctness of the transformation, a new constraint expressing the primary key property is added to the new model:

$$A.allInstances() \rightarrow size() = A.allInstances() \rightarrow collect(akey) \rightarrow size()$$

This must be maintained by the constructor, for example:

```
A(att1x : T1, att2x: T2, akeyx: Integer)
  pre:  akeyx /: A.allInstances()->collect(akey)
  post: akey = akeyx and att1 = att1x and att2 = att2x
```

ζ is the identity interpretation.

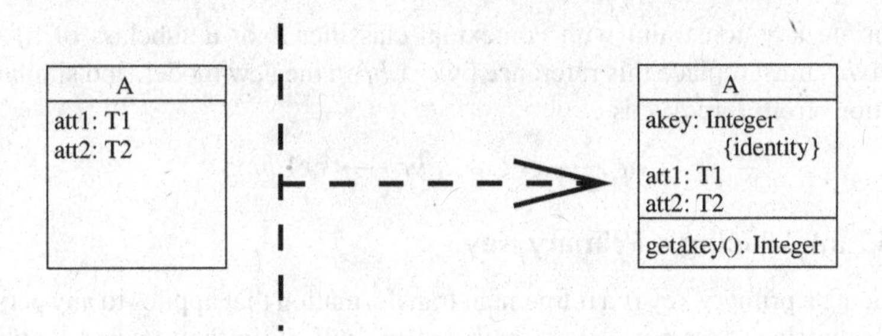

FIGURE 14.11 Introducing a primary key.

14.4.6 Replacing Association by a Foreign Key

Replacing association by a foreign key is a refinement transformation that expresses, as a UML class diagram transformation, the representation of associations by foreign keys in a relational database schema. It applies to any explicit many–one association between persistent classes. It assumes that primary keys already exist for the classes linked by the association. It replaces the association by embedding values of the key of the entity at the "one" end of the association into the entity at the "many" end.

This is an essential step for implementation of a data model in a relational database. The transformation is shown in Figure 14.12. The L constraint is

$$
\begin{aligned}
&r : \ \mathit{Association} \\
&r.\mathit{stereotypeNames}{\rightarrow}\mathit{includes}(\text{``}\mathit{explicit}\text{''}) \\
&r.\mathit{memberEnd}{\rightarrow}\mathit{at}(1).\mathit{upper} \ = \ 1 \\
&r.\mathit{memberEnd}{\rightarrow}\mathit{at}(2).\mathit{upper} \ > \ 1
\end{aligned}
$$

(together with the case that the member ends are in the opposite order). In the new model a copy of the primary key of the first $r.\mathit{memberEnd.type}$ class is added as a foreign key to the second $r.\mathit{memberEnd}$ class.

For instances $a : A$, $b : B$, $b.\mathit{akey}$ is equal to $a.\mathit{akey}$ exactly when $a \mapsto b$ is in the original association. This correspondence must be maintained by implementing *addbr* and *removebr* operations in terms of the foreign key values.

To ensure semantic correctness, navigation from an A instance to its associated br set must be replaced by

$$B.\mathit{allInstances}(){\rightarrow}\mathit{select}(B :: \mathit{akey} = A :: \mathit{akey})$$

in the new model, corresponding to an SQL *SELECT* statement, and similarly for navigation from B to A.

The ζ interpretation is therefore

$$
\begin{aligned}
br \ &\longmapsto \ B.\mathit{allInstances}(){\rightarrow}\mathit{select}(B :: \mathit{akey} \ = \ A :: \mathit{akey}) \\
ar \ &\longmapsto \ A.\mathit{allInstances}(){\rightarrow}\mathit{select}(B :: \mathit{akey} \ = \ A :: \mathit{akey}){\rightarrow}\mathit{any}()
\end{aligned}
$$

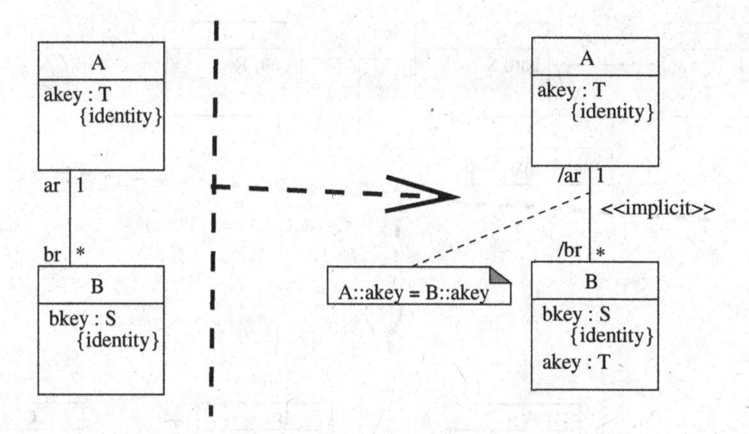

FIGURE 14.12 Replacing association by a foreign key.

14.4.7 Replacing a Global Constraint by Local Constraints

Replacing a global constraint by local constraints is a transformation that refines a class diagram by replacing a constraint that spans n classes, $n > 1$, by constraints that are local to m classes, $m < n$. Local constraints are usually easier to implement than global constraints.

L in this case is

$$c \;:\; Constraint$$
$$c.constrainedElements \rightarrow size() \quad > \quad 1$$

A specific form of localization is when some global constraint can be replaced by one or more (more local) constraints, which together ensure the global constraint (Figure 14.13).

For example, in the case of integer-valued attributes *aatt*, *batt*, *catt*, the predicate $P(aatt, catt)$ could be $aatt < catt$, $Q(aatt, batt)$ is $aatt < batt$, and $R(batt, catt)$ is $batt \leq catt$. This transformation is semantically correct because the refined model establishes all the properties of the original model: The local constraints imply the global constraint when combined. Other transformations to simplify constraints are given by Giese and Larsson [17].

14.4.8 Weakening Preconditions or Strengthening Postconditions

An operation precondition can be weakened (so that it is able to be applied in more situations without error) and/or its postcondition strengthened (so that its effect is determined more precisely) [31]. Both potentially move the method closer to implementation. Figure 14.14 shows a general situation. The semantic correctness of this transformation is shown in [27].

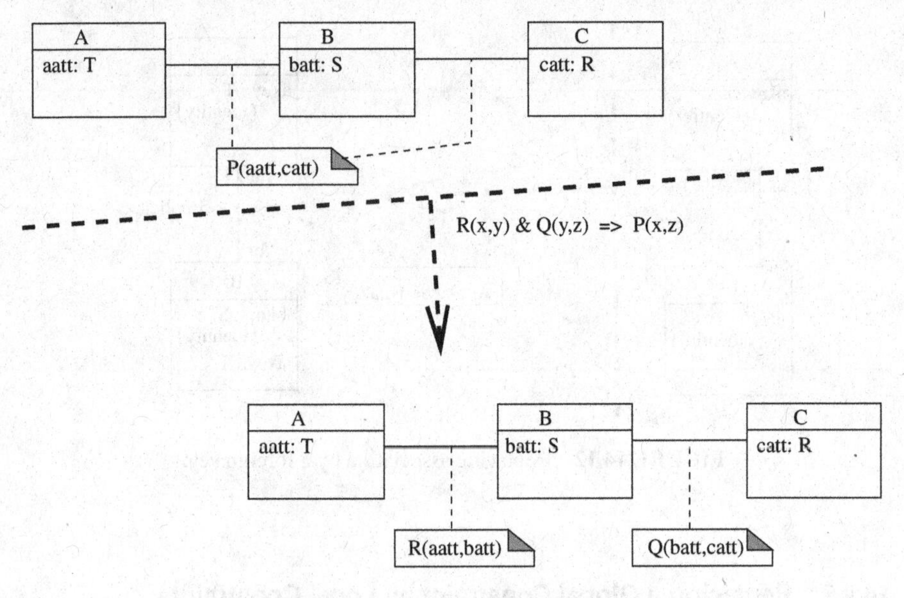

FIGURE 14.13 Localizing constraints.

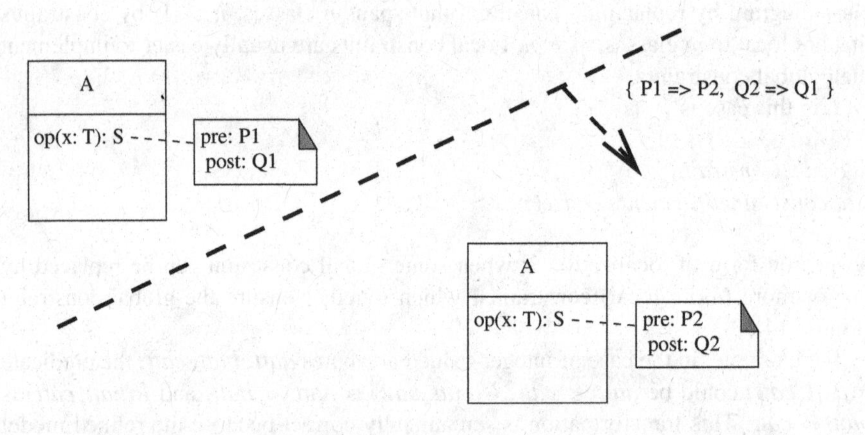

FIGURE 14.14 Weakening preconditions/strengthening postconditions.

14.4.9 Refining an Attribute into an Entity

Refining an attribute into an entity is a refinement transformation that replaces an unstructured attribute *att* : *T* of a class *C* by a new entity *CT* and an association to this (Figure 14.15). This is a common form of evolution that may occur during development of a system, when a property of an entity that was originally modeled as a simple value attached to each object of the class representing the entity is later recognized to have internal structure and properties of its own, and so must be modeled as an entity in its own right [9].

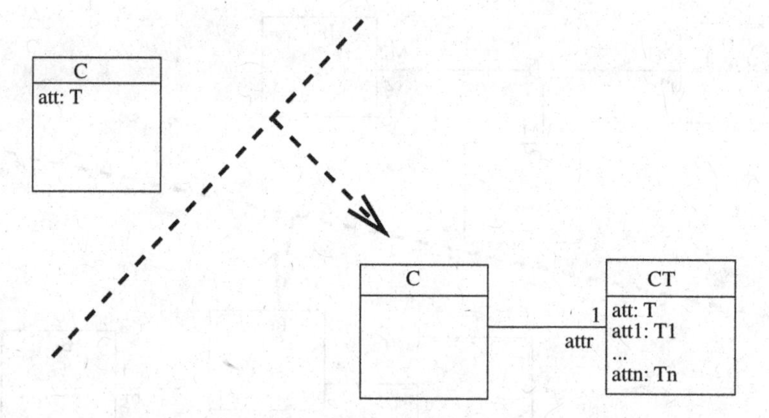

FIGURE 14.15 Refining attribute to entity.

To ensure semantic correctness, references to *att* in constraints of the source model should be replaced by *attr.att* when these constraints are restated in the target model. The ζ interpretation is

$$att \longmapsto attr.att$$

14.4.10 Removing Ternary Associations

It is possible to define ternary associations in UML class diagrams, associations that consist of triples (x, y, z) of objects, from three classes. These cannot be directly implemented in a normal object-oriented programming language and must be refined into a class and three new associations (Figure 14.16).

For objects $b : B$, $c : C$, the association end $(b, c).r1$ in the original model is replaced by $R.allInstances()\rightarrow select(br = b \text{ and } cr = c)\rightarrow collect(ar)$ in the new model, and similarly for $r2$ and $r3$. Associations of higher arity are handled similarly.

14.4.11 Other Class Diagram Refinement Transformations

Some further refinement/specialization transformations on class diagrams are:

- Decompose an attribute into two or more parts (e.g., a *name* into *forename*, *surname*). This is Blaha and Premerlani's "Transform a multi-valued attribute" [8].
- Replace an enumeration-valued attribute by a set of boolean-valued attributes plus a constraint to express that only one of these booleans can be true [8]. For example, *gender* with values *male* and *female* replaced by two boolean attributes *isMale*, *isFemale* and the constraint

$$isMale = true \ implies \ isFemale = false$$

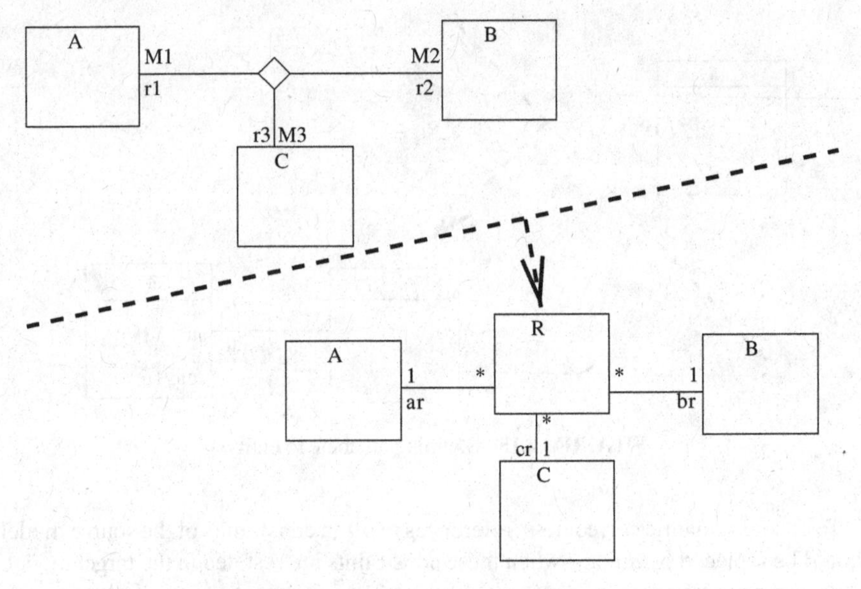

FIGURE 14.16 Removing ternary associations.

This transformation also applies in the reverse direction.

14.4.12 Replacing Transition Postconditions by Actions

Replacing transition preconditions by actions is a refinement transformation on a state machine model that can be used to implement a protocol state machine by a behavior state machine. Figure 14.17 shows an example. For each protocol transition

$$s_1 \rightarrow_{op(x)[Pre]/[Post]} s_2$$

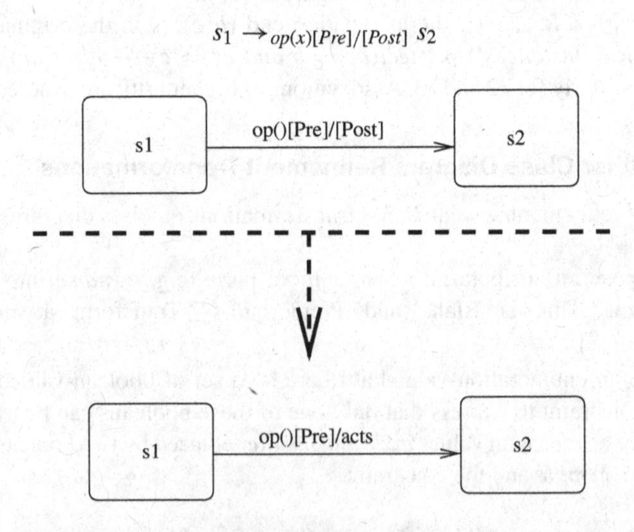

FIGURE 14.17 Refining a protocol to a behavior state machine.

the corresponding behavior transition is

$$s_1 \rightarrow_{op(x)[Pre]/acts} s_2$$

where *acts* are actions that establish *Post*,

$$Inv_{s_1} \wedge Pre \implies [acts]Post$$

and do not change any other features except those modified in *Post*. ζ in this case is the identity interpretation.

14.4.13 Source Splitting

The source splitting transformation refines the behavior of a state machine by introducing substates of a state s and splitting a transition from s into cases for each of these substates. The motivation for this transformation is that a simple behavior may need to be refined into subcases, in particular if a new attribute or other structural feature is introduced in a class.

A simple case with two states is shown in Figure 14.18. Any number of new states and corresponding transitions can be introduced. The logical interpretation ζ is the identity interpretation. To ensure semantic correctness, all new substates of s must be sources of new transitions derived from the transition of s. These new transitions

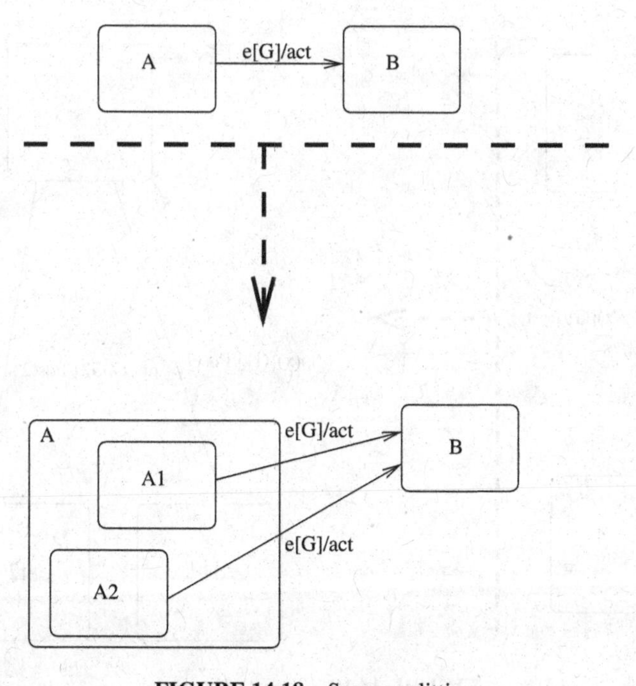

FIGURE 14.18 Source splitting.

can have additional postconditions/actions, but must have the same trigger and guard as the original transition. The targets of the new transitions can be substates of the original target. This transformation is due to Cook and Daniels [10].

14.4.14 Target Splitting

Target splitting is a transformation that replaces a single transition in a state machine by two or more transitions distinguished by disjoint firing conditions, and with possibly distinct actions and target states. It is used to refine behavior by making distinct different cases which were amalgamated in the abstract model. It can be used to define a state machine for a subclass so that the subclass state machine is behaviorally compatible with the superclass machine.

Figure 14.19 shows the structure of this transformation in the case of a split into two transitions. One state of the source model is split into two, and any transition into the state is also split in two, such that $G \equiv G1 \vee G2$ and $G1 \implies \neg G2$. Postconditions can be strengthened:

$$Post1 \implies Post$$
$$Post2 \implies Post$$

In behavior state machines, additional actions can be added in parallel to the existing actions of the transition. Any number of new substates of t can be introduced. This transformation is also due to Cook and Daniels [10].

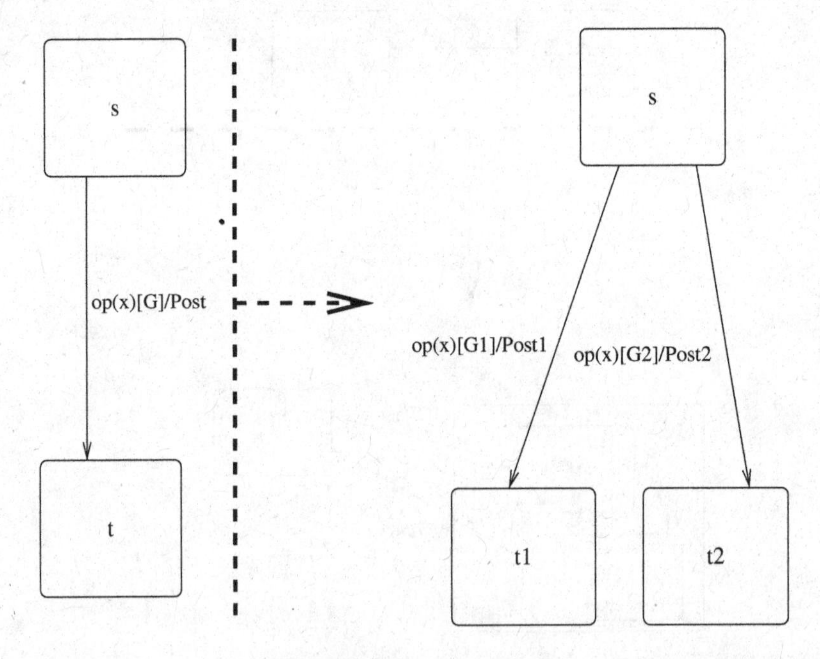

FIGURE 14.19 Target splitting.

14.4.15 Expressing a State Machine in Pre- or Postconstraints

Expressing a state machine in pre- or postconstraints is a transformation that expresses the protocol state machine *SM* of a class *C*, which only has call triggers on its transitions, as new data and pre/post conditions of *C*. A new enumerated type, $States_C$, is introduced, with an element for each basic state configuration of the state machine, and an attribute $stateC : States_C$ of *C*, together with operation pre- and postconditions (e.g., in OCL) expressing the behavior of all the state machine transitions.

If operation $\alpha(p)$ has transitions $t\alpha_1, \ldots, t\alpha_{n\alpha}$ from state configurations $s\alpha_1, \ldots, s\alpha_{n\alpha}$ to state configurations $p\alpha_1, \ldots, p\alpha_{n\alpha}$ with guards $G\alpha_1, \ldots, G\alpha_{n\alpha}$ and postconditions $Post\alpha_1, \ldots, Post\alpha_{n\alpha}$, the precondition of α is augmented with the condition

$$(stateC = s\alpha_1 \; and \; G\alpha_1) \; or \; \ldots \; or \; (stateC = s\alpha_{n\alpha} \; and \; G\alpha_{n\alpha})$$

and the postcondition is augmented by the conjuncts

$$(stateC@pre = s\alpha_i \; and \; G\alpha_i@pre) \; implies \; stateC = p\alpha_i \; and \; Post\alpha_i$$

for $i = 1, \ldots, n\alpha$. Each state invariant Inv_s of a state *s* becomes a new class invariant,

$$stateC = s \; implies \; Inv_s$$

and each attribute of *SM* becomes an attribute of *C*.

The encoding of the state machine as explicit data and updates to this can facilitate the generation of executable code to ensure that objects of the class obey the dynamic behavior it describes. This transformation is defined in UML superstructure 2.1.1 [34], together with other transformations, such as adding an orthogonal region to a state.

14.4.16 Flattening a State Machine

Flattening a state machine is a transformation that removes composite states and expresses their semantics in terms of their substates instead. A transition from a composite state boundary becomes duplicated as a transition from each of the enclosed states (if they do not already have a transition for that event). A transition to the composite state boundary becomes a transition to its default initial state.

The transformation reduces the complexity of the constructs used to express dynamic behavior, making this behavior easier to verify, although the size of the model will be increased. Some results suggest that elimination of composite states may nonetheless improve the comprehensibility of a model for nonexpert users [12].

Figure 14.20 shows a typical case of elimination of a composite state, and Figure 14.21 shows the elimination of a concurrent composite state.

In the case of flattening, ζ expresses a composite state of the original model as a condition defined as the disjunction of all the state memberships of the flattened states of which it is composed. In Figure 14.20, for example, *in A* is interpreted by *in A1 or in A2 or in A3*.

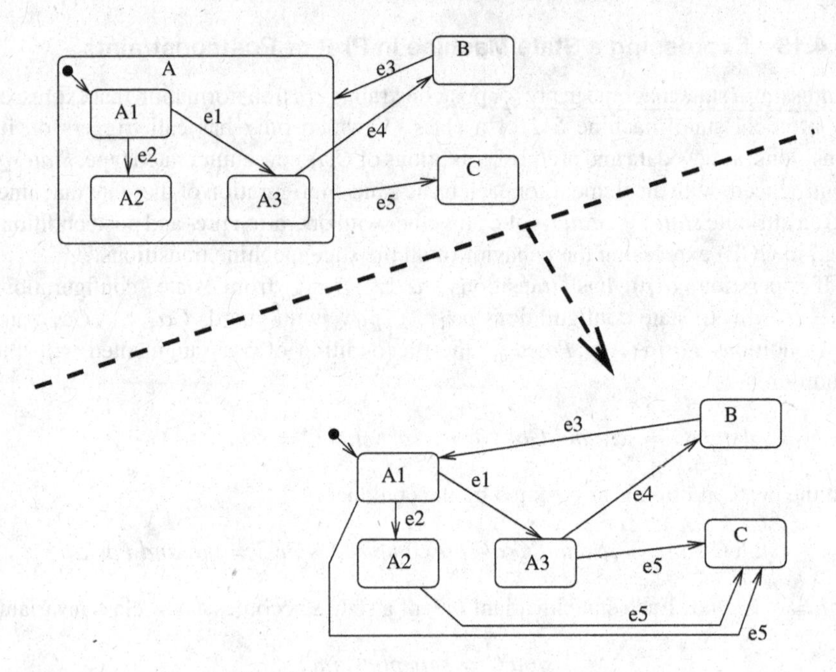

FIGURE 14.20 Eliminating a composite state.

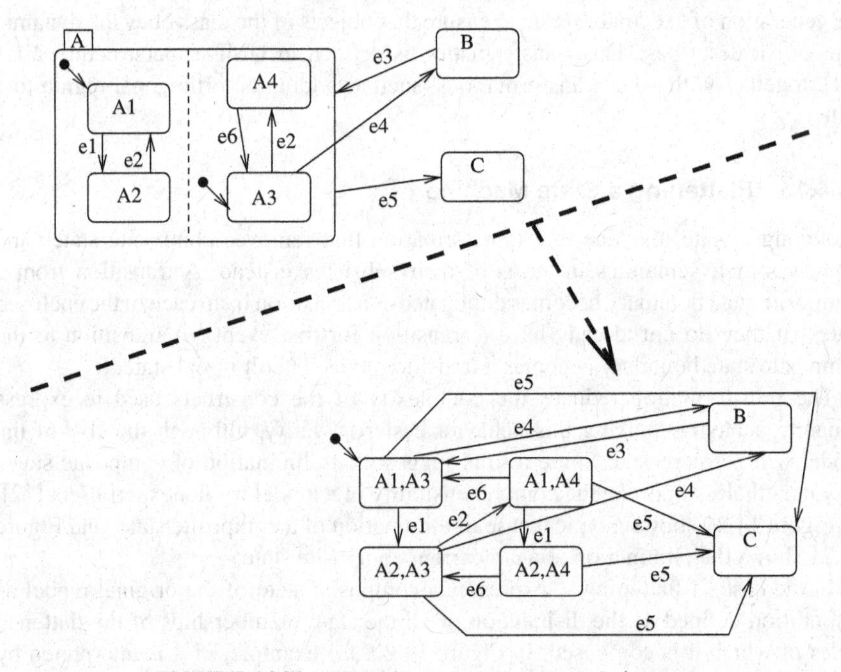

FIGURE 14.21 Flattening a concurrent composite state.

14.5 QUALITY IMPROVEMENT TRANSFORMATIONS

Quality improvement transformations do not change the abstraction level of a model, but rationalize and improve its structure and elements to make the model more flexible, concise, comprehensible, or complete. The concept of *slicing* transformation as defined in [19] also falls into this category, since these transformations aim to reduce some complexity measure of the model while preserving the core semantics of the model.

One subcategory of quality improvement transformation is that of *factoring* and *refactoring* transformations. Factoring transformations introduce a new element that captures commonalities between elements of the original model, which had no distinct representation in that model. Inheritance in class diagrams, and state inclusion in state machines, are typically used to carry out this factoring. Some design patterns, such as template method, facade, and session facade [11], can also be seen as factoring quality improvement transformations. Refactorings reorganize existing structure to improve the factorization in the model instead of introducing new elements [15].

A second subcategory is the removal of redundancy from a model by removing elements that duplicate information already present in the model. Transformations that remove spurious elements of a model such as unreachable states in a state machine can be employed to "clean up" a model after a transformation that may introduce such elements (e.g., a slicing transformation).

14.5.1 Introducing a Superclass

Introducing a superclass is a quality improvement transformation that introduces a superclass of several existing classes, to enable common features of these classes to be factored out and placed in a single location. In general, this transformation should be applied if there are several classes $A, B, \ldots$ which have common features and there is no existing common superclass of these classes, and similarly if there is some natural generalization of these classes that is absent in the model. It is particularly useful for reorganizing and rationalizing a class diagram after some change to a system specification [9].

Figure 14.22 shows a generic example where the existing classes have common attributes, operations, and roles.

The features that are placed in the superclass must have the same intended meaning in the various subclasses, rather than an accidental coincidence of names.

The properties of the features in the superclass are the disjunction of their properties in the individual subclasses. For common roles, this means that their multiplicity on the association from the superclass is the "strongest common generalization" of their multiplicities on the subclass associations. For example, if the subclass multiplicities were $m1..n1$ and $m2..n2$, the superclass multiplicity would be $min(m1, m2)..max(n1, n2)$. For common operations, the conjunction of the individual preconditions can be used as the superclass operation precondition, and the disjunction of the individual postconditions as the superclass operation postcondition.

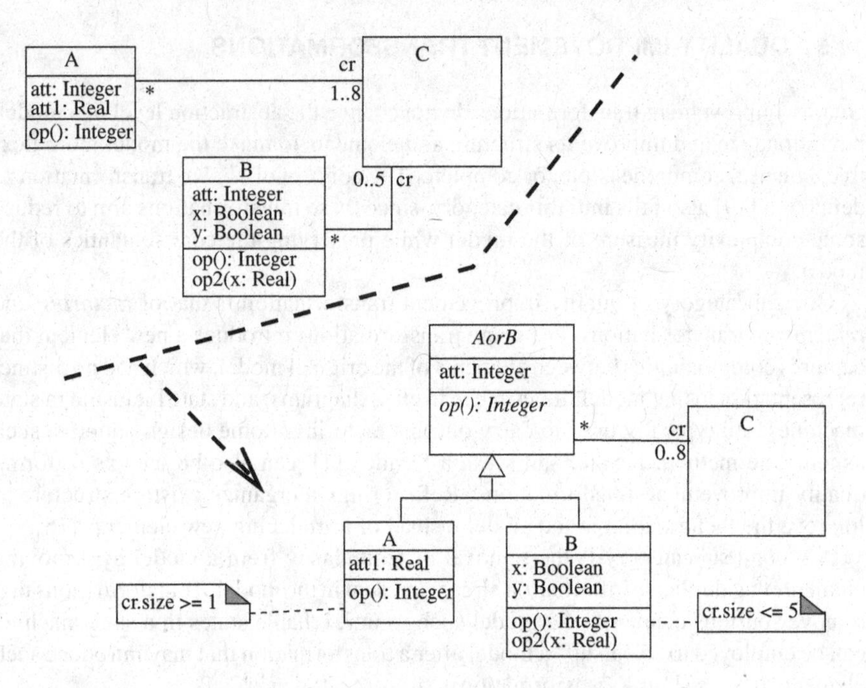

FIGURE 14.22 General superclass introduction.

Common constraints of the subclasses can also be placed on the superclass. In subclasses the original properties of roles and other features which are now owned features of the superclass must be expressed as constraints, as with the restrictions on $cr \rightarrow size()$ in Figure 14.22.

Variations include situations where a common superclass already exists but some common features of its subclasses are missing from it. In this case the common features are simply moved up to the superclass. The pull-up method of refactoring [15] is one example of this situation.

Other quality improvement refactorings of a class diagram, to rationalize class hierarchies and remove optional association ends, are described by Lano and Bicarregui [23].

14.5.2 Introducing Entry Actions of a State

Introducing entry actions of a state is a quality improvement transformation (Figure 14.23) that factors out common actions from all incoming transitions of a particular state and makes them into an entry action of the state. If all transitions $t_1, \ldots, t_n$ into a state s have the same final sequence *act* of actions, remove these actions from the transitions and add *act* as the first actions of the entry action of s. Similarly, if all outgoing transitions from a state have the same initial actions, these can be made into exit actions of the state.

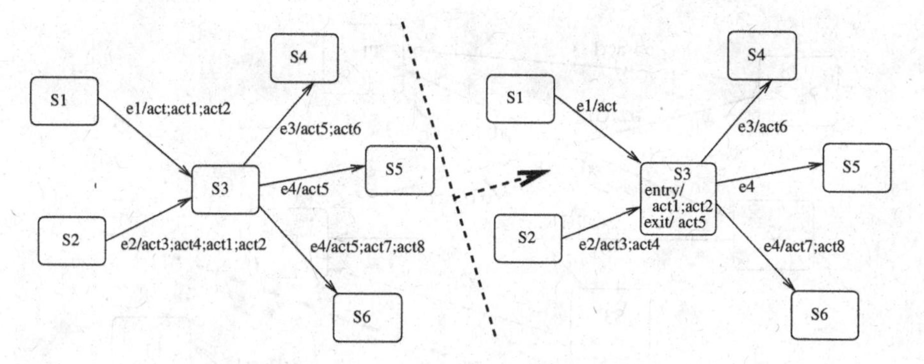

FIGURE 14.23 Introducing entry and exit actions.

The new model has semantics identical to that of the original model, according to Lano's semantics [27]. The transformation is described with other UML refactorings by Sunyé et al. [42].

14.5.3 Introducing a Superstate

If states $s_1, \ldots, s_n$ of a statechart all have a common set of outgoing transitions, that is, for a nonempty set $\alpha_1, \ldots, \alpha_m$ of events they have transitions $t_{s_1,\alpha_1}, \ldots, t_{s_n,\alpha_1}$, etc., such that for a given j, the t_{s_i,α_j} all have the same guards, actions, and target states, introduce a new superstate s of the s_i, and replace the t_{s_i,α_j} by new transitions t_{s,α_j} from s to the common target of the t_{s_i,α_j}, and with the same guard and actions. Common invariants of the substates can be placed on the superstate. s is an abstract superstate of the s_i: Membership of s implies membership of one of the s_i.

This transformation reduces the complexity of the diagram [the number of transitions is reduced by $(n-1)m$] and may identify a conceptually significant state that was omitted from the original model.

Figure 14.24 shows an example of this transformation.

A formal description of this transformation is split into two cases: (1) there already exists a common superstate s of the s_i, in which case the duplicated transitions are moved up to s, or (2) there is no such state, and it is created before applying (1).

For (1), the L predicate is

$$\begin{array}{l}
sts : Sequence(State) \\
ts : Sequence(Transition) \\
r : Region \\
sts{\rightarrow}size() = ts{\rightarrow}size() \\
sts{\rightarrow}asSet(){\rightarrow}size() > 1 \\
ts{\rightarrow}asSet(){\rightarrow}size() > 1 \\
(1..sts{\rightarrow}size()){\rightarrow}forAll(i \mid ts{\rightarrow}at(i).source = sts{\rightarrow}at(i)) \\
ts.target{\rightarrow}asSet(){\rightarrow}size() = 1 \\
ts.effect{\rightarrow}asSet(){\rightarrow}size() = 1
\end{array}$$

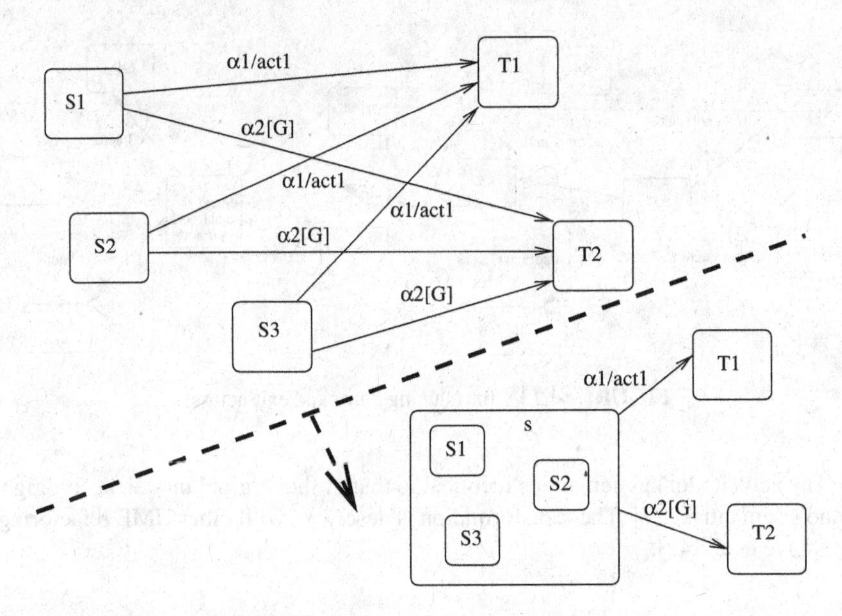

FIGURE 14.24 Introducing a superstate.

$$ts.guard \rightarrow asSet() \rightarrow size() = 1$$
$$r.subvertex = sts \rightarrow asSet()$$
$$r.state.region \rightarrow size() = 1$$

The *R* predicate specifies the creation of a new transition *t* from *r.state*, replacing the t_i:

$$t : Transition$$
$$t.source = r.state$$
$$t.target = ts \rightarrow at(1).target$$
$$t.effect = ts \rightarrow at(1).effect$$
$$t.guard = ts \rightarrow at(1).guard$$
$$Transition.allInstances() = (Transition.allInstances()@pre - ts \rightarrow asSet()) \rightarrow including(t)$$

ζ is the identity interpretation.

14.5.4 Removing an Unreachable State

If a basic state has no incoming transitions, it cannot be reached from the initial state of a state machine, so no object can ever be in the state. This transformation eliminates such states together with all outgoing transitions from the state.

The L predicate is

$$
\begin{aligned}
&s \; : \; State \\
&s.region{\rightarrow}size() \; = \; 0 \\
&s.incoming{\rightarrow}size() \; = \; 0
\end{aligned}
$$

The R predicate is

$$
\begin{aligned}
&Element.allInstances(){\rightarrow}excludes(s) \\
&Element.allInstances(){\rightarrow}excludesAll(s.outgoing)
\end{aligned}
$$

14.5.5 Extending State Invariants

If a state s in a state machine has invariant Inv_s, and a transition from this state to a state t has guard G and no actions/postconditions, then Inv_s *and* G is an invariant of t if t has no other incoming transitions (and t is noninitial). This transformation is useful when a state machine is used to represent an algorithm, and a loop invariant needs to be carried over to the terminal states of the algorithm, to establish a postcondition. The correctness of the transformation can be shown using the semantics of Chapter 8 to deduce that an object can enter state t only via a transition from s.

14.5.6 Simplifying Guards Using Invariants

Simplifying guards using invariants is a quality improvement transformation that simplifies a guard G on a transition exiting a state s by taking account of the fact that the invariant Inv_s of s will be true when the condition G is tested. Therefore, G can be replaced by G_1, where

$$Inv_s \textit{ and } G_1 \equiv Inv_s \textit{ and } G$$

Figure 14.25 shows an example of this transformation. This and other state machine refactoring transformations are defined by Lano and Bicarregui [23].

14.5.7 Disaggregation

A class may become large and unmanageable, with several loosely connected functionalities. It should be split into several classes, such as a master/controller class and helper classes, which have more coherent functionalities and data.

Figure 14.26 shows a typical example.

The transformation can be applied to a class C if the state machine for C is divided into two or more concurrent components CM, CS_1, ..., CS_n, where CM is a client of the CS_i: it queries the states of these components and invokes operations upon them, but the CS_i do not refer to CM.

The helper/component objects must always exist when the master object delegates operations to them. Constraints of A which refer to the attributes that have been placed in auxillary classes must replace the attribute reference by a suitable navigation expression: for example, $att1$ replaced by $ar1.att1$ in Figure 14.26. The state machine of A will be factored into orthogonal regions for each new subordinate class. This transformation is related to "extract class" 15] and "partition class" [8].

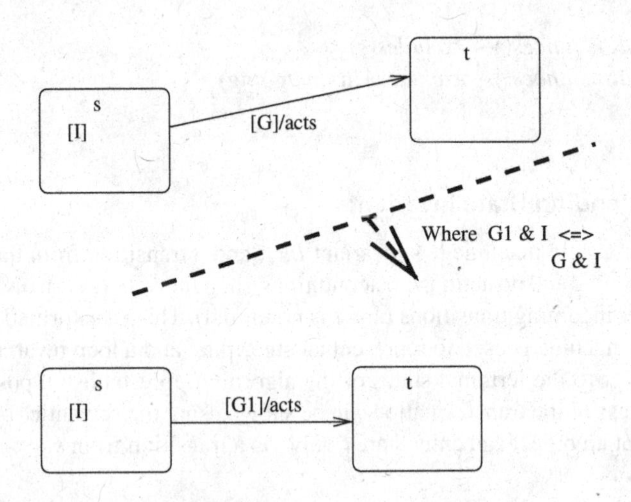

FIGURE 14.25 Simplifying guards.

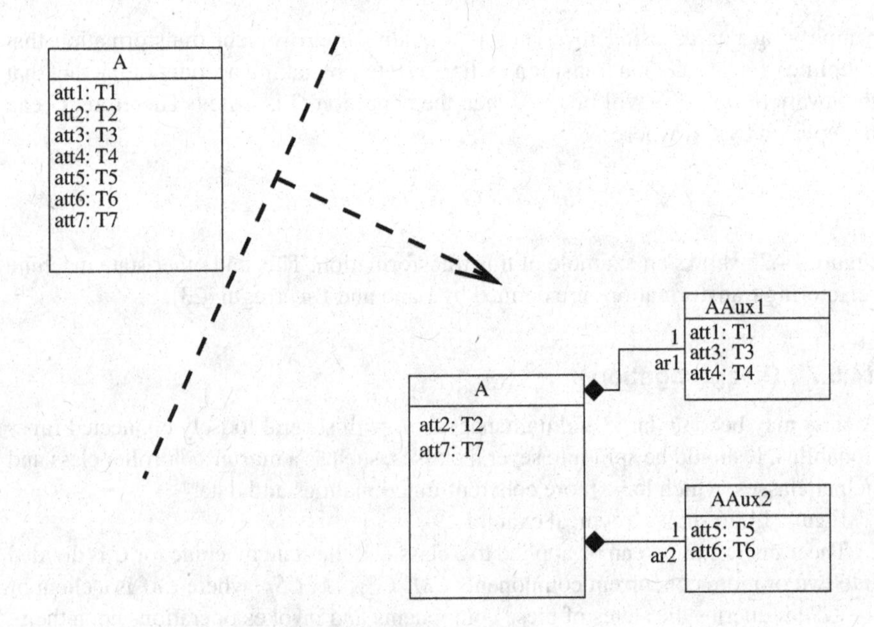

FIGURE 14.26 Disaggregation.

14.5.8 Factoring out a Parameter Group

Factoring out a parameter group is a transformation that replaces a group p_1: T_1, ..., p_n: T_n of parameters to an operation *op* of a class *C*, by a single parameter $p : D$, where *D* is a new class which has attributes $p_1 : T_1$, ..., p_n: T_n and public set and get operations for each parameter.

The transformation reduces the number of parameters of the operation. If several operations use the same group of parameters, this factoring simplifies the interface of the class significantly.

The group of parameters should have coherent meaning as an entity. References to p_i in the pre- and postconditions of the operation should be replaced by $p \cdot p_i$. Calls $op(px_1, \ldots, px_n)$ of *op* are replaced by *op*(*p*), where $p \cdot p_1 = px_1$, ..., $p \cdot p_n = px_n$.

The transformation is related to the Value Object pattern of [11], which introduces a class to package up a group of data items which are passed between different subsystems of an application to make this data transfer more efficient. It is also known as Access Bean [40].

14.5.9 Factoring Out Suboperations

An operation may involve complex or repeated subcomputations. These can be factored into private helper operations of the same class, invoked from the operation. Figure 14.27 shows a generic example where a complex expression *exp* is factored out into a separate operation *m*1.

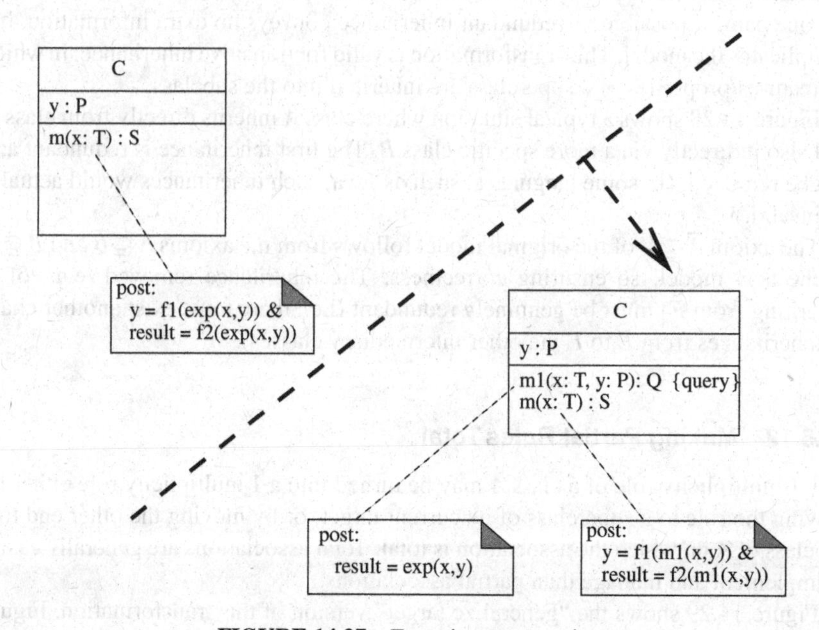

FIGURE 14.27 Factoring an operation.

Before they are created, it should be checked that the helper operations do not already exist in the class or in other classes. The helper operations should be query operations.

This transformation, combined with "introduce superclass," gives the template method pattern in the case that methods in two separate classes have the same remainder after their helper method code is factored out.

A similar transformation introduces derived features:

14.5.10 Introducing Derived Features

An expression e built from local features of a class, which reoccurs several times in a specification, is replaced by a new derived feature f of the class, plus the constraint $f = e$.

Complex repeated expressions lead to inefficient implementations. A derived feature representing the expression need only be recomputed when one of its defining features changes value.

The interpretation ζ is the identity. Properties $\varphi(e)$ of the initial model can be proved from the corresponding properties $\varphi(f)$ of the new model because of the defining equality of f.

14.5.11 Eliminating a Redundant Inheritance

If a class inherits another by two or more different paths of inheritance, remove all but one path, if possible. A redundant inheritance conveys no extra information, but complicates the model. This transformation is valid for transitive inheritance, in which all features/properties of a superclass are inherited into the subclass.

Figure 14.28 shows a typical situation where class A inherits directly from class C and also indirectly via a more specific class B. The first inheritance is redundant and can be removed. (In some languages, such as Java, such inheritances would actually be invalid.)

The axiom $\overline{A} \subseteq \overline{C}$ of the original model follows from the axioms $\overline{A} \subseteq \overline{B}$ and $\overline{B} \subseteq \overline{C}$ of the new model, so ensuring correctness. The inheritance removed (e.g., of E inheriting from F) must be genuinely redundant (i.e., there must exist another chain of inheritances from E to F via other intermediary classes).

14.5.12 Making Partial Roles Total

A 0..1 multiplicity role of a class A may be turned into a 1 multiplicity role either by moving the role to a superclass of its current target, or by moving the other end to a subclass of A on which the association is total. Total associations are generally easier to implement and manage than partial associations.

Figure 14.29 shows the "generalize target" version of this transformation. Figure 14.30 the "specialize source" version.

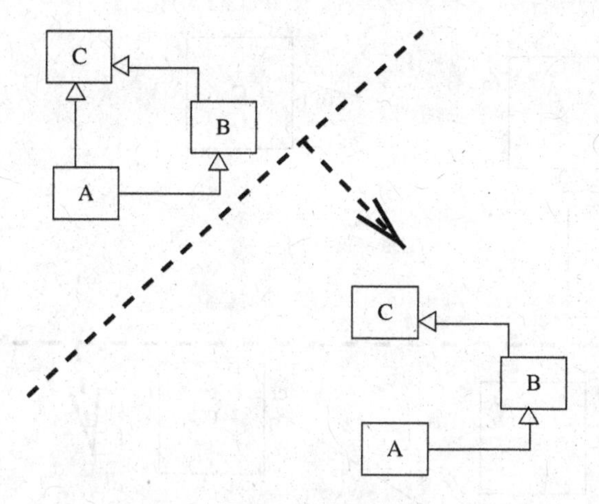

FIGURE 14.28 Redundant inheritance removal.

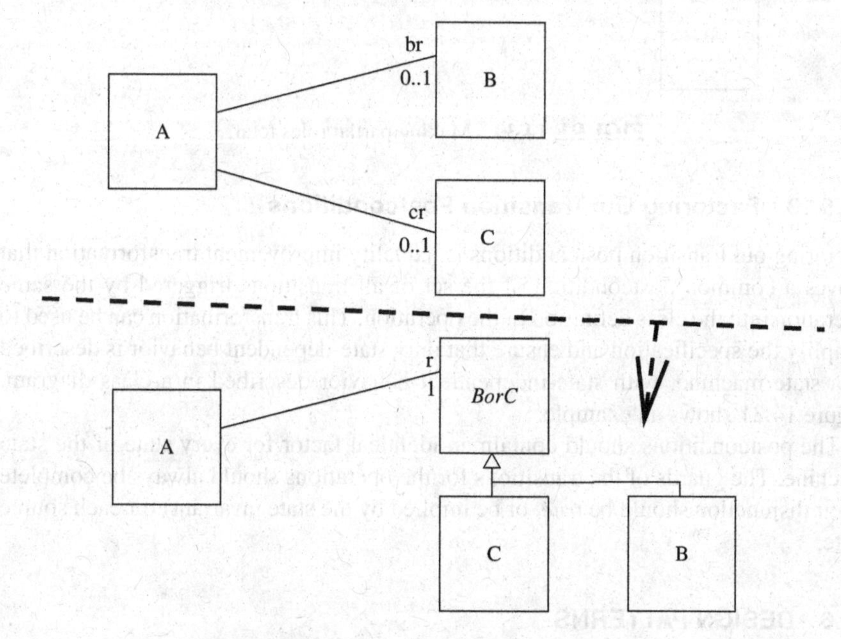

FIGURE 14.29 Making partial roles total.

In the first version we need the condition

$$br \rightarrow isEmpty() \ \ implies \ \ not(cr \rightarrow isEmpty())$$

r is the union of br and cr. In the second we need that

$$bx.cr \rightarrow size() = 1$$

for $bx : B$, and cr is otherwise empty.

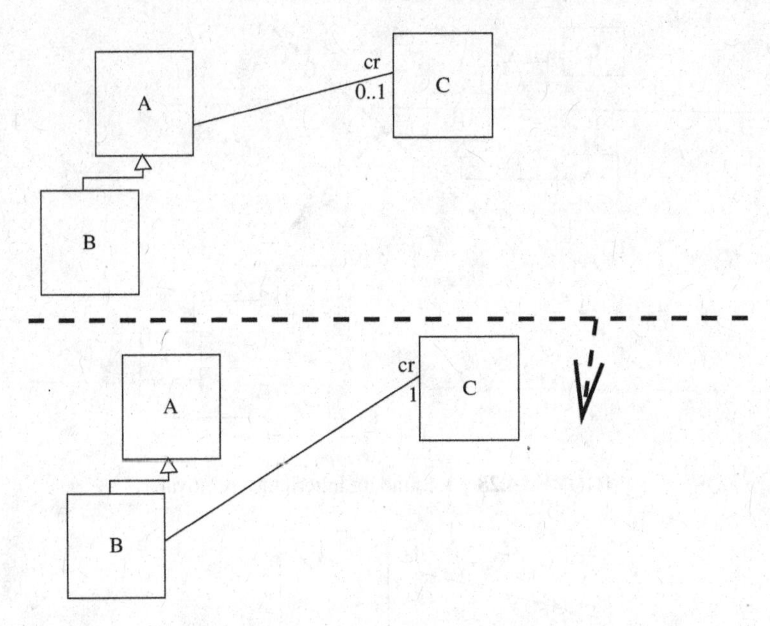

FIGURE 14.30 Making partial roles total.

14.5.13 Factoring Out Transition Postconditions

Factoring out transition postconditions is a quality improvement transformation that moves a common postcondition of the set of all transitions triggered by the same operation into the class definition of the operation. This transformation can be used to simplify the specification and ensure that only state-dependent behavior is described in a state machine, with state-independent behavior described in a class diagram. Figure 14.31 shows an example.

The postconditions should contain an identical factor for every state of the state machine. The guards of the transitions for the operations should always be complete (their disjunction should be *true*, or be implied by the state invariant) for each source state.

14.6 DESIGN PATTERNS

Introducing a design pattern by reorganizing the elements of a model to conform to the pattern can be regarded as a model transformation [26]. The L predicate of these transformations expresses the conditions in which the pattern is relevant and should be introduced. The R predicate expresses the structure of the system after introduction of the pattern [6].

In some cases these transformations will be quality improvement transformations; in other cases, refinements [41]. The Abstract Factory, Adapter, State, Mediator, and Observer patterns are analyzed as transformations by Lano [26]. Here we consider Facade and Singleton.

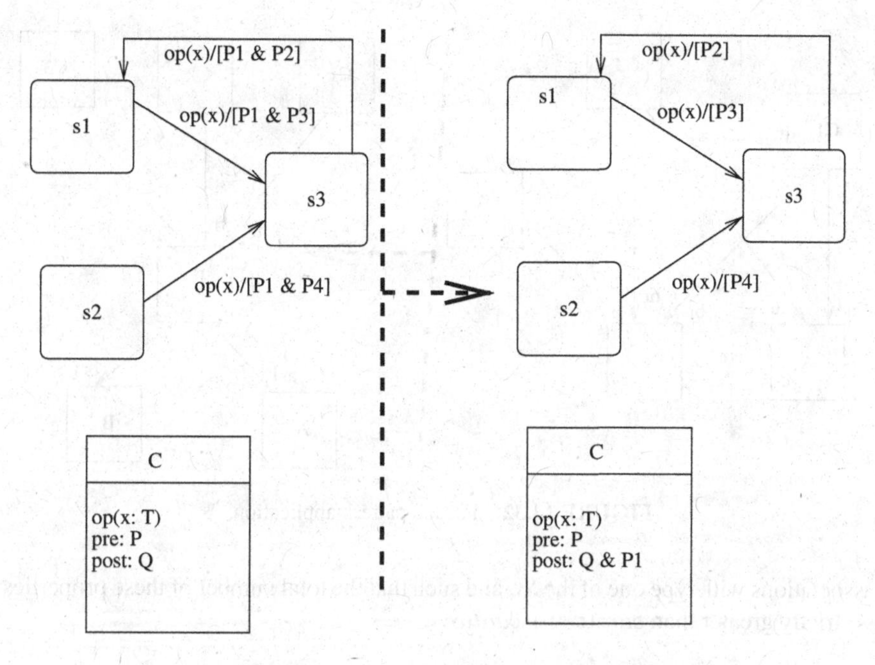

FIGURE 14.31 Factor transition postconditions.

14.6.1 Introducing a Facade Pattern

This structural pattern is defined in [16]. It has the aim of reducing direct dependencies between classes. It is an example of a factoring quality improvement transformation.

A generic facade with three client classes and two suppliers would be represented as a transformation from the original model, which simply contains these five classes, to a new model, where communication is via a facade class (right-hand side of Figure 14.32). Classes A and B are factored out into a new subsystem, which has boundary (interface) class F.

The original $C1 :: br$ role is implemented by the composition $C1 :: fr.F :: br1$ in the new model, and similarly for the other suppliers and clients. ζ is

$$C :: ar \longmapsto C :: fr.F :: ar1$$

for each client class C and role ar from C to a supplier.

The significant effect of the transformation is that invocations $br.op(x)$ in operation definitions of clients $C1$, $C2$, and $C3$ in the original model become invocations $fr.op(x)$ in the new model, and op on F is defined to call the original op in A or B.

The number of dependencies in the model is potentially reduced, from $C * S$ to $C + S$, where C is the number of client classes, and S the number of suppliers. The L predicate specifies that there is a set Cs of classes, and a (disjoint) set Ss of classes, such that the elements of Cs have one or more owned properties which are ends of

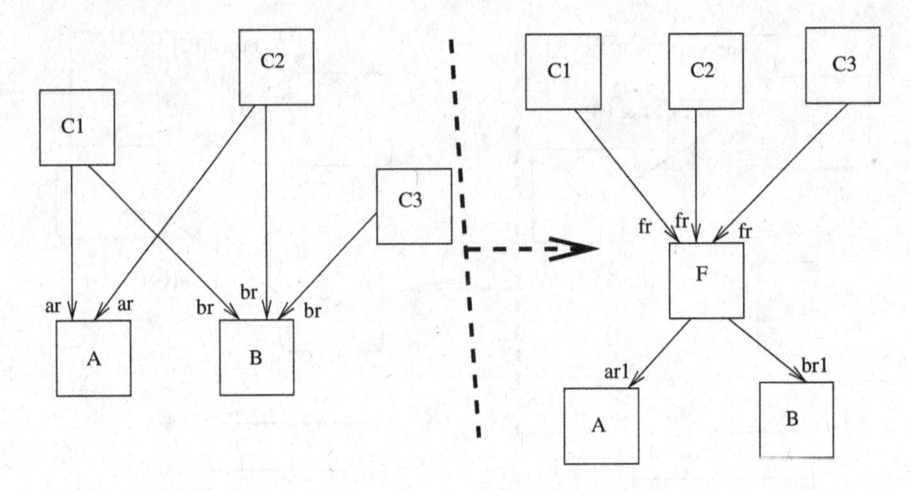

FIGURE 14.32 Facade pattern application.

associations with type one of the *Ss*, and such that the total number of these properties is strictly greater than $card(Cs) + card(Ss)$.

14.6.2 Introducing a Singleton Pattern

The Singleton pattern gives a standard design for a class which must have only one object instantiation. This pattern is a refinement transformation which implements a constraint

$$C.allInstances() \rightarrow size() \leq 1$$

for a class C.

Figure 14.33 shows the structure of a typical Singleton class after application of this pattern. The constraint is ensured by the definition of the constructor as private and by the *getInstance*() operation.

14.7 ENHANCEMENT TRANSFORMATIONS

Enhancement transformations extend a model in a monotonic manner such that all existing elements of the model remain in the new model, but new elements are added. For example, new classes, associations, and attributes can be added, association multiplicities made more precise, operation postconditions strengthened, targets of transitions made more specific, and so on. The primitive transformations "Add construct," "Assert construct is derived" (together with the constraint that defines the derivation), and "Reorder attributes" of Blaha and Premerlani [8] are further examples.

Not all additions to a diagram are valid enhancements. For example, adding a new element to an enumerated type falsifies the semantics of the original model, as does adding a new direct substate to a composite state with a single region. In both cases

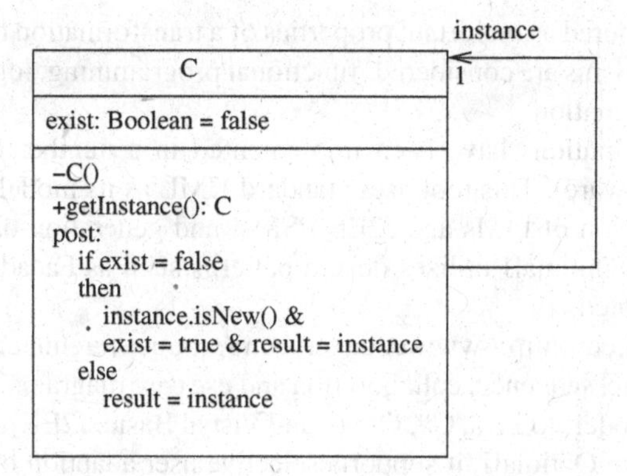

FIGURE 14.33 Introduction of a Singleton class.

the extended element already had an axiom expressing that it was complete in the original model (although UML allows an alternative semantics for composite states which does not enforce completeness).

14.7.1 Introducing a Constructor for a Class

Introducing a constructor for a class is an enhancement transformation that adds a new constructor to a class based on the class invariant. If the class C has attributes $att_1 : T_1, \ldots, att_n : T_n$, and class invariant Inv_C, a constructor $create_C(att_1 : T_1, \ldots, att_m : T_m)$ can be defined, where $m \leq n$:

$$
\begin{aligned}
&create_C(attx_1 : \ T_1, ..., \ attx_m : \ T_m) \\
&\texttt{pre: } \exists \ attx_{m+1} : T_{m+1}; \ \ ...; \ attx_n : \ T_n \ \cdot \ Inv_C[attx/att] \\
&\texttt{post:} \ Inv_C[attx_1/att_1, ..., \ attx_m/att_m] \ and \\
&\quad att_1 \ = \ attx_1 \ and \ \ ... \ and \ att_m \ = \ attx_m
\end{aligned}
$$

In other words, the condition for the constructor to execute normally is that there do exist values for the other attributes of the class which satisfy the invariant when the values supplied for the first m attributes are assigned to these. The effect of the constructor is to carry out these assignments and to choose values for the other attributes so that the invariant holds true.

14.8 IMPLEMENTATION OF MODEL TRANSFORMATIONS

Alternative implementation techniques and languages for implementing model transformations are considered in [30]: The ability of tools to provide guidance on the selection of appropriate transformations to apply to a particular model is considered desirable, as is the ability for a user of the tool to customize existing transformations and define new ones. The ability to group and compose transformations and to verify them is also considered as important properties of a transformation tool. Three implementation mechanisms are considered: functional programming, logic programming, and graph transformation.

Model transformations have been implemented in a number of tools, such as OptimalJ (Compuware). This tool uses standard UML as its modeling notation, and supports construction of PIMs and J2EE PSMs, and generation of executable Java code from PSMs. OptimalJ utilizes design patterns such as Facade to structure the code that is generated.

Codagen Architect (http://www.codagen.com/products/architect/) supports UML class, state machine, sequence, collaboration and use case diagrams, and code generation from UML models to Java, C#, C++, and Visual Basic. J2EE and .Net platforms are supported. Like OptimalJ, it supports selective user adaption of generated code, to enable manual maintenance of some sections of code.

SosyInc Modeler and Transformation Engine (http://www.sosyinc.com) use UML-like notation to define class diagrams, from which code in Visual Basic or Java can be generated automatically. It includes a specification of behavioral logic in a functional model so that complete executable code can be produced.

UML2Web [25] supports transformations for UML class and state machine diagrams, for refinement and quality improvement. Transformations are specified as pairs of predicates L, R, and the transformations which are applicable to a given model (class diagram or state machine) are identified by evaluating the L predicates of the transformations on the model. When an applicable transformation is selected by the user, the R predicate of the transformation is then applied to the model to modify it. New transformations can be defined by the user, although there is no mechanism to verify these transformations (the predefined transformations have been already verified as correct). The control of the ordering and application of transformations is achieved by using state machines, as shown in Figure 14.5.

In general however the transformations supported by transformation tools are 'hard coded' into the tools, and it is not possible to add new transformations or extend the transformations provided. The Together Architect tool for QVT (http://www.borland.com) and the Converge system of Tratt [43] do permit a general definition of transformations and their implementation, via the use of pattern-matching and pattern-transformation facilities. Together Architect uses the QVT notation of Section 14.3 to define transformations. These are then applied to the elements of the model until no elements that match the LHS of the transformation rule remain in the source model. Kermeta (http://www.kermeta.org) is similar in style. The iterative approach of these tools (applying rules to elements, one by one) can produce a different result to the pure relational view of a transformation, which operates simultaneously on all elements that satisfy the applicability condition. In particular, the iterative approach may not terminate.

Other important aspects of transformation implementation are change propagation and bidirectionality [43]. *Change propagation* means that a transformation can be used to maintain consistency between a source and a target model under some changes to the source, without needing to reapply the transformation to the entire source model. *Bidirectionality* means that this also operates in the target-to-source direction.

These are related to the monotonicity and invertability properties at the transformation specification level: If a transformation is monotonic, extensions of the source model that do not alter the elements matched by the transformation and do not affect the application of the transformation can be copied to the target model without reexecuting the transformation. Invertability with a functional inverse transformation means that a transformation can be executed in reverse from the transformed model to obtain the original model.

Approaches to support these implementation properties generally use tracing information to identify exactly how a target model was produced from, and depends upon, the source [36,37,43].

Automated application of transformations is generally desirable to improve the efficiency of development; however, in some cases human intervention may be necessary to resolve choices: for example, in the "introduce superstate" transformation, there may be alternative (conflicting) ways of grouping states together based on their outgoing transitions.

14.9 SUMMARY

We have defined a systematic representation and classification of model transformations, with all forms of model transformation being defined as relations at the metamodel level. Different specification approaches have been described, and a large number of common transformations have been defined, including examples of their application and details of their use. The verification of transformations has been shown, using the concept of a logical interpretation from the source language to the target language.

REFERENCES

1. K. Androutsopoulos. Verification of reactive system specifications using model checking. Ph.D. dissertation, King's College, London, 2004.
2. D. Akehurst and S. Kent. A relational approach to defining transformations in a metamodel. In Proceedings of UML 2002. Lecture Notes in Computer Science, vol. 2460. Springer-Verlag, New York, 2002.
3. D. Bämer et al. Role object. *In Pattern Languages of Program Design*. Addison-Wesley, Reading, MA, 2000.
4. S. Markovic and T. Baar. Refactoring OCL annotated class diagrams. *In MoDELS 2005*. Lecture Notes in Computer Science, vol. 3713. Springer-Verlag, New York, 2005.
5. S. Markovic and T. Baar. *Refactoring OCL Annotated UML Class Diagrams, MoDELS 2005 Proceedings*. Lecture Notes in Computer Science, vol. 3713. Springer-Verlag, New York, 2005.
6. I. Bayley and H. Zhu. On the composition of design patterns. QSIC 2008. IEEE Computer Society, Los Alamitos, CA, 2008.

7. C. Batini, S. Ceri and S. Navathe. *Conceptual Database Design: An Entity-Relationship Approach*. Benjamin-Cummings, Redwood City, CA, 1992.
8. M. Blaha and W. Premerlani. A catalog of object model transformations. Presented at the 3rd Working Conference on Reverse Engineering, Monterey, CA, 1996.
9. G. Booch, M. Engel, and B. Young. *Object Oriented Analysis and Design with Applications*. Addison-Wesley, Reading, MA, 2007.
10. S. Cook and J. Daniels. *Designing Object Systems*. Prentice Hall, Upper Saddle River, NJ, 1994.
11. J. Crupi, D. Alur, and D. Malks. *Core J2EE Patterns*. Prentice Hall, Upper Saddle River, NJ, 2001.
12. J. Cruz-Lemus, M. Genero, M. Esperanza Manso, and M. Piattini. Evaluating the effect of composite states on the understandability of UML statechart diagrams. *In MoDELS 2005*. Lecture Notes in Computer Science, vol. 3713, Springer-Verlag, New York, 2005.
13. K. Czarnecki and S. Helsen. Feature-based survey of model transformation approaches. IBM Systems Journal, special issue on model-driven software development, 45(3): 621–645, 2006.
14. T. Mens, K. Czarnecki, and P. Van Gorp. A Taxonomy of model transformations. *Dagstuhl Seminar Proceedings* vol. 04101, 2005.
15. M. Fowler. *Refactoring: Improving the Design of Existing Code*. Addison-Wesley, Reading, MA, 2000.
16. E. Gamma, R. Helm, R. Johnson, and J. Vlissides. *Design Patterns: Elements of Reusable Object-Oriented Software*, Addison-Wesley, Reading, MA, 1994.
17. M. Giese and D. Larsson. Simplifying transformations of OCL constraints. *In MoDELS 2005*. Lecture Notes in Computer Science, vol. 3713. Springer-Verlag, New York, 2005.
18. M. Grand. *Patterns in Java*. Wiley, New York, 1998.
19. M. Harman, D. Binkley, and S. Danicic. Amorphous program slicing. *Journal of Systems and Software*, 68(1): 45–69, Oct. 2003.
20. A. Knapp and J. Wuttke. Model-checking of UML 2.0 interactions. *In Proceedings of the 5th International Workshop on Critical Systems Development Using Modelling Languages (CSDUML)*. Telenor Report 20/2006, 2006.
21. S. Kim and D. Carrington. A formal mapping between UML models and object-Z specifications. *In ZB 2000*, Lecture Notes in Computer Science, vol. 1878. Springer-Verlag, New York, 2000.
22. K. Lano. *The B Language and Method*. FACIT Series. Springer-Verlag, New York, 1996.
23. K. Lano and J. Bicarregui. Semantics and transformations for UML models. Presented at the UML'98 Conference, Mulhouse, France, 1998.
24. K. Lano. *Transformational program analysis. Journal of Software Testing Verification and Reliability*, 4: 155–189, 1994.
25. K. Lano. *Constraint-driven development. Information and Software Technology*, 50: 406–423, 2008.
26. K. Lano. *Formalising design patterns as model transformations*. Chapter VIII in T. Taibi, ed., *Design Pattern Formalisation Techniques*. IGI Publishing, Hershey, PA, 2007.
27. K. Lano. A compositional semantics of UML-RSDS. *SoSyM*, 8(1): 85–116, Feb. 2009.
28. S. Markovic and T. Baar. Refactoring OCL annotated class diagrams. In *MoDELS 2005*. Lecture Notes in Computer Science, vol. 3713. Springer-Verlag, New York, 2005.

29. S. Markovic and T. Baar. Semantics of OCL specified with QVT. *Software and Systems Modelling*, 7(4), Oct. 2008.
30. T. Mens, K. Czarnecki, and P. Van Gorp. A taxonomy of model transformations. *Dagstuhl Seminar Proceedings*, vol. 04101, 2005.
31. B. Meyer. Applying design by contract. *IEEE Computer*, pp. 40–51, Oct. 1992.
32. C. Morgan. *Programming from Specifications*. Springer-Verlag, New York, 1990.
33. OMG. Model-driven architecture. http://www.omg.org/mda/, 2007.
34. OMG. *UML Superstructure, Version 2.1.1*. OMG Document Formal/2007-02-03. Object Management Group, Needham, MA, 2007.
35. OMG. *UML Infrastructure Version 2.1.2*. OMG Document Formal/2007-11-04. Object Management Group, Needham, MA, 2007.
36. OMG. *Query/View/Transformation Specification*. Technical Report ptc/05-11-01. Object Management Group, Needham, MA, 2005.
37. I. Porres. Rule-based update transformations and their application to model refactorings. *Software and Systems Modelling*, 4(4), 2005.
38. D. Schmidt and C. Cranor. Half-sync/half-async: an architectural pattern for efficient and well-structured concurrent I/O. In *Proceedings of the 2nd Annual Conference on the Pattern Languages of Programs*, Monticello, IL, pp. 1–10, Sept. 1995.
39. C. Snook and M. Butler. U2B: a tool for translating UML-B models into B. In J. Mermet, ed., *UML-B Specification for Proven Embedded Systems Design*. Chapter 6. Springer-Verlag, New York, 2004.
40. Sun Microsystems. Core J2EE patterns. http://www.java.sun.com, 2008.
41. G. Sunyé, A. Le Guennec, and J. M. Jézéquel. Design patterns application in UML. In *ECOOP 2000*, Lecture Notes in Computer Science, vol. 1850, Springer-Verlag, New York, pp. 44–62, 2000.
42. G. Sunyé, D. Pollet, Y. Traon, and J.-M. Jézéquel, Refactoring UML models. In *Proceedings of UML 2001*. Lecture Notes in Computer Science, vol. 2185. Springer-Verlag, New York, 2001.
43. L. Tratt. Model transformations and tool integration. *SoSym*, 4(2): 112–122, May 2005.
44. D. Varro, and A. Pataricza. *Automated formal verification of model transformations*. Presented at the CSDUML 2003 Workshop.

INDEX

Printed in the United States
By Bookmasters